PREFACE TO 1832

This opportunity to produce the Checklist has been provided by a number of persons, known and unknown, who were (or are) involved with the project. The effort began, in large part, because of the initiative, energy, and eclectic interests of Douglas C. McMurtrie, who directed much of the work of the American Imprints Inventory: that part of the Work Projects Administration that did the survey which forms the basis for this entire series. McMurtrie, a massive man of more than 400 pounds who wrote or edited over 700 items during his life, guided his imprints work through the bureaucratic web of the WPA. His energies then made the raw materials available today.

Those who worked for the Inventory deserve recognition. Often trained only by studying McMurtrie's Manual of Procedure (Chicago, The Historical Records Survey, 1938), these persons worked diligently in an attempt to find every fugitive imprint. Witness, for example, the following excerpt from a series of memos found buried in the WPA files. The particular problem discussed involved the verification and a "style A description" for an item reported to the Inventory's central office.

> TO: Mrs. Maxwell   September 9, 1940.
> FROM: F. C. Calkins
> SUBJECT: Style A Imprints.
>
> ... Amos Blanchard, American Military and Naval Biography, Walker Library. Miss Williams, the librarian, joined me in a search for this volume. No trace of it. She has an index by names of authors and another by names of volumes and no mention of Amos Blanchard.... One thing makes me think you have the wrong library is that at Walker all shelves are on cardinal points of the compass. [On each card done by the WPA the exact physical location, such as northwest wall, bindery table, duplicate exchange room, etc. , was given for the item when the card was produced.] ... there is no 'n. w. wall. '

iii

Although the search continued through several months to four other libraries, the item was not found in Tallahassee but, using its national organization, the Inventory did locate a copy of Blanchard in a private library in Marshall, Missouri.

Spot-checking today's remainder with the corpus available thirty-five years ago would be an impossible task without the aid of several persons. Among these we would like to acknowledge the help of Dr. Roger W. Moss, Jr., Secretary and Librarian of the Athenaeum of Philadelphia. Because of his invitation, the total holdings of "PPA" appear, for the first time, in this volume of the Checklist. Vital, too, was the aid of the American Antiquarian Society and especially the counsel and assistance of Mary Brown of that institution who led us to many uncatalogued pamphlets as well as to previously undiscovered almanacs. It is anticipated that these holdings of "MWA" will strengthen this and future volumes of the Checklist.

It goes without saying that the continuing interest of Scarecrow Press is paramount to this work. We would be remiss if we did not also note the significant and continuing support of Shippensburg State College. Its library has acquired the major tools needed to complete this type of bibliographical research. In addition, the college has seen fit to provide a sabbatical leave during 1978 to push forward the work on 1833 and 1834.

Without these resources and support, both present and past, this organized access to the record of nineteenth century American publishing would not have been possible.

Shippensburg, Pennsylvania   Scott Bruntjen
December, 1976   Carol Bruntjen

Abbot Female Academy. Andover, Mass.
Catalogue of the trustees, instructors and students of the Abbott Female Academy, Andover, Mass., Pr. by Flagg, Gould and Newman, Dec. 1832. 8 p. MAnA.								10776

Abbott, Benjamin, 1732-1796.
Experience and gospel labours of the Rev. Benjamin Abbott;... New York, B. Waugh and T. Mason for the Methodist Episcopal church, 1832. 282 p. CtY; CtMW; IEG; MoJMC; MnHi.								10777

Abbott, Jacob, 1803-1879.
Cousin Lucy's Stories. Stories told to Rollo's Cousin Lucy when she was a little girl. Boston, 1832. 180 p. MWA.								10778

---- A description of the Mount Vernon school in 1832. Being a brief account of the internal arrangements and plans of the institution. Addressed to a new scholar... By Jacob Abbott, principal. Boston, Pr. by Peirce & Parker [pref. 1832]. 72 p. DLC; ICBB; MeB; OO; RPB.								10779

---- The young Christian; or, A familiar illustration of the principles of Christian duty. By Jacob Abbott... Boston, Peirce & Parker, 1832. 323 p. CtY; KyWA; MWA; MWA; RPB; ViU.								10780

Abercrombie, James, 1758-1841.
The Mourner Comforted; a selection of extracts, consolatory on the death of friends from the writing of the most eminent divines and others, by James Abercrombie. Steubenville, Ohio, J. Wilson, 1832. 404 p. CSmH; IaMp; KyWA; MoS; OClWHi.								10781

Abercrombie, John, 1780-1844.
Extracts from Inquiries concerning the intellectual powers, and the investigation of truth, on the uncertainty of medicine. Baltimore, By J. Lucas & E. K. Deaver, for the Botanic Medical Society of Baltimore, 1832. 12 p. DLC; MiD; MiDW-M.								10782

---- ... Inquiries concerning the intellectual powers, and the investigation of truth. By John Abercrombie... From the 2d Edinburgh ed. New-York, J. & J. Harper, 1832. 349 p. CtY; ICP; LNB; MB; PPA; ViU.								10783

Abernathy, Lunenburg Co., comp.
Laughable anecdotes;-Both ancient and modern selected from the Funny companion, Jemmy Twitcher's jests, The Gridiron, The Post chaise companion and other sources, many of which were never before in print- By Lunenburg C. Abernathy.... Frankfort, Pr. at the Kentuckian and Commentator office, 1832. 348 p. ICU;

2   Abernethy

KyHi.   10784

Abernethy, John, 1764-1831.
Surgical observations on the
constitutional origin and treatment of local diseases and on
aneurisms. Boston, Stimpson &
Clapp, 1832. 140 p. CSfCMS;
MBM.   10785

Abrantes, Laure Saint-Martin
[Permon] Junot, duchesse d',
1784-1838.
Memoirs of the Duchess D'-
Abrantes, (Madame Junot) com-
plete in one volume. New York,
J. & J. Harper, 1832. 445 p.
CtY; MBL; PPA; PU; ScCC; ViU.
                               10786
The Academic Pioneer and Guard-
ian of Education. Pub. by an as-
sociation of Teachers. Vol. 1.
Cincinnati, 1832- 40 p. KyLc;
NNC-T; OCHP; OC.WHi; PPL;
PPULC.   10787

Academie de medecine, Paris,
France.
Report of the Royal Academy
of Medicine, to the Minister of
the Interior, upon the cholera-
morbus. Pub. by order of the
French Government. Tr. from
the French by John W. Sterling
...New York, Samuel Wood and
Sons, 1832. 234 p. CtY; MBM;
MeB; P; PPA; VtU.   10788

An account of the origin, symptoms, and cure of the influenza
or epidemic catarrh; with some
hints respecting common colds
and incipient pulmonary consumption. Philadelphia, H. H.
Porter, 1832. 80 p. CtMW;
DLC; NhD; PHi; PPA; WuU.
                               10789
An account of the rise and progress of the Indian or spasmodic
cholera. With a particular description of the symptoms attending the disease. Illustrated
by a map, showing the route and

progress of the disease from
Jessore near the Ganges, in
1817, to Great Britain in 1831.
New-Haven, L. H. Young, 1832.
48 p. DLC; DNLM; MB; MWA;
NNNAM; PPCP.   10790

Adair, James.
Prince Owen Roe. By James
Adair. Philadelphia, Clarke,
1832. 203 p. PWW.   10791

Adam, Alexander, 1741-1809.
An abridgment of Adam's Latin grammar. Designed for the
use of beginners. A new ed.,
cor. and improved. Cambridge,
Brown, Shattuck and company;
Boston, Hilliard, Gray and company, 1832. 158 p. CtSoP; DLC;
ICU; MH; WaPS.   10792

---- Adam's Latin grammar,
with some improvements, & the
following additions: rules for the
right pronunciation of the Latin
language; a metrical key to the
odes of Horace; a list of Latin
authors arranged according to the
different ages of Roman literature... by B. A. Gould. Boston,
Hilliard, Gray, Little, and Wilkins, 1832. 284 p. ICU; MB; NN;
PPA; PPULC.   10793

---- ---- New York, W. Kerr
and Co. , [1832?] MH.   10794

---- Handbuch der romischen al-
terhimer. Ans dem englischen
nach der zweiten vermehrten ausgabe von J. I. Meyer. 4. verbes-
serte und vermehrte auflage.
Erlangen, 1832. 2 vol. CtY; MII;
PPG; PPULC.   10795

---- [Rudiments of Latin and
Eng. grammar.] Abridgement.
New ed. Cambridge, 1832. DLC;
MB.   10796

Adams, Catherine Lyman, d. 1879.
Parlor lectures on the New

Testament. By the author of parlor lectures on scripture history. Augusta, Me., Brinsmade and Dole, 1832. 227 p. CSmH; MeAug.   10797

Adams, Charles L.
A concise view of North and South America. C. L. Adams. Boston, [1832?] Broadside. MHi.
10798

Adams, Daniel, 1773-1864.
Adams' new arithmetic; arithmetic in which the principles of operating by number are analytically explained and synthetically applied... Keene, N.H., J. and J. W. Prentiss, 1832. MH; PP.
10799

---- Geography; or, A description of the world. In three parts. ...By Daniel Adams, A.M. ... 14th ed. Boston, Lincoln & Edmands, 1832. 321 p. KgHi; NNC.
10800

Adams, Hannah, 1755-1832.
A memoir of Miss Hannah Adams, written by herself. With additional notices, by a friend. Boston, Gray and Bowen, 1832. 110 p. CSmH; IEG; MHi; RNR; TNV.   10801

Adams, John, 1750?-1814.
Flowers of ancient history; comprehending, on a new plan, the most remarkable and interesting events, as well as characters, of antiquity. Designed for the improvement and entertainment of youth. By the Rev. John Adams... Baltimore, J. N. Lewis, 1832. 288 p. DLC; MdHi; OrALc; PLFM; PWaybu. 10802

Adams, John Quincy, 1767-1848.
Dermot Mac Morrogh, or, The Conquest of Ireland. ...By John Quincy Adams. 2d ed. Boston, Carter, Hendee & Co., 1832. 108 p. CoD; MH; MeB; MWA; NjP; OO.   10803

---- Letter from Mr. Adams to Andrew Stevenson, speaker of the House of Representatives of the United States, 11 July, 1832. [Washington, 1832] 2 p. CU; PPL.   10804

---- Letters on masonry addressed to William L. Stone, esq. of New York, by John Quincy Adams, late President of the United States. Lancaster, Pa., Pr. at the office of the Examiner, 1832. 15 p. DLC; MH; NN; PPL; RNHi.
10805

---- Letters on the entered apprentice's oath. By John Quincy Adams. ... Boston, Young Men's Antimasonic Association, 1832. 24 p. NNFM; WHi.   10806

---- Letters... to Edward Livingston on Masonry. Philadelphia, 1832. PPL-R.   10807

---- Notice of Mr. Adams' eulogium on the life and character of James Monroe. [Washington, 1832] 36 p. MWA; PHi; ViU.
10808

---- Remarks of Mr. Adams in the House of Representatives, Feb. 8, 1832, on the ratio of representation; the question being on a motion to strike out 48,000, and insert 44,000 as the ratio. n.p., [1832]. MH.   10809

Adams, John Watson, 1796-1850.
A discourse, delivered at the Presbyterian church, Syracuse, on Sabbath afternoon, July 22, 1832, by Rev. J. W. Adams... Syracuse [N.Y.], Pr. by W. S. Campbell, 1832. 17 p. CSmH; N; NNtoA; NSy; PPPrHi. 10810

Adams, Nehemiah, 1806-1878.
Remarks on the Unitarian belief; with a letter to a Unitarian friend on the Lord's supper. Boston, Peirce & Parker, 1832. 175 p. CtY; GDccCT; MeBat;

NNUT; RPB.   10811

Adams, Thomas Boylston.
Catalogue of (his) library,
sold. Boston, 1832. MBAt.
                                    10812
Address and proceedings of the
Ohio State Convention. . . at Co-
lumbus, Ohio, January 9, 1830. . .
See under Ohio. Convention. Co-
lumbus, 1832.

Address before the teachers of
the Howard Sunday School, September, 1832. By a teacher.
Boston, Green, 1832. 18 p. DLC;
MB; MWA.   10813

An address delivered before the
teachers of the Hancock Sunday
School, on the removal of that
school to the vestry of the Second Church. Boston, Benjamin H.
Greene, 1832. 25 p. MWA.
                                    10814
An address, delivered in the Representative Hall before the General Assembly of the State of Alabama, and the citizens of Tuscaloosa, December 7, 1832, in
commemoration of the death of
Charles Carroll of Carrollton. . .
Tuscaloosa, E. Walker, 1832.
DU.   10815

The address of a farmer to the
honest men of all parties. . . See
under Burges, Tristam 1770-
1853.

The address of the carriers of
the Boston Press, to their pa-
trons, with the compliments of
the season. Boston, 1832.
Broadside. MB.   10816

Address of the Free People of
Color of the Borough of Wilmington, Delaware. Signed by: Abraham D. Shad, Peter Spencer,
Wm. S. Thomas. [Boston, Garrison and Knapp, 1832]. DHU;
DLC; MHi; NN; NN-Sc.   10817

Address of the young men of the
National Republican party, of the
Fifth congressional district, to
the young men of the state of
Maryland. [Baltimore, Pr. by
Sands & Neilson, 1832]. 10 p.
DLC; MWA; MiU-C; NN; OClWHi;
WHi.   10818

Address to the citizens of Penna.
by a Democrat. Philadelphia,
1832. 12 p. PPL.   10819

Address to the Community on the
necessity of legalizing the study
of anatomy. By order of the Medical Society of Maine. Brunswick,
Joseph Griffin, 1832. 2 p. MeB;
MeLewB.   10820

An address to the Freemen of
Massachusetts. See Allen,
George, 1792-1883.

An address to the freemen of
Rhode Island on the subject of the
spring elections, 1832, by a Republican farmer. Providence,
1832. 16 p.   10821

Address to the Liberal and Humane. Philadelphia, 1832. 4 p.
MWA.   10822

Address to the master mechanics,
journeymen, and apprentices. . . By
a brother mechanic. Philadelphia,
T. W. Ustick, 1832. 16 p. MWA.
                                    10823
Address to the people of Maine.
Against the re-election of Andrew
Jackson to the presidency in 1832.
Portland, October 25, 1832.
Broadside. MH.   10824

Address to the people of Massachusetts, Virginia [etc.] by a convention of the people of South Carolina, declaring that the act of
Congress, approved May 19, 1828,
and the act approved July 14,
1832, altering the acts imposing
duties on imports are unconstitu-

tional and void, and that a protecting tariff shall be no longer enforced in South Carolina]. [n.p., 1832?] 10 p. MB. 10825

Address to the people of the United States by the Convention of the people of South Carolina. [1832] MBAt; MWA; PHi; PU; ScU. 10826

An address to the people of the United States, on the subject of the presidential election; comprising a comparative view of the character and administration of Andrew Jackson. By a freeman of the United States... Washington, 1832. 35 p. DLC; IaU; MWA; NjR; OClWHi. 10827

Adlum, John, 1759-1836. History of a Philadelphia Chestnut tree. n.p., 1832. 2 p. PPULC; PU; PU-B; PU-BZ. 10828

The adventures of a bodkin. By the author of 'The gold thimble', 'Jane Courtney,' 'The little wanderers', 'The contrast', 'Contentment', 'Edwin', 'The flower girl', etc. Boston, Cottons and Barnard, 1832. 30 p. CtY; MB. 10829

The adventures of a school-boy. Boston, Greene, 1832. CtY. 10830

The adventures of Count D'Orveau. A Romance.... Philadelphia, G. M. & W. Snider, 1832. 180 p. CtY; MH; NcD; NjP; PKit. 10831

Aesopus, 619-564 B. C. Forty-nine of Aesop's fables; illustrated with large plates. For the use of schools. New Harmony, Ind., 1832. 53 p. ICN; InNBW; InNhW; InU. 10832

Affecting scenes; being passage from the diary of a physician. New York, J. & J. Harper, 1832. 2 Vols. MBoy; MII; PPL; RJa;

ViU. 10833

The affecting story of Mary Davis... New York, Mahlon Day, 1832. 17 p. DLC; MHaHi. 10834

An affectionate invitation to the communion. Dover, 1832. 8 p. MH; MH-AH. 10835

Affection's gift; or a holiday present. New-York, J. C. Riker, 1832. 288 p. CtMW; DLC; NN; NjR; RPB. 10836

Agnew, John Holmes, 1804-1865. An inquiry into the institution, perpetual obligation, change of day, utility, and duties of the Sabbath, by John Holmes Agnew. Pittsburg, Pr. by D. and M. Maclean, 1832. 108p. InCW; NjP; NjPT; PWW; PPi. 10837

Agnew, Margaret. The conspiracy acknowledged and defended; in a letter to the Rev. William W. Phillips, D. D. ... New York, 1832. 30 p. CtY; MH; NN; PPL. 10838

---- The conspiracy explained and defended; in a letter to the Rev. William W. Phillips. 2d ed. New York, n.p., 1832. 30 p. MB; MH; NjR; PPULC; PPrHi. 10839

---- Letter to Rev. William W. Phillips. New York, 1832. CtY; PPL. 10840

Agricola [pseud.] The Virginia Doctrines, not Nullification. By Agricola. Published in the Richmond Enquirer, between the 17th of August and the 15th of September, 1852... Richmond, Pr. by Samuel Shepherd & Co., 1832. 52 p. CtY; DLC; ScU; TxU; ViL. 10841

Agricultural almanac for 1833. Lancaster, John Bear [1832]

MWA.   10842

Ainsworth, Luther.
   Ainsworth's practical, mercantile arithmetic. Providence,
W. Marshal and A. S. Beckwith,
etc., 1832. 306 p. CtHW-W.
                              10843
Ainsworth, Robert, 1660-1743.
   A new abridgment of Ainsworth's dictionary, English and
Latin... Into this edition are introduced several alterations and
improvements for the special
purpose of facilitating the labour
and increasing the knowledge of
the young scholar, by John Dy-
mock. 1st Amer. ed., with corrections and improvements by
Charles Anthon. New York, H.
C. Sleight, etc., etc., 1832.
CtY; MH; MnSM.   10844

---- ---- Philadelphia, Carey &
Lea, 1832. 405 p. DLC; IEG;
IaAs; NcD; PU.   10845

---- ---- 3d Amer. ed. with
corrections and improvements, by
Charles Anthon... New York, H.
C. Sleight; Boston, Richardson,
Lord, and Holbrook, 1832.
IaMH; MiU.   10846

Alabama.
   Acts passed at the thirteenth
annual session of the General Assembly of the state of Alabama,
begun and held in the town of
Tuscaloosa, on the third Monday
in November, one thousand eight
hundred and thirty-one. John
Gayle, governor. James Jackson,
president of the senate. James
Penn, speaker of the house of
representatives. Tuscaloosa, Pr.
by Wiley, M'Guire & Henry,
state printers, 1832. 120 p. AU;
DLC; In-SC; MiU-L; NNB; NNLI.
                              10847
---- Journal of the House of
Representatives of the State of
Alabama. Begun and held at the

Town of Tuscaloosa on the first
Monday in November, 1832. Tus-
caloosa? E. Walker, 1832. 48 p.
A-SC; AB.   10848

---- Journal of the House of Representatives of the State of Alabama. Begun and held at the
Town of Tuscaloosa, on the Third
Monday in November, 1831. Tuscaloosa, Wiley, M'Guire and Henry, 1832. 246 p. A-SC.   10849

---- Journal of the Senate of the
State of Alabama. Begun and held
at the Town of Tuscaloosa, on
the first Monday in November,
1832. Tuscaloosa, E. Walker,
1832. 40 p. A-SC.   10850

---- ---- Begun and held at the
Town of Tuscaloosa, on the third
Monday in November, 1831. Tuscaloosa, Wiley, McGuire and
Henry, 1832. 207 p. A-SC.
                              10851
---- Memorial of the legislature
of Alabama on behalf of sundry
individuals belonging to the Creek
Indians, praying for assistance
from the government. February
15, 1832.   10852

---- Reports of cases argued and
determined in the Supreme Court of
Alabama, embracing the decisions
made in the year 1829 and those
made at the January Term of the
year 1830. By George N. Stewart,
Reported appointed by the Court...
Tuscaloosa, E. Walker, 1832.
526 p. AU; DLC; LNL-L; MH-L;
PU-L.   10853

The Albany quarterly. no. 1-
Albany, N.Y., 1832-   CtY; MB;
NjR; OClWHi; PPPrHi.   10854

Albany Sacred Music Fund Society.
   Constitution of the Albany Sac-
red Music Fund Society. Instituted
October, 1831. Albany, 1832. 14 p.
N; BrMus.   10855

The Album; or Ladies' common-place book devoted to literature. Lowell, Alfred Gilman, 1832-33. 200 p. (No. 1, 1832-Oct. 12, 1833) RPB.   10856

Alcott, A[mes] B[ronson], [1799-1858]
On the nature and means of early education, as deduced from experience... delivered before the American Institute of Instruction, Boston, 1832. MDeeP.   10857

Alcott, William Andrus, 1798-1859.
Essay on the construction of schoolhouses, to which was awarded the prize offered by the American Institute of Instruction, August, 1831. By William A. Alcott. With an appendix. Boston, Hilliard, Gray, Little and Wilkins, and Richardson, Lord and Holbrook, 1832. 66 p. CtY; IaU; MWA; MHi; NjR; ScCC; TxU.   10858

---- A historical description of the first public school in Hartford, Conn., now under the superintendence of J. Olney... with a particular account of its methods of instruction and discipline. Accompanied by general remarks on common schools. By Wm. A. Alcott. Hartford, D. F. Robinson & Co., 1832. 102 p. CtY; DLC; ICJ; MiD; NN.   10859

Alexander, Archibald, 1772-1851.
An address to candidates for the ministry on the importance of aiming at eminent piety in making their preparation for the sacred office. Philadelphia, Russell and Martin, 1832. 194 p. DLC; NjPT.   10860
---- Annals of the Jewish nation during the period of the second temple. New York, Jonathan Leavitt; Boston, Crocker & Brewster, etc., 1832. 355 p. GDecCT; ICU; RKi; TNT. 10861

---- The evidences of the Christian religion. By Archibald Alexander, D. D. 6th ed. New York, Jonathan Leavitt; Boston, Crocker and Brewster, 1832. 258 p. GDecCT; LNB; NjPT; OMC; ViRut.   10862

---- A pocket dictionary of the Holy Bible, containing a historical and geographical account of the persons and places mentioned in the Old and New Testaments ... Revised by the Committee of publication. 25th ed. Philadelphia, American Sunday School Union, 1832. 546 p. CtHWalk; OO; PPWe.   10863

---- Selection of hymns... 3d ed. New York, Leavitt, 1832. 524 p. MH-AH; NjP; PPULC; PPPrHi.   10864
---- Suggestions in vindication of Sunday-Schools, but more especially for the improvement of Sunday-School books, and the enlargement of the plan of instruction. By Archibald Alexander. Princeton, N. J., 1832. 30 p. CtY; MB; MnU; NjP.   10865

Alfieri, Carlo.
De Porquet's Italian phrases... Boston, See Fenwick de Porquet, Louis Philippe R.

Alger, Israel, 1787-1825.
Orthorpical guide to the Eng. tongue. Boston, 1832. MB.   10866
Alleine, Joseph, 1634-1668.
The saints pocket-book, containing the voice of the herald before the Great King. 1st Amer. ed. New York, 1832. MH; MH-AH.   10867

Allen, Benjamin, 1789-1829.
Memoir of the Rev. Benjamin Allen... By his brother the Rev. Thomas G. Allen. To which is added, the funeral sermon deliv-

ered in St. Paul's church, for the improvement of the death of Mr. Allen, by the Rev. Gregory T. Bedell, D. D. Also, the history of the Bible classes of St. Paul's church, which was written by Mr. Allen... Philadelphia, Latimer & Co., 1832. 547 p. DLC; GDecCT; MiD; NN; PChW. 10868

Allen, Elizabeth.
The silent harp; or, Fugitive poems. Burlington, E. Smith, 1832. 119 p. CtMW; CtY; MB; NcD; VtU.   10869

[Allen, George] 1792-1883.
An address to the Freemen of Massachusetts. By a Freeman. Worcester, Pr. by M. Spooner & Co., 1832. 16 p. CSmH; MBC; NN; PPAmP; WHi.   10870

---- A freeman on freemasonry. (Boston, 1832?) 8 p. CtY; MB; RPB; BrMus.   10871

Allen, Joseph, 1790-1873.
Easy Lessons in History and Geography. By Joseph Allen. Boston, Hillard, Gray, Little and Wilkins, 1832. 116 p. CtHWatk; MB; MH; NNC.   10872

---- Questions on select portions of the four Evangelists. 4th ed. Boston, C. Bowen, 1832. MH
                                   10873
Allen, William, 1770-1843.
Thoughts on the Importance of Religion (with extracts from Job Scott). Ed. 4? Philadelphia, 1830. PHi.   10874

Allen, William, 1784-1868.
An American biographical and historical dictionary, containing an account of the lives, characters, and writings of the most eminent persons in North America from its first settlement, and a summary of the history of the several colonies and of the

United States. By William Allen. ... 2d ed. Boston, W. Hyde & co., 1832. 800 p. DLC; MnH; NjP; PPA; PU; RNB; TxU.   10875

---- Freedom conferred only by the Gospel: a sermon preached in New York, Oct. 3, 1832, before the American board of commissioners for foreign missions, at their twenty-third annual meeting. Boston, Pr. by Crocker & Brewster, 1832. 38 p. ICT; MBAt; NjPT; PLT; RPB; WHi.
                                   10876
---- The minister's warfare and weapons. A sermon, preached at the installation of Rev. Seneca White at Wiscasset, April 18, 1832. By William Allen, D. D. Brunswick [Me.], Press of Joseph Griffin, 1832. 31 p. CSmH; CtY; MH; MWA; RPB.   10877

---- Sermons of John VIII; 36. Preached in New York. Oct. 3, 1832... New York, 1832. 15 p. MeB.   10878

Allen, Zachariah, 1795-1882.
The practical tourist, or Sketches of the state of the useful arts, and of society, scenery, &c. &c. in Great-Britain, France, and Holland... By Zachariah Allen. Providence, A. S. Beckwith; Boston, Richardson, Lord & Holbrook, and Carter and Hendee, 1832. 2 vols. CtY; ICU; MeB; NjR; PPA; PPAmP; RNR. 10879

Allyn's Anti-Masonic Almanac. Philadelphia, Pa., John Clarke [1832] MWA.   10880

Alpha Delta Phi.
Chapters of Alpha Delta Phi. Boston, Pr. by Samuel Chism, Franklin Printing House, for Calkins, Reed & Bangs, 1832. 126 p. MB; MeB; MsFM.   10881

Ambrose, Isaac, 1604-1664.

Looking unto Jesus: a view of the everlasting gospel; or, the soul's eyeing of Jesus.... Pittsburgh, Luke Loomis & Co., 1832. 715 p. InUpT; KyLoP; OWof; WaPS; WU.   10882

American Academy of Fine Arts. New York.
    Catalogue of paintings. New York, 1832. 15 p. MB.   10883

---- A descriptive catalogue of the paintings, by the ancient masters... New York, Pr. by W. Mitchell, 1832. 32 p. MB; NNUT.
                                    10884
American advertising directory for manufacturers and dealers in American goods for the year 1832-3. New York, Pr. by Hezekiah Howe, New Haven, for Jodelyn Darling & Co., 1832. 400 p. ICMcHi; MHi.   10885

American Almanac, 1833. Calendar by Charles F. Egelmann. Baltimore, Joseph N. Lewis, 1832. 1 v. DLC; MWA.   10886

---- Boston, Gray & Bowen, [1832] 312 p. IaHA; MWA. 10887

American almanac and repository of useful knowledge. Boston, Gray and Bowen [1832] MWA.
                                    10888
---- 2nd ed. Boston, David Williams [1832] MWA.   10889

American Baptist Foreign Mission Society. Burmah Mission.
    Brief History. Philadelphia [1832] 36 p. MBC.   10890

American Baptist Home Mission Society.
    Annual report... v. 1- 1832-New York City, American Baptist Home Mission Society, 1832. DLC; ICU; MiU; PHi; TxU.   10891

---- Proceedings of the convention held in the city of New York, on the 27th of April, 1832, for the formation of the...society... accompanied by an address of the executive committee to the Baptist churches of the U.S. New York, Pub. at office of the A.B. H.M.S., 1832. 16 p. IAIS; KyLeS; MnHi; ViRU; WHi.   10892

---- Reports. New York, 1832-MBC.   10893

American Board of Commissioners for Foreign Missions.
    Abstract of the twenty-second annual report of the American Board of Commissioners for Foreign Missions, for the year ending Aug. 31, 1831. Boston [Pr. by Crocker & Brewster] 1832. 36 p. WHi.   10894

---- Constitution, laws and regulations of the board with instructions to missionaries. Boston? 1832.   10895

---- The Missionary herald, containing the proceedings at large of the American board of Commissioners for foreign missions; with a general view of other benevolent operations. For the year 1832. Boston, Pr. by Crocker and Brewster [1832] KWiU; MA; TxHuT.   10896

---- Monthly paper. Boston, 1832-ArU; CtY; MBC; PCA.   10897

---- Report of the American board of commissioners for foreign missions, read at the thirty-third annual meeting, which was held in the city of New York, Oct. 3, 4, and 5, 1832. Boston, Pr. for the board by Crocker and Brewster, 1832. 192 p. CSPSR; IAIS; ICP; MeB; MeBat.   10898

American Colonization Society.
    ... Address of the managers

of the American Colonization Society, to the people of the United
States. Adopted at their meeting, June 19, 1832... Washington, Pr. by J. C. Dunn, 1832.
16 p. DLC; KyU; InU; OClWHI;
PHi; ScU.   10899

---- American Colonization Society, and the Colony at Liberia.
Boston, Pr. by Perkins & Marvin
for the Massachusetts Colonization Society, 1832. 16 p. KHi; M;
MWA; MiD-B.   10900

---- Office of the Colonization
Society, Washington, July 7,
1832. Dear Sir:-- ... [signed]
R. R. Gurley, Secretary, [Wash-
ington, 1832] Broadside. MiU-C.
                             10901
The American Comic Almanac,
1833, with whims, scraps, and
oddities. Baltimore, Cushing &
sons, 1832. 46 p. MWA; NjR.
                             10902
---- New York, David Felt; Boston, Charles Ellms, [1832] 48 p.
MWA; OHi.   10903

---- Philadelphia, Grigg & Elliot
[1832] MWA; NN; PHi.   10904

American Comic Almanack, 1833.
Boston, Charles Ellms & Willard
Pelt & Co. [1832] MHa; MLunHi;
MWA.   10905

American Education Society.
Illinois Branch.
    First annual report of the di-
rectors of the Illinois branch of
the American Education Society,
presented at the annual meeting
held in Jacksonville, August 14,
1832. Jacksonville, Pr. by James
G. Edwards, 1832. 17 p. ICHi;
IHi; WHi.   10906

American Engineer and Railroad
Journal. See Railway locomotives and cars.

American Farmers' Almanac for
1832. Calculations by Horace
Martin Auburn, Pub. by J. C. Iv-
ison & Co. , 1832- NBuG.
                             10907
American Farmer's Almanack,
1833. Calculated by Charles F.
Egelmann. Hagerstown, Md. ;
J. Gruber [1832] MWA.   10908

American Institute of the City of
New York.
    Charter of the American Insti-
tute of the City of New York. In-
corporated May 2, 1829. Accom-
panied with the by-laws. Adapted
May, 1830. New York, Elliott &
Hegeman, 1832. 8 p. MH-BA;
MWA; PHi.   10909

The American jest book: being a
chaste collection of anecdotes, bon
mots, and epigrams, original and
selected, for the amusement of
the young and old of both sexes.
By the author of the American
Chesterfield. Philadelphia, J.
Howe, 1832. 216 p. CoFS; IU;
NBuG; PP; PPA.   10910

The American Letter-Writer; containing select models of letters,
on friendship, love, business, &c.
&c. Interesting and essential to
every American citizen to which
is prefixed, An Essay on Epistolary correspondence. Lewistown,
Pa. , Charles Bell & Sons, 1832.
288 p. CSmH; ICBB.   10911

American Lyceum, or the Society
for the Improvement of Schools,
and Diffusion of Useful Knowledge.
Proceedings July 1832. No. 1.
New York, Collins & Hannay; Boston, Carter and Hendee, 1832-
CtY; DLC; MB; PHi; PP. 10912

The American miniature almanac
for the year...1833. (Allen's ed.)
Boston, Allen & co. [1832] (32) p.
MB; MHi.   10913

---- New York, William Minns, & Co., [1832] DLC.   10914

The American monthly review. v. 1-4; Jan. 1832-Dec. 1833. Cambridge, Hilliard & Brown; Boston, Hilliard, Gray & Co.; [etc., etc.] 1832-33.   CU; ICN; MB; NhD; OO.   10915

...The American quarterly review versus the state of New York. [Albany, 1832] 8 p. DLC; NN; PPL.   10916

American railroad journal. Philadelphia. See Railway locomotives and cars.

The American sentinel. Democratic daily newspaper. Philadelphia, 1832-41. PCDHi; PHi; PPL; PPULC.   10917

American Sunday School Union.
    American Sunday-school psalmody; or Hymns and music, for the use of Sunday schools and teachers' meetings; with a manual of instruction. Arranged for the American Sunday School Union, by E. Ives, Jun. Revised by the Committee of publication. Philadelphia, American Sunday School Union, 1832. 156 p. ICN; ICRL; NBuG; NNUT; PP. 10918

---- Election Day; written for the American Sunday School Union, and revised by the committee of publication... Philadelphia, American Sunday School Union, 1832. 100 p. ICBB; MiU; WaU; WHi.   10919

---- A help to the Acts of the apostles, adapted to the lesson system of reading and teaching the scriptures...revised by the Committee of Publication of the American Sunday School Union. Philadelphia, American Sunday-School Union [1832] 2 v. in 1.

DLC; MTop; NcRSh; ViU. 10920

---- Hints to aid in the organization and support of Sabbath schools in the country. 7th ed. Philadelphia, American Sunday School Union, 1832. 10 p. DLC; OCIWHi.   10921

---- History of the First Christians, prepared for the Sunday School Union, and revised by the Committee of Publication. American Sunday School Union. Philadelphia, 1832. ICartC; ICMcHi; OMC.   10922

---- Jane Scott... Philadelphia, American Sunday School Union, 1832. 36 p. DLC; NNU-W.   10923
---- The kind little boy. Philadelphia, American Sunday School Union, 1832. 16 p. MiHi. 10924

---- The knife-grinder. Philadelphia, American Sunday-School Union, [1832] NN; NNC. 10925

---- The life of President Edwards. Written for the American Sunday School Union and revised by the committee of publication. Philadelphia, American Sunday School Union, 1832. 143 p. CtY; GAU; PU; ScCoT; WBeloHi.   10926
---- Little Patrick the Weaver's Son. American Sunday School Union, Philadelphia, 1832. BrMus. 10927
---- New Sunday-school hymn book. Philadelphia, American Sunday School Union, 1832. 159 p. AmSSchU; NjPT.   10928

---- The nursery book, for a child that loves to learn. Revised by the Committee of publication. Philadelphia, American Sunday School Union, 1832. 24 p. DLC.   10929
---- A picture book for little

boys and girls. Written for the
American Sunday-school Union,
and revised by the Committee of
Publication. Philadelphia, American Sunday School Union [1832]
16 p. DLC; NRU.   10930

---- Popular superstitions. Writ-
ten for the American-Sunday-
School Union, and revised by the
Committee on Publication. Phila-
delphia, American Sunday-School
Union, [c 1832] 95 p. FTU;
MBMU; MOWgT; OO.   10931

---- Six-penny glass of wine.
1832. AmSSchU.   10932

---- Teacher's assistant in the
use of the fourth volume of union questions. Written for the
American Sunday School Union
and revised by the Committee of
Publication. Philadelphia, American Sunday School Union [1832]
276 p. ICN; KRu; WHi.   10933

---- The teacher's assistant in
the use of the third volume of
union questions. Philadelphia,
American Sunday School Union,
1832. 213 p. DLC; GDecCT; MH.
                          10934
---- The Teacher's Parting Gift,
to a Sunday School Boy. Phila-
delphia, American Sunday School
Union, 1832. PPeSchw; PPULC.
                          10935
---- The two prodigals. Written
for the American Sunday School
Union. And revised by the Committee of Publication. Philadelphia, American Sunday School
Union [c 1832] 52 p. BrMus.
                          10936
---- The Two Sunday School
Boys; or, The History of Thom-
as and Joseph. By a Sunday
School Teacher. pp. 36. Printed
for the Author: London (1820?)
(Another edition.) The History of
Thomas and Joseph. Revised by
the Committee of Publication.

pp. 36. Philadelphia, American
Sunday School Union, 1832.
BrMus.   10937

---- Union Fragen über auser-
lesene Bibelabschnitte aus dem
Neuen Testamente, für die Americanische Sonntagsschulen Union
geschrieben und durchgesehen
übersetzt von dem Ehrw. T. H.
Dreyer. Philadelphia, Americanische Sonntagsschulen Union,
1832. 246p. NN; PAtM; PPL-R;
PPULC.   10938

---- Union questions, on select
portions of scripture, from the
New Testament. Prepared for the
American Sunday School Union,
and revised by the committee of
publication. Philadelphia, American Sunday-School Union, 1832.
128 p. KyBgW; MdHi; PCA.
                          10939
---- The Young Soldier. Revised
by the Committee of Publication.
Philadelphia, American Sunday
School Union, 1832. BrMus.
                          10940
American Temperance Almanac
for 1833. New York, L. D. Dewey [1832] MWA.   10941

American Tract Society. Indiana
Branch.
   First annual report of the Indiana Branch Tract Society, auxiliary to the American Tract Society. Madison, Pr. by Arion &
Lodge, 1832. 16 p. OCHP.
                          10942
The American Unitarian Association.
   The Apostle Peter as a Unitarian. n.p., 1832. PPL; RP.
                          10943
---- Essays written for American Unitarian Association... Boston, C. Bowen (etc.) [1832-
1852?] ICU.   10944

---- The Faith once delivered to
the Saints. 4th ed. Pr. for the

American Unitarian Association.
Boston, Gray & Bowen, 1832.
24 p.   CBPac; ICMe; MeB;
MB-FA; RP.   10945

---- Tracts of the American Uni-
tarian Association.... Boston,
Gray & Bowen, 1832. 28 p.
ICMe; IEG.   10946

Americanische Stadt und Land
Calender for 1833. Philadelphia,
Conrad Zentler [1832] 29 p. CtY;
InU; MWA; PReaHi; RPB.   10947

The American's guide: comprising the Declaration of independence; the Articles of confederation; the Constitution of the
United States, and the constitutions of the several states com-
posing the Union... Philadelphia,
Towar & Hogan; Pittsburgh, D.
M. Hogan, 1832. 430 p. CtY;
GDecCT; LNP; NBuG; ScHi.
                             10948
Der Amerikanisch-Teutsche Haus-
freund und Baltimore Calender.
Auf das Jahr 1833... zum drey-
zehntenmal herausgegeben. Baltimore, Johann T. Hanzsche
[1832] 36 p. Mistake of the publisher, this is the 12th and not
the 13th ed. of the calender.
MWA; PHi.   10949

[Ames, Nathaniel] d. 1835.
Nautical reminiscences. By the
author of 'A mariner's sketches.'
Providence, W. Marshall; Hartford, W. Marshall & Co., 1832.
216 p. CtY; DLC; MWA; NcD;
PU.   10950

Amherst Academy.
Catalogue of the trustees, in-
structors and students; during the
year, ending August 23, 1832.
Amherst, J. S. and C. Adams,
1832. 8 p. MB; MH; OClWHi.
                             10951
Amherst College
(Appeal for funds. n.p., 1832)

DLC; MH.   10952

---- Catalogue of the corporation,
faculty, and students. November,
1832. Amherst, Pr. by S. and C.
Adams & Co. [1832?] 16 p. ICN;
MH; MeB; NN; NNC.   10953

---- Laws of Amherst college.
[Amherst? Mass., 1832?] 27 p.
DHEW; IU; M.   10954

--- Order of exercises at commencement, MDCCCXXXII, August 22, 10 o'clock, A. M. Amherst, Mass., Pr. by J. S. & C.
Adams, [1832] 4 p. MA; MH.
                             10955
---- Order of exercises at summer exhibition, 1832. MH. 10956

Ammah Philom, pseud.
Address to the people of New
England.... To educate indigent
young men for the ministry of the
gospel.... Listen to Ammah Philom. New-York, Reprinted from
an ed. of 1817, 1832. 85 p.
CSmH; MeBa.   10957

---- History of defection in New
England. To which is now added
an address to the people of New
England.----1832. New York?
n.p., 1832. CSmH; Ct; MH; MWA;
WHi.   10958

The ancient Christians' principle,
or, Rule of life set forth. To
which is added an extract from
Anthony Benezet's Preface to the
plain path to Christian perfection.
Philadelphia, [Pr. by Thomas
Kite & co.] for Tract Association
of Friends of Philadelphia, 1832.
12 p. MeB; NjR.   10959

Anderson, John, 1748-1830.
A Catechism, setting forth the
principles of public convenanting as
practised in the Secession church.
Albany, Packard, Hoffman & White,
1832. 80 p. MWA; UaHA; IaHA.
                             10960

Anderson, Rufus, 1796-1880.
Memoir of Catharine Brown, a
Christian Indian of the Cherokee
nation. Prepared for the Ameri-
can Sunday School Union, by Rev.
Rufus Anderson, and revised by
the Committee of publication.
Philadelphia, American Sunday-
School Union, 1832. 138, 4 p.
AU; DLC; OKU.   10961

Anderson, Thomas A.
The female's practical moni-
tor, or Guide to health. By
Thomas A. Anderson A.M. M.D.
1st ed. Pub. and sold by Z.
Jayne, of Philadelphia, Monroe
County, T. Nelson & Harding, prs.
Knoxville, T. , 1832. 118 p. T.
                         10962
Andover, Massachusetts.
Expenses of the Town of And-
over from March 4, 1831 to Mar.
2, 1832. Broadside. MH-AH.
                         10963
Andover (Mass.) Theological
Seminary.
Catalogues of the officers and
students. Jan. 1832. Andover,
1832. 12 p. CtY; NNC.   10964

---- Revival Associations.
Publications of the revival as-
sociation in the Theological Semi-
nary, Andover. v. 1, no. 1.
Andover, May, 1832- IEG; ICP;
MoSpD; OClWHi.   10965

Andral, Gabriel, 1797-1876.
A treatise on pathological an-
atomy, by G. Andral ... Tr.
from the French by Richard
Townsend... and William West...
New York, S. Wood & sons, 1832.
2 v. DSG; GFU; LNOP; MH; NhD.
                         10966
Anecdotes of missionary worth-
ies in the Moravian church.
Philadelphia, 1832. 114 p. DLC;
GDecCT; NjP; PHi; PPULC.
                         10967
Angel, William G. , 1790-1858.
Speech on the resolution to ap-

point a committee by ballot, to
investigate the affairs of the Bank
of the United States. Washington,
Pr. at the Globe Office by F. P.
Blair, 1832. 8 p. DLC; MBC;
MiD-B; RPB.   10968

Angell, Joseph Kinnicut, 1794-
1857.
A treatise on the law of private
corporations aggregate. By Joseph
K. Angell and Samuel Ames. Boston, Hilliard, Gray, Little & Wilkins, 1832. 539 p. CU; DLC;
MdBJ; NNLI; PP.   10969

Angell, Oliver, 1787-1858.
The report of a committee on
the subject of schools, with a
table shewing the number of
schools in Rhode Island, the sums
expended for their support, and
the number of scholars taught in
them. Submitted May 17, 1832.
Providence, Pr. by J. Knowles,
1832. 11 p. MWA.   10970

Annals of the United States. [New
York? 1832?] Broadside. NN.
                         10971
Annette Warington, or Sequel to
the Black Velvet Bracelet. By
the author of Early Impressions,
Temptation, etc. Boston, B. H.
Greene, 1832. 221 p. DLC; MH;
PP; TxU.   10972

Annual catalogue of fruit and hardy
ornamental trees, shrubs, herb-
aceous plants... cultivated and for
sale at the nursery of William
Kenrick in Newton, near Boston
... Boston, Pr. by I. R. Butts,
1832. 30 p. MoSB.   10973

Anti-Masonic almanack, for the
year 1833: by Edward Giddins.
Utica, William Williams [1832]
72 p. MBFM; MHi; MWA; N; NHi;
PPFM.   10974

Anti-masonic convention.
Extract from the proceedings

of the... convention. Mr. Spencer's report. Utica, William Williams, 1832. 58 p. MWA.
10975
Anti-Masonic Republican Convention of Massachusetts.
Proceedings of Anti-Masonic Republican Convention of Massachusetts. Boston, 1832. 55 p. MWA.
10976

Antimasonic State Convention of Maine, 1832.
Address before the Anti-Masonic State Convention at Maine. Hallowell, 1832. 32 p. MWA.
10977
---- Addresses of the Anti-Masonic Convention held at Augusta, July 4, 1832, to the people of Maine. [n.p.] 1832. 8 p. IaCrM.
10978

Antimasonic State Convention of Massachusetts, 3d, Worcester, 1832.
Address of the Antimasonic Republican Convention, to the people of Massachusetts. [Held at Worcester, Sept. 5th and 6th, 1832.] [Worcester, 1832] 8 p. CSmH; MWA; MiD-B; PPFM.
10979
---- Anti-Masonic pamphlets, No. 1. Memorial against the Masonic incorporations of Connecticut; together with the report and some of the debates, in the General Assembly, May session, 1832. 8 p. PPFM.
10980

---- ... Antimasonic Republican convention, of Massachusetts, held at Worcester, Sept. 5th & 6th, 1832, for the nomination of candidates for electors of president and vice president of the United States, and for governor and lt. governor of Massachusetts. Proceedings, resolutions, and address to the people. Boston, Pr. by Perkins & Marvin, 1832. 55 p. DLC; ICU; MeB;

PHi: RPB.
10981
---- ... Reply to the Declaration of 1200 Masons. [Boston, 1832] 8 p. CSmH.
10982

Anti-Masonic State Convention of Pennsylvania, Harrisburg, 1832.
Proceedings of the Democratic Anti-Masonic State Convention held at Harrisburg, Feb. 22, 1832. [Harrisburg, T. Fenn, 1832?] MWA; MnU; N; PHi.
10983
Anti-Masonic Sun. Philadelphia, By William Collum, J. Clarke [1832] InU; MWA; OClWHi; PP.
10984
Anti-Tariff Convention, Milledgeville, 1832.
Proceedings of the Anti-tariff Convention of the state of Georgia, held in Milledgeville, 1832. Milledgeville, M. J. Slade, 1832. 28 p. CtY; GU; GU-De.
10985

... An appeal to the people on the question what shall we do next? ... Columbia, Free Trade and State Rights Association, 1832. 12 p. NN; NcD; ViU.
10986
The apple girl. From the Boston juvenile miscellany. (Signed: D**.) New-York, Mahlon Day, 1832. 17 p. NN.
10987

Appleton, Nathan, 1779-1861.
Minimum duties. Remarks of Mr. Appleton, of Massachusetts, on Mr. Bouldin's resolution of inquiry, into the nature of minimum duties. Washington, Pr. at the office of Jonathan Elliot, 1832. 12 p. DLC; ICU; MH-BA; MWA; NN.
10988

---- Speech of Mr. Appleton of Massachusetts, in reply to Mr. McDuffie, of South Carolina, on the tariff. Delivered in the House of Representatives U.S. on the 30th of May, 1832. Washington, Pr. by Gales & Seaton, 1832. 24 p. CtY; DLC; MBC; OClWHi; ScCC.   10989

Application of abstract reasoning of the Christian doctrines. Originally published as an introduction to Edwards on the Will. Boston, Crocker, 1832. 163 p. IGK.   10990

Arago, Dominique Francois Jean, 1786-1853.

Tract on Comets; and particularly on the Comet that is to intersect the earth's path in October, 1832. By M. Arago, attached to the Royal Observatory at Paris. Transl. from the French, by John Farrar. Boston, Hilliard, Gray & Co., 1832. 89 p. MH; MWA; PPAmP; PSC; RPB.   10991

Aram, Eugene, 1704-1759.

The genuine account of the trial of Eugene Aram; who was convicted, at York Assizes, Eng. Aug. 5, 1759, of the murder of Daniel Clark... 1st Amer. from 11th English ed. Boston, B. Franklin Edmands, 1832. 34 p. DLC; MH; MWA (40 p.); N-L; RPB; WHi.   10992

---- Trial of Eugene for the murder of Daniel Clark, convited at York Assizes, England, Aug. 5, 1759. Boston, 1832. PPB; PPULC.   10993

Arblay, Mme. Frances (Burney) d', 1752-1840.

Evelina; or, The history of a young lady's introduction to the world. By Miss Burney. New York, J. & J. Harper, 1832. 2 vols. CtY; LU; MH; NPtW; PPULC.   10994

Archer's tower; or, The Stanhope family. New-York, Pr. by G. F. Bunce, for J. M. Morgan & Co., 1832. 68 p. MBevHi; PPULC.   10995

The Argus, Albany.

Address to the Republican State Convention... [Albany, 1832?] 24 p. IEN.   10996

Aristides, pseud.

The prospect before us; or, Strictures on the late message of the president of the United States and the report of the secretary of the treasury, in a series of letters. By Aristides... Charleston, S. C., 1832. 24 p. GU; ICU; MH; RPB; WHi.   10997

Arkansas.

Acts, passed at the seventh session of the General Assembly of the Territory of Arkansas: which was begun and held at the town of Little Rock, on Monday, the third day of October, and ended on Monday, the seventh day of November, one thousand eight hundred and thirty-one. Little Rock, Pr. by Charles P. Bertrand, pr. to the Territory, 1832. 102 p. ArL; ArU; DLC; Ia; TxU. 10998

---- Journals of the Seventh Session of the General Assembly... Pr. by Charles P. Bertrand, pr. to the Territory, 1832. 328 p. ArHi; ArL; DLC; IaU; MH-L; TxU.   10999

Armistead, Robert Alexander.

Grammatical applications of the English language; or a lucid system of keys and schemes, exemplifying the principles of Lindley Murray's English grammar, adapted to the different classes of learners and constituting a uniform standard of parsing on a plan entirely original. 1st ed. Norfolk, Pr. by T. C. Broughton, 1832. 24 p. DLC.   11000

Armstrong, John, 1758-1843.

Notice of Mr. Adams' eulogism on the life and character of James Monroe. [Washington, 1832] 36 p. DLC; MBAt; MiD-B; PHi; ScU.   11001

Arndt, Johann, 1555-1621.
Des geist-und troftruchen seligen Johann Arndst weiland Gen-
eral-Superintendenten des Fursten-
thums Lüneburg... Philadelphia,
Georg W. Mentz und Sohn, Buch-
handler, 1832. 232 p. MoInRC;
PHi. 11002

---- Paradiesgärtlein, voller
christlichen Tugenden, wie solche
zur Uebung des wahren Christen-
thums durch geistreiche Gebete in
die Seelen zu pflanzen; dem bey-
gefüget vierzehn Wundergeschich-
ten welche sich mit diesem Buch
begeben; ingleichen Morgen- und
Abendsegen auf alle Tage in der
Woche, wie auch ein dreyfaches
Register, so den Nutzen und Gebrauch dieses Buches weiset.
Philadelphia, G. W. Mentz und
Sohn, 1832. 232 p. MH; PPULC;
PHi. 11003

---- Sechs Bücher vom Wahren
Christenthum... mit beigefügtem
Lebenslauf des sel. Autors...
Philadelphia, Herausgegeben von
Georg W. Mentz und Sohn... 1832.
939, 230 p. MH; PHi; PLFM;
PReaHi. 11004

The Assembly's Shorter Catechism see Westminster Assembly of Divines.

Associate Reformed Church of
North America.
The constitution and standards
of the Associate-Reformed Church
in North America. Pittsburg,
Johnston & Stockton, 1832. 478 p.
GDecCT; KyLoP; NcU; PPPrHi;
VU. 11005

Associate Reformed Synod of the
West.
Letters of Warning, to the congregations and people under the
care of the Associate Reformed
Synod, at its Meeting... Ohio, October 1832. On revivals. St.

Clairsville, O., Pr. by Horton J.
Howard, [1832] 23 p. CSmH;
PPPrHi. 11006

Associated Friends of Ireland.
The constitution, by-laws, and
list of members of the Associated
Friends of Ireland in the city of
Baltimore, and the speech of Ro-
bert Emmett, Baltimore, James
Myres, 1832. 23 p. MdBLC.
11007
Association of Friends for the In-
struction of Poor Children.
Origin and Proceedings... Phil-
adelphia, 1832. PHi. 11008

Association of Master Carpenters,
Lexington, Ky.
Bill of prices of the association
of master carpenters, of the City
of Lexington. Adopted May 15,
1832. Copyright secured. Lexington, Ky., H. Savary & Co., book
and job printers, 1832. 35 p.
KyLx. 11009

Association Reformed Congregation.
Lectures on the general principles of moral government, as they
are exhibited in the first three
chapters of Genesis. Pastor of the
Association Reformed Congregation of Baltimore. Baltimore,
Cushing and sons, 1832. 376 p.
IaMp. 11010

An astronomical diary for 1833.
New York, David Felt [1832]
CtY; NHi. 11011

Atkins, Dudley, 1798-1845, ed.
Reports of hospital physicians,
and other documents in relation
to the epidemic cholera of 1832...
New York, G. & C. & H. Carvill,
1832. 200 p. CtY; DLC; Ia;
LNOP; MnU. 11012

Atkins, Sarah
Memoirs of John Frederic Ob-
erlin, pastor of Waldbach, in the
Bau de la Roche; from the 3d

London ed. with an introduction
by the American ed., for Cambridge, Hilliard, 1832. MA.
                            11013
---- ---- 1st Amer. ed., with a
dedication on translations by the
Rev. Luther Halsey... Pittsburgh, Luke Loomis & Co., 1832.
246 p. CtHC; ICU; MWA; PCA;
PPL.   11014

An atlas of the United States of
North America, corrected to the
present period, accompanied by
a condensed view of the history &
geography of each state compiled
from the latest official documents... London, Simpkin & Marshall; Philadelphia, T. Wardle,
1832. [58] p. MiD-B; OClWHi.
                            11015
Auber, Daniel François Esprit,
1782-1871.
   My sister dear. From the opera of Masaniello. (Song. T. The
accomp.) arranged for the Spanish guitar by L. Meignen. Philadelphia, Willig, 1832. [2] p. MB.
                            11016
Auburn.   Benevolent Association.
Constitution of the Benevolent
Association, Auburn. [Auburn,
1832] [4] p. NAuT.   11017

Auburn Theological Seminary.
   Catalogue of the officers and
students of the Theological Seminary, at Auburn, New York, January, 1832. Auburn, Pr. by Henry Oliphant, 1832. 8 p. MH;
MWA; NAuT.   11018

Audubon, John James, 1780-1851.
   Ornithological biography, or,
An account of the habits of the
birds of the United States of
America; accompanied by descriptions of the objects represented
in the work entitled The birds of
America, and interspersed with
delineations of American scenery
... manners. Vol. 1, Philadelphia;
E. L. Carey & A. Hart; vol. 2,

Boston, Hilliard, Gray & Co.; vol.
3-5, Edinburgh, A. & C. Black,
1832-1849. 5 vols. DLC; ICJ;
KyU; MH; PPULC.   11019

[Austen, Jane] 1775-1817.
   Elizabeth Bennet, or, Pride
and Prejudice: a novel... By the
author of "Sense and Sensibility"
...1st Amer. from 3rd London
ed. Philadelphia, Carey & Lea,
1832. 2 Vols. DLC; InU; MB; MH;
PPA; PPULC.   11020

---- Mansfield park: a novel.
By Miss Austen, author of "Pride
and Prejudice," "Emma," &c.
&c. Philadelphia, Carey & Lea,
1832. 2 Vols. PPULC; PU; TNP.
                            11021
---- Persuasion. By Miss Austen... Philadelphia, [Pr. by Griffs
& Dickinson] Carey & Lea, 1832.
2 vols. CtHT; ICBB; MB; NjR;
PU.   11022

Authentic obituaries of Sabbath
school children. Boston, Massachusetts Sabbath School Union,
1832. 24 p. MB.   11023

Averill, Chester, 1804-1836.
   An address delivered before a
branch of the American Associa-
tion, at Schenectady. By Chester
Averill. Schenectady, Pr. by S.
S. Riggs, 1832. 22 p. CtY; MH;
NjPT; OClWHi; PPL.   11024

---- Facts regarding the disinfecting powers of chlorine: with
an explanation of the mode in
which it operates, and with directions how it should be applied for
disinfecting purposes: in a letter
from Chester Averill, A.M. to the
Hon. John I. De Graff... Schenectady, Pr. by S. S. Riggs, 1832.
23 p. CtHT; DSG; MB; NBMS;
PPL-R.   11025

Aydelott, Benjamin Parham,
1795-1880.

(The) Rev. B. P. Aydelott in
answer to the Rt. Rev. P. Chase.
Cincinnati, 1832. 45 p. IHi; MBC;
NNG; OCHP; PPL.   11026

B

Babbage, Charles, 1792-1871.
   On the economy of machinery
and manufactures. By Charles Babbage. Philadelphia, Carey & Lea,
1832. 282 p. GU; IaU; LU; NNF;
RNR; ViU.   11027

Babcock, Rufus, 1798-1875.
   Sermons on various subjects,
etc. Portland, Zion's Advocate,
1832. Williamson.   11028

Bache, A[lexander] D[allas]
1806-1867.
   Notice of experiments on electricity developed by magnetism.
Communicated to the Journal of the
Franklin Institute, by A. D. Bache.
Philadelphia, J. Harding, pr.,
1832. 8 p. DLC; PPL; PPULC.
                               11029
---- On the diurnal variation of the
horizontal needle. [Philadelphia,
1832] NN; PPAmP; PU.   11030

---- Safety apparatus for steam
boilers, by A. D. Bache... With an
account of the experiments made
upon it, by the Committee on explosions of the Franklin institute...
[Philadelphia? 1832?] 11 p. DLC;
MH.   11031

Bache, Richard, 1794-1836. A
view of the valley of the Mississippi... See under Baird, Robt.
1798-1863.

Bacheler, Origen, and Robert Dale
Owen.
   Discussion on the existence of
God, and the authenticity of the Bi-
ble. Between Origen Bacheler, and
Robt. Dale Owen. 2 Vols. New
York, Pub. by the authors, 1832.
ICP; OC; OCIW; OSW; PPM.
                               11032

Bachi, Pietro, 1787-1853.
   Comparative view of the Italian
and Spanish languages, by Pietro
Bachi. Boston, Cottons and Bar-
nard, 1832. CtY; MBAt; MH;
NNC; RP.   11033

---- Rudiments of the Italian language: or, Easy lessons in spelling and reading, with an abridgment of the grammar; adopted to
the capacity of children. By Pietro Bachi... Boston, Carter,
Hendee and co., 1832. 136 p.
CtY; KyBC; MH; ScCC; TxU-T.
                               11034

Backus, Henry T.
   An oration, delivered on the
centennial anniversary of the birth
of Washington... Feb. 22, 1832.
Norwich [Conn.] J. Dunham, 1832.
CSmH; DLC; MBAt; NN.   11035

Backus, Samuel.
   "Man a living soul:" a sermon
preached at the installation of
Rev. Charles Fitch over the
church and society in Western,
Mass., June 6, 1832. Brookfield,
Mass., E. Merriam & Co., 1832.
27 p. DLC; M; MAnP; RPB.
                               11036
[Bacon, David Francis] 1813-1866.
   Missionary museum; or, An ac-
count of missionary enterprises.
in conversations between a mother
and her children... New Haven,
J. L. Cross, 1832. 2 vols. CtY;
ICBB; MH-AH; NNMr; NcD.
                               11037
Bacon, Francis, Viscount St. Al-
bans, 1561-1626.
   Moral, Economical and Politi-
cal Essays. A new ed. Boston,
C. D. Strong, 1832. MshM.
                               11038
Bacon, Leonard, 1802-1881.
   The Christian doctrine of stew-
ardship in respect to property.
A sermon, preached at the re-
quest of the Young Men's Benevo-
lent Society, of New Haven,
Conn., by Leonard Bacon, pastor

of the First Church in New-
Haven. New Haven, Nathan Whit-
ing, 1832. 20 p. CtY; ICP; MH;
NjR; PPPrHi.   11039

---- The hopefulness of efforts
for the promotion of peace. A
discourse, pronounced in the
Centre Church in Hartford, at the
celebration of the anniversary of
the Hartford County Peace Society; on the evening of the Lord's
day, June 10, 1832. By Leonard
Bacon, pastor of the First
Church in New Haven. Hartford,
Pr. by Philemon Canfield, 1832.
26 p. CSmH; CtY; MAnP; MH;
MH-AH; MWA; NN; NNC; NjR.
                               11040
Badger, Willard.
    A circular in regard to es-
tablishing a building for mechanics, with a cast iron foundry,
and the sale of stock. Boston,
Nov. 1, 1832. [1] p. MHi. 11041

La Bagatelle; intended to intro-
duce very young children to some
knowledge of the French lan-
guage. Boston, Carter & Hen-
dee, 1832. 152 p. MB; MH.
                               11042
Bailey, Ebenezer.
  . The young ladies class book.
By Ebenezer Bailey... Boston,
Lincoln & Edmonds, New York,
Collins & Hanney (etc., etc.)
1832. 408 p. ICU; MH; Nh;
RPB; TxGR.   11043

Bailey's Franklin Almanac for
1833. Calculated by Joshua
Sharp. Philadelphia, Lydia R.
Bailey [1832] MWA.   11044

Baillie, Joanna, 1762-1851.
    The complete poetical works
of Joanna Baillie. 1st Amer. ed.
Philadelphia, Carey & Lea, 1832.
574 p. CtY; DLC; GHi; ICMe;
OMC; PPA; RNR.   11045

[Baird, Robert] 1798-1863.
    View of the valley of the Mis-
sissippi: or, The emigrant's and
traveller's guide to the West...
Philadelphia, H. S. Tanner, 1832.
341 p. CtHT; IaU; NjR; OO;
WaS.   11046

[Baker, Artemas]
    Circular, to the Honorable the
Representatives of the people of
Ohio in the Congress of the
United States. n. p. [1832] 16 p.
MB; OClWHi.   11047

Baker, Joseph, b. 1788.
    The natural physician's book
of remedies, containing a patent
right for doctoring. 2d ed. Chil-
licothe, O., 1832. 172, 16 p.
N; OCLloyd; OClWHi; OOxM.
                               11048
Baker, Pacificus, 1695-1774.
    The devout communicant...
Baltimore [1832] DLC.   11049

Baker, William Deal, 1812-1876.
    The Saturniad: being a full &
true account of the rise, progress & downfall of the University
of Quilsylvane, in three cantos,
by Hyton Hosmot. Philadelphia,
1832. 63 p. CSmH; CtY; DLC;
PHi; PU.   11050

Baldwin, Abraham Chittenden,
1804-1887.
    A sermon, preached in the
Unitarian Congregational Church
in Northborough, at the funeral
of Isaac B. Davis, who died, January 7, 1832, aged 22. By Abraham C. Baldwin, pastor of the
Evang. Congregational Church in
Berlin, Mass. Boston, Peirce
& Parker, 1832. CoCsC; CtY;
MHi; RPB.   11051

Baldwin, Henry.
    Hypocrisy unmasked in letters
to Stephen Simpson... Philadelphia, Probasco, 1832. PPiU;

PPULC. 11052

Baldwin, John Dennison, 1809-1883.
A scriptural view of the Messiah: being the substance of a sermon delivered in the Methodist Chapel, Dighton, Mass.... May 27, 1832. Taunton, Edmund Anthony, 1832. 16 p. MBC; MBNMHi; MHi; MnHi. 11053

Baldwin, Theron, 1801-1870.
Historical sketch of the origin, progress, and wants of Illinois College. New York [J. T. West] 1832. 16 p. CtY; ICHi; MBC; PPPrHi. 11054

---- ---- 2d. ed. New York, Pr. by John T. West, 1832. 16 p. CtY; ICN; NNUT; PPPrHi; RPB. 11055
Baldwin-Lima-Hamilton Corporation.
Description of Philadelphia and Eddystone plant. 1832. 11056

Baldwin Locomotive Works. See Baldwin-Lima-Hamilton Corporation.

Balfour, Walter, 1776-1852.
An inquiry into the Scriptural import of the words Sheol, Hades, Tartarus, and Gehenna: all translated Hell,...3d ed. By Walter Balfour. Boston, B. B. Mussey, 1832. 347 p. IAIS; KyLoP; MeB; NjP; OHi; PHi; TNM. 11057

[Ball, Charles]
Life of a Negro slave. [n. p., n. d.] 32 p. "this account is abridged from a lengthy narrative published in New York in 1832." CtY; IEN; TNF. 11058

---- Slavery in the U. S. a narrative of the life & adventures of Charles Ball, a black man, who lived forty years in Maryland, South Carolina, & Georgia, as a slave. New York, John S. Taylor, 1832. CtY; NIC. 11059

Ball, Eli.
A connected view of a correspondence between Eli Ball...and John Hersey, on the subject of Baptism. Baltimore, Armstrong, 1832. 36 p. NcD; NcWfC; NcWsW. 11060

Ballou, Adin, 1803-1890.
An argument on "Punishment and forgiveness, and the doctrines of penalty and pardon" between Revs. Adin Ballou and Barton Ballou. Providence, Pr. by H. H. Brown, 1832. 32 p. MBC; MBUPH; MHope; MMeT-Hi. 11061

Ballou, Hosea, 1771-1852.
Great sermons delivered on various occasions, from important passages of scripture. Boston, 1832. 350 p. OO. 11062

---- Notes on the Parables of the New Testament. Scripturally illustrated and argumentatively defended. By Hosea Ballou...5th ed. stereotyped. Revised by the author. Boston, Marsh, Capen & Lyon, 1832. 297p. GDecCT; MBAt; MiU; NjPT; VtFah. 11063

---- Select Sermons, delivered on various occasions, from important passages of scripture by Hosea Ballou, pastor of the Second Universalist Society in Boston. Boston, Marsh, Capen and Lyon, 1832. 350 p. DLC; GDecCT; ICP; MBAt; TNM. 11064

---- A series of lecture sermons ... By Hosea Ballou ...2d ed. Stereotyped. Revised by the author. Boston, Marsh, Capen & Lyon, 1832. 375p. DLC; GDecCT; ICBB; MMeT-Hi; NjPT. 11065

---- Sermon delivered in Hingham, at the funeral of Mrs.

Mary Gardner. By Rev. Hosea
Ballou. Boston, Pr. at the office of the Universalist, 1832.
16 p. ICN; MMeT-Hi; RPB.
                                    11066
---- Sermons on Important Doctrinal Subjects. By Hosea Ballou,
... To which are added critical
and explanatory notes. Together
with a brief memoir of the Author, written by himself. Boston,
Pr. B. W. Bazin, pub. at the
Trumpet Office, 1832. 176 p.
CtY; ICP; KyLxT; MH; NhPet.
                                    11067
---- A treatise on atonement;
the necessity and nature of atonement, and its glorious consequences in the final reconciliation of all men to holiness and
happiness. 4th ed. Boston,
March, Capen & Lyon, 1832.
228p. CtY; DLC; GDecCT;
MBC; NNUT.   11068

Baltimore. City Council. First
Branch.
    Journal of the proceeding of the
first branch of the city council of
Baltimore. January session, 1832.
Baltimore, Sands and Neilson,
1832. 371 p. MdBB; MdHi. 11069

---- ---- Second Branch.
    Journal of the proceedings of
the second branch of the city council of Baltimore. January session,
1832. Baltimore, Sands & Neilson, 1832. 131 p. MdBE; MdHi.
                                    11070
---- Mayor.
    Mayor's communication, Jan-
uary 2, 1832. Baltimore, J. Robinson, 1832. 9 p. DLC; IU; Md-
LR; NN.   11071

---- Ordinances, etc.
    The Ordinances of the Mayor
and City Council of Baltimore,
passed at the extra session in
1831, and at the January session,
1832. To which is annexed,

sundry acts of Assembly, passed
Dec. session. 1831; A list of the
officers of the Corporation, the
summary of the Register, and
the annual Reports and Returns
of the officers of the corporation.
Baltimore, J. Robinson, 1832.
154 + 148 p. ICJ; MH-L; MdBB;
MdHi; NNLI.   11072

Baltimore and Ohio Railroad
Company.
    Communication from the pres-
ident of the Baltimore and Ohio
Railroad Company, to the legislature of Maryland, enclosing surveys and estimates of the railroad from Baltimore to Washington. Annapolis, Jeremiah Hughes,
1832. 13 p. NN.   11073

---- Memorial of, for a subscription to its stock. [Washington?
1832] CtY; IU; MBAt; MWA;
NjP.   11074

---- Report from the president
and directors of the Baltimore
and Ohio rail road company, to
the executive of the state of
Maryland. December, 1832. 6 p.
MdHi.   11075

---- Report of the city directors
of the Baltimore and Ohio Rail
Road, to the mayor and city council of Baltimore, n. p. [1832?]
MiU-T; NN.   11076

---- Report of the managers of
the Baltimore and Ohio Rail Road
Company, to the executive of Maryland. Annapolis, J. Hughes,
1832. 8 p. NN.   11077

Baltimore and Port Deposits Railroad Company.
    An act to incorporate the Balti-
more and Port Deposits Railroad
Company. Baltimore, James Lucas & E. K. Deaver, 1832. 15 p.
MdHi; NN; NNE.   11078

Baltimore Life Insurance Company.

Proposal and rates of the Baltimore Life Insurance Company ... Baltimore, Pr. by John D. Fay, 1832. 26 p. DLC; MH-BA; MdHi; MHi; NjP.   11079

Baltimore Typographical Society.
Constitution and by-laws of the Baltimore Typographical Society. Adopted June 2, 1832; to which is added, the list of prices. Baltimore, Pr. by W. Woody, 1832. 19 p. DLC.   11080

Baltimore Young Men's Society.
An address to the young men of Baltimore; with the constitution, by-laws and standing rules, instituted May, 1832. Baltimore, Sands & Neilson, 1832. 15 p. MdBLC.   11081

Bancroft, Aaron, 1755-1839.
To young householders in the Second Congregational Society, Worcester [1832] 20 p. ICN; MH-AH; MWA; MHi; NN. 11082

Bangs, Nathan, 1778-1862.
An authentic history of the missions under the care of the missionary society of the Methodist Episcopal Church. By Nathan Bangs... New York, J. Emory & B. Waugh, 1832. 258 p. CSmH; ICU; NB; OCHP; WHi.   11083
---- A discourse on the death of the Rev. Dr. Adam Clarke, delivered in Green-street church, in the city of New-York, on the evening of October 30, 1832. By Nathan Bangs, D.D. ...New York, B. Waugh & T. Mason, 1832. 28 p. CtY; ICP; MdBJ; TxDaM; PPPrHi.   11084

---- History of missions under the care of the Methodist Church. By Nathan Bangs. New York, n.p., 1832. NjMD; ODW. 11085

---- The life of the Rev. Freeborn Garrettson: Compiled from his printed and manuscript journals, and other authentic documents. By Nathan Bangs...3d ed., revised and corr. New York, Emory & Waugh, 1832. 342 p. CtY; ICN; NcD; NN; NjR; OO.   11086

---- ---- 5th ed. New York, Carlton & Lanahan (etc., etc.) 1832. 294 p. IEG; MB; NNUT; NRed.   11087

[Banim, John] 1798-1842.
Damon and Pythias, a tragedy, in five acts. By Richard Shiel, Esq., author of The Apostate, &c. As performed at the Covent Garden and Baltimore Theatres. Baltimore, J. Robinson, 1832. 70 p. MWA; NN.   11088

---- The smuggler: a tale. By the author of "Tales by the O'-Hara family," etc. New York, J. & J. Harper, 1832. 2 v. MB; MdBP; NCH; NNS; Vi.   11089

Bank of America, New York.
Abstract of the Charter...With a synopsis of the Laws concerning & regulating Banks. New York, Pr. by Prior & Bowne, 1832. 8 p. NNC; PHi; PPULC.   11090

Bank of the United States.
Documents from N. Biddle, president of the Bank of United States, to Hon. G. M. Dallas, Chairman of the Select committee of the Senate on the memorial of the Bank of the United States in reply to the resolutions offered by Mr. Benton and adopted by the Senate on the 31st January, 1832. [Washington, 1832] DLC; MH.   11091
---- Questions "on the influence of the Bank of the United States upon trade." [1832] PPULC; PHi.   11092

---- Questions on the subject of branch bank notes and drafts. [1832] PPULC; PHi.   11093

---- Reports of the committee of inquiry... Washington, 1832. PPL; PPULC; PHi.   11094

---- Select Committee to examine the books & proceedings.
Minority report... Washington, Gales, 1832. 29 p. PPULC; PU.   11095
Banks and a paper currency...
See Ronaldson, Richard.

Banner of truth.   Lexington, Ky. volume 1, no. 1-5, November 1832-March 1833.   ICU; KyLxT.   11096
Baptist Education Society of New York.
Fifteenth annual meeting... at Hamilton, June 5, 1832. Utica, From press of Bennett & Bright, 1832. 22 p. CSmH; MB; NRCR; PCA.   11097

Baptist Education Society of Ohio.
Annual meeting of the Ohio Baptist Education Society and of the trustees of the Granville Literary & Theological Institution, October 6, 1832. Cincinnati, Pr. by Whetstone & Johnson, 1832. 23 p.   PCA.   11098

Baptist Education Society of the Young Men of Providence.
Constitution... formed December 2, 1831. [Providence, 1832] 4 p. RHi.   11099

Baptists.   Alabama. Alabama Association.
Minutes of the Thirteenth Annual Session of the Alabama Baptist Association, begun and held at Mount Pleasant Meeting House, Dallas County, Alabama...1832. [Montgomery] Planter's Gazette Office, 1832. 11 p. Ar.   11100

---- ---- Bethlehem Association.
Minutes of the Bethlehem Baptist Association convened at the Murder Creek Church, Conecuh County...1832. Cahawba [Ala.] Pr. by G. W. and W. W. Gayle, 1832. 11 p. Ar.   11101

---- Connecticut. State Convention.
Proceedings of the Connecticut Baptist convention, Connecticut Baptist Education Society, Connecticut branch of the Baptist General Tract Society, and the Connecticut Baptist Sunday School Society, at their annual meetings held at Middletown, June, 1832. Hartford [Pr. by Philemon Canfield] 1832. 34 p. NRAB; PCA.   11102
---- ---- Stonington Union Association.
Minutes of the fifteenth anniversary of the Stonington North-Stonington, June 20 and 21, 1832. 8 p. NHC-S; PCA.   11103

---- ---- Union Association.
... Anniversary of the Union Baptist Association ...23d. 1832. [Danbury? Conn.] Pr. at the Repository office [1832] 1 vol. CSmH.   11104

---- Georgia. Convention.
Minutes 1832-1840 [Washington, News office, 1832-40]. 3 v. GMilvC.   11105

---- ---- Flint River Association.
Minutes of the Flint River Association, convened at Shoal Creek, Pike County, on the 20th, 21st, 22d, and 23d days of October, 1832. 8 p. NRAB.   11106

---- Illinois. Blue River Ass'n.
New Association... Contains minutes of a meeting held with the Mount Zion Church, Pike County, Illinois, November 10-12, 1832, for the organization of the

body which was later named the
Blue River Association of United
Baptists. [Jacksonville, 1832]
IAlB; ISBHi.   11107

---- ---- Illinois Association.
Minutes of the Illinois United
Baptist Association, began [sic]
and held at Elkhorn Church
Meeting House, Washington Co.
Ill. Oct. 6, 7, and 8, 1832. [Ed-
wardsville? 1832] 4 p. ISBHi;
NRAB.   11108

---- Illinois and Missouri.
Friends to Humanity.
Minutes of three separate as-
sociations, held by the Baptized
Churches of Christ, Friends to
Humanity, in Missouri & Illinois,
for the year 1832. [Rock Spring,
1832] 8 p. ISBHi; NRAB.   11109

---- Indiana. Coffee Creek Association.
Minutes. Sixth annual meeting
of the Coffee Creek Baptist Association, begun and held at Ebenezer meeting house, Jackson
county, Indiana, 1st, 2d and 3d
days of September, 1832. [Pr.
by Arion & Lodge, Madison] 1832.
4 p. InFrlC; NRCR-S.   11110

---- ---- Convention.
Proceedings... v.1- 1832-
Indianapolis, 1832- ICU; MiD-B;
OClWHi; NRAB; PCC.   11111

---- ---- Flat Rock Association.
Minutes of the Flat Rock Association of Baptists, begun and
held at Flat Rock meeting house,
Bartholomew county, Indiana, the
first Friday, Saturday, and Sunday in October, eighteen hundred
and thirty-two. [Pr. by Douglass
& Maguire, Indianapolis] 1832.
7 p. InFrlC; TxDaHi.   11112

---- ---- Indianapolis Association.
Minutes of the Indianapolis

Association, held at Friendship
church, Morgan county, Indiana,
on the 24th, 25th, and 26th days
of August, 1832. [Pr. by Douglass & Maguire] 1832. 7 p. ICU;
NRCR-S; PCA.   11113

---- ---- Laughery Association.
Minutes of the fifteenth annual
meeting of the Laughery Association of Baptists, held at Bear
Creek meeting house, Dearborn
Co. Ind., in 3d Friday, September
1832. 4 p. InFrlC.   11114

---- ---- Lost River Association.
Minutes of the seventh annual
meeting of the Lost River Association, held at Union meeting-
house, Washington county, Indiana,
on the first Saturday, Lord's day,
and Monday in September, 1832.
4 p. InFrlC.   11115

---- ---- Madison Association.
Minutes. 1832- PCA. 11116

---- ---- Union Association.
Minutes of the eighth annual
Union Association of Baptists,
held at Little Flock church meeting house, Sullivan county, Indiana convened on Friday the 14th
day of September, 1832. [Pr. at
the office of the Vincennes Gaz.]
1832. 4 p. InFrlC.   11117

---- ---- White River Association.
Minutes of the White River
Association, held at Indian Creek
meeting house, Lawrence county,
on the 2d Saturday in August,
1832. 4 p. InFrlC.   11118

---- Kentucky. Convention.
Minutes of the First Session
of the Kentucky Baptists Convention, held in Bardstown, on the
29th, 30th, and 31st days of
March, 1832. Frankford, Ky.,
Pr. by A. G. Hodges & Wm. M.

Todd, 1832. 8 p. ICU; PCA.
                                11119
---- ---- West Union Association.
    Minutes. 1832- PCA. 11120

---- Maine, Bowdoinham Association.
    Minutes of the 46th anniver-
sary of the Bowdoinham Association, holden in Litchfield, Wednesday and Thursday, Sept. 26 and
27, 1832. 8 p. PCA.   11121

---- ---- Cumberland Association.
    Minutes of the 21st anniversary
of the Cumberland Baptist Association, held at the meeting house
of the First Baptist Church in
Brunswick, Me., on Wednesday
and Thursday, Aug. 29 and 30,
1832. Portland, Pr. at the office
of Zion's Advocate, 1832. 10 p.
PCA.   11122

---- ---- Eastern Maine Association.
    Minutes of the 14th anniver-
sary of the Eastern Maine Association. Holden in the Baptist
Meeting-house in Franklin, on
Wednesday and Thursday, September 5 and 6, 1832. Ellsworth,
Robert Grant, 1832. 16 p. PCA.
                                11123
---- ---- Lincoln Association.
    Minutes of the Lincoln Asso-
ciation held with the Third Baptist Church. Thomaston, Geo. W.
Nichols, 1832. 8 p. MiD-B.
                                11124
---- ---- Oxford Association.
    Minutes of the 4th anniversary
of the Oxford Baptist Association,
held at the Baptist meeting-house
in Livermore, on Wednesday and
Thursday, Oct. 3 and 4, 1832.
Norway, Wm. E. Goodnow, 1832.
12 p. PCA.   11125

---- ---- Penobscot Association.
    Minutes of the 7th... held at
the Baptist meeting-house in

Parkman, 1832. Bangor, Burton
& Carter, 1832. 16 p. MeBa.
                                11126
---- ---- Waldo Association.
    Minutes... held at Hope... Hal-
lowell, Me., Glazier, Masters &
Co., 1832. 8 p. MNtcA; PCA.
                                11127
---- ---- York Association.
    Minutes of the York Baptist
Association, holden at the Baptist
meeting-house in Sanford, Me.,
June 13 and 14, 1832. Together
with an exhibit of the state of the
churches. Portland (Me.), Zion's
Advocate, 1832. 22 p. ICN.
                                11128
---- Maryland. Baltimore Associ-
ation.
    Minutes of the Baltimore Bap-
tist Association, held by appoint-
ment, with the Warren Church,
Baltimore County, May 17, 18,
19 & 20, 1832. [Washington, D.C.,
Pr. by S. C. Ustick, 1832] 12 p.
PCA; ViRU.   11129

---- Massachusetts.
    Minutes of a convention held in
the Federal Street Baptist Meeting-
House, Boston, May 30, 1832, to
form a Sabbath school union in the
Baptist denomination in Massachusetts. Boston, Pr. by J. Howe,
1832. 12 p. MWA; PCA. 11130

---- ---- Barnstable Association.
    Minutes. 1832- PCA. 11131

---- ---- Berkshire County Association.
    Minutes of the fifth anniversary
of the Berkshire county Baptist
Association, held at North Adams,
Mass., May 30, 1832. 8 p. MPiB.
                                11132
---- ---- Boston Association.
    Twenty-first anniversary. Min-
utes of the twenty-first anniversary of the Boston Baptist Association held at the Baptist meeting
house, Newton, on Wednesday and
Thursday, Sept. 19 & 20, 1832.

Boston, Pr. by Lincoln & Edmands [1832?] 32 p. CBB; IAIS; LNB; MNtCA; MiD-B. 11133

---- ---- Convention.
Minutes of the Massachusetts Baptist Convention, held in Springfield, October 31st and November 1st, 1832. Eighth anniversary. Worcester, Pr. by Moses W. Grout, 1832. 32 p. NRAB. 11134

---- ---- General Association.
Minutes of the General Association of Massachusetts at their meeting in Northampton, June 1832 with the narrative of the state of religion and the pastoral address. Boston, Pr. by Crocker and Brewster, 1832. 19 p. IEG. 11135

---- ---- Salem Association.
Minutes of the fifth anniversary of the Salem Baptist Association, held at... Amesbury Mills... September 26 and 27, 1832. Boston, Pr. by Lincoln & Edmands [1832] 24 p. CSmH; IAIS; MBevHi; MiD-B. 11136

---- ---- Worcester County.
Articles of faith and covenant, adopted by several Baptist churches in the County of Worcester. Worcester, Pr. by Moses W. Grout, 1832. 23 p. ICN; MWA; MiD-B; NRAB; RNHi. 11137

---- Michigan. Saint Joseph River Association.
Minutes. 1832- PCA. 11138

---- Mississippi. Pearl River Association.
Minutes of the... convened at Hebron Church, Lawrence County, on Saturday, September 8th, 1832. Monticello [sic] J. R. Chambers, 1832. 13 p. LNB. 11139

---- Missouri. Salem Association.

Minutes of the Salem Association, held at Fulton, Callaway County, Mo. on the 1st, 2d and 3d September, 1832. Columbia, Mo., N. Patten [1832] MoHi. 11140

---- New Jersey.
.... Of the Central New Jersey Baptist Association, held in the meeting-house of the Baptist Church of Nottingham Square, October 17th and 18th, A. D. 1832. 8 p. PCA. 11141

---- ---- State Convention.
Minutes of the third annual meeting of the New Jersey Baptist State Convention for missionary purposes; held at the meeting house of the Highstown Baptist Church, November 7, 1832. Trenton, Pr. at the Union Office, 1832. 12 p. PCA. 11142

---- New York.
Minutes of a convention held at Stephentown, Rennselaer County, May 1st, 1832, for the purpose of organizing a new Baptist Association. Kinderhood, Pr. by E. Pitts, 1832. 8 p. NRAB. 11143

---- ---- Black River Association.
Minutes of the Twenty-third Anniversary of the Black River Baptist Association, convened at Adams, Jefferson County, N.Y., June 13th and 14th, 1832. Watertown, Pr. by Knowlton & Rice, 1832. 12 p. PCA. 11144

---- ---- Bottskill Ass'n.
Minutes of the Bottskill Baptist Association held at Kingsbury, August 22 and 23, 1832; together with their circular. Union Village, Pr. by W. Lansing, 1832. 8 p. NRCR. 11145

---- ---- Cayuga Baptist Association.
Thirty-second session of the

Cayuga Baptist Association held
in Throopsville, Cayuga County,
N. Y. On the 19th and 20th of
September, 1832. Containing their
circular and corresponding letters
... Auburn, Pr. by H. Oliphant,
1832. 12 p. NHC-S; PCA. 11146

---- ---- Holland Purchase Association.
Minutes of the Annual Meeting
of the Holland Purchase Baptist
Association; held with the church
in Eden, August 22d and 23d,
1832 with their Circular and Corresponding Letters. Buffalo, Pr.
by Steele & Faxon, 1832. 16 p.
NHC.   11147

---- ---- Hudson River Association.
The Seventeenth Anniversary of
the Hudson River Baptist Associ-
ation--statement of belief--held in
the Meeting-House of the First
Baptist Church, Albany, June 20
& 21, 1832. New York, Pr. by
G. F. Bunce, 1832. 16 p. ICU;
PCA.   11148

---- ---- Madison Association.
On the Scripture qualification
for partaking of the Lord's Supper. Being the annual circular
letter of the Madison Baptist Association for 1832. Utica, From
the Press of Bennett & Bright,
1832. 8 p. PScrHi.   11149

---- ---- Missionary Convention.
Minutes of the Eleventh Anniversary of the Baptist Missionary Convention of the State of
New York; held at Rome, Oct 17,
& 18, 1832; with the Proceedings
and Report of the Board, an account of the State of Religion
within the Bounds of its operations, as an address to the
Churches, Treasurer's Report,
&c. Utica, Pr. by Bennett &
Bright, 1832. 32 p. InHi; MWA;
PCA.   11150

---- ---- New York Association.
Minutes of the Forty-Second
Anniversary of the New-York
Baptist Association, held in the
Meeting-House of the Baptist
Church, Scotch-Plains, New-Jer-
sey, May 29, 30, 31-1832. 20 p.
PCA.   11151

---- ---- Ontario Association.
Minutes of the Nineteenth An-
niversary, of the Ontario Baptist
Association, convened at Benton,
Yates County, on Wednesday and
Thursday, September 26 & 27,
1832. Seneca Falls, Pr. by Wm.
Child, 1832. 16 p. PCA.   11152

---- ---- Otsego Association.
Minutes of the thirty-seventh
anniversary of the Otsego Baptist
Association, held at Salisbury,
Herkimer County, N. Y., Wednes-
day & Thursday, Aug. 29th & 30th,
1832. Utica, Pr. by Bennett &
Bright, 1832. 20 p. NHC-S;
NRC-R; PCA.   11153

---- ---- Seneca Association.
Minutes of the tenth annual session... in Elmira, Tioga County,
N. Y. ...September 5th and 6th,
1832. [Ithaca, Mack & Andrus,
1832] 8 p. NN.   11154

---- ---- Union Association.
Twenty-Third Anniversary of
the Union Baptist Association,
held with the Second Baptist
Church in Danbury, Conn. September 5th and 6th, 1832. 8 p.
PCA.   11155

---- North Carolina. Beulah Association.
Minutes. 1832- PCA. 11156

---- ---- Free-Will Association.
Minutes of the Free-Will Baptist Association, for the year
1832, held at Avary's Creek Meeting-House, Buncombe County,
N. C. October 5, 6 & 7, 1832.

Rutherfordton, Pr. by Roswell Elmer, Jr., 1832. 8 p. MoSM.
11157

---- Ohio. Bethel Association.

Minutes of the Bethel Baptist Association, held at Bethel Meeting House, on the 21st and 22nd of September, 1832. Together with their circular letter. Batavia, O., Pr. by David Morris, 1832. 6 p. NHC-C; OClWHi.
11158

---- ---- Cleveland Assocation.

Minutes of the 1st meeting, 1832. Cleveland, 1832. DLC; OCl; OClWHi; OO.
11159

---- ---- East Fork of the Little Miami Association.

Minutes of the East Fork of the Little Miami Baptist Association, held at East Fork Meeting House, Clermont County, Ohio, on the 31st of August, and the two following days [1832] 8 p. OClWHi; PCA.
11160

---- ---- Huron Association.

Minutes of the eleventh annual meeting of the Huron Baptist Association, held at Henrietta, Lorain County, Ohio, August 24, 25 & 26, 1832. Together with circular letter, and minutes of the Huron Baptist Missionary Society. Norwalk, Ohio, Pr. by S. Preston & Co., 1832. 8 p. OClWHi.
11161

---- ---- Little Miami Union Regular Assocation.

Looker & Reynolds, Printers. Cincinnati. Minutes of the Little Miami Union Regular Baptist Association, held at the Little Miami Meeting House, Columbia Township, Hamilton Co., O., on 24th, 25th, & 26th August, 1832. The Introductory Sermon was preached by Elder Hezekiah Smith, from Acts, 11 chap. and last part of the 23d verse. After which letters from the following

churches were received and their Messengers' names enrolled...
[1832] 4 p. OClWHi.
11162

---- ---- Meigs'-Creek Association.

Minutes of the seventh anniversary of Meigs-Creek Baptist Association, held by appointment, with the Marietta Church, at the Newport, Washington County, Ohio. On the 16th, 17th, 18th, and 19th days of August, A.D. 1832. Marietta, Pr. by R. Prentiss, 1832. 8 p. PCA.
11163

---- ---- Miami Association.

Minutes of the Miami Baptist Association; held at Bethel Meeting House, Warren County, Ohio, on the 7th, 8th and 9th of September 1832. 8 p. OClWHi; PCA.
11164

---- ---- Rocky Mountain Association.

Minutes. 1832. PCA.
11165

---- ---- Rocky River Association. See Baptists. Ohio. Cleveland Association.

---- ---- Salem Baptists Association.

Minutes...held at Troy Church; Athens Co., on the 6th, 7th and 8th days of October, 1832. Athens, Pr. by Maxon, 1832. 8 p. NHC-S; OClWHi.
11166

---- Pennsylvania. Central Union Association.

Minutes of the Central Union Association, formed in Philadelphia, July 31st, 1832. Philadelphia, Pr. for the Association, by Martin & Boden, 1832. 12 p. PCA; PCC.
11167

---- ---- Centre Association.

Second Annual Publication, Minutes of the Centre Baptist Association, held in the meeting-house of the Birmingham Church,

Huntingdon County, Pennsylvania,
August 17, 18, 1832. Bellefonte,
Pa., Pr. by John Bigler, 1832.
8 p. PCA.   11168

---- ---- Philadelphia Association.
Minutes of the Philadelphia
Baptist Ass'n., held by appointment at Southampton, Bucks County, October 2nd, 3rd, & 4th,
1832. 16 p. PCA.   11169

---- ---- State Annual.
Minutes of the fifth annual
meeting of the Baptist Missionary Association of Pennsylvania
held at the meeting-house of the
First Baptist Church of Philadelphia, in Second Street, June 5,
1832, with the Constitution and
the annual report of the Board of
Managers, etc. Philadelphia, Pr.
by T. W. Ustick, 1832. 16 p.
PCA.   11170

---- Rhode Island.
Minutes of the Rhode Island
Baptist anniversaries. Providence, 1832. RHi; RPB.   11171

---- ---- Charitable Baptist Society.
Charter and by-laws of the
Charitable Baptist Society in
Providence. Providence, Pr. by
H. H. Brown, 1832. 8 p. RHi;
RP; RPB.   11172

---- ---- Conference.
Minutes of the Baptist yearly
conference, in the ancient order
of the six principles of the doctrine of Christ and his apostles,
held at the Baptist meeting house
in Richmond, R. I. September 7,
8, and 9 A. M. 1832. Providence,
Pr. by H. H. Brown, 1832. 8 p.
RHi.   11173

---- ---- State Convention.
Minutes of the Baptist convention of the state of Rhode Island

and vicinity, held in Fall River
April 10, 1832. Seventh anniversary. Providence, H. H. Brown,
1832. 12 p. RHi; RPB.   11174

---- ---- Warren Association.
Sixty-fifth anniversary. Minutes of the Warren Baptist Association, held at the Baptist meeting house in Warren, on Wednesday and Thursday, September 12
and 13, 1832. Providence, Pr.
by H. H. Brown, 1832. 16 p.
PCA, RHi.   11175

---- South Carolina. Welsh Neck
Assocation.
Minutes. 1832- PCA. 11176

---- Vermont. Shaftsbury Association.
Minutes of the fifty-second anniversary of the Shaftsbury Baptist Association held at the meeting house of the first church in
Shaftsbury, Vermont, June 6 and
7, 1832. Bennington, J. C. Haswell [1832?] 16 p. PCA. 11177

---- ---- State Convention.
Proceedings of the seventh annual meeting of the Baptist Convention of the State of Vermont,
held at the Baptist meeting house
in Barnet, on Wednesday and
Thursday, October 24 & 25, 1832.
Brandon, Vermont Telegraph Office, 1832. 24 p. VtMiS. 11178

---- ---- Vermont Central Association.
Minutes of the Barre Baptist
Association, held at the meeting
house in Post Mills Village,
Thetford, on Wednesday and Thursday, September 12 & 13, 1832.
Brandon, Vermont Telegraph Office, 1832. 11 p. PCA.   11179

---- ---- Woodstock Association.
Minutes of the Woodstock Baptist Association, held at the Union Meeting house in Weston, on

Wednesday and Thursday, September 26 & 27, 1832. Windsor, Pr. at the Chronicle Press, 1832. 12 p.   11180

---- Virginia. Columbia Baptist Association.
Minutes of the 13th annual meeting of the Columbia Baptist Association, held, by appointment, at Bethlehem meeting house, Prince William Co., Va. Aug. 23, 24, 25, & 26, 1832. Washington, Pr. by Stephen C. Ustick, 1832. 12 p. NbHi; ViRu.   11181

---- ---- Ebenezer Association.
Fifth annual meeting. Minutes. ...25th & 26th of May, 1832. Woodstock, Va., Pr. by J. H. Darlington, 1832. 12 p. NRAB.
                                      11182
---- ---- Goshen Association.
Minutes of the Goshen Baptist Association, held at Good-Hope Meeting-house, Spotsylvania County, Virginia, commencing on the 22d of September, 1832. Fredericksburg, Va., Pr. at The Herald Office, [1832] 15 p. ViRu.
                                      11183
---- ---- Ketocton Baptist Association.
The 66th annual publication. Minutes of the Ketocton Baptist Association, held by appointment at North Fork, Loudoun County, Va. August 16, 17 & 18, 1832. Winchester, Pr. at the office of the Winchester Republican, 1832. 8 p. ViRU.   11184

---- ---- Pig River District Association.
Minutes of the Pig River District Baptist Association, held at Story Creek and Leatherwood Churches, 1831-2. Danville, Va., Pr. at the Reporter Office, 1832. 7 p. ViRu.   11185

Baraga, Frederic.
Otawa anamie-misinaigan.

Mojag tashamiam, ka wika tadebenimossim; giikitogoba Jesos. Lud. 18, 1 Wawiyatanong (i. e. Detroit, Mich.) Geo. L. Whitney, Ogimisinakisan manda misinaigan, 1832. 207p. MBAt; MiDC; MnHi.   11186

Barbaroux, C[harles] O[gé].
L'histoire des Etats-Unis d'-Amérique. Par C. O. Barbaroux ... Ed. rev. et cor. pour l'usage des écoles. Boston, Carter, Hendee & co.; Philadelphia, Key, Mielke & Biddle, 1832. 304p. ICU; MH; OFH; RNR; ViU.11187

Barbauld, (Mrs.) Anna Letitia (Aikin) 1743-1825.
A discourse on being born again. 3rd ed. 1st series. no. 13. Pr. for the American Unitarian Association. Boston, Gray & Bowen, 1832. 12 p. CBPac; ICMe; MB-HP; MMeT-Hi; MeBat.
                                      11188
---- Gl'inni Giovenili della Signora Anna Letizia Barbauld, tr. in italiano... Boston, C. E. Hendee, 1832. 110 p. CtY; DLC; MB; MH; TNV.   11189

---- Hymns in prose for children. In Italian. Boston, 1832. 110 p. MWA.   11190

---- Lessons for children with engravings and four original tales. New York, P. Hill, 1832. MH; PPULC.   11191

Barber, John Warner, 1798-1885.
Account of the most important and interesting religious events, which have transpired from the commencement of the Christian era to the present time with a short biographical sketch of persons distinguished in religious history. New Haven, Young, 1832. 404 p. CtHT; CtY; NbCrD; Nh; NSyHi.   11192

---- Chronological compendium of important and interesting events which have occurred from the commencement of the Christian era to the present time. Constructed and compiled from the most approved authors by J. W. Barber. Hartford, S. B. & V. M. Sheldon, 1832. Broadside. MHi.   11193

---- Interesting events in the history of the United States. New Haven, J. W. Barber, 1832. 324 p. CtHWatk; DLC; MWA; Nj; NSYU.   11194

---- Metamorphosis; or a transformation of a picture representing... See under title.

Barber, Jonathan, 1784-1864.
    Grammar of elocution; containing the principles of the arts of reading & speaking: illustrated by appropriate exercises & examples... (as) taught in Harvard University. New Haven, A. H. Maltry, 1832. 346 p. AMob; ICP; LNL; RPB; TxH.   11195

[Barber, William, Wesleyan]
    Memorials of the late Mrs. Barber, of Longford Academy, near Gloucester, obit. Aug. 20, 1822, aetat ann. 21. Gloucester, Pr. by J. Roberts, 1832. MH.
                                 11196
Barclay, Robert, 1648-1690.
    An apology for the true Christian divinity. Being an explanation and vindication of the principles and doctrines of the people called Quakers. By Robert Barclay. 3rd stereotype ed. New York, Sam Wood & Sons, for the Trustees of Obadiah Brown's Benevolent Fund, 1832. 587 p. CSmH; MHi; PHC; RLa; WaPS.   11197

---- On the Universality and efficacy of Divine Grace. Philadel-
phia, Pr. by Thomas Kite & Co., for the Tract Association of Friends, 1832. 16 p. InRchE; MeB; OClWHi.   11198

Bard, William, 1777-1853.
    A letter to David E. Evans, esquire, of Batavia, on life insurance... December 1st, 1832. New York, Pr. of W. Van Norden, 1832. 17, [3] p. DLC; MB; MWA; NjR; NN.   11199

Barker, James Nelson, 1784-1858.
    Ode, written at the request of the printers of Philadelphia, for the Centennial Celebration of the birth day of Washington! [Philadelphia, 1832] Broadside. CSmH.   11200

Barnabas, pseud.
    Plain hints, which may be useful to some of the "New school" theologians. By Barnabas, a friend. Princeton, N.J., Pr. by D'Hart & Connolly, 1832. 24 p. CtHC; CtY; NjPT; PPPrHi; PPULC.   11201

Barnard, Daniel Dewey, 1797-1861.
    Address before Adelphic Union Society of Williams College. Williamstown, 1832. 36 p. CtY; MWA.   11202

No entry   11203

Barnes, Albert, 1798-1870.
    Development of the Christian character. New York, 1832. 16 p. MH-AH.   11204

---- Question on the historical book of the New Testament, designed for Bible classes and Sunday schools. New York, Harper & Bros. [1832] DLC; GEU; MH; NN.   11205

---- ---- New York, J. Leavitt, 1832. NjMD; OO.   11206

Barnes, John Harbeson.

Tariff, or, rates of duties, from & after the third day of March, 1833, on all goods, wares, & merchandise imported into the United States of America... by J. H. Barnes & E. A. Carroll. Philadelphia, Russel, 1832. 91, 88 p. ICF; MH; PHi; PPAmP; OHi.
11207

Barnes, William.

A few words in defense of the reformed Catholic church (established in these realms). A sermon preached July 12, 1831. 2d ed. Richmond, 1832. 39 p. MBAt.
11208

Barney, Mrs. Mary [Chase].

A biographical memoir of the late Commodore Joshua Barney: from autographical notes and journals in possession of his family, and other authentic sources. Ed. by Mary Barney... Boston, Gray & Bowen, 1832. 328 p. CSmH; KHi; LN; PPA; PPAmP; WHi.
11209

Barnum, H. L.

The American farrier; containing a minute account of the formation of every part of the horse, from the extremity of the head to the hoof. With a description of all the diseases to which each part is liable; the best remedies to be applied in effecting a cure; and the most approved mode of treatment for preventing disorders: accompanied with a copious alphabetical list of medicines, describing their qualities and effects when applied in different cases; and a complete treatise on rearing and managing the horse from the foal to the full grown active laborer.... Illustrated with numerous engravings, and arranged on a new improved plan. By H. L. Barnum. Cincinnati, H. L. Barnum; Philadelphia, U. Hunt, 1832. 255p. CSmH; MdBP; NjR; OO; TNP.
11210

---- The child's second book of spelling and reading; connected with the elements of writing; with fifty five engravings. Boston, Carter, Hendee & Co., 1832. 31 p. DLC.
11211

---- The Farmer's Own Book; or, Family Receipts for the Husbandman and Housewife;... By H. L. Barnum... Boston, Carter, Hendee & Co., 1832. 165 p. MWA; Nh; OMC; PPM; ScCMe.
11212

---- The first book of geography, connected with spelling, reading and writing; illustrated by thirty maps... By H. L. Barnum. Boston, Carter, Hendee & Co., 1832. 60 p. CtHWatk; DLC; ICU; MH; NNC.
11213

---- Specimen of Barnum's introductory school-books. Lancaster, Mass., Pr. by Carter, Andrews & Co., 1832. MH.
11214

Barrett, Eaton Stannard, 1786-1820.

The heroine; or, Adventures of Cherubina, by Eaton Stannard Barrett, Esq. ... Baltimore, J. Robinson, 1832. 2 v. in 1. CSmH; MdBP; NcD; PU.
11215

Barrett, Samuel, 1795-1866.

The Apostle Peter a Unitarian. Boston, Gray & Bowen, 1832. 23 p. DLC; ICMe; MH-AH; Nh.
11216

---- ---- 2d ed. Pr. for the American Unitarian Association. Boston, Gray & Bowen, 1832. 23 p. DLC; ICMe; Meb; Nh; PPL.
11217

---- Excuses for the Neglect of the Communion considered. 3d ed., 1st series, no. 22. Pr. for the American Unitarian Association. Boston, Gray & Bowen, 1832. 24 p. CBPac; ICMe; MB-FA; MeB; Nh.
11218

---- A sermon, preached in the

Twelfth Congregational Church, Boston, Thursday, August 9, 1832, the day appointed for fasting, humiliation, and prayer, on account of the approach of the cholera. By Samuel Barrett, Minister of that church. Pub. by request. Boston, Hilliard, Gray & Co., 1832. 18 p. DLC; MBAt; MiD-B; MWA; NN.   11219

Barrington, George, 1755-1804.
    The London spy; or, The frauds of London detected... By G. Barrington... Boston, n.p., 1832. 216 p. DLC; ICU; MH; NjR.   11220

[Barrow, Sir John] 1764-1848.
    ... Description of Pitcairn's Island and its inhabitants, with an authentic account of the mutiny of the ship Bounty, and of the subsequent fortunes of the mutineers. New York, Harper, 1832. 303 p. CtHT; KyDC; MnHi; OClWHi; RPB; ViU.   11221

Barry, William Taylor, 1785-1835.
    Reply to the request of the committees of the board of alderman and of the common council for information on the importance to the post office department of the re-establishment of the bridge across the Potomac. [Washington, 1832] DLC.   11222

[Bartlett, James] 1792-1837.
    Probate forms, for the use of executors, administrators, &c. ... Dover [N. H.] Pr. by John Mann, 1832. 129 p. CSmH; MH-L; Nh-Hi.   11223

Bartlett, John, 1784-1849.
    Sacred Concert. John Bartlett respectfully informs the Ladies and Gentlemen of Dedham and vicinity that the members of his School will give a Concert of Sacred Music... Dedham, March

29, 1832. Broadside. MHi.   11224

Bartlett [Josiah?] 1768-1838.
    Speech of Mr. Bartlett, at a meeting of citizens opposed to the re-election of Andrew Jackson, holden at Portsmouth, N. H., Oct. 15, 1832. [Portsmouth?] Pr. by Miller & Brewster [1832] 23 p. DLC; NhDo.   11225

Bartlett, Montgomery Robert.
    The Clinton primer: a series of first lessons with cuts for little children; designed to prepare them for entering upon the study of the first part of the National school manual... Philadelphia, Carey & Lea, 1832. 48 p. DLC; MiU-C; NN.   11226

---- The national school manual; a regular and connected course of elementary studies... Comp. from the latest and most approved authors. By M. R. Bartlett... Philadelphia, Carey & Lea, 1832. 4 v. DLC; MB; MoU; OO; PWW.   11227

Barton, Bernard, 1784-1849.
    Poems: By Bernard Barton... A new edition including his poems to the year 1832. Boston, Munroe & Branch, 1832. 278 p. IrRchE; KyBC; MB; PPL; ScCoB. 11228

Barton, Edward Hall, d. 1859.
    The application of physiological medicine to the diseases of Louisiana. Philadelphia, Skerrett, 1832. 55 p. DNLM; DSG.   11229

Barton, Lucy, 1808?-1898.
    Bible letters for children. By Lucy Barton; with concluding verses by Bernard Barton... Philadelphia, Latimer & Co., 1832. 162 p. DLC; ICBB; PPULC; PSC-Hi.   11230

Barton, William Paul Crillon, 1786-1856.
    Engravings of fifty medicinal

plants indigenous to the United
States; made after original draw-
ings from nature. Philadelphia,
Coll. of Pharm., 1832. 2 p.
PPAN; PPCP.   11231

---- Programe[!] of the courses
of instruction. (At the Therapeutic institute, Philadelphia),
1832. See Therapeutic Institute
of Philadelphia.

Bascom, Chauncy.
    Guide to chirography in a se-
ries of writing books. Hallowell,
Glazier, Master & Smith Co.,
1832. NHD; NN; NNC.   11232

[Bascom, Henry Biddleman] 1796-
1850.
    Address on temperance pub-
lished by order of the General
Conference of the Methodist Episcopal church. New York Tract
Society of the Methodist Episcopal Church [1832] 11 p. CtMW.
                               11233
Bates, William, 1625-1699.
    The four last things, namely:
death, judgment, heaven and hell.
Practically considered and applied in several discourses. With
a biographical notice of the author. By William Bates... Burlington, Chauncey Goodrich,
1832. 550 p. ICU; KWiU; MWA;
NNUT; PU.   11234

---- The harmony of the divine.
Attributes in the contrivance and
accomplishment of man's re-
demption, by William Bates,
D.D. With an introductory essay
by A. Alexander, D.D. New York,
Jonathan Leavitt; Boston, Crocker
& Brewster, 1832. 348 p.
CSansS; KyLoP; NjP; OO; TKC;
WHi.   11235

Battle of the Potomac with the
Malays. Written by one of the
crew. [Boston, J. G. & H. Hunt,
1832?] Broadside. MHi; WHi.
                               11236

Bauern und Handwerksmannes
Calender .... Philadelphia, Herausgegeben von Georg M. Mentz
und sohn [1832] 35 p. NjP.
                               11237
Baxter, George Addison, 1771-
1841.
    Inaugural address of the Rev.
G. A. Baxter, D.D. on his in-
duction into the professorship of
Christian theology, in Union Theo-
logical Seminary. Delivered at the
College Church, Prince Edward
County, Virginia, April 11, 1832;
with the charge to the professor,
by Rev. W. Hill, D.D. First
Vice-President of the Board of
Directors. Pub. by request of the
board of directors of the semi-
nary. Richmond, Pr. by J. Mac-
Farlan, 1832. 26 p. CSmH; NcU;
PPULC; RPB; ViU.   11238

Baxter, Richard.
    A call to the unconverted. By
Richard Baxter. Boston, Lincoln
& Edmands, 1832. 163 p. MeB;
PReaAT.   11239

Bayley, Kiah, 1770-1857.
    Impenitent sinners in a deplor-
able situation. A sermon preached
at Campton, N.H., 1831, and
printed at the request of a member who heard it delivered. Boston, 1832. 14 p. MBC; MH-AH,
RPB.   11240

Bazeley, Charles W.
    The examiner; comprehending
questions and exercises on the
history of South and North America, particularly the United States;
with a synopsis of the celebrated
persons connected with its history
and a chronological series of
events from its discovery to the
cession of Florida. Designed for
the use of schools and private
students. By Charles W. Bazeley.
Philadelphia, M'Carty & Davis,
1832. 72 p. DLC; MH.   11241

36 Beach

Beach, Ephraim.
Report on the survey of a
route for the proposed Susquehanna & Delaware railroad...
See under Susquehanna and Delaware Railroad Co.

Beach, Wooster, 1794-1868.
The American Practice of
Medicine; being a treatise on
character, causes, symptoms,
morbid appearances and treatment
of disease, on vegetable and botanic principles... New York,
Betts and Anstice, 1832. 3 v.
PPHa; PPULC.   11242

[Beaconsfield, Benjamin Disraeli,
1st earl of, 1804-1881]
Contarini Fleming. A psycho-
logical autobiography. By the author of "Vivian Grey," "The
young duke," &c. New-York, Pr.
and pub. by J. & J. Harper, and
sold by principal booksellers
throughout the United States,
1832. 183 p. PPA.   11243

Bean, James.
The Christian minister's affec-
tionate advice to a new married
couple. By Rev. James Bean,
A.M. Boston, Christian Register
Office, 1832. 108 p. DLC; ICMe;
MB; NcD; OC.   11244

Beard, John Reilly.
Sermons accompanied by suitable prayers designed to be used
in families. 1st Amer. from 1st
and 2d London eds. In 2 vols.
Boston, Leonard C. Bowles, 1832.
2 vols. CSansS; IEG; KWiU; MNF;
PLT.   11245

Beardsley, Samuel, 1790-1860.
Speech of Mr. Beardsley, of
New-York, in the House of Representatives of the United States,
May 9 and 10, 1832, upon the
power of the house to punish for
an alleged Contempt and Breach
of Privilege. [n.p., 1832] 1-16 p.

DLC; N; NLitf; NN; NUtHi.
                           11246
---- Speech...on the resolution
proposing to examine into the af-
fairs of the Bank of the U.S.
Washington, 1832? 8 p. DLC; N.
                           11247
Beaumont, Charles C.
Campbell. An American tale.
New York, N.Y., 1832. 84 p.
RPB.   11248

Beaumont's Mississippi and Lou-
isianna [sic] almanac, for the year
of our Lord and Savior Jesus
Christ, 1833; ... Natchez, Franklin Beaumont, [1832] 20-35, 36 p.
Ms-Ar; MsJs.   11249

Beauties of the children's friend.
Boston, Lincoln & Edmands; Cincinnati, Hubbard & Edmonds,
1832. 252p. MWHi.   11250

The beautiful garden, or A fath-
er's instructions to his children.
By the author of The Mother's
Garland. Boston, James Loring,
1832. 108 p. ICBB; NNU-W;
PPULC.   11251

Beck, John Brodhead.
A letter on the establishment
of a new medical school in con-
nection with Columbia college...
by John B(rodhead) Beck, M.D.
New-York, Pr. by G. P. Scott &
co., successors to J. Seymour,
1832. 8 p. CtY; MB; NNN.
                           11252
Beddeford, Maine. First Congre-
gational Church.
Account of the dealings with A.
Norwood, Jr. Sacco, William
Condon, 1832. 80 p. MBC.11253
Bedell, Gregory Townsend, 1793-
1834.
Christ crucified; a sermon.
New York, Wm. Vn Norden,
1832. 18 p. DLC; MH.   11254

---- It is Well or Faith's Esti-

Bedford 37

phia, French & Perkins, 1832.
109 p. IEG; MBC; NPlaK; PP;
PPULC.   11255

---- The life of Moses. By G.
T. Bedell... Written for the
American S. Union and revised by
the committee of Publication.
Philadelphia, American Sunday
School Union, 1832. 210 p. DLC;
NN; ViU.   11256

---- (The) religious souvenir...
for 1832. See under title.

---- Way-marks; or, Directions
to persons commencing a religious life... By Gregory T. Bedell... Philadelphia, Key,
Mielke, & Biddle, 1832. 80 p.
CBCDS; GDC; MH; NjP.   11257

Bedford, Gunning S., 1806-
1870.
   Eulogy on the late James M.
Pendleton, M.D. Delivered by
appointment of the New-York city
and county Medical Society, in
the hall of Columbia College,
February 9th, 1832.... New
York, Pr. by J. Watt, 1832.
16 p. CtY; DLC; MBAt; NN;
OCHP; WHi.   11258

Beecher, Catherine Esther,
1800-1878.
   Arithmetic simplified...in
three parts...by Catherine E.
Beecher. Hartford, D. F. Rob-
inson & Co., 1832. 273 p.
CtHT-W; CtY; DAU; DHEW;
DLC; ICN.   11259

No entry   11260

Beecher, Lyman, 1775-1863.
   Dependence and Free Agency.
A sermon delivered in The Chap-
el of The Theological Seminary,
Andover, July 16, 1832. By
Lyman Beecher, D. D. Boston,
Pr. by Perkins & Marvin, 1832.

40 p. CtSoP; IaGG; MH; NjR;
PPL.   11261

---- A plea for the west, by Lyman Beecher, D.D. Cincinnati,
Truman and Smith, 1832. 172 p.
CtY; InCW; MH; OMC; Vt.
                          11262
Beechey, Frederick William,
1796-1856.
   Narrative of a voyage to the Pacific and Bering's Strait, to co-
operate with the polar expeditions:
performed in His Majesty's ship
Blossom, under the command of
Captain F. W. Beechey...in the
years 1825, 26, 27, 28... Philadelphia, Carey & Lea, 1832.
493 p. InCW; LNT; NjPT; PPA;
PU; ScC.   11263

Beethoven, Ludwig von, 1770-
1827.
   Credo [From his first mass.]
Boston, 1832. 12 p. MB. 11264

---- Glory to God [Chorus from
his first mass.] [Accomp. for or-
gan] [Boston, 1832] 11 p. MB.
                          11265
---- The Mount of Olives. Boston, 1832. 19 p. MB.   11266

Begg, James A.
   The Scriptural argument for the
coming of the Lord at the commencement of the millennium; derived from the literal fulfilment
of prophecy, and the views held
in the Apostolic age concerning
the millennial kingdom. Pittsburgh, Begg, 1832. 23 p. KyU;
PPPrHi; PPULC.   11267

---- True cause of the prevalence of pestilence. Paisley,
1832. MWA.   11268

Belfast, Maine. Fire Engine
Company.
   By-laws of the Belfast Fire Engine Company. Adopted September
5, 1829. Belfast, W. M. 's Advocate

Press, August, 1832. 11 p.
                                11269
Belfrage, Henry.
    Memoir of John Watson and
sister of Linlithgow, Scotland.
Exemplifying the loveliness of early
piety. Boston, James Loring,
1832. 108 p. MWHi.   11270

Bell, Henry Glassford, 1803-1874.
    Mary, Queen of Scots. New
York, J. & J. Harper, 1832. 2 v.
AzPh; MB; ViU.   11271

Bell, Jared, 1799-1876.
    Considerations for young men.
By the author of "Advise to a
young Christian"... New York, Jon-
athan Leavitt; Boston, Crocker &
Brewster, 1832. 205 p. GDecCT;
MB; NcCJ; OO; TxHR.   11272

Bell, John, 1796-1872.
    All the material facts in the
history of epidemic cholera: being
a report of the College of Physicians of Philadelphia, to the
Board of Health: and a full account of the causes, post mortem
appearances, and treatment of
the disease. By John Bell...
and by D. Francis Condie... Philadelphia, T. Desilver, jun., 1832.
127 p. CSt-L; LU; PU; RPM;
ViU.   11273

---- ---- 2d ed. Philadelphia,
Thomas Desilver, Jun., 1832.
188 p. DLC; KyU; MiU; NcD-MC;
PP.   11274

Bell, John, 1797-1869.
    Speech of John Bell of Tennes-
see on the tariff, delivered in
the house of representatives, June
15, 1832. Washington, Blair, 1832.
51 p. DLC; MWA; PPAmP; TxU;
WHi.   11275

[Bellini, Vincenzo] 1801-1835.
    The pirate; a melodrama in
two acts as performed at the
Richmond-Hill theatre. (Words

by Romani). New York, L. da
Ponte, 1832. 71 p. CtY; MH.
                                11276
Beman, Nathaniel Sidney Smith,
1785-1871.
    A discourse, delivered at the
opening of the General Assembly
of the Presbyterian Church, on
the 17th of May, 1832. Philadelphia, Geddes, 1832. 16 p. MWA;
NCH; OCHP; PHi; PPM.   11277

---- The influence of ardent spirits in the production of the cholera. Letter to the mayor and
common council of the city of
Troy. Troy, N. Tuttle [1832] 8 p.
NN.   11278

--- Sacred lyrics: or, Select
hymns, particularly adapted to
revivals of religion, and intended
as a supplement to Watts. By
Nathan S. S. Beman. Troy, Pr.
by N. Tuttle, 1832. CtY. 11279

Benedict, H. T. N.
    Murray's English grammar, re-
vised, simplified, and adapted to
the inductive and explanatory
mode of instruction. See Murray,
Lindley, 1745-1826.

Benjamin, Asher, 1773-1845.
    The practical house carpenter:
being a complete development of
the Grecian orders of architecture... 3d ed. Boston, 1832.
119 p. KEmT; MH; NNC; NjP;
RP.   11280

Benjamin, Park, 1809-1864.
    A poem on the meditation of
nature, spoken September 26th,
1832, before the Association of
the Alumni of Washington College.
Hartford, F. J. Huntington, 1832.
23 p. CtY; DLC; MB; NIC; RPB.
                                11281
Bennett, Caleb P. b. 1758.
    Sketch of Major Bennett's life.
Major C. P. Bennett, having been
presented to the consideration of

his fellow citizens, as a candidate for the office of Governor of this State, it is thought that a brief sketch of his life and character would prove acceptable to them. He was born... 11th Nov. 1758. [Delaware, n.p., 1832?] Broadside. DLC.   11282

Bennett and Walton's almanac for the year of our lord...1833. Philadelphia, 1832. CtY; InU; MWA; NjR; PHi.   11283

Bennington Academy. Bennington, Vermont.
Catalogue for the year, ending August 7, 1833. Bennington, J. C. Haswell [1832] 4 l. CSmH.   11284

Bennington Seminary. Bennington, Vermont.
Catalogue for the year ending October 10, 1832. [Bennington? 1832?] 12 p. VtU.   11285

Bentley, Rensselaer.
The American instructor;... To which is added a comprehensive abridgement of English grammar. By Rensselaer Bentley ... 4th ed. Albany, Oliver Steele, 1832. 238 p. IaNowd; NNC.   11286
---- The Derivative Expositor; containing Rules for spelling Derivative words, etc. Boston, Richardson, Lord & Holbrook, 1832. 72 p. CtHWatk; ICP.   11287

---- English spelling book, containing the rudiments of the English language... By Rensselaer Bentley. Poughkeepsie, P. Potter & Co., 1832. 124 p. ICU; NP.   11288

Benton [Thomas Hart] 1782-1858.
Mr. Benton's speeches on the amendments to the bill to recharter the Bank of the United States, and on the question to engross the bill for the third

reading; in the Senate of the United States, May and June, 1832. City of Washington, C. H. Barron, 1832. 36 p. DLC; MH; PPL; T.   11289

---- Speech of Mr. Benton, of Missouri, on the introduction of a resolution on the state of currency. Delivered in the Senate of the United States, Jan. 20, 1832. Washington, Pr. by F. P. Blair, at the Globe office, 1832. 24 p. DLC; MWA; OClWHi; NbU; Sc.   11290

---- Speech on the reduction of the renewal and regulation of commerce, delivered in Senate, March 15, 1832. [Washington] 1832. 16 p. DLC; PHi; PPAmP; WHi.   11291

Berens, Edward, 1777?-1859.
Pastoral advice to young men, particularly those in country villages, in seven sermons. By the Rev. Edward Berens... New York, Swords, Stanford & Co., 1832. 83 p. NBuG; NNUT.   11292

---- Village sermons on the chief articles of faith, &c. on the Christian character, and on some of the relative duties; to which is added pastoral advice to young men, particularly those in country villages, in seven sermons. By the Rev. Edward Berens... New York, Swords, Stanford & Co., 1832. 375 p. CtY; NNUT; ODa; ViAl; WHi.   11293

Bernard, John, 1756-1828.
Retrospections of the stage. By the late John Bernard... Boston, Carter & Hendee, 1832. 2 vols. in 1. DLC; MH; PPL; TU; UPB.   11294

Bernard, Stephen.
A new grammar of the French language, divided into forty les-

40 Bernays

sons, with an introduction; the whole followed by a complete treatise on the regular, irregular and defective verbs... By Stephen Bernard... Richmond [Va.], Pr. for the author, 1832. 147, 95 p. CSmH; DLC; MdBS; NcD; ViU; Vi. 11295

Bernays, Adolphus, d. 1864.
Bernays' Compendious German grammar, with a dictionary of prefixes and affixes, and with alterations, additions, and references to an "Introduction to the study of the German language." By Hermann Bokum... Philadelphia, Hogan and Thompson, 1832. 61 p. CtY; GDecCT; MH; NhD; PU. 11296

[Berquin, Arnaud] ca. 1749-1791.
The looking-glass for the mind, or, Intellectual mirror. Being an elegant collection of the most delightful little stories and interesting tales. Chiefly translated from that much admired work L'Ami Des Enfans. With elegant engravings on wood, by Anderson... Philadelphia, Alexander Towar, etc., 1832. 216 p. DLC; ICN; NUt; RNHi; ViW. 11297

Berry, Henry.
The speech of, in the House of Delegates of Virginia, on the Abolition of Slavery. It is due to Mr. Berry to state that his speech on the abolition of slavery, has been published in its present form, by gentlemen favorable to the views which he has advocated --not by himself. Richmond, January 11, 1832. 8 p. CSmH; MB; NcU; PHi; Vi. 11298

Berzelius, Jons Jakob, 1779-1848.
Chemical nomenclature. An essay on chemical nomenclature, prefixed to the treatise on chemistry; by J. J. Berzelius. Tr. from the French with notes by

A. D. Bache... [Philadelphia, Pr. by C. Sherman & Co., 1832] 31 p. DLC; PPULC; PU; PU-S. 11299

Bethune, Joanna [Graham] 1770-1860.
The infant school grammar consisting of elementary lessons in the analytical method; 2d ed. enlarged and improved. New-York, R. Lockwood and A. W. Carey, 1832. 140 p. AmSSchU; ICBB; MH; NN; NNC. 11300

[Bethune, John Eliot Drinkwater] 1801-1851.
... Life of Galileo Galilei: with illustrations of the advancement of experimental philosophy. Boston, W. Hyde & Co., 1832. 307 p. CtMW; DLC; ICMe; MBL; PPL-R. 11301

Bible.
The apocryphal New Testament. Being all the Gospels, Epistles, and other pieces now extant attributed in the first four centuries to Jesus Christ. His apostles and their companions, and not included in the New Testament. By its compiler. From the last London ed. Boston, N. H. Whitaker, 1832. 290 p. CtY; KyLoP; MB; OCl; WHi. 11302

---- ---- Ravenna, O., Pr. by W. Coolman, Jr., 1832. 348 p. IEG; OClWHi; OO. 11303

---- La biblia Sagrada, a saber; el Antiguo y el Nuevo Testamento, traducidos de la Vulgata latine en espanol, por el Rmo. P. Felipe Scio de S. Miguel... Nueva ed., a costa de la Sociedad americana de la Biblia. Nueva-York, Edicion esterectipica por A. Chandler, 1832. 753, 251 p. DLC; MB; NN; PHi. 11304

---- The Comprehensive Bible... with the various readings and marginal notes usually printed

Bible   41

therewith.... Hartford, Andrus
& Judd, 1832. 1460 p. NNAB.
                            11305
---- A concordance to the Holy
Scriptures [by Rev. John Brown]
... New York, J. & J. Harper,
1832. DLC; MBC.   11306

---- The Daily Commentary;
being a selection from the Exposition of Matthew Henry. Compiled and arranged by Rev.
Joseph Wilson, New York, John
P. Haven, 1832. 451p. MH-AH;
Nh; OO; PPM; ScCliP.   11307

---- The English Version, of the
Polyglott Bible, containing the
old and new testaments; with original selections of references to
parallel and illustrative passages; and marginal readings;
together with other valuable additions; the whole designed to
facilitate the acquisition of scripture knowledge in Bible classes,
sunday schools, etc. Baltimore,
Armstrong & Plaskitt, 1832.
920, 281 p. CtY; MB; NBuG;
PPL; VtU.   11308

---- ---- Philadelphia, Key,
Mielke, and Biddle, 1832. ICU;
MBC; NN; PP.   11309

---- Harmony of Kings & Prophets: or unarrangement of hist. in
the books of Kings & Chron. with
writings of Prophets in chronological order fr. revolt of Ten
Tribes to Malachi, by S. Merrill. Boston, Massachusetts
Sabbath School Society, 1832?
463 p. ICP; InIBU; MoS; OO.
                            11310
---- Harmony of the four Gospels in English. According to
the Common version. Newly arranged, with explanatory notes.
By Edward Robinson. Boston,
Crocker & Brewster, 1832. 216 p.
ViRu.   11311

---- The Holy Bible containing
the Old and New Testament connected in the history of the Jews
from the declension of the kingdoms of Israel and Judah to the
time of Christ. 2d Amer. from
20th Lond. ed. Baltimore, 1832.
2 v. OO.   11312

---- The Holy Bible, containing
the Old and New Testaments,
translated out of the original
tongues. Boston, Carter, Hendee
& Co., 1832. 1003, 321 p.
MMhHi; MToP; NN.   11313

---- ---- Boston, Gaylord, 1832.
486, 162 p. MB; MWA; NN;
PPL; WHi.   11314

---- ---- Boston, J. A. Ballard.
[1832]   11315

---- ---- Concord, N.H., Moses
G. Atwood, 1832. 792 p. MB;
NN.   11316

---- ---- Cooperstown [N.Y.],
stereotyped, pr. and pub. by H.
& E. Phinney, 1832. 576, [4],
99 p. CSmH; ICN; THi.   11317

---- ---- Hartford, Conn., Andrus & Judd, 1832. 11-729, 225 p.
CtY; NNAB.   11318

---- ---- Hartford, Hudson &
Skinner, 1832. Unpaged. NN.
                            11319
---- ---- Hartford, Silas Andrus,
1832. 729, 225, 70 p. MB; MiU.
                            11320
---- ---- Lunenburg (Mass.),
Edmund Cushing, 1832. 930 p.
NNAB.   11321

---- ---- Middletown, Conn.,
William H. Niles, 1832. 824,
251 p. NN.   11322

---- ---- New York, Pr. by W.
E. Dean, for Collins and Hannay,
1832. 3 v. LN; MB; NjP; OO;

ViU. 11323

---- ---- New York, Pr. by D. Fanshaw, for The American Bible Society, 1832. NMaril. 11324

---- ---- New York, Daniel D. Smith, 1832. 811,3 p. NN; NNAB. 11325

---- ---- New York, J. Emory and B. Waugh, 1832. 6 v. LNB; T; ViU. 11326

---- ---- New York, J. Leavitt, stereotyped by T. H. Carter & Co., Boston Type and Stereotype Foundry, 1832. 6 v. GHi; IJI. 11327

---- ---- New York, N. & J. White, stereotyped by J. Howe, Philadelphia, 1832. CtY-D; ICP; ViU. 11328

---- ---- Philadelphia, Alexander Towar, also Hogan & Thompson, Stereotyped by L. Johnson, 1832. 819, 256, 82 p. ICN; NN; NRSB; OHi; PPLT. 11329

---- ---- Philadelphia, James Kay Jr. & Co., Stereotyped by L. Johnson, 1832. 1425 p. MHingHi. 11330

---- ---- Philadelphia, M'Carty & Davis, 1832. 1076 p. NN. 11331

---- The Holy Bible... The text corrected according to the standard of the American Bible Society. Stereotyped by James Conner. Brattleboro, Pub. by the Brattleboro Bible Co., Peck & Steen & Co., agents, 1832. 827, 168, 14 p. NNAB; NjP. 11332

---- The Holy Bible, translated from the Latin Vulgate... The Old Testament was first published by the English college at Doway, A.D. 1609: And the New Testament, by the English college at Rheims, A.D., 1582. With an-

notations, and etc., by the Rev. Dr. Challoner: together with references, and an historic and chronological index. Revised and corrected according to the Clementine edition of the Scriptures. Baltimore, F. Lucas, Jr., 1832. 789, 5-235 p. DGU; NN; NNAB. 11333

---- ---- Philadelphia, Eugene Cummiskey, Stereotyped by J. Howe, 1832. DGU. 11334

---- ---- Philadelphia, Jas. B. Smith & Co., 1832. 436, 162 p. 11335

---- Das neue testament unsers Herrn und Heilandes Jesu Christi nach der uebersetzung Doctor Martin Luthers, mit kurzen inhalt eines jeden capitels und vollstandiger wie auch aller sonn und festtagigen Episteln und Evangelien. Philadelphia, Herausgegeben von Georg W. Mentz, Buchbandier, 1832. 504 p. MH; PP. 11336

---- A new concordance to the Holy Scriptures. Being the most comprehensive and concise of any before published... By the Rev. John Butterworth.... A new ed., with considerable improvements. By Adam Clarke, LL.D. Stereotyped at the Boston Type and Stereotype Foundry. Boston, Crocker & Brewster; New York, Jonathan Leavitt, 1832. 516 p. NbOM; OW; ViU; WHi. 11337

---- The New Testament of Our Lord and Saviour, Jesus Christ, translated out of the original Greek... Baltimore, J. N. Lewis, 1832. 344 p. PPL. 11338

---- ---- Baltimore, John J. Harrod, 1832. 259 p. MdHi. 11339

---- ---- Brattleboro, Brattleboro Bible Co., 1832. 335 p. VtMiM; VtMiS. 11340

---- ---- Concord, N. H. , Luther Roby, 1832. 335 p. MBo-T.
11341

---- ---- Elizabethtown, N. J. , B. F. Brookfield, 1832. 344 p. MH.
11342

---- ---- Hartford, S. Andrus, 1832. 222 p. NN.
11343

---- ---- New York, American Bible Society, 1832. 340 p. CtHT; MWA; PP.
11344

---- ---- New York, Pr. by J. Collord, for B. Waugh and T. Mason, 1832. 2 v. PCA; PMA.
11345

---- ---- New-York, John C. Riker, 1832. CSmH; KWiU; MeBD; NN.
11346

---- ---- New York, Jonathan Leavitt; Boston, Crocker & Brewster, 1832. 546 p. NT; PPL; PU.
11347

---- ---- Newark, Olds, 1832. NcD.
11348

---- ---- Philadelphia, Alexander Tower, 1832. 256 p. NNAB; PPPrHi.
11349

---- ---- Philadelphia, Harmstead, 1832. PPL.
11350

---- ---- Utica, William Williams, 1832. 237 p. MBC; N; NN; NUt; PPL.
11351

---- ---- Windsor, Simeon Ide, 1832. 372 p. NN.
11352

---- ---- Woodstock, Nahum Haskell, 1832. 335 p. VtMiM; VtMiS.
11353

---- Le nouveau Testament de notre seigneur Jesus Christ. Imprimée sur l'edition de Paris, de L'année 1805. A' New York, Imprime avec des planches solides par D. Fanshaw, aux frais de la Société Biblique Americaine, 1832. 207 p. PPPrHi; RNR.
11354

---- Old and new testaments. Boston, Hale's Steam Press, prs. Stereotyped at the Boston Type & Stereotype Foundry, late T. H. Carter & Co. Pub. by Nathan Hale, Stimpson & Clapp, Hilliard, Gray, Little and Wilkins, Richardson Lord & Holbrook, Lincoln & Edmands, Crocker & Brewster, Munroe and Francis, and R. P. and C. Williams. 1832. 687, 134, 212 p. MEab; NN.
11355

---- A paraphrase and notes on the epistles of St. Paul to the Galatians, First and Second Corinthians, Romans, Ephesians. To which is prefixed an essay for the understanding of St. Paul's epistles, by consulting St. Paul himself. By John Locke. Cambridge, Brown, Shattuck; Boston, Hilliard, Grey & Co., 1832. 455 p. CBPac; GDecCT; ICMe; MBL; OCY.
11356

---- Psalms in metre, selected from the Psalms of David, with hymns... Baltimore, J. N. Lewis, 1832. 48 p. MdBE.
11357

---- ---- New Haven, Durrie & Peck, 1832. 505 p. IaDL; MH; OCH; PU; ViRU.
11358

---- ---- Philadelphia, Hogan & Thompson, 1832. PPL.
11359

---- The Sacred Writings of the Apostles and Evangelists of Jesus Christ, commonly styled the New Testament. Translated from the Original Greek, by Doctors George Campbell, James Macknight, and Philip Doddridge. With Prefaces, Various Emendations, and an Appendix, etc. 3d ed. , rev. and enl. Bethany, Brooke Co. , Va. ,

Alexander Campbell, 1832. 517,
100 p. & maps. CSmH; GEU-T;
InU; LNB; NcD.   11360

---- La Sainte Bible...imprimée
sur l'edition de Paris, de
L'année 1805. Edition stéréotype,
rev. et cor. avec. soin d'après
les textes hébreu et grec. New
York, Aux freis de la Société
biblique américaine, par Daniel
Fanshaw, 1832. 788 p. KyU;
MBC; NN; PP; RNR.   11361

---- A selection of passages of
Scripture, for young persons to
commit to memory. By the Rev.
Wm. Brown, M.D. Philadelphia,
1832. CtY.   11362

Bible Association of Friends in
America.
   An appeal to the Society of
Friends in behalf of the Bible
Association of Friends in Amer-
ica. Philadelphia, W. Brown,
1832. 72 p. MH; PHC; PPAmP;
PHi.   11363

Bible dictionary. See Smith,
William.

Bickersteth, Edward, 1786-1850.
   The Christian student designed to assist Christians in
general in acquiring religious
knowledge... 3d ed., corr. by
the Rev. E. Bickersteth. Cincinnati, Seeley & Allbach, 1832.
672 p. IaPeC.   11364

---- Treatise on prayer designed
to assist in the devout discharge of that duty. Philadel-
phi Key, Mielke, and Biddle,
1832. 240 p. MBGCT; NN; PPLT.
                             11365
---- The works of Rev. E. Bickersteth...containing Scripture
help, Treatise on prayer, The
Christian hearer, The chief concerns of man for time and eter-
nity, Treatise on the Lord's

supper, and the Christian student... New York, D. Appleton;
Boston, Crocker & Brewster;
[etc., etc.] 1832. 655 p. DLC;
MeB; OCIW; PPP; ViU.   11366

Biddle, Charles.
   Senator Grundy's Political Con-
duct Reviewed. By Charles Bid-
dle. Nashville, Republican and
Gazette Office, 1832. 25 p.
CSmH; DLC; LNH; MBAt; MH;
T.   11367

Biddle, James Cornell, 1795-
1838.
   Annual oration...before the
Philomathean society of the Uni-
versity of Pennsylvania...James
C. Biddle. Philadelphia, Pr. by
John Young, 1832. 12 p. GHi;
MH; NjR; PPAmP.   11368

Biddle, John.
   A discourse, delivered on the
anniversary of the Historical Society of Michigan, September,
1832. Detroit, Pr. by Geo. L.
Whitney, 1832. 31 p. DLC; MH;
MiD-B; Oc; PHi.   11369

Bigelow, Andrew, 1795-1877.
   Christians called unto liberty;
a sermon preached at Derry, N.H.,
Sept. 30, 1832. Occasioned by
the gathering of a Unitarian Congregation in that place... Boston,
Leonard C. Bowles, 1832. 21 p.
DLC; ICN; MBAt; RPB; WHi.
                             11370
Bigelow, Erastus Brigham, 1814-
1879.
   The self-taught stenographer,
or, Stenographic guide; explaining the principles and rules of
the art of short-hand writing,
illustrated by appropriate plates
and examples. Compiled and improved from the latest European
and American publications, by E.
B. Bigelow, stenographer. Lancaster (Mass.), Pr. by Carter,
Andrews & Co., 1832. 25 p.

CtY; MB; MH; NN.   11371

Bigelow, Jacob.
Elements of technology, taken chiefly from a course of lectures delivered at Cambridge, on the application of the sciences to the useful arts. By Jacob Bigelow. 5th ed. Boston, Hilliard, Gray, Little & Wilkins, 1832. 507 p. MH-AH.   11372

[Bigelow, Josiah]
Review of "An address to the workingmen of New England, on the state of education and on the condition of the producing classes in Europe and America..." By Seth Luther... Boston, Pub. by the author, 1832. Cambridge, Pr. by E. W. Metcalf & Co., for the author, 1832. 31 p. DLC; MB; MH; MH-BA.   11373

Bigland, John, 1750-1832.
A natural history of animals. Philadelphia, John Grigg, 1832. PPAmP.   11374

---- A natural history of birds, fishes, reptiles, and insects.... Philadelphia, J. Grigg, 1832. 179 p. CSmH; MBilHi; MH; MdBlC; NjN.   11375

Bilby, Thomas, 1794-1872.
The infant teacher's assistant, for the use of schools and private families; or, Scriptural and moral lessons for infants with observations on the manner of using them. By T. Bilby and R. B. Ridgway... Boston, Munroe & Francis, 1832. 116 p. AmSSchU; DLC; NjR; PP; PPULC.   11376

Binaghi, O. A.
Opinion upon the epidemic choleramorbus observed at Warsaw. Transl. from the Italian by Wm. Sampson. New York, P. Hill, 1832. 27 p. DLC; NN; PaHosp; RPM; ScU; VU.   11377

Bingham, Caleb, 1757-1817.
The American preceptor improved; being a new selection of lessons for reading and speaking. By Caleb Bingham...8th imp. ed. Boston, J. H. A. Frost; New York, Collins & Hannay (etc., etc.) c 1832. 228 p. CtEhad; MB; MH; MiD.   11378

---- The Columbian orator, containing a variety of original and selected pieces, together with rules; calculated to improve youth and others in the art of eloquence. Boston, J. H. A. Frost, Lincoln & Edmands, Stimpson & Clapp, etc., 1832. 300 p. InKoHi; MH; NBuG; OSW; PPiU.   11379

Binney, Horace, 1780-1875.
Speech delivered by Horace Binney, esq. at the Anti-Jackson meeting, held in the State House yard, Philadelphia, October 20, 1832. 8 p. DLC; IU; MWA; NjR; WHi.   11380

Biographical sketches of eccentric characters. Boston, N. H. Whitaker, 1832. 448 p. CtB; LNH; MH; NN; RPB.   11381

Biography of Martin Van Buren. See Butler, Benjamin Franklin, 1795-1858.

Biography of pious persons; abridged for youth. Springfield, Merriam, Little & Co., 1832. 336 p. CSmH; DLC; GDecCT; ICBB; MNBedf.   11382

Bishop, Robert Hamilton, 1777-1855.
An address delivered to the graduates of Miami University, September 26, 1832... Oxford [O.] Pr. by W. W. Bishop, 1832. 15 p. CSmH; KyLx; MHi. 11383

Blackford, Martha, pseud. See Stoddart, Isabella [Wellwood] d. 1846.

Blackstone, William, 1723-1780.
An analytical abridgment of the commentaries of Sir William Blackstone on the laws of England. In four books. Together with an analytical synopsis of each book. To which is prefixed, an essay on the study of law... By John Anthon. 2d ed. Philadelphia, P. H. Nicklin and T. Johnson, 1832. 347 p. Ct; DLC; MB; PPB; WM.   11384

---- Commentaries of the laws of England: in four books; with an analysis of the work. By Sir William Blackstone, Knt... New York, Collins & Hannay, etc., Philadelphia, Collins & Co., J. White, Grigg & Elliot, 1832. 2 v. Ct; DLC; NCH; OCX; WaPS.
11385

Blair, Hugh, 1718-1800.
An abridgement of lectures on rhetoric. By Hugh Blair... New ed., with appropriate questions to each chapter, by a teacher of Philadelphia. Philadelphia, C. Bell [1832] 230 p. MoU.   11386

---- ---- Philadelphia, Key, Mielke & Biddle, 1832. 230 p. NN; PHi; PPULC.   11387

---- Lectures on rhetoric and belles lettres: chiefly from the lectures of Dr. Blair. By Abraham Mills, A.M. New York, James Conner, 1832. 360 p. CLCM; ICU; MH; OkU; OSW.
11388

---- ---- New York, Lockwood, 1832. 360 p. ICMcHi; MBC; OO; PP; PPULC.   11389

Blaisdale, Silas.
First lessons in intellectual philosophy: or, A familiar explanation of the nature and operations of the human mind. From a London copy, ed. by Rev. Silas Blaisdale. 2d ed. Boston, Lincoln & Edmands; Cincinnati, Hub-

bard and Edmands, 1832. 358 p. CtSoP; DLC; GMM; ICU; MH; MMidb.   11390

---- Primary lessons in geography; consisting of questions adapted to Worcester's and Woodbridge's Atlases. 4th ed. rev. By Silas Blaisdale. Boston, Marsh, Capen, & Lyon, 1832. 36 p. M; MH; NNC.   11391

Blake, John Lauris, 1788-1857.
Conversations on the evidences of christianity; in which the leading arguments of the best authors are arranged... & connected with each other. Adapted to the use of schools & families. Boston, Carter, Hendee & Co., 1832. 274 p. MdW; OMC; PPM; PU; RPB.
11392
---- Evidences of Christianity; a first classbook for Sunday Schools; arranged by Rev. J. L. Blake, A.M. Rector of St. Matthew's Church, Boston. Boston, Lincoln & Edmands, 1832. 86 p. DLC; IaHA; MB-W; MiHi; Nh-Hi.
11393
---- Family cabinet and juvenile encyclopedia of useful knowledge. Boston, New York, 1832-33. 240 p. MH; MWA; MWBorHi.
11394
---- First book in astronomy... Boston, Lincoln and Edmunds; New York, R. Lockwood; etc., etc. [1832] KyBgW; PWcHi.
11395
---- The first book in natural philosophy; illustrated mostly by experiments, which may be performed without regular apparatus. Adapted to the use of American schools. By the Rev. J. L. Blake, A.M. New York, Collins & Hannay, 1832. 271 p. NRHi.
11396
---- The high school reader, designed for a first class book. Consisting of extracts in prose and poetry.... Boston, William

Hyde & Co. , 1832. 408 p. DLC;
ICU; OWorP; MLy; Nh-Hi. 11397

---- The historical reader, designed for the use of schools and
families on a new plan. By Rev.
J. L. Blake, A. M. Boston, Rochester, New York, Hoyt, Porter
& Co. , 1832. 302 p. NCanHi;
NN; NRHi.   11398

Blake, Louisa.
  Poems. Boston, Carter Hen-
dee and Co. , 1832. 138 p. CtY;
DLC; ICN; MHi; MPiB; NN;
NjP; PPULC.   11399

Blanchard, Amos, comp.
  American military and naval
biography: containing the lives
and characters of the officers of
the revolution... To which are
added the life and character of
Benedict Arnold and... the capture,
trial and execution of Major Andre. Compiled by Amos Blanchard. Cincinnati, A. Salisbury,
1832. 604 p. FTa; LNB; OAU;
PP; TNP.   11400

---- Book of Martyrs. See
Foxe, John.

Blanchard, Ira Henry Thomas.
  The Christian Doctrine of Re-
generation. I. H. T. Blanchard, of
Harvard, Mass. Boston, Leonard
C. Bowles, and B. H. Greene,
1832. 81 p. MB; MH; MWA; MeB;
NHCS.   11401

Blanchard, W.
  On statutes of limitations.
Philadelphia, 1832. NN.   11402

Blane, Gilbert, 1749-1834.
  Elements of medical logick.
Hartford, Huntington & Hopkins,
1832. 319 p. MiDW-M.   11403

Blunt, Joseph, 1792-1860.
  An examination of the relations
between the Cherokee and the

Government of the United States.
... New York, Clayton & Van
Norden, 1832. 15 p. MdHi; PHi;
PPULC.   11404

---- The merchant's and ship-
master's assistant; containing information useful to the American
merchants, owners, and masters
of ships... Together with the tariff for 1832... New-York, E. & G.
W. Blunt, 1832. 474 p. CU; CtY;
NN; PPAmP; RPJCB.   11405

Blythe, C.
  Oration delivered at the organ-
ization of Pennsylvania College at
Gettysburg. Gettysburg, Pr. by
H. C. Neinstedt, 1832. 19 p. MH;
MoKU; NcU; NNU-W.   11406

Blythe, James, 1765-1842.
  A summary of gospel doctrine
and Christian duty, being a sermon delivered to the church and
congregation of Pisgah on the res-
ignation of the pastoral charge...
Lexington, Ky. , Pr. by Thomas
T. Skillman, 1832. 16 p. CSmH;
ICP; NcMHi; PPULC; PPPrHi.
                                   11407

Boardman, John, 1795-1841.
  The presence of Christ, the
glory of His house. A sermon delivered... in West Boylston, August 22, 1832. Salem, Pr. by Warwick Palfray, jun. , 1832. 31 p.
CtY; DLC; MWA; MiD-B; RPB.
                                   11408

Boeuf, Joseph F. A.
  A new and complete grammar
of the French tongue. 2d ed. ,
corr. , enl. and improved. New-
York [Ludwig & Tolefree] 1832.
MBC; MH; NBuG; NCH.   11409

Boisseau, Francois Gabriel,
1791-1836.
  On cholera morbus, tr. by G.
S. Bedford. New York, 1832.
NN.   11410

---- On fevers...translated by J.

R. Knox, M. D. Philadelphia,
1832. ICU-R; MB; PPL; PPULC.
                              11411
---- Physiological pyretology; or,
A treatise on fevers: according
to the principles of the new medical doctrine. By Francois Gabriel Boisseau... Philadelphia,
Carey & Lea, 1832. 504 p. CU;
GU-M; NjR; PPCP; TNV. 11412

---- A treatise on cholera mor-
bus; or, Researches on the
symptoms, nature, and treatment
of the disease; and on the differ-
ent means of avoiding it. By F.
G. Boisseau... Tr. from the
French, by G. S. Bedford... New
York, Collins & co., 1832. 148 p.
CSt; IEN-M; MeB; NBuG; PPCP;
ViU.   11413

Bokum, Hermann, 1807-1878.
    Anleitung zur erlernung der
englischen sprache, enthaltend
auszüge aus den besten deutschen
schriftstellern, mit einer englischen wörtlichen und freien uebersetzung und einer sorgfältigen
abhandlung über die englische
aussprache... Von Hermann Bokum... Philadelphia, G. W.
Mentz und sohn [etc.] 1832. 199 p.
DLC; PPG; PPULC.   11414

---- Bernays' Compendious German Grammar... See Bernays,
Adolphus, d. 1864.

---- An introduction to the study
of the German language, comprising extracts from the best
German prose writers, with...
translations... notes, and a treatise on pronunciation... By Hermann Bokum... 2d ed. cor. and
improved. Philadelphia, Hogan &
Thompson; Pittsburg, D. M. Hogan, 1832. 199 p. CtHW;
GDecCT; MH; OUrC; PMA; PU.
                              11415
---- An introductory lecture delivered in the University of Penn-

sylvania, on the 5, May, 1832.
n. p., n. d. 16 p. PPAmP;
PPULC; PU; ScCC.   11416

Bolling, Philip A.
...The speeches of Philip A.
Bolling, (of Buckingham) in the
House of delegates of Virginia,
on the Policy of the state in re-
lation to her colored population;
delivered on the 11th and 25th of
January, 1832... Richmond, Pr.
by T. W. White, 1832. 16 p.
CSmH; IU; NcD; PPAmP; TxU;
Vi.   11417

Bolmar, A.
    A collection of colloquial
phrases, on every topic necessary
to maintain conversation; arranged under different heads...
Philadelphia, Carey & Lea, 1832.
DLC; ICU; MeBat; OO; ViU.
                              11418
Bonar, Horatius, 1808-1890.
    Morning of joy; a sequel to
The night of weeping. New York,
1832. RPB.   11419

[Bonnycastle, John]
    [Bonnycastle's introduction to
algebra] New York, James Ryan,
1832. TxConT.   11420

Book of Martyrs. See Foxe,
John

A book of ornithology, for youth.
Embracing descriptions of the
most interesting & remarkable
birds in all countries, with particular notice of American birds.
Boston, W. Hyde & co., 1832.
322 p. CtY; ICJ; MiGr; OClW;
PU.   11421

The book of prayer, and administration of the sacraments, and
other rites and ceremonies of the
church... New York, Elam Bliss,
1832. 250, 122 p. TNM.   11422

Boston, Thomas, 1676-1732.

Human nature in its fourfold state of primitive integrity, entire depravation, begun recovery, & consumate happiness or misery in the parents of mankind in Paradise, the unregenerate, the regenerate, all mankind in the future state; in several practical discourses. 5th ed. Philadelphia, Towar, 1832. 400 p. KKcBT; OHi; PU; PWW; ScCC.   11423

---- ---- Pittsburgh, Hanna, 1832. 400 p. GAU; InAS; OO; PPins.   11424

Boston, Mass. City Council.
(Ordered, that a board of commissioners of health be appointed with full powers to carry into execution all the authority vested in the city council by the laws of the Commonwealth and the ordinances of the City, for the purpose of preventing the introduction and limiting ravages of Cholera, June 20, 1832.) Boston, 1832. 8 p. CtY; MB; MBM; NN.
                                         11425
---- ---- [Report of the joint committee of the City council to whom was referred a communication from the auditor of accounts, embracing an estimate of appropriations necessary for the expenditures of the financial year. Boston, 1832] 8 p. DLC. 11426

---- ---- Committee on Ordinances.
Report on the subject of watering streets. Boston, 1832. 107 p. MCM.   11427

---- Clarendon Street Baptist Church.
The declaration of faith, with the church covenant, and list of members of the Federal Street Baptist Church, Boston, constituted July 16th, 1827. 3d ed. Boston, Putnam & Damrell, 1832.

34 p. PCA.   11428

---- Common council.
Rules and orders of the Common Council of the city of Boston. The city charter, the city ordinances, and the laws of the commonwealth... Boston, Eastburn, 1832. 64 p. DLC.   11429

---- ---- Standing committee on House of reformation for juvenile offenders.
Report of the Standing committee of the Common Council, on the subject of the House of reformation for juvenile offenders... [Boston, Pr. by J. H. Eastburn, 1832. 84 p. CtY; DLC; MB; NBLiHi; PPULC.   11430

---- Congregational Church [Green Street]
The Articles of Faith, and Form of Covenant, of the Congregational Church in Green-street, Boston... Boston, Crocker and Brewster, 1832. 14 p. DLC; M; MWA.   11431

---- Farm and Trade School, Thompson's Island.
Report on a farm school. [Boston, Mass., 1832?] 8 p. M; MBAt; MWA; NIC.   11432

---- Federal Street Baptist Church. See Boston. Clarendon Street Baptist Church.

---- Health Department.
General abstract from the bill of mortality for the city of Boston, from Jan. 1, 1831 to January 1, 1832. Broadside. MHi.
                                         11433
---- ---- ... [Report of the Committee of the Board of health commissioners, appointed to consider measures for the care and treatment of the sick. Boston, 1832] 3 p. CSmH; MWA.   11434

---- ---- ... To the Board of
health commissioners of the city
of Boston: The medical deputa-
tion appointed... to visit New York
for the purpose of making observations relative to the disease now
prevailing in that place, respectfully report: ...[Boston, 1832]
4 p. CSmH; DLC; MB; NN.
                              11435

---- Independence Day.
Order of Service, Boston,
July 4, 1832. [Boston, 1832]
4 p. MHi.   11436

---- Latin school.
A catalogue of the scholars...
Oct. 1832. Boston, Frost, 1832.
40 p. PPAmP.   11437

---- South Boston Evangelical
Congregational Church.
Articles of faith and form of
covenant adopted by the church.
Boston, n.p., 1832.   11438

---- Sunday School Society.
Annual report of the Sunday
school society read at the second
public meeting of the society,
May 30, 1832. Boston, 1832.
21 p. WHi.   11439

---- Young Men's Anti-Masonic
Association.
Constitution of the Young Men's
Anti-masonic Association for the
diffusion of truth. Boston, 1832.
10 p. MB; WHi.   11440

---- Young Men's Christian Association.
Address, to the young men of
Boston; to which is annexed the
constitution of the society. Boston, Garrison, 1832. 13 p.
NCH.   11441

Boston and Barre Company.
Acts of incorporation and by-
laws of the Boston and Barre
Company. Boston, Pr. by Perkins & Marvin, 1832. 15 p.

MH-BA; MWA.   11442

Boston and Providence Railroad
Corporation.
Report of the board of directors to the stockholders of the
Boston and Providence rail road
company, submitting the report of
their engineer... to which are annexed the acts of incorporation.
Boston, J. E. Hinckley & Co.,
1832. 87 p. CSt; MBAt; MeHi;
OClWHi; RHi.   11443

---- Report on the surveys, with
the estimates of cost, for a railroad from Boston to Providence
and Taunton, by the engineer, to
the president and directors of the
company, 1832. [Boston, 1832]
87 p. NN.   11444

Boston and Worcester Railroad
Corporation.
Annual Report of the Boston &
Worcester Rail-Road Corporation
...number 1. Boston, 1832. CSt;
IU; MCM.   11445

---- [Notice of a meeting of the
stockholders in Boston, March
28th, 1832. Boston, 1832] 1 p.
MB; MH-BA; NN.   11446

---- Report of directors of the
Boston and Worcester rail-road
corporation to the stockholders
together with the Report of John
M. Fessendin, esq., civil engineer, and a plan and profile of
the location of the railroad. Boston, From the Steam power press
office, Pr. by W. L. Lewis,
1832. 40 p. CU; DLC; ICJ; M;
PU.   11447

---- Report [to the legislature of
Massachusetts.] [1st] Boston,
1832- CSt; DBRE; M; NjP;
PPULC.   11448

Boston Asylum for Indigent Boys.
An account of the Boston Asy-

lum for Indigent Boys, the Act
of Incorporation, Bye-Laws, and
the Rules and Regulations adopt-
ed By the Board of Managers.
Also, an Extract from the First
Anniversary Sermon, by the Rev.
Mr. Lowell. Boston, Pr. by
Nathaniel Willis, 1816. 3d ed.
Boston, 1832. 38 p. DLC; MB;
MH; MiD-B; NN.   11449

Boston Athenaeum.
    Catalogue of the sixth exhibi-
tion of paintings in the Athenaeum
gallery. Boston, Pr. by J. H.
Eastburn, 1832. 8 p. MB; MBAt;
MHi; MNF.   11450

Boston Daily Advocate, January
3, 1832- December 1838. CSmH;
DLC; MBAt; MWA; WHi.   11451

Boston Daily Atlas, July 2, 1832-
Dec. 31, 1860, Jan.-June, 1861.
[Boston] John H. Eastburn & Co.,
[etc.] 32 vols. MBAt; MTaHi.
                        11452
The Boston Literary Magazine.
Edited by W. G. Hanaford and H.
Bourne. Vol. 1, no. 1. May 1,
1832-April 1, 1833. Boston,
1832-33. ICU; MHi; OClWHi.
                        11453
Boston Lying-In Hospital.
    Act of Incorporation, by-laws,
trustees, regulations, and offi-
cers of the Boston Lying-In Hos-
pital. Boston, J. E. Hinckley, &
Co., 1832. 20 p. DLC; DNLM;
MB; MH; MWA.   11454

Boston Mechanic and Journal of
the Useful Arts and Sciences.
Boston. 1832 [February, 1836]
DLC; MB; MBC; MWA; NjR.
                        11455
Boston Port Society.
    An Account of the Port Society
of the City of Boston and its vicinity, and of the proceedings at
it's Third Annual Meeting. Boston, Pr. by S. W. Dickinson,
1832. 24 p. MB; MH; MWA;

MHi; NjR; OO.   11456

Boston Relief Association.
    Regulations of the Boston Re-
lief Association, with a list of
members. Boston, Pr. by I. R.
Butts, 1832. 29 p. MHi; MWA.
                        11457
---- Report, Aug. 13, 1832.
[Boston, 1832] MBAt.   11458

Boston Society for the Promotion
of Temperance.
    One hundred and thirty ques-
tions on the use of ardent spirits.
Boston, 1832. MB; MBAt. 11459

Boston Society of Natural History.
    Act of incorporation, constitu-
tion and by-laws. Boston, Eastburn, 1832. 16 p. MB; MBAt;
MHi; PPL; PPULC.   11460

Boston Young Men's Temperance
Society.
    Address of the Young Men's
Temperance Society to the young
men of Boston; to which is an-
nexed the Constitution of the So-
ciety. Boston, Pr. by Garrison
and Knapp, 1832. 13 p. MBAt;
NNUT; PPPrHi; TxHi; WHi.
                        11461
Bostwick, Henry, 1787-1836 or 7.
    Historical and classical atlas.
New York, 1832. PPULC; PPWa.
                        11462
Boswell, James, 1740-1795.
    The life of Samuel Johnson,
LL. D., including A journal of a
tour of the Hebrides. By James
Boswell, esq. A new ed. With
numerous additions and notes by
John Wilson Croker... Boston,
Carter, Hendee & Co., 1832.
2 v. CtHT; GEU; MdBP; PPA;
ScC.   11463

Botanick Sentinel and Enquirer.
Rochester, N. Y.
    First Botanick Society in Mon-
roe County, 1832. NN.   11464

Botham, P. E. Bates.
The common school arithmetic, in which the rules are explained in the plainest and most concise methods extant, with many important improvements, containing proofs in each rule with demonstrations from the most simple and evident principles; together with reasons for every rule, accompanied with a series of questions on the nature and application of the same. To which is added a dictionary of arithmetical terms not found in any other treatise. By Bates Botham. Hartford, H. Benton, 1832. 228 p. CtHT-W; CtHWatk; DLC; MBU-E.   11465

Bouldin, Thomas Tyler, 1772-1834.
Speech of Mr. Thomas T. Bouldin of Virginia, on the bill proposing a reduction of the duties on imports. Delivered in the House of Representatives, June, 1832. Washington, Pr. by Duff Green, 1832. 29 p. DLC; PPAmP; ScU; Vi; ViU.   11466

Bourrienne, [Louis Antoine Fauvelet] de, 1769-1834.
The life of Napoleon Bonaparte, by M. de Bourrienne, his private secretary. With notes, now first added, from the dictation of Napoleon at St. Helena, from the memoirs of the Duke of Rovigo, of General Rapp, of Constant, and numerous other authentic sources. Philadelphia, Carey & Lea, 1832. 669 p. CSmH; GU; MiU; PU; ScCC; WHi. 11467

Bowditch, Nathaniel.
The new American practical navigator: being an epitome of navigation;... with an appendix, ...By Nathaniel Bowditch, L. L. D. 7th stereotype ed. New-York, E. & G. W. Blunt, 1832. 618 p. ICart; IaDaM; MB; MCH; NNC.
11468

Bowdoin College.
Catalogue of the officers and students of Bowdoin College and the Medical School of Maine. April, 1832. Brunswick, Joseph Griffin, 1832. 24 p. Me; MeB; MeBat; MeHi; OC.   11469

---- Catalogue Senatus Academici, et eorum qui munera et Officia Gesserunt, quique alicujus gradus laurea donati sunt, in Collegic Bowdoinenai, Brunswick, in republica mainensi. Brunsvici, E. Typhis Griffin et wold, 1832. 16 p. MeB.   11470

---- Laws of Bowdoin College in the State of Maine. Brunswick, Joseph Griffin, 1832. 30 p. MeB.   11471

Bowie, Alexander.
An oration delivered on the 4th July, 1832, before Capt. Andrew Miller's company of "Jeffersonian Nullifiers" in Abbeville district. By Col. Alexander Bowie. Pub. at the request of the company. Abbeville, Pr. by John Taggart, 1832. 12 p. NN.   11472

Bowler, Leonard C.
Catalogue of books, stationary, cutlery, and fancy goods, for sale by Leonard C. Bowler... Boston, Pr. by Leonard C. Bowles, 1832. 8 p. CBPSR.
11473
Bowles, Magdalene [Wade]
Characters and incidents of village life, mostly founded upon fact... by Mrs. Bowles...2d ed. New York, Swords, Stanford & Co., 1832. 168 p. NNG.   11474

The boy in prison...Written for the American Sunday School Union... Philadelphia, American Sunday School Union, 1832. 22 p. DLC.   11475

Boyer, Abel, 1667-1729.

French dictionary; comprising all the additions and improvements of the latest Paris and London editions, (etc.) Boston, Hilliard, Gray, Little & Wilkins, 1832. Vol. 2 has an English-French dictionary, designed as a second part to the Boston ed. of Boyer's French dictionary, with Tardy's pronunciation. Boston, Hilliard, Gray & co., 1832. 2 vols. in 1. IaHoL; MH; OO; TMeV; WvLeGC; ViAl.
11476

[Brackenridge, Henry Marie] 1786-1871.
The history of the late war between the United States and Great Birtain containing a brief recapitulation of the events which led to the declaration of war, its progress, and an account of the various brilliant land and naval victories including the battle of New Orleans, New York, Lomax & Mitchell, 1832. 144 p. CSmH; DLC; MiD; OSW; PP.
11477

---- Judge Brackenridge's letters (Washington 1832) concerning his removal by Gen. Jackson from the territorial judiciary for Florida. [Washington, 1832] 15 p. DLC; KyHi; MiD-B; OClWHi; TxU.
11478

Bradford Junior College, Bradford, Mass.
Catalogue of the officers and students of Bradford Academy, female department, Bradford, Massachusetts, October, 1832. Haverhill, Pr. by C. P. Thayer & Co., 1832. 12 p. MHa.
11479

Bradford, Mass. First Church.
Articles of faith and covenant, adopted by the First Church of Christ in Bradford, Massachusetts... Haverhill, Pr. by A. W. Thayer, 1832. 22 p. ICN; MBC; MBradJ; MHaHl; Nh.
11480

Bradley, Eliza, b. 1783.
An authentic narrative of the shipwreck and sufferings of Mrs. Eliza Bradley, the wife of Captain James Bradley, of Liverpool, Eng., commander of the British ship Sally, which was wrecked on the coast of Barbary, in June, 1818. ...Written by herself. Boston, John Page, 1832. 108 p. MH; MiU-C; NNUT; NjR.
11481

---- ---- New York, J. H. Tunney, 1832. 108 p. IaHA; MPiB; NPU; NUt.
11482

---- ---- Utica, N.Y., Alexander Cameron, 1832. 106 p. NUt.
11483

[Brainard, John Gardiner Calkins] 1796-1828.
The Fort Braddock letters, a tale of the old French war; or, The adventures of Du Quesne, Dudley, and Van Tromp: with the capture of Captain Kidd. Peekskill, Pr. by Huestis & Brewer, 1832. 128 p. DLC; MB; NN; PPULC.
11484

---- The literary remains of John G. C. Brainard, with a sketch of his life... by J. G. Whittier. Hartford, P. B. Goodsell [1832] MA.
11485

Braintree [Mass.] Union Religious Society.
Constitution of the temperance association, in the Union Religious Society, of Braintree and Weymouth. Dedham Patriot Office, Pr. by Herman Mann, Jr., 1832. 12 p. MBNEH; MWey; MWeyHi.
11486

Braman, Isaac.
Centennial discourse delivered at the reopening of the Congregational meeting-house in New-Rowley, September 6, 1832. Haverhill, C. F. Thayer & Co., 1832.

16 p. MHa.   11487

Brannon, John.
Official letters of the military
and naval officers of the United
States during the war with Great
Britain, in the years 1812, 13,
14, and 15, with some additional
letters and documents elucidating
the history of that period. Washington, Pr. by Way & Gideon,
for the author, 1832. 510 p.
AMob.   11488

Brashears, Noah.
The satirist; with miscellane-
ous pieces in verse and prose.
Washington, Pr. by C. H. Bar-
ron, for the author, 1832. 59 p.
CSmH; MH; MdBP; NhPoA; RPB.
                               11489
Bray, Joseph.
Slavery. Copy of a letter from
Mr. Joseph Bray...28th April,
1832... Broadside. OClWHi.
                               11490
Brazer, John, 1787-1846.
The efficacy of prayer, first
published in the Unitarian Advo-
cate. Boston, Christian Register
Office, 1832. 31 p. MWA; MeB;
MiU.   11491

---- On the value of the public
exercises of our religion. [Bos-
ton, D. Reed, 1832] 24 p. MH.
                               11492
---- The Power of Unitarianism
over the affections. By John
Brazer. 2d ed. 1st series. no.
27. American Unitarian Association. Boston, Gray & Bowen,
1832. 24 p. CBPSR; ICMe;
MeB; MeBat; NjPT.   11493

The bread of deceit. From the
London ed., rev. Philadelphia,
Latimer & co., 1832. 146 p.
DLC.   11494

Breckinridge, John, 1797-1841.
[Catholic controvers between
J. Breckinridge and J. Hughes.

Philadelphia, 1832-33?] 326 p.
NN.   11495

Breckinridge, Robert Jefferson,
1800-1871.
An address delivered before
the Temperance Society in the
Woodford Ch., on the 13th of
November 1831... Lexington, Ky.,
Skillman, 1832. 11 p. MH-AH;
PPPrHi.   11496

Breese, Sidney.
To the voters of the 1st Con-
gressional district, composed of
the counties of Macoupin, Madi-
son, St. Clair, Bond, Clinton,
Washington, Monroe, Randolph,
Perry, Jackson, Franklin, Union,
Alexander, Johnson, Pope & Gal-
latin... Fellow citizens: Sidney
Breese. Camp near Fort Will-
burn, June 21, 1832. Broadside.
ICHi.   11497

Brewster, David, 1781-1868.
Letters on natural magic ad-
dressed to Sir Walter Scott, bart.
By Sir David Brewster... New
York, Harper & bros., 1832. 314
p. ArCH; CtY; NcD; TNP; VtU.
                               11498
---- ... The life of Sir Isaac
Newton. By David Brewster,
LL. D., F. R. S. ...New-York,
J. & J. Harper, 1832. 323 p. Ct;
LNH; MHi; NPtw; TMeT.   11499

Bridge, Bewick, 1767-1833.
A treatise on the elements of
algebra. By the Rev. B. Bridge
... 1st Amer. rev. and corr.
from the 6th London ed. Philadelphia, Key, Mielke & Biddle, 1832.
199 p. DLC; GU; IaU; MBAt; PU.
                               11500
Bridge, William, 1600?-1670.
The Refuge, containing the
righteous man's habitation in the
time of plague and pestilence: being a brief exposition of the 91st
Psalm. New York, Daniel Appleton, 1832. 120 p. LNH; MH; NjPT;

OO; PHC.   11501

Bridgeport, Conn. , First Congregational Church.
     Manual for the communicants
of the First Congregational church
in Bridgeport, compiled Jan. 1,
1832... New Haven, 1832. 36 p.
ICN; NBLIHi.   11502

A brief history of the reformation in Germany; with a sketch of
the life of Martin Luther. B[os-
ton] 1832. 36 p. MH.   11503

Brigham, Amariah, 1798-1849.
     Remarks on the influence of
mental cultivation and mental excitement upon health. Hartford,
F. J. Huntington, 1832. 116 p.
CtSoP; IaDa; MB; OO; PCC.
                           11504
---- A treatise on epidemic
cholera; including an historical
account of its origin and progress to the present period, compiled from the most authentic
sources. Hartford, Huntington,
1832. 368 p. CtY; DLC; MdBJ;
NBuG; ViRM.   11505

Brigham, John C[lark].
     Nuevo sistema de geografia...
Por Juan C. Brigham y Sidney
E. Morse. Nueva York, N. Y.
J. White, 1832. MH.   11506

Bristol, Rhode Island.
     By-Laws of the Town of Bris-
tol. August 28, 1832. Broadside.
                           11507
British Drama. A collection of
the most esteemed tragedies,
comedies, operas and farces in
the English language. Philadelphia, Woodward, 1832. 2 v. CtY;
IaGG; MH; NcU; TxU; WHi.
                           11508
The British essayists, containing
the spectator with notes and general index; and the tatler and
guardian, with notes and index, in
two volumes. Stereotype ed. Pr.

verbatim, from the original London ed. Philadelphia, J. J. Woodward, 1832. 2 vols. P; ViR.
                           11509
Broad grins; or, Fun for the new
year 1832. Boston, Arthur Ainsworth [1832] 45 p. MB; MWA;
MiD-B.   11510

Brodnax, William H. , 1786-1834.
     The speech of William H.
Brodnax, (of Dinwiddie) in the
House of Delegates of Virginia, on
the policy of the State with respect to its colored population delivered Jan. 19, 1832. Richmond,
Pr. by Thomas W. White, 1832.
44 p. CSmH; IU; NcD; PPAmP;
ViU.   11511

Bronson, Henry, 1804-1893.
     Observations on the chlorides
and chlorine... preventives of
cholera. By Henry Bronson, M. D.
Boston, Clapp & Hull, 1832. 12 p.
CtHWatk; MBAt; MWA; NN.
                           11512
Brooke, Henry, 1703-1783.
     Fool of quality; or, The history
of Henry, Earl of Moreland; 3d
Amer. from 3d London ed. Balti-
more, M'Dowell, 1832. 2 v. CtMW;
NICLA; NcU.   11513

Brookes, Richard, fl. 1750.
     A new universal gazetteer, con-
taining a description of the principal nations, empires, kingdoms,
states... of the known world...
Originally composed by Brookes.
The whole re-modelled and the
historical and statistical department brought down to the present
period by John Marshall... With
numerous additions by the American ed. ...A description of the
various Indian tribes in North
America... New York, W. W.
Reed & Co. , 1832. 899 p. DLC;
FMU; MiU; PP; TBiK.   11514

Brooks, Charles.
     Prayers for individuals. Bos-

ton, 1832. 39 p. MDeeP; MH-
AH.   11515

Brooks, Thomas, 1608-1680.
Apples of gold for young men
and women and a crown of glory
for old men and women, by
Thomas Brooks. New York, C.
Wells, 1832. 221 p. MNtCA;
NBuU; NjMD; NNG.   11516

---- The precious remedies
against Satan's devices. By
Thomas Brooks... ed. by Staunton
Stevens Burdett. 1st Amer. ed.
New Haven, N. W. Whiting,
1832. 264 p. NcD; OMC; TJaU;
TxU.   11517

Brothers in Unity, Yale College
Library. See Yale University.
Library.

Broussais, Francois Joseph Victor, 1772-1838.
Cholera. Two clinical lectures
upon the nature, treatment and
symptoms, of spasmodic cholera,
by J. F. V. Broussais. Delivered during the prevalence of the
disease in Paris. New York,
W. Stodart, 1832. 28 p. CSt-L;
IEN-M; MB; NNN.   11518

---- Principles of physiological
medicine, in the form of propositions; embracing physiology,
pathology, and therapeutics, with
commentaries on those relating
to pathology. By F. J. V. Broussais... Tr. from the French by
Isaac Hays, M. D., and R. Eglesfeld[!], Griffith... Philadelphia,
Carey & Lea, 1832. 594 p. CSt-
L; ICJ; MnU; PPC; ViU.   11519

---- A treatise of physiology applied to pathology... Tr. from the
French, by John Bell, M. D. ...
and R. LaRoche, M. D. 3d Amer.
ed. Philadelphia, Carey & Lea,
1832. GEU-M; ICJ; KyU; OO;
PPM; TNV.   11520

Brown, Bartholomew, 1772-1854.
Temple carmina. Songs of
the temple; or, Bridgewater collection of sacred music. 22d ed.
Boston, Carter, Hendie & Co.,
1832. 349 p. CtMW; ICN; MH;
RPB.   11521

Brown, Benjamin Boyer.
Notes on various subjects connected with medicine by Benj. B.
Brown, student of medicine in the
University of Pennsylvania, Philadelphia, 1830. [Philadelphia]
1832. 185 [29] p. CSt-L.   11522

Brown, Erastus.
The trial of Cain, the first
murderer, in poetry, by rule of
court; in which a predestinarian,
a Universalian, and an Arminian,
argue as attornies at the bar; the
two former as the prisoner's
counsel, the latter as attorney
general. Hartford, Loren Hills,
1832. 48 p. NBuG; RPB.   11523

Brown, Goold, 1791-1857.
The institutes of English grammar methodically arranged, with
examples for parsing, questions
for examination, false syntax for
correction, exercises for writing,
observations for the advanced student, and a key to the oral exercises: to which are added four
appendixes. Designed for the use
of schools, academies, and private learners... Stereotype ed.
rev. by the author. New York,
Wood; Boston, Ticknor & Co.
[1832] 311 p. CtY; IEG; MB;
OCIWHi; PLFM.   11524

---- A key to the exercises for
writing, contained in the Institutes of English grammar. Designed for the aid of teachers and
private learners. New York, S.
S. and W. Wood [1832] 48 p.
NN.   11525

Brown, James.

The American grammar. By
James Brown. Prepared for the
use of schools by the author.
Auburn, Pr. by H. Oliphant,
1832. 84 p. NCH.   11526

Brown, John, 1722-1787.
A brief vew of the figures,
and explanations of the Meta-
phors contained in Scriptures.
By Rev. John Brown. 2d Amer.
ed. Middlebury, Vt., A. Cotton,
1832. 480 p.   CU; IEG; MWA;
NcC; VtHi.   11527

---- A concordance to the Holy
Scripture of the Old and New
Testaments...See under Bible.

---- A dictionary of the Holy
Bible... The whole comprising
whatever important is known...
By the Rev. John Brown...From
the 12th and latest Edinburgh ed.
Complete in 1 vol. New York,
J. J. Harper, 1832. 534, 26 p.
InCW; NBLISH; NNMHi; NjP.
                           11528
---- The shorter catechism for
young children. Philadelphia, L.
Johnson, 1832. 32 p. AmSSchU;
MH; NcD; NPot; OMC.   11529

---- Two short catechisms mutu-
ally connected. The question of
the former being generally supposed and omitted in the letter...
Pittsburgh, Johnston, 1832.
PPPrHi; PPULC.   11530

Brown, John Thompson.
The speech of John Thompson
Brown, in the House of Delegates of Virginia, on the abolition of slavery. Delivered Wednesday, Jan. 18, 1832. Richmond, Pr. by Thomas W. White,
1832. 32 p. DLC; ICN; NIC;
PHi; Vi.   11531

Brown, M.
Memoir of Rev. Obadian Jen-
ings...By Rev. M. Brown.

Pittsburgh, n.p., 1832. 27 p.
NjPT.   11532

Brown, Matthew, 1776-1853.
An address delivered to the
graduates in Jefferson college,
Pa., at the anniversary com-
mencement, Sept. 27, 1832...
Pittsburgh, Pr. by D. & M.
Maclean, 1832. 12 p. CSmH;
DLC; PWW.   11533

Brown, William, 1783-1863.
Selection of passages of scripture for young persons... Philadelphia, French and Perkins,
1832. 176 p. CtHWatk; CtY;
MBC; MeBat.   11534

Brown University.
Catalogue of the officers and
students of Brown University, for
the academical year, 1831-32.
Providence, H. H. Brown, 1832.
16 p. DLC; ICJ.   11535

---- Catalogue of the officers
and students of Brown University,
for the academical year, 1832-
33.   Providence, Pr. by H. H.
Brown, 1832. 18 p. Ct; NRAB;
PCA.   11536

Browne, Daniel Jay, b. 1804.
The etymological encyclopaedia
of technical words and phrases
used in the arts and sciences...
By Daniel Browne.   Boston,
Wm. Hyde & Co., Lyceum
Press, Geo. W. Light and Co.,
1832. 258 p. ANA; CtHWatk;
MH; OO; WGr.   11537

---- First lessons in natural history; geology comprising the elements of the science in its present advanced state, designed for
the use of schools & private
learners... Boston, Hyde, 1832.
108 p. CtHWatk; MH; PPULC; OO;
PU.   11538

---- The sylva Americana; or,

A description of the forest trees
indigenous to the United States,
practically and botanically considered. Illustrated by more
than one hundred engravings.
Boston, William Hyde & Co.,
1832. 408 p. CtY; DLC; MWA;
MPiB; NjP; PPA; WaU.   11539

Brownell, Thomas Church, 1779-
1865.
   An address upon the occasion
of the annual commencement of
the General theological seminary
of the Protestant Episcopal church
in the United States; delivered in
the chapel of St. Peter's church,
June 29, 1832. New York, Pub.
by request of Board of Trustees,
Pr. at the Protestant Episcopal
church, 1832. 12 p. CtHT; MWA;
NNUT; PHi; WHi.   11540

---- A charge to the clergy of
the Protestant Episcopal Church
in the state of Connecticut. Delivered... the 6th of June, A.D.
1832. By Thomas Church Brownell. New Haven, L. H. Young,
1832. 17 p. CtY; MWA; MiD-B;
NNG; OClWHi; PPL.   11541

---- A farewell address to the
students of Washington College,
delivered in the college chapel
on the sixteenth of December,
1831, by the Rt. Rev. T. C.
Brownell, on his retiring from
the presidency of the institution.
Hartford, Pr. by P. Canfield,
for H. & F. J. Huntington, 1832.
19 p. CtHT; MWA; NjR; PHi;
RPB.   11542

Bryan, John A.
   Address delivered at Columbus, Ohio, on the anniversary of
the Victory of N. Orleans... January 9, 1832. [Columbus? 1832]
8 p. OClWHi.   11543

Bryant, William Cullen, 1794-
1878.

Poems, by William Cullen
Bryant. New-York, E. Bliss,
1832. 240 p. CSt; DLC; MBAt;
NjP; PPA; RNR.   11544

---- Selections from the American poets. New York, Harper,
1832. PPULC; PPGi.   11545

---- Tales of Glauber-Spa. By
several American authors...[Ed.
by W. C. Bryant] New York, J.
& J. Harper, 1832. 2 v. AU;
CtHT; MB; NIC; TNP.   11546

Buchan, William, 1729-1805.
   Domestic Medicine, or A treatise on the prevention and cure
of diseases, by regimen and simple medicines:...By William Buchan, M.D. ...Exeter, J. & B.
Williams, 1832. 495 p. InVal;
NN; Nh.   11547

Buck, Charles, 1771-1815.
   Anecdotes, religious, moral
and entertaining. New York, J.
H. Turney, 1832. 2 v. in 1.
ABBS; IEG; MS; NCabs; OO.
                        11548
---- A theological dictionary...
By the late Rev. Charles Buck.
Woodward's new ed. Pub. from
the last London ed. Philadelphia,
J. J. Woodward, 1832. 624 p.
CLU; MH; PHi; ScDue; TNP.
                        11549
Buckingham, Joseph Tinker.
   Trial: Commonwealth vs J. T.
Buckingham, on an indictment for
a libel on John O. Moffit, before
the municipal court of the city of
Boston, December term, 1822.
5th ed. Boston, 1832. 27 p. ICU.
                        11550
Buckner, Alexander, d. 1833.
   Speech... on the resolution pro-
posing to purchase sixty copies of
the History of the bank of the
United States, March 1832. Wash-
ington, 1832. 8 p. PPM; WHi.
                        11551

Buckstone, John Baldwin, 1802-
1879.
The breach of promise; or,
Second thoughts are best. A
comedy, in two acts. By J. B.
Buckstone. New York, Samuel
French [1832] 40 p. C; OCl.
11552
---- The pet of the petticoats.
An opera, in three acts, by J.
B. Buckstone. New York, Sam-
uel French, [1832] 36 p. OCl.
11553
Buffalo, New York.
An Act to incorporate the City
of Buffalo, passed April 20,
1832. Buffalo, Pr. by David M.
Day, 1832. 24, 26 p. DLC;
NBu; NBuG. 11554

---- Laws and Ordinances of The
Common Council of the City of
Buffalo, passed June 20, 1832.
Pub. by order of the Common
Council. Buffalo, Pr. by David
M. Day, 1832. 24 p. NBuG.
11555
Buffon, Georges Louis Leclerc,
Comte de, 1707-1788.
Buffon's natural history of
quadrupeds, birds, fishes, ser-
pents, reptiles and insects...
New York, C. Wells, 1832. 285 p.
MB; MWA; NIC-A; NcAS; PPA.
11556
Buist, Robert, 1805-1880.
The American flower garden
directory, containing practical
directions for the culture of plants
in the hot-house, garden house,
flower garden, and rooms or par-
lours, for every month in the
year. Instructions for erecting a
hot-house... with lists of annuals,
biennials, and ornamental shrubs
...By Hibbert & Buist. Philadelphia, A. Waklie, 1832. 375 p.
DLC; GU; NcU; PHi; ViU. 11557

Bulfinch, Stephen Greenleaf,
1809-1870.
Contemplations of the Saviour;
a series of extracts from the
gospel history, with reflections,
and original and selected hymns.
Boston, Carter & Hendee, 1832.
155 p. CBPac; GMM; IEG; MH;
OCoC; RPB. 11558

Bulgarin, Faddei Venediktovich,
1789-1859.
Ivan Vejeeghen; or, Life in
Russia. By Thaddeus Bulgarin...
[Tr. from the Russian by George
Ross] Philadelphia, Carey & Lea,
1832. 2 v. CSmH; CtY; MB; NNS;
PPA; T. 11559

Bullard, Henry Adams, 1788-1851.
Speech on the Tariff in the
Committee of the Whole House on
the State of the Union, June 15,
1832. [Washington, 1832] 16 p.
CtHWatk; DLC; MBAt; MH.11560

Bunker Hill Monument Association.
Report of the president, vice-
presidents, and several directors
... (From June 1831 to June
1832) Boston, Boston Daily Advocate, 1832. 15 p. CtY; IaU; MeB;
RPB; WHi. 11561

Bunyan, John, 1628-1688.
Eines Christen Reise Nach der
Seligen Ewigkeit Johann Bunyan
Harrisburg, Gustav S. Peters,
1832. 2 v. in 1. KyDC; P; PHi;
PPULC; PSt. 11562

---- The holy war made by King
Shaddai upon Diabolus, to regain
the metropolis of the world; or,
The losing and taking again of the
town of Mansoul. By John Bunyan
...New ed. with explanatory, ex-
perimental, and practical notes.
By the Rev. G. Burder... New-
York, J. H. Turney, 1832. 252 p.
DLC; MBevHi; OMC; TNS. 11563

---- Pilgerreise. Harrisburg,
G. S. Peters, 1832. PPeSchw.
11564
---- The pilgrim's progress.

With a life of John Bunyan, by
Robert Southey. Boston, Crocker
& Brewster; New York, Jonathan
Leavitt, 1832. 348 p. CtY; KAS;
MB; MH; OCIW.   11565

---- The pilgrim's progress from
this world, to that which is to
come. Delivered under the sim-
ilitude of a dream. In two parts.
Cincinnati, H. M. Rulison, Queen
City Pub. House [1832] 216 p.
MWA; OC; OUrC.   11566

---- ---- Hartford, Silas And-
rus, 1832. xv, 360 p. CtHT-W;
IGK; KBB; KyBgW; ViLxW.
                                11567
---- ---- New York, R. Worth-
ington, 1832. 572 p. PReaAT.
                                11568
---- The works of that eminent
servant of Christ, John Bunyan
... Philadelphia, J. Locken,
1832. 2 v. CtY; GDecCT; KU;
MeB; PHi.   11569

Burdekin, Richard.
   An historical account of the
plague and other pestilential dis-
tempers, which have appeared in
Europe, more especially England,
from the earliest period. ...
New York [1832] 78 p. MBM.
                                11570
Burder, George.
   Village Sermons; or, One hundred and one plain and short discourses, on the principal doctrines of the Gospel... By George
Burder... To which is added to
each sermon, a short prayer...
New York, M'Elrath & Bangs,
1832. 476 p. IaDmU; MoS; OMC;
ViAl.   11571

---- ---- Philadelphia, J. Grigg,
1832. 476 p. InID; MH; OCX;
PPEB; ViAl.   11572

Burford, Robert.
   Description of the panorama of
the superb city of Mexico, and
the surrounding scenery, painted
on twenty-seven hundred square
feet of canvass, by Robert Burford, esq. from drawings made
on the spot, at the request of the
Mexican government, by Mr. W.
Bullock, junior. Now open for
public inspection. Washington,
1832. 16 p. CLO; DLC; MB; P;
PPAmP.   11573

Burges, Tristam, 1770-1853.
   The address of a farmer to the
honest men of all parties in the
State of Rhode-Island and Provi-
dence plantations [1832] 16 p.
PPFM.   11574

---- Address to the citizens of
R. I. statement... upon principles
and measures adopted by General
Jackson in his administration of
the National Government. Providence, 1832. 12 p. RHi.   11575

---- A brief sketch of the remarks delivered at East Greenwich, at a convention of National
Republicans,... Providence, Pr.
by Wm. Marshall & Co., 1832.
15 p. MWA; MiD-B; RP.   11576

---- Soldiers of the revolution.
Rhode Island, May 26, 1832
[Rhode Island 22d Cong. 1st sess.
Doc. no. 246] RP.   11577

---- Speech in the case of Samuel Houston, charged with a violation of the rights and powers of
the House by assaulting the Hon.
William Staberry, a member of
Ohio, for words spoken in debate. House of Representatives,
May 11, 1832. Washington, 1832.
32 p. DLC; MH; OCIWHi; RHi;
TxU.   11578

---- Speech of Mr. Burges of
Rhode Island, on the leading principles of the American System...
House of Representatives June 1,
1832. Providence, Pr. by Wm.

Marshall & Co., 1832. 48 p.
ICU; MWA; NjR; NyPL; RP.
11579
---- Statement of some leading
principles and measures adopted
by Gen. Jackson, See Robbins,
Asher, 1757-1845.

Burke, Francis.
Trial of Francis Burke, be-
fore Baltimore city court, on an
indictment for manslaughter, by
administering to Benjamin M.
Hazelip certain Thomsonian rem-
edies. Baltimore, J. Lucas &
E. K. Deaver, 1832. 108 p.
DNLM; MBS; MdBE; MdHi; PHi;
PPULC.   11580

Burke, William.
The rudiments of Latin grammar, founded on the definitions
and rules of Thomas Ruddiman;
to which is annexed a complete
system of prosody; the whole
compiled from the best authorities, and affectionally inscribed
to his pupils. Richmond [Va.],
Sheperd, 1832. 186 p. CSmH;
CtY; ICU; MH; NjR; Vi.   11581

Burlamaqui, Jean Jacques, 1694-
1748.
The principles of natural and
politic law... by J. J. Burlamaqui... tr. into English by Mr. Nu-
gent. 7th ed. cor. Philadelphia,
P. H. Nicklin & T. Johnson,
1832. 2 v. in 1. DLC; InHuP;
MoU; OAlM; PPL.   11582

Burnap, Uzziah Cicero, 1794-
1854.
Youth's ethereal director; or,
A concise & familiar explanation
of the elements of astronomy...
designed for the use of schools &
academies, & especially for such
young ladies & gentlemen as are
unacquainted with the higher
branches of the mathematicks.
Middlebury, Vt., Coepland, 1832.
95 p. PPULC; PU.   11583

Burnet, Gilbert, 1643-1715.
Incidents in the life of Matthew Hale; exhibiting his moral
and religious character, with Baxter's Recollections of Hale. Boston, Loring, 1832. 112 p. CtSoP;
DLC; ICMe; MB; MBoy.   11584

---- Lives, characters, and an
address to posterity, by Gilbert
Burnet... With the two prefaces
to the Dublin editions... Ed. with
an introduction, and notes, by
John Jebb...1st Amer. ed. New
York, Protestant Episcopal Press,
1832. 344 p. OCl.   11585

Burnett, William.
An address on the subject of
temperance, delivered in the
chapel of Jefferson College, Canonsburg, Pa. on the 4th of July
1832. By William Burnett, a
member of the Senior Class.
Pittsburgh, Pr. by D. & M. Maclean, 1832. 16 p. PWW.   11586

---- An oration delivered before
the Phile Literary Society of Jefferson College, Pa., at the dedication of their hall at Canonsburg,
June, 1832. Pittsburgh, Pr. by
J. P. Butler, 1832. 12 p. PWW.
11587
Burns, John, 1774-1850.
Principles of midwifery; including the diseases of women
and children. With improvements
and notes by T. C. James. From
5th Lond. ed. Philadelphia,
Parker, 1832. 592 p. PPC; PPCF;
PPULC.   11588

Burns, Robert, 1759-1796.
The works of Robert Burns:
with an account of his life, and
criticism on his writings. To
which are prefixed some observations on the character and condition of the Scottish peasantry. By
James Currie, M. D. A new ed.,
with many additional poems and
songs, from the latest London edi-

tions, embellished with thirty-three engravings on wood. New York, Pr. by J. Booth and sons, 1832. 2 pts. in 1 v. DLC; FSa; MB; NR.   11589

---- ---- New-York, Pr. by W. Pearson, 1832. 425, 13 p. ArBaA; DLC; LNT; MiD; NjR.
11590

---- ---- Philadelphia, J. Crissy and J. Grigg, 1832. 2 pt. in 1 v. ArPb; DLC; NjP; PP; ViU.
11591

Burr, David H., 1803-1875.
The steamboat, stage, and canal register, etc. etc. etc. for the year 1832. New York, The Author, 1832. 16 p. MiD; MoSHi.   11592

Burroughs, Stephen, 1765-1840.
Memoirs of the notorious Stephen Burroughs: containing many incidents in the life of this wonderful man, never before published. Stereotype ed., newly cor. and rev. Boston, C. Gaylord, 1832. 2 v. in 1. CtMW; MWA; NcD; PHi; ViU.   11593

---- Sermon, delivered in Rutland, on a haymow, to his auditory, the Pelhamites, at the time when a mob of them after pursuing him to Rutland... shut him into a barn into which he ran for asylum... Boston, Pr. for the publisher, 1832. 8 p. MBAt; MH; MWA; Nh; OClWHi; VtU.   11594

Burrowes, John Frecklaton, 1787-1852.
...A companion to the Thorough--base primer, being fifty preliminary exercises, consisting of a base and melody, corresponding with the explanations, and intended to precede each exercise in that work. To which is added a key to the exercises. By J. F. Burrowes. 1st Amer. (from 2d

London) ed. New York, Firth & Hall (1832). 116 p. ICN; NRUMus.   11595

[Burrows, Silas E.] 1810-1860.
To the honest independent Jackson electors of New York, who are opposed to the establishment of a Spanish inquisition in America. New York, 1832. 8 p. WHi.
11596

Burton, Warren, 1800-1866.
Cheering views of man and providence, drawn from a consideration of the origin, uses, and remedies of evil. By Warran Burton. Boston, Carter, Hendee & Co., 1832. 264 p. CtY; IaB; MDeeP; NBu; PCA.   11597

---- My Religious Experience at My Native Home. By Warren Burton. No. 65. Pr. for The American Unitarian Association. Bost_n, Gray & Bowen, Nov. 1832. 32 p. CBPac; ICMe; MeB; Nh-Hi; PPL.   11598

Bush, George, 1796-1859.
The life of Mohammed; founder of the religion of Islam, and of the Empire of the Saracens. By the Rev. George Bush, A. M. New York, Pr. by J. & J. Harper, 1832. 261, 6 p. CU; ICR; LNB; MMe; NcU.   11599

---- Questions & notes, critical & practical, upon a Book of Exodus... New York, Haven, 1832. 240 p. CtY; IEG; MBAt. NN; PPPrHi; OO.   11600

---- A treatise on the millennium; in which the prevailing theories on that subject are carefully examined; and the true scriptural doctrine attempted to be elicited and established. By George Bush... New York, J. & J. Harper, 1832. 277 p. ArCH; CtY; ICP; MiD; ScDuE.   11601

Butler, Benjamin Franklin, 1795-1858.
Biography of M. Van Buren. Washington, Jonathan Elliot, 1832. 15 p. DLC; NN; NdU; PPL. 11602

---- Speech of Benjamin F. Butler, at the great meeting at the capitol, of which Simeon De Witt was chairman, October 18, 1832. Albany, N. Y., 1832. 19 p. MBC; NbU; PPL; ScU. 11603

Butler, Samuel, 1612-1680.
Hudibras; in three parts, written in the time of the late wars, with a life of the author annotations, and an index. Hartford, S. Andrus & Sons, 1832. 312 p. MBC; MH. 11604

Butler, Samuel, 1774-1839.
An atlas of ancient geography. By Samuel Butler, D. D. ... Philadelphia, Carey & Lea, 1832. 34 p. DLC; IaGG; MeB; TxHuT; WaPS. 11605

Byron, George Gordon Byron, 1788-1824.
Don Juan, by George Gordon Byron Byron, 6th baron, in sixteen cantos. Campe's ed. Nurnberg and New-York, Frederick Campe & Co. [1832] MH. 11606

---- Works, including the suppressed poems, by George Gordon Byron Byron, 6th baron, also a sketch of his life by J. W. Lake. Philadelphia, Key, Mielke & Biddle, 1832. 8 vol. IU; MB; MH; NjP; ViU. 11607

C

Cabinet of American History. Philadelphia, 1832. DLC. 11608

The cabinet of curiosities; or, Wonders of the world displayed, forming a repository of whatever is remarkable in the regions of nature & art, extraordinary events, & eccentric biography... New York, M'Elrath, 1832-33. 2 v. in 1. DLC; CLU; PP; PPULC. 11609

The Cabinet of literature, designed as a companion for leisure hours: containing, illustrations of American history... with upwards of thirty engravings... New York, A. & R. Hoyt, 1832. 284 p. CSmH; DLC; IC. 11610

Caesar, C. Julius.
C. Julii Caesar's quae extant, interpretatione et notis, illustravit Johannes Godvinus, professor Regius, in usum Delphin. The notes and interpretations translated and improved by Thomas Clark. 8th ed. Philadelphia, Thomas Desilver, 1832. 410 p. KyLo; MH; NStC; ScU; ViU. 11611

---- Caii Julii Caesaris commentarii de bello gallico ad codices Parisinas recenseti a N. L. Achaintre atque index historious et geographicus. Curorit F. P. Lererett. Bostoniae, Hilliard, Gray, Little et Wilkins, 1832. 220 p. CtHWatk; DLC; ICU; MWH; OBerB; RPB. 11612

Cain, John, 1805-1867.
The officer's guide and farmer's manual, containing a comprehensive collection of judicial and business forms adapted to the jurisprudence of Indiana... by John Cain. Indianapolis, Douglass & Maguire, 1832. 347 p. CSmH; DLC; In; InCW; InHi. 11613

Caldwell, Charles, 1772-1853.
A discourse on the advantages of a National University, especially in its influence on the union of the states: delivered, by request, to the Erodelphian Society of Miami University, September 25th,

1832. Cincinnati, E. H. Flint,
1832. 57 p. DNLM; MB; MWA;
OClWHi; OU; PPPrHi.   11614

---- A discourse on the first
centennial celebration of the
birthday of Washington, delivered
by request to the citizens of Lexington on the 22d of February,
1832. By Charles Caldwell, M. D.
Lexington, Ky. , Pr. by N. L.
Finnell & J. F. Herndon, 1832.
56 p. CSmH; DLC; ICU; KyU;
MWA; OC.   11615

---- Thoughts on the means of
preserving health in hot climates;
being an introductory lecture, delivered on the 6th day of November, 1832. OCGHM.   11616

Caldwell, Joseph, 1773-1835.
    Letters on popular education,
addressed to the people of North-
Carolina. Hillsborough, 1832.
54, 48p. NcHiC; NcU; NcWfC;
NcU; P; Vi.   11617

Caldwell, Merritt, 1806-1848.
    An address delivered before
the Readfield Temperance Society at their first anniversary
July 4, 1832. Hallowell, Advocate Office, 1832. 23 p.
MBNMHi; MeHi; MiD-B;
PPPrHi.   11618

Caledonia County Grammar
School. Lyndon, Vermont.
    Catalogue, Lyndon Academy.
For quarter ending November 23,
1832. St. Johnsbury, Pr. by S.
Eaton, Jr. 1832. 6 p. MH.
                          11619
Calender eines Christen Philadel-
phia, Conrad Zentler, [1832] MWA.
                          11620
Calhoun, John Caldwell, 1782-
1850.
    Important correspondence on
the subject of state interposition
between His Excellency Gov.
Hamilton and Hon. John C. Cal-

houn...Charleston, A. E. Miller,
1832. 27 p. MBAt; NCH; ScCC;
ScU.   11621

Calhoun, William B.
    Report of case of contempt in
the House of Representatives of
Massachusetts. Boston, Carter,
1832. 144 p. DLC; OCLaw.
                          11622
A calm appeal to the citizens of
the state of New York, on the ex-
pulsion of the Rev. James R.
Wilson, from the House of Assembly as one of their chaplains
... By a citizen of Albany. Albany, the author, 1832. 22 p.
CtY; DLC; MB; NcD; ViU. 11623

Calmet, Augustin, 1672-1757.
    Dictionary of the Holy Bible,
as published by the late Mr.
Charles Taylor, with the frag-
ments in corporated... American
ed. Rev. , with large additions,
by Edward Robinson...Illustrated
with maps, and engravings on
wood. Boston, Crocker and Brewster; New York, J. Leavitt, 1832.
1003 p. CSt; KyLo; NNUT; RPB;
ViU.   11624

Calvert, George Henry, 1803-
1889, ed.
    Illustrations of phrenology; be-
ing a selection of articles from
the Edinburgh phrenological journal, and the Transactions of the
Edinburgh phrenological society.
With twenty-six wood cuts. Ed.
by George H. Calvert. With an
introduction by the editor. Baltimore, W. & J. Neal, 1832. 192 p.
CSmH; ICBB; MdHi; PPA; TxGR.
                          11625
Cambridge, Massachusetts.
    Extracts from the Act author-
izing the Town of Cambridge to
establish a Board of Health; with
the Rules and Regulations of said
Board. [Cambridge, 1832] Broadside. MH.   11626

Camden and Amboy Railroad.
Acts relative to the (Company).
n.p., n.p., 1832. DLC.   11627

Cameron, Lucy Lyttelton (Butt)
1781-1858.
The holiday queen. By Mrs.
Cameron... New-York, M. Day,
1832. 23 p. DLC.   11628

---- The warning clock, or, The
voice of the new year. By the
author of "The two lambs," &c.
New-York, Pr. & sold by Mahlon
Day, 1832. 16 p. DLC.   11629

Campbell, Alexander, 1788-1866.
Delusions; an analysis of the
book of Mormon, with an examination of its internal and external
evidences, and a refutation of its
pretences to divine authority; with
prefatory remarks, by Joshua V.
Himes. Boston [Benjamin H.
Green] 1832. 16 p. CU; IaU;
KyRE; MHi; PU.   11630

---- [Psalms hymns. 1832]
Psalms, hymns, and spiritual
songs. Adapted to the Christian
religion, selected by Alexander
Campbell. 4th ed., Bethany, B.
C. Virginia, 1832. 192 p. InIB;
MoU; NNUT; NjMD; TNDC.
11631
Campbell, George, 1719-1796.
Lectures on systematic theol-
ogy and pulpit eloquence. By the
late George Campbell.. To which
are added, Dialogues on eloquence,
by M. De Fenelon... [New ed.],
Ed. by Henry J. Ripley... Boston,
Lincoln & Edmonds, 1832. 206,
102 p. CU; GHM; ICMe; NNUT;
ScDuE.   11632

Campbell, Thomas, 1777-1844.
Poetical works of Thomas
Campbell, consisting of The
pleasures of hope, Gertrude of
Wyoming, Theodric, and other poems, written at different periods
from the year 1799-1832. New

ed. Boston, Munroe and Francis,
1832. 300 p. CtB; MB; NOg.
11633
Canandaigua, N.Y. Board of
Health.
To the citizens of Canandaigua.
The recent appearance of the Asi-
atic or malignant cholera... in
Canada... June 28, 1832. Broad-
side. NN.   11634

The cannibals: or, A Sketch of
New Zealand. By the author of
The Naval Chaplain, etc... Rev.
by the publishing Committee. Bos-
ton, Massachusetts Sabbath School
Union, 1832. DLC; ICP; MNS;
MSaP; PPAmS.   11635

Capen, Lemuel, 1788-1858.
A Discourse on The Character
of Mr. John Hawes, preached before the Hawes Place Society, at
South Boston, February 1, 1829.
By Lemuel Capen. Boston, Leonard C. Bowles, 1832. 24 p. CtY;
ICMe; MBC; MWA; PHi; WHi.
11636
Cardell, William Samuel, 1780-
1828.
The happy family; or, Scenes
of American life, designed for
well instructed children of seven
years old and upwards. 3rd ed.
Philadelphia, Uriah Hunt, 1832.
215 p. DLC; ICBB; PPPrHi.
11637
---- The moral monitor; consisting of reading lessons, moral, instructive, and amusing. Designed
for children in families and
schools. Rochester, Marshall &
Dean, 1832. NIC; OHi.   11638

---- ... Story of Jack Halyard,
the sailor boy: or, The virtuous
family... 13th ed., with appropriate questions, by M. T. Leaven-
worth, esq. Philadelphia, Uriah
Hunt, 1832. 232 p. CSmH; DLC;
PReaHi.   11639

Carden, Allen D.

The Missouri harmony, or A choice collection of psalm tunes, hymns, and anthems... together with an introduction to grounds of music, the rudiments of music, and plain rules for beginners... rev. and improved. Cincinnati, Morgan and Sanxay, 1832. CtY; OClWHi.   11640

Carey, Mathew, 1760-1839.
Address to the Liberal and Humane. See under title.

---- Advertisement. n.p. [1832] 2 p. MWA.   11641

---- Advices and suggestions to increase the comforts of persons in humble circumstances. Philadelphia, 1832. 1 p. MH; MWA; NBuU; PPAmP; PPULC.   11642

---- The crisis. An appeal to the good sense of the nation, against the spirit of resistance and dissolution of the Union... 2d ed. Philadelphia, Pr. by W. F. Geddes, 1832. 28 p. CtY; DLC; MH; MWA; PPULC.   11643

---- ---- 3d ed. Philadelphia, W. F. Geddes, 1832. 26 p. MH; NN.   11644

---- ---- 3d ed., corr. Philadelphia, W. F. Geddes, 1832. 28 p. DLC; InU; MH; NCH; ViU.
                                  11645
---- ---- 4th ed. corr. Philadelphia, 1832. 12 p. InU; MBAt; MHi; PU; WHi.   11646

---- ---- 5th ed. [Philadelphia, 1832] 17 p. CSmH; DLC; MB; MWA.   11647

---- Cursory Views of the Literal and Restrictive Systems of Political Economy; with an Examination of Mr. Huskinson's System of Duties on Imports. By a Citizen of Philadelphia. 2d ed., greatly enl.

and imp. Philadelphia, 1832.
                                  11648
---- The dissolution of the Union. A sober address to all those who have any interest in the welfare, the power, the glory, or the happiness of the United States. By a Citizen of Pennsylvania (pseud.). Philadelphia, John Bioren, 1832. 20 p. CSmH; DLC; MWA; PHi; PPL.   11649

---- ---- 2d ed. Philadelphia, J. Bioren, 1832. 20 p. CtY; InU; MBAt; NNC; PHi.   11650

---- ---- Philadelphia, Pr. by J. Bioren, 1832. (paged continuously) 36 p. DLC; MH; MHi.   11651

---- ---- By a Friend of Union and Liberty... With a Preface by the Publisher. 1st Charleston ed. Charleston, S. C., W. Estill, 1832. 24 p. DLC; MHi; MiD-B; NNC; NcAS.   11652

---- Epitaph of the constitution of the United States [in case of a dissolution of the union in two forms anon.] accompanied by a political balance. Philadelphia, 1832. 4 p. DLC; MBAt.   11653

---- ---- 4th ed. Philadelphia, 1832. 4 p. MWA.   11654

---- Essay on the dissolution of the union, threatened by the nullifiers of South Carolina. 2d part. 3d ed. imp. Philadelphia, Pr. by L. Johnson, Oct. 3, 1832. 36 p. IEN; MB; NN; PPL; TxU.   11655

---- Extracts from the Olive Branch, No. 3, on the Protecting System. In Letters to Hon. W. Drayton and Hon. H. Middleton. [Philadelphia, 1832] 68 p. CU; MdHi; OCl; PPAmP.   11656

---- Infant schools. [Philadelphia? 1832?] 3 p. MWA; OCl.   11657

---- Letters on the Colonization Society; with a view of its probable results... addressed to the Hon. C. F. Mercer, M. H R. U. S. By M. Carey. Hartford, P. Gleason & Co. [1832] 32 p. DLC; MHi; PHi; PPULC. 11658

---- ---- 2d ed. enl. and improved. Philadelphia, Young, pr., 1832. CU; MBAt; OO; PHi; TxU. 11659

---- ---- 3d ed., enl. and improved... Philadelphia, Pr. by Young, 1832. iv [5]-32 p. front., map. CtY; ICJ; MiD-B; NNUT; RPB. 11660

---- ---- 4th ed., greatly enl. and improved... Philadelphia, Stereotyped by L. Johnson, 1832. 32 p. CSmH; DLC; MdHi; NjR. 11661

---- ---- 5th ed. Philadelphia, Stereotyped by L. Johnson, 1832. GDecCT; MH; MWA; MiD-B; NGH. 11662

---- ---- 6th ed. Philadelphia, Stereotyped by L. Johnson, 1832. MB. 11663

---- ---- 7th ed. Philadelphia, Stereotyped by L. Johnson, 1832. 32 p. M; MBAt; MHi; MiU. 11664

---- Letters to Messrs. Abbott Lawrence... (etc. Signed M. Carey and dated Philadelphia, Nov. 8-17, 1832.) 16 p. CtY; MB; MiU-C; PPL; PPULC. 11665

---- A looking glass for Nullifiers consisting in full perfection (and view of the tariff of 1832). [Philadelphia, 1832] 4 p. CtY; ICN; MWA; MiU-C. 11666

---- The olive branch no. III or, An inquiry whether any arrangement is practicable between the friends and opposers of the protecting system... With a view of

the strong probability of a secession, at least of S. C., unless a compromise take place... in a series of letters addressed to the Hon. W. Drayton and the Hon. H. Middleton. Philadelphia, Clark, March, 1832. 62 p. ICU; MB; NcU; PPL; ScU. 11667

---- ---- No. IV. Philadelphia, [n. p.] 1832. 4 p. DLC; MWA; MiU; NBL; ViU. 11668

---- A plea for the poor. No. 1-3 n. d. Philadelphia, 1831 and 1832. 3, 4 p. MWA. 11669

---- Prospects beyond the Rubicon. Philadelphia [1832-3]. MiU-C. 11670

---- Prospects on the Rubicon. Part II. Letters on the prevailing excitement in South Carolina. On the Means employed to produce it. On the Causes that led to the Depreciation of the Great Staple of the State, and on the Misconception of the Effects of the Tariff. Addressed to the Hon. H. Clay... By the Author of the Olive Branch. 2d ed. Philadelphia, Clark & Raser, 1832. 5-52 p. CtY; MH; MWA; NcD; TxU; ViU. 11671

---- Reflections on the causes that led to the formation of the Colonization Society; with a view of its probable results, under the following heads: the increase of the coloured population; the origin of the Colonization Society; the manumission of slaves in this country;... the advantages to the free coloured population by emigration to Liberia, etc. Philadelphia, W. F. Geddes, 1832. 19 p. DLC; MWA; NN; PPWa; ScCC. 11672

---- Should the nullifiers succeed... the following will be an appropriate epitaph. (By Mathew

Carey). Philadelphia, 1832. 4 p.
MWA; PPL; PPULC.   11673

---- Signs of the times. South
Carolina toasts. [Philadelphia?
1832?] 15 p. DLC; ICU; MBAt.
                          11674
---- To the public. Philadelphia,
1832. 4 p. MWA.   11675

---- The Tocsin: A solemn
warning against the dangerous doctrine of Nullification; in other
words, dissolution of the Union
containing a view of the doctrines
held by Judge Cooper in 1813,
contrasted with his doctrines in
1824, and 1827... To which is
added a review of the tariff of
1832. 3d ed. corr. Philadelphia,
Pr. by William F. Geddes, 1832.
16 p. MBAt; MWA; NNC; PHi;
ScU; TxU.   11676

---- ---- 4th ed. corr. Philadelphia, W. F. Geddes, 1832.
ICU; MBAt; MWA; MHi; PPULC.
                          11677

Carnahan, James, 1775-1859.
   ...Bondage of sin; freedom by
the gospel...By James Carnahan
... Pittsburg, n.p., 1832. 64 p.
NjP; NjR.   11678

Carpenter, Lant, 1780-1840.
   The Beneficial tendency of Uni-
tarianism. By Lant Carpenter,
LL.D., of England. 2d ed...Bos-
ton, Gray & Bowen, 1832. 32 p.
CBPac; ICMe; MB-FA;MiGr; PPM.
                          11679
---- The Scripture Doctrine of
Redemption by Christ Jesus. By
Lant Carpenter...2d ed. Boston,
Gray & Bowen, 1832. 12 p.
ICMe; MB-HP; Nh; PPLT.   11680

Carroll, Charles, 1737-1832.
   State of Maryland: I, Charles
Carroll of Carrollton, of Anne Ar-
undel County, in the said state, do
make this my last will and testament... Baltimore, 1832.   11681

Carroll, Daniel Lynn.
   Funeral sermon occasioned by
the death of the Rev. Joseph Sanford, of Philadelphia; delivered
in the First Presbyterian Church,
Brooklyn, L.I., Jan. 1, 1832.
New York, J. T. West, 1832.
30 p. ICP; NBLiHi; PPPrHi.
                          11682
Carson, Alexander, 1776-1844.
   Baptism in its mode and subject considered and the arguments
of Mr. Ewing and Dr. Wardlaw
refuted by Alexander Carsons,
A.M. New York, C. C. P. Crosby, 1832. 395 p. CtY; LNB;
MBC; RnR; TxH.   11683

Cartee, Cornelius Sowle, 1806-
1885.
   New and extensive series of
geographical questions. Providence, Cory & Brown; Boston,
Richardson, Lord & Holbrook,
1832. 116 p. CtHT-W.   11684

Carter, James Gordon, 1795-
1849.
   Copy of the answer of Deacon
James G. Carter to a vote of
the Church of Christ in Lancas-
ter, under the pastoral care of
Rev. Nathaniel Thayer, request-
ing him to resign his office of
Deacon of the Church...n. imp.,
[Lancaster, Mass.] 1832. 16 p.
CtY; MB; MH-AH; MWA; MiD-B.
                          11685
---- Records of the church in
Lancaster, Mass., in the case
of Deacon J. G. Carter. See un-
der Lancaster, Mass., Church of
Christ.

Cartwright, Samuel Adolphus,
1793-1863.
   Some account of the Asiatic
cholera asphyxia or pulseless
plague; with a sketch of its pathology and treatment from the best
authors, and some original remarks; also, advice, relative to
its prevention on plantations, and

its mitigation, premonitory symptoms and treatment should it occur. By Saml. A. Cartwright... Natchez, Miss., Pr. at "The Natchez" office, 1832. 34 p. DLC; MBM; NNNAM; NRU-M.
11686

Carver, William.
A Letter to the Rev. E. Burn, Minister at St. Mary's Church, Birmingham, England... together with a sacred fragment... Boston, 1832. 24 p. MHi.   11687

Cary, Freeman Grant.
Address, delivered before the Hamilton County Agricultural Society, at a special meeting held at Mount Pleasant, Aug. 11, 1832, by Mr. Freeman G. Cary. Cincinnati, Pr. by L. R. Lincoln, for the Society, 1832. 16 p. MWA.
11688

Casender, Pedro.
The Lost Virgin of the South. An historical novel, founded on facts. Connected with the Indian war in the South, in 1812 to '15. By Don Pedro Casender. Courtland, Ala., M. Smith, 1832. 2 vols. A-Ar; AB.   11689

Castillo y Lanzas, Joaquin Maria de, 1781-1878.
La Victoria de Temaulipas; Canto publicado en Veracruz en 1832. Filadelfia, Clark and Roser, 1832. 71 p. C-S; CtY.11690

Castle, Thomas, 1804?-1870?
A manual of surgery, founded upon the principles and practice lately taught by Sir Astley Cooper. 3d ed., ed. by Thomas Castle. Pr. for E. Cox, St. Thomas St. 3d ed. Boston, Repub. by Munroe and Francis and Charles S. Francis, 1832. 463 p. KyLxT; LNOP; MBC; NPV; TU-M. 11691

Castleton Medical College. Castleton, Vermont.
Triennial catalogue of the offi-

cers, corporation, instructors, graduates and students, of the Vermont Academy of Medicine, Castleton [Vermont Statesman pr.] November, 1832. 19 p. VtU.
11692

Catel, Charles Simon, 1773-1830.
A treatise on harmony written and composed for the use of the pupils at the Royal Conservatoire of Music, in Paris: By Catel... Boston, J. Loring, 1832. 156 p. CtY; IaGG; MBAt; PPL; RPB; VtB.   11693

Catholic Almanac. Baltimore, James Myres. [1832] MWA.
11694

Catholic Almanac, and Laity's Director for the year of our Lord, 1833. Baltimore, F. Lucas, Jr., 1832. 130 p. MdW; NRSB. 11695

Caton, Richard.
A brief statement of facts in the management of the late Mr. Carroll of Carrollton's moneyed estate. By Richard Caton, his agent... [Baltimore, 1832] CSmH; MdBJ-G; PHi.   11696

Cavallo, Tiberius, 1749-1809.
The elements of natural or experimental philosophy, by Tiberius Cavallo, F.R.S. &c. 5th Amer. ed. with additional notes, selected from various authors, by F. X. Brosius. Philadelphia, Hogan & Thompson, 1832. 2 vols. in 1. AMob; CtY; KyU; MnU; ViU.
11697

Caverno, Arthur, 1801-1876.
An address, delivered to the free-will Baptist church in Hopkinton, N.H. Feb. 2, 1832. By Arthur Caverno... Limerick, Me., D. Marks, 1832. 28 p. MeLewB; NNUT; Nh-Hi.   11698

Cazenave, Pierre Louis Alphée, 1802?-1877.
A practical synopsis of cutaneous diseases, from the most cele-

brated authors, and particularly
from documents afforded by the
clinical lectures of Dr. Biett...
By A. Cazenave...& H. E. Sche-
del...Tr. from the French, with
notes, 2d Amer. ed. Philadelphia, Carey & Lea, 1832. 400 p.
ArU-M; CtY; KyLxT; NhD; PPC.
                                11699
Central Hickory Club, Washington, D. C.
    Address of the Central Hickory
Club to the Republican citizens of
the United States... City of Washington, n. p. , 1832. 8 p. DLC;
NjR; OCHP; PU.   11700

Chadwick, Jabez, b. 1779.
    New light on the subject of
Christian baptism, presented in
three parts...Ithaca[N. Y.]Mack,
1832. 204 p. CU; DLC; MiU;
NBuG; PPULC.   11701

Chalmers, Thomas, 1780-1847.
    The efficacy of prayer; a ser-
mon preached at St. George's
Church, Edinburgh, Mar. 22,
1832, being the day appointed for
a national fast on account of the
prevalence of cholera. Boston,
1832. 24 p. DLC; NjR; PPULC;
RPB; MBAt; ScU.   11702

---- On political economy in con-
nexion (sic) with the moral state
and moral prospects of society.
New York, Daniel Appleton and
Jason Leavitt; Boston, Crocker &
Brewster; Philadelphia, Grigg &
Elliot; Baltimore, Armstrong &
Plaskett; Richmond, R. I. Smith;
Cincinnati, Corey & Fairbanks,
1832. v, 405 p. CtY; KyLx;
NcD; PPA; ScU; ViRut.   11703

Chamberlain, John.
    Sketches of mission scenes in
India, compiled from the journals
of the Rev. John Chamberlain.
Boston, James Loring, 1832.
108 p. GDecCT.   11704

Chambers, T. J.
    Prospectus for translating in-
to English and Publishing a Compilation of the Laws in force in
the State of Coahuila and Texas
...to be interwoven with a Compendium of the Spanish Code: the
whole to be illustrated with notes
and references. By T. J. Chambers...[Austin? 1832?] 3 p.
TxU.   11705

Chandler, John A.
    The speech of John A. Chand-
ler of Norfolk Co. in the House
of Delegates of Virginia on the
policy of the state with respect to
her slave population. Delivered
January 17, 1832. Richmond, Pr.
by Thomas W. White, 1832. 10 p.
CtY; MWA; NjP; OClWHi; PHi;
ViU.   11706

Channing, William Ellery, 1780-
1843.
    A discourse on religion. Bos-
ton, Gray & Bowen, 1832. 134 p.
IaPeC.   11707

---- ...A discourse on the evidences of revealed religion, by
William E. Channing. 4th ed. Pr.
for the American Unitarian Association. Boston, Gray & Bowen,
1832. 35 p. ICMe; MBAU; NNUT;
PPLT; RHi.   11708

---- Discourses. Boston, Richard,
Lord & Holbrook, 1832. 17 p.
MBAt; MNH; RPB; RPAt. 11709

---- Discourses. Eleven discourses by William Ellery Channing. Boston, Charles Bowen;
Cambridge, E. W. Metcalf & Co. ,
prs. to the University, 1832.
279 p. MA; MWH; MeB; RPB;
PPAt.   11710

Chapin, Graham H.
    An oration delivered at Lyons,
Wayne County, N. Y. on the fourth
day of July, 1832. By Graham H.

Chapin. (Pub. by request.) Lyons, Pr. at the Office of the Western Argus, 1832. 22 p. CSmH; CtY; N.   11711

The Chaplet; a selection of buds and blossoms from the garden of knowledge and virtue... New-York, A. Hawley, Lomax & Mitchell, 1832. DLC.   11712

Chapman, George, fl. 1833.
A discourse on religious liberty, delivered in the Unitarian Church, in Louisville, July 4th, 1832. By George Chapman. Pr. by request. Louisville, Ky., Pr. at J. G. Dana's office, 1832. 19 p. CSPac; ICME; MBAU; MH; MWA.   11713

---- A lecture on the uses of knowledge; delivered before the Louisville Lyceum, by George Chapman. Pr. by request of the Lyceum. Louisville, K., Pr. at the Herald Office, 1832. 19 p. ICU; MH; MWA.   11714

Chapman, George Thomas, 1786-1872.
Sermons upon the ministry, worship, and doctrines of the Protestant Episcopal church, and other subjects; by G. T. Chapman... Burlington, Goodrich, 1832. 324 p. ICU; NB; NhD; RPB; Vt.   11715

---- ---- 2d ed. Burlington, Chauncey Goodrich, 1832. 324 p. GHi; IEG; MCET; NcU; PPM; ViU.   11716

Chapman, Jonathan.
Addresses before the Young Men's Temperance Society at Boston. Boston, Garrison and Knapp, 1832. MWA.   11717

Chapman, Lucretia.
Trial of Lucretia Chapman... jointly indicted with Lino Amelia Esposy Mina for the murder of William Chapman... prepared for publication by William E. DuBois. Philadelphia, Mentz, 1832. 213 p. DLC; MWA; MoU; NNN; PPB.   11718

Chapone, Hester (Mulso).
Letters on the improvements of the mind; addressed to a lady. By Mrs. Chapone. Boston, Bowles, 1832. 176 p. MB; MoSpD; NjP; PU.   11719

Charles Seymour; or, The good aunt and the bad aunt, a Sunday story. New York, Betts & Anstice, 1832. NPV.   11720

Charlestown [Mass.] Female Seminary.
Charlestown Female Seminary instituted in Charlestown, Mass. March, 1831. Design of the Charlestown Female Seminary, board of Examiners etc. ... Boston, Pr. by I. Howe, 1832. 20 p. MBB; MWo; NBuG.   11721

Charlestown, Mass. Second Congregational Church.
A statement of proceedings, against Mrs. Emily Richardson, in the Second Congregational church in Reading. Charlestown, William W. Wheildon, 1832. 38 p. NNUT.   11722

Charleston, S. C. College of Charleston.
Catalogue of the Trustees, Faculty, and Students... June, 1832. Charleston, 1832. 12 p. MHi.   11723

---- Medical Society.
Report of Medical Society; July 17, 1832. Charleston, Riley, 1832. DSG.   11724

---- Ordinances.
A Collection of the Ordinances of the City Council of Charleston, from... October, 1826, to...

March 1832. To which are added, the Acts of the Legislature of South-Carolina, relating to the Corporation of Charleston, passed in and since December, 1825. Charleston, Pr. by A. E. Miller, 1832. 90 p. DLC; IU; MH-L; NN.   11725

---- State rights and free trade convention, 1832.
... Proceedings of the State rights & free trade convention, held in Charleston (S. C.) on the 22d and 25th February, 1832.
... Charleston, State rights and free trade association, 1832. 16 p. Ct; DLC; MB; NN; ScU.   11726

[Chase, Philander] 1775-1852.
Bishop Chase's defence of himself against the late conspiracy at Gambier, Ohio in a series of letters to his friends. n. p. [1832?]   60 p. CSmH; MHi; NNG; OCHP.   11727

Chase, Samuel.
Remarks upon recent publications against the Rt. Rev. Philander Chase, D. D. Steubenville, O., Pr. by James Wilson, 1832. 28 p. CSmH; IHi; MBD; MH; MWA; OCIWHi.   11728

Chautauque County almanac for 1833. Jamestown, A. Fletcher [1832] 11 l. NRU.   11729

Cheever, George Barrell, 1807-1890.
The American Common-place Book of Poetry... By George B. Cheever. Boston, Pr. by Hiram Tupper, for Carter & Hendee, 1832. 405 p. DLC; ICN; MeLewB; MiU; PPL.   11730

---- The American common-place book of prose, a collection of eloquent and interesting extracts from the writings of American authors... Boston, Carter

and Hendee, 1832. 468 p. CtY; MB; PPM; TSewU; ViU.   11731

---- Remarks on the Life, Character, and Writings of Archbishop Leighton. By George B. Cheever. Boston, Peirce & Parker, 1832. 50 p.   11732

Chesapeake & Ohio Canal Company.
The memorial of the Chesapeake and Ohio canal company, to the general assembly of Maryland, December 31, 1832. Washington, Gales & Seaton, 1832. 55 p. MdHi; NN; NNC; Vi. 11733

---- Proceedings of the president and directors... for the joint construction of the canal and railroad from the "point of rocks" to Harper's Ferry... together with the proceedings of the General meeting of the stockholders... Washington, Gales & Seaton, 1832. DLC; ICJ; MH-BA; NN.   11734

---- Report of the Committee appointed on the 28th April, 1832, by the Stockholders on the Resolution of the General Assembly of Maryland, relative to the joint construction of the Chesapeake & Ohio Canal and the Baltimore & Ohio Railroad, between the "Point of Rocks" and Harper's Ferry. Washington, Gales & Seaton, 1832. 21 p. DLC; DBRE; ICU; MiU-T; NN.   11735

---- Report on a survey and estimate for the improvement of the navigation of Goose Creek, Little River, and Beaver Dam in Loudon County, Va., made by order of the president and directors of the Chesapeake and Ohio canal Company. November 1832. [Washington? 1832] 12 p. DLC; PHi; PPULC; ViU.   11736

---- The reports of the president

to the directors of the Chesapeake and Ohio canal company, on the present state of the finances of the company, and an extension of the navigation of the Potomac to a point nine miles above the town of Cumberland, on a plan consistent with the present charter. Washington, Gales & Seaton, 1832. 14 p. DLC; MdHi; PHi; PPULC; ViU. 11737

Chester County almanac. West Chester, by Hannum and Rutter, Denny & Whitehead [1832] DLC; InU; MWA. 11738

Chester County Cabinet of Natural Science.
Constitution. West Chester, Pa., C. Hannum & J. A. Hemphill, 1832. 11 p. PPAmP. 11739

Chester, S. C. Citizens.
Proceedings of a general meeting, held at Chester Courthouse, November 18, 1831. Columbia, Landrum, 1832. 16 p. MHi; NcD; PPL; ScU. 11740

Chesterfield, Philip Dormer Stanhope, 4th earl of.
The chronicles... See Nathan ben Saddi.

[Cheves, Langdon] 1776-1857.
... Call of the legislature...
[Charleston? 1832?] 8 p. ViU. 11741
---- Letters to the Hon. Langdon Cheves. [Pendleton? S. C., 1832] 7 p. GU. 11742

---- Occasional reviews. (State rights). No. I-III. Charleston, J. S. Burges, 1832. 3 v. in 1. ICU; MHi; NcD; ViU. 11743

Child, David Lee, 1794-1874.
Report of the case of alleged contempt, and breach of the privileges of the House of Representatives of Massachusetts, tried be-fore said House, on complaint of William B. Calhoun, speaker, against David L. Child, a member. With notes by the latter. Boston, Carter & Hendee, 1832. CU-Law; DLC; MBAt; MWA; NN; PHi. 11744

Child, Lydia Maria (Francis), 1802-1880.
The American frugal housewife, dedicated to those who are not ashamed of economy. 8th ed. Boston, Carter & Hendee, 1832. 130 p. MB; MW; MWA. 11745

---- ---- 10th ed. Boston, Carter & Hendee, 1832. 130 p. MH; MWA. 11746

---- ---- 11th ed. Boston, Carter & Hendee, 1832. MB; MWA. 11747
---- ---- 12th ed., enl. and corr. by the author. Boston, Carter, Hendee and co., 1832. 130 p. MBeHi; OU; NNMuCN. 11748
---- Appeal in favor of the class of Americans called Africans. Boston, Allen, 1832. 232 p. PPPrHi. 11749

---- The biographies of Lady Russell, and Madame Guyon, by Mrs. Child. Boston, Carter, Hendee & Co., 1832. 264 p. CSmH; DLC; MnHi; NhD; RNR. 11750

---- The biographies of Madame de Staël, and Madame Roland. By Mrs. Child... Boston, Carter & Hendee, 1832. 265 p. CSmH; FMF; GEU; MBL; RNR. 11751

---- Biography of good wives. Boston, Carter & Hendee, 1832. CSmH; DLC. 11752

---- The coronal. A collection of miscellaneous pieces, written at various times... Boston, Carter & Hendee, 1832. 285 p. CSmH;

DLC; IUC; MB; NjP.   11753

---- The little girl's own book. Boston, 1832. MB.   11754

---- Memoirs of Madame de Staël and of Madame Roland. Boston, 1832. CtY.   11755

---- The Mother's Book. By Mrs. Child, author of "The Frugal Housewife," "The Girl's Own Book,"...3d ed. Boston, Carter & Hendee, 1832. 169 p. MHoly; MnU; NBLIHi; NjP.   11756

---- ---- 4th ed. Boston, Carter & Hendee, 1832. 169 p. MB; MWH; MBev; MnU; PPi.   11757

Childhood, a poem. January 1, 1832. Cortland Village, New York, C. W. Gill, 1832. 6 p. CSmH.   11758

Children in the wood.
    The children in the wood. To which is added, My mother's grave, a pathetic story. New York, Mahlon Day, 1832. 23 p. CtY; NN.   11759

Child's Albany directory and City register for the years 1832-3. Compiled by Edmund B. Childs containing an alphabetical list of the inhabitants, and much other useful and interesting matter. Albany, Pr. by E. B. Child, 1832. 450 p. NAl.   11760

Child's assistant...5th ed. Springfield, Merriam, Little & Co., 1832. MH.   11761

The Child's cabinet. v. 1; 1832. New-Haven, Conn., J. L. Cross, 1832. 156 p. AmSSchU; DLC; PPAmP; PPULC.   11762

The Child's cabinet, containing a variety of pretty stories, with one hundred and fifty pictures. Concord, John W. Moore & Co., 1832. 194 p. CtY.   11763

The Child's Library, of useful knowledge; containing a variety of entertaining and familiar stories; well adapted to the capacities of children; with the history of birds and animals. Pittsburgh, Cramer and Spear, 1832. 112 p. MB.   11764

The child's own book of tales and anecdotes about dogs, with engravings. Boston, Carter, Hendee, and Co., 1832. 108 p. DLC.   11765

Chitty, Joseph.
    A practical treatise on the criminal law, with comprehensive notes...Containing precedents of indictments, &c. By Joseph Chitty...From the 2nd and last London ed., cor. and enl. by the author. With notes and corrections, by Thomas Huntington...Brookfield, E. Merriam & Co.; Philadelphia, Grigg & Elliott; New York, Collins & Hannay, 1832. 3 v. CtY; InIBA; MoU; NcD; ViU; WaU.   11766

Chivers, Thomas Holley, 1809-1858.
    The Faith of Sorrow, or, The Lament of Youth: A Poem. By Thomas H. Chivers, M. D. Franklin [Tenn.] The Author, 1832. 132 p. CtY; PHi; RPB; ViRut; ViU.   11767

Choate, Rufus, 1799-1859.
    Speech of Mr. Choate of Massachusetts, on the bill to alter and amend the several acts imposing duties on imports. Delivered in committee of the whole on the state of the Union. House of Representatives, U. S. June 13, 1832. n.p., n.p. [1832] 16 p. MB; MH; MWA; MdHi; NNC; TxU.   11768

A choice collection of hymns, and spiritual songs designed for the devotions of Israel, in prayer, conference, and camp-meetings. Also, a suitable pocket companion for Christians of every denomination, although not numbered among the regular tribes... 3d ed. Concord, N.H., Moses G. Atwood, 1832. 192 p. CSmH; MBU-T; NN; RPB. 11769

The cholera bulletin. Conducted by an association of physicians. Vol. I. New-York, July 6, 1832. no. 1-24. July 6-Aug. 31, 1832. 192 p. DNLM; NN; NNN; PR; ScU. 11770

Cholera gazette. v. 1, no. 1-16. July 11, Nov. 21, 1832. Philadelphia, Carey, Lea and Blanchard, 1832. CSmH; DNLM; MoSU-M; NcD; PU. 11771

Christian almanac for Connecticut...1833...Hartford, Pub. for the Connecticut Branch of the American Tract Society [1832] 36 p. CtHi; InU; MWA; NjR; WHi. 11772

The Christian almanac, for Indiana, for the year of our Lord and Savior Jesus Christ, 1833: Being the first after bissextile, or leap year, and the fifty-seventh of the independence of the United States. Calculated for the meridian of Madison. Madison, Indiana Branch of the American Tract Society [1832] 36 p. InHi. 11773

The Christian almanac, for Kentucky [1832] ICU. 11774

Christian Almanac for Maryland and Virginia, 1833. Baltimore, Md., American Tract Society [1832] MWA. 11775

The Christian Almanac, for New England for the year 1832. Boston, Gould, Lincoln & Edmands, 1832. 36 p. MPeaHi; NjR; PCA; RNHi; WHi. 11776

Christian Almanac for Pennsyl-

vania, Delaware and West New Jersey for 1833. Philadelphia, Pennsylvania Branch of the American Tract Society [1832] DLC; MWA; PHi; PPFM. 11777

Christian almanac for South Carolina. Charleston, South Carolina Branch of the American Tract Society [1832] MWA. 11778

Christian almanac for Tennessee, for the year of Our Lord and Savior Jesus Christ, 1832... Calculated for the meridian of Knoxville... Knoxville, American Tract Society [1832] T. 11779

The Christian almanac for the western district for 1833. Rochester, American Tract Society; Levi A. Ward; Geneva, Warren Day, [1832] 18 l. ICHi; NRMA; NRU. 11780
---- Utica, Pub. for American Tract Society, and sold by Edward Vernon [1832] 36 p. CtY; MWA; NCH; NIC. 11781

Christian almanac for Virginia, for 1833. Richmond, R. J. Smith, 1832. MB; MWA; Vi; ViHi; ViW. 11782
Christian Almanack for 1833. Boston, Lincoln & Edmands, [1832] MWA; NCH; RNHi. 11783

Christian Almanack for New York, Connecticut and New Jersey for 1833. New York, American Tract Society [1832] CtY; DLC; IU; MWA; WHi. 11784

Christian and Farmer's Almanac for 1833. By Zadock Thompson. Burlington, Vt., E. & T. Mills [1832] MWA. 11785

The Christian economy, translated from the original Greek of an old manuscript found in the island of Patmor, where St. John wrote his book of Revelations. Boston, J.

Gay and A. C. Demerit, 1832.
94 p. MH; MWA; N.   11786

Christian Library, comprising a
Series of Standard Works in Religious Literature. Philadelphia
and New York, 1832-1835. 4 vols.
OClW.   11787

The Christian magazine... Conducted under the supervision of
the Associate Reformed synod of
New York by the Rev. J. F. M'-
Laren, editor. Geneva [N. Y.]
1832-1842. Vol. 1-11 [1832-
1842?] ICN; NBuG; OOxM;
PPPrHi; RPB.   11788

The Christian monitor, and common people's Boston advisor, V.
1-2 no. 9; Apr. 17-1832-Aug. 12,
1833. Brooklyn, Conn., J. Holbrook [etc.] 1832-33. 2 v. in 1.
DLC; MB-W.   11789

The Christian offering and churchman's annual. New York, 1832-
1839. PP.   11790

The Christian Offering, for 1832.
Boston, Lincoln and Edmands,
and B. Franklin Edmands, 1832.
231 p. DLC; GEU-T; MBilHi;
NjP; RNHi; WU.   11791

Christian Palladium. Devoted to
the improvement and happiness
of mankind. Union Mills, N. Y.,
Pub. under direction of the Christian General Book Association,
1832-1860? v. 1-29. DLC; ICM;
MH-AH; NN; NcD.   11792

A Christian's word of warning
and comfort, in regard to that
alarming scourge, the cholera.
Tr. from the German... Harrisburg, J. Baab, 1832. 12 p.
MiU.   11793

Christmas, C. W.
    Lands of Seneca and Big Spring
Reservations. Wooster, 1832.

12 p.   11794

The Churchman's Almanac for
1832... calculated for the Meridian of New York by D. Young,
with a table... by F. R. Hassler,
F. A. P. S. New York, New York
Protestant Episcopal Press, 1832.
36 p. OrPD; WHi; WNaE. 11795

Cicero, Marcus Tullius.
    M. Tullii Ciceronis ad Quini-
um fratrem dialogi tres de ora-
tore. Cum excerptis ex notis var-
iore. Novi Portus: Sumtibus H.
Howe, Novi Portus, et Collins &
Hannay, Novi Eboraci, 1832.
260 p. DLC; InHi; NjP; PU; ViU.
                         11796
---- M. Tullii Ciceronis De clar-
is oratoribus liber qui dicitur
Brutus. Ex editionibus Oliveti et
Ernesti. Cantabrigiae, (Mass.),
sumtibus Brown, Shattuck, et soc.,
1832. 88 p. CtY; MB; MH.11797

---- M. T. Ciceronis Orationes
Quaedam Selectae, Notis illustratae. In usum Academiae exonien-
sis. Editio Stereotypa. Zabulis
analyticis instructa... Bostoniae,
Sumptibus Hillard, Gray, et Soc.,
1832. 278 p. ICU; KMK; MB;
TxU-T; VU.   11798

Cincinnati, Ohio. Board of Education.
    Common School Report. To
the Honorable the City Council
of the City of Cincinnati: The
Board of Trustees and Visitors
of the Common Schools within the
City of Cincinnati, in submitting
to the City Council their Annual
Report of the state and prospects
of the Institutions entrusted to
their supervision... Cincinnati
[1832] WHi.   11799

Cincinnati and St. Louis railroad
Company.
    Charter of the Cincinnati & St.
Louis R. R. Company, passed

Feb. 8, 1832. Cincinnati, Pr. at the office of the Evangelist, 1832.   11800

Cincinnati Historical Society.
    Act of incorporation and by-laws of the Historical and Philosophical Society of Ohio. [Columbus? 1832?] 8 p. OClWHi.   11801
---- Circular... To In Mss.[?], Doctor Droke Columbus, Ohio? 1832? 8 p. WHi.   11802

Cincinnati University. College of Medicine.
    Annual circular of the Medical college of Ohio. Cincinnati, Pr. by Lodge & L'Hommedieu, 1832. 7 p. OCHP.   11803

---- Catalogue of the library of the Medical College of Ohio and the rules adopted by the trustees in relation thereto, also extracts from the college regulations for the government of the medical class. Cincinnati, Corey & Fairbank, 1832. 26 p. OCHP. 11804

Citizen's Almanack for 1833. Philadelphia, Pa.; Griggs & Dickinson, for Key, Mielke & Biddle [1832] MWA; PPL.   11805

Citizen's and Farmers' Almanac. By C. F. Englemann. Baltimore, Cushing & Sons [1832] MWA.   11806
---- Baltimore, J. T. Hanzsche, [1832] MWA.   11807

---- Baltimore, Plaskitt & Co.; Philadelphia, Griggs & Dickinson [1832] IClHi; MWA.   11808

Citizens and Farmers' Yearly Messenger. No. 9. 1833. Baltimore, J. T. Hanzsche [1832?] 30 p. MH; MWA.   11809

Claggett, Rufus.
    The juvenile speaker. Provi-

dence, H. H. Brown, 1832. 36 p. RHi.   11810

Claims of the Africans; or, History of the American colonization society. By the author of Conversations on the Sandwich Islands mission, etc. ... Rev. by the publishing committee. Boston, Massachusetts Sabbath School Union, 1832. 252 p. DLC; GDecCT; MH-AH; OO; TxH.   11811

Clapp, Samuel Capen, 1810-1831.
    Selections, in prose and verse, from the writings of Samuel Capen Clapp, of Dorchester. Boston, Clapp & Hull, 1832. 52 p. MB; MBNEH; MH; MWA; TxU. 11812

Clark, Ansel Russel.
    A sermon delivered before the Auxiliary education society of Norfolk County, at their annual meeting in Walpole. June 13, 1832... Boston, Pr. by Perkins & Marvin, 1832. 24 p. CtY; MeHi; NhD; OClWHi; RPB.   11813

Clark, Guy C.
    Sketch of the life and adventures of Guy C. Clark, who, on the 11th of December, 1831, was sentenced to be hung on the 3d day of Feb. 1832, for the murder of his wife, Mrs. Fanny Clark; together with the minutes of his trial, etc. Ithaca, 1832. 15 p. MH-L; N; NIC; NN.   11814

Clark, John Alonzo, 1801-1845.
    The final meeting of the pastor and his people. A farewell sermon, to the parishioners of Christ church. By the Rev. John A. Clark, A. M. New York, N. B. Holmes, 1832. 32 p. CBCDS; DLC; MWA; NNG; P; RPB.
                        11815
Clark, Lucius Fayette.
    The child's expositor and sabbath school teacher's and scholar's assistant. First part. 3d ed.

Hartford, D. F. Robinson & Co.,
1832. 128 p. MH; MH-AH;
VtMidSM.   11816

---- Scripture geography adapt-
ed to Child's expositor; by L. F.
Clark. 3d ed. Hartford, D. F.
Robinson & Co., 1832. 31 p.
MH-AH; WFta-M.   11817

---- Topics and references designed to assist in the study of
Woodbridge's Universal geography; by L. F. Clark. 3d ed. Hartford, Cooke & Co., 1832. 15 p.
NjR.   11818

Clark, Matthew St. Clair.
    Legislative and documentary
history of the Bank of the United
States. Washington, Gales & Seaton, 1832. 832 p. MiD.   11819

Clarke, Adam, 1760-1832.
    Discourses on various sub-
jects relative to the Being and
Attributes of God and his works
in creation, providence and grace.
By Adam Clarke, LL.D. etc.
Vol. 11. On the Decalogue,
Lords prayer, etc. New York, B.
Waugh & T. Mason, 1832. 3 v. in
1. GDecCT; IEG; LNB; MB;
TNT.   11820

---- ---- 7th ed. New York, M'-
Elrath & Bangs, 1832. 3 vol.
KBB; NjMd; OSW; PMA.   11821

---- Memoirs of the Wesley
family; collected principally from
original documents. By Adam
Clarke ... New York, J. Emory & B. Waugh, for the Methodist Episcopal church, 1832.
350 p. CtMW; IEG; MWA; OO;
PLT.   11822

---- "Sermons." New York, B.
Waugh and T. Mason, 1832. 3 v.
IBLeW.   11823

Clarke, Amos.

The grace of our Lord Jesus
Christ. A discourse preached at
Sherburne, Mass. March 21,
1819 (sic) (1830). By Amos Clarke.
Pub. by request. Boston, Press of
Independent Messenger, Pr. by
Edwin M. Stone, 1832. 15 p.
ICN; MB; MH; MWA; VtHidbC.
                                11824
---- A letter addressed to the
Rev. Samuel Lee, Minister of the
Evangelical Church in Sherburne,
by Amos Clarke, Minister of the
First Parish and Church in Sher-
burne. Cambridge, E. W. Met-
calf and Co., 1832. 30 p. CtY;
ICN; MBC; MWA; VtMidbC.
                                11825
Clarke, James, 1793-1859.
    A catechism of the rudiments
of music designed for the assist-
ance of teachers of the piano-forte
...from the 2d Lond. ed. with
corr. and additions. Baltimore,
J. Cole, 1832. 83 p. IEG; MB;
MdBS; NRUmus.   11826

Clarke, John.
    An Answer to the Question,
Why are you a Christian? By
John Clarke, D.D. 2d ed. 1st se-
ries, no. 51. American Unitarian
Association. Boston, Gray &
Bowen, 1832. 34 p. IEG; MB-HP;
MH; MeB; NUt.   11827

Clarke, Matthew St. Clair.
    Legislative and documentary
history of the Bank of the United
States: including the original Bank
of North America. Comp. by M.
St. Clair Clarke, & D. H. Hall.
Washington, Pr. by Gales & Sea-
ton, 1832. 808p. CtY; MBAt;
NcD; OCHP; PPA; RPL.   11828

Clarke, Pitt.
    An explanation of John 1: 1. in
a discourse. By Pitt Clarke...
Boston, Carter & Hendee, 1832.
21 p. CtY; DLC; ICMe; MH;
MWA; NjR.   11829

Clarke, Samuel, 1684-1750.
A collection of the sweet as-
suring promises of scripture, or
the believers' inheritance. By
Samuel Clarke, D. D. Revised by
J. J. Harrod. Baltimore, Pub.
by Joseph N. Lewis, Stereotyped
by H. Simmons & co., 1832.
250 p. OBerB.   11830

---- Daily scripture promises to
the living Christians. By Samuel
Clarke, D.D. ... Boston, James
Loring, 1832. 190 p. CtMW; MB;
NN; NNG; PCA.   11831

Clarks Saving Company.
Constitution of the Clarks Saving Company, in Washington,
1832. Washington, Pr. at the
Globe Office, by F. P. Blair,
1832. PPi.   11832

Classes of hazards, and rates of
premium, adopted by the fire insurance companies, for the city
of New York and Brooklyn. New
York, Pr. by Swords, 1832. 16 p.
Mi.   11833

Clay, Clement Claiborne, 1819-
1882.
Speech of C. C. Clay, of Alabama, on the tariff. Delivered in
the House of Representatives, on
the 12th June, 1832. Washington,
F. P. Blair, 1832. 24 p. Ct; DLC;
PPAmP.   11834

Clay, Henry, 1777-1852.
Debate in the United States
Senate on the return of the bank
bill with Gen. Jackson's veto. n. p.
1832. 36 p. DLC; ICN.   11835

---- Speech of Henry Clay in de-
fence of the American system;
delivered in the Senate of the
United States, February 2, 3,
and 6th, 1832. Hartford [Conn.]
Samuel Hanmer, 1832. 25 p.
CSmH; MH-BA; NN; OClWHi;
ViU-M.   11836

---- ---- Washington, Pr. by
Gales & Seaton, 1832. 43 p. CtY;
DLC; KyDC; LNH; MWA; ScU.
                                 11837
Clayton, Augustin Smith, 1783-
1839.
Speech of Mr. Clayton, of
Georgia, on the Bank of the United
States, House of Representatives,
March 2, 1832. [Washington,
1832?] 39 p. DLC; GEU; GU-De;
TxU.   11838

---- Speech of Mr. Clayton, of
Georgia, on the bill proposing a
reduction of the duties on im-
ports. Delivered in the House of
Representatives, June 10, 1832.
Washington [D. C.] Pr. by Duff
Green, 1832. 43 p. A-Ar; CSmH;
DLC; GEU; PPAmP.   11839

Clayton, John Middleton, 1796-
1856.
Speech of Mr. Clayton, of Delaware, on the bill for the apportionment of the representation in
Congress. Delivered in the Senate of the United States, April
25th, 1832. Washington, Pr. at
the office of J. Elliot, 1832. 24 p.
DLC; MH; MWA; MdHi; PPM.
                                 11840
Clayton, W. H.
A collection of psalms and
hymns. 3d ed. Boston, Gray,
1832. MB.   11841

Cleishbotham, Jedediah.
Tales of My Landlord, Fourth
and Last Series, collected and arranged by Jedediah Cleishbotham
... Philadelphia, Carey & Lea,
1832. 3 vols. KyU; MdBS; NcEd;
PHi; TNP.   11842

Cleveland, A. B.
Studies in poetry and prose:
consisting of selections principally from American writers, and
designed for the highest class in
schools. By A. B. Cleveland,
M. D. Baltimore, W. & J. Neal,

1832. 480 p. CtHWatk; Ia; InGr;
MB; MdBE.   11843

Cleveland, Charles Dexter, 1802-
1869.

The National orator; consisting
of selections adapted for rhetorical recitation, from the parlia-
mentary...3d ed. New York, N.
& J. White, 1832. 297 p.
CtHWatk; NjR; OWorP; PPeSchw;
RPB.   11844

---- To My Friends. (A statement concerning Dickinson College, 1832.) 39 p. CtY.   11845

Cleveland, Richard Falley.

Abstract of an Address before
the Peace Society of Windham
county, at its annual meeting in
Brooklyn, August 22, 1832. By
Rev. Richard F. Cleveland.
Brooklyn [Conn.] Pr. by Charles
Webber, 1832. 16 p. CSmH; MeB.
                            11846

Clinton, DeWitt.

Early dredging appliances and
steam dredges. (Extracts from
report of De Witt Clinton...to
Lieut. Col. John J. Abert...
1832) DES; MiU; OU.   11847

---- ... Hampshire and Hampden
and Farmington canal. Letter
from the Secretary of War, transmitting a report on the examination of the...canal. February 14,
1832... [Washington, 1832] 7 p.
CtY.   11848

---- [Report to the joint committee on fire and water on the best
sources and means of transportation of an inexhaustible supply of
pure and wholesome water for the
city of New York.] Board of Aldermen, Doc. No. 61. Nov. 10,
1832. [New York, 1832] 120 p.
DNLM; NN.   11849

Clowes, John.

The Golden Wedding Ring or

observations on the institution of
marriage by a clergyman of the
Church of England. Boston, John
Allen, 1832. 48 p. MB; MH;
MLanc; NNUT; OUrC.   11850

Cobb, Alvan, 1788-1861.

God's culture of his vineyard.
A sermon, delivered at Plymouth
...on the 22d of December, 1831.
By Alvan Cobb...Taunton [Mass.]
E. Anthony, 1832. 24 p. CSmH;
ICN; MB; MiD-B; MPlyP.   11851

Cobb, Daniel J.

The family adviser; calculated
to teach the principles of botany.
Compiled with a strict regard for
logic. Containing directions for
preserving health, and curing diseases. For use of families and
private individuals. New Bedford,
Benjamin T. Congdon, 1832. 131 p.
MNBedf.   11852

Cobb, Jonathan Holmes, 1799-
1882.

A manual containing information
respecting the growth of the mulberry tree... Boston, Carter &
Hendee, 1832. 68 p. CtY; MB;
MWA; NjR; TxSaI.   11853

Cobb, Lyman, 1800-1864.

Cobb's explanatory arithmetick,
no. 1...By Lyman Cobb...New
York, Collins & Hannay; Ithica,
Mack & Andrus, 1832. 104 p.
CtHWatk; CtY; DLC; N; NIC.
                            11854

---- Cobb's explanatory arithmetick, no. 2...To which is annexed
a practical system of book-keeping. Ithaca (N. Y.) Mack & Andrus;
Baltimore, Joseph Jewett, 1832.
216 p. CSmH; CtY; MB; NIC;
NNC.   11855

---- ---- New York, Collins &
Hannay, 1832. 216 p. CtY; DAU;
DLC; MH; NN.   11856

---- ---- Philadelphia, Desilver,

Thomas & Co. [etc., etc., 1832] 213 p. MH; NN.   11857

---- Juvenile reader No. 1; containing interesting, moral & instructive reading lessons... designed for the use of small children in families & schools. New York, Chapman & Flagler; Philadelphia, T. L. Bonsal; 1832. 72 p. CSmH; OClWHi; PPULC; PPeSchw.   11858

---- Juvenile reader No. 2, containing interesting, moral, and instructive reading lessons, composed of works of one, two, and three syllables designed for the use of small children. Ithaca, Mack & Andrus, 1832. 216 p. NIC.   11859

---- ---- Oxford, N.Y., Chapman & Flagler, 1832. 144 p. MiD-B; NRMA; WHi.   11860

---- ---- Philadelphia, Thomas L. Bonsal, 1832. 144 p. OCoC; PatM.   11861

---- Juvenile reader, No. 3, containing interesting, historical, moral, and instructive reading lessons composed of words of a greater number of syllables than the lessons in no. I and no. II;... By Lyman Cobb... Oxford, N.Y., Chapman & Flagler, 1832. 212 p. CtY; MH; NPV; OTifH; PU-Penn.   11862

---- Sequel to the juvenile readers; comprising of lessons in prose and poetry, from highly esteemed American and English writers. By Lyman Cobb. Baltimore, Joseph Jewett, 1832. 215 p. InI.   11863

---- ---- Chambersburg, Pa., Hickok & Blood, 1832. PPM.   11864

---- ---- Havana, N.Y., Henry W. Ritter, 1832. 215 p. CtY; WHi.   11865

---- ---- Indianapolis, Henkle & Chamberlain [1832] 216 p. InMuB.   11866

---- ---- Pittsburgh, Luke Loomis [1832] 212 p. OClWHi.   11867

---- ---- St. Clairsville, Ohio, Horton J. Howard, 1832.   11868

Cobb, Sylvanus, 1798-1866.
    A discourse delivered at the First Church in Malden, Mass. April 5, 1832, by Sylvanus Cobb. Boston, Pr. by G. W. Bazin, 1832. 18 p. MBUPH.   11869

---- Reply to the letter of Dr. Ephraim Buck, to Rev. Sylvanus Cobb, in answer to his Review of Dr. Dwight's Tract delivered in the First Church in Malden, Mass. May 20, 1832. By Sylvanus Cobb, pastor. Boston, Pr. by G. W. Bazin, 1832. 39 p. MBUPH; MMeT; MMeT-Hi; MWA; NCaS.   11870

---- A sermon, delivered in the meeting house of the First parish in Malden, Mass., January 1, 1832. By Sylvanus Cobb, pastor. Boston, Marsh, Capen & Lyon, 1832. 20 p. MBC; MBUPH; MiD-B; NNUT; OClWHi.   11871

---- Simplicity of the Gospel. A sermon delivered in the First Church in Malden, Mass., on Sunday, Sept. 2, 1832. By Sylvanus Cobb, pastor. Boston, Pr. by G. W. Bazin, Trumpet Office, 1832. 16 p. MMeT-Hi; MWA.   11872

Cobbett, William, 1763-1835.
    A French grammar; or plain instructions for the learning of French. In a series of letters. By William Cobbett. New York, J. Doyle; Providence, R.I., T. Doyle, 1832. CtY; ICU; LN; MdBP; PPA; RPB.   11873

---- A grammar of the English language in a series of letters. Intended for the use of schools and of young persons in general; but, more especially for the use of soldiers, sailors, apprentices, and ploughboys. By William Cobbett. To which are added, six lessons, intended to prevent statesmen from using false grammar, and from writing in an awkward manner. New York, J. Doyle, 1832. 213 p. CtY; MoSW; NjR; RJa; ScU; TxU-T.   11874

---- A history of the Protestant reformation, in England and Ireland...in a series of letters, addressed to all sensible and just Englishmen. By William Cobbett. New York, John Doyle, 1832. 2 vols. CtMW; NjR; OO; PU; RNR; TxU.   11875

Cochecho Aqueduct Association, Dover, N.H.
    The act of incorporation and by-laws of the Cochecho aqueduct association. Dover [N.H.] Enquirer press, Pr. by Geo. Wadleigh, 1832. 13 p. CSmH; Nh-Hi.
                                       11876
Cochrane, James.
    Address delivered at Medina, on the fourth of July, 1832, before the Medina Temperance Society, and now published at their request. Medina, Pr. for the society by D. P. Adams, 1832. 16 p. CSmH.   11877

Codman, John, 1782-1847.
    The faith of the Pilgrims. A sermon delivered at Plymouth, on the twenty-second of December, 1831. By John Codman, D.D. Boston, Perkins & Marvin, 1832. CtY; ICN; MWA; NjPT; PLT.
                                       11878
Coffee, Thomas J.
    To the freemen of Rankin County... [Brandon, 1832] Broadside. Ms-Ar.   11879

Cogswell, William, 1787-1850.
    The Theological Class Book; containing a system of divinity in the form of questions and answers, accompanied by scripture proofs. Designed for the benefit of theological classes and the higher classes in Sabbath Schools. By William Cogswell. Boston, Crocker & Brewster; New York, Jonathan Leavitt, 1832. 172 p. CtMW; IaHi; KyBC; MeBat; Nh.   11880

Colburn, Warren, 1793-1833.
    First lessons in arithmetic. Bellows Falls, Vt., Pr. for the publishers by S. H. Taylor, 1832. 172 p. VtU.   11881

---- First lessons in reading and grammar. Boston, Hilliard, Gray & Co., 1832. MH.   11882

---- Intellectual, arithmetic, upon the inductive method of instruction. By Warren Colburn... Boston, Hilliard, Gray, Little & Wilkins, 1832. 172 p. NcAS; NWattJHi.   11883

---- An introduction to algebra upon the inductive method of instruction. By Warren Colburn... Boston, Hilliard, Gray, Little and Wilkins, 1832. 276 p. CtY; ICP; LU-E; MB; OClWHi. 11884

---- Second lessons in reading and grammar for the use of schools chiefly from the works of Miss Edgeworth. Selected and prepared by Warren Colburn. MH.
                                       11885
---- Third lessons in reading and grammar, for the use of schools; chiefly from the works of Miss Edgeworth. Selected and prepared by Warren Colburn... Boston, Hilliard, Gray & co., 1832. 139 p. DLC; MH; WU.
                                       11886
Colby College, Waterville, Maine.
    Catalogue of the officers and

students of Waterville College, and the Clerical School of Medicine, at Woodstock, Vt. , connected with the college. Hallowell, Glazier, Masters & Co. , 1832. 12 p. MeHi.   11887

---- Constitution of the Manual Labor Association, connected with Waterville College; with an address to the public. Augusta, Eaton and Severance, 1832. 12 p. MH; MeHi; NN.   11888

---- Laws of Waterville College. Waterville, 1832-53. 5 v. in 1. MB.   11889

Cole, George F.
     The Baltimore Centennial march, as performed at the celebration in 1832, in honour of the birth of Washington. The music arranged from the opera of Cinderella and dedicated to Col. John Thomas... (For pianoforte) Baltimore, Cole [1832] 3 p. CSmH; MB.   11890

Coleman, Lyman.
     A sermon delivered at Belchertown, Mass. , September 9, 1832, upon the dissolution of his pastoral relation with the church in that place. Belchertown, 1832. 15 p. CtY; MNF; MWA; MiD-B.   11891

Coleridge, Samuel Taylor, 1772-1834.
     The poetical works of Coleridge, Shelly and Keats, complete in one volume. Philadelphia, L. J. Grigg, 1832. 607 p. CtY; GDecCT; LNT; TNP; WHi. 11892

---- The statesman's manual; or The Bible the best guide to political skill and foresight: a lay sermon, addressed to the higher classes of society. By S. T. Coleridge, esq. Burlington, C. Goodrich, 1832. 231 p. CtY; DLC; OHi; PPM; RNR.   11893

Coles, L. B.
     Cole's pocket edition of Psalms, containing most of the tunes used in the different churches of New York, by L. B. Coles. New York, I. P. Cole, 1832. 96 p. KMK; MWHi; NjMD.   11894

Colesworthy, Daniel Clement, 1810-1893.
     Common incidents. Recommended by the Book Committee of Maine Sabbath School Union. By Philo-Paidos. Portland, G. Hyde & Co. , 1832. 108 p. MH; MeB; MeBa.   11895

Coley, H.
     Poisons & Asphyxia. New York, 1832. MB.   11896

Coley, Henry.
     A treatise on medical jurisprudence. Part I. Comprising the consideration of poisons and asphyxia. By Henry Coley.New York, W. Stodart, 1832. 72 p. CSt-L; MBM; MiD; NbU-M; PPCP.   11897

A collection of interesting tracts, explaining several important points of Scripture doctrine. Published by order of the general conference. New York, Carleton & Porter [1832] 378, 4 p. CtHC; InNomanC.   11898

A collection of psalms, hymns, anthems, etc. (with the evening office) for the use of the Catholic church throughout the United States. 2d ed. Washington, Thompson & Homans, 1832. 289 p. DGU; MdBD; MdW; PPcHi.   11899

College of Physicians of Philadelphia.
     Material facts in the history of epidemic [Cholera]. Philadelphia, 1832. MB.   11900

---- Report of the College of Physicians of Philadelphia, to the

Board of health, on epidemic cholera. Philadelphia, T. Desilver, jun., 1832. 36 p. DLC; ICP; MB; NNNAM; PPL.   11901

Collier, John Allen, 1787-1873.
   Speech of Mr. Collier, of New York, upon Mr. Clayton's resolution, that a committee be appointed to examine into the affairs of the United States Bank. Delivered in the House of Representatives, U.S., 13th March, 1832. Binghamton, Pr. by Canoll & Evans, 1832. 16 p. CtY; N; NN; NUtHi; RNR; TxU.   11902

Collier, William R.
   An Essay on Currency and Banking. Being an attempt to shew their true nature, and to explain the difficulties that have occurred in discussing them. With an application to the currency of this country. Philadelphia, Pr. by Jesper Harding, 1832. 76 p. DLC; ICJ; MWA; PPL; ScU.   11903

---- Remarks on the protective system; being an extract from an address delivered July 4, 1832. By W. R. Collier. Andover, Mass., 1832. 12 p. MB; MWA; PPL-R; ScCC; ScU.   11904

Collins, Gabriel.
   The Louisville directory, for the year 1832: to which is annexed, lists of the municipal, county and state officers; with a list of various societies and their officers. Also, an advertiser. Louisville, R. W. Otis, 1832. 198 p. ICU; MB; OCHP; OClWHi; PPL; WHi.   11905

Collins, Isaac.
   Prose and poetry selected for a mourner. Philadelphia, 1832. PPL; PPL-R; PPULC.   11906

Collot, Alexander G., b. 1796.
   Choix d'anecdotes ou faits mémorables, saillies et bonsmots, tirés De la Vie des Hommes Illustrés, de l'Histoire de Napoléon, de la Révolution d'-Amérique, &c.... Philadelphia, Grigg & Elliot, 1832. 162 p. KyLoP; MH.   11907

---- Dialogues arrangés pour faciliter l'étude de la langue française. Par A. G. Collot. Première série. Philadelphia, M. Herte, 1832. 75 p. DLC.
                                11908
---- Dialogues, gradués par ordre de difficultés, pour faciliter l'étude de la langue Française... par A. G. Collot. Première série. Philadelphia, Carey & Lea, 1832. 105 p. MH; PPM; ScCMu; TxU-T.
                                11909
Colman, George, 1732-1794.
   The deuce is in him:... Philadelphia [1832] MH.   11910

Colman, Henry, 1785-1849.
   An address to the Essex Agricultural Society, delivered at Andover, Massachusetts, 29th Sept. 1831. At their annual cattle show. By Henry Colman. Pub. at the request of the Society. [Andover, Mass.] Gazette Office, 1832. 22 p. MWA; MNe.   11911

---- ---- Salem, 1832. MDeeP.
                                11911a
Colonization laws of Mexico, Coahuila and Texas, which were in force before the declaration of independence by Texas [1832] TxH.   11912

Colonization of the free colored population of Maryland, and of such slaves as may hereafter become free... Baltimore, managers appointed by the state of Maryland, Robinson, pr., 1832. 16 p. CSmH; DLC; MA; MH.   11913

Colonization Society of Virginia.
First annual report of the
Board of Managers of the Coloni-
zation Society of Virginia. Rich-
mond, Pr. at the office of the
Southern Churchman, 1832? CtY;
MB; PHi; TxU; Vi; ViU.   11914

---- Proceedings...and report of
the managers, presented June 9th,
1831...Added, the Constitution
... Richmond, White, 1832. 14 p.
CSmH; MB; TxU.   11915

Colton, Charles Caleb, 1780? -
1832.
Lacon; or, Many things in few
words; addressed to those who
think...Rev. ed. New-York,
Charles Wells, 1832. 2 v. in 1.
CtY; GDecCt; NIC; PPAmP;
ScNC.   11916

Columbian Almanac for 1833.
Philadelphia, Pa., Jos. M'Dow-
ell [1832] DLC; MWA; PHi;
WHi.   11917

The Columbian calendar of New
York and Vermont Almanac, for
...1833...By a successor to
Andrew Beers. Troy, Francis
Adancourt [1832] 12 p. CLU; InU;
M; MWA; OClWHi; VtHi.   11918

The Columbus almanac for 1833.
By William Lusk. [Columbus] Pr.
by David Smith [1832] 48 p. OHi.
                           11919
The Comet... V.1-2; Apr. 19,
1832-July 28, 1833. New York,
H. M. Duhecqet, 1832/33-34. 2
vols. CtY; DLC; IEG; MH; NIC.
                           11920
[Comfort, Silas] 1808-1868.
An essay on the demoniacs of
the New Testament. Boston,
1832. MH; MH-AH.   11921

The Comforter; or, Extracts selected for the consolation of
mourners, under the bereave-
ments of friends and relations.

By a village pastor. New York,
J. & J. Harper, 1832. 203 p.
ABBS; CSoonsS; MBC; PLT;
PPAt.   11922

Comic tales, sketches, and anecdotes, original and selected.
Philadelphia, G. M. & W. Snider,
1832. 224 p. IU; MW; NNC; TxU.
                           11923
Comic Token...A companion to
the Comic Almanac for 1833.
Boston, Mass., Charles Ellms
and Willard Felt and Co. [1832]
48 p. MB; MHi; MWA; RWe;
WHi.   11924

Comly, John, 1773-1850.
English grammar, made easy
to the teacher and pupil originally
compiled for the use of the West-
town Boarding School, Pennsylvania. By John Comly. 15th ed.,
corr. and much improved. Philadelphia, Kimber & Sharpless,
1832. 216 p. CtHWatK; ICBB;
MdW; PSC-Hi; PU.   11925

---- An Epistle, or Salutation in
Gospel Love: with a word of encouragement to all who believe
in the light... Also some views
and remarks intended for the promotion of the peace and harmony
of society, and the quiet and sol-
emnity of our religious meetings
... Philadelphia, J. Richards,
1832. 36 p. MH; MWA; PHC;
PPL; PSC-Hi.   11926

Commercial advertiser and Essex
county Journal. April 4, 1832.
Ct; MBAt; MWA.   11927

The common almanac for 1833.
Buffalo, R. W. Haskins [1832]
12 l. NBuHi.   11928

---- Watertown, Knowlton and
Rice [1832] 12 l. DLC; MWA; NHi;
NN.   11929

Communication forwarded from

San Felipe de Austin, relative to
late events in Texas. Mobile, Pr.
at the office of the Patriot, 1832.
11 p. CtY; TxU.   11930

The complete Grocer; being a series of very valuable receipts for
distilling and mixing cordials of
all kinds, Brandy, Rum and Gin,
by an old Distiller. New York,
Pr. by John H. Turney, 1832.
204 p. N; RNR.   11931

A compliment for the season.
New York, N. B. Holmes [1832]
216 p. MB; MBAt; RPB.   11932

Comstock, Andrew, 1795-1874.
    Rhythmical reader, being a
selection of pieces in prose &
verse presented under a system
of rotation which exhibits the
measure of speech, the quantities
of syllables & the just admeas-
urement of pauses. Philadelphia,
Brown, 1832. 300 p. DLC; PPL;
PPULC; PU.   11933

Comstock, Franklin G.
    A digest of the law of execu-
tors and administrators, guardian
and ward, and dower. By Franklin Comstock. Hartford, H. F.
Sumner & Co., 1832. 504 p. Ct;
DLC; MH-L; NcD; PPB.   11934

Comstock, John Lee, 1789-1858.
    Elements of chemistry; in which
the recent discoveries in the science are included and its doctrines
familiarly explained. Illustrated by
numerous engravings, and designed
for the use of schools and academies. By J. L. Comstock, 3d ed.
Hartford, Robinson & Co., 1832.
356 p. CaBVaU; IEN-M; IaDuU;
MH.   11935

---- An introduction to mineralogy; adapted to the use of schools
and private students; illustrated
by nearly two hundred wood cuts.
By John L. Comstock. 2d ed. im-

proved. Hartford, Pr. [by P.
Canfield] for B. B. Barber, 1832.
343 p. CtMW; DLC; MH; PU;
ScSp; ViU.   11936

---- An introduction to the study
of botany; in which the science is
illustrated by examples of native
and exotic plants... Designed for
the use of schools and private
students. By J. L. Comstock.
Hartford, D. F. Robinson & Co.,
1832. 260 p. CSmH; DLC; MiU.
                           11937
---- A system of natural philosophy; in which the principles of
mechanics, hydrostatics, hydraul-
ics, pneumatics, acoustics, op-
tics, astronomy, electricity, and
magnetism are familiarly explained. Illustrated by more than
two hundred engravings. To which
are added questions for the examination of pupils. By J. L. Comstock. 3d stereotyped ed. Hartford, D. F. Robinson & Co., 1832.
295 p. CtY; MB; MH; NNC; PMA;
PP, PU.   11938

Concert at the capitol by Mr.
Blisse, the Tyrolese minstrel...
Detroit, June 21, 1832. Broad-
side. MiD-B.   11939

Condition and character of females
in pagan and Mohammedian countries. Stereotype ed. Boston,
1832. 12 p. MH; MWA; PHi.
                           11940
The conduct of the Administration.
Boston, Stimpson and Clapp,
1832. 86 p. MWA.   11941

Cone, Spencer Houghton, 1785-
1855.
    The Bible, its excellence. New
York, n.p., 1832. 48 p. NHCS.
                           11942
Confessions and execution of the
pirates, Gibbs & Wansley, on Ellis Island the 22nd April 1831.
7th ed. New York, Pr. by C. B.
C. Brown, 1832. 28 p. MH.
                           11943

Congregational Board of Publication.
The publications of the American doctrinal tract society. Boston, Pub. by the Society. Perkins & Marvin, agents. 1832. 255 p. MHans; NjPT. 11944

Congregational Churches in Connecticut. Association and Consociation of the Eastern District of Fairfield County.
Rules of the Association and Consociation of the Eastern District of Fairfield County adopted by December 9, 1831, with an appendix. New Haven, Pr. by Baldwin & Treadway, 1832. 23 p. Ct; NNUT. 11945

---- First Congregational Church of Bridgeport.
Manual for the communicants of the First Congregational Church of Bridgeport, Connecticut. Compiled Jan. 1, 1832. New Haven, 1832. 36 p. ICN; NBLiHi. 11946

---- First Congregational Church of Waterbury, Connecticut.
Articles of Faith and church covenant with embers. New Haven, 1832. 32 p. CtSoP. 11947
---- General Association.
Proceedings of the General Association of Connecticut, June, 1832. Hartford, P. B. Gleason & Co., 1832. 28 p. IEG; MoWgT. 11948

Congregational Churches in Maine.
Minutes of the general conference of Maine, at their annual meeting at Wiscasset, June 26, 1832. Portland, Arthur Shirley, 1832. 32 p. IEG; M; MeBat. 11949

Congregational Churches in Massachusetts, Worcester County, Paxton. Paxton, Mass. Congregational Church.
Articles of faith and form of covenant adopted by the Congregational Church in Paxton, October 11, 1832. Pr. by order of the Church, for the use of its members. Moses Winch, Pastor. Worcester, Pr. by S. H. Colton & Co., Spy Office, 1832. 8 p. MPax. 11950

Congregational Churches in Vermont. General Convention.
Extracts from the minutes of the General Convention at Congregational and Presbyterian ministers in Vermont, at their session at Middlebury, 1832. Windsor, Pr. at the Chronicle Press, 1832. 20 p. MiD-B. 11951

Congress of Nations.
Dissertation on...n.p., 1832. 28 p. MWA. 11952

A congress of nations, for the amicable adjustment of national differences. By a friend of peace ... Richmond [Va.] Pr. by J. MacFarlan, 1832. 24 p. CtY; DLC; OCl; OCIWHi. 11953

No entry. 11954

Connecticut. Governor.
The annual message of the Governor to the Legislature in the May session, 1832. New Haven, Pr. at the Office of the Palladium and Republican, 1832. 12 p. CSmH. Ct. 11955
---- ---- By his excellency John S. Peters, governor of the state of Connecticut, a proclamation as a day of humiliation, prayer and fasting... March 1, 1832. Signed John Peters [n.p., 1832] Broadside. MiU-C. 11956

---- Laws, statutes, etc.
An act for the greater security of banking institutions. [Hartford, 1832] 7 p. CtY.   11957

---- ---- The code of 1650; being a compilation of the earliest laws and orders of the General Court of Connecticut; also, the constitution, or civil compact, entered into and adopted by the towns of Windsor, Hartford, and Wethersfield in 1638-9, to which is added some extracts from the laws and judicial proceedings of New Haven colony, commonly called blue laws. Hartford, Silas Andrus, 1832. 119 p. CtY; DLC; MB; NN; NT; P.   11958

---- ---- The public statute laws of the state of Connecticut, passed at the session of the General Assembly in 1832. Hartford, Pub. by authority of the General Assembly, under the direction and superintendence of the Secretary of State, Pr. by Charles Babcock, 1832. 369-412 p. Ct; CtY; IaU-L; Nv.   11959

---- Legislature.
Report of the Joint Committee. ... "Growth of the mulberry tree and the culture of silk," with a bill for a public act, printed by the order of the Senate. New Haven, Pr. by J. Barber, 1832. 7 p. NjR.   11960

---- State Medical Society.
Proceedings of the president and fellows of the Connecticut Medical Society... May 1832. New Haven, Pr. by Hezekiah Howe, 1832. 16 p. CtY; NNNAM; PPL.   11961

Connecticut annual register and United States calendar for 1833 ... to which is prefixed an almanac ... New-London [Conn.] Pub. by Samuel Green, [1832] 160 p. IaHi; Mi.   11962

Connecticut Doctrinal Tract Society.
Prospectus [of the Evangelical magazine. Hartford, 1832] 2 p. Ct.   11963

Connecticut Peace Society.
Annual report, 1st. Hartford, 1832. 2 p. MB.   11964

Conrad, Timothy Abbot, 1803-1877.
Fossil shells of the tertiary formations of North America. Illustrated by figures drawn on stone, from nature. By T. A. Conrad, member of the Academy of Natural Science of Philadelphia. Vol. I. Philadelphia, 1832. 56 p. A-GS; CoU; In; MdBJ; PPAN.   11965

Considerations for young men
See Bell, Jared, 1799-1876.

The Contrast. By the author of "The gold thimble,"... Boston, Cottons & Barnard, 1832. 60 p. DLC; MB.   11966

Convention of delegates, elected by the citizens of the different districts interested in the connexion of the Susquehanna and Lehigh rivers, by a canal through the valley of the Nescopeck, and in the navigation of the Lehigh, on equitable terms. Proceedings. [n. p.] 1832. 16 p. ICJ; IU; MiU-C; NN; ViU.   11967

Convention of republican delegates from the several states in the Union for the purpose of nominating a candidate for... vice-president of the United States... Albany, Packard, 1832. 8 p. NN; NNC; PU.   11968

Conversation between R., once a Baptist minister, and B., a congregational minister, on the mode of baptism, and on the subject of close communion. Boston, Peirce

& Parker, 1832. 23 p. LNB;
MBC; MLow; NNUT; NjPT.
11969
Conversations on Common Things;
...by a teacher. 4th ed. , rev. ,
cor. and stereotyped. Boston,
Munroe & Francis, 1832. 288 p.
CtY; ICBB; MWinchrHi; MdAA;
VtMidSM.   11970

Conversations on the Sandwich is-
lands' mission. By a lady...2d
ed. Boston, Mass. , Sabbath
School Union, 1832. 216 p.
GMiluC; InCW; MH-AH; NNMr;
PU; ViRut.   11971

Converse, A.
Scriptural view of the mode of
baptism in a letter to an inquirer. By Rev. A. Converse.
Richmond [n.p. , n.pr.] 1832. 38
p. NjPT.   11972

Converse, John Kendrick, 1801-
1880.
A discourse, on the moral,
legal and domestic condition of
our colored population, preached
before the Vermont Colonization
Society, at Montpelier, Oct. 17,
1832. By. J. K. Converse. ..
Burlington [Vt.] E. Smith, 1832.
32 p. DLC; MWA; OO; RPB;
TNF.   11973

Conyngham Town, Pa. Citizens.
The proceedings of a convention of delegates, elected by the
citizens of the different districts
interested in the connexion of the
Susquehanna and Lehigh rivers,
by a canal through the valley of
the Nescopeck, and in the navigation of the Lehigh, on equitable
terms. Held at Conyngham Town,
Luzerne County, on the 20th and
21st days of December, 1832.
[Conyngham, Pa. , 1832?] 16 p.
MH; NNC; P.   11974

Cooke, Eleutheros, 1787-1864.
Speech of Mr. Cooke, of Ohio,

in the case of Samuel Houston,
charged with a contempt and
breach of the privileges of the
House, by assaulting the Hon.
Wm. Stanberry...delivered in the
House of Representatives...8th
May, 1832. Washington, Gales
& Seaton, 1832. 19 p. DLC;
OClWHi; MWA.   11975

Cooke, Parsons, 1800-1864.
Remarks on a sermon of the
Rev. Mr. Backus, delivered at
an installation in Western....
[Boston, 1832] 16 p. CBPac; ICN;
NIC; PPPrHi; RPB.   11976

---- A sermon preached at Williamstown, Mass. Oct. 28, 1832,
by Parsons Cooke... Boston, Pr.
[by Geo. W. Light & co.] Lyceum
Press, 1832. 12 p. MBAt; MBC;
MH-AH; NjPT; PPPrHi.   11977

Cooke, Thomas, Rev.
The new and complete letter-
writer, or, New art of polite
correspondence: containing a
course of interesting original letters...and a set of complimentary
cards... To which are added,
forms of mortgages, deeds, bonds,
powers of attorney, indentures,
&c. ...Also, the usual style of
address for the principal public
officers in the United States. New-
York, Pub. for the trade, 1832.
105 p. CtY; MiToC; NN. 11978

The cook's oracle. New York, J.
& J. Harper, 1832. 431 p. MWA;
RPB.   11979

Cook's own book: being a complete culinary encyclopedia...by
a Boston housekeeper...See Lee,
N. K. M.

Cooper, Astley Paston, bart. ,
1768-1841.
Treatise on dislocations and
on fractures of the joints by Sir
Astley Cooper, bart, F. R. S....

2d Amer. from 6th London ed.,
rev. and greatly improved...
Boston, Lilly & Wait and Carter
& Hendee [etc, etc.] 1832. 516 p.
DLC; KyU; LNOP; RNR; ViU.
11980
[Cooper, James Fenimore] 1789-
1851.
    The bravo: a tale. By the au-
thor of "The spy," "The Red
rover," "The water-witch," &c...
In 2 vols. Philadelphia, Carey &
Lea, 1832. 2 vols. TNP. 11981

---- The Heidenmauer; or, The
Benedictines. A legend of the
Rhine. Philadelphia, Carey &
Lea, 1832. 2 vols. CtY; DLC;
MWA; NN.   11982

---- The last of the Mohicans;
...4th ed. Philadelphia, H. C.
Carey & I. Lea, 1832. 2 vols.
MDeeP; MH.   11983

---- Lionel Lincoln; or, The
Leaguer of Boston.... by the au-
thor of "The Spy." In 2 volumes.
Vol. II. 5th ed. Philadelphia,
Carey & Lea, 1832. 2 v. DLC;
ICU; MOra; NPla; ViRVal. 11984

---- Notions of the Americans;
picked up by a travelling bachelor,
in two volumes. Philadelphia,
Carey & Lea, 1832-1833. MB;
MeB; NSmB; TNP.   11985

---- The Pilot: a tale of the sea.
By the author of "The Pioneer"
5th ed. Philadelphia, Carey & Lea,
1832. 2 vols. MH.   11986

---- The Pioneers, or, The
Sources of the Susquehanna; a de-
scriptive tale. By the author of
"The Spy." Philadelphia, Carey &
Lea, 1832. 2 vols. DLC; IaScT;
LNH; MdBJ; WU.   11987

---- The prairie. New York, F.
M. Lupton Pub. Co., 1832. 358 p.
GAM; IaBl; KNB; OO; PHC. 11988

---- The red rover, a tale....
Philadelphia, Carey, Lea and
Carey, 1832. 2 v. in 1. IU; OU;
NcAS; ViAl.   11989

---- The Spy: a tale of the neu-
tral ground.... By the author of
"Precaution." 6th ed. Philadelphia, Carey & Lea, 1832. 2 vols.
TNP.   11990

---- The Wept of Wish-Ton-Wish.
Philadelphia, Carey, Lea & Carey,
1832. 2 vols. DLC; MWA; PU.
11991
Cooper, James G.
    Essay on comets, containing a
short account of the principal
comets, a new theory for the solution of the cometic phenomena;
& a refutation of previous theories. Philadelphia, Young, 1832.
40 p. ICBB; MB; NjR; PPAmP;
PPL-R; PU; RPB.   11992

Cooper, Mary (Hanson), 1786-
1812.
    Memoirs of the late Mrs. Mary
Cooper of London...by Adam
Clarke. New York, Pub. by B.
Waugh & T. Mason, for the Meth-
odist Episcopal Church, 1832.
CtY-D; DLC; MNS; ViRU. 11993

Cooper, Samuel, 1780-1848.
    A dictionary of practical sur-
gery, comprehending all the most
interesting improvements, from
the earliest times down to the
present period...by Samuel Cooper. With numerous notes and additions, by David Meredith Reese,
M.D. From the 6th London ed.,
rev., cor. and enl. New York,
J. & J. Harper, 1832. 2 vols.
KyLxT; MdBS; NNN; NcD;
WU-M.   11994

Cooper, Thomas, 1759-1839.
    The case of Thomas Cooper,
submitted to the Legislature and
the people of South Carolina. Dec.
1831. 2d ed. Columbia, S.C., Pr.

at the Times & Gazette office,
1832. 31, 14, **4 p.** MH; NIC;
NcD; PPAmP; PPL; ScU.   11995

---- Hints, suggestions, and contributions toward the labours of
a convention. Columbia, S. C.,
at the Telescope office, 1832.
17 p. A-Ar; NN; ScU.   11996

---- Memoirs of a nullifier; written by himself. See Johnston,
Algernon Sidney, 1801-1853.

---- To any member of Congress.
3d ed. First pub. in 1829. Columbia, S. C., Pr. at the Times
& Gazette office, 1832. 15 p.
IEN-M; MH; PPL; ScU.   11997

Copeland, Melvin.
When does the Sabbath begin?
A careful examination of the passages of scripture which are
thought to favor the beginning of
the Sabbath on Saturday evening,
at sunset; and also, of the passages which are thought to teach
a different practice. Hartford,
Pr. by G. F. Olmsted for D. F.
Robinson & Co., 1832. 18 p.
CSmH; CtY; MBC; OClWHi;
PPPrHi.   11998

Corbett, M.
The sisters' budget; a collection of original tales in prose and
verse. By the authors of "The odd
volume"... with contributions from
Mrs. Hemans, Miss Mitford, Miss
Jewsbury... By M. Corbett. Baltimore, W. & J. Neal, 1832. 2 v.
DLC; ICBB; MAnP; NjP.   11999

Corbyn, Frederick.
A treatise on the epidemic Cholera, as it has prevailed in India.
together with the reports of the
medical officers, made to the medical boards of the presidencies of
Bengal, Madras, and Bombay...
Calcutta, Pr. at the Baptist mission press; Philadelphia, Carey,

Lea & Carey, 1832. 389 p. DLC;
ICJ; MB; OClM; PPA; PU.
   12000
Cornardo, Luigi, 1475-1566.
Discourses on a sober and tem-
perate life, wherein is demonstrated by his own example, the
method of preserving health to ex-
treme old age. New ed. With in-
trod. and notes, by Sylvester
Graham [New York, Day, 1832]
MB; NRU; RPB.   12001

Cornelius, Elias, 1794-1832.
The little Osage captive. An
authentic narrative...2d ed. Boston, Sabbath School Society, 1832.
72 p. CtHWatk; DLC; MH-AH;
MiD-B.   12002

Correspondence between the First
Church and the Tabernacle Church
in Salem. See Salem, Mass.
First Church.

Corte, Hernando.
Tales from American History,
chiefly relating to the conquest of
Mexico and Peru, by Hernando
Cortez and Francisco Pizarro...
New York, William Burgess, 1832.
MC; Md-B.   12003

Cortland Academy.
Catalogue of the trustees, instructors, and students... for the
year ending December, 1832.
Homer Village, 1832. 7 (1) p. NN.
   12004
Cotterill, Thomas.
Family prayers, composed
principally in expressions taken
from the Holy Scriptures and from
established services of the Church
of England. By the Rev. Thomas
Cotterill, A. M., Perpetual Curate
of Lane-End, Staffordshire; and
late fellow of St. John's College,
Cambridge. 3d Amer. ed. New
York, Swords, Stanford & Co.,
1832. 256 p. CtHT; NjPT; ScCMu.
   12005
Cottin, Marie (Risteau).

The Saracen, or Matilda and
Maleh Adhel,... From the French
of Madame Cottin, with an historical introduction, by J. Mich-
and... Exeter, J. & B. Williams,
1832. 238 p. DLC; MeB; NPV;
Nh.   12006

Cottom's Virginia and North Caro-
lina almanack for 1833. Richmond,
P. Cottom [1832] 36 p. DLC; NcD;
NcU; Vi; ViW.   12007

The cotton manufacturer's useful
assistant. Philadelphia, J. Metcalfe and Co., 1832. 20 p. DLC.
                               12008
The Court and Camp of Bonaparte.
New York, J. & J. Harper, 1832.
389 p. LNH; MB; NNS; PPA; RPB;
ViU.   12009

Cousin, Victor, 1792-1867.
    Introduction to the history of
philosophy, by Victor Cousin...
Tr. from the French by Henning
Gotfried Linberg. Boston, Hilliard, Gray, Little, & Wilkins,
1832. 458 p. CU; GDecCT; KyDC;
MH; OHi; PPA.   12010

Coventry, Thomas, 1797-1869.
    An analytical digested index to
the common law reports from the
time of Henry III. To the commencement of the reign of George
III. With tables of the titles and
names of cases. By Thomas Coventry and Samuel Hughes. Philadelphia, R. H. Small, 1832. 2 v.
In-SC; KyLxT; LNT-L; OCLaw;
PU.   12011

Cowell, Benjamin, 1781-1860.
    An address delivered before
the anti-Masonic Convention,
holden at Providence, Nov. 2,
1832. By Benjamin Cowell. Pub.
by request of the Convention.
Providence, Pr. by Edward and
J. W. Cory, 1832. 20 p. MB;
RWe.   12012

---- Ancient documents relative
to the Old Grist Mill, with some
remarks on the opinion of Messrs.
Hunter and Greene, counsel employed by the town to examine the
same.   Providence, Herald Office,
1832.   12013

Cowgill, John.
    The Key of Nature, by which
the Mysteries therein are unfold-
ed with some new and sublime
ideas on astronomy and philosophy, and some pieces of sublime
poetry. The whole carefully revised and corrected in proof
sheets, by the author, John Cowgill. Nashville, Pr. for the author, 1832. 72 p. T; TNP. 12014

Cowley, Hannah Parkerhouse,
1743-1809.
    Who's the Dupe? A farce in
two acts. (In British drama)
Vol. 2. Philadelphia, J. J. Woodward, 1832. 164-173 p. IaGG;
MH.   12015

Cowper, William, 1731-1800.
    The Works of Cowper and
Thomson, including many letters
and poems never before published
in this country, with a new and
interesting memoir of the life of
Thomson.   Philadelphia, J. Grigg,
1832. 133 p. MH; MS; Md; O;
TNP.   12016

[Cox, John]
    On the argument, in reference
to the bridge bill, prepared by
Judge Cranch and Doctor May,
which the honorable chairman of
the committee of the Senate, has
transmitted to the mayor of
Georgetown; the following remarks
are respectfully submitted. n. p.
[1832] 27 p. MWA; PPL; ScU.
                               12017
Cox, John Redman, 1773-1864.
    Letter to John Vaughan, 1832.
Ms. communication to the APS.
Vol. on medicine, anatomy and

physiology. PPAmP.   12018

Cox, Ross, 1793-1853.
Adventures on the Columbia
River, including the narrative of
a residence of six years on the
western side of the Rocky Mountains, among various tribes of
Indians hitherto unknown: together
with a journey across the American continent. By Ross Cox.
New-York, J. & J. Harper, 1832.
335 p. CoD; KyLx; MiD; PPWi;
ViU.   12019

Cox, William, d. 1851.
Crayon sketches. By an ama-
teur. Edited by T. S. Fay. New
York, Harper & Bros., 1832. 2
vols.   12020

Crabb, George, 1778-1851.
English synonyms, with copi-
ous illustrations and explanations
... A new ed. enl. By George
Crabb, M.A. New York, J. & J.
Harper, 1832. 535 p. DLC; LU;
NPV; ScNC; ViRut.   12021

Craigengelt, Arthur, pseud.
...Fashionable satires. Rho-
doshake's visit from the moon; a
poem; in two cantos. By Arthur
Craigengelt. New York, Peabody
& Co., 1832. 63 p. CSmH; DLC;
MWA; NjR; RPB.   12022

Cramer's Magazine almanac. See
also Loomis' magazine almanac.

Cramer's magazine almanack, on
a new and improved plan, for the
year of our Lord 1833: the first
after bissextile, or leap-year, and
after the fourth of July, the fifty-
eighth year of American independence. Pittsburgh, Cramer &
Spear, [1832] 58 p. MWA;
OClWHi; PPi.   12023

Cramer's Pittsburgh almanac on
a new and improved plan, for the
year of our Lord 1833: the first

after bissextile, or leap-year,
and after the fourth of July, the
fifty-eighth year of American independence. Pittsburgh, Cramer
& Spear [1832] 36 p. MWA;
OClWHi; OHi; PPiU.   12024

Crane, Joseph Halsey, 1782-1851.
Speech of Mr. Crane, of Ohio,
in the case of Samuel Houston,
tried for a breach of the privileges of the House of Representatives of the United States. Delivered May 9th, 1832. Washington,
Jonathan Elliot, 1832. 12 p. DLC;
ICP; O; OClWHi.   12025

Crawford, George William.
Slavery! Captain Yorke's views
on the subject of colonial slavery,
refuted in two letters, by the Rev.
G. W. Crawford, together with
Captain York's (sic) attempted defense. Cambridge, Weston Hatfield, 1832. 11 p. DHU.   12026

Crawford, Thomas Hartley, 1786-
1863.
Speech of T. Hartley Crawford,
of Pennsylvania, in opposition to
the bill, entitled "a bill to reduce
& equalize the duties upon imports"
& in favor of the American system. Delivered in the House of
Representatives U.S. on the 29th
& 30th of May, 1832. Washington,
Gales & Seaton, 1832. 16 p. Ct;
DLC; NN.   12027

---- ---- Washington, 1832. 30 p.
DLC.   12028

Cressy, Benjamin C.
An appeal in behalf of the Indi-
ana Theological Seminary, located
at South Hanover, Indiana. Boston,
Pr. by Peirce & Parker, 1832.
16 p. CtY; IEG; InHi; MH; NbOP.
                           12029
Cries of London.
The new cries of London. New
York, Mahlon Day, 1832. 23 p.
DLC.   12030

The Crisis, or Nullification un-
masked. With the Union and
States Rights Party of South Carolina. By an exposition of the
real designs clumsily counter-
feited, by the disseminators of
that anarchical doctrine.
Charleston, 1832. 16 p. ICN;
MHi; PHi; ViU.   12031

Croly, George, 1780-1860.
    ...Life and times of His late
Majesty George the Fourth. With
anecdotes of distinguished persons of the last fifty years. By
the Rev. George Croly. New and
improved ed. New York, J. & J.
Harper, 1832. 414 p. CtMW;
IEG; MHi; NcU; TNP.   12032

Cross, Nathaniel.
    An address delivered before
the Young Men's Temperance
Society of Basking-Ridge, N.J.
January 1st, 1832. Morristown,
[N.J.] S. P. Hull [1832] 17 p.
T.   12033

Croswell, Harry.
    Sermon to Children by Harry
Croswell. New Haven, 1832.
10 p. IEG.   12034

Crozet, Claudius, 1789-1864.
    Report of C. Crozet, Esqr.,
engineer, to the president and
directors of the Portsmouth and
Roanoke Rail Road Company.
Norfolk, Shields and Ashburn,
prs., Beacon Office, 1832. 16 p.
MCM; MWA; NcU; NNP.   12035

Cumberland Almanac, for the
year of our Lord 1833, being the
first after bissextile or leap year,
and the 57th and 58th of American Independence. Containing the
motions of the sun and moon--
the true phases and aspects of
the planets--the rising and setting of the sun--the rising and
setting of the moon--solar and
lunar eclipses, &c. Calculated

for the horizon of Nashville,
Ten. Latitude about 36°n. and
longitude 87°w. of London, and
10° of Washington, and with slight
variation, will answer for Kentucky and Alabama. Nashville,
Tenn., Hunt, Tardiff & Co., at
the Whig & Banner Office [1832]
36 p. MWA.   12036

Cumberland [Maine] District Medical Society.
    By-laws and system of police
of the Cumberland District Medical Society. Portland, Arthur
Shirley, 1832. 18 p. MeHi.
                              12037
Cuming, Francis Higgins.
    Catechism of sacred geography
and history: designed for Sunday
and other schools. Part 1...Le-
Roy [N.Y.] E. Starr, pr., 1832.
NRU.   12038

---- The spiritual character of
the liturgy of the Protestant
Episcopal church. By the Rev.
F. H. Cuming...3d ed. New-
York, The Protestant Episcopal
Press, 1832. 24 p. DLC; MWA;
MdBD; NjR; PPPrHi.   12039

Cumings, Samuel.
    Western pilot; containing charts
of the Ohio river & of the Mississippi from the Missouri to the
Gulf of Mexico...with directions
for navigating the same & a gazeteer... Cincinnati, Guilford, 1832.
151 p. DLC; Ia; MiD-B; PPi;
TxD-W.   12040

Cumming, Hooper, 1788-1825.
    The essential doctrines of the
Gospel. An introductory sermon,
delivered...June 1, 1823. New
York, Seymour, 1832. 27 p.
PPPrHi.   12041

Cummings, Asa, 1791-1856.
    A memoir of the Rev. Edward
Payson, D.D., late pastor of the
Second church in Portland. By

Asa Cummings... 5th ed. Boston, Crocker & Brewster; New York, J. Leavitt, 1832. 400 p. CtY; ICN; OO; RNR; ViU.   12042

Cunningham, Allan, 1784-1842.
... The lives of the most eminent British painters and sculptors. By Allan Cunningham... [Harper's stereotype ed.] New York, Harper & bros., 1832. 3 vols. LN; LNH; MoK; WvW.
                                  12043
---- Some account of the life and works of Sir Walter Scott... Boston, Stimpson & Clapp, 1832. 106 p. DLC; ICBB; MBAt; RPB; WM.
                                  12044
Cunningham, J. P.
Man's interest in the Sabbath. A sermon, delivered in Concord church, Greene county, December 25, 1831. By J. P. Cunningham, pastor. Tuscaloosa, Ala., Pub. by request, Pr. by Robinson & Hampton, 1832. 24 p. AU; ICU.
                                  12045
Cunningham, John William, 1780-1861.
Sancho, or The proverbialist ... Philadelphia, 1832. NjP.
                                  12046
---- A world without souls. By J. W. Cunningham, A. M. Boston, James Loring, 1832. 108 p. PWaybu.   10247

Curtis, Benjamin Robbins.
An address delivered at the centennial celebration of the birthday of Washington, at Deerfield, Mass. Feb. 22d, 1832. By Benjamin R. Curtis. Pub. by request. Greenfield, Mass., Pr. by Phelps & Ingersoll, 1832. 23 p. CSmH; MBAt; MH; MWA; NjR.
                                  10248
Cushing, Caleb.
An oration delivered before the citizens of Newburyport, on the fifty-sixth anniversary of American independence. By Caleb Cushing. Newburyport, T. B. & E. L.

White, 1832. 56 p. CSmH; MeBaT; Nh-Hi; PHi; RPB. 12049

[Cushing, Caroline Elizabeth (Wilde)] d. 1832.
Letters, descriptive of public monuments, scenery, and manners in France and Spain... Newburyport, Pr. by E. W. Allen & co., 1832. 2 v. CtY; DLC; MBAt; OO; PP.   12050

[Cuthberson, Catherine] fl. 1803-1830.
Santo Sebastiano, or The Young Protector. By the author of "The Romance of the Pyrenees." Boston, Carter & Hendee, 1832. 3 v. CtY; MBAt; MH; PP; RPB.
                                  12051
Cutter, Benjamin Clarke.
Sermon in behalf of the New-York Protestant Episcopal City-mission Society... By Benjamin C. Cutler... New-York, Protestant Episcopal Press, 1832. 16 p. DLC; MdBD; NNG; PHi; RPB.
                                  12052
Cutter, Calvin, 1807-1872.
Treatise on anatomy, physiology and hygiene... Rev. ed. Boston, 1832. Nh.   12053

Cuvier, Georges, 1769-1832.
The animal kingdom, arranged in conformity with its organization. By the Baron Cuvier... Tr. from the French, and abridged for the use of schools, &c. by H. M'Murtrie... New York, G. & C. & H. Carvill, 1832. 532 p. CtY; MiU; PU; TNL; WU.   12054

D

[Dabney, Jonathan Peele]
Selection of hymns and psalms for social and private worship. 11th ed. Boston, Munroe & Francis, 1832. 24 p. IEG; MBC.
                                  12055
Daboll, Nathan, 1750-1818.

96 Daily

Daboll's schoolmasters assistant, improved and enlarged being a plain practical system of arithmetic... By Nathan Daboll. With the addition of the farmers and mechanics best method of bookkeeping, designed as a companion to Daboll's arithmetic. By Samuel Green. Utica, Hastings & Tracy, 1832. 240 p. CtY; KyBC; MH; NUt; PSorHi.   12056

Daily express. Philadelphia, 1832. PPL; PPL-R.   12057

Daily food for Christians, being a promise, and another Scriptural portion, for every day in the year. Together with the verse of a hymn, New York, American Tract Society [1832] MH.   12058

Daily intelligencer. Dec. 1, 1832-August 1, 1833. Philadelphia [1832] PHi.   12059

Dallas, George Mifflin, 1792-1864.
Speech of George Mifflin Dallas, delivered in the Senate of the United States, upon the subject of the tariff, on the twenty-seventh of February, 1832. Philadelphia, Peter Hay & Co., 1832. 40 p. Ct; DLC; MWA; NN; OCHP.   12060

---- Speech upon the bill to modify and continue the charter of the Bank of the United States, delivered in the Senate U.S. May 22, 1832. Washington, Pr. by Gales & Seaton, 1832. 8 p. MH; MdHi; MnHi; PHi; PPAmP.   12061

Dalzel, Andrew, 1742-1806.
Anaekta'Hellenika Meizona; sive, collectanea Graeca majora, ad usum academicae Juventutis, accomodater cum notis philologicis, quas partin collegit, partim scripsit. A. Dalzel. Boston, Hilliard, Gray, Little, et. Wilkins,

1832.   ArCH; InU; LNT; MiD; RNR.   12062

---- ... Collectanea Graeca majora... Bostoniae, Hilliard, Gray, Little, et Wilkins, 1831. 4th Amer. ed. Boston, Hilliard, Gray, Little & Wilkins, 1832. 2 vols. CtY; InU; MH; NN; OClStM.   12063

Damon, David, 1788-1843.
The means of attaining religion. ...Pr. for the Union Ministerial Association, Dover, Mass., 1832. 16 p. CBPac; Nh-Hi.   12064

Damon, Ivory.
Lectures on the Unity of God and the Character of the Messiah, by Ivory Damon. Leominster, Mass.   Fitchburg, Gazette Press, 1832. 24 p. MWA.   12065

Dana, Daniel, 1771-1859.
Conversion the work of God. A sermon delivered Dec. 31, 1831; A day devoted by several churches in Newburyport and its vicinity, to united praise for the spiritual blessings of the year. By Daniel Dana, D.D. Pub. by request. Newburyport, W. & J. Gilman, 1832. 24 p. CBPSR; MH; Nh-Hi; OMC; RPB.   12066

---- A sermon occasioned by the death of Mrs. Harriet Putnam, wife of the Rev. Israel W. Putnam, Portsmouth, and delivered June 17, 1832.... Portsmouth [N.H.] Pr. by Miller & Brewster, 1832. 23 p. CSmH; MB; MH; RPB.   12067

---- Speaking the Truth in Love. A sermon preached at the ordination of the Rev. John C. March as Colleague Pastor over the church in Belleville. March 1, 1832. By Daniel Dana, D.D. ... Newburyport, Charles Whipple, 1832. 18 p. CtSoP; ICT; MNe; Nh-Hi; RPB.   12068

Dana, Edmund P.

A few impartial remarks and observations, on both sides of the question, on the approaching presidential election; with a brief description of the characters of Clay, Wirt, Calhoun, Jackson, Adams, McDuffie, R. M. Johnson, and Poindexter; on the rejection of the nomination of Martin Van Buren, by the Senate of the United States... Baltimore, Pr. by Sands & Neilson, 1832. 16 p. MB; OClWHi.   12069

D'Anbigne, Merle.

Discourse on the study of the history of Christianism, and its usefulness at this epoch, delivered at Geneva January 2, 1832. ...Trans. from the French, by Thos. S. Grimke. Charleston, 1832. 22 p. MHi.   12070

Dann, Joseph.

Liber primis; or a first book of Latin exercises... Boston, 1832. 192 p. DLC.   12071

Danvers, (Mass.) Second Universalist Society.

By laws of the Second Universalist Society in Danvers. Salem, Pr. at the Advertiser Press, 1832. 14 p. MPeaHi.   12072

Danville and Pottsville Railroad Co.

Laws and by-laws of the Danville and Pottsville Rail-road Company. Philadelphia, Pr. by Lydia R. Bailey, 1832. 28 p. DBRE; NN; NbO.   12073

Da Ponte, Lorenzo, 1749-1838.

Versi compositi nel la morte d'Anna Celestina Ernestina, sua consorte. New-York, J. H. Turney, 1832. 36 p. MH; MiU; PPL.   12074

Darby, William, 1775-1854.

A new gazetteer of the United States of America... including...

geographical, historical, political, and statistical information; with the population of 1830. By William Darby and Theodore Dwight, jr. New York, E. Hopkins, 1832. 630 p. CSmH; MdBP; NN; OO; ViU.   12075

---- The United States reader or Juvenile Instructor...No. 2. Baltimore, 1832- DLC.   12076

Darlington, William.

A catechism of mythology; containing a compendious history of the heathen gods and heroes. By William Darlington. Baltimore, William R. Lucas, 1832. 305 p. DLC; ICartC; LNH; MH; OUrC.   12077

Daru, [Pierre Antoine Noël Bruno] 1767-1829.

Volney's Ruins; or, Meditation on the Revolution of Empires. Transl. under the immediate inspection of the author from the 6th Paris ed., to which is added, the Law of Nature, and A short Biographical Notice, by Count Daru: also, the Controversy between Dr. Priestly and Volney. Boston, Charles Gaylord, 1832. 216 p. Md-B.   12078

Dauphin and Susquehanna Coal Company.

An act to incorporate the Dauphin and Susquehanna Coal Company. Passed the fifth day of April, 1826. Philadelphia, Clark & Raser, 1832. 8 p. NN; NbO; PPM.   12079

[Daveis, Charles Stewart] 1788-1865.

The north-eastern boundary of the United States. Boston, Pr. by Peirce & Parker, 1832. 100 p. CtY; DLC; MBAt; MeU; Nh.   12080

Davenport, Bishop.

History of the United States, containing all the events necessary to be committed to memory; with the declaration of independence, constitution of the United States, and a valuable table of chronology... by B. Davenport.... Philadelphia, Uriah Hunt, 1832. 144 p. NjR.   12081

---- A new gazetteer, or Geographical dictionary, of North America & the West Indies. Complete from the most recent & authentic sources. Baltimore, G. M. Dowell & Son, 1832. 471 p. DLC; InU; MiU; NcD; PPAmP; TNV.   12082

Davenport, Richard Alfred, 1777?-1852.
A dictionary of biography; comprising the most eminent characters of all ages, nations and profssions... By R. A. Davenport, 1st Amer. ed., with numerous additions, corr. and improvements. And illustrated by two hundred fine portraits, on wood. Boston, Gray & Bowen, 1832. 527 p. MiU; PPL-R; TxU; ViU; WHi.   12083

---- ---- Exeter, J. & B. Williams, 1832. 527 p. OO; ViU.   12084

Davidson, Mary Crawford.
Dying Exercises of Mary Crawford Davidson. Tuscaloosa [1832?]   12085

Davidson, Samuel C.
Camp meeting songster; or A collection of hymns and spiritual songs, with a few pieces never before published; designed principally, for camp meetings. By Samuel C. Davidson. Knoxville, Tenn., Pr. by F. S. Heiskell, 1832. 120 p. MoS.   12086

Davies, Charles, 1798-1876.
Elements of descriptive geometry, with their application to spherical trigonometry, spherical projections, and warped surfaces.

By Charles Davies...2d ed. New York, Harper, 1832. 174 p. CtMW; InCW; KU; PU; ScCC.   12087

---- A treatise on shades and shadows and linear perspective. By Charles Davies. New York, Pr. & pub. by J. & J. Harper, 1832. 157 p. CoD; ICN; LNL; PPi; TNP.   12088

Davies, Richard, 1635-1708.
An account of the convincement, exercises, services, and travels, of that ancient servant of the Lord, Richard Davies: comprising some information relative to the spreading of the truth in North Wales. From the 6th London ed. Philadelphia, Nathan Kite, 1832. 138 p. CtHT; ICN; OClWHi; PHi; TxU.   12089

Davies, Samuel.
Memoir of the Rev. Samuel Davies, formerly President of the College of New Jersey, revised... Boston, Massachusetts Sabbath School Society, 1832. 131 p. DLC; InCW; MH; MeB.   12090

Davis, Elnathan, 1807-1881.
Eulogy on Thomas Crocker. Bound up with Outline of the Course of Study in the Department of Christian Theology. Lancaster, Carter, Andrews & Co., 1832. 8 p. DLC; MB; OClW.   12091

Davis, Emerson.
The Franklin intellectual arithmetic: for the use of schools. By E. Davis, A.M., principal of Westfield Academy. Springfield, G. & C. Merriam, 1832. 108 p. DLC; NbCrD.   12092

Davis, Gustavus Fellows, 1797-1836.
A brief treatise on the duty of courtesy between those who differ in opinion. Addressed to all religious denominations & to all po-

litical parties. By Gustavus F. Davis. Hartford, F. J. Huntington, 1832. 36 p. Ct; CtW; DLC; MBC; MWA. 12093

Davis, J. A. G.
A lecture on the constitutionality of protecting duties, delivered in the University of Virginia. By J. A. G. Davis. Charlottesville, Pr. by Cary & Watson, 1832. 24 p. TxU; ViL. 12094

Davis, Paris M.
The four principal battles of the late war. Being a full detailed account of the battle of Chippeway, fall and destruction of the city of Washington, battles of Baltimore, and New-Orleans. By Adjutant P. M. Davis... Harrisburg, Pr. by J. Baab, 1832. 32 p. CtY; KHi; MBC; PHi; WHi. 12095

Davis, Warren Ransom.
Speech of Warren R. Davis, of South Carolina, on the great pension bill. Delivered on the 4th and 5th of April, 1832, in the House of Representatives, in committee of the whole on the state of the union, Mr. L. Condict, of New Jersey, in the chair. Washington, Pr. by Duff Green, 1832. 16 p. A-Ar; DLC; ICN; NcD; PPAmP; ScU. 12096

Davisson, Josiah.
The splendid horse, [cut of horse and groom] Kentucky Snap, will stand the present season, at my stable in the town of Xenia, ...Xenia, Ohio, Pr. at the office of the Xenia Free Press [1832] broadside. 12097

[Davy, Sir Humphry] 1778-1829.
Salmonia: or, Days of fly fishing. In a series of conversation; with some account of the habits of fishes belonging to the genus Salmo. By an angler... 1st Amer.

from the 2d London ed. Philadelphia, Carey & Lea, 1832. 312 p. CU; GU; MoU; OClW; ViU. 12098

Dawson, William, 1773-1841.
Memoirs of the Rev. David Stoner; containing copious extracts from his diary & epistolary correspondence. 1st Amer. from 2d English ed. New York, Emory & Waugh, 1832. CtW; DLC; MoS; NBuG; ViU. 12099

[Day, Edward] 1759?-
The independent credenda in theology, accompanied by annotations and explanatory observations... compiled in part, from the works of many celebrated authors... historical, polemic and theological... Prepared for the private use of the writer, A. D. 1832. ...By a Country layman aged 73 years. Baltimore, for the author, 1832. 58 p. DLC; MdBP; MdHi. 12100

Day, Jeremiah, 1773-1867.
An introduction to algebra. Being the first part of a course of mathematics adapted to method of instruction in the American colleges. By Jeremiah Day, president of Yale College. 8th ed. New Haven (Conn.), Hezekiah Howe, 1832. 332 p. IaB; LUT; MB; MH. 12101

---- ---- 9th ed. New Haven, H. Howe & Co., 1832. ANA; MH; ODW. 12102

Day, Thomas, 1748-1789.
The history of Sandford & Merton. By Thomas Day, Esq. Baltimore, William & Joseph Neal, 1832. 391 p. DLC; MBL; MH; OMC; PAtM. 12103

Day's Academy, Wrentham, Mass.
Catalogue of the officers and students of Day's Academy, Wrentham, November 23, 1832... Dedham, Pr. by Ebenezer Fish,

[1832] broadside. MH.   12104

Day's New York Pocket Almanac
for 1833. New York, M. Day
[1832] DLC; IaB; LNHT; MH;
MWA.   12105

Days of sickness, by the author
of The Talisman. Boston, L. C.
Bowles, 1832.   69 p.   DLC.
                           12106

Dayton, Ohio.
    The ordinances of the common
council of the town of Dayton; to
which are prefixed the several
acts of incorporation. [Dayton?]
Van Cleve & Comly, 1832. 47 p.
OClWHi.   12107

De La Beche, Henry Thomas,
1796-1855.
    A geological manual. Philadel-
phia, Carey & Lea, 1832. 535 p.
CU; GU; NcU; PPA; TxU;
WaS.   12108

[Dean, Christopher, C.]
    Claims of the Africans. See
under title.

---- Hugh Clifford: or, Prospectus missions on the North-west
coast, and at the Washington Islands... Boston, Massachusetts
Sabbath School Union, 1832. 102 p.
ICP; WaU.   12109

Dean, Paul, 1789-1860.
    An address delivered before
the Boston encampment of Knights
Templars, at the public installa-
tion of its officers, on the evening
of the 28th of Feb. A.D. 1832.
By Paul Dean. Boston, Moore &
Sevey-Cornhill, 1832. 11 p. CtY;
PPFM.   12110

---- Course of lectures in defense
of the final restoration, delivered
in the Bulfinch Church, Boston...
Boston, Edwin M. Stone; Press of
the Independent Messenger, 1832.

10-180 p. CSmH; ICN; MH;
MeBat; NNUT.   12111

---- A discourse delivered at the
annual election, January 4, 1832,
before his Excellency Levi Lin-
coln, Governor; his Honor Thomas
L. Winthrop, Lieutenant-Governor;
the Honorable Council, and the
Legislature of Massachusetts. By
Paul Dean. Boston, Dutton &
Wentworth, 1832. 38 p. CBPac;
ICT; MH-AH; MNe; MWA;
NIC.   12112

Debate in the Senate on the nomination of Martin Van Buren, to
be Minister of the United States
to Great Britain. This debate took
place mainly on the 24th and 25th
of January, 1832, and, according
to the rules of the Senate, in secret session. After the question
was decided, the injunction of
secrecy was removed, by a vote
of the Senate, from the debates
as well as the proceedings in
this case. In consequence of which,
the following proceeding and authentic sketches of speeches delivered in that debate were published in the National Intelligencer
and other papers, etc. [Washing-
ton, 1832] 55 p. MWA; MdHi;
MnHi; PHi; PPL; ScU.   12113

Debate in the U.S. Senate on return of the bank bill with Gen.
Jackson's veto, 1832. PPL.
                           12114
DeCharms, Richard, 1796-1864.
    The true nature of a Religious
Profession: A discourse delivered before the western convention
of the New Jerusalem church, Assembled in the City of Cincinnati,
on the 13th Oct., 1832. Cincinnati, Pr. by L. R. Lincoln, 1832.
19 p. CSmH; OUrC; PBa. 12115

The declaration of seventy-five
physicians of Boston. Albany,
Packard & Benthuysen, 1832. 1 l.

DNLM.   12116

---- [Boston] Ford & Damrell,
Temperance Press, Wilson's
lane [1832] broadside. MB;
MBAt; MH; OCHP.   12117

Defence of the convention of the
Protestant Episcopal Church, in
the state of Massachusetts against
certain editorial statements of the
paper called 'the Banner of the
Church' Boston, Stimpson & Clapp,
1832. 44 p. MWA.   12118

Delaware.
   Laws of the state of Delaware,
passed at a session of the General Assembly commenced and
held at Dover, on Tuesday the
third day of January, 1832...
George Town, James S. M'Calla,
1832. 85-199 p. DLC; In-Sc; Nj;
R; T.   12119

Delaware and Hudson Canal Company.
   Charter of the Delaware and
Hudson Canal Co. with the several acts supplementary to the
same published by order of the
board of managers. New York,
Pr. by Elliott & Palmer, 1832.
58 p. DLC; DBRE; IU; N. 12120

Delaware and Lackawanna Railroad. Report on the preliminary
survey... See under Hudson
and Delaware Railroad.

Delaware and Maryland almanac
for 1833. Wilmington, P. B.
Porter [1832] NHi.   12121

Democratic Party. Massachusetts. Convention, 1832.
   Proceedings... holden at Concord. Concord, Hill & Barton,
1832. 10 p. DLC; MWA.   12122

---- National Convention, Baltimore, 1832.
   Proceedings of a convention of

Republican delegates, from the
several states in the Union, for
the purpose of nominating a candidate for the office of vice-
president of the United States.
Baltimore, S. Harker, 1831
[1832] DLC; NbU; PPL; ViL.
                         12123

---- ---- Summary of the proceedings of a convention of Republican delegates... for... nominating
a candidate for... vice-president
of the United States; held at Baltimore...1832: with an address...
Albany, Pr. by Packard & Van
Benthuysen, 1832. 24 p. CSmH;
DLC; ICU; MiU; WHi.   12124

---- New Hampshire. Conven-
tion, 1832.
   Proceedings of the Democratic
Republican State Convention, hold-
en at Concord, June 20, 1832.
(Pub. by order of the Convention)
Concord, Hill & Barton, prs.,
1832. 10 p. NNC.   12125

---- New York (City).
   Democratic festival, to take
place Monday, four o'clock, November 26, at Tammany Hall...
New-York, November 19, 1832.
broadside. MH.   12126

---- New York (State) Convention.
1832.
   Address of the Republican
State Convention [assembled at
Herkimer]... For president, And-
rew Jackson. For vice-president,
Martin Van Buren. For governor,
William L. Marcy, For Lieut.
governor, John Tracy...[Albany,
Albany Argus, 1832] 24 p. CtY;
N; OClWHi; ViU.   12127

---- ---- Legislative Caucus.
   Resolutions and address of the
Republican members of the Legislature of the State of New-York.
1832. Albany, Pr. at the office
of the Albany Argus, 1832. 7 p.
MBC; NbU.   12128

---- ---- Tompkins County.
Proceedings of a General
Meeting of the Republican Me-
chanicks of the Town of Ithaca
[n.p. , 1832] 8 p. NbU.   12129

---- North Carolina. Jackson
central committee.
An address to the friends of
General Andrew Jackson, in
North-Carolina; and to the sup-
porters of his administration of
the affairs of the general government. Raleigh, Pr. at the office
of the Constitutionalist, 1832.
14 p. DLC; NcU.   12130

---- Pennsylvania. Convention,
1832.
Proceedings of the Democrat-
ic convention held at Harrisburg,
Pennsylvania. March 5, 1832...
Harrisburg, H. Welsh, 1832. 24 p.
DLC; ICU; NbU; P; PPT.   12131

---- ---- Lebanon County. Committee of Correspondence.
Beweise von der Mitwirkung
und den Handlungen des Joseph
Ritner bey der Einfuhrung des
"Innerlichen Verbesseruns-Sys-
tems" durch welches dieser Staat
in Schuldan perieth, und das Volk
num jetzigen Tax verpflichtet
warde. Auszuge von antlichen
Becorden. Auf Befehl der Demo-
cratischen correspondenz Committee von Libanon County be-
kannt gemacht. [Lebanon? 1832?]
24 p. MH.   12132

---- ---- Philadelphia. Committee of Correspondence.
The missionaries and the state
of Georgia. Address of the Democratic Committee of Correspondence for the City of Philadelphia.
[Philadelphia, 1832] 4 p. DLC;
PPL.   12133

---- Vermont.
An address to the freemen of
Vermont by their delegation to

the National Republican convention, holden at Baltimore, Maryland. In December, 1831. Middlebury, Vt. , Pr. by H. H.
Houghton, [1832?] 16 p. CSmH;
Vt; VtU.   12134

---- Virginia. Accomac Co.
... Address. [Snow-Hill, Md. ,
Pr. at the Messenger office,
1832] 10 p. Vi.   12135

Democratic Republicans. National Convention. See Democratic
Party.

Demosthenes.
The orations of Demosthenes
translated by Thomas Leland.
New York, J. & J. Harper, 1832.
2 vols. CtY; KyLoS; IaCrM; Nh;
PPA.   12136

---- ---- New York, W. Burgess, 1832. 199 p. CtHT; KyU;
NcAS; NjP; PPA; TBriK.   12137

Denison University, Granville, O.
Annual meeting of the trustees
of the Granville literary and theological institution, and of the
Ohio Baptist Education Society.
Cincinnati, Columbia, 1832-1837.
6 v. CSmH; Nh; OClWHi.   12138

[Denniston, Isaac, d. 1853]
The last will and testament of
Isaac Denniston of the City of Albany. Considering the uncertainty
of life...I do make and publish
this my last will and testament
...this twenty third day of August, one thousand eight hundred
and thirty two. Isaac Denniston.
[Albany, 1832] broadside. WHi.
                          12139
[Derenzy, Margaret Graves] d.
1829.
A whisper to a newly-married
pair from a widowed wife. Philadelphia, E. L. Carey, 1832.
103 p. MBC; NIC.   12140

Dermot McMurrough; or The Conquest of Ireland... See Adams, John Quincy, 1767-1848.

Description of Pitcairn's Island and its inhabitants... See Barrow, Sir John.

Desilver, Robert.
Der letzte Wille des am 26. December 1831 verstorbenen Herrn Stephan Girard, zufolge offentlicher Beglaubigung; nebst einer Kurzen Lebensbeschreibung. Nach Desilver's englischer Ausgabe. Philadelphia, 1832. 33 p. PHi.   12141

Desilver's United States Register and Almanac for 1833. Calculated by Seth Smith. Philadelphia, Pa., R. Desilver, T. Desilver & J. Grigg [1832] 56 p. CtY; DLC; MWA; PPiU; WHi.   12142

Detroit, Michigan.
Instructions by the Board of Health of the City of Detroit, for the prevention of the Asiatic cholera... Detroit, 1832. broadside. MiD-B.   12143

Detroit Association for the Suppression of Intemperance.
Second annual report of the Detroit Association for the Suppression of Intemperance, with an appendix, containing extracts from the fourth annual report of the American Temperance Society. Detroit, the Association, February, 1832. 24 p. MiD-B. 12144

Devises, bequests, and grants to the corporation. Philadelphia, 1832. MB.   12145

[Devonshire, Charles] 1783-1851.
The Tri dead, a tale; with other pieces in verse by a mechanic... Salem, Indiana, John Wilson, 1832. 31 p. CSmH; MH; MiU; NjP; RPB.   12146

Dew, Thomas Roderick, 1802-1846.
Review of the debate [on the abolition of slavery] in the Virginia legislature of 1831 and 1832. By Thomas R. Dew... Richmond, Pr. by T. W. White, 1832. 133 p. A-Ar; CtY; LU; ScCC; Vi.   12147

Dewees, William Potts, 1768-1841.
A compendious system of midwifery chiefly designed to facilitate the inquiries of those who may be pursuing this branch of study. Illustrated by occasional cases. With many engravings. 5th ed., with additions and improvements. By William P. Dewees. Philadelphia, Lea & Carey, 1832. CSt-L; NBMS; PPCP; TNV; ViU.   12148

---- A treatise on the physical and medical treatment of children. By William Potts Dewees... 4th ed., with cor. Philadelphia, Blanchard & Lea, 1832. CtY; ICJ; NcD; PU; TxU.   12149

Dewey, Chester, 1784-1867.
The acquisition of truth: a discourse delivered before the Young Men's Society in Pittsfield, Mass., on Sabbath evening, Aug. 26, 1832. New York, H. Mason, 1832. 34 p. MWiW; PPPrHi.
                                  12150

---- An appeal to the friends of temperance, delivered in Pittsfield, Mass., on Sabbath evening, October 7, 1832. By Rev. C. Dewey. Pittsfield, Pr. by P. Allen & son [1832] 24 p. CSmH; CtY; DLC; MH; PPPrHi. 12151

Dewey, Orville, 1794-1882.
On Tests of true religion. 2d ed. Boston, Gray & Bowen, 1832. 20 p. ICMe; MB-HP; MeB; MeBat; MMeT-Hi.   12152

---- The Pulpit, as a field of
exertion, talent and piety. A
sermon delivered... in Providence, by Orville Dewey. New-
Bedford, Pr. by Benjamin Lind-
sey, 1832. 36 p. CSmH; ICMe;
MH; NjP; RPB.   12153

---- A sermon on the Moral
Uses of the Pestilence... Delivered on Fast-Day, August 9,
1832. By Rev. Orville Dewey,
... in New-Bedford. Pub. by request of the Society. New-Bedford, Pr. by Benjamin T. Congdon, 1832. 20 p. CBPac; ICMe;
MB; MH; RPB.   12154

---- Working out our salvation
a practical work. Boston, 1832.
14 p. DLC; MH; MH-AH. 12155

DeWitt, John, 1789-1831.
    The Scripture doctrine of re-
generation defended: a sermon
by the Rev. John DeWitt, D.D.
... New York, n.p., 1832. 22 p.
ICN; MBC; NjPT; OO; PPPrHi.
                             12156
DeWitt, Susan (Linn), 1778-1824.
    The pleasures of religion; a
poem. New York, T. Harris,
1832. 72 p. IU; MH; NIC; RPB;
ViU.   12157

Dialogue between a Merchant and
a Planter. Part II. ... Columbia, States rights and free trade
association, 1832. 12 p. MBAt;
MHi; ViU.   12158

A dialogue of the gods. Being a
comparison between ancient mythology and modern theology. According to the best historical records. Dedicated to the freemen
of the United States... By a physician. Boston, Pub. at the office
of the Investigator, 1832. 12 p.
DLC.   12159

Dialogues and recitations in
prose and verse. Watertown,

N.Y., Knowlton & Rice, 1832.
MH; NjNbR.   12160

Dibdin, Charles, 1745-1814.
    The Quacker; a comic opera
in two parts. Philadelphia, 1832.
24 p. MB.   12161

Dibdin, Thomas, 1771-1841.
    The Two Gregories, or Luck
in a name; an operatic farce.
Philadelphia, Turner & son
[1832?] 22 p. HCL; MH.   12162

Dick, Thomas, 1774-1857.
    Celestial scenery; or the won-
der of planetary system displayed;
illustrating the perfection of Deity
and a plurality of words. By
Thomas Dick, LL.D. ... New
York, Harper & Bros., 1832.
422 p. LCPNA.   12163

---- The Philosophy of religion;
or An illustration of the moral
laws of the universe... New York,
King, 1832. 391 p. ICN; MiD;
NCH; ODaB; PPLT.   12164

Dickens, Charles, 1812-1870.
    The life and adventures of
Nicholas Nickleby by Charles
Dickens, (Boz.) author of "Pick-
wick Papers" etc., with numerous illustrations by Phiz. Philadelphia, 1832. 403 p.   12165

Dickerson, Mahlon, 1770-1853.
    Observations of Mr. Dickerson,
of New Jersey, on The Bill for
the Apportionment of the Representation in Congress. Made in
the Senate of the United States,
March 12, 1832. Washington, Pr.
at the Office of Jonathan Elliot,
1832. 12 p. DLC; MB; MH; WHi.
                             12166
---- Speech on the reduction of
the tariff delivered Jan. 23, 1832,
in the Senate of the United States,
on a motion to amend Mr. Clay's
resolution. Washington, J. Elliott
[1832?] 31 p. MBAt; NbU;

OClWHi; ScC; ScCC.   12167

Dickinson College, Carlisle, Pa.
Union Philosophical Society.
   Catalogue of the members of
the Union Philosophical Society
of Dickinson College from...
1788, to...1836. Carlisle,
Philips, 1832. PCarlD; PPPrHi.
                             12168
Dickson, John, 1783-1852.
   Speech of Mr. Dickson, of
New-York in the case of Samuel
Houston, tried for a breach of the
privileges of the House of Repre-
sentatives of the United States.
Delivered, May 11th, 1832.
Washington, J. Elliot, 1832. 16 p.
CSmH; Ct; MWA; WHi.   12169

Dickson, Samuel Henry.
   An address delivered before
the Horiticultural Society of
Charleston, at the anniversary
meeting, July 11th, 1832.
Charleston, Pr. by A. E. Miller,
1832. 18 p. MHi; MiD-B; NN;
ScCC; ScHi.   12170

Dilworth, Thomas, d. 1780.
   The Federal calculator; or,
American schoolmaster's assistant and young man's companion.
Being a compendium of federal
arithmetic, both practical and
theoretical. In five parts. Altered from Dilworth's Arithmetic, and adapted to the currency
of the United States, by Daniel
Hawley. Rev., cor. and greatly
improved. By William Stoddard,
teacher of the Troy Grammar
School. New York, Collins &
Hannay, 1832. 223 p. DAU.
                             12171
Dimmick, Luther Fraseur, 1790-
1860.
   A call to seek first the kingdom of God: a sermon, occasioned by the death of Mr. Amos
Pettingell, who departed this life
at New Haven, Con. Nov. 30,
1831, aged twenty seven years.

Delivered in the Brick church,
Newburyport. Also, in the First
church in Newbury... By L. F.
Dimmick. Newburyport, C.
Whipple, 1832. 16 p. CtY; ICN;
MBC; RPB; Vt; WHi.   12172

---- A memorial of the year
eighteen hundred thirty-one. A
sermon, delivered in Newburyport, Dec. 31, 1831, on occasion
of a public thanksgiving of several of the churches, for the spiritual mercies of the past year. By
L. F. Dimmick. Newburyport,
Ephraim W. Allen & Co. [1832?]
20 p. Ct; CtY; MB; MNe; RPB.
                             12173
Diocesan Sunday-School Society
of Pennsylvania. Auxiliary to the
General Protestant Episcopal
Sunday School Union.
   Constitution, July 9, 1832.
Philadelphia, 1832. 8 p. PHi.
                             12174
Directions to persons just commencing a religious life. With a
momento of affection from Christian pastors... Boston, Benjamin
H. Greene, 1832. 16 p. MWA.
                             12175
A directory for the city of Buffalo; containing the names and
residence of the heads of families and householders, in said
city, on the first of July, 1832.
To which is added a sketch of
the history of the village, from
1801 to 1832. Buffalo, L. P.
Crary, 1832. 122 p.   12176

Disbrow, Levi.
   Advertisement of a proposition for ward companies to supply New York with rock water.
New York, Clayton & Van Norden,
1832. 23 p. DSG; MBAt; MH; NN;
WHi.   12177

Discussion of the scripture doctrine of regeneration. Dover
[N. H.] IaHi; MH; Nh; Nh-Hi.
                             12178

A dissertation of employing emulation to encourage literary excellence. Cambridge, Brown, Shattuck and Co., 1832. 41 p. MWA.   12179

The dissolution of the Union. Serious reflections for the citizens of South Carolina. Charleston, S.C., William Estill, 1832. 24 p. MWA.   12180

Dix, Dorothea Lynde, 1802-1887.
American moral tales, for young persons. By the author of 'Evening hours,' 'Conversations on common things,' &c. With ten engravings. Boston, Leonard C. Bowles, and B. H. Greene, 1832. 281 p. CSmH; MBAt; MH; NNC.
                    12181
---- Conversations on common things, or Guide to knowledge, with questions. By a teacher. 4th ed., rev., cor. and stereotyped. Boston, Munroe & Francis, 1832. CtY; MH.   12182

Doane, George Washington, 1799-1859.
Episcopal charges or the churchman. Boston, Stimpson & Clapp, 1832. OMC.   12183

---- The Gospel in the church: A sermon, delivered, by appointment, at the opening of the annual convention in the Commonwealth of Massachusetts, at Christ Church, Boston, Wednesday, June 20, 1832, by George Washington Doane, Rector of Trinity Church, Boston. Pr. by request. Boston, Stimpson and Clapp, 1832. 40 p. InID; MHi; NjR; PHi; RPB.   12184

A doctrinal guide for the convert and the anxious inquirer by a clergyman... New York, Jonathan Leavitt; Boston, Crocker and Brewster, 1832. 294 p. CtY; DLC; GDecCT; MiU; PPPrHi.
                    12185

Documents in proof of the climate and soil of Florida, particularly the southern section (containing a "Brief account, &c of R. S. Hackley's lands.") New York, Peter Van Pelt, 1832. 28 p. CtY; MWA; MiU-C; NN.   12186

Doddridge, Philip, 1702-1751.
The life of the honorable Col. James Gardiner, who was slain at the Battle of Prestonpans, 21st September, 1745... Baltimore, J. J. Harrod, 1832. 173 p. IU; MdHi; NPalK.   12187

---- The Rise and Progress of Religion in the Soul. Illustrated in a course of serious and practical addresses, suited to persons of every character and circumstance. With a devout meditation or prayer subjoined to each chapter. By Philip Doddridge, D.D. Baltimore, Joseph Lewis, 1832. 304 p. PPPrHi; ViU.   12188

---- ---- New York, J. H. Turney, 1832. 252 p. NcGv.   12189

---- ---- Philadelphia, Key, Mielke & Biddle, 1832. 326 p. MH; OOxM; ViU.   12190

---- Sermons to young persons. By Philip Doddridge, D.D. to which are added the Balm of Gilead with several other sermons selected from the writings of eminent Divines. Also the Crook in the Lot. Revised and cor. with biographical sketches of the authors, 1st Amer. ed. Charlottesville, Joseph Martin, 1832. 336 p. ILM; MsJS; OHi-C; ScCliTO; ViU.
                    12191
Doddridge, Philip, 1772-1832.
Speech of Mr. Doddridge, in the case of Samuel Houston, charged with a contempt and breach of the privileges of the House, by assaulting the Hon. William Stanberry, a member

Dods 107

from the state of Ohio, for
words used in debate. Delivered
in the House of Representatives,
May 9, 1832. Washington, Pr. by
Gales & Seaton, 1832. 32 p. A-
Ar; DLC; NNNG; PU; Tx; WHi.
                              12192
Dods, John Bovee, 1795-1872.
    The second death illustrated.
A sermon delivered... in Taunton,
Mass. ...Feb. 12, 1832. By
John B. Dods, pastor... Taunton,
Pr. by Edmund Anthony, 1832.
24 p. MBUPH; MMeT-Hi; MTaHi;
PPL; RPB.   12193

---- Twenty-four short sermons,
on the doctrine of universal salvation. Boston, Pr. by G. W.
Bazin, 1832. 214 p. MHi;
MMeT-Hi; NCaS.   12194

Dodsley, Robert, 1703-1764. The
chronicles... See Nathan ben-Saddi.

---- The economy of Human life.
Translated from an Indian manu-
script. To which is prefixed an
account... Lewistown, Pa.,
Charles Bell & sons, 1832. 248 p.
NN; OClWHi; PHi.   12195

Does baptism mean immersion?
No. 2, or, The scripture use of
baptizo, sustained by classic authors; with some remarks in reply
to the "review" of the "key" to the
New Testament meaning of baptism. Newbern, Watson, 1832.
18 p. CtY; NcU.   12196

Doggert, Henry.
    Life and campaigns of Napoleon
Buonaparte (sic) Emperor of
France. &c. By Henry Doggert.
Baltimore, John G. Hanzsche,
1832. 286 p. DLC; MdBP; NjR;
NNC; WMDSC.   12197

Donnegan, James, fl. 1841.
    A new Greek and English lexi-
con; principally on the plan of the
Greek and German lexicon of

Schneider... by James Donnegan
...1st Amer. from 2d London ed.
rev. and enl., by R. B. Patton.
Boston, Hilliard, Gray & co.;
New York, G. & C. & H. Carvill,
1832. 1413 p. CLSU; DLC; MH;
NjP; PPAN.   12198

---- ---- Philadelphia, Carey &
Lea, 1832. 838 p. C-S; LNH;
MiD; PWbo; TxU-T.   12199

Dorchester [Mass.] Academy.
    Catalogue of the trustees,
teachers, and pupils of Dorchester
Academy, for the quarter ending
Sept. 25, 1832. Boston, Pr. by J.
Ford, 1832. 10 p. MBAt; MH;
MiD-B.   12200

Dorchester and its environs, during the British, Roman, Saxon,
and Norman periods. Dorchester,
1832. CaBVaU; MBC.   12201

Dorr, Benjamin, 1796-1869.
    The Church and Her Holy Sea-
sons Vindicated. A sermon,
preached in Trinity Church, Utica,
on the Sunday after Christmas Day,
January 1st, 1832. By Benjamin
Dorr... Utica, Pr. by E. A. Maynard, 1832. 32 p. CU; MBAt;
MdBD; NUt; NjR.   12202

---- On knowing each other in the
world of spirits; a sermon
preached in Trinity Church, Utica,
New York. New York, Van Norden, 1832. 12 p. CtHT; NGH;
NUt.   12203

Dorset, Catharine Ann, 1750?-
1817?
    Think before you speak; or,
The Three Wishes; a poetic tale.
1st Amer. from 2d London ed.
Philadelphia, Wm. W. Weeks for
Morgan & Sons, 1832. 16 l. NN;
PP; RPR.   12204

Dorsey, John L.
    A treatise on the American law

of insolvency; containing a compilation of the insolvent laws of Maryland, and the laws in relation to insolvent debtors, of the United States, by John L. Dorsey ... Baltimore, E. J. Coale & J. S. Littell, 1832. 243,177 p. DLC; MdBP; PU-L.   12205

Dover, George James Welbore Agar-Ellis, 1st baron, 1797-1833.
The life of Frederic the Second, King of Prussia. By Lord Dover... New York, J. & J. Harper, 1832. 2 vols. CtMW; LNH; NjP; PPA; TU; ViU. 12206

Dow, Lorenzo, 1777-1834.
A cry from the wilderness, a voice from the East, a reply from the West, trouble in the North, exemplifyed in the South; intended as a timely and solemn warning to the people of the United States. By Lorenzo Dow. New York, United States, n. pub. 1832. 167 p. CU; ICN; IU; NjMD; OU.   12207

Drake, Daniel, 1785-1852.
An account of the epidemic of cholera, as it appeared in Cincinnati. By D. Drake. Cincinnati, Ohio, Pr. at the Chronicle office, E. Deming, 1832. 46 p. CSt-L; ICJ; MH; NNNAM; ScU.   12208

---- Practical essays on medical education, and the medical profession in the United States. By Daniel Drake... Cincinnati, O., Roff & Young, 1832. 104 p. KyLo; OClWHi; PPL; ScU; TNV.
12209

---- A practical treatise on the history, prevention, and treatment of epidemic cholera, designed both for the profession and the people. By Daniel Drake, M.D. Cincinnati, Corey & Fairbank, 1832. 180 p. DLC; MH; OCHP; TNV; ViRA.   12210

Drake, Samuel Gardner, 1798-1875.
Indian biography, containing the lives of more than two hundred Indian chiefs; and a history of their wars... By Samuel Gardner Drake. Boston, Josiah Drake, 1832. 348 p. DLC; MNF; RPB; ScC; WHi.   12211

Draper, Bourne Hall.
Bible illustrations; or A description of manners and customs peculiar to the East, especially of the Holy Scriptures. Amer. ed. Baltimore, 1832. 215 p. MB; MNan; MWA.   12212

---- ---- Boston, Carter, Hendee & co., 1832. 215 p. CBPac; MeSaco.   12213

---- ---- Philadelphia, French, 1832. 215 p. KyMay; MShi; PU.
12214

---- Bible stories; or, A description of manners and customs peculiar to the East, especially explanatory of the Holy Scriptures. Philadelphia, Thomas, Cowperthwait & Co. [1832] 215 p. DLC; GDecCT; MBC; MNan; ViU.
12215

---- The Sunday School Story-Book. Philadelphia, 1832. BrMus.
12216

Drayton, William, 1776-1848.
Address to the people of the congressional district of Charleston. By the Hon. William Drayton. Charleston, Pr. at the Charleston press by W. Estill, 1832. 17 p. DLC; InHi; MBAt; NN; PHi.   12217

A dream of the nineteenth century. Taunton, Anthony, 1832. CSmH.   12218

[Dresser, Horace] 1803-1877.
Constable's Guide; being a concise treatise on the powers and duties of a constable and collector

in the state of New York... By a member of the Bar. Binghampton, 1832. 236 p. M; MH-L; N; NN; WU-L.   12219

Dreyer, J. H.
Biblische erzahlungen urbersetzt. Philadelphia, 1832. PPL-R.   12220

Droz, Joseph, 1773-1850.
The art of being happy: from the French of Droz, 'Sur l'art d'être heureuse'; in a series of letters from a father to his children; with observations and comments. By Timothy Flint... Boston, Carter & Hendee, 1832. 313 p. CtY; MoU; NhD; PPA; RPB; ScC.   12221

Drury, Luke, d. 1845.
An address delivered before the Bristol association for the promotion of temperance, March 23, 1832. By Luke Drury. Providence, Pr. by Weedon & Knowles, 1832. 28 p. DLC; MB; NNUT.
                                 12222
Dryden, John, 1631-1700.
All for Love, or The World well lost.... Philadelphia, J. J. Woodward, 1832. IaGG.   12223

Drysdale, Isabel.
Evening Recreations: a series of dialogues on the history and geography of the Bible. 4 pt. Philadelphia, 1832. BrMus.
                                 12224
The Dublin penny journal. v. 1-4; June 30, 1832-June 25, 1836. Dublin, John S. Folds; New York, Wardle & Dobson, Philadelphia; Gray & Bowen, Boston (etc.) 1832-36. OKHi.   12225

Duffield, George, 1794-1868.
An address delivered in the Presbyterian Church, before the Young men's temperance society of Carlisle... Carlisle [Pa.] Fleming, 1832. 12 p. MH-AH;

MiU.   12226

---- The divine power exerted in a sinner's regeneration; two discourses. By George Duffield... Carlisle [Pa.] Pr. by G. Fleming, 1832. 26 p. DLC; IU; MiU; OClWHi.   12227

---- Remarks upon the Carlisle Presbytery's Report on Duffield on Regeneration; with additional extracts from the minutes. Philadelphia, 1832. 40 p. MBC; NCH; NNG; PHi.   12228

---- Spiritual life; or, Regeneration, illustrated in a series of disquisitions relative to is author, subject, nature, means, etc. By George Duffield... Carlisle [Pa.] Fleming, 1832. 613 p. CtY; ICP; MiD-B; NNUT; PHi; OkU. 12229

[Duignan, James A.]
Reflections on the relics of ancient beauty, and the pleasing retirements in the South of France. To which is added a lecture upon natural philosophy in letters addressed to a friend in New York. By J. A. D. New York, W. Applegate, 1832. DLC; LNH; NNU-W.   12230

Duncan, John Mason, 1790-1851.
Lectures on the general principles of moral government as they are exhibited in the first three chapters of Genesis... Baltimore, Cushing & Sons, 1832. 376 p. CtY; ICP; MdHi; NbOP; ViRu.   12231

Dunglison, Robley, 1798-1869.
Elements of hygiene. Philadelphia, 1832. PGenlHos.   12232

---- Human physiology... By Robley Dunglison... Philadelphia, Carey & Lea, 1832. 2 v. CtY; GEU-M; MeB; NNN; PPA; TxU-M.   12233

[Dunham, Samuel Astley] d. 1858.
... History of Spain and Portugal... Philadelphia, Carey & Lea, 1832-33. 5 v. CtMW; ICU; MB; PPA; ViU; WvW.   12234

Dunlap, Andrew, 1794-1835.
An oration delivered at the request of the Washington Society at the city of Boston, July 4, 1832. By Andrew Dunlap. Boston, True & Greene, prs., 1832. 21 p. CSmH; CtSoP; MDeeP; MeB; NNC.   12235

Dunlap, William, 1766-1839.
A history of the American theatre. By William Dunlap... New York, J. & J. Harper, 1832. 420 p. CtY; MH; PHi; PPA. ScU; WaS.   12236

Dunn, William.
The morning of life, or history of a young man who left the home of his childhood. A narrative of facts. Revised American ed. Boston, James Loring, 1832. 108 p. ICBB.   12237

Duponceau, Peter Stephen, 1760-1844.
An historical discourse delivered before the Society for the commemoration of the landing of William Penn, 24 Oct. 1832; being the one hundred and fiftieth anniversary of that event. By Peter S. Duponceau... Philadelphia, James Kay, Jun. & Co., 1832. 32 p. ICN; LNH; MdHi; OCHP; WHi.   12238

Durfee, Job, 1790-1847.
Whatcheer; or, Roger Williams in banishment: a poem.... Providence, R.I., Cranston and Hammond, 1832. 200 p. CtY; ICT; MH; RWe; WHi.   12239

Duties of children. Wendel, J. Metcalf, 1832. 18 p. ICU; MA.   12240
The duty of prayer. Addressed by the Middlesex North Association of Ministers, to the congregations under their pastoral care. Lowell, R. Meacham, 1832. 12 p. MWA.   12241

The duty of the church in relation to Sunday schools... Philadelphia, Pr. by Martien and Russell, 19 p. NjR; PPL.   12242

Dwight, Edwin Welles, 1789-1811.
Memoir of Henry Obookiah, a native of the Sandwich Islands... New York, Pr. by D. Fanshaw, for the American Tract Society, 1832. 124 p. IEG; MnM.   12243

Dwight, Harrison Gray Otis, 1803-1862.
A dictionary of the New Testament, and vocabulary of proper names for Sabbath School teachers and scholars. Rev. and enl. by J. P. Cowles. Stereotyped. New York, also Boston, 1832. 2 maps. CtY; ICBB; MB; MH-AH; Mhotn.   12244

Dymond, Jonathan, 1796-1828.
On the applicability of the pacific principles of the New Testament to the conduct of states, and on the limitations which those principles impose on the rights of self-defence... 1st Amer. ed. from the 2d London ed. Brooklyn, Pr. by A. F. Lee, People's press, 1832. 19, 4 p. CtY; DLC; IU; MWA; PPPrHi.   12245

E

Early, Jacob M.
To the public. In Mr. Stuart's speech of Satuday last, at Mr. Hill's mill on Sugar Creek, he gave the lie to a certificate of mine, published in the circular of Mr. Calhoun... [Signed] J. M. Early, Springfield, August 9th, 1832. [Springfield, 1832] Broadside. IHi.   12246

East, Timothy.
The Evangelical Rambler. A series of tracts published in London. Revised by the Rev. G. T. Bedell--in four volumes. 3d Amer. ed. Philadelphia, George Latimer & Co., 1832. 4 vols. InU; MWA; NcD; PHi; TNJ-R.
12247

Eastman, Francis Smith, 1803-1846 or 7.
A history of the state of New York, from the first discovery of the country to the present time: with a geographical account of the country, and a view of its original inhabitants. ...A new ed. New York, Augustus K. White, 1832. 455 p. CSmH; MiU; MnHi; NUt; OHi.
12248

Eaton, Amos, 1776-1842.
Geological text-book, for aiding the study of North American geology...2d ed...Albany, Websters & Skinners; New York, G. and C. and H. Carvill, [etc., etc.] 1832. 134 p. CSt; ICU; MnU; OO; PU; VtMidbC.
12249

---- Manual of botany for North America: containing generic and specific descriptions of the indigenous plants and common cultivated exotics, growing north of the Gulf of Mexico. By Prof. Amos Eaton...With the addition of the most approved natural arrangement of genera: also their etymologies and accentuation. 6th ed. Albany, Steele, 1832. 401 p. NBronC; NYBT.
12250

Eaton, John Henry, 1790-1856.
Memoirs of Andrew Jackson. Late major general and commander in chief of the Southern division of the army of the United States. Compiled by a citizen of Massachusetts. Philadelphia, n.p., 1832. 334 p. OC.
12251

Eaton's anti-masonic almanack

for the year of the Christian era, 1833. By Edward Giddins. Danville, E. Eaton & Captain Ira White [1832] 36 p. CtY; IaCrM; MWA; PPFM.
12252

Eberle, John.
Annual announcement of lectures, &c. By the trustees and professors of Jefferson Medical College, Philadelphia, for the year 1832. Philadelphia, Pr. by Clark & Raser, for the medical faculty, 1832. 16 p. GU-M.
12253

Eddy, William.
The result of an Ex-Parte Council, convened in Providence June 19, 1832, by letters missive from aggrieved members of the Richmond Street Church; with a brief history of the origin and progress of the difficulties which led to the convocation of said Council. Providence, H. H. Brown, 1832. 24 p. DLCL LNB; MH; PPL; RHi.
12254

Edgeworth, Maria, 1767-1849.
The knapsack; a tale... Boston, 1832. ICN.
12255

---- The little merchants. A story for children. By Maria Edgeworth. With colored engravings. Franklin press ed. 2d ed. New York, R. Schoyer, 1832. 78 p. MPiB.
12256

---- Moral tales for young people. By M. Edgeworth. New York, Pendleton & Hill, 1832. NPV.
12257

---- Tales and novels by Maria Edgeworth. Eighteen volumes bound in nine. New-York, J. & J. Harper, sold by the principal booksellers throughout the United States. 1832-33. CtY; MH; NCH; PPA; ViU.
12258

Edinburgh Encyclopedia.
The Edinburgh Encyclopaedia, conducted by David Brewster,

with the assistance of Gentlemen eminent in science and literature. The 1st Amer. ed...cor. & impr. by the addition of numerous articles relative to the institutions of the American continent... Philadelphia, Joseph & Edward Parker, 1832. 18 v. in 36.   CU; IU; MeB; PPA; PU; WaPS.   12259

Edmands, Benjamin Franklin.
   Boston school atlas. 5th ed. Boston, Lincoln & Edmands, [1832] CtY; DLC; MB; MH; NNU-W.   12260

Edwards, Bela Bates, 1802-1852.
   Biography of self-taught men; with an introductory essay. By B. B. Edwards. Boston, Perkins & Marvin, 1832. 312 p. DeWi; GDC; MBAt; NhD; PHi; ViAl.
                                          12261
---- The Eclectic Reader, designed for Schools and Academies. Boston, Perkins & Marvin, 1832. 324 p. CtHWatk; MB; MeB; Nh; OMC.   12262

---- The missionary gazetteer; comprising a geographical and statistical account of the various stations of the American and foreign Protestant missionary societies of all denominations... Boston, W. Hyde & Co., 1832. 431 p. CSmH; ICP; MnU; NjP; TxH; ViRut.   12263

---- Sketch of the life and character of the Rev. E. Cornelius. Boston, 1832. 26 p. MH-AH; MHi; MiD-B; MWA.   12264

Edwards, Charles, 1797-1868.
   Feathers from my own wings. [Including Tecumseh, a poem, with historical notes; The Indians, etc.] New York, William, Stodart, 1832. 200 p. CtY; ICU; MeB; RPB; TxU; WHi.   12265

---- A practical treatise on parties to bills and other pleadings in chancery; with precedents. By Charles Edwards... New York, Gould, Banks & co., Albany, W. & A. Gould & Co., 1832. 360 p. CU; MH-L; Nj; RPL; WaU.
                                          12266
Edwards, Jonathan, 1703-1758.
   Edwards on revivals: containing a faithful narrative of the surprising work of God in the conversion of many hundred souls in Northampton, Massachusetts, A.D. 1735. Also, Thoughts on the revival of religion in New England, 1742.... with introductory remarks, and a full general index, prepared by the present editor. New York, Dunning & Spalding, 1832. 424 p. CtY; LNB; MHi; NcD; TxH.   12267

---- A narrative of many surprising conversions in Northampton and vicinity. Written in 1736. Together with some thoughts on the revival in New England, written in 1740. To which is added an account of the conversion of the author. By Jonathan Edwards.... Worcester, Moses W. Grout, 1832. 382 p. CtSoP; ICNBT; MNe; PHi; RBr.   12268

Edwards, Jonathan, 1745-1801.
   The injustice and impolicy of the slave trade and of the slavery of Africans; illustrated in a sermon preached in New Haven, September 15, 1791...3d ed. New Haven, Anti-Slavery Society, 1832. 40 p. MH.   12269

The Efficacy of Prayer. First pub. in the Unitarian Advocate. Boston, Christian Register Office, 1832. 31 p. MA.   12270

Eight stories for Isabel. Concord, J. W. Moore & Co., 1832. 3-14 p. DLC.   12271

Eliot, William Harvard, 1796-1831.

Catalogue of the library of the late William H. Eliot, Esq., which will be sold by public auction at the office of J. L. Cunningham. Boston, Pr. by J. H. Eastburn, 1832. 42 p. CtY; MHi; NIC.   12272

Elizabeth Bennet; or, Pride and Prejudice: A Novel. In two volumes. By the author of "Sense and Sensibility," &c. 1st Amer. from 3d London ed. Philadelphia, Carey & Lea, 1832. 2 vols. ICMcHi; RJa.   12273

Elkinton, John A.

Notes on the practice pursued with cholera patients at the hospitals in New York; Facts and observations of a practical nature. By John A. Elkinton, M. D. Read before the Sanitary Committee of the Northern Liberties, August 2nd, 1832, by John A. Elkinton, M. D., who visited New York, during the prevalence of epidemic cholera, and spent one week among the hospitals while the disease was at its height. [Philadelphia, 1832] 12 p. DLC; DNLM; NNNAM; PHC.
                                 12274

Ellenwood, Henry S.

A lecture on elocution, particularly with reference to the art of reading; delivered, agreeably to appointment, before the North Carolina Institute of Education, at their annual meeting, June 20th, 1832. By Henry S. Ellenwood... Newbern, Pr. by John I. Pasteur, 1832. 16 p. NN; NcU; PHi.
                                 12275

Elliot, Jonathan, 1784-1846.

The Virginia & Kentucky resolutions of 1798-99... See under title.

Elliot's pocket almanac and annual register of the federal and state governments for 1832...

Washington, Pr. by J. Elliot, jr. [1832] NCH.   12276

Elliott, William.

Address to the people of St. Helena parish... Charleston, S. C., Pr. by W. Estill at the Charleston press, 1832. 15 p. ICU; MB; NcD; PU; TxU. 12277

Ellis, William R.

Brief narrative of his religious experience, with poems. Utica, 1832. N.   12278

Ellison, William.

Address delivered on the 11th November, 1831, at Chester Court-House, before the Citizens of Chester District. By William Ellison. Pub. by request of the Committee of Arrangements. Charleston, Pr. by James S. Burges, 1832. 20 p. MWA.
                                 12279

Ellsworth, William W., 1791-1868.

Speech in the case of Samuel Houston, charged with a contempt and breach of privileges of the house, by assaulting the Hon. William Stanbery, a member from the state of Ohio, for words used in debate, delivered in the House of Representatives, May 9, 1832. Washington, 1832. 32 p. CtY; NjR; OCIWHi; TxU; WHi.   12280

Emerson, Benjamin Dudley, 1781-1872.

Introduction to the national spelling book with easy and progressive reading lessons; designed for the use of primary schools by B. D. Emerson author of the national spelling book. Boston, Carter & Hendee & Co., 1832. MH.
                                 12281

---- The National spelling-book, and pronouncing tutor; containing rudiments of orthography and pronunciation on an improved plan... Designed for the use of schools in the United States... Boston, Carter, Hendee & Co., 1832. MH; Nh.   12282

Emerson, Frederick, 1788-1857.
... The North American arithmetic. Part second, uniting oral and written exercises, in corresponding chapters... Boston, Lincoln & Edmands; New York, Collins & Hannay [etc., etc.] 1832. 190 p. includes A Key... Boston, Lincoln & Edmands; New York, Collins & Hannay, etc., etc. 1832. 54 p. DLC; ICU; NNC; OClWHi; PPA; TxU-T.   12283

---- ---- Cincinnati, Hubbard & Edmands, 1832. 190 p. MoU.
                                 12284
---- ---- Windsor, N.C., Nathan C. Goddard, 1832. 216 p. MB; NNC; RPB.   12284a

Emerson, Joseph, 1777-1833.
The poetic reader, containing selections from the most approved authors... By Joseph Emerson... Wethersfield (Conn.), 1832. 95 p. CSt; ICU; MH; NNC; OO.   12285

---- Questions adapted to Whelpley's Compend of history. 10th ed. Boston, Richardson, Lord & Holbrook, 1832. MB; MH.   12286

---- Questions and supplement to Goodrich's History of United States. By Joseph Emerson... 3d ed. typed. Boston, Carter, Hendee & Co., 1832. 204 p. DLC; IaDmD; MNBedf; OO.   12287

Emerson, Ralph Waldo, 1803-1882.
Letter from the Rev. R. W. Emerson, to the second church and society. 1st ed. Boston, by I. R. Butts [1832] 8 p. CSmH; MBAt.
                                 12288
Emery, Stephen.
Report delivered before Oxford County Lyceum. By Stephen Emery. Paris, Maine, Horatio King, 1832. 7 p. MeHi.   12289

The emigrants travel guide to the west. See Baird, Robert, 1798-1863. View of the valley of....

Emmet, Robert, 1778-1803.
The speeches of celebrated Irish orators. By Robert Emmet. Philadelphia, Key, Mielke & Biddle. 1832. 370 p. MBrigStJ.   12290

Emmons, Ebenezer, 1799-1863.
Manual of mineralogy and geology. By Ebenezer Emmons, M.D... 2d ed. Albany, Webster and Skinners, 1832. 299 p. CU; DLC; MH; NNC; TNV.   12291

Emmons, Richard, b. 1788.
The Fredoniad; or, Independence preserved. An epic poem on the late war of 1812. By Richard Emmons, M.D. ... 3d ed. Philadelphia, W. Emmons, 1832. 4 v. CoD; KyDC; MoSHi; NBu; OClWHi.
                                 12292
Emmons, Samuel Bulfinch.
The grammatical instructor, containing an exposition of all the essential rules of English grammar, with their variations carefully arranged under their respective parts of speech. The whole interspersed with a variety of familiar and entertaining illustrations, well adapted to impart a thorough and critical knowledge of the science. By Samuel B. Emmons... Boston, Waitt & Dow, 1832. 160 p. DLC; CtHWatk; NNC.   12293

Emmons, [William].
Authentic biography of Richard W. Johnson, of Kentucky. Boston, Proprietor, 1832. 92 p. DLC.
                                 12294
Encyclopaedia americana, a popular dictionary. Philadelphia, Carey & Lea, 1832. KyLx; OM. 12295

Enfield, William, 1741-1797.
Institutes of natural philosophy theoretical and practical...
With some corrections and
change in the order of branches.
5th Amer. ed., with imp. Boston, Hilliard, Gray, Little & Wilkins, 1832. 216 p. CU; IaGG; MH;
TU; WHi.   12296

England, John, 1786-1842.
A Discourse delivered before
the Anti-duelling Society of
Charleston, S. C. in the Cathedral Church of St. Finbar, 1828.
Charleston, William S. Blain,
1832. 32 p. NN.   12297

---- Oration delivered on the an-
niversary of the Literary and
Philosophical Society of South
Carolina, on Wed. the 9th of
May, 1832, in the Cathedral
Church of St. Finbar, in the city
of Charleston... Baltimore, J.
Myres, 1832. 48 p. InNd; LNH;
MBAt; MdW; ViU.   12298

---- ---- Charleston, Pr. by
William S. Blain, 1832. 44 p.
CtY; MiD-B; NNC; PPL; ScU.
                           12299
---- The substance of a dis-
course... in the City of Washing-
ton... By Rt. Rev. John England,
D.D.; 2d ed. Charleston, Wm. S.
Blain, 1832. 50 p. NjR.   12300

Entick, John, 1703?-1773?
Entick's English-Latin dictionary, containing all the words and
phrases proper for reading the
classics in both languages, accurately collected from the most
approved Latin authors. To which
is prefixed, a Latin-English dictionary, carefully compiled from
the most celebrated English writers. To this edition has been annexed an etymological paradigm.
For the use of grammar schools
and private education... vol. 2.
[Baltimore, n.p., 1832] CtY.
                           12301

---- Tyronis Thesaurus. Baltimore, 1832. MB.   12302

The Eolian songster, a choice
collection of the most popular
sentimental, patriotic, naval, and
comic songs. With music. Cincinnati, U. P. James [1832] 252 p.
OC; OMC.   12303

Episcopalian.
An examination of Mr. Howell's review, and A postscript
to the "Second Letter." A second letter to Mr. Howell. See
under title.

Erasmus, Desiderius.
The complaint of peace, etc.,
Tr. from the Latin American
reprint. Boston, 1832. RP.
                           12304

Erie almanac for 1833. Erie,
O. Spofford [1832] MWA; NHi.
                           12305

Erie Public Library and Erie
Public Museum.
Annual Report. Erie, Pa.,
1832. PHi.   12306

Errors in fact, advanced by
Senator Hayne, in his Anti-tariff speech; and the evil results
his policy must produce, exposed, for the good of the people. Philadelphia, Henry Young,
1832. 8 p. MWA.   12307

Erskine, Thomas.
Remarks on the internal evi-
dence of the truth of revealed
religion by Thomas Erskine...
Philadelphia, 1832. 171 p. ViW.
                           12308
No entry.   12309

Essays on the philosophy of instruction, or the nurture of young
minds. Greenfield, Mass., A.
Phelps, 1832. 41 p. MWA.
                           12310

Essex Agricultural Society.
Essay on the cultivation of the
mulberry trees and the culture
of silk; (by the committee on
that subject.) Salem, Press of
Foote & Brown, 1832. 106 p.
MB; MBAt; MWA; NNC.   12311

---- Transactions of the Essex
Agricultural Society for 1831. Salem, Press of Foote & Brown,
1832. 120 p. MAm.   12312

Estill's Almanac, calculated for
the Carolinas and Georgia, for
the year 1833, being the first after bissextile or leap year. Containing all the useful astronomical calculations, and local information. Charleston, S.C., Wm.
Estill [1832] 36 p. ScHi.   12313

Estradas de Mina, Caroline Al-
malic, 1809-1832.
The life and confessions of
Caroline Estradas de Mina, executed at Doylestown, June 21,
1832 for poisoning with arsenic
William Chapman. Translated
from the original in Spanish, by C.
G. Philadelphia, Robert Desilver,
1832. 50 p. MH; MoU; NIC; PHi;
PPL-R.   12314

Evangelical Association.
Doctrine & discipline together
with the design of their union, tr.
from the German. New-Berlin,
Pa., Evangelical Assoc., 1832.
147 p. PReaAr; PU.   12315

Evangelical Lutheran Church.
General Synod.
Hymns, selected and original
for public and private worship.
Published by the General Synod of
the Evangelical Lutheran Church.
3d ed. Baltimore, James Lucas,
and E. K. Deaver, 1832. 535 p.
IEG; PPLT.   12316

Evangelical Lutheran Ministerium
of Pennsylvania and Adjacent States.

Erbauliche Lieder-Sammlung
zum gottesdienst-lichen Gebrauch
in den Vereinigten evangelisch-
lutherischen Gemeinen in Pennsylvanien und den benachbarten
Staaten. Gesammelt, eingerichtet
und zum Druck befordert durch
das hiesige Deutsche evangelisch-
lutherische Ministerium.
Philadelphia, W. G. Mentz [1832]
512 p. CSt; MH.   12317

---- Minutes of the German Evangelical Lutheran Synod of Pennsylvania; convened in Wommelsdorf, Berks County, in Trinity
Week, 1832. Philadelphia, Conrad
Zentler, 1832. 20 p.   12318

Evanglical Lutheran Synod of
Pennsylvania.
Verhandlungen der deutchen
evangelisch lutherischen Synede
van Pennsylvanien, gehalten in
Wommelsdorf, Berks County, in
der Trinitatisweche, 1832. Philadelphia, Gedruckt bei Conrad Zentler, in der Zveiten Strasn, unter-
halt der Rehs-strasse. 1832. 20 p.
PAtM.   12319

Evangelical Lutheran Synod of
Virginia.
Auszug aus den Verhandlungen
der dritten Evangelisch Lutherisch-
en Synode und des Ministeriums
von Virginien, welde in der Zion-
kirche, Botetourt Caunty, in October, 1831 gehalten wurde. Neu-
Market, S. Henkel...1832. 24 p.
C; NBuG; Vi; ViNnT; ViU. 12320

Evangelical Lutheran Synod of
West Pennsylvania.
Liederbuch für sonntagesschul-
en. Herausgegeben von einer com-
mittee der Ev. Luth. synode von
West-Pennsylvanien. Gettysburg,
Gedruckt bey R. C. Neinstedt,
1832. 94 p. PPLT; PSt.   12321

Evangelical Magazine. July, 1832-
June 1836. Hartford, P. B. Glea-

son & Co. [1832]-36. 4 v.
CtY-D; DLC; MHi; MNBedf;
OMC.   12322

Evangelical Ramber. See East,
Timothy.

Evans, David.
    Calumny refuted, and the
members of the Miami monthly
meeting of Friends defended
against the wanton and malicious
charges and foul reproaches cast
upon them by their quondam
brethren, in a late publication,
entitled "A testimony of Miami
monthly meeting of Friends concerning Joseph Claud." Richmond,
Indiana, Thos. J. Larsh, 1832.
12 p. In; InHi; PSC-Hi.   12323

Evans, George, 1797-1867.
    Speech of George Evans, of
Maine, in support of the Protec-
tive System. Delivered in the
House of Representatives, June 11,
1832. Washington, Pr. by Gales
& Seaton, 1832. 30 p. Ct;
MBAt; MH; ScCC; WHi.   12324

Evans, J.
    The Believer's Pocket Com-
panion. By J. Evans. 1st Amer.
ed. With additions and corrections.
By an American Clergyman. Buffalo, Steele & Faxon, 1832.
                                  12325
Evans, John, 1767-1827.
    A sketch of the denomination
of the Christian world, to which
is prefixed an outline of atheism,
deism, theophilanthropism, Ma-
hometanism, Judaism, and Christianity... Amhurst, J. S. & C.
Adams, prs., 1832. 273 p.
CtMW; MBC; NjR; OClWHi;
RPAt.   12326

Evans, Oliver.
    The young mill-wright and
Miller's guide. Illus. by twenty-
eight descriptive plates. 7th ed.
with additions and corrections...

and a description of an improved
merchant flour-mill, with engravings, by C. & C. Evans, engineers. Philadelphia, Carey & Lea,
1832. 383 p. NjPat; VtMidSM.
                                  12327
Evans, Richard.
    Love and patriotism, a poem,
pronounced at Bowdoin college on
the annual commencement, Sept.
5, 1832. Portland, n. p., 1832.
8 p. MB; NjPT.   12328

Evans, Robert Wilson, 1789-1866.
    The Rectory of Valehead. By
the Rev. Robert Wilson Evans,
M. A. ... 1st Amer. from the 6th
ed. Philadelphia, Carey & Lea,
1832. 324 p. CtHT; InCW; MdBP;
NNUt; RPAt.   12329

---- ---- 2d Amer. from 6th
London ed. Philadelphia, 1832.
CSd; CtY; NcC; NSchU.   12330

Evans, Thomas.
    Condensed view of the cholera
in Europe, with its introduction
in America; to which is added
forty-seven days' experience in a
cholera hospital. With a list of
names of those who were admitted and who died. By Thomas
Evans and James C. Kent. New
York, The Authors, 1832. 21 p.
DLC; MH-M; NN.   12331

[Everett, Alexander Hill] 1790-
1847.
    The conduct of the administra-
tion... Boston, Stimpson & Clapp,
1832. 86 p. CtY; IaU; MnU; PPL;
WHi.   12332

---- Memorial of the New York
convention, to the Congress of
the United States. Presented
March 26, 1832 and referred to
the committee on manufactures.
In convention of the Friends of
Domestic Industry assembled at
New York, Oct. 26, 1832... Baltimore, By order of the perma-

nent committee of the New York convention, 1832. 23 p. DLC; MB. 12333

---- Strictures on nullifications; from the N. Amer. review. Boston, 1832. CtY; InU; MBAt; OCLaw; RP; TxU. 12334

Everett, Edward, 1794-1865.
An address delivered as the introduction to the Franklin lectures, in Boston, November 14, 1831. By Edward Everett. Boston, Gray & Bowan, 1832. 24 p. CtHT; MBAt; NjR; OO; PHi; PPAmP. 12335

---- The progress of Reform in England. Boston, 1832. PPL. 12336

---- Remarks in the House of Representatives, May 17, 1832, on the apportionment bill. [Washington, 1832] 9 p. CtY; MH; MWA; NIC; ViU. 12337

---- Speech... on the proposed adjustment of the tariff delivered in the House of Representatives of the United States, on the 25th June, 1832. Washington, Pr. by Gales & Seaton, 1832. 38 p. CtHWatk; MHi; PPAmP; ScCC. 12338

Everett, L. S.
To the Public. Slander exposed and refuted. [Buffalo? H. A. Salisbury? 1832] 36 p. DLC. 12339

Evidences of the Truth of the Christian Religion, deduced from the miracles of our Lord and Saviour Jesus Christ. No. 25. Tract Association of Friends, Philadelphia, 1832. OClWHi. 12340

Ewing, James.
A treatise on the office and duty of a justice of peace, sheriff, coroner, constable and of executors, administrators and guardians... 2d ed. Trenton, N. J., D. Fenton, 1832. 508 p. IU; Nj;

NjN; NjP; NjR. 12341

Ewing, Thomas, 1789-1871.
Speech of Mr. Ewing, of Ohio, in favor of the protecting system. Delivered in the Senate of the United States. February 17 and 20, 1832. Washington, Gales & Seaton, 1832. 22 p. Ct; MWA; OCHP; PPAmP; WHi. 12342

---- Speech of Mr. Ewing, of Ohio, on the bill providing for the distribution of the process of the sales of the public lands, for a limited time. Delivered in the Senate of the United States, June 28, 1832. Washington, Gales & Seaton, 1832. 14 p. DLC; OCIW; OClWHi. 12343

An examination of Mr. Howell's review of Dr. Ducachet's letter of "The office of sponsors in baptism" in a letter to the reviewer, from an Episcopalian. 55 p. MB; MWA; MdBD; NjPT. 12344

Examination of the Indian question. [Cherokee Indians] From the Globe, March 31, 1832. [Washington? 1832] 16 p. CtY; DLC; GU-De; NN; WHi. 12345

Exeter, N.H., First Congregational Church.
The confession of faith and the covenant. Exeter, 1832. 16 p. MBC; MH. 12346

Experience of a Green Mountain girl; to which is added, The experience of another [in verse] written in honour of their Lord. [n.p.] Pr. for the Publisher, 1832. RPB. 12347

An expose. In order to do justice to an injured woman, whose conduct and motives have been so greatly misrepresented, her friends have determined to give publicity to the following correspondence. The separation took place in April, 1832. [Cortland, Ala. , 1832]   12348

An exposition of the unequal, unjust and oppressive operation of the present tariff system, in relation to iron, wool, hemp, paper, and the manufactures thereof... Philadelphia, Pr. by Mifflin & Parry, 1832. 68 p. DLC; LNH; MWA; NjR; PPL-R; TxU.
12349

Extracts from the Journal of a city missionary. New York, Morgan & Burger, 1832. 11 p. MH; NjR.   12350

F

Facts for the people (against Gen. Jackson). Philadelphia, 1832. PPL.   12351

---- [2d ed.] Frankfort, Ky. , 1832. [8] p. ICU; KyU; MWA.
12352

Fairfield, Sumner Lincoln, 1803-1844.
    The last night of Pompeii; a poem: and Lays and legends. By Sumner Lincoln Fairfield. New-York, Pr. by Elliott & Palmer, 1832. 309 p. CtHT; MH; NNUT; RPB; WHi.   12353

Fairfield, New York. College of Physicians and Surgeons of the Western District.
    Circular and catalogue of the faculty and students, of the College of Physicians and Surgeons of the western district of the state of New-York, in Fairfield, Herkimer County, for 1831-32. Utica, Pr. by Hastings and Tracy, 1832. 11, [1] p. CtY; MH-M; NN; NbU.   12354

Fairhaven Institution for Savings.
    Charter and by-laws of the Fairhaven institution for savings.

New Bedford, Benjamin T. Congdon, 1832. 11 p. MNBedf. 12355

Falsehood and slander refuted and exposed. [New York, 1832] 8 p. DLC.   12356

Familiar dialogues between Benjamin and Peter, on the subject of close communion. By Anti-delta. Philadelphia, Pr. by Russell & Martien, 1832. 47 p. NbOP; NjPT; PCA.   12357

Family Cabinet. See Blake, John Lauris.

Family cabinet atlas. 1st Amer. rev. ed. , corr. & enl. Philadelphia, Carey & Lea, 1832. 100 p. PPA.   12358

The Family lyceum. Designed for instruction and entertainment, and adapted to families, schools and lyceums. v. 1-2 no. 5 July 28, 1832. Dec. 7, 1833. Boston, G. W. Light & co. , 1832-33. 2 v. DLC; OClWHi; WaU.   12359

Farley, Frederick Augustus.
    An explanation of the words "By nature children of wrath," found in Ephesians 11.3. (Anon) 2d ed. Boston, Grey and Bowen, 1832. 12 p. ICMe; MB-FA; MeBat; MMeT-Hi;MNBedf. 12360

---- Two tracts. First on the origin of the Doctrine of the Trinity. Second on the Genuineness of the text of "The Three Heavenly Witnesses." Brooklyn, 1832. 23 p. RHi.   12361

(Old) Farmer's Almanac. Calculated by Robert B. Thomas, 1832. Boston, Richardson, Lord & Holbrook, 1832. PHi; RNHi. 12362

Farmer's almanac for 1833. New York, R. Bartlett and S. Raynor [1832] 36 p. MHi; MWA.   12363

---- New York, Daniel D. Smith,
[1832] 18 p. NjHi; NN.   12364

---- Philadelphia. By John Ward,
M'Carty and Davis [1832] CU;
DLC; MWA; NCH; PHi.   12365

---- Portland, Me., G. Hyde &
co., 1832. [58] p. ICMcHi;
MeHi; NbHi.   12366

---- Poughkeepsie, P. Potter &
Co., [1832] 24 p. DLC; M; MWA.
                            12367
The Farmer's Almanack, for the
year of our lord, 1832...Adapted
to the meridian of Buffalo, Erie
Co., New York...Astronomical
calculations by the successor of
Oliver Loud... Buffalo, R. W.
Haskins [1832] 24 p.   12368

The (old) farmers' almanack for
1833. By Robert Thomas. Boston, Carter, Hendee & Co., etc.,
etc. [1832] CoD; GU; MWA; PPT;
RWe; TxU.   12369

---- By Samuel Burr, Philom.
Cincinnati, N. & G. Guilford,
1832. OHiHL.   12370

---- By Zadock Thompson. Burlington, Pr. by E. & T. Mills
[1832] 24 p. DLC.   12371

The farmer's and mechanics almanac... [1st] 1833- Montgomery, N.Y. [1832] DLC; NBuG;
NBLiHi.   12372

The farmer's and mechanics Al-
manack for 1833. By Charles
Egelmann. Philadelphia, George
W. Mentz and son, [1832] 18 l.
CLU; KHi; MWA; PHi; ViU.
                            12373
Farmers' and Planters' Almanac
for 1833. Salem [1832] 18 p.
NcD.   12374

The Farmer's diary, or Western
Almanack for 1833... Ithaca,

Mack & Andrus [1832] 24 p.
CSmH; MWA; NCH; NIC; NUtHi.
                            12375
The Farmers family almanac; or
New York Farmer's almanac for
the year of Our Lord and Saviour,
1833. New York [1832] MWA;
NPalk.   12376

The farmer's guide, and western
agriculturist, by several eminent
practical farmers of the west,
and published under the patronage
of the Hamilton county agricultural society. Cincinnati, Buckley,
Deforest and co., 1832. 367 p.
CtHWatk; InLPU; MH; OClWHi;
NPV.   12377

Farmer's, mechanic's and gentleman's almanack for 1833. By Nathan Wild. Keene, J. & J. W.
Prentiss [1832] CLU; InU; MWA;
(NHHS); WHi.   12378

Farr, Jonathan.
    Counsels and consolations, con-
taining meditations and reflections
on sixty two passages of Scripture, with particular reference to
those in trouble and affliction.
To which are added four sermons.
Boston, L(eonard) C. Bowles,
1832. 206 p. IU; MBAU; MH;
MWA; NhPet.   12379

The Fashionable American letter
writer, or The art of polite cor-
respondence... Newark, N.J.,
Benjamin Olds, 1832. MBE; MH.
                            12380
Faulkner, Charles James, 1806-
1884.
    The Federal Union, its origin
and value. Address delivered by
Charles Faulkner, Esq., in the
Lutheran Church, in Martinsburg,
July 4th, 1832. [Martinsburg,
W. Va. 1832?] 12 p. NcD.12381

---- The speech of Charles Jas.
Faulkner, (of Berkeley) in the
House of delegates of Virginia,

on the policy of the state with respect to her slave population. Delivered January 20, 1832. Richmond, Thomas W. White, pr. 1832. 22 p. ArU; IU; LU; MWA; P; PHC.   12382

[Fay, Theodore Sedgwick] 1807-1898.
Dreams and reveries of a quiet man; consisting of the Little genius and other essays. By one of the editors of the New-York Mirror. In two vols. New York, J. & J. Harper, 1832. 2 vols. CtY; ICU; NcD; RPB; TNP.
                                       12383
Fear not: for behold I bring you good tidings of great joy, which shall be unto all people. Woodstock, Press of the Universalist Watchman, Pr. by W. W. Prescott, 1832. 12 p. MMeT-Hi; NCaS.   12384

Feltham, Owen, 1602?-1668.
Resolves, Moral, Political. With some account of the Author and his Writings. Cambridge, Mass., Hilliard & Brown, 1832. 315 p. CtY; ICMe; KyDC; MH-AH; TNP.   12385

Female Bethel Flag Society of Philadelphia.
Constitution of the Society. Philadelphia, 1832. 6 p. PHi.
                                       12386
Fenelon, Francois de Salignac de La Mothe-, 1651-1715.
Les aventures de Télémaque, fils d'Ulysse. Par M. Fenelon. Nouvelle edition. Soigneusement revue et corrigée sur l'édition de Didot à Paris. Par A. Bolman... Philadelphia, Carey & Lea, 1832. 222 p. MH; OSW; PPL; PWcT; ViU.   12387

---- Dialogues concerning eloquence in general and particularly that kind which is proper for the pulpit. By M. de Fenelon. Tr.

from the French, and illus. with notes and quotations by William Stevenson. Boston, Lincoln and Edmands, 1832. 102 p. CBPac; InGrD; MA; OCX; TJaL.   12388

---- The first eight books of the adventures of Telemachus the son of Ulysses. See his Les Aventures de Télémaque.

---- Key to the first eight books of the Adventures of ... see his Les Aventures de Télémaque.

---- Petit Télémaque ou précis des aventures de Télémaque fils d'Ulisse. New ed. par A. Bolmar ... Philadelphia, Carey, 1832. 323 p. MB; PPL; PU; ViU.
                                       12389

Fenwick de Porquet, Louis Philippe R.
De Porquet's Italian Phrases; or, Il fraseggiatore toscano. A copious choice of Italian sentences to facilitate a knowledge of the formation of the verbs and syntax of that elegant tongue... 3d ed. rev. and cor... By Carlo Alfieri... Imp. by the American editor. Boston, S. Burdett & co., 1832. 120 p. CtMW; DLC; MB; MH; NIC.
                                       12390
Fergus, John Freeland.
History and treatment of the malignant cholera, as it prevailed at Vienna... By John Freeland Fergus, esq., surgeon. From the London lancet of June, 1832... New-York, Charles S. Francis, 1832. 23 p. MH; NNN; PaHosp.
                                       12391
Ferguson, John, fl. 1831.
Sermon delivered Dec. 16, 1831, occasioned by the death of Mr. Ebenezer Daggett, Jr., ... of Attleborough, etc. Dedham, 1832. 12 p. MBAt; Mw; NBLiHI. 12392

Ferguson, Walter. An only son. See Kennedy, William.

Fessenden, Thomas Green, 1771-1837.
... The New American gardener, containing practical directions on the culture of fruits and vegetables; including landscape and ornamental gardening, grapevines, silk, strawberries, &c., &c. By Thomas G. Fessenden... 6th ed. Boston, Carter, 1832. 306 p. MdBS; MH; Nh-Hi; IaHI; OO; PHC.   12393

---- New England farmers' almanac... See under title.

Feurbach, Paul Johann Anselm, ritter von, 1775-1833.
Caspar Hauser. An account of an individual kept in a dungeon, separated from all communication with the world, from early childhood to about the age of seventeen. Drawn up from legal documents. By Anselm von Feuerbach... Trans. from the German. Boston, Allen & Ticknor, 1832. 178 p. CtY; Ia; MWA; NjPT; PPA; PPP.   12394

Fidler, Isaac.
Observations on professions, literature, manners, and emigration in the United States and Canada... by the Rev. Isaac Fidler... New York, J. & J. Harper, 1832. 248 p. DLC; ICRL; MHi; NdHi; TNP.   12395

Field, Barnam, 1796-1851.
The American School Geography... with an atlas, by Barnam Field, A.M. Revised ed. Boston, Wm. Hyde & Richardson, Lord & Holbrook, 1832. 13 p. CTHWatk; ICU; MH; MeHi. 12396

---- Atlas designed to accompany the American school geography... Boston, W. Hyde & co., 1832. MH; NNC.   12397

Field, Joseph, 1772-1869.

On Zeal. By Joseph Field. 2d ed. No. 57. Pr. for The American Unitarian Assoc. Boston, Gray & Bowen, 1832. 19 p. CBPac; ICMe; IEG; MeB; RNR.
                              12398

Fielding, Henry, 1707-1754.
Select works of Henry Fielding. With a memoir of the life of the author, by Sir Walter Scott; and an essay on his life and genius, by Arthur Murphy, Esq. Containing "The history of Tom Jones." Philadelphia, Carey & Lea, 1832. 2 vols. IaU; LNL; MBBC; PU; TNP.   12399

[Fillmore, Millard] pres. U.S., 1800-1874.
An examination of the question, 'Is it right to require any religious test as a qualification to be a witness in a court of justice?' ... Buffalo, Pr. by C. Faxon, 1832. 14 p. Ct; DLC; MiU; NN; OCl; TxU.   12400

[Finley, Anthony]
Map of Ohio and the settled parts of Michigan. [Philadelphia] 1832. MH.   12401

---- A new general atlas, comprising a complete set of maps, representing the grand divisions of the globe, to-gether with the several empires, kingdoms and states in the world; compiled from the best authorities and connected by the most recent discoveries. Philadelphia, A. Finley, 1832. MH.   12402

Finney, Charles Grandison, 1792-1875.
Review... or an examination... See Wisner, Benjamin Blydenburg 1794-1835.

Firemen's Insurance Company of Cincinnati.
Charter of the Firemen's Insurance Company of Cincinnati. In-

corporated by Act of Assembly, in 1832. Cincinnati, Pr. by Wood & Stratton, 1832. 12 p. MiU-C; OCHP.   12403

The first and second coming of Jesus Christ; with appropriate texts. New-York, Pr. by George P. Scott & co., 1832. 12 p. NNG.   12404

First principles of arithmetic. For the use of very young children. Gallipolis, Ohio, Pr. at the Phoenix Office, 1832. 30 p. NN; NNT-C.   12405

Fish, Phineas, 1785-1854.
   The coming of the kingdom of God. A sermon preached at Orleans, Oct. 1832, on the occasion of the ordination of Rev. Samuel Munsen as a missionary to the heathen. Barnstable, Pr. by Thompson & Underwood, 1832. 22 p. MBNEH; PLT; RPB. 12406

Fisher, Charles, 1789-1849.
   Address of Mr. Fisher to the Anti-Tariff Meeting held in Salisbury, of the Request of a Jackson Meeting. Pr. by Western Carolinian, Salisbury, 1832. 16 p. GU; NcD; NcU; ViU.   12407

---- Address to the citizens at Rowan County. N.p. [1832?] NcU.   12408

Fisk, Theophilus.
   The nation's bulwark, An oration, on the freedom of the press, delivered at the Court house in Danbury, Con. ...Dec. 5, 1832. On the liberation of P. T. Barnum...from imprisonment, for an alleged libel... New-Haven, Office of the Examiner and watch tower of freedom [1832?] 16 p. DLC; ICU; MH; MnU; PU. 12409

Fisk, Wilbur, 1792-1839.
   Address to the members of the Methodist Episcopal church on the subject of temperance. New York, Waugh, 1832. 16 p. CtMW; CtY; MoS; MnU; MWA.   12410

---- A discourse on predestination and election, preached on an especial occasion at Greenwich, Mass. New-York, J. Emory and B. Waugh, for the Methodist Episcopal Church, at the Conference, 1832. 36 p. CtSoP; MWiW; MiD-B.   12411

---- The science of education: an inaugural address, delivered at the opening of the Wesleyan university, in Middletown, Connecticut, September 21, 1831. By the Rev. Wilbur Fisk, D.D., president of the University. New York, Pr. by M'Elrath & Bangs, 1832. 24 p. CtSoP; IEG; KyDC; MBC; NjR.   12412

Fiske, Nathan Welby, 1798-1847.
   Bible class book; designed for Bible classes, Sabbath schools, and families. Prepared for the Massachusetts Sabbath School Union, by N. W. Fiske. Revised by the publishing committee. Boston, Massachusetts Sabbath School Union, 1832. 36 p. DLC; ICP; NNUT.   12413

Fitch, Eleazar Thompson, 1791-1871.
   A vindication of the divine purpose in relation to the existence of sin. New Haven, Baldwin & Treadway, 1832. 48 p. CtHC; CtY; MBC; OO.   12414

Fitz, Gideon.
   Instructions for surveying the lands of the United States, in the state of Mississippi. Prepared by Gideon Fitz. Natchez, Pr. by Robert Semple, 1832. 36 p. DNA; MsSM.   12415

Fleetwood, John.
   The life of our Lord and Saviour

Jesus Christ; containing a full
and accurate history, from his
taking upon himself our nature,
to his crucifixion, resurrection,
and ascension; together with the
lives, transactions, and suffering
of his Holy Evangelists, Apostles,
and other primitive martyrs: to
which is added the history of the
Jews. New Haven, Nathan Whiting,
1832. 606 p. CtY; ICU; MWA;
MiD; PU.   12416

Fletcher, James.
The history of Poland; from
the earliest period to the present
time. By James Fletcher, esq....
with a recent narrative of events
...New York, J. & J. Harper,
1832. 339 p. MB; MNtCA; NjR;
NPtw; PPD.   12417

[Fletcher, John William] 1729-
1785.
An appeal to matter of fact and
common sense; or, A rational
demonstration of Man's corrupt
and lost estate... New York, B.
Waugh & T. Mason, for the Methodist Episcopal Church, Pr. by J.
Collard, 1832. 165 p. CtMW;
MBAt; MsJMC; NcD; TxU. 12418

---- Sermons on various religious
and moral subjects, by the Rev.
John Fletcher... From the first
English ed. Baltimore, J. Myres,
1832. 412 p. IaDuMtC; MdBS;
MWH; NNF; NPStA.   12419

Fleury, Claude, 1640-1723.
Manners of the ancient Israel-
ites: Containing an account of
their peculiar customs and cere-
monies...Written originally in
French by Claude Fleury...By
Adam Clarke, LL. D., F. S. A....
New York, J. Emory & B. Waugh,
1832. 283 p. GAuP; IEG; MnSH;
OHi; WaPS.   12420

Flint, Corporal.
Sketches from American his-

tory; containing the stories of
Sergeant Jasper and the boy
Gwinn. New York, Morgan &
Burger, 1832. 79 p. DLC; MH;
NBuG.   12421

Flint, Jacob, 1767-1835.
An address on the character
and services of George Washington delivered to the people of Co-
hasset, Feb. 22, 1832, being the
hundredth birthday of that illustrious benefactor of his country,
by Jacob Flint. First Church, Co-
hasset. Boston, Leonard C.
Bowles, 1832. ICMe; MBC; MWA;
MdHi; NN.   12422

Flint, Timothy, 1780-1840.
The art of being happy. See
Droz, Joseph, 1773-1850.

---- The history and geography
of the Mississippi valley. To which
is appended a condensed physical
geography of the Atlantic United
States and the whole American
continent. 2d ed. Cincinnati, E.
H. Flint & E. R. Lincoln, 1832.
2 v. GAU; KyU; MiU; PMA; WaU.
                            12423
---- The United States and other
divisions of the American continent. In two volumes. Cincinnati,
E. H. Flint & L. R. Lincoln, 1832.
2 v. MoSB; MsJS; PWCHi; WLacT.
                            12424

Flint, Waldo, 1794-1879.
An Address delivered before the
Worcester Agricultural Society, Oc-
tober 10, 1832; being their four-
teenth anniversary Cattle Show and
Exhibition of Manufactures. By
Waldo Flint. Worcester, Pr. by
S. H. Colton & Co., 1832. 16 p.
Ct; IaDa; MWA; OClWHi; OO.
                            12425
Flinter, George Dawson, d. 1838.
Examen del Estado actual de
los Esclavos de la Isla de Puerto
Ricobago el Gobierno Espanol: en
que se manifiesta la impolitica...
de la premature emancipacion de

los esclavos de la India Occiden-
tal, etc. Neuva York, 1832.
124 p. CU-B; DLC; MBAt; MH;
NN.   12426

Floral magazine and botanical
repository. v. 1- Philadelphia,
D. & C. Landreth, 1832. ICF;
MdBJ; NcU; OU; PPAmP. 12427

Florida.
   Acts of the Legislative council
of the territory of Florida,
passed at their 10th session, commencing January 2d and ending
February 12th, 1832. Tallahassee, Pr. by Wm. Wilson, 1832.
162 p. DLC; F; In-SC; Mi-L; Nj.
                             12428
---- A journal of the proceedings
of the legislative council of the
territory of Florida, 10th-16th
session. Tallahassee, Pr. by
Dyke & Carlisle, 1832 [-1836].
136 p. DLC; FU-L; MH; NcD;
ViU.   12429

Flowers of wit; or the laughing
philosopher, and budget of comi-
calities. Embellished with numerous quantity of copper plate and
wood engravings, plain and colored. Baltimore, C. V. Nickerson, 1832. 108 p. MB; MdHi.
                             12430
Floyd, Benjamin.
   The Lowell directory... By
Benjamin Floyd. Lowell, Pr. by
Theo. Billings, 1832. MBNEH;
MLow.   12431

Follen, Charles Theodore Christian, 1796-1840.
   Funeral oration: delivered before the citizens of Boston assembled at the Old South Church,
Nov. 17, at the burial of Gaspar
Spurzhein... Boston, March, Cap-
en, & Lyon, 1832. 32 p. CBPac;
ICMe; MeHi; OCHP; WHi. 12432

Follen, Eliza Lee (Cabot), 1787-
1860.

Sequel to "The well-spent
hour." or, The birthday. Boston,
Carter & Hendee, 1832. 154 p.
DLC; MH; MH; MiU-C; NcD.
                             12433
---- The well spent hour. 3d ed.
cor. and enl. Boston, Carter &
Hendee, 1832. 160 p. DLC; ICU.
                             12434
---- Words of truth. Cambridge
(Mass.) 1832. 249 p. DLC;
ICartC; MB.   12435

Foot, Joseph Ives.
   Co-operation; a sermon
preached in North Woodstock,
Conn., at the dedication of the
meeting house and the ordination
of the Rev. Orson Cowles... April
25, 1832. Brookfield (Mass.), E.
Merrian & Co., 1832. 18 p.
CtSoP; IEN; MiD-B; RPB. 12436

Foot, Lundy.
   A few words of plain truth.
In reply to a misstatement of
facts and misinterpretations of
Scripture contained in a letter to
the Hon. and Rev. G. Noel. By
a Unitarian. Bridgeport, 1832.
BrMus.   12437

Foot, Samuel Alfred, 1790-1878.
   An address delivered before
the Euglossian and Alpha Phi Del-
ta societies of Geneva college,
August 1, 1832. Subject- Conver-
sation as a branch of education.
By Samuel A. Foot, of New York.
Geneva, Pr. by J. C. Merrell &
Co., 1832. 23 p. CSmH; CtY;
MB; NGH; NN.   12438

Forbes, Gerritt Van Husen.
   Green Mountain annals, a tale
of truth. By G. V. H. Forbes...
New York, Burnett & Smith,
1832. 140 p. DLC; MH; MWA;
NGH; RPB; Vt.   12439

The Forget-me-not. Hudson,
N. Y., A. Stoddard, 1832. 8 p.
RPB.   12440

Forsyth, John, 1780-1841.
Rough sketch of speeches delivered in secret session by Mr. Forsyth, of Georgia, on the nomination of Mr. Van Buren. Washington, Blair, 1832. 6 p. CtY; MB; NCH.   12441

---- Speech in the secret session of the Senate, on the nomination of Mr. Van Buren (to be minister to England). Washington, F. P. Blair, 1832. 8 p. DLC; MB.   12442

Foster, Benjamin Franklin.
Practical penmanship, being a development of the Carstairian system: comprehending an elucidation of the movements of the fingers, hand and arm, necessary in writing.... Illustrated by 24 engravings; shewing (sic) the position of the fingers in holding the pen, process of pen making .... By B. F. Foster. Albany (N. Y.), O. Steele, 1832. 112 p. IaHi; GSAJC; MH; NCaS; RPB.
                                     12443
Foster, Elijah.
Brief examination of the mode and subjects of Christian baptism. Addressed to Pedobaptists. By E. Foster. 2d ed. Salisbury, New-England Chronicle Press, Pr. by J. Caldwell, 1832. 52 p. MB; MBC; NHCS; NjPT; OClWHi.
                                     12444
---- God's judgements are to be deprecated. A sermon, addressed to his people, on fast day... By Elijah Foster.... Newburyport, Pr. by W. & J. Gilman, 1832. 16 p. MNtcA; PCA.   12445

Foster, Thomas Flournoy, 1790-1848.
Speech... on a memorial, and certain resolutions therewith submitted, relative to the missionaries, (Worcester and Butler) who are imprisoned under a judgment of a state court in Georgia. De-

livered in the House of Representatives, U. S., June 11, 1832. Washington, D. Green, 1832. 16 p. A-Ar; CtY; GU-De; MHi; MWA.
                                     12446
Foulke's Almanac for 1833. By Joseph Foulke. Philadelphia, Pa., John Richards [1832] InU; MWA; NjR; PP; PPM.   12447

Fowle, William Bentley.
The French first class book; being a new selection of reading lessons: in four parts.... The whole calculated to interest as well as improve the learner. By William B. Fowle... Boston, Crocker & Brewster; New York, Jonathan Leavitt, 1832. CtHWatk; ICU; MH; RPB; TxU-T.   12448

Fowler, William Chauncey, 1793-1881.
Sermon preached at the ordination of the Rev. Robert Southgate, as Pastor over the First Congregational Church and Society, in the north parish of Woodstock, Vt., January 4, 1832. Woodstock, Pr. by Rufus Colton, 1832. 23 p. CSmH; MBAt; MH-AH; PPPrHi; VtU.   12449

Fox, George, 1624-1691.
A Journal of historical account of the life, travels, sufferings, Christian experiences, and labour of love, in the work of the ministry, of that ancient, eminent, and faithful servant of Jesus Christ. George Fox. Philadelphia, Pr. by Thos. Kite & Co., 1832. 672 p. OCl; PPF; RLa; TxDaM; ViU.
                                     12450
Fox, Thomas Bayley, 1808-1876.
An oration, delivered at the request of the Washington Light Infantry Company, in Newburyport, Feb. 22, 1832; at the centennial celebration of the birthday of Washington. By Thomas B. Fox. Newburyport, White, 1832. 22 p. CBPac; MHi; NCH; PHi; RPB.   12451

Foxe, John, 1516-1587.
Book of martyrs. Compiled from Foxe's by A. Blanchard. Cincinnati, O., 1832. 540 p. 12452

---- Book of martyrs; or a history of the lives, sufferings and triumphant deaths, of the primitive as well as Protestant Martyrs; Originally composed by the Rev. John Foxe, A.M. and now improved by important alterations and additions by Rev. Chas. A. Goodrich. Embellished with numerous engravings. Cincinnati, Roff & Young, 1832. 597 p. IaG; NN; NcU; OMC; WBeloC. 12453

---- ---- 3d ed. Cincinnati, Pr. by Robinson & Fairbanks, 1832. 540 p. CtHT; MiToC; OHi-C. 12454

---- ---- 7th ed. Cincinnati, A. P. Robinson, 1832. 540 p. NWatt. 12455

---- ---- Hartford, Eli Hall, 1832. 597 p. KyCovV; MnS; MTyn; OClWHi; REd. 12456

---- ---- New York, W. W. Reed & co., 1832. 400 p. GEU; ICT; MTemNHi; PPT; PPTU. 12457

---- ---- Philadelphia, Key Mielke & Riddle, 1832. 2 vols. MeBat; NcU; OO; PU; ViRU. 12458

Framingham, Mass. First Church.
The confession of faith and covenant adopted by the First Church of Christ, Jan. 1832. Boston, Peirce & Parker, 1832. 11 p. MBC; MH. 12459

---- Review of the confession of faith & covenant of the First Church of Christ in F. Boston, Leonard C. Bowles, 1832. 24 p. CtY; MWA; MiD-B; NNUT. 12460

Francestown (N.H.). First Congregational Church of Christ.
Confessions of faith, with the covenant, regulations, resolutions, and a sketch of the history. Amherst, R. Boylston, 1832. 20 p. Nh-Hi. 12461

Francis, Convers, 1795-1863.
The Christian change, described by the Apostle Peter, by Convers Francis, printed for the American Unitarian Association. Boston, Gray & Bowen, 1832. 16 p. DLC; MBAU; MH; MCon; MHing; MeBat. 12462

---- ---- 2d ed. Boston, James Munroe & Co., 1832. 16 p. CBPac; ICMe; MNBedf. 12463

---- A discourse delivered at Plymouth, Mass. Dec. 22, 1832, in commemoration of the landing of the fathers. By Convers Francis, Congregational Minister of Watertown. Pub. by request of the committee of the First Parish. Plymouth, Pr. by Allen Danforth, 1832. 56 p. DLC; MiD-B; MNBedf; NNUT; OOxM; VtMidbC. 12464

Francis, John W.
Letter on the cholera asphyxia ...addressed to James Bond Read, M.D. ...by John W. Francis, M.D. New-York, Pr. by George P. Scott & Co., 1832. 35 p. IEN-M; MB; MHi; NNNAM; WU-M. 12465

Franklin, pseud.
Philadelphia library. [Philadelphia, 1832] 10 p. NN; PSt. 12466

Franklin, Benjamin, 1706-1790.
The way to wealth as clearly shown in the preface of an old Pennsylvania almanac, entitled, "Poor Richard improved." By Dr. Benjamin Franklin. New-Harmony (Ind.), J. O. Watles, 1832. 15p. CtY; In; InNhW; MiU. 12467

---- The works of Dr. Benjamin consisting of essays humorous moral and literary with his life written by himself. Exeter, J. & B. Williams, 1832. 256 p. CtY; DLC; MWA; OC; PP.   12468

Franklin almanac. By John Ward. Philadelphia, M'Carty and Davis [1832] 18 ll. PHi; PPL; PPeSchW.
                                    12469

Franklin Family Almanac for 1832. Calculations by John Armstrong. Pittsburgh, Pa., Johnston & Stockton, [1832] 60 p. No. 15. MWA; OManS; PPiU.   12470

Franklin Institute. Philadelphia.
     Address of the committee on premiums and Exhibitions, (of the) Franklin Institute of Pennsylvania for the Promotion of the Mechanic Arts. Philadelphia, J. Harding, 1832. 8 p. CoU; KU; MBAt; NBuB; PHi.   12471

Free Trade and State Rights Association.
     Political Tract number 12. An appeal to the people on the question what shall we do next? Columbia, The Association, 1832. 12 p. MWA.   12472

Free Trade Convention, Philadelphia, 1831.
     Memorial of the committee appointed by the "Free Trade Convention" held at Philadelphia, in September and October, 1831, to prepare and present a memorial to Congress, remonstrating against the existing tariff of duties. New York, Pr. by W. A. Mercein, 1832. 87 p. A-Ar; CtY; MWA; NNC; TxU.   12473

Freeman, Frederick.
     Religious Liberty. A discourse delivered in the Congregational Church at Hanson, on the Fourth of July, 1832. By F. Freeman, Pastor of the 3d Church in Ply-

mouth, Plymouth, Mass., Pr. by Benjamin Drew, Jr., 1832. 32 p. CBPSR; IEG; MeBat; MWA; PPL; RPB.   12474

Freeman, James.
     Sermons and charges, by James Freeman. New ed. Boston, Carter, Hendee & Co., 1832. 428 p. CtHT; ICMe; MB; NNG; RNR; MMeT.   12475

The Freeman's Almanack for the year of our Lord, 1833...by Samuel Burr, Philom....Cincinnati, N. & G. Guilford [1832] [46] p. ICU; MWA; MiD-B; OHi; WHi.   12476

Freemasons. Alabama. Grand Lodge.
     Proceedings of the Grand Lodge of the state of Alabama, at its annual communication in December, 1831. Tuscaloosa, Pr. by E. Walker, 1832. 22 p. AMFM; DSG; InCrM; MBFM; OCM.   12477

---- Boston. Knights Templars. Boston Commandery.
     Order of exercises of the installation of the officers of the Boston encampment...Feb. 28, 1832. [Boston, 1832] Broadside. MB.   12478

---- Connecticut. Grand Lodge.
     Proceedings of the Grand Lodge of Connecticut, at their annual communication at New Haven, on the ninth day of May, A. L. 5852. New Haven, Pub. by order of the Grand Lodge, 1832. 33 p. NNFM.   12479

---- Indiana. Grand Lodge.
     Proceedings of the Grand Lodge of...Masons, of the state of Indiana, at its annual communication, held at Salem, on Monday, the 1st day of October, A. L. 5832. Most Worshipful Woodbridge Parker, G.M. Right Worshipful Austin

W. Morris, G. S. Indianapolis, Pr. by Douglass & Maguire, 1832. 20 p. IaCrM; MBFM; NNFM. 12480

---- Kentucky.

Proceedings of the Grand Chapter and of the Grand council of the state of Kentucky, at a grand annual convocation, begun and held at Mason's hall in the city of Lexington. Frankford, Pr. by A. G. Hodges, 1832. 15 p. NNFM. 12481

---- ---- Grand Lodge.

Proceedings of the Grand Lodge of Kentucky, at a grand annual communication, in the city of Lexington, commencing on the 27th, of August. 5832. Lexington, Pr. by Finnell & J. F. Herndon, 1832. 30 p. KyLx; NNFM. 12482

---- Louisiana. Grand Lodge.

Extract from the proceedings of the Grand Lodge of Free and Accepted Masons of the state of Louisiana, held in the city of New Orleans. New Orleans, Pr. at the Tribune Office, 1832. 18 p. NNFM. 12483

---- Maine. Grand Lodge.

Proceedings of Grand Lodge of the most Ancient and Honorable Fraternity of Free and Accepted Masons of the state of Maine. Augusta, I. Berry & Co., 1832. 16 p. IaCrM; NNFM. 12484

---- ---- ---- Proceedings of Masonic Lodge, in Maine, meeting held in 1832. Augusta (Me.) I. Berry & Co., 1832. 16 p. IaCrM. 12485

---- Massachusetts.

Grand Royal Arch Chapter of Massachusetts. Boston, December 1832. Boston, Pr. by companion E. G. House, 1832. 12 p. NNFM. 12486

---- Mississippi. Grand Lodge.

Extract from the proceedings of the Grand Lodge of the state of Mississippi at a grand annual communication... the city of Natchez, on the 20th of February, A. D. 1832, A. L. 5832. Natchez, Pr. at "The Natchez" office, 1832. 23 p. IaCrM; MBFM; MsMFM; NNFM. 12487

---- New York.

Abstract of the proceedings of the worshipful Grand Lodge of the state of New York, and of the Grand Stewards' Lodge, from August 31st, 5831, to June the 8th, 5832, inclusive, New York, Pr. by Wm. A. Mercein, 1832. 47 p. NNFM; OCM. 12488

---- ---- Grand Lodge.

The constitution of the Ancient and Honourable Fraternity of Free and Accepted Masons, containing all the particular ordinances and regulations of the Grand Lodge, of the state of New York... New York, Pr. by Peter Crawford, 1832. 80 p. IaCrM; NNFM; ODaM; PPFM. 12489

---- ---- ---- Proceedings of Grand Lodge of Masonic Lodge, in New York State; Meeting held in 1832. New York, Wm. A. Mercein, 1832. 47 p. IaCrM. 12490

---- North Carolina. Grand Lodge.

Proceedings of the Grand Lodge of Ancient York Masons of North Carolina.... Raleigh, Pr. by Lawrence & Lemay, 1832. 7 p. IaCrM; OCM. 12491

---- Ohio.

Journal of the proceedings of the Grand Royal Arch Chapter of the state of Ohio.... Columbus, January 4, 1832. Columbus, Pr. by companion John Bailhache, 1832. 7 p. NNFM. 12492

---- ---- Grand Lodge.

Proceedings of the Grand

Lodge of... Masons in... Ohio, at
the Annual Grand Communication,
A. L. 5832. Most Worshipful
Charles Anthony, Grand Master.
Zanesville, Pr. by Bro. Adam
Peters, 1832. 11 p. IaCrM;
MBFM; NNFM; OCM.   12493

---- Pennsylvania.
    Annual publication, the Grand
Lodge of the most Ancient and
Honourable Fraternity of Free and
Accepted Masons of Pennsylvania
and Masonic jurisdiction thereunto
belonging. Michael Nisbit, Right
Worshipful Grand Master. Phila-
delphia, Pr. by Thomas S. Man-
ning, March 1832. 32 p. PPFM.
                        12494
---- ---- Proceedings of Grand
Lodge of Masonic Lodge, in Penn-
sylvania; meeting held in 1832.
Philadelphia, Thomas S. Manning,
1832. 28 p. IaCrM; PPFM.
                        12495
---- Rhode Island. Grand Lodge.
    Extracts from Masonic oaths
and penalties as sworn to by the
Grand Lodge of Rhode Island.
Providence? 1832? WHi.   12496

---- ---- ---- Proceedings of the
Grand Lodge, of the state of
Rhode Island and Providence plan-
tations, at the annual meeting,
holden at Mason's hall in Newport,
June 25, A. L. 5832. Providence,
Pr. by Cranston & Hammond,
1832. 8 p. IaCrM; NNFM. 12497

---- Tennessee. Grand Chapter.
    Proceedings of the Grand Royal
Arch Chapter of Tennessee at a
grand annual convocation, begun
and held at the Masonic Hall,
Nashville. On Monday the 8th October A. D. 1832, Y. D. 2372,
A. L. 5832 Nashville, Pr. at the
Republican and Gazette Office,
1832. 12 p. MBFW.   12498

---- ---- Grand Lodge.
    Proceedings of the Grand

Lodge of the State of Tennessee,
at a grand annual communication
held at the Masonic Hall in the
town of Nashville, on Monday,
Oct. 1st, A. L. 5832, A. D. 1832.
Nashville, Hunt, Tardiff & co.,
prs., 1832. [3], 4-15 p. IaCrM;
MBFM; T; TxU.   12499

---- ---- ---- Knights Templars.
Proceedings of the Grand Lodge
of the State of Tennessee at a
Grand Annual Communication held
at the Masonic Hall in the Town
of Nashville, on Monday, Oct.
1st, A. L. 5832, A. D. 1832. Nashville, Pr. by Hunt, Tardiff & Co.,
1832. 15 p. T.   12500

---- Virginia. Grand Lodge.
    Proceedings of a Grand Annual
Communication of the Grand
Lodge of Virginia, begun and held
in the Mason's hall, in the city of
Richmond, December 10th, A. D.
1832. Richmond, Pr. by John
Warrock, 1832. 31 p. NNFM.
                        12501
The Freewill Baptist Register and
Saint's visiter for 1833. Portland
[1832] 36 l. ICU; NhHi. 12502

Free-will Baptists.
    Hymns for Christian melody.
Selected from various authors.
Boston, Pub. by David Marks, for
the Free-will Baptist Convention,
1832. 608 p. MTaHi; PCA.
                        12503
Frelinghuysen, Theodore, 1787-
1862.
    Resolutions to protect the Indi-
ans Feb. 2, 1832. [Washington,
1832] 1 p. GU-De.   12504

Frey, Joseph Samuel Christian
Frederick, 1771-1850.
    Narrative of the Rev. Joseph
Samuel C. F. Frey... 9th ed. New
York, Pr. for the Author, 1832.
10-151 p. KyLxT; MnU; NHC-S.
                        12505

Friends, Society of. Baltimore
Yearly Meeting.
Epistle from the Yearly Meeting, held in Baltimore, by adjournments, from the 29th of the
Tenth month to the 31st of the
same, inclusive, 1832. To the
quarterly and monthly Meetings
within its limits and to its members individually. Baltimore, Pr.
by Wm. Wooddy, 1832. 6 p.
PHC.   12506

---- Indiana Yearly Meeting.
Minutes of Indiana yearly
meeting. At Indiana yearly meeting of Friends, held at White-
Water, in Wayne county, Indiana,
on the 8th day of the tenth month,
1832. [Richmond? 1832] 28 p. In;
InHi; InRchE; InU; WHi.   12507

---- London Yearly Meeting.
The epistle from the yearly
meeting held in London...1832.
Mountpleasant, Ohio, Pr. by E.
Bates, 1832. 12 p. OClWHi.
                           12508
---- Miami Monthly Meeting.
A testimony of Miami monthly
meeting of Friends, concerning
Joseph Cloud: containing some ac-
count of his early religious exer-
cises, left by him in manuscript.
Richmond, Indiana, Pr. by T. J.
Larsh, 1832. 24 p. CtY; In;
InHi; InRchE; InU.   12509

---- New York Yearly Meeting.
Memorials concerning de-
ceased Friends, published by di-
rection of the yearly meeting of
New York. New York, Isaac T.
Hopper, 1832. 45 p. MBC; MH;
NBuG; NNFL; PHC.   12510

---- ---- Memorials concerning
deceased Friends, published by
direction of the yearly meeting of
New York. New York, I. T.
Hopper, 1832. BrMus.   12511

---- Ohio Yearly Meeting.

The discipline of the Society of
Friends of Ohio yearly meeting;
printed by direction of the meeting, held at Mountpleasant, in the
year 1819. Reprinted...1832...St.
Clairsville, Horton J. Howard,
1832. OClWHi.   12512

---- ---- A minute of advice of
Ohio yearly meeting, Mountpleas-
ant, O., E. Bates, 1832. 8 p.
OCHP; OClWHi.   12513

---- Philadelphia Yearly Meeting.
An epistle from the yearly
meeting of Friends held in Philadelphia, by adjournments from the
ninth day of the 4th month to the
14th of the same, inclusive, 1832,
to the free people of colour residing in Pa., N.J., and parts
adjacent. Philadelphia, J. Richards, 1832. 8 p. CU-A; DLC;
MB; NN; NjR.   12514

---- ---- Extracts from the minutes of the Yearly Meeting of
Friends, held in Philadelphia. By
adjournments from the 9th of the
4th month to the 14th of the same,
inclusive, 1832. Philadelphia, Pr.
by J. Richards, 1832. 11 p.
PPFr; ViRut.   12515

Friends of American Industry.
See Friends of Domestic Industry.

Friends of Domestic Industry.
General convention of the
Friends of Domestic Industry, as-
sembled at New York October 26,
1831. [Baltimore, 1832] 198 p.
CtY; MnU; OO; TxU; Vi.   12516

---- Memorial of the New-York
convention on the 25th of October,
(1831), asking congress to continue the duties on imported foreign articles which were intended
for the protection of domestic
manufacturers. [Boston, 1832]
48 p. ICRL; MH; MHi; WHi.
                         12517

---- Memorial of the New York convention to the Congress of the United States, Presented March 26, 1832, and referred to the committee on manufactures. Baltimore, [1832] [23] p. DLC; MH-BA; OCIWHi.   12518

---- Report on the currency. [Baltimore, 1832?] 49-63 p. CtY; DLC; MdBP; PU.   12519

---- Report of the Production and Manufacture of Cotton, (by a Convention of Friends of American Industry). Boston, Pr. by J. T. & E. Buckingham, 1832. 20 p. MB; MBAt; MiD-B; PPL; WHi.
                             12520

---- To the friends of peace, good order, and the union of the states. [N.p. 1832?] 32 p. NSchU.   12521

---- Committee on Iron.
    Report of the Committee on iron. Assembles at New York, Oct. 26, 1831. Baltimore, n.p., 1832. DLC; ICU; TxU.   12522

---- Committee on the manufacture of cotton.
    Report, 1832. 15 p. OCIW.
                             12523

Friends of Education in Greece, Hartford, Conn.
    School at Athens. [A circular inviting subscriptions. Hartford, 1832] BrMus.   12524

Friends of Protection to American Industry.
    A large and respectable meeting of the... from Berwick and South Berwick, Maine, and Somersworth, New Hampshire, was held at the town house in South Berwick, June 11, 1832. Broadside. DNA.   12525

Friend's United States Almanac. Philadelphia, Pa., Marcus T. C. Gould, 1832. MWA; PHi. 12526

Friendship's offering, and winter's wreath.
    Friendship's Offering. A literary album & Christmas & New Year's present for 1832. New York, W. Jackson, 1832. 384 p. OrC.   12527

Frost, Henry Rutledge, 1790-1866.
    Address... before the Young Men's Temperance Society. Charleston, W. Estill, 1832. 20 p. DLC; ScCC.   12528

Frothingham, Nathaniel Langdon.
    Barabbas Preferred; A sermon. By N. L. Frothingham, Minister of the First Church, in Boston. Boston, Christian Register Office, 1832. 118, 8 p. ICMe; MBAt; MHi; MWA.   12529

Fry, Caroline.
    The Listener. See Wilson, Caroline (Fry) 1787-1846.

Fryer, Michael, of Reeth.
    The trial and life of Eugene Aram... Richmond, Pr. by and for M. Bell, 1832. 124 p. CtY; IEN; MiD-B; NcD; TxU.   12530

A full account of the operation of injecting the veins with aqueous and saline liquids, for the cure of malignant cholera, in the most hopeless cases... New York, Peter Hill, 1832. 13 (1) p. MB; MH; NN; NNNAM; ScU.   12531

A full report of the evidence given on the conspiracy case; with the appeals made to the jury. By Messrs. Seldon, Shankland, Maxwell, and Hoffman; and the recorder's charge. New York, William Stodart, 1832. 37 p. NN; NjR.   12532

Fuller, Allen.
    The Gospel of Christ; a dialogue between a minister and an

inquirer after truth. Columbia, S. C., Pr. for the author, 1832. 24 p. MMeT; NcD; ViU.   12533

---- ---- 6th ed. Cincinnati, Roff & Young, 1832. 218 p. OCHP; T.   12534

Fuller, Andrew, 1754-1815.
An inquiry into the nature, symptoms, and effects of religious declension with the means of recovery. By Andrew Fuller. Philadelphia, N. Kite, 1832. 137 p. NN; PHC.   12535

---- Letters to Mr. Vidler, on the doctrine of universal salvation;...Washington, O., Pr. by Yeoman & Lydy, 1832. 115 p. CSmH; IaU; OC.   12536

---- Memoirs of the late Rev. Samuel Pearce, A. M. with extracts of some of his most interesting letters. Compiled by Andrew Fuller, D. D., Philadelphia, Baptist General Tract Society [1832] 300 p. MoWgT.   12537

Fuller, Cyrenus Metcalf.
A selection of hymns from the most approved authors. Particularly designed to be used in, and for the promotion of, Revivals of Religion, in Christian conference meetings. Together with the articles of faith & church covenant of the Elbridge Baptist Church. By C. M. Fuller, Pastor of the Baptist Church in Elbridge. 2d ed. Auburn, H. Ivison & Co., 1832. 212 p. MH-AH; NCanHi; NIC.   12538

Fuller, J. G.
Conversations...In which the principal arguments in favor of the latter practice, are stated, as nearly as possible, in the words of its most powerful advocate, The Rev. Robert Hall. With Mr. Griffin's letter on communion and the review of it by Professor Ripley of Newton. 2d

ed. Boston, Lincoln, 1832. [25]-288 p. GMM; ICU; KyDC; MBC; OO.   12539

The Fulness of Christ, from the remarks of W. Romaine and others. Millbury, Mass., Jonathan Grout [1832] 96 p. DLC; MWA; NN.   12540

A funeral address, delivered at the interment of Amelia Bloom, who was a member of the Sunday School of St. Clement's Church, New-York, on the evening of Christmas day, 1831. By the Rector of that church. New-York, Pr. at the Protestant Episcopal Press, 1832. 8 p. NGH.   12541

Funk, Joseph, 1777-1862.
A compilation of genuine church music, comprising a variety of metres, all harmonized for three voices; together with a copious elucidation of the science of vocal music. By Joseph Funk...Winchester [Va.], Pr. by J. W. Hollis, at the office of the Republican, 1832. 208 p. CSmH; InGo; ViU.   12542

Furness, William Henry, 1802-1896.
The genius of Christianity. By William H. Furness. 3d ed. Boston, Gray & Bowen, for the American Unitarian Association, 1832. 212 p. FDeS; IEG; MeBat; NbU; PPLT.   12543

---- On prayer. (A sermon.) Boston, 1832. MH.   12544

---- A sermon, delivered in the First Congregational Unitarian Church, on the evening of the Lord's day, January 1, 1832. By William Henry Furness...Philadelphia, J. Harding, 1832. 15 p. ICMe; MRev; PHi; PP; ViU.   12545

G

Gahan, William, 1730-1804.
A compendious abstract of the
history of the church of Christ,
from its first foundation to the
eighteenth century... with several
other remarkable events and oc-
curances... by the Rev. William
Gahan, O. S. Philadelphia, Eugene Cummiskey, 1832. 369 p.
MB; WOccR.   12546

Gaither, Nathan.
Address by the Hon. Gaither
to his constituents, upon the subject of the veto by the President,
of the bill to recharter the Bank
of the United States. [Washing-
ton? 1832?] 22 p. MdHi.   12547

Gales's North Carolina Almanac,
for the year of our Lord 1833.
...Raleigh, Pr. by J. Gales &
Son [1832] 36 p. MWA; NcD;
NcU.   12548

Gallatin, Albert, 1761-1849.
An essay on currency and
banking. Philadelphia, 1832.
PPL.   12549

Gallaudet, Thomas Hopkins, 1787-
1851.
The child's book on the soul.
2d ed. Hartford, Cooke & Co.,
1832. 158 p. numbered plates.
MH; RPB.   12550

---- ---- 3d ed., improved.
With questions adapted to the use
of Sunday schools, and of infant
schools. Hartford, Cooke & Co.,
1832. 2 v. CtSoP; DLC.   12551

---- ---- 4th ed., with questions. Hartford, Cooke & co.,
1832. 126 p. DLC; IaHA; NPot;
MHi.   12552

---- Jacob and his sons; or,
The second part of a conversa-
tion between Mary and her moth-
er. Prepared for the American
Sunday School Union by Rev.
Thomas H. Gallaudet... Revised
by committee of publication.
Philadelphia, American Sunday
School Union, 1832. 103 p. DHU;
DLC; OO; TxBradM.   12553

---- Natural theology. New York,
1832. 231 p. MWA; UU.   12554

---- Simple scripture biographies;
or, His third part of a conversation between Mary and her mother
prepared for the American Sunday
School Union. Philadelphia, American Sunday School Union, 1832.
162 p. NUt; PU; ScCliTO. 12555

---- The youth's book on natural
theology, illustrated in familiar
dialogues, with numerous engravings. By Rev. T. H. Gallaudet,
late principal of the American
Asylum for the Deaf and Dumb.
Hartford, Cooke & Co., 1832.
248 p. DLC; GDecCT; NhPet;
PU; ViU.   12556

---- ---- New York, The American Tract Society [1832] 231 p.
DLC.   12557

Galt, John, 1779-1839.
The life of Lord Byron, by
John Galt, esq., New York, J.
& J. Harper, 1832. KyDC;
MDeeP; MH; NPtw; PPD. 12558

---- Memoirs of the Early Life
of, by John Galt. 2d ed. Boston,
1832.   12559

---- The progress of genius; or,
Authentic memoirs of the early
life of Benjamin West... compiled
from materials furnished by himself, by John Galt, abridged for
use of young persons, by a lady.
2d ed. Boston, Leonard C.
Bowles, 1832. 88 p. ICU; MWA;
MiD-B; PU-S; VtU.   12560

Gambold, John, 1711-1771.
   The Martyrdom of Ignatius. A
tragedy. By John Gambold...
Wrote in 1740, published after
his death by Rev. Benjamin La
Trobe...[Philadelphia?] Pr. by
I. Ashmead & Co., for J.
Wright, 1832. 82 p. DLC;
MBBC; MH; NN.   12561

Gannett, Ezra Stiles, 1801-1871.
   An essay on the Demoniacs of
the New Testament. Boston,
Leonard C. Bowles, 1832. 50 p.
CtY; MB; MBAU; MH-AH; WHi.
                          12562
---- Sermon on death of Thom-
as Tarbell May 2, 1832. Boston,
1832. 16 p. PHi.   12563

Garden, Alexander, 1685-1756.
   Regeneration and the testimony
of the spirit: being the substance
of two sermons, preached in St.
Philip's, Charlestown: by The
Rev. Alex. Garden, A.M. Rector
of said Parish, and commissary
of the Bishop of London in South-
Carolina. Dedicated to the inhab-
itants of Charlestown, 1740.
Charleston, "The Protestant
Episcopal Society for the Ad-
vancement of Christianity in
South-Carolina." 1832. 23 p.
DLC.   12564

Gardiner, William, 1770-1853.
   The music of nature; or, An
attempt to prove that what is
passionate and pleasing is the art
of singing, speaking, and per-
forming upon musical instruments,
is derived from the sounds of the
animated world. With curious
and interesting illustrations, by
William Gardiner. Boston, Pr.
by Ditson, 1832. 505 p. CLCo;
IaGG; KU; MiOC; MPeaI; MW.
                          12565
Gardiner Lyceum. Gardiner, Me.
   Report of the Committee on
Literary Institutions of the petition
of the trustees of Gardiner Lyce-

um, February 26, 1832. Pr. by
order of the Senate. Augusta, I.
Berry & Co., 1832. 6 (2) p.
MeU.   12566

Gardner, C.
   Articles of faith, held at the
First Congregational Church, in
Lowell, examined, in a discourse
delivered in Lowell,...February
26, 1832... Lowell [Mass.?] Pr.
by Thomas Billings, 1832. 18 p.
NN.   12567

Garrison, William Lloyd, 1805-
1879.
   An address on the progress of
the abolition cause; delivered before the African abolition free-
hold society of Boston, July 16,
1832... Boston, Pr. by Garrison
and Knapp, 1832. 24 p. CtY;
OClWHi; PSC-Hi; RP; TNF.
                          12568
---- Thoughts on African Colonization: or, An impartial exhibition of the doctrines, principles
and purposes of the American
Colonization Society, together with
the resolutions, addresses and
remonstrances of the free people
of color, by Wm. Garrison and
Knapp, 1832. 160 p. ICU; KHi;
NcD; PPM; TNF; ViHal.   12569

Gaston, William.
   Address delivered before the
Philanthropic and Dialectic Soci-
eties at Chapel-Hill, June 20,
1832. Raleigh, Pr. by Jos. Gales
& Son, 1832. 16 p. NN; NjR;
OClWHi; PPPrHi; ScCC.   12570

---- ---- 2d ed. Richmond, 1832.
22 p. MB; MBAt; MH; PHi.
                          12571
Gavin, Anthony, fl. 1726.
   A master-key to popery; giving
a full account of all the customs
of the priests and friars and the
rights and ceremonies of the pop-
ish religion...To which is added
an account of the inquisition of

God... Cincinnati, B. Crosby,
1832. 420 p. IEG; KyLoP; MoK;
OClWHi; TxH.   12572

Gebauliche Lieder-Sammlung.
Philadelphia, George M. Mentz
and Co., 1832. PPeSchw.   12573

Des Geist-und troflreichen selig-
en Tohann arndts, meiland Gen-
eral-Superintendenten des Furft-
enlhums Luneburg, Paradiesgart-
leen, mie folche zur Uebung des
mahren Chriftenthums Durch
Geiflreiche Ceberte in de Geelen
zu pflanzen, dem bengefuget
Bierzehn Wundergefchichten
melche fich mit diefem Buch be-
geben, ingleichen Morgen-und
Ubendifegen auf alle Lage in der
Boche, mie auch ein drenfaches
Regifter, fo den Ruben und Ceb-
rauch dieses Buches meiset.
Philadelphia, Serausgegeben bon
Georg B. Mentz und Cohen, Buch-
handler, 1832. 224 p. ScCeT.
                               12574
Gemeinintzige Landwirth-Shafts
Calender. Lancaster, William
Albrecht [1832] MWA; PDoBHi;
PHi; PPL.   12575

Das Gemeinschaftliche gesang-
buch, zum gottesdienstlichen
gebrauch der lutherischen und reformirten gemeinden in Nord-
America. Auf verlangen der mei-
sten prediger beyder benennungen
gesammelt, und von den commit-
teen. Zweyer ministerien geprüft
und genehmiget. 6 aufl. Philadelphia, G. B. Mentz und sohn, 1832.
374 p. MH-AH; PloWyT; PReaHi;
TxU.   12576

General Theological Seminary of
the Protestant Episcopal Church
in the United States.
    The Act of Incorporation, Con-
stitution, and Statutes of, New
York, 1832. 22 p. MH.   12577

---- Proceedings of the board of

trustees, held in Trinity-Church,
New-York, October 10, 1832.
Published by order of the board.
New-York, Pr. by order of the
board, 1832. 42 p. CtHT; InID;
NNC.   12578

Genesee Sabbath School Union.
    Hymns for Sabbath schools.
Pub. by the Genesee Sabbath
School Union. 3d ed. Rochester,
Pr. by Hoyt, Porter & Co., 1832.
21 p. NRHi.   12579

Genesee Wesleyan Seminary,
Lima, New York.
    Officers, course of study, and
laws of the Genesee Wesleyan
Seminary, Lima, Livingston County, New-York. Canandaigua, Pr.
by Morse and Harvey, 1832. 15 p.
NLG.   12580

Genest, John, 1764-1839.
    Some account of the English
stage, from the restoration in
1660 to 1830. [Anon.] Boston,
1832. 10 v. IC.   12581

Gentleman's almanac and Pocket
Companion for 1833. Philadel-
phia, Thomas T. Ash [1832]
MWA.   12582

George Talbot; or, Samuel re-
formed. New Haven, Sidney's
Press; S. Babcock, 1832. 24 p.
CtY; MB; Mi.   12583

Georgia.
    Acts of the General Assembly
of the State of Georgia, passed
in Milledgeville at an annual session in November and December,
1831. Pub. by authority. Milledgeville, Pr. by Prince & Ragland,
1832. 344 p. G.   12584

---- Cherokee question. Report
of the Committee on the State of
the Republic, presented to the
Legislature of Georgia, December 15, 1831. Reprinted. [New

York, 1832] 8 p. NN.   12585

---- Journal of the House of Representatives of the State of Georgia, 1832. 432 p. G; GMilvC.
                              12586
The Georgia Almanac for 1833. By David Young. Augusta, Richards and Ganahl. [1832] 18 l. GEU.   12587

Gerando, Joseph Marie de, baron, 1772-1842.
  Self-education; or the means and art of moral progress. Tr. from the French of M. le baron Degarando. Boston, Carter and Hendee, 1832. 386 p. DLC; OMC; PPI; RP.   12588

---- The visitor of the poor; tr. from the French of the Baron Degerando, by a lady of Boston. With an introduction, by Joseph Tuckerman. Boston, Hilliard, Gray, Little and Wilkins, 1832. 211 p. DLC; MBAt; MH; NcD; ODW; PPA.   12589

Gerb, George.
  Retour de gloire. Rondo, pour le pianoforte. By George Gerb, Professor of Music. Philadelphia, George Willig, 1832. 4 p. MBNEC.   12590

Gerhard, William Wood, 1804-1872.
  Observations on the cholera of Paris by G. W. Pennock and W. W. Gerhard. Philadelphia, Skerrett, 1832. 76 p. NBMS; PPAN; PPN; PHi.   12591

Germain, R. I.
  An address, delivered July 4th, 1832, before the trustees and students of Canandaigua Academy. By R. I. Germain, (a student of the same.)... Canandaigua, Pr. by Morse & Harvey, 1832. 8 p. NCanHi; NCH.   12592

German Reformed Synod.
  Proceedings of the German Reformed Synod of Pennsylvania & adjacent States, held at Mechanicsburg, Cumberland Co., September 2nd, 3rd, 4th, and 5th. 1832. Reading, Pr. by John Ritter & Co., 1832. 23 p. PLT.
                              12593
German Society of Maryland.
  Constitution of the German Society of Maryland. Baltimore, John T. Hanzsche, 1832. 22 p. DLC; MdHi.   12594

---- Verfassung der Deutschen Gesellschaft in Maryland. Baltimore, J. T. Hanzsche, 1832. 22 p., 15 cm. Text in English and German. DLC; MdHi.   12595

Gessner, Solomon, 1730-1788.
  The death of Abel. In five books, from the German of Solomon Gessner. Baltimore, J. E. Harrod, 1832. 191 p. MdBD.
                              12596
Gettysburg College.
  Miscellaneous papers. Gettysburg, Pa., Pr. by H. C. Neinstedt, 1832-53. PPLT.   12597

---- Philomathaean Society.
  Catalogue of the Philomathaean Society of Pennsylvania College. Gettysburg, Pa., Pr. by H. C. Neinstedt, 1832. 72 p. NjP.
                              12598
Gibbs, Charles, 1794?-1831.
  Lives and trial of Gibbs and Wansley, executed for piracy. Boston, 1832. 310-328 p. MWA.
                              12599
Gibbs, Josiah Willard.
  A manual Hebrew and English lexicon, including the Biblical Chaldee. Designed particularly for beginners. 2d ed. rev. and enl. New-Haven, E. Howe; New-York, J. Leavitt, (etc., etc.) 1832. 236 p. CBPac; ICP; LU; NjR; PU.
                              12600

Gibson, John Mason.
A condensation of matter upon the anatomy, surgical operations and treatment of diseases of the eye... By John Mason Gibson... Baltimore, W. R. Lucas, 1832. 204 p. CtMW; ICJ; NNNAM; PU; RPB.   12601

Gibson, Robert, 1793-1837.
Strictures on a Pamphlet, published by a minority of the Eastern Subordinate Synod, of the Reformed Presbyterian Church. By Robert Gibson, Pastor of the Second Reform Presbyterian Church, in the city of New-York. New-York, Pr. at the Greenwich Printing Office, 1832. 26 p. NjR; PPPrHi.   12602

Gibson, Robert.
The theory and practice of surveying: containing all the instructions requisite for the skilful practice of this art, with a new set of accurate mathematical tables, by Robert Gibson. Illustrated by Copper-Plates. Newly arranged, improved, and enl., with useful selections, by James Ryan, New York, J & J. Harper, 1832. 248 p. MH; NvU; PBlv; ViU.   12603

Gibson, William, 1788-1868.
The institutes and practice of surgery: being the outlines of a course of lectures... 3d ed., with additions. Philadelphia, Carey & Lea, 1832. 2 v. CtY; GU-M; LUT-M; MBM; OU.   12604

Gilbert, Ann [Taylor] 1782-1866.
Hymns for infant minds chiefly by the author of original poems, rhymes for the nursery.... Rev. by the committee of publication of the American Sunday School Union. Philadelphia, American Sunday School Union, 1832. 85 p. ICBB; IaCrM.   12605

Gillpatrick, James, 1801?-1865.
The nature and remedy of intemperance. An address... by James Gillpatrick... Boston, Lincoln & Edmands, 1832. 19 p. MBAt; MeHi; NN; NNNAM.   12606

Gilly, William Stephen, 1789-1855.
A memoir of Felix Neff, pastor of the High Alps. By William Stephen Gilly... From the London ed., with notes. Boston, W. Hyde & co., 1832. 318 p. GDecCT; LNB; PU; ViU; WHi.   12607

---- ---- Philadelphia, Carey & Lea, 1832. 320 p. PPA.   12608

Gilman, Charles R.
Hints to the people on the prevention and early treatment of spasmodic cholera, by C. R. Gilman, M.D.   New York, Charles S. Francis, 1832. 15 (1) p. NjR; NNNAM; RNR.   12609

Gilmor, Robert, 1774-1848.
Catalogue of a collection of autographs in the possession of Robert Gilmor, of Baltimore, 1832. [Baltimore? 1832?] 52 p. MB; MH; MdHi; PPL.   12610

Gilpin, Henry D.
Address of Democratic Committee of Correspondence for city of Philadelphia. "The Missionaries and State of Georgia." Oct. 29, 1832. 4 p. PHi; PPL. 12611

Gilpin, Joshua.
Statements made to Congress in relation to a post road from Philadelphia to Baltimore. Washington, 1832. PPL.   12612

Girard, Stephen, 1750-1831.
The will of the late Stephen Girard, esq., procured from the office for the probate of wills, with a short biography of his life ... Philadelphia, T. and R. De-silver, 1832. 36 p. CtY; KHi;

MBC; ScCC; WHi.   12613

Girard almanack, for the year of
our Lord 1833, being the first
after Bisextile, or leap year, and
the 57th and 58th of American Independence. Carefully calculated
for the latitude meridian of Philadelphia, by Joseph Cramer.
Philadelphia, Thomas L. Bonsal
[1832] 34, [2] p. InU; MWA;
PPFM; WHi.   12614

Girard bank, Philadelphia.
    An Act to incorporate the Gi-
rard bank, of the city of Philadelphia. Approved April 3, 1832.
Philadelphia, Peter Hay & Co.,
prs., 1832. 44 p. MB; ScU.
                         12615
---- By-laws and rules of the
Girard bank in the city of Philadelphia. n.p., n. pub., Pr. by
Young, 1832. 8 p. NjR.   12616

Girard College.
    Under authority of resolutions
.... Philadelphia, 1832. Broadside. PPAmP.   12617

Girard journal of wealth, and
record and depository of benevolence. v. 1-Feb. 8, 1832-Phila-
delphia, 1832- MH.   12618

Girard Trusts.
    Ordinance for the management
of the Girard Trusts: September
15, 1832. Philadelphia, 1832.
12 p. PHi.   12619

---- Report of the committee,
appointed by the Select and Common Councils of Philadelphia to
digest a plan for the management
of the bequests of Stephen Girard.
Philadelphia, 1832. 6 p. PHi.
                         12620
The girls best ornament; with
other sketches, by the author of
the beautiful garden. Boston, J.
Loring, 1832. 107 p. DLC. 12621

Gleig, George Robert, 1796-1888.
    History of the Bible. New-
York, Harper, 1832. 2 v. MH;
Nj; OMC; RHi.   12622

Glover, Stephen E., d. 1869.
    The cradle of liberty: or, Bos-
ton in 1775... Correctly marked
and arranged by J. B. Wright...
New York, S. French, 1832. 39
p. C.   12623

Gobinet, Charles.
    The Instruction of Youth in
Christian Piety; taken out of the
Sacred Scriptures and Holy Fathers; from the French of Charles
Gobinet... Philadelphia, Cummiskey, 1832. 161-170 p. 2 vol. in
1. MdBS; MdW; OCX; PV. 12624

Goldsmith, Oliver, 1728-1794.
    The Grecian history, from the
earliest State to the death of Alexander the Great. By Dr. Goldsmith. Revised and corr., and
a vocabulary of proper names appended; with prosodial marks to
assist in their pronunciation. By
William Grimshaw. Philadelphia,
John Grigg, 1832. 2 v. in 1.
InEvC; KMK; MdW; MiD-B.
                         12625
---- The history of Rome from
the foundation of the city of Rome
to the destruction of the Western
empire... New York [1832] 258 p.
IU.   12626

---- A history of the earth and of
animals, in general. Chambersburg, Pa., Repub. by T. J.
Wright, 1832. 388 p. OSW; PHi;
TxU.   12627

---- The miscellaneous works of
Oliver Goldsmith, with an account
of his life and writings stereotyped from the Paris edition, edited by Washington Irving. Complete
in one vol. Philadelphia, J. Crissy
and J. Grigg, 1832. 527 p. LNT;
MiU; MSMer.   12628

---- Pinnock's improved edition of Dr. Goldsmith's history of England, from the invasion of Julius Ceasar to the death of George II. With a continuation to the year 1832...16th Amer., cor. and rev. from 24th Eng. ed. Philadelphia, Thomas Cowperthwait & Co., 1832. 468 p. PLFM.
12629

---- Roman history. For the use of schools; rev. and corr., and a vocabulary of proper names appended; with prosodial marks, to assist in their pronunciation. By William Grimshaw. Improved ed. Philadelphia, Grigg, 1832. 235 p. IaMpI; MdM; MoS; POilc. 12630

Gooch, Robert, 1784-1830.
An account of some of the most important diseases peculiar to women. By Robert Gooch, M.D. From 2d London ed. Philadelphia, E. L. Carey & A. Hart, 1832. 326 p. ArU-M; ICJ; KyLxT; MdBJ; WMAM. 12631

---- A practical compendium of midwifery; being the course of lectures on midwifery, and on the diseases of women and infants, delivered at St. Bartholomew's Hospital, by the late Robert Gooch, M.D. Prepared for publication by George Skinner... Philadelphia, E. L. Carey & A. Hart, 1832. 319 p. CSt-L; ICJ; LNOP; MdBJ; ViU. 12632

Good, John Mason, 1764-1827.
The book of nature...from the last London ed., to which is now prefixed a sketch of the author's life. Hartford, Belknap & Hamersley, 1832. 467 p. PBa; WGr.
12633

The Good Boy. Wendell, Mass., John Metcalf, 1832. 8 l. DLC; MA; MWA; PP. 12634

The good child's little hymn book. New York, Mahlon Day, 1832.

4 p. DLC. 12635

Good examples for children... New-York, Mahlon Day, 1832. 18 p. MH. 12636

The good-natured little boy. Norwich, N.Y., Pr. by Hubbard & Johnson, 1832. 12 p. DLC.
12637

Goode, William O.
The speech of William O. Goode, on the Abolition of Slavery; delivered in the House of Delegates of Virginia, on Tuesday, January 24, 1832. Richmond, Pr. by Thomas W. White, 1832. 33 p. MB; NcD; PHi; PPAmP; ViL.
12638

Goodheart, Mrs. (pseud.)
Progressive primer; adapted to infant school instruction. Concord, Moses G. Atwood, 1832. 35 p. MHi; Nh-Hi. 12639

Goodrich, Charles Augustus, 1700-1862.
Atlas accompanying C. A. Goodrich's Outlines of modern geography. Hartford, S. G. Goodrich [1832] unpaged. MH. 12640

---- The child's book on the creation: the first of a series of works on the Bible, on a similar plan. 2d ed. New Haven, Durrie, & Peck, 1832. CtHWatk; ICU; KyBC; MH; NBuG. 12641

---- Child's history of the United States designed as a first book of history for schools, illustrated by numerous anecdotes. [2d ed.] Boston, Carter & Hendee, 1832. 150 p. MNBedf; OCHP. 12642

---- A history of the United States of America, on a plan adapted to the capacity of youth... By Rev. Charles A. Goodrich. Bellow Falls, Vt., J. I. Cutler and Co., 1832. 296, 20 p. Ct; DLC; MShF; OClWHi. 12643

---- ---- 17th ed. Bellows Falls, James I. Cutler & Co. [1832] ICRL.   12644

---- ---- Hartford, D. F. Robinson & Co., 1832. 432 p. LJMac; WaPS.   12645

---- ---- 35th ed. Boston, Richard, Lord & Holbrook; New York, R. Lockwood; etc., etc. 1832? CtY; DLC; MB; MH; WaWW.   12646

---- Lives of the signers to the Declaration of independence, by ... Charles A. Goodrich. 2d ed. New York, T. Mather, 1832. 460 p. CU; IU; MdHi; NbU; Vi.
                                12647
---- ---- 3d ed. New York, T. Mather, 1832. 460 p. DLC; FMU; PMA.   12648

---- A new family encyclopedia; or, Compendium of universal knowledge. Ed. by Rev. Chas. A. Goodrich. 3d ed. Philadelphia, 1832. 468 p. CtY; MBC; MS; CU; WBelCHi.   12649

---- Outlines of modern geography, on a new plan, carefully adapted to youth, with numerous engravings of cities, manners, and curiosities, accompanied by an atlas, by Rev. Charles A. Goodrich... Boston, Richardson, Lord, & Holbrook [etc.] 1832. 252 p. MdBE; Tx.   12650

---- Religious ceremonies and customs; or The forms of worship... On the basis of the work of Bernard Picart. To which is added a brief view of minor sects which exist at the present day. Hartford, 1832. 576 p. PPDrop.   12651

Goodrich, Chauncy Allen, 1790-1860.
     Exercises in elocution. n.p.,

[183-?] 84 p. MH.   12652

---- Lessons in Greek parsing: or, Outlines of the Greek Grammar... By Chauncey A. Goodrich ...2d ed. New-Haven, Durrie & Peck, 1832. 138 p. IaAS; MH; NCH; OMC; TxU-T; WHi. 12653

---- Lessons in Latin parsing; containing the outlines of the Latin grammar, divided into short portions and exemplified by appropriate exercises in parsing. By Chauncey A. Goodrich, professor of rhetoric and oratory in Yale college. New Haven, Durrie & Peck, 1832. 197 p. CSt; DLC; MH; Nh; OO.   12654

Goodrich, Samuel Griswold, 1793-1860.
     Atlas designed to illustrate the Malte-Brun School geography... Hartford, F. J. Huntington, 1832. 21 p. CtY; MB; MH; NN; PHi.
                                12655
---- A book of Mythology, for youth... Boston, Richardson, Lord and Holbrook, 1832. 121 p. CtY; DLC; MB; Nh; PU-Penn; RPB.
                                12656
---- A Book of ornithology, for youth. See under title.

[----] A book of quadrupeds, for youth, embracing descriptions of the most interesting and remarkable quadrupeds in all countries, with particular notices of those in America... New York, P. Hill, 1832. 324 p. DLC; MB; MiGr.
                                12657
[----] The child's book of American Geography; designed as an easy and entertaining work for use of beginners... Boston, Carter, & Hendee [etc.] 1832. 64 p. CTHWatk; CtY; MH; NNC; P.
                                12658
---- Child's botany. 5th ed. Boston, Carter & Hendee, 1832. 103 p. MH; MSaP; NIC.   12659

[----] The child's geology. By the author of "The child's botany." Rev. and enl. by Mrs. Almira H. L. Phelps... Brattleboro, G. H. Peck & Co. [etc., etc.] 1832. 132 p. CSmH; MH; NNB; RPB; VtBT.   12660

---- Les contes de Pierre Parley sur l'Amérique ... Boston, Carter & Hendee, 1832. 144 p. CtY; MH; NNG; MnU; OHi.   12661

[----] The first book of history. For children and youth by the author of Peter Parley's tales... Boston, Richardson, Lord and Holbrook, 1832. 180 p. MH; NN; OCIW.   12662

[----] ---- New York, Collins & Hannay [etc., etc.] 1832. 180 p. NN.   12663

[----] ---- Philadelphia, Key & Meilke & Biddle, 1832. DLC; ICU.   12664

[----] A new Universal Pocket Gazeteer, containing descriptions of the most remarkable empires, kingdoms, nations, states, tribes, cities, towns, villages, mountains, islands, rivers, seas, lakes, cataracts, canals, and railroads, in the known world, With notices of manners, customs, religion, governments, laws, arts, commerce, manufactures, and population. Boston, William Hyde & Co., and Richardson, Lord & Holbrook, 1832. 297 p. CoCsC; CtY; In; MB; OCHP; PU.   12665

---- Outlines of chronology, ancient and modern; an introduction to the study of history, on the plan of Rev. D. Blair; accompanied by a chart. Boston, Richardson, Lord & Holbrook, 1832. CSmH; IaGG; NN; PU.   12666

---- Peter Parley's book of curiosities, natural and artificial. Illustrated by one hundred engravings. Boston, Richardson, Lord & Holbrook [etc.] 1832. 224 p. DLC; MH; ViU.   12667

---- ---- New York, Collins and Hannay; Boston, Richardson, Lord & Holbrook; etc., etc., 1832. 224 p. DLC.   12668

---- Peter Parley's juvenile tales ...Boston, Carter & Hendee & Gray & Bowen, 1832. 91 p. MFiHi.   12669

[----] Peter Parley's method of telling about geography to children. New York, Collins & Hannay, 1832. MH.   12670

[----] Peter Parley's method of telling about the history of the world to children. Illustrated by seventy five engravings. Hartford, F. J. Huntington, 1832. [10]-144 p. DLC.   12671

[----] Peter Parley's Tales about ancient and modern Greece... New York, Collins & Hannay; Boston, Richardson, Lord & Holbrook, etc., etc. [1832] 202 p. DLC; MH; MWA; TU; TxU.   12672

[----] Peter Parley's tales about Great Britain; including England, Wales, Scotland, and Ireland... Baltimore, J. Jewett, 1832. 160 p. DLC; NjP; OU; ViU.   12673

[----] Peter Parley's tales about South America... Baltimore, J. Jewett, 1832. 172 p. DLC; NNC; ViU.   12674

[----] Peter Parley's tales about the state and city of New York. Illustrated by a map and many engravings. For the use of schools. New York, Pendleton & Hill, 1832.

DLC; MH; NjR; PP; T.   12675

[----] Peter Parley's tales of animals; containing descriptions of 300 quadrupeds...2d ed. with many corrections and improvements, and adapted to the use of schools. Boston, Carter & Hendee, 1832. 343 p. DCU; MH; ViU.   12676

[----] Peter Parley's tales of the sea with many engravings. Boston, Gray & Bowen and Carter & Hendee, 1832. 144 p. MiHi.   12677

[----] The second book of history, including the modern history of Europe, Africa and Asia, Designed as a sequel to the "First book of history." Baltimore, Cushing and sons, 1832. ICRL; MH; OOxM.   12678

---- ---- Baltimore, J. J. Harrod, 1832. 180 p. MH; OOxM.   12679

---- ---- Boston, Carter, Hendee & Co., 1832. 180 p. DLC; MB; MH.   12680

---- ---- New York, Collins & Hannay, 1832. MH.   12681

---- ---- Philadelphia, Key, Meikle and Biddle, 1832. 180 p. MH; NjR.   12682

---- A system of school geography, chiefly derived from Malte-Brun, and arranged according to the inductive plan of instruction. By S. Griswold Goodrich. 2d ed. Hartford, F. J. Huntington [etc., etc.] 1832. 288 p. AU; CSt; MB; OClWHi; RPB; TxU.   12683

---- A system of universal geography, popular and scientific, comprising...the world and its various divisions; Baltimore, W. & J. Neal, 1832. 920 p. MAm; MdHi; PU.   12684

---- ---- Boston, Carter, Hendee & Co., 1832. 920 p. CtHWatk; MBAt; MH; MeBa; Nh.   12685

---- ---- Cincinnati, Roffe & Young, 1832. 920, (2) p. DLC; NIC; NRU; O.   12686

---- ---- New York, Collins & Hannay, 1832. [9]-920 p. NcD; OSW; ViU; WBeloC.   12687

---- ---- Philadelphia, Key, Mielke & Biddle, 1832. 920 p. KyLo; MB; N; PPM; ScSp. 12688

[----] The tales of Peter Parley, [pseud.] about America. 13th ed. Boston, Carter & Hendee and Gray & Brown, 1832. MBAt; MH.   12689

[----] The universal school atlas, arranged on the inductive plan, and designed to render the study of geography both easy and instructive... Baltimore, J. Jewett, 1832. 45 p. CtY; MH.   12690

---- Ton Paidion e geographia. Upo Petrou tou Omiletou. Melite, 1832. 112 p. OO.   12691

Goodwin, Philo Ashley, 1807-1873.
    Biography of Andrew Jackson, president of the United States, formerly major general in the army of the United States; by Philo A. Goodwin. Hartford, Clapp & Benton, 1832. 422 p. CtY; DLC; KyU; WaU; ViW.   12692

Goodwin, Stephen A.
    An oration delivered at Auburn, Cayuga C. (N. Y.) on the fourth day of July, 1832, by Stephen A. Goodwin. Auburn, Pub. at the office of the Cayuga Patriot, 1832. 16 p. CSmH; CtMW; MBC; NCH.   12693

Gordon, Alexander.
    Catalogue of fruit trees, ornamental trees, ornamental shrubs, flowering plants, kitchen garden,

herb, and flower seeds, for sale
at the Rochester nursery, on
Main Street, by Alexander Gordon. Rochester, Pr. by Hoyt,
Porter & Co., 1832. 16 p. N.
                              12694
Gordon, Thomas Francis, 1787-
1860.
   A gazetteer of the state of
Pennsylvania. Part first; contains
a general description of the state,
its situation and extent, general
geological construction, canals and
railroads, bridges, revenue expenditures, public debt. Part second; embraces ample descriptions
of its counties, towns, cities, villages, mountains, lakes, rivers,
creeks. Alphabetically arranged.
By Thomas F. Gordon. To which
is added a table of all the post offices in the state, their distances
from Washington and Harrisburg,
and the names of the Post Masters. With a map of the state.
Philadelphia, By T. Belknap,
1832. 500 p. CoD; DLC; MWA;
NN; PP; PPA.   12695

---- The history of America. By
Thomas F. Gordon. Volumes first
and second, containing the history
of the Spanish discoveries prior
to 1520... Philadelphia, Pr. for
the author, 1832. 2 v. ICN; NNA;
NjR; PPL; TNP.   12696

---- The history of ancient Mexico; from the foundation of that
empire to its destruction by the
Spaniards...By Thomas F. Gordon...Philadelphia, The author,
1832. 2 v. CU; MH; NbOM;
PPA; PU; TxDa.   12697

Gosden, J. I.
   I ne'er will forsake thee.
Adapted to Count de Gallenburg's
celebrated waltz. Written, ar-
ranged, and dedicated to Miss Mc-
Evers, by J. I. Gosden. Balti-
more, John Cole, 1832. 2 p.
ViU.   12698

Gottfried, Geshe Marg.
   Life of Geshe Marg Gottfried.
Trans. by E. Friederici. Gettys-
burg, Pa., n.p., 1832. 79 p.
PHi.   12699

Gould, Hannah Flagg, 1789-1865.
   Poems by Miss H. F. Gould.
Boston, Hilliard, Gray, Little &
Wilkins [1832] 174 p. IU; MWA;
NNUT; RPB; TxU.   12700

Gould, James, 1770-1838.
   A treatise on the principles of
pleading in civil actions, by James
Gould. Boston, Lilly & Wait, 1832.
536 p. FTU; IU; NNLI; RPB; WU-
L.   12701

Gould, Marcus Tullius Cicero,
1793-1860.
   The art of shorthand writing;
comp. from the latest European
publications, with sundry improvements...Stereotype ed. Cincinnati,
H. L. Barnum, 1832. 45, 3 p.
MiU-C; OCIWHi; PU; WaSp.
                         12702
Gould, Nathaniel Duren, 1781-
1864.
   National church harmony, designed for public and private devotion, in two parts. Music arranged for the organ and piano
forte, by introducing small notes.
Edited by N. D. Gould. Boston,
Lincoln & Edmands, and Crocker
& Brewster [etc., etc.] 1832.
289 p. CtY; ICN; MB; MH; NN.
                         12703
---- ---- 2d ed. Boston, Lincoln
& Edmands, 1832. 289 p. CtY;
MB; NRES; RPB; WHi.   12704

---- Penmanship; or, The beauties of writing. Hartford, Andrew Dodd, 1832. PPM.   12705

Gowen, James.
   Irish eloquence. Speeches of
Mr. James Gowen, and Mr. Haly,
at the Irish Anti-Jackson meeting
held in Philadelphia on the 6

August, 1832. n.p. 1832. 12 p.
MdBP; NN.   12706

Graham, David, 1808-1852.
A Treatise on the Practice of
the Supreme Court of the State of
New-York. By David Graham, Jun.
Counsellor at Law. New York,
Gould Banks & Co. , and W. & A.
Gould & Co. , Albany, 1832. 848 p.
CU; MiD; NbCrD; NcD; NRAL.
                                  12707
Graham, Samuel L.
Revivals of religion: a ser-
mon... before the Synod of North
Carolina, at Hillsborough, N.C. ,
Oct. 15, 1831. Hillsborough, 1832.
20 p. MBC; NcU.   12708

Granger, Arthur.
Divine truth practically illus-
trated. A sermon preached at the
dedication of the Orthodox Congre-
gational Meeting House in Med-
field, April 17, 1832. By Arthur
Granger, Minister of the Gospel.
Pub. by request. Boston, Pr. by
Peirce & Parker, 1832. 24 p.
MBC; MeBat; MWA; RPB;
VtMidbC.   12709

Granger, Ralph.
Address made to the Agricultural Society of Geauga County, at
its annual meeting, in September,
1832... [Painesville, O. , Henry
Sexton] 1832? 16 p. OClWHi.
                                  12710
Granville, Augustus Bozzi, 1783-
1872.
A catechism of facts, or Plain
and simple rules respecting the
nature, treatment, and prevention
of Cholera. By A. B. Granville...
Baltimore, G. M'Dowell & sons,
1832. 108 p. CtY; DLC; DNLM;
DSG.   12711

---- ---- Philadelphia, E. L.
Carey & A. Hart, 1832. 11-108 p.
DLC; MeB; NBMS; PPCC; PPL.
                                  12712
Gray, Francis Calley, 1790-1856.

Discourse delivered before the
American institute of instruction
at the opening of their third course
of lectures, Aug. 23, 1832. By
Francis C. Gray. Boston, Carter,
Hendee & co. , 1832. 21 p.
CSansS; MB; MH; MHi; PPmP.
                                  12713
---- Oration delivered before the
legislature of Massachusetts... on
the hundredth anniversary of the
birth of George Washington... Boston, Dutton & Wentworth, prs. to
the state, 1832. 80 p. ICU; KHi;
PU; ScCC; WHi.   12714

[Gray, Frederick Turell]
An address delivered before
the teachers of the Howard Sunday
School, September, 1832. By F.
T. Gray. Boston, Benjamin H.
Green, 1832. 18 p. ICMe; M; MB;
MBAt.   12715

---- The Sunday school teacher's
reward: An address delivered before the teachers of the Hancock
Sunday School, on the removal of
that school to the Vestry of the
Second Church, March 31, 1832,
by F. T. Gray. Boston, Benjamin
H. Greene, S. G. Simpkins, 1832.
25 p. ICMe; MB; MBAt; MH; MHi.
                                  12716
Gray, John F.
The policy of chartering colleges of medicine; being an introductory lecture to a course on the
theory and practice of physic, delivered Monday, November 5, 1832,
by John F. Gray. New York, Henry Ludwig, 1832. 31 p. NBMS.
                                  12717
Great Britain. Court of King's
Bench.
Reports of cases argued and
determined in the Court of King's
Bench, with tables of the names
of the cases and the principal
matters. By George Maule and
William Selwyn, Esqs. Ed. by
Theron Metcalf. Boston, Lilly,
Wait, Colman & Holden, 1832.

6 vol. in 2. Ct; LNB; NcD; OO;
WaU.   12718

---- Courts.
Reports of some recent decisions by the Consistorial court of
Scotland, in actions of divorce,
concluding for dissolution of mar-
riages celebrated under the English law. By James Fergusson,
[1811-1817]. Philadelphia, P. H.
Nicklin and T. Johnson, 1832.
ICLaw.   12719

---- Parliament. House of Com-
mons. Select Committee on
Steam Carriages.
Report on Steam Carriages,
by a Select Committee of the
House of Commons of Great Brit-
ain: with the Minutes of Evidence
and Appendix. Reprinted by order
of the House of Representatives.
[U. S.] Washington, Pr. by Duff
Green, 1832. 346 p.   CtHT; MBL;
PPAPU; ScCC; ViL.   12720

Great meeting of Irishmen at
Philadelphia. The call and proceedings of the naturalized Irish
citizens of Philadelphia City and
county, in the state house yard,
August 6, 1832, to adopt measures to prevent the re-election of
Andrew Jackson, to the presidency
of the United States; because of
his utter abandonment of those
principles which had induced them
heretofore to support him. [Phila-
delphia] Bragh, 1832. 24 p.
MBAt; PHi; ScU.   12721

Green, Jacob, 1790-1841.
A monograph of trilobites of
North America; with coloured
models of the species.... By
Jacob Green, M. D. ... Philadel-
phia, Joseph Brano 1832. 93 p.
CtY; ICU; MiU; PPA; TxU; WHi.
                            12722
---- Text-book of Chemical Phi-
losophy. Philadelphia, 1832. NN.
                            12723

The Green Mountain repository;
for the year 1832. Ed. by Z.
Thompson... Burlington, Pr. by
E. Smith, 1832. 284 p. CtY; DLC;
MB; OHi; VtU.   12724

Greenfield (Mass.). Boarding
School for Young Men.
Report of the teachers of the
Greenfield Boarding School for
Young Men, conducted on the
self-supporting system of educa-
tion. Greenfield, Phelps, 1832.
10 p. CtHW; MWA; ScCC. 12725

---- High School for Young
Ladies.
Outline of Plan of Education
at ---- with catalogue for 1831-
32. Greenfield, 1832. CtHWatk;
OCHP.   12726

Greenhow, Thomas Michael, 1791-
1881.
Cholera, as it recently appeared
in the towns of Newcastle and Gat-
ishead; including cases illustrative
of its physiology and pathology,
with a view to the establishment
of sound principles of practice.
By T. M. Greenhow... Philadelphia,
Carey & Lea, 1832. 168 p. CtMW;
MB; Nh; PPCP; TNV.   12727

Greenwood, Francis William Pitt,
1797-1843.
The Christian and national
church, a sermon preached at the
installation of the Rev. James W.
Thompson over the Independent
Congregational church in Salem
March 7, 1832. Boston, Gray,
1832. 39 p. CtSoP; ICMe; NHi;
NjR; PPAmP.   12728

---- A collection of psalms and
hymns for Christian worship. 5th
ed. Boston, Carter & Hendee,
1832. IEG; IU; MH-AH; MHi;
MMeT.   12729

---- ---- 6th ed. Boston, Carter
& Hendee, 1832. IEG; MB. 12730

---- ---- 7th ed. Boston, Carter
& Hendee, 1832. (560 hymns).
MBNMHi; MWHi; RBr.   12731

---- ---- 8th ed. Boston, 1832.
[428] p. MH-AH; MHi.   12732

---- Prayer for the sick. A sermon preached at King's chapel,
Boston, on Thursday, Aug. 9,
1832, being the Fast day appointed by the governor of Massachusetts, on account of the appearance of cholera... Boston, Bowles,
1832. 13 p. CBPac; DLC; ICMe;
MWA; NjR.   12733

Gregory, George, 1754-1808.
Dr. Gregory's history of the
Christian church; from the earliest periods to the present time.
Rev. and imp., with numerous
additions... exhibiting the present
state and prospects of the Christian world. By Martin Ruter...
Cincinnati, Roff & Young, 1832.
637 p. DLC; In; NcD; UPB; WU.
                        12734
Gregory, John, 1724-1773.
A father's legacy to his daughters, with a biographical sketch
of the author. A mother's advice
to her absent daughters, with an
additional letter, on the management and education of infant children, by Lady Pennington. Boston, Bowles, 1832. CtY; MWA.
                        12735
---- ---- Worcester, 1832.
148 p. MWA; RPJCB.   12736

Gregory, Olinthus Gilbert, 1774-
1841.
Letters to a friend on the evidences, doctrines & duties of the
Christian religion. New York,
American Tract Society, 1832.
480 p. P.   12737

Grew, Henry, 1781-1862.
A tribute to the memory of the
apostles, and an exhibition of the
first Christian churches. Hart-

ford, Pr. by G. W. Kappel, 1832.
69 p. CtSoP; MBAt; PPL; ScCC;
WHi.   12738

[Grierson, Miss]
Pierre and his family; or, A
story of the Waldenses...Rev. by
the committee of publication.
Philadelphia, American Sunday
School Union, 1832. 214 p. NcD;
NjP; PPT.   12739

---- ---- Richmond (Va.), Pub.
by E. Thompson Baird [1832]
192 p. NcD; NcMHi; ScCliTO.
                        12740
Griffin, Edward Dorr.
A letter to the Rev. Ansel D.
Eddy, of Canandaigua, N.Y. on
the narrative of the late revivals
of religion, in the Presbytery of
Geneva. Williamstown, Pr. by
Ridley Bannister, 1832. 12 p.
CtHC; ICU; MH-AH; NN; PPPrHi.
                        12741
---- A letter to the Rev. Dr.
William B. S. Sprague: published
in the appendix of his volume of
lectures on revivals. Albany,
Packard & Van Benthuysen, 1832.
17 p. CtY-D; MH-AH; MWiW;
NjPT; PPPrHi.   12742

Grigg, John, 1792-1864.
Grigg's southern and western
songster, being a choice collection
of the most fashionable songs,
many of which are original. New
ed., greatly enl. Philadelphia, J.
Grigg, 1832. 324 p. CtY; DLC;
MB; MH; ScU.   12743

[Grim, Charles Frederic]
An essay towards an improved
register of deeds. City and county
of New York. To December 31,
1799, inclusive. New York, Gould,
Banks & co., 1832. 371 p. C;
MiD-B; NBuG; NNLI. WHi.
                        12744
Grimke, Thomas Smith, 1786-
1834.
Address at the celebration of

the Sunday school jubilee; or,
The fiftieth year from the institution of Sunday schools by Robert Raikes, delivered at
Charleston, S. C. ... Sept. 14,
1831. By Thomas Smith Grimke.
Philadelphia (n. p. , n. p.) 1832.
20 p. CtY; NbOP; NjPT; PHi;
PPPrHi.   12745

---- Address on the truth, dig-
nity, power and beauty of the
principles of peace, and on the
unchristian character and influence of war and the warrior delivered...at New Haven...At the request of the Connecticut Peace
Society... the 6th of May, 1832;
By Thomas S. Grimke... Hartford, Pr. by G. F. Olmsted,
1832. 56 p. CtHC; ICU; NjR;
PPL; TxU.   12746

---- A letter to the Hon. John
C. Calhoun, Vice President of
the United States, Robert Y.
Hayne, Senator of the United
States, George McDuffie of the
House of Representatives of the
United States, and James Hamil-
ton, Jr. Governor of the State of
S. Carolina. By Thomas S. Grim-
ke. Philadelphia, Pr. by Thos.
Kite & Co. , 1832. 17 p. ArU;
CtY; IaPeC; MdHi; NjR.   12747

---- ---- 2d ed. Charleston, Pr.
by James S. Burges, 1832. 15 p.
CtY; MBC; MiD-B; OCHP; PHi.
                               12748
---- Oration on the duties of
Youth to instructors and them-
selves: on the importance of the
art of speaking, and of debating
societies: delivered by appointment, before the Euphradion Society of the College of Charleston,
on Monday 13th August, 1832, in
the College Chapel. Charleston,
Miller, 1832. 28 p. CSansS; KHi;
NcD; ScC; TxU.   12749

---- To the people of South Car-

olina. Charleston, 1832. 16 p.
IEG; MH; PHi; ScU; ViU.   12750

Grimshaw, William, 1782-1852.
   History of England, from the
first invasion by Julius Caesar,
to the ascension of William the
Fourth. By William Grimshaw.
Philadelphia, Grigg & Elliot,
1832. 318 p. IU; MsCliM; Nh-Hi;
NjR; PWaybu; TBrik.   12751

---- The history of France,
from the foundation of the mon-
archy to the death of Louis XVI.
Interspersed with entertaining
anecdotes, and biographies of
eminent men. By William Grimshaw, author of A History of the
United States, &c. Baltimore,
Joseph Jewett, 1832. 302 p. CtY;
ICBB; PHi.   12752

---- History of the United States,
from their first settlement as
colonies, to the period of the fifth
census, in 1830... By William
Grimshaw... Philadelphia, Grigg
& Elliott, 1832. 326 p. IU; MiD;
NNC; TxU; ViL.   12753

---- Key, adopted to the Question
for Ramsay's Life of Washington,
as revised... Baltimore, Jewett,
1832. 40 p. DLC; NN.   12754

---- The life of Napoleon, with
the history of France, from the
death of Louis XVI to the year
1821...Baltimore, J. Jewett
[c. 1829] 1832. ICBB; OSW; PHi.
                               12755
---- Questions adapted to Ramsay's life of Washington, as revised and enl. by William Grimshaw... Baltimore, J. Jewett &
Cushing & Sons, 1832. 41 p.
DLC.   12756

Griscom, John.
   School discipline essay...read
before the American Lyceum, May
5, 1832. [Boston, 1832] IU; NN.
                               12757

Grosch, George.
Das neue allgemeine gesang-
büchlein, zum gebrauch aller
aufrichtigen Christen. Aus den
besten autoren zusammen getragen
und nach der neuern Kirchen-
Musik eingerichtet. Von George
Grosch und Jacob Meyers. 1. aufl.
Lancaster [Pa.] J. Bär, 1832.
MiU-C; NN; PPL; PSt; RPB.
                                    12758
Grosh, Aaron Burt, 1803-1884.
Zion's Property; A sermon,
delivered in Norwich, Chenago
County, New-York, Sunday, No-
vember 4th, 1832. Being the day
recommended by many Universal-
ists as a day of public Thanks-
giving. Pub. by request of the
Congregation. Utica, Pr. [by
Grosh & Hutchinson] 1832. 12 p.
MMeT.   12759

Grou, Jean Nicholas, 1731-1803.
The portraiture of true devotion, written originally in French
by the Abbe Grou, new translation and arrangement... Baltimore, F. Lucas, 1832. viii,
195 p. DCU; MdBS; MdW; MoSU.
                                    12760
Groves, John.
A Greek and English dictionary,
comprising all the words in the
writings of the most popular
Greek authors; with the difficult
inflections in them and in the Sep-
tuagint and New Testament: designed for the use of schools and
the undergraduate course of a
collegiate education. By the Rev.
John Groves, with corrections
and additional matter, by the
American editor. Boston, Hilliard, Gray, Little, & Wilkins,
1832. 615, 102 p. MA; MdLuW;
MdW; NbOP; OCl.   12761

Grund, Francis Joseph, 1805-
1863.
An elementary treatise on
geometry, simplified for beginners not versed in algebra. Part

1, containing plane geometry,
with its application to the solution of problems. By Francis J.
Grund. 3d ed. stereotyped. Boston, Carter & Hendee, 1832.
190 p. KWiU; MH; RPB.   12762

---- ---- Part II, containing solid geometry, with its application
to the solution of the problems,
by Francis J. Grund. 2d ed.
Boston, Carter, Hendee & co.,
1832. 159 p. InNd; MdHi; PPM;
RPB; TxU-T.   12763

---- Elements of natural philosophy, with practical exercises...
Boston, Carter & Hendee, 1832.
278 p. CtMW; GHi; MH; NjP;
RP.   12764

Grundy, Felix, 1777-1840.
Speech of the Honorable Felix
Grundy, (of Tennessee) on the
tariff. Delivered February 15,
1832, in the Senate of the United
States, on Mr. Clay's resolution.
Washington, n.p., 1832. 27 p.
KyDC; NcH; ScU; TxU; WHi.
                                    12765
Guide to Piety: A memento of
affection from Christian pastors.
Newburyport, Charles Whipple,
1832. 96 p. DLC; MNe; NN.
                                    12766
Gulliver, Verigull, pseud.
A fragment of the voyages of
Mr. Verigull Gulliver, (grandson
to the celebrated traveller) to the
island of Ae-ri-si-ter, in the
lake of Spe-cul, situated in the
province of Fo-li, a part of China
hitherto unexplored, &c. (Middle
Hill Press, 1832.) 5 p. DLC;
MH.   12767

Gummere, John, 1784-1845.
A treatise on surveying, containing the theory and practice:
to which is prefixed a perspicuous
system of plane trigonometry. The
whole clearly demonstrated and illustrated by a large number of ap-

propriate examples, particularly
adapted to the use of schools.
By John Gummere... 6th ed. , im-
proved. Philadelphia, Kimber &
Sharpless, 1832. 216 p. DLC;
InNd; MdW; OO; PU.   12768

Gurley, Ralph Randolph, 1797-
1872.
    Letter on the American coloni-
zation society, and remarks on
South Carolina opinions on that
subject. By R. R. Gurley.
[Washington? 1832] 16 p. CtY;
DLC; ICN; RP; ScU.   12769

Gurney, Joseph John, 1788-1847.
    Observations on the religious
peculiarities of the Society of
Friends... 2d Amer. ed. Phila-
delphia, N. Kite, 1832. 331 p.
CSansS; InRchE; MnU; NIC; PPi.
                            12770
Guy, Joseph, 1784-1867.
    Guy's elements of astronomy,
and an abridgment of Keith's
New treatise on the use of the
globes. New Amer. ed. , with
additions and improvements...
Philadelphia, Key, Mielke &
Biddle, 1832. viii, 136, 173 p.
DLC; InNd; MBAt; PU; TxD-T.
                            12771

                  H

Hackley, Philo.
    Partial description of his
steam generator. Herkimer,
N.Y., 1832.   12772

Hadley, Alfred.
    The infantile instructor. Indi-
anapolis, Pr. by Douglas & Mc-
Guire, 1832. 18 p. In.   12773

Hadley, Mass. First Church.
    First Church in Hadley. Con-
fession of faith, and catalogue of
members. April 1, 1832. Northampton, Pr. by T. W. Shepard,
1832. 24 p. DLC; MHad.   12774

The Hagerstown Town and Country almanack for 1833. By
Charles F. Egelmann. Hagerstown, J. Gruber [1832]   12775

[Hale, James W.]
    An historical account of the
Siamese twin brothers, from ac-
tual observations... 5th ed. New
York, Pr. by Elliott & Palmer,
1832. 16 p. CtY; DLC; MNe;
NCH; NcD.   12776

---- ---- 6th ed. New York, Pr.
by Elliott & Palmer, 1832. 16 p.
DNLM; PMA.   12777

---- ---- 7th ed. New York, Pr.
by Elliott & Palmer, 1832. 16 p.
OCHP; TxU.   12778

---- ---- 9th ed. New York, Pr.
by Elliott and Palmer, 1832.
16 p. ScCMu.   12779

[Hale, Salma] 1787-1866.
    History of the United States,
from their first settlement as
colonies, to the close of the War
with Great Britain in 1815. To
which is added questions, adapted
to the use of schools. Keene,
N.H., J. & J. W. Prentiss, 1832.
298 p. MH; ViU.   12780

---- An oration delivered at
Keene, N.H. February 22, 1832,
being the Centennial Anniversary
of the Birth-Day of Washington.
By Salma Hale. Keene, N.H.,
Geo. Tilden, 1832. 28 p. DLC;
MBAt; MH; Nh; ViW.   12781

Hale, Sarah Josepha (Buell),
1788-1879.
    Flora's interpreter: or, The
American book of flowers and
sentiments. By Mrs. S. J. Hale
... Boston, Marsh, Capen &
Lyon, 1832. 223, [3] p. CtY;
ICU; MB; NcD; RNR.   12782

---- ---- 2d ed. , rev. Boston,

Marsh, Capen & Lyon, 1832.
14-224 p. MB; NN.   12783

Hall, B. F.
A discourse on Christian Union, delivered in Little Rock,
A. T., July 4th, 1832. By B. F.
Hall.... Little Rock, Pr. for
the author, by Wm. E. Woodruff,
1832. 42 p. TxU.   12784

Hall, Charles.
The daily expositor for the
Acts. New York, Haven, 1832.
2 v. in 1. MBC; NCH; NNUT.
                          12785

Hall, Edward Brooks.
What is it to be a Unitarian?
By Edward B. Hall. Pr. for the
American Unitarian Association.
Boston, Gray & Bowen... Pr. by
I. R. Butts, 1832. DLC; ICMe;
MB; MeB; MMeT-Hi.   12786

---- ---- 2d ed. Boston, L. C.
Bowles, 1832. 24 p. CBPac;
ICMe; MB-HP; MH; RPB. 12787

Hall, James, 1793-1868.
Legends of the West. By
James Hall... Philadelphia, H.
Hall, 1832. 265 p. CSmH; IGK;
MBAt; NNS; OClWHi.   12788

Hall, John.
The life of Rev. Henry Martyn
with some account of Abdool Mes-
seeh, a Hindoo convert. Rev. by
the committee of publication.
Philadelphia, American Sunday
School Union, 1832. 246 p.
KyLoP; NjT; OO; PPPrHi. 12789

Hall, Robert, 1764-1831.
The works of the Rev. Robert
Hall, A. M. Memoir and a sketch
of his literary character, by the
Rt. Hon. Sir J. Mackintosh, LL. D.
M. A. and a sketch of his char-
acter as a theologian and a
preacher, by the Rev. John
Foster... New York, J. & J.
Harper, 1832. 3 vols. GHi;

LNB; OMC; PPL; TNT.   12790

Hall, Samuel Read, 1795-1877.
The arithmetical manual. By
S. R. Hall... Andover [Mass.]
Flagg, Gould & Newman, 1832.
288 p. DLC; IAlS; MAnP; NhD;
OMC.   12791

---- The Child's Instructer (sic)
or lessons on common things.
By S. R. Hall. Andover, Flagg
and Gould, 1832. 140 p. CtY;
MDovC; OClWHi.   12792

---- The Grammatical Assistant
containing definitions in Etymology, rules of syntax, and selections for passing. By S. R. Hall.
Springfield, Merriam, Little & co.,
1832. 130 p. CoGrS; CtHWatk;
DLC; MBAt; MH.   12793

---- Lectures on school-keeping;
4th ed. By Samuel R. Hall...
Boston, Richardson, Lord & Holbrook, 1832. 100 p. DHEW; MWA;
NBuG; OO; WbeloC.   12794

---- Lextures to female teachers
on school-keeping. By S. R. Hall,
Boston, Richardson, Lord & Holbrook, 1832. 179 p. ICU; MiU;
NjR; OO; TxU.   12795

Hall, William McClay, 1801-1851.
Address... to the Mifflin Coun-
ty Temperance Society, on Tues-
day, evening, February 28, 1832.
Lewistown, Pa., Pr. by Geo. W.
Patton, 1832. 16 p. CSmH; PHi;
PPPrHi.   12796

Hallet, Benjamin Franklin, 1797-
1862, ed.
A legislative investigation into
masonry being a correct history
of the examination, under civil
oath of more than fifty adhering
and seeding masons, before a
committee of the General Assembly of Rhode Island, held at Providence and Newport, between De-

cember 7, 1831 and January 7,
1832...[Boston] Office of the Boston daily advocate, 1832. 85 p.
DLC; IaCrM; MHi; ScU; WHi.
                                    12797
[Hambden, pseud.]
    Strictures on Mr. Lee's Ex-
position of evidence on the sugar
duty, in behalf of the committee
appointed by the Free-trade Convention. [Boston, Mass., 1832]
18 p. GEU; MWA; NN.   12798

Hamburger Familien Kalender
auf 1833. Fremont, Stausmyer's
Park, Drug store [1832] 32 p.
OFH.   12799

Hamilton, James, 1786-1857.
    ... Important correspondence
on the subject of state interposition, between His Excellency Gov.
Hamilton, and Hon. John C. Calhoun, vice-president of the United
States...Charleston, Pr. by A. E.
Miller for the association, 1832.
27 p. CtY; ICU; MBAt; NcU;
ScCC; WHi.   12800

Hamilton, William T.
    Grounds of thanksgiving: A
discourse delivered in the First
Presbyterian Church, Newark,
N.J. December 8, 1831, on the
occasion of public thanksgiving.
By William T. Hamilton, A.M.,
pastor of said church. Newark,
Pr. by W. Tuttle & Co., 1832.
20 p. OClWHi; PPPrHi.   12801

Hamlin, Lorenzo F.
    English grammar in lectures:
designed to render its principles
easily adapted to the mind of the
young learner, and its study entertaining. By L. F. Hamlin.
Stereotype ed. Boston, Munroe &
Francis; New-York, Lockwood
[etc., etc.] 1832. 108 p. CtY;
KU; MB; MH; NNC.   12802

---- ---- Brattleboro, Vt., Peck,
Steen & co. (Brattleboro power

press office), 1832. 108 p. MB;
MPiB; OO; VtHi; WU.   12803

Hammond, Jabez Delano.
    An address delivered at Cherry-
Valley on the fourth day of July,
1832. Utica, Pr. by William Williams, 1832. 19 p. MiD; N; NN;
NNC.   12804

Hampden, pseud.
    ...Essays of Hampden; Rights
of "The States," and of "The
people"...Richmond [n.d.] 88+ p.
[With The Virginia and Kentucky
resolutions of 1798 and '99.
Washington, 1832] ViU.   12805

Hampden [Mass.] Mechanic Association.
    Constitution of the Hampden
Mechanic Association. Instituted
Feb. 5, 1824...Springfield, from
the press of S. Bowles, 1832.
12 p. MWA.   12806

Hancock, Thomas, 1783-1849.
    The principles of peace, ex-
emplified in the conduct of the
Society of Friends in Ireland, during the rebellion in the year
1798; with preliminary and concluding observations...From the
London 2d rev. and enl. ed.
Providence, Pr. by H. H. Brown,
for the trustees of Obadiah
Brown's Benevolent Fund, 1832.
215 p. CtY; DLC; NjN; OU; PHC.
                                    12807
---- ---- 2d Amer. ed. Philadelphia, Pr. by Thomas Kite &
Co., for Nathan Kite, 1832. 171,
8 p. GDecCT; InRchE; MBC;
NNG; OMC.   12808

Handel and Haydn Society. Boston.
    Collection of church music; be-
ing a selection of the most approved psalm and hymn tunes,
anthems, sentences, chants, &c.
Together with many beautiful extracts from the works of Haydn,
Mozart, Beethoven, and other

eminent composers. Edited by
Lowell Mason. 11th ed., with
additions & improvements. Boston, Richardson, Lord & Holbrook, 1832. 357 p. IEG; MH;
NBuG; RPB; ViU.   12809

---- ---- 12th ed. with additions
and improvements. Boston, Richardson, Lord & Holbrook, 1832.
357, (3) p. MBAt; MeLewB;
NUtHi; OO; RPB.   12810

Hanning, John.
   Sermon on beneficence of uni-
versal charity preached in Repub-
lican Township Jefferson co.,
Ind.... Lexington, Ky, 1832.
PPPrHi.   12811

Hansen, Edward Richard.
   Centennial tribute. A grand
march offered to the memory of
the birthday of the immortal
Washington. (For pianoforte) Boston, Bradlee [1832] 3 p. MB;
MiU-C.   12812

Hanson, Mass. Congregational
Church.
   The Confession of faith and
covenant.... Plymouth, 1832. 11 p.
MBC.   12813

The happy cottagers; or, The
breakfast, dinner, & supper: to
which is added The shepherd's
boy reading to the poor widow.
New York, Mahlon Day, 1832.
16 p. DLC.   12814

The Harbinger of the Mississippi
Valley. v. 1. No. 1-2, March-
April, 1832. Frankfort? Ky.,
1832. CSmH; ICP; MoSHi; OU;
PPPrHi.   12815

Harding, Alpheus.
   Address delivered in Green-
field, June 25, 5832, before the
Franklin R. A. Chapter, and a
collection of Companions and
Brethren of the Masonic Family,

in commemoration of the birth of
John the Baptist. By Alpheus Hard-
ing, A.M., Pastor of the Church
in Newsalem. Wendell, Pr. by
John Metcalf, 1832. 16 p. MDeeP;
MWA; NNUT; PPFM.   12816

Hardy, James F. E., 1802-1882.
   Second annual address delivered
before the Asheville Temperance
Society with the executive committee's first annual report. Rutherfordton, Roswell, 1832. 12 p.
NcU.   12817

Harper, William, 1790-1847.
   Communication of William
Harper and T. R. Dew in relation
to the memorial of the committee
of the free trade convention
against the tarriff. 1832. 11 p.
RPB.   12818

---- ... Judge Harper's speech,
before the Charleston state rights
and free trade association, at
their regular meeting, April 1,
1832, explaining and enforcing the
remedy of nullification... Charleston, The State rights and free
trade association, 1832. 12 p.
ICU; MWA; NcD; PHi; ScC.
                         12819
---- ... The remedy by state interposition, or nullification; explained and advocated by Chancellor Harper in his speech at Columbia, (S. C.) on the twentieth
September, 1830... Charleston,
State rights and free trade association, 1832. 24 p. DLC; ICU;
MWA; NcD; PU; TxU; WHi.
                         12820
Harris, David.
   Real facts stated, and misstatement corrected. A Reply to
a Pamphlet, entitled, "An Injured
Minister's Character vindicated,
by James Upton,..." Kingston,
1832. 51 p. CtY.   12821

Harris [Thaddeus William]
   A discourse delivered before

the Massachusetts Horticultural
Society, on the celebration of its
fourth anniversary, October 3,
1832. Cambridge, E. W. Metcalf,
1832. 96 p. CU; DLC; IU; MHi;
PPAmP.   12822

Harris, Thomas.
    Modern Entries, or Approved
Precedents, of Declarations,
Pleadings, Entries, and Writs (6
lines cont) By Hugh Davey Evans,
of the Baltimore Bar. Vol. II.
Baltimore, James Lucas and E.
K. Deaver, 1831-1832. 2 vols.
DLC; In-SC; MdBB; NNU; OCoSc.
                                12823
Harrisburg and Lancaster Rail-
road.
    Charter... passed June 9, 1832.
[Harrisburg, 1832?]   12824

Harrison, Thomas.
    Correspondence between Thom-
as Harrison, Esq. Comptroller
General of South Carolina, and
the accounting officers of the
Treasury Department, of the
South Carolina claim. Washington,
1832. 39 p. A-Ar; MBAt. 12825

Harrod, John J. , comp.
    The academical reader, com-
prising selections from the most
admired authors, designed to promote the love of virtue, piety,
and patriotism... 4th ed. Baltimore, Phoenix N. Wood & co. ,
1832. 324 p. CU; MdHi; NN.
                                12826
Harry Winter; the shipwrecked
sailor boy. To which is added the
oak at home. New York, Mahlon
Day, 1832. 23 p. DLC.   12827

Hart, Louis.
    The national jubilee of the
"Great Columbus!" and the new
era of the bright morning star of
America. Baltimore, n. p. , 1832.
4 p. DLC; MdHi.   12828

Hart, Nathaniel C.

Documents relative to the
House of Refuge... See Society
for the Reformation of Juvenile
Delinquents in the City of New
York.

Hartford, Conn.
    By laws of the city of Hart-
ford relative to fire, and names
of the officers of the fire department. Hartford, 1832. 19 p.
CtHT-W.   12829

---- Baptist Church.
    Articles of faith and covenant
... together with the names of the
members. [Hartford, 1832] 12 p.
CtY.   12830

---- North Church.
    A brief history of the forma-
tion of the North Church in Hartford, Connecticut, together with
a summary of Christian doctrine,
and a form of covenant adopted
by the church and publicly read
on the admission of members.
Hartford, Pr. by Goodwin & Co. ,
1832. 19 p. Ct; CtY; DLC;
NBLiHi; NNG.   12831

Hartwell, Abram.
    A brief history of a most de-
structive and tremendous fire
which has been enraging in Shirley for months. By Abram Hartwell. Lunenburg, Mass. , 1832.
14 p. CtY; MWA.   12832

Harvard University.
    A catalogue of the officers and
students of Harvard University,
for the academical year 1832-3.
Cambridge, Brown, Shattuck &
co. , 1832. 32, 4 p. KHi. 12833

---- Statement of the pecuniary
concerns of the college. 1832.
27 p. RPB.   12834

---- Statutes and laws of Harvard
University relative to undergraduates. Cambridge, E. W. Metcalf

& Co., 1832. 40, 7 p. CtY;
DLC; MWA; N; RPB.   12835

---- Institute of 1770.
Catalogue of the... Institute of
1770.... Cambridge, E. W. Metcalfe & co., 1832. CtY; DLC;
MHi; MWA; OClWHi.   12836

---- Law School.
Reports of cases argued and determined at Cambridge Law School,
1832. J. Rand. [Cambridge, Mass.,
1832-33] 143 p. MB; MH-L.
                          12837

---- Library.
Circular from the Librarian.
Circular relating to the Univer-
sity Library. Aug. 29, 1832. 3 p.
MHi.   12838

---- Pierian Sodality.
Catalogue of the honorary and
immediate members of the Pierian Sodality of Harvard University,
instituted 1808. Cambridge, E. W.
Metcalf & Co., 1832. 15 p. MH.
                          12839

Harvest. Written for the American Sunday-school Union, and
rev. by the committee of publication. Philadelphia, American
Sunday-school Union, 1832. 47 p.
DLC; MH; NjP; ScCliTO.   12840

Harvey, Joseph, 1787-1873.
Letters on the present state
and probable results of theological speculations in Connecticut.
By an Edwardean. n. p. 1832.
40 p. ICN; MoSpD; NRCR;
PPPrHi; WHi.   12841

Haskins, Roswell Willson.
An historical eulogy of M. le
Marquis de La Place, pronounced
in the public session of the Royal
Academy of Sciences, at Paris,
June 15, 1829, By M. le Baron
Fourier, perpetual secretary.
Trans. from the French by Ros-
well Willson Haskins, of Buffalo,
N. Y. [Batavia? 1832?] 14 p.

DLC; MH; NBuG; NBuHi; NN;
NjR; WHi.   12842

Haslam, John.
A few brief observations on
the foot of the horse, and on
shoeing... Baltimore, Pr. by
Samuel Harker, 1832. 14 p. DSG;
MdHi.   12843

Hassler, Ferdinand Rudolph,
1770-1843.
... Comparison of weights and
measures of length and capacity,
reported to the Senate of the
United States by the Treasury
department in 1832, and made by
Ferd. Rod. Hassler, M. A. P. S.
Washington, Pr. by D. Green,
1832. 122 p. CtHT; MoU; PPi;
RNR; ScU.   12844

---- Elements of Arithmetic, theoretical and practical; adapted to
the use of schools, and to private
study. A new stereotype ed., rev.
& corr. 8th ed. New York, C. &
C. & H. Carvill, 1832. 219 p.
DLC; InU; NNC; PBL.   12845

Hastings, Thomas, 1784-1872.
The juvenile instructor; for the
use of teachers in infant, Sabbath
and primary schools. Utica, Wm.
Williams, 1832. NNUT.   12846

---- Musica sacra, or Utica and
Springfield collections united: consisting of psalm and hymn tunes,
anthems, and chants, arranged for
two, three, or four voices, with
a figured bass for the organ or
piano forte. By Thomas Hastings
and Solomon Warriner. 9th rev.
ed. --with additions and improvements. Utica, W. Williams, 1832.
300 p. CtY; DLC; ICP; NUt;
NNUT.   12847

---- Spiritual songs for social
worship, adapted to the use of
families & private circles... missionary meetings... words & music

arranged by Thomas Hastings...
& Lowell Mason... Utica, Hastings & Tracy and W. Williams,
1832. 162 p. CtMW; ICU; MWA;
NNUT; OClWHi.   12848

Hatch, Julius Wells, 1801-1882.
A compendium of astronomy,
designed to accompany a course
of popular lectures upon that science. By J. W. Hatch. Utica,
Pr. by Hastings & Tracy, 1832.
35 p. MWA; NUt.   12849

Hatfield, S.
She lives in hopes; or, Caro-
line. Hingham, Gill, 1832. 2 v.
DLC; ICBB; OHi.   12850

Hathaway, Joshua W.
An oration delivered at Ellsworth, July 4, 1832. At the
celebration of the fifty-sixth anniversary of American independence. Ellsworth, R. Grant, 1832.
16 p. MH; MeBat; MeHi; NN.
                                 12851
Hatsted, O.
A full and accurate account of
the new method of curing dys-
pepsia discovered and practiced
by O. Hatsted with some observations on diseases of the diges-
tive organs. 2d ed, with plates
and explanatory notes. New York,
O. Hatsted, 1832. 155 p. OMC.
                                 12852
Haupt-inhalt der Christlichen
lehre, nebst einer kurzgefassten
Kirchen geschichte. Reading,
Gedruckt bei Johann Ritter und
Co., 1832. 38 p. CSmH; PHi;
PReaHi.   12853

Havenden, John Eykyn.
A general treatise on the
principles and practice by which
courts of equity are guided as to
the prevention or remedial correction of fraud, with numerous
incidental notices of collateral
points, both of law and equity.
By John Eykyn Hovenden... 1st

Amer. ed.; with notes, and references to American decisions,
by Thos. Huntington. New York,
Collins & Hannay, 1832. 2 v. in
1. CoU; IaU-L; Ky; PPL; WaU.
                                 12854
Hawes, Joel, 1789-1867.
Lectures to young men on the
formation of character, etc. Originally addressed to the young men
of Hartford and New Haven, and
published at their united request.
6th ed. with an additional lecture
on reading. By Joel Hawes, pastor of the First Church in Hartford, Ct. Hartford, Cooke &
Co., stereotyped by A. Chandler, 1832. 172 p. CtSoP; MA;
MH; NR; PPM.   12855

---- A sermon preached at the
funeral of the Rev. Elias Cornel-
ius, corresponding secretary of
the A. B. C. F. M. who died in
Hartford, Conn., Feb. 12, 1832,
aged 37; by Joel Hawes, pastor
of the First Church in Hartford.
Hartford [Pub. at the united re-
quest of the Commissioners for
Foreign Missions and the Execu-
tive Committee of the Auxiliary
Society for Foreign Missions of
Hartford County] Pr. by Hudson
& Skinner, 1832. 31 p. Ct; CtY;
DLC; IEG; MB; MBAt; MBC;
MWA.   12856

Hawker, Robert.
The true Gospel; no yea and
nay Gospel, a tract, affectionate-
ly recommended to the people of
God in the present low state of
the church. By Robert Hawker...
New York, n. p., n. pr., 1832.
12 p. NjR.   12857

[Hawks, Francis Lister] 1798-
1866.
The early history of the southern states: Virginia, North and
South Carolina, and Georgia. Illustrated by tales, sketches, anecdotes, and adventures, with

numerous engravings. By Lambert Lilly, schoolmaster [pseud.] Philadelphia, Key, Mielke & Biddle, 1832. 192 p. AU; DLC; KyU; NcU; WaS.   12858

Hawley, William.
    Funeral discourse on the death of Mrs. Marcia Van Ness, consort of the Hon. John P. Van Ness, mayor of the city of Washington; by the Rev. William Hawley... City of Washington, Pr. by F. P. Blair, 1832. 39 p. DLC; MdBD; NNG; PPAmP.   12859

Haxall, Robert William, 1802-1872.
    Prize essay, on fistula lachrymale's [sic]... By Robert W. Haxall, M.D., of Richmond, Va. Richmond, John H. Nash, 1832. 41 p. DNLM; NNNAM; Vi. 12860

Hay, William, 1793-1870.
    Isabel Davalos the maid of Seville; or Female heroism and fidelity; a concise poem. By its author. (16 lines poetry quoted.) Glen's Falls, Pr. by Abial Smith, for the author, 1832. 96 p. CtHWatk; DLC; NBuG; NGlf; RPB.   12861

Hayden, B. R.
    Description of the Picture of Christ's Entry into Jerusalem. Philadelphia, 1832. 7 p. MHi.
                                          12862
The haymaker. Written for the American Sunday-school Union, and revised by the committee of publications. Philadelphia, American Sunday-school Union, 1832. 16 p. DLC; NNC; OClWHi. 12863

Hayne, Robert Young, 1791-1839.
    Errors in fact, advanced by Senator Robert Y. Hayne, in his Anti-Tariff Speech and the evil results his policy must produce, exposed, for the good of the people. Philadelphia, Pr. by Henry

Young, 1832. 8 p. MBAt; MWA; MiD-B.   12864

---- Letter of Robert Y. Hayne, to a committee of the State rights and free trade party, embracing a reply to Col. Drayton's late address. Charleston, Pr. by E. J. Van Brunt, 1832. 30 p. CU; ICU; NcD; RPB; WHi.   12865

---- Remarks on the third reading of the tariff bill. [Washington, 1832] 8 p. DLC; NN; NcD; OOC; ScU.   12866

---- Speech in reply to the Hon. Henry Clay in Senate, Monday, January 16, 1832. n.p., n.p. [1832] 18 p. MHi; NcD; ScU.
                                          12867

---- Speech of Mr. Hayne, of South Carolina, in support of his amendment to Mr. Clay's resolution proposing to reduce the duties on imports. In Senate, Jan. 16, 1832. [Washington, 1832] 20 p. CU; DLC; MiD-B; NcWfC; PHi; TxU.   12868

---- Speech of the Hon. Robert Y. Hayne, (of South Carolina,) on the reduction of the tariff. Delivered Jan. 9, 1832, in the Senate of the United States, on a motion to amend Mr. Clay's resolution. Washington [1832] 47 p. A-Ar; MH; NcD; OCHP; ScC.   12869

Hays, Henry H.
    Addresses before the Young Men's Jefferson Society, 4th July, 1832. New York, Pr. by R. Stevenson & R. Holstead, [1832?] 12 p. DLC; MnHi; PPL; TU.
                                          12870
Hayward, John, 1781-1862.
    A view of the United States: historical, geographical, and statistical. November 1832 by John Hayward. New York, J. & W. Day, 1832. 20 l. CtHC; DLC; IU;

MB; NN.   12871

Hazen, Edward.
The speller and definer, or
classbook No. 2. New York,
M'Elrath & Bangs, 1832. IaDaP;
MH.   12872

Health almanac for 1833. Philadelphia, Key, Meilke & Biddle
[1832] InU; MWA; NjR; PP.
                           12873
Healthside. v. 1-52, no. 6; Sept.
1832-Dec. 1884. Columbus, O. ,
Jarvis Pike & co.; Cincinnati,
O. , William H. Cook, 1832-1884.
52 v. MiU; OHi; PPC; VW.
                           12874
Healy, William.
A brief account of (his) life
and adventures (written by himself). B(oston), 1832. 17 p. MH.
                           12875
Heath, Jesse.
Psalms, hymns and spiritual
songs, selected... By Jesse Heath
and Elias Hutchins. See Watts,
Isaac, 1674-1748. An arrange-
ment of the psalms...

Heber, Reginald, 1783-1826.
The life of Rt. Rev. Jer. Tay-
lor, D. D. Lord Bishop of Down,
Connor, & Dromore...1st Amer.
from 3d London ed. Hartford, F.
J. Huntington, 1832. 368 p.
GDecCT; MBC; NNG; ViU; WNaE.
                           12876
Hedge, Levi.
Elements of logic; or A sum-
mary of the general principles and
different modes of reasoning. By
Levi Hedge...Stereotyped. Boston,
Hilliard, Gray & Co. , 1832.
178 p. LNT; OCIW; PEaL. 12877

Heinrich, Anton Philipp, 1781-
1861.
The first labour of Hercules,
un pezzo di gran brauura à la
valse austriaco per lo forte piano,
da A. P. Heinrich, composto...
a parlgi... [Boston, 1832?] 15 p.

NN; NcU.   12878

---- The four pawed kitten dance.
N. p. [183-?] MB.   12879

Heirs of Patrick Ward vs. Pat-
rick Gaffnay and Michael Foley,
Before the Baltimore County
Court [1832] 8 p. MWA.   12880

Helfenstein, J. C. Albertus.
A collection of choice sermons,
by the Rev. J. C. Albertus Helfenstein. Trans. from the German by I. Daniel Rupp, Carlisle,
Rev. Chas. Helfenstein, 1832.
261 p. KyDC; MdHi; PHi; OSW;
ViAl.   12881

Helps to the study of the prophecies; or, An inquiry into the
original of the figurative or met-
aphoric language thereof, with a
view to the more easy interpre-
tation of the same; to which is
added an application of the subject, in an explanation of the first
part of the 9th chapter of the
Apocalypse. Baltimore, Young,
1832. 88 p. KyLoP; MdBP; NGH;
PPLT; OCH.   12882

Hemans, Felicia Dorothea (Browne)
1793-1835.
The poetical works of Hemans,
and Pollok. Complete in one vol-
ume. Stereotyped by J. Crissy
and G. Goodman. Philadelphia,
John Grigg, 1832. 348 p. ICU;
GHi; MWA; PPL; TBriK; ViU.
                           12883
---- ---- Philadelphia, Thos. T.
Ash, 1832. 2 vol. in 1. CtY;
MH; MBev; WaSpG.   12884

Hemphill, Joseph, 1770-1842.
Remarks in the Pennsylvania
legislature in House committee,
on his amendment to insert "Columbia in the York & Maryland
line railroad bill; Jan. 1832.
Harrisburg, 1832. 15 p. PHi.
                           12885

Henderson, Jacob, 1681-1751.
The Rev. Mr. Jacob Henderson's fifth letter, to Daniel Dulany, Esq.; in relation to the case and petition of the clergy of Maryland. [Philadelphia] Pr. for the author, 1832. 41 p. CtY.
12886

Henderson, Thomas, 1789-1854.
The physician's first steps in professional life: an address delivered at the medical commencement in Washington, March 7, 1832. By Thos. Henderson, Washington, 1832. 16 p. DNLM; DSG; MdHi.   12887

Hendrickson, Joseph
The decision... See Wood, George.

Henry, John Flourney, 1793-1873.
A letter on the cholera as it occurred in Cincinnati, Ohio, in October, 1832, addressed to Dr. Short of Lexington, Ky. [Lexington, Ky., 1832] 29 p. DNLM; OC; OHi.   12888

Henry, Joseph, 1797-1878.
On a disturbance of the earth's magnetism, in connexion with the appearance of an aurora borealis, as observed at Albany, April 19, 1831. Communicated to the Albany Institute, January 26, 1832. [Albany, 1832?] 15 p. DNLM; DSG; NN.   12889

Henry, Matthew, 1662-1714.
A method for prayer, with scripture expressions proper to be used under each head. ... Philadelphia, Towar & Hogan, 1832. 233 p. MoSpD; NNC; NjP; PMA; ScCliTO.   12890

Henry, William, 1774-1836.
An estimate of the philosoph[y] ...of Dr. Priestley; by William Henry... Read to the first meeting of the British Association, for the promotion of Science, at York,

September 28th, 1831. York, Pr. by T. Wilson and sons, 1832. 15 p. CtY; IEN-M; PPAmP; PSt.   12891

Henshaw, John Prentiss Kewley, 1792-1852.
Preface to the first American stereotype edition of Saurin's sermons. Baltimore, n.p. 1832. 3 p. RPB.   12892

---- The selection of hymns for the use of social religious meetings, and for private devotions, by J. P. K. Henshaw. 5th ed. Baltimore, Armstrong & Plaskitt, 1832. 320 p. CBB(B); IEN; MdBD; RPB; ViRut.   12893

---- A sermon preached on the 4th July, 1832, appointed by the Governor of Maryland to be observed as a day of humiliation & prayer... Baltimore, W. R. Lucas, 1832. 32 p. CtY; MdHi; NcD; NjR; VtMidbC.   12894

Herbert, John Carlyle.
An address delivered at the first anniversary meeting of the Maryland state temperance society, on the 5th January, 1832. Pub. by request of the society. Annapolis, Pr. by J. Green, 1832. 15 p. MdBLC; MdHi.   12895

Hersey, John, 1786-1862.
The Christian's duty or importance of strict economy and unanimity of effort among the followers of the Lord Jesus Christ. Baltimore, Jas. Lucas & E. K. Deaver, 1832. 24 p. MH; MnH; MnHi.   12896

---- An inquiry into the character and condition of our children; and their claim to a participation in the privileges and blessings of the redeemer's kingdom on earth, examined and established. Also some remarks on the mode of administering the ordinance of baptism. By John Hersey. Richmond, Pr. by Samuel Shepherd & Co., 1832. 36 p. MWA; NcD; NcU; PPPrHi.   12897

Hervey, James, 1714-1758.
Meditations and contemplations by the Rev. James Hervey. Containing Meditations among the tombs, Reflections on a flowergarden, Descent upon oration... together with the life of the author. Cincinnati, Roff & Young, 1832. 2 v. in 1. ICU; MBC; NcWilA; OHi; OO.   12898

Hewett (D.).
Universal traveller and commercial and manufacturing directory... Philadelphia, 1832. MWA.   12899

[Hewson, John]
Christ rejected... Written by a believer in Christ, under the accused name of Captain Onesimus... Philadelphia, Pr. by J. Rakestraw, for the author, 1832. 444, (4) p. DLC; NjPT; PPC; TxDaM; UPB; WHi.   12900

Hickok, John Hoyt, 1792-1841.
The sacred harp, containing part first... the rules and principles of vocal musick, Part second, a collection of the most approved church tunes... Lewistown, Pa., Shugert & Cummings, 1832. 141, [3] p. IEG; NBuG; NNUT; OClWHi; PPi.   12901

Hicks, Elias, 1748-1830.
Journal of the life and religious labours of Elias Hicks, written by himself. New York, Hopper, 1832. 451 p. CtY; DLC; MiD; NjPT; TxU.   12902

---- ---- 2d ed. New York, Isaac T. Hopper, 1832. 451 p. IC; MdBJ; NcD; NjP; PHi; TxU.   12903

---- ---- 3d ed. New York, I.

T. Hopper, 1832. 451 p. NNUT; OO; PHi; RPB; WaPS.   12904

---- ---- 5th ed. New York. I. T. Hopper, 1832. 451 p. DLC; ICU; MW; MiU; NNS; PHi. 12905

Hildreth, Hosea.
A view of the United States, for the use of schools and families. By Rev. Hosea Hildreth. 3d ed. Boston, Carter & Hendee, 1832. 160 p. DLC; KU; MB; MHi; MLow.   12906

Hill, Benjamin Munro, 1793-1881.
Hymns of Zion: being a selection of Hymns for social worship, compiled chiefly for the use of Baptist Churches by Benjamin M. Hill. New Haven, Durrie & Peck, 1832. 255 p. CtY-D; MB; NHC-S; RNHS; RNHi.   12907

[Hill, Henry Aaron]
A collection of hymns for the use of native Christians of the Mohawk language; to which are added, a number of hymns for Sabbath schools. New York, Pr. by M'Elrath & Bangs, 1832. 146 p. MB; MH; WHi.   12908

Hill, Isaac, 1788-1851.
Proceeding to the demise of Isaac Hill at the Eagle Coffee House. Concord, N.H. Aug. 8, 1832. [Concord? 1832] 16 p. MH.   12909

---- Speech in Senate, May 10, 1832 on Mr. Bibb's amendment to the bill for establishing post roads, proposing the abolition of postage on newspapers. [Washington, 1832?] 12 p. DLC; IU.   12910

---- Speech of Mr. Hill, of New Hampshire, on the subject of Mr. Clay's Resolutions in relation to the Tariff... [Washington, 1832?] 24 p. MBAt; NbU; NcU; NN; PPL.   12911

Hilliard, Gray & Co.
A list of new works in press,
and books published... Boston,
July, 1832. 4 p. NN.   12912

Hilliard, Henry Washington, 1808-
1892.
An address delivered before
the Erosophic Society, at its first
anniversary, May 26, 1832. By
Rev. Henry W. Hilliard, professor of elocution in the University
of Alabama. Tuscaloosa, Pub. at
the request of the society, Pr. by
Wiley, M'Guire & Henry, 1832.
16 p. CtHWatk; NcD; TxU.12913

---- An address delivered in the
Representative hall before the
General Assembly of the State of
Alabama, and the citizens of Tuscaloosa, December 7, 1832, in
commemoration of the death of
Charles Carroll, of Carrollton.
By Prof. Hilliard, of the University of Alabama. Tuscaloosa, Pr.
by E. Walker, state pr., 1832.
10 p. NcD; TxU.   12914

Hind, John, 1796-1866.
A digested series of examples
in the applications of the principles of the differential calculus.
By John Hind. Cambridge, Pr.
by J. Smith, 1832. CU; DLC; MiU;
OAU; PU.   12915

---- The principles and practice
of arithmetic, designed for the
use of students in the university
... Cambridge, W. Metcalf, 1832.
332 p. DAU; MB.   12916

Hinds, John.
The veterinary surgeon, by
John Hinds, with considerable
additions and improvements...
by Thos. M. Smith. Philadelphia,
Grigg, 1832. 224 p. CtY; IaU;
NBuU-M; NcWfc; OClM.   12917

Hingham Temperance Society.
Address of the... Society on

the evil effects of intemperance.
Hingham, Mass., J. Farmer,
1832. 36 p. MBC; MH.   12918

Hints for those who purpose attending the meeting at Exeter-
Hall, on Wednesday, 15th August,
1832. 8 p. OClWHi.   12919

The History of birds, Concord,
John W. Moore & Co., 1832. 16
p. CtY.   12920

The History of Jesus, drawn up
for the instruction of children.
New York, J. Emory & B. Waugh,
1832. 76 p. NjMD; NN.   12921

History of lying, by the author
"Phebe Bartlet"...Boston, Massachusetts Sabbath School Union,
1832.   12922

History of nations spoken in the
Old Testament... Boston, Peirce
and Parker, 1832. 144 p. CtHC;
DLC.   12923

A history of the Bible. Providence, 1832. 192 p. RHi. 12924

A history of the Black Hawk War.
By an old resident of the military
tract. Fort Armstrong, 1832.
63 p. DLC; ICarbS.   12925

History of the church in the fifth
century. Compiled by the American Sunday School Union, and revised by the Committee of publication. Philadelphia, American
Sunday School Union, 1832. 106 p.
DLC.   12926

History of the Delaware and Iro-
quois Indians, formerly inhabiting
the middle states; with various
anecdotes, illustrating their manners and customs...written for
the American Sunday School Union
and revised by the committee of
publication. Philadelphia, American Sunday School Union, 1832.

153 p. DLC; ICU; NBuHi; OHi; WHi.   12927

History of the giants. Philadelphia, W. Johnson, 1832. 15 p. DLC; NN; NNC.   12928

History of the orphan asylum in Philadelphia, with an account of the fire in which 23 orphans were burned. Philadelphia, American Sunday School Union, 1832. 68 p. DLC; PPeSchw; PP; PU.   12929

History of the proceedings of the Carlisle Presbytery in relation to a work, entitled Duffield on regeneration; in a series of lectures from a person present to his friend. Philadelphia, Wm. F. Geddes, 1832. 31 p. CtY; DLC; MWA; MiU; NjPT; PPM; ViRut.
                             12930
History of the United States in the French language, for the use of schools. Boston, Carter, Hendee & Co., 1832. 304 p. IAlS.
                             12931
History of Widow Gray and her family; or, Things as they often are, by the author of "The military blacksmith" &c. ... New York, General Protestant Episcopal Sunday School Union, 1832. 44 p. DLC; MMedHi.   12932

Hitchcock, David, 1773-1849.
    Christ; not the minister of sin; or, The absurdity of believing that all men will finally be saved. Illustrated in a dialogue between a Universalist and his neighbor ... Hartford, Pr. for the author, 1832. 35 p. MBBC; MChB; MWA.
                             12933
Hitchcock, Edward, 1793-1864.
    Geological map of Mass. See under Massachusetts Geological Society.

---- Report of a geological survey of Massachusetts made under an appointment by the governor, and

pursuant to a resolve of the legislature of the state. Pt. I. Amherst, J. S. & C. Adams, 1832. 70 p. CtHT; DGS; ICJ; MHi; PPL.
                             12934
Hitchcock, Ira Irvine, 1793-1868.
    Key of Hitchcock's new method of teaching bookkeeping. Baltimore, Pub. by the author, 1832. 56 p. DLC; MH; MeHi; NNC; PPF.   12935

---- Ledger of Hitchcock's new method of teaching book-keeping. Baltimore, Author, 1832. MH; PPFrankI.   12936

---- A new method of teaching book-keeping. 7th ed. Baltimore, Pub. by the author, 1832. 42 p. MB; MH; PPFrankI.   12937

Hoar, Samuel.
    Argument in the Brookfield church case. Boston, 1832. See Massachusetts. Supreme Judicial Court.

Hobart, John Henry, 1775-1830.
    The altar: a companion to the altar. By Rt. Rev. J. Henry Hobart. Together with prayers and meditations, selected from the works of Bishops Beveridge, Taylor, and others. Philadelphia, Richard McCauley, 1832. 89 p. MdBD.   12938

---- The churchman. The principles of the churchman stated and explained in distinction from the corruptions of the church of Rome, and from the errors of certain Protestant sects in charge, delivered to the clergy of Connecticut and New York, T. & J. Swords; repr. Boston, 1832. 25 p. InID; MB; NBu.   12939

---- Companion for the altar; or, Week's preparation for the holy communion... New York, Swords, Stanford & co., 1832. 244 p.

NBuDD; NjP; ScCMu; WNaE.
12940
---- The high churchman vindicated: in a charge to the clergy of the Protestant Episcopal Church in the state of New York, by John Henry Hobart, D. D. New York, J. & J. Swords. Repr. Boston, 1832. 100 p. InID; MB; MH. 12941

---- The posthumous works of the late Rt. Rev. John Henry Hobart ...with a memoir of his life by the Rev. William Berrian...New York, Swords, Stanford & Co., 1832-1833. 3 v. CtY; MH; NNUT; PU; VtU. 12942

---- A word for the Church: consisting of "The Churchman," and "The High Churchman Vindicated"; two Episcopal Charges by the Rt. Rev. John Henry Hobart...By Geo. W. Doane, Boston, Stimpson & Clapp, 1832. 100 p. CtY; DLC; MHi; NNUT; PPPD. 12943

Hobbs, Benedict H.
To the members of the Presbyterian Church in Fleming County, Ky. 1832. PPPrHi. 12944

Hobby, Wensley.
Speech of, delivered at the celebration dinner, at Appling, Columbia County, Georgia, July 4, 1832. 16 p. GU; MHi; NcD.
12945

Hobson, Samuel.
The Christian schoolmaster, or, Conversations on various subjects, between a village schoolmaster and his neighbours, by the Rev. Samuel Hobson... Norwich, Pr. by T. Webster [1832] 190 p. CtY; DLC. 12946

Hoch Deutsch Americanische Calender for 1833. Germantown, Pa., Michael Billmeyer [1832] InU; MWA; NjR; PHi; PPL.
12947

Hoch-Deutsches Lutherisches A B C und Namen-Büchlein für Kinder welche anfangen zu lernen. Philadelphia, Georg W. Mentz und Sohn, 1832. PPeSchw. 12948

Hodge, James.
The grace of God in the gift of the Holy Spirit. Pittsburgh, 1832. NjR. 12949

Hoffman, David, 1784-1854.
A lecture, being the 9th of a series of lectures, introductory to a course of lectures (on Roman civil law) now delivering in the University of Maryland. Baltimore, Toy, 1832. 41 p. DLC; MWA; MdHi; NCH; PHi. 12950

Hoffman, Ogden, 1793-1856.
An address delivered before the association of the alumni of Columbia College, at their anniversary, May 2, 1832. By Ogden Hoffman. Pub. at the request of the association. New York, G. & C. & H. Carvill, 1832. 28 p. CtY; DLC; MBAt; NNC; PU.
12951

Hofland, Barbara Wreaks.
The son of a genius: A tale for the use of youth. New and imp. ed. New York, J. & J. Harper, 1832. 213 p. MB; MH; NNC; RJa; TNP. 12952

[Hogg, James] 1770-1835.
Songs, by the Ettrick shepherd, (pseud.) Now first collected. 1st Amer. ed. New-York, W. Stodart, 1832. 311 p. CoD; DLC; NjP; RPB; TxU. 12953

Holbrook, Josiah, 1788-1854.
Easy lessons in geometry, intended for infant and primary schools, but useful in academies, lyceums and families...5th ed. Boston, Carter, Hendee & Babcock, 1832. 36 p. CtY; ICU; MB; MiU; NN. 12954

---- ---- 8th ed. Boston, Carter, Hendee & co., 1832. 36 p.
CtHWatk; MB; MH; NNC; RPB.
                                12955
Holdich, Joseph, 1804-1893.
    Bible history: or, The princi-
pal events of the Old Testament
...J. Holdich. New York, Carlton & Lanahan; Cincinnati,
Hitchcock & Walden [1832?] 186
p. TNT.   12956

---- Questions on historical parts
of Old Testament. New York, B.
Waugh & T. Mason, 1832. 192 p.
NSyU.   12957

Holmes, John, 1773-1833.
    Speech of Mr. John Holmes,
of Maine, on the Tariff. In...
Jan. 30, 1832. The Resolution
submitted by Mr. Clay being under consideration, with the
amendment proposed by Mr.
Hayne [1832?] 16 p. DLC; InU;
LU; MWA.   12958

---- Speech...on the annual appropriation bill, against the policy
of the administration...delivered
in the Senate of the United States,
April 9, 10, and 11, 1832. [Wash-
ington, 1832] 24 p. DLC; KHi;
MWA; MeHi; WHi.   12959

Holmes, Oliver Wendell, 1809-
1894.
    History of elementry school-
books. In New England magazine.
Boston, 1832. CSt.   12960

Holmes, Sylvester.
    On the death of Godly and
faithful men. A sermon occa-
sioned by the death of Gen. Shep-
ard Leach, delivered at Easton,
Sept. 23, 1832. By Sylvester
Holmes, Pastor of the North
Church in New Bedford. Boston,
Pr. by Perkins & Marvin, 1832.
29 p. A-Ar; CtSoP; MB; MBC;
NBLiHI.   12961

Home, John, 1722-1808.
    Douglas, a tragedy. Philadel-
phia, 1832. MH.   12962

Homerus.
    ....Homeri Ilias, ex recen-
sione C. G. Heynii fere impressa;
cum notis Anglicis, in usum schol-
arum; curante J. D. Ogilby. Novi
Eboraci: Excudit Gulielmus E.
Dean. Sumtibus Collins et Hannay,
Collins et co., et N. & J. White,
1832. 414, [1] p. IaGG; PU;
TNJU.   12963

Homo, pseud.
    Practical musings, for courte-
ous readers both laical and clerical. By Homo. New York, John
P. Haven, 1832. 172 p. IaB; InID;
KyLoP; MB; NNG.   12964

Hood, Thomas, 1799-1845.
    Dreams of Eugene Aram, the
murderer....New York, Peabody,
1832. 21 p. CSmH; DLC; MB;
MH; MWA.   12965

[Hook, Theodore Edward] 1788-
1841.
    Plebeians and Patricians. By
the author of "Old maids" "Old
bachelors,"...Philadelphia, 1832.
2 v. CtY.   12966

---- Sayings and doings, a ser.
of sketches from life. Philadelphia, 1832. 2 vols. PPL-R.
                               12967
Hooker, Mary Ann (Brown),
1796-1838.
    The life of David, King of Is-
rael. By the author of 'Bible
Sketches.' Illustrated with a variety of original cuts; a map of
the travels of David; and an appendix of references, written for
the American Sunday School Union, and revised by the Committee of Publication. Philadelphia,
American Sunday School Union,
1832. 275 p. AmSSchU; DLC;
MPeaHi; MWA; MWinchrHi.
                               12968

Hooper, Robert, 1773-1835.
Examinations in anatomy,
physiology, practice of physic,
surgery, chemistry, obstetrics,
materia medica, pharmacy and
poisons...from last London ed.
New York City, Collins, 1832.
190 p. MdBM; Nh; PU;
RPB.   12969

---- Lexicon medicum; or, Med-
ical dictionary. 4th Amer. ed.
New York, Harper, 1832. 2 vol.
in 1. IJI; NcCJ; PPC; PPHa.
                                12970
Hooper, William, 1792-1876.
A lecture on the imperfection
of our primary schools, and the
best method of correcting them;
delivered before the North Caro-
lina institute of education at
Chapel Hill, June 20th, 1832. By
William Hooper...Newbern, J. L.
Pasteur, 1832. 28 p. NcHiC;
NcU; NN; TxU.   12971

Hooton, Robert Treat.
Life and frolics of Major Stevens, the wonderful dwarf...his
numerous adventures...his perils
in Rhode Island by "Flood and
Field"... Boston, the author,
1832. 28 p. MB; MH; MiU-C.
                                12972
[Hope, Thomas] 1770?-1831.
...Anastasius; or, Memoirs of
a Greek. Written at the close of
the eighteenth century. New York,
J. & J. Harper, 1832. 2 vols.
DLC; MeBa; TNP; TxU-T. 12973

Hopkins. Caleb.
...Easy lessons...New-York,
M'Elrath & Bangs, 1832. 180 p.
DLC; ICarbS.   12974

---- School library of useful and
general knowledge; consisting of
easy lessons, juvenile tales, natural history, anecdotes, &c. in
different volumes...By Caleb
Hopkins. ...New York, M'Elrath
& Bangs, 1832. vol. II, III, IV,

V. DLC; ICardS.   12975

---- Story of Frank... New
York, M'Elrath & Bangs, 1832.
180 p. DLC.   12976

[Hopkins, John Henry] 1792-1868.
Defence of the convention of
the Protestant Episcopal church,
in the state of Massachusetts,
against certain editorial state-
ments of the paper, called 'The
Banner of the church.' Boston,
Stimpson & Clapp, 1832. 44 p.
CtHT; DLC; MBAt; NNUT;
OClWHi.   12977

---- The pleasures of luxury, un-
favorable to the exercise of
Christian benevolence. A sermon
...by Rev. John H. Hopkins...
Boston, Perkins & Marvin, 1832.
20 p. CtSoP; ICMe; MHi; NNG;
PHi.   12978

---- Religious education, the
safest means of ministerial in-
crease. A sermon preached...
Hartford, Sept. 26th, 1832, by
Rev. John H. Hopkins, Boston,
Stimpson & Clapp, 1832. 32 p.
CtHT; IEG; MiD; NNG; RPB.
                                12979
---- A sermon...in the Old South
Church, Boston, Jan. 18, 1832,
before the Harvard Benevolent
Society... Boston, Perkins & Mar-
vin, 1832. 20 p. MH-AH; MiD-
B.   12980

Hopkins Academy, Hadley, Mass.
Catalogue of the trustees, instructors, and students, during
the year ending Nov. 20, 1832.
Northampton, John Metcalf, 1832.
8 p. MWA.   12981

Hopkinson, John P.
Engravings of the arteries.
Philadelphia, Gibbons, 1832. 15
p., plates. MH-M; NbU-M;
PPCP.   12982

---- Remarks on the pathology
and treatment of the disease
termed malignant cholera, by J.
P. Hopkinson, M. D. ...Extract-
ed from the American journal of
the medical sciences for Aug.
1832. Philadelphia, Pr. by Jos.
R. A. Skerrett, 1832. 16 p. DSG;
NNNAM; PPL; ScU; ViU.   12983

Hopkinson, Joseph, 1770-1842.
   Lecture upon the principles of
commercial integrity, and the duties subsisting between a debtor
and his creditors. Delivered to
the Mercantile Library Company,
Mar. 2, 1832. Philadelphia,
Carey & Lea, 1832. 24 p. DLC;
MH; OCHP; PHi; ScU.   12984

Hopper, Isaac Tatem, 1771-1852.
   Narrative of the life of Thom-
as Cooper. New York, Isaac T.
Hopper, 1832. 36 p. DHU; NcU;
OO; RP.   12985

Hoppus, John, 1789-1875.
   Account of (Lord Bacon's)
Novum organon. Boston, 1832.
64 p. MBM.   12986

Hordynski, Jozef.
   History of the late Polish revolution... Boston, Carter & Hendee, 1832. 406 p. CU; MHi; NN;
OC; ViU.   12987

Horn, Charles E.
   The Mermaids Cave. Sung by
Miss Hughes, with enthusiastic
applause. Written by Miss H. F.
Gould (of Newburyport). Com-
posed by Charles E. Horn. New
York, Dubois & Stodart, c1832.
7 p. MB; MH; NN; ViU.   12988

Horner, J. M.
   The modern emigrant; or,
Lover of liberty: being a dis-
course, delivered in the city of
New York, by the Rev. J. M.
Horner, author of 'immersion,
the only Scriptural mode of bap-

tising;' of 'modern persecution,
a poem;' and of 'hymns and spiritual songs, collected, arranged,
and composed for the use of the
Union Baptists.' New-York, Pr.
by W. Mitchell, 1832. 18 p.
CtHC; DLC; MBC; NN; PCA.
                         12989
Horner, William Edmonds, 1793-
1853.
   Catalogue of the anatomical
museum of the University of
Pennsylvania, with a report to
the museum committee of the
trustees Nov. 1832. 2d ed. Philadelphia, Bailey, 1832. 51 p.
DLC; MdBi; NNNAM; IEN-M;
PHi; PaHosp.   12990

Horton, Mary Lambert.
   Poetical and prose composition.
By Mary L. Horton. Salem, W.
& S. B. Ives, 1832. 88 p. DLC;
ICU; MB; MH; MnU.   12991

House, Erwin.
   A treatise vindicating infant
church-membership...also, on
the mode of baptism...Rochester,
N. Y., Marshall & Dean, 1832.
84 p. MBC; N; NjPT.   12992

The house that Johnathan built,
or Political primer for 1832...
With twelve cuts... Philadelphia,
P. Banks, 1832. 16 p. CtY; IU;
MiD-B; OClWHi; PHi.   12993

Hovenden, John Eykyn.
   A general treatise on the principles & practice by which courts
of equity are guided as to the
prevention or remedial correction of fraud: with incidental
notices of collateral points... by
J. E. Hovenden...1st Amer. ed.
by T. Huntington. New York,
Collins & Hannay, 1832. 2 v. in
1. DLC; Mi-L; TxU; ViU-L;
WaU-L.   12994

How, Samuel Blanchard, 1790-
1868.

The use of the means of grace
... Being the third in a series of
lectures now delivering by different clergymen in the Sixth Presbyterian Church, Philadelphia.
Philadelphia, Russell & Martien,
1832. 104 p. DLC; PPPrHi.
                              12995
How to be good: or Practical lessons on the great science of human life... Springfield, G. & C.
Merriman, 1832. 112 p. DLC.
                              12996
Howard, Edward, d. 1841.
    Outward Bound; or, A mer-
chant's adventures, by the author
of Rattlin, the reifer... Philadelphia, E. L. Carey & A. Hart,
1832. 2 vols. RPB.   12997

Howard, Horton.
    An improved system of botanic
medicine, founded upon correct
physiological principles, embracing a concise view of anatomy and
physiology; together with an illustration of the new theory of medicine. By Horton Howard... Columbus, The Author, 1832. 2 vols.
DLC; KyLxT; PPiAM; RPM; TxU.
                              12998
---- A treatise on the complaints
peculiar to females: embracing a
system of midwifery; the whole in
conformity with the improved system of botanic medicine. By Horton Howard. Columbus, Pr. by
Chas. Scott, for the author, 1832.
172 p. IEN-M; In; MOSW-M;
OCHP; TU.   12999

Howard, N. G.
    To the people of Rankin County
...[Brandon, 1832] Broadside.
Ms-Ar.   13000

Howe, George.
    An address delivered at Colum-
bia (S.C.) March 28, 1832, at the
inauguration of the author, as professor of biblical literature, in
the theological seminary of the synod of South Carolina and Georgia.

Charleston, Observer office press,
1832. 27 p. MBC; NcD; NNUT;
PPPrHi; TxU.   13001

Howe, John, 1630-1705.
    Blessedness of the righteous:
treatise on Psalm 17:15 & the
vanity of this mortal life, or of
man, considered in his present
mortal state. Burlington, Goodrich, 1832. 315p. CtHC; IEG;
InCW; OO; OrPD.   13002

[Howell, John] 1788-1863.
    The life and adventures of Al-
exander Selkirk, the real Robinson Crusoe. A narrative founded
on facts... New York, Mahlon
Day, 1832. 23 p. CtY; MH; MWA.
                              13003
Howell, Robert Boyte Crawford,
1801-1868.
    A letter to the Rev. Henry W.
Ducachet, in reply to his "Examination of Mr. Howell's review"
under the signature of "An Episcopalian" by R. B. C. Howell,
pastor of the Baptist church in
Cumberland St., Norfolk, Va.
Norfolk, Pr. by Shields & Ashburn, 1832. 44 p. DLC; NjPT.
                              13004
---- Notes of annual pastoral dis-
courses preached in Norfolk, Va.,
Nashville, Tenn., and Richmond,
Va., 1832-67. MH; MH-AH.
                              13005
[Howland, Avis C.]
    Tales of old times. By the au-
thor of "Rhode Island tales"...
New-York, M. Day, 1832. 60 p.
CtY; OU; PHC.   13006

Howland, John, 1757-1854.
    Notices of the military services
rendered by the militia, as well
as by the enlisted troops, of the
state of Rhode Island, during the
Revolutionary war. [Providence?
1832] 11 p. MiU-C; NN; RPB;
RHi.   13007

Howland, Mary W.

The infant school manual, or, Teacher's assistant... A variety of useful lessons: for the use of teachers. By Mrs. Howland. 5th ed., rev., imp. and enl. Boston, Richardson, Lord & Holbrook, 1832. 274 p. MH; NNC.   13008

Hubbard, Henry, 1784-1857.
Speech of Mr. Hubbard, of New Hampshire, in the House of Representatives, on the Apportionment Bill. Washington City, Pr. by F. P. Blair at the Globe office, 1832. 8 p. DLC; MWA; PHi; TxU.   13009

---- Speech... upon the bill making further provisions for persons engaged in the land and naval service of the U.S. during the revolutionary war... House... Feb. 29, 1832. Washington, Pr. by F. P. Blair at the Globe office, 1832. 29 p. CtHWatk; DLC; MB; MH; MiD-B.   13010

Huchings' Improved Almanac for ...1833 by David Young. New York, John C. Totten, [1832] 18 p. M; MWA.   13011

Huchings' Revived Almanack for ... 1833... by David Young. New York, John C. Totten [1832] 18 p. NHi; P.   13012

Hudson, Charles, 1795-1881.
A history of the town of Westminster, from its first settlement to the present time. Mendon, Mass., Pr. by G. W. Stacy, 1832. 42 p. DLC; ICN; MBAt; NN; WHi.   13013

---- Primary questions on select portions of scripture. Designed for sabbath schools. Boston, Independent messenger, 1832. 45 p. DLC.   13014

---- Questions on select portions

of Scripture designed for the higher classes in Sabbath Schools. By Charles Hudson, of Westminster, Mass. A new ed. with alterations and additions, by Otis A. Skinner, pastor of the Fifth Universalist Society, Boston. Boston, J. M. Usher, 1832. 167 p. DLC; MBUGC; MBUPH.   13015

Hudson and Delaware Railroad.
Report of the preliminary survey of the route of the Hudson and Delaware and Delaware and Lackawanna railroads, by Henry G. Sargent, Esq., of Fort-Ann, Washington County, N.Y. Together with some general observations on the advantages of the undertaking and the act of incorporation. Pub. for the commissioners of the Hudson and Delaware and Delaware and Lackawanna railroad corporation. Newburgh, Pr. by Parmenter & Spalding, 1832. 51 p. NRU.
                                13016

Huger, Alfred.
Letter of Alfred Huger, Esq. In answer to the Resolutions of a Meeting in St. Thomas' Parish. Pendleton, S.C., 1832. 8 p. GU; MBAt.   13017

---- A letter to the people of Spartanburgh District. By Alfred Huger, member of the late state convention. Columbia, [S.C.] 1832. 8 p. GU.   13018

Hughes, John, Abp., 1797-1864.
Controversy between Rev. Messrs. Hughes and Beckinridge, on the subject "Is the Protestant religion the religion of Christ?" (1832-1833). 3d ed. Philadelphia, Cummiskey, 1832. 472 p. CSrD; ILM; NYScJ; PPPrHi; ViRU.
                                13019

Hull, Amos Gerald.
Dr. Hull's patent truss. Extracts from the opinions of distinguished surgeons, and late

medical authors... of Dr. Hull's newly invented instrument for... disease of hernia, or rupture. [New York, Philip French, 1832] 8 p. NNNAM.   13020

Humboldt, Alexander freiherr von, 1769-1859.
The travels and researches of Alexander von Humboldt; being a condensed narrative of his journeys in the equinoctial regions of America and in Russia; together with analyses of his more important invetigations, by W. Mac-Gillivray. With a map of the Orinoco, and engravings. New York, Harper & bros., 1832. 367 p. CSal; GMM; LNH; MB; NN.   13021

Hume, David, 1711-1776.
The history of England, from the invasion of Julius Caesar, to the revolution in 1688. By David Hume, esq. With notes and references, exhibiting the most important differences between this author and Dr. Lingard. Philadelphia, M'Carty & Davis, 1832. 2 vols. AFlT; GDecCT; NcU; OHi; TNV.   13022

Hume, George Henry.
Canada, as it is. Comprising details relating to the domestic policy, commerce and agriculture, of the upper and lower provinces... Especially intended for the use of settlers and emigrants. By George Henry Hume. New York, W. Stodart, 1832. 173 p. CSt; CtMW; MH; OTifH.   13023

Humphreys, Hector, 1797-1857.
An inaugural address by the Rev. Hector Humphreys, President of St. John's College, delivered at the Annual Commencement, February 25, 1832. Annapolis, Pr. by J. Hughes, 1832. 20 p. CtY; InID; MdBLC; NNG; PHi.   13024

Hunter, Henry, 1741-1802.
Sacred biography; or, The history of the Patriarchs; to which is added the history of Deborah, Ruth and Hannah, and also the history of Jesus Christ. Philadelphia, J. J. Woodward, 1832. 596 p. CtHC; KyDC; MeB; PPLT; TChu.   13025

Hunter, John H.
Sermon occasioned by the death of Mrs. Susannah Hull... delivered at Fairfield, Jan. 15, 1832. New Haven, 1832. 16 p. CtSoP; CtY; MH; NjPT.   13026

Huntington, John Whiting, 1809-1832.
A dissertation on employing emulation to encourage literary excellence. Cambridge, Brown, Shattuck & Co., 1832. 41 p. CtY; MB; MHi; MNF; N.   13027

Hunt's Philadelphia Almanack for 1833. By Joseph Cramer. Philadelphia, Pa., Uriah Hunt [1832] CtY; DcU; MWA; NjR; PHi.
13028

Hurlbutt, Ralph.
Difference between the wicked and the righteous. Discourse at funeral of Mrs. Lucy Bradford, Esq., Aug. 20, 1831. New London, 1832. 7 p. MBNMHi. 13029

Hurlgate and the proposed canal. (Project for cutting a ship canal across Hallet's Point, to avoid passing through Hurl Gate, i. e. Hell Gate. With a memorial to Congress, and the Acts of Incorporation of the Hallet's Cove Railway Company.) n. t. p. [New York, Snowden, 1832] 20 p. NN.
13030
---- New York, J. Dick [1832] 18 p. P.   13031

---- Poughkeepsie, P. Potter and Co. [1832] N; NHi.   13032

Hutchings, Elizabeth C. , 1813?-
Memoir of Charles L. Winslow,
Ceylon, January 12, 1821, died
in New York, May 24, 1832...by
Mrs. Hutchings. New York, Amer-
ican Tract Soc. , [1832?] 107 p.
CtW; ICP; NN; OO.   13033

Hutchings' Almanac for...1833 by
David Young. New York, D. D.
Smith [1832] 18 p. MWA.   13034

---- New York, N. B. Holmes,
[1832] 17 p. NN.   13035

---- New York, S. Marks & Son,
[1832] 18 p. DLC.   13036

---- Poughkeepsie, Edward M'-
Whood [1832] 18 p.   13037

Hutchins' Improved Almanac for
...1833...Published and sold
wholesale and retail by R. Bartlett & S. Raynor and Newburgh
by Sneden & Hathaway [1832]
18 p. MWA.   13038

Hutchins' improved family alman-
ac for 1833. New York, N.Y.,
Alexander Ming [1832] MWA.
                          13039
Hutchins' revised almanac. By
David Young. New York, Holmes,
1832. DLC; MWA; PHi.   13040

Hutchins' revised almanac for...
1833 by David Young. New York,
John C. Totten [1832] 18 p. NN.
                          13041
Hutton, Joseph.
Unitarians entitled to the name
of Christians. By Joseph Hutton,
LL. D. American Unitarian Assn.
1st series, no. 64. Boston, Pr.
by I. R. Butts, Gray & Bowen,
1832. 24 p. DLC; ICMe; MHi;
MeB; PPL.   13042

Hutton, William.
Hutton's book of nature laid
open. Adapted to the use of families and schools. 2d ed. By Rev.

J. L. Blake. Boston, Waitt &
Dow, 1832. 267 p. NBuG; OO.
                          13043

Hyde, Charles.
A sermon, preached at the
funeral of the Rev. Alfred Mitchell, pastor of the Second Congregational Church in Norwich,
December 22, 1831. By Rev.
Charles Hyde, Pastor of the
church at Norwich Falls. Norwich, Pub. by request of the So-
city, J. Dunham, 1832. 17 p.
CtNwchD; MBC; MiD-B; NN;
RPB.   13044

Hyde, William.
Boston Bookstore. Catalogue of
Christmas Gifts, and New Year's
Presents, for 1832. For sale by
William Hyde. n. p. [1832?] 18 p.
MHi.   13045

                 I

Illinois.
[Manual of the House of Representatives for 1832-3. Vandalia?
1832?]   13046

---- Message from the governor
of the state of Illinois, to both
Houses of the General Assembly.
Pr. by order of the Legislature.
Vandalia, M. Greiner, pub. pr. ,
1832. 16 p. IHi.   13047

Illinois Advocate. Edwardsville.
Illinois Advocate. Extra, general orders. To Col. (Nathaniel]
Buckmaster: you are hereby
commanded to cause your regiment of militia to convene...[6
lines] to meet without fail at
Beardstown on the 22d inst. to
repel an invasion of the Indians.
John Reynolds, Com. in Chief.
April 16, 1832. [Edwardsville,
1832] Broadside. IHi.   13048

Illinois College. Jacksonville.
Catalogue of the officers and

students in Illinois College, 1832-1833. [Jacksonville? 1832] 8 p. MHi; MWA.   13049

---- Historical sketch of the origin, progress, and wants, of Illinois college, June 1832. 2d ed. New York, Pr. by John T. West, 1832. 16 p. IJI; NNUT.
13050

Illinois Farmers' almanac for 1833...No. II. Calculated for the meridian of Vandalia, state of Illinois...By Benaiah Robinson. Edwardsville, Pr. & sold by John Y. Sawyer [1832] [24] p. IHi.   13051

Illinois Herald. Springfield.
Illinois Herald Extra. Springfield, April 20, 1832. The following letter was received by Gen. Neale and Col. Henry, last evening, by express. We have thought proper to lay it before the public without delay, together with the annexed communications to the Governor, received about the same time in an extra from the office of the Illinois Advocate...[136 l. in 2 col.] Broadside. IHi.   13052

Illinois. State Lyceum.
Circular. Bluffdale, Greene Co., Illinois, Sir: Herewith I send you the Constitution of the Illinois State Lyceum, of which you have been duly elected a member. ...n.p., The Lyceum, [1832?] 4 p. IHi.   13053

Illustrations of the four first degrees of female masonry... Boston, 1832. 32 p. DLC. 13054

Imitatio Christi. English.
An extract of Christian's pattern; or, A treatise on the Imitation of Christ written in Latin by Thomas à Kempis. By John Wesley, A.M. Baltimore, Jos. N. Lewis, 1832. 208 p. ICLaw;

MdBAHi; MdHi.   13055

---- ---- Boston, Lincoln & Edmands, 1832. 228 p. CSmH; MB; NcU.   13056

---- ---- New York, C. Wells, 1832. MBC; NBuG; NNG; NjNbS; PPL.   13057

---- The imitation of Christ. In three books. By Thomas à Kempis. Rendered into English from the original Latin, by John Payne. With an introductory essay, by Thos. Chalmers. A new ed., ed. by Howard Malcom. Boston, Lincoln & Edmands, 1832. 228 p. CSmH; MB; NcU.   13058

The import duties considered in relation to the happiness of the people and prosperity of the union. By a friend of the administration. Philadelphia, January 14, 1832. 10 p. MWA; MiD-B; NNC.
13059

Important facts for the people. 2d ed. From Poulson's American daily advertiser. Jackson and his veto. Philadelphia, Sept. 1832. 8 p. MWA; NjR; T.   13060

Improved roll book for superintendants of Sunday schools...2d ed. 1832. PPAmS.   13061

Indiana.
Journal of the House of Representatives of the state of Indiana, being the seventeenth session of the General Assembly, begun and held at Indianapolis, in said state, on Monday the 3d day of December, A.D. 1832. Indianapolis, N. Bolton, state pr., 1832. 640 p. In; InU; N.   13062

---- Journal of the Senate of the state of Indiana, during the seventeenth session of General Assembly, commenced at Indianapolis, on Monday the 3d of December,

1832. Indianapolis, A. F. Morrison, pr. to the Senate, 1832. 489 p. In; InU; N.   13063

---- Laws of the State of Indiana, passed and published at the sixteenth session of the General Assembly; held at Indianapolis, on the first Monday in December, one thousand eight hundred and thirty-one. By authority. Indianapolis (Ind.), Pr. by Douglass & Maguire, 1832. 302 p. Ar-SC; IaHi; MdBB; Nj; RPL.   13064

Indigent Widows' and Single Woman's Society of Philadelphia.
Constitution, with rules for the regulation of the board of managers and for the government of the asylum. Philadelphia, L. R. Bailey, 1832. 12 p. MB.
                                  13065
The infallibility of the Church of Christ. Hartford, Conn., Office of the United States Catholic Press, 1832. 16 p. MoFloSS.
                                  13066
The infant preacher, or, The story of Henrietta Smith. Sabbath breaking, a dialogue between two Sunday scholars. Ann Wood: and other pieces. Newburyport, C. Whipple [1832?] 36, 23 p. NN.
                                  13067
The infant school grammar, consisting of elementary lessons in the analytical method; illustrated by sensible objects and actions... 2d ed, enl. and imp. New-York, R. Lockwood & A. W. Corey, 1832. 9-140 p. DLC.   13068

Infant school primer, and arithmetical tables in verse, with a simple catechism for infant schools; containing the first principles of the Christian religion ...New York, Mahlon Day, 1832. 24 p. DAU.   13069

Infant School Society of the City of Boston.

Juvenile concert in Bowdoin Street Church, June 13, 1832. [Boston, 1832] 12 p. DLC. 13070

Infantry drill, being an abridgement of the tactics for the U.S. published by the Department of War, under the Act of March 22, 1829. Baltimore, n.p. [1832?] 192 p. CtHWatk; PHi.   13071

Ingalls, William, 1769-1851.
An essay on the ganglionary system of nerves in the cavity of the cranium, and its use. Boston, Marsh, Capen & Lyon, 1832. 15 p. DLC; MB; MH-M; DNLM; Nh.
                                  13072
Ingersoll, Charles Jared, 1782-1862.
Oration delivered before the Philadelphia Association for Celebrating the Fourth of July, without distinction of Party. By Chas. J. Ingersoll. July 4, 1832. Philadelphia, Pub. by order of the Association, 1832. 24 p. DLC; MBAt; MWA; NNC; PHi.   13073

Ingersoll, Charles M.
Conversations on English grammar, explaining the principles and rules of the language; illustrated by appropriate exercises; adapted to the use of schools. By Charles M. Ingersoll...10th ed. Boston, Wm. Hyde, 1832. 251 p. MB.   13074

---- ---- 11th ed. Boston, Wm. Hyde & Co., 1832. 377 p. Ct; MH; MoS; TxD-T; WU.   13075

Ingraham, Joseph Wentworth, 1799-1848.
Letters to Sunday scholars, on the geography & of the places mentioned in...the account of the nativity of our Saviour, and the season of Advent. New York [1832] 107 p. DLC; MH-AH.
                                  13076
Innes, William, 1770-1855.

Instruction for young inquirer:
being a series of addresses, intended to explain and enforce the
leading doctrines of the word of
God. By William Innes. Carefully revised. Boston, James Loring,
1832. 108 p. DLC; GDecCT.
13077
Interesting history of the September riots in 1831, the adoption of
a municipal form of government
in June, 1832. [Providence, 1832]
7 p. RP. 13078

Interrogative grammar; in a series of progessive and practical
questions: illustrating the principles of the English language, and
the mode of syntactical parsing
... Boston, Hilliard, Gray, Little, & Wilkins, 1832. 70 p.
CtHWatk; DLC; MB; MH; NNC.
13079
Ipswich Female Seminary.
Catalogue of the officers, and
members of Ipswich Female
Seminary. Salem, Pr. by Warwick Palfray, Jun., 1832. 10 p.
ICU. 13080

Iriarte y Oropesa, Tomás de,
1750-1791.
Fábulas literarias de d. Tomás de Iriarte, conteniendo todas
las fábulas literaries póstumes
del autor. Reimpreso de la edicion de Madrid de 1830... En
seguida se hallará la obra maestra
dramática, intitulade El si de las
niñas de d. Leandro Fernandez
de Moratin. Reimpresa de la última ed. corr. por el autor antes
de su fallecimiento. Preparado
...por F. Sales. Boston, Burdett,
1832. 144, 95 p. CtY; DLC; IU;
MH; MNBedf; OClW. 13081

---- Literary Fables of Don
Thomas De Iriarte. Boston, S.
Burdett & Co., 1832. 95 p. MH;
MeB. 13082

Irish eloquence. See also

Gowen, James.

Irish eloquence: the speeches of
the celebrated Irish orators, Philips, Curran and Grattan. To
which is added the powerful appeal of Robert Emmett, at the
close of his trial for high treason. Selected by a member of
the bar. Philadelphia, Key,
Meilke and Biddle, 1832. 370 p.
CSmH; GDecCT; Nj; OClW; ViU.
13083
Irving, Christopher, d. 1856.
A catechism of Botany...
adapted to the use of schools in
the United States. By C. Irving.
With engraved illustrations. 5th
Amer. ed., rev. and corr. New
York, Collins & Hannay, 1832.
82 p. NcWsS. 13084

---- A Catechism of Jewish antiquities; containing an account of
the classes, institutions, rites,
ceremonies, manners, customs,
etc. of the ancient Jews... By C.
Irving, LL.D... 5th Amer. ed.
New York, Collins & Hannay,
1832. 71 p. MH; MH-AH;
MRoxAND; MdBD; NcU. 13085

---- A catechism of mythology;
being a compendious history of
the heathen-gods, goddesses, and
heroes... By C. Irving... 5th Amer.
ed.; rev. & cor. New York, Collins & Hannay, 1832. 80 p. NjR.
13086
---- A catechism of universal
history. 5th Amer. ed., rev.
and cor. New-York, Collins &
Hannay, 1832. MB; MH; NjR.
13087
[Irving, Washington] 1783-1859.
The Alhambra: a series of
tales and sketches of the Moors
and Spaniards. By the author of
The sketch book... [1st ed.]
Philadelphia, Carey & Lea, 1832.
2 v. AU; DLC; InU; MA; OU;
PPA. 13088

---- A History of New York from
the beginning of the world to the
end of the Dutch dynasty, containing among many surprising
and curious matters, the unutter-
able ponderings of Walter the
doubter, the disastrous projects
of William the testy, and the chiv-
alric achievements of Peter the
headstrong, the three Dutch gov-
ernors of New-Amsterdam...7th
Amer. ed., by Diedrich Knickerbocker. Philadelphia, Carey &
Lea, 1832. 2 vols. CtY; KyLo;
MH; NN; PU.   13089

---- The Rocky Mountains; or,
Scenes, incidents, and adventures
in the far West; digested from
the journal of Capt. B. L. E.
Bonneville...and illustrated from
various other sources, by Washington Irving... Philadelphia,
Carey, Lea, & Blanchard, 1832-
1835. 2 v. CtY.   13090

---- The Sketch-Book. By Irving,
Washington. Philadelphia, Carey
& Lea, 1832. 2 v. IEG; MPlyA;
NN; PPL.   13091

---- Tales of a traveller. By
Washington Irving. 3d Amer. ed.
Philadelphia, Carey & Lea, 1832.
2 v. CtY; ICU; MeU; NNUT;
PPL.   13092

Isabel Waltz. arranged for the
guitar by L. Meignen. Philadelphia, Willig, 1832. 1 p. MB.
                           13093
Ithaca and Owego Railroad Company.
    Prospects of the Ithaca &
Owego rail road company. [n.p.]
Pr. by Hosford & Wait [1832?]
14 p. DBRE; MB; MiU; NN;
PPL.   13094

Iucho, Wilhelm.
    New-York gallopade. New
York, 1832. CtY.   13095

Ives, Elam, 1802-1864.
    The American elementary sing-
ing book, designed as the first
book for the study of music.
Hartford, F. J. Huntington, 1832.
108 p. CtMW; DLC; ICHi; MB;
PHi; RPB.   13096

---- American Sunday-school
psalmody: or, Hymns & music
for the use of Sunday schools &
teacher's meetings. Philadelphia,
American Sunday School Union,
1832. 56 p. AmSSchU; CtMW;
ICP; KyLoP; NNUT; PP.   13097

Ives, Levi Silliman.
    A sermon at the opening of the
first convention...delivered in St.
Paul's Church, Edenton, N.C.,
May 1832: by the Rt. Rev. Levi
Silliman Ives. New-York, Pr. at
the Protestant Episcopal Press,
1832. 26 p. CSmH; InID; MWA;
MdBD; MWA; NcD.   13098

Ivimey, Joseph.
    John Milton: life and times,
by Joseph Ivimey. New York, D.
Appleton & co., 1832. GMM.
                           13099

J

J. Parker and Company.
    Stage arrangements for 1832.
East & west from Utica...[Utica,
Pr. by William Williams for J.
Parker & Co., 1832] Broadside.
NBuHi.   13100

Jackson, Andrew.
    An address to the friends of
General Andrew Jackson, in
North-Carolina: and the support-
ers of his administration in the
affairs of the general government. Raleigh, Pr. at the office
of the Constitutionalist, Oct.
1832. 14 p. NcHiC; PPL. 13101

---- The Claims of Andrew Jackson to the Office of President, impartially examined. New-York, Pr. by John M. Danforth, 1832. 12 p. BrMus. 13102

---- Message at the opening to the second session of the twenty-second Congress. [Washington, 1832] Broadside. MH. 13103

---- President Jackson's proclamation against the nullification ordinance of South Carolina, December 11, 1832. Washington, 1832. 20 p. A-Ar; NiU; PHi; T; TxDaM. 13104

---- Proclamation by Andrew Jackson, President of the United States...Done at the city of Washington, this 10th day of December...1832...Ed. Livingston, Secy. of State. [Washington, D.C., 1832] Broadside. DLC; MB; MH; WHi. 13105

---- Veto message from the President of the United States, returning the bank bill, with his objections &. To the Senate: ...Andrew Jackson. Washington, July 10, 1832. Broadside. CtSoP; ICN; MH; MHi; RNHi. 13106

[Jackson (Charles)]
Report on the establishment of a Farm School. See under Boston. Farm and Trade School, Thompson's Island.

Jackson, Charles Thomas, 1805-1880.
Remarks on the mineralogy and geology of the peninsula of Nova Scotia, accompanied by a colored map, illustrative of the structure of the country, and by general views of its scenery, by Charles Thomas Jackson and Francis Alger. Cambridge, Metcalf, 1832. 116 p. CtY; ICU; MH; Me; PPAN. 13107

Jackson, Daniel, b. 1790.
Alonzo and Melissa; or The unfeeling father. An American tale. Sanborton [N.H.?] D. V. Moulton, 1832. 253 p. MB; NjR; OClWHi; OU; ViU. 13108

Jackson, Isaac Rand, d. 1843.
A sketch of the life and public service of W. H. Harrison. New York, Pr. by Harper & bros., 1832. 32 p. NN. 13109

Jackson, James, 1810-1834.
Cases of cholera collected at Paris, in the month of April, 1832, in the wards of MM. Andral and Louis, at the hospital, La Pitié. By James Jackson, jr. Boston, Carter, Hendee & Co., 1832. 212 p. DLC; MB; PPAmP; RPB; TxU. 13110

Jackson, Samuel, 1787-1872.
The Principles of Medicine, founded on the structure and functions of animal organism. By Samuel Jackson, M.D. ... Philadelphia, Carey & Lea, 1832. 630 [28] p. CoCsE; CtY; DLC; PPA; PU; ViRA. 13111

Jackson and liberty! Republicans awake. The Republicans of the towns of Augusta, Vernon, Verona, and their vicinities, in the county of Oneida, are requested to meet at the inn of Capt. Ichabod Hand, in the town of Vernon, on Thursday next, at 1 o'clock in the afternoon, to adopt such measures as shall be deemed expedient in relation to the approaching election. [Utica? 1832] Broadside. NBuHi. 13112

Jacob, William, 1762?-1851.
An historical inquiry into the production and consumption of the precious metals. By William Jacob... Philadelphia, Carey & Lea, 1832. 427 p. CtY; GHi; ICU; MiD; PPA; WU. 13113

Jacob and his sons; or, The second part of a conversation between Mary and her mother. Prepared for the American Sunday School Union by Rev. Thos. H. Gallaudet... Philadelphia, American Sunday School Union, 1832. 103 p. DLC.   13114

Jacobs, Frederick Wilhelm, 1764-1847.
Greek reader. 6th New York from 9th German ed. with imp., additional notes and corrs. by David Patterson. New York, Collins & Hannay, etc., 1832. 258, 78 p. CtHT; NcHpC; RWe; ViSwc.   13115

---- ...Jacob's Latin reader. First part. With a vocabulary and English notes. For the use of schools, academies, etc. Boston, Hilliard, Gray, Little & Wilkins, 1832. 264 p. KAStB; MH; NNC; PMA; RNR.   13116

Jahn, Johann, 1750-1816.
Jahn's Biblical archaeology, translated from the Latin, with additions and corrections, by Thos. C. Upham...3d ed. Andover, Flagg & Gould, 1832. 532 p. NNUT; PBa; PPDroP; RNR; ViU.   13117
---- ---- Andover, Mark Newman, 1832. 573 p. CBPac; IaGG; KyU; MH; MeB.   13118

---- ---- New York, J. Leavitt, 1832. 573 p. CtB; DLC; IEG; MWA; OO.   13119

James, Edwin.
Chippewa First Lessons in spelling and reading. By Edwin James, M.D. Pub. by the Baptist Board of Missions. Boston, Lincoln & Edmands, 1832. 16 p. MBGCT; MWA; NN.   13120

James, George Payne Rainsford, 1799?-1860.

Henry Masterton: or, The adventures of a young cavalier. By the author of "Richelieu," "Philip Augustus," &c....New York, J. & J. Harper, 1832. 2 v. LNH; MBAt; MHa; NBLIHI; NN; PPA.   13121
---- The history of chivalry. By G. P. R. James, Esq. New York, J. & J. Harper, 1832. 342 p. KyLo; MHi; NBuG; PLT; RPA; TxU.   13122

James, John Angell, 1785-1859.
The family monitor; or, A help to domestic happiness. Concord, N.H., Oliver Sanborn, 1832. 216 p. MnU.   13123

---- The Sunday school teacher's guide. By J. A. James. Philadelphia, American Sunday School Union, 1832. 87 p. GDecCT; ICBB.   13124

James, Thomas P.
Musci Cestrici the anophytes of Chester county, Pa. Philadelphia, 1832. PWcT.   13125

James, William.
Last will of W. James. [Albany, 1832] 19 p. MB.   13126

Jameson, Anna Brownell (Murphy) 1794-1860.
Characteristics of women. New York, Saunders, 1832. PNt.   13127
---- Diary of an ennuyee. Memoirs of celebrated female sovereigns. New York, 1832. 2 v. MdBP.   13128

---- Legends of the Madonna as represented in the fine arts. Boston, 1832. 483 p. MW. 13129

---- Memoirs of celebrated female sovereigns. By Mrs. Jameson...New York, Harper, 1832. 2 v. CtHT; LNT; NcU; PHC; PPA; ViU.   13130

---- Shakespeare's characters of the passions and imagination. New York, Leavitt & Allen bros., 1832. 158 p. MSwe. 13131

Jameson, Horatio Gates, 1778-1855.
An epitome of the epidemic cholera; in which is exhibited an inquiry into the character, nature and prevention of the disease, its treatment, etc. By H. G. Jameson... Baltimore, Pr. by W. Wooddy, 1832. 78 p. MnU. 13132

Jameson, Robert, 1774-1854.
Narrative of discovery and adventure in Africa, from the earliest ages to the present time: with illustrations... By Prof. Jameson, James Wilson and Hugh Murray. New York, Harper, 1832. 359 p. AU; MHi; OrCS; TxHR; WvW. 13133

Jane and her teacher. Philadelphia [1832?] BrMus. 13134

Jane Courtney. By the author of 'The gold thimble.' 'The adventures of a bodkin.'... Boston, Cottons & Barnard, 1832. 54 p. plates. [Boston, 1832] MB. 13135

Jane Scott. See American Sunday School Union.

Jaquith, Moses.
An appeal to the public: in a case of cruelty, inflicted on a child of Mr. Jaquith, at the Mayhew school in Hawkins-st. by Wm. Clough... Boston, Pub. for the benefit of the public, 1832. 24 p. DLC; MH; NN. 13136

[Jardine, David] 1794-1860.
... Criminal trials. v. 1- Boston, 1832- 1 v. CtY; MDeeP; NCH; PU-L; RP. 13137

Jay, William, 1769-1858.
The Christian Contemplated; in a course of lectures, delivered in Argyle Church, Bath. By Wm. Jay... Philadelphia, Key, Mielke & Biddle, 1832. 264 p. CBCDS; ICBB; KWiU; MHoly; NbOP; PU. 13138

---- An essay on marriage; or, The duty of Christians to marry religiously... From the 2d London ed. Philadelphia, W. S. Young, 1832. 34 p. PPLT; PPM. 13139

---- Evening exercises for the closet: for every day in the year ... New York, Daniel Appleton, 1832. 2 vols. in 1. CtY; IAIS; NN; NPlaK; WNaE. 13140

---- Exercises for the closet, for every day in the year, by Wm. Jay... Stereotyped by D. Fanshaw. New York, John P. Haven, 1832. 2 vols. in 1. CSmH; GEU-T; ICU; NN; TxShA. 13141

---- Prayers for the use of families; or, The domestic minister's assistant. Hartford, Silas Andrus, 1832. 266 p. AFlT, CtSoP; NCH. 13142

---- ---- Philadelphia, Hogan & Thompson, 1832. 249 p. KyLxT; MH. 13143

---- Sermons by William Jay, to which is annexed an essay on marriage. 3d Amer. from 2d London ed. Philadelphia, Wm. S. Young, 1832. 240, 22 p. CSansS; KyLxT; OMC; PPLT; ScCoT. 13144

---- Standard works of Rev. Wm. Jay; of Argyle Chapel, Bath. Comprising all his works known in this country; and also several which have not heretofore been presented to the American public. Baltimore, Plaskitt & Co., 1832. 3 v. CSansS; InID; LNB; NNUT; PWW. 13145

---- Thoughts on marriage... Boston, 1832. 240 p. MH; MWA. 13146

---- Works. By Rev. Wm. Jay.
Baltimore, n.p., n.pr., 1832.
3 vols. NjPT.   13147

Jefferson, Thomas.
   Notes on the state of Virginia.
By Thos. Jefferson. Boston,
Lilly and Wait, 1832. 280 p. CtY;
ICMe; MHi; TNP; ViU.   13148

---- Observations on the writings
of Jefferson... See under Lee,
Henry, 1787-1837.

Jefferson College. Canonsburg,
Pa.
   A catalogue of books belonging
to the Franklin Literary Society
of Jefferson College. Pittsburgh,
Pr. by D. & M. Maclean, 1832.
13 p. PWW.   13149

---- Catalogue of the officers
and students of Jefferson College,
Canonsburg. July, 1832. Pittsburgh, Pr. by D. & M. Maclean
[1832] 12 p. PHi; PWW.   13150

Jefferson College. Washington,
Miss.
   Improved river land. Apply to
the undersigned at Washington,
Mississippi. B. L. C. Wailes,
agent of Jefferson College. 20th
December 1832. Pr. by Andrew
Marschalk [Natchez? 1832]
Broadside. Ms-Ar.   13151

---- (Prospectus). 1832. MH.
                                 13152
---- Washington, Miss. Oct. 10,
1832. [Natchez, 1832] Broadside.
Ms-Ar.   13153

---- Washington, Miss. 1st. Dec.
1832. Sir: [Natchez? 1832]
Broadside. Ms-Ar.   13154

Jefferson Medical College, Philadelphia.
   Annual announcement of lectures, &c. &c. &c. by the trustees and professors of Jefferson

Medical College, Philadelphia:
for the year 1832. Philadelphia,
Pr. for the Medical faculty, by
Clark & Raser, 1832. 16 p. CtY;
DLC; MB; NjP; OCHP; P.   13155

Jenkins, Charles, 1786-1831.
   Sermons by the late Charles
Jenkins, pastor of the Third Con-
gregational Church. Portland, A.
Shirley, 1832. 407 p. CtY; DLC;
MH-AH; OO; USI.   13156

Jenks, Benjamin, 1646-1724.
   Prayers and offices of devo-
tion for families and for particu-
lar persons upon most occasions.
Altered and imp. by the Rev.
Charles Simeon. New York,
Swords, 1832. 300 p. CSmH;
CtHT; MiToC.   13157

Jennings, Obadiah, 1778-1832.
   Debate on Campbellism; held
at Nashville, Tennessee, in which
the principles of Alexander Campbell are confuted, and his conduct examined, by Obadiah Jennings. To which is prefixed, A
memoir of the author. Pittsburgh,
Pr. by D. & M. Maclean, 1832.
252 p. DLC; ICN; KyDC; NN; OO;
PPi; T.   13158

Jennison, Timothy Lindall
   Description of a foveat and
compressor, an improved mode of
preparing and using fomentations
in cases of sickness and surgery.
Cambridge, 1832. MBAt.   13159

Jerram, Charles, 1770-1853.
   Conversations on infant bap-
tism. By Chas. Jerram. Phila-
delphia, Latimer & co., 1832.
GAGTh; GDecCT; ICT; LN; PPLT.
                                 13160
---- A tribute of affection to the
memory of a beloved daughter
(Hannah Jerram) containing some
hints on the religious education.
Baltimore, n.p., 1832. 28 p.
CtHT.   13161

Jerrold, Douglas William, 1803-1857.
...The rent day, a domestic drama, in three acts. As performed at the Theatre Royal, (Drury Lane) and American Theatre, (Bowery). By Douglas Jerrold...Pr. from the acting copy, with stage directions. New-York, E. B. Clayton and C. Neal, [1832] 48 p. C; MB; MH; OCl.
                                        13162

Jesse, Edward, 1780-1868.
Gleanings in natural history; with local recollections. By Edward Jesse, Esq. Philadelphia, 1832. PPL-R.   13163

Jewett, Charles, 1807-1879.
An address delivered before the Richmond and Exeter Union Society for the Promotion of Temperance, June 10, 1832. Providence, Pr. by J. Knowles, 1832. 16 p. NN; RP.   13164

[Jewett, Isaac Appleton] 1808-1853.
...A brief history and defence of the drama. [Cincinnati? 1832?] 69 p. DLC; MH; NNC.   13165

Jewett, Paul.
The New-England Farrier; or, a Compendium of Farriery, in four parts; wherein most of the diseases to which horses, neat cattle, sheep and swine are incident, are treated of; with Medical and Surgical Observations thereon. The Remedies in general, are such as are easily procured, safely applied, and happily successful; being the result of many years experience--and first production of the kind in N.E. To which is added an Appendix, never before published, etc. 2d ed., enl. Exeter, John J. Williams, 1832.   13166

Jewsbury, Maria Jane, 1800-1833.

Letters to the young. 3d ed. Philadelphia, Presbyterian Board of Publication [1832?] 232 p. CSansS; PHi.   13167

Johnson, Alexander Bryan.
A discourse on language. Utica, Wm. Williams, book pr., 1832. 28 p. CSmH; MB; MnHi; NjR; PPAmP.   13168

Johnson, Edwin Ferry, 1803-1872.
...Method of conducting the canal surveys in the state of New York... [Middletown, Conn., 1832] 10 p. MH-BA.   13169

Johnson, Evan M.
Parish details; containing a statement of the parish statistics of St. John Church, Brooklyn, L.I., prepared for the use of the congregation, to Jan. 14, 1832. by Evan M. Johnson, Rector. New York, Protestant Episcopal Press, 1832. 14 p. MdBD; NBLiHi.   13170

Johnson, N. E.
An address delivered in Homer, at the annual meeting of the Cortland Co. Temperance Society, January 24, 1832. Homer, N.Y., Kinney, 1832. PPPrHi.   13171

Johnson, Oliver, 1809-1889.
A dissertation on the subject of future punishment...By Oliver Johnson. Boston, Peirce & Parker, 1832. 32 p. ICMe; MB; MBC; OO.
                                        13172

Johnson, Samuel, 1709-1784.
Johnson's English dictionary, as improved by Todd, and abridged by Chalmers; with Walker's pronouncing dictionary, combined: to which is added, Walker's key to the classical pronunciation of Greek, Latin, and scripture proper names. Boston, Joseph A. Ballard; Hillard, Gray & Co.; and Perkins & Marvin, 1832. 1156 p. MH; MW; TxSaO.   13173

---- The works of Samuel Johnson. New York, A. V. Blake,
[1832] 2 v. CtY; NN.   13174

---- ---- with an essay on his
life and genius, by Arthur Murphy, esq. 1st complete Amer.
ed. New York, G. Dearborn,
1832. 2 v. in 1. IEN; NcU;
OCIW; TU; ViU.   13175

---- ---- 3d complete Amer. ed.
New York, Harper & Bros.
[1832?] 2 vols. MHab; MMal;
NbU; OWoC.   13176

Johnson, Samuel Roosevelt,
1802-1873.
    An address by the Rev. Sam-
uel R. Johnson, on moving the
acceptance of the twenty-third
annual report of the New-York
Protestant Episcopal Tract Society in St. John's chapel, October
4, 1832. (New York, New York
Protestant Episcopal Tract Society, 1832) 8 p. NNG.   13177

Johnson, W[alter] R[ogers] 1794-
1852.
    A concise view of the general
state of education in the United
States... [Philadelphia, W. F.
Geddes, 1832] 9 p. DLC;
OCIWHi.   13178

---- Description on the rotoscope
for exhibiting several phenomena
and illustrating certain laws of
rotary motion. New Haven, 1832?
18 p. DLC; MH.   13179

---- Experimental inquiries respecting head and vapor; with
some practical applications, by
Walter R. Johnson [New Haven,
1832?] 54 p. DLC; MH.   13180

---- ---- Philadelphia, 1832.
PPAN; PPL; PPM.   13181

---- Observations and experiments on the rapid production of
steam in contact with metals at
a high temperature. (With additions.) New Haven, etc.? 1832?
54 p. MH.   13182

---- On the utility of visible illustrations... Delivered before
the American Institute of Instruction. Boston, 1832. MDeeP.
                           13183
---- ...Remarks on the strength
of cylindrical steam boilers. By
Walter R. Johnson, prof. of nat.
philosophy in the Franklin Institute, Philadelphia. Read before
the Institute...July 26, 1832.
[New Haven? 1832?] 12 p.
CSmH; DLC; MB; MH; PPAN.
                           13184
---- ---- Philadelphia, Pr. by
J. Harding, 1832. 8 p. CSmH;
DLC; MB; PPAN.   13185

Johnson, William Cost, 1806-1860.
    Speech of William Cost John-
son, in the Legislature of Maryland, December session, 1832,
on the bill reported by him for
regulating the admission of attornies (sic) to the bar of the
courts of the state. Frederick,
n.p., 1832. 24 p. DLC; MWA;
MdBE; NjR; OCLaw; PPAmP.
                           13186
---- To the citizens of the United
States against nullification by a
native of Maryland. Baltimore?
n.p., 1832? 24 p. PPL.   13187

Johnson's almanac. By William
Collom. Philadelphia, Willard
Johnson [1832] MWA; NN. 13188

Johnston, Algernon Sidney, 1801-
1853.
    Memoirs of a nullifier; writ-
ten by himself. By a native of
the South. (Thos. Cooper) Columbia, S.C., The Telescope office,
1832. 110 p. CSmH; MWA; NIC;
OCIWHi; RP.   13189

Johnston, David Claypole.

Scraps; designed, engraved, and published by D. C. Johnston. Boston, Johnston, 1832. 4 p. CLCM; DLC; MB; PPL.   13190

Johnston, Josiah Stoddard, 1784-1833.
Remarks relative to certain charges against the bank of the United States, in reply to Mr. Benton. [Washington, 1832?] 10 p. DLC; MH-BA; MH-L.   13191

Johnston, William.
The age of enquiry. Consisting of several letters, on the authenticity of the Scriptures. Addressed to the Rev. Andrew Murphey... Pub. by the Liberal tract and free press association of Chester County, Pennsylvania. Wilmington, Del., Pr. at the Free Press Office, 1832. 28 p. CSmH; NN.
                                    13192

Johnstone, Christian Isobel, 1781-1857.
... Lives and voyages of Drake, Cavendish, and Dampier; including an introductory view of the earlier discoveries in the South Sea and the history of the buccaneers... New York, J. & J. Harper, 1832. 332 p. CtY; IP; OM; RP; ViAL.   13193

Jones, Abner, 1772-1841.
Melodies of the Church; a collection of psalms and hymns, adapted to publick and social worship, seasons of revival, monthly concerts of prayer, and various similar occasions. Selected from Watts and other authors... By Abner Jones. New York, Henry C. Sleight, 1832. CtY; InCW; NNUT; PPi; Vi.
                                    13194

Jones, Charles Colcock, 1804-1863.
The religious instruction of the negroes. A sermon, delivered before associations of planters in Liberty and M'Intosh counties,

Georgia, by the Rev. Charles Colcock Jones, of Savannah. 4th ed. Princeton, N.J., Pr. by D'-Hart & Connolly, 1832. 38 p. MH; NcD; PHC; PPPrHi.   13195

Jones, Elizabeth C.
The infant speaker. By Miss E. C. Jones. Boston, F. B. Callender, 1832. 32 p. DLC. 13196

Jones, Isaac Dashiell.
An address, delivered before the Somerset County colonization society; at their first annual meeting, July 4, 1832. By Isaac D. Jones, esq. Pub. by order of the society. Princess-Anne, Md., Pr. by J. S. Zieber, 1832. 16 p. DLC; MdHi; MdToH; PHi; PWW. 13197

[Jones, Miss]
The False Step, and The Sisters. New York, J. & J. Harper, 1832. 2 v. NCH; NN; RPB; ViLxW.   13198

Jones, Talbot.
Helps to the study of the prophecies. See under title.

Jones, Thomas P., 1774-1848.
New conversations on chemistry, adapted to the present state of that science; wherein its elements are clearly and familiarly explained. With one hundred and eighteen engravings... appropriate questions; a list of experiments, and a glossary. On the foundations of Mrs. Marcet's "Conversations on chemistry." By Thos. P. Jones...J. Grigg, Philadelphia, 1832. 332 p. A-GS; CtHWatk; MiU; OU; PPAN; TxSoU.
                                    13199

Jones, William, 1762-1846.
The history of the Christian church from the birth of Christ to the 18th century: including the very interesting account of the Waldenses and Albigensis...2 v. in 1. 3d Amer. from 5th London

ed. Philadelphia, R. W. Pomeroy, 1832. 607 p. CtY; GMW; NNUT; PLT; MH; WHi.   13200

---- Letters from a tutor to his pupils. By the Rev. Wm. Jones. (New ed.)... New-York, 1832. CtY; MAm; MBC; NNG; RPB.
13201

Josephus, Flavius.
The works of Flavius Josephus. The learned and authentic Jewish historian and celebrated warrior. With three dissertations concerning Jesus Christ. John the Baptist... to Abraham, etc. and explanatory notes and observations. Trans. by Wm. Whiston A. M. Complete in one vol., Stereotype ed. Baltimore, Armstrong & Plaskett and Plaskett & Co., 1832. 648 p. CtY; ICU; MBev; NCaS; TJaL.   13202

---- ---- Philadelphia, J. Grigg, 1832. 2 vols. IAlS; MiDU; NDunk; OClWHi.   13203

Josse, Augustin Louis, 1763-1841.
A grammar of the Spanish language, with practical exercises... By M. Josse, revised, amended, imp. and enl. by F. Sales. 5th Amer. ed. Boston, 1832. 2 vol. in 1. CtYL LNL; MHi; NNC; PPAmP.   13204

Journal of the Institute at Flushing, for October, 1832. Jamaica, I. F. Jones & Co., 1832? NN; NSmb.   13205

Judson, Adoniram, 1788-1850.
Christian baptism. A sermon, preached in the Lal bazar chapel, Calcutta: on Lord's day, Sept. 27, 1812: previous to the administration of the ordinance of baptism. With many quotations from Pedobaptist authors. By Adoniram Judson, jun., A.M. 4th Amer. ed., cor. and enl. Boston, Lincoln & Edmands; Hartford, F. J.

Huntington; [etc., etc.] 1832. 64 p. DLC; NNUT; OClWHi; RPB; ViU.   13206

---- ---- 5th Amer. ed. By Adoniram Judson. Boston, 1832. 64 p. NjPT.   13207

---- A letter, addressed to the female members of the Christian church, in the United States of America. New Haven, Baldwin & Treadway, 1832. 12 p. Ct; MBC; NCH-S; OO; RWe.   13208

---- Letter of Rev. A. Judson, (Baptist missionary at Burmah) to the female members of the Christian churches in the United States of America. New York, Sleight & Robinson, 1832. 8 p. MB.   13209

---- Letter to female members of Christian churches in United States. 2 ed. Providence, 1832. 12 p. OO; RP; RPB.   13210

---- Letter to the female members of Christian churches in the United States of America. Providence, Pr. by H. H. Brown, 1832. 12 p. Ct; MBC; MWA; NN; PCA; RPB.   13211

Julia changed; or, The true secret of a happy Christmas. Written for the American Sunday School Union and rev. by the Committee of Publication. Philadelphia, American Sunday School Union, 1832. 71 p. DLC. 13212

Junius, pseud.
Peacock; parallel between an address by John Smith, of Portsmouth, N. H. and addresses delivered by chief justice Story, Hon. Daniel Webster, and Hon. Edward Everett. Boston, 1832. 8 p. Nh-Hi.   13213

Junot, Laure Permon, Duchesse-

d'Abrantes.
Memoirs. New York, 1832.
MB; MdBP.   13214

Juvenalis, Decimus Junius.
Decimi Junii Juvenalis et Auli
Persii Flacci Satirae expurgatae,
notis illustratae. Curavit F. P.
Leverett. Bostoniae, Hilliard,
Gray, Little et Wilkins, 1832.
252 p. GU-M; KyLoS; LNT; RNR;
TNP.   13215

---- Satirae expurgatae; notis
illus. curavit F. P. Leverett.
Bostoniae, Hilliard Gray et al,
1832. 1828 p. IaMvC; OSand;
PPM.   13216

Juvenile biography; or, Brief
memoirs of Ann Town, Sarah
Colby, and others... Boston, Pr.
by Waitt & Dow's press, for C.
D. Strong, 1832. 6 v. FNp; ICU;
NNC; NNU-W.   13217

The Juvenile library by Mrs.
Tuthill and others. Boston, Cros-
by, Nichols & Co., 1832. ICU;
KyBgW.   13218

Juvenile pastimes, or sports for
the four seasons. Part I (Spring,
Summer) Embellished with 28 neat
copperplate engravings. Providence, Cory, Marshall and Hammond (1832). 8 l. DLC; PP.
                                       13219
---- Part II (Autumn, Winter)
Embellished with 28 neat copperplate engravings. Providence,
Cory, Marshall and Hammond
[1832] 8 l. MB; PP.   13220

Juvenile Poems. Wendell, Mass.,
J. Metcalf, 1832. 18 p. ICU;
MH.   13221

Juvenile Rambler; or, family and
school journal. Vol. 1- Jan. 4,
1832- Boston, Allen & Goddard,
etc., 1832- DLC; MB; NN; OO;
RPB.   13222

The juvenile rollin; or conversations on ancient history. By a
Mother. Boston, Hyde, 1832.
242 p. DLC; NNU-W.   13223

K

Kane, Elias K.
Speech of Mr. Kane of Illinois,
upon the arrangement of the colonial trade with Great Britain. Delivered in the Senate of the United
States, on the 8th of April, 1832.
Washington, F. P. Blair, 1832.
28 p. CtSoP; DLC; MeB; NNC;
PPl-R.   13224

Kappa lambda society, New York.
Report of the committee of the
K. A. society, appointed for the
purpose of preparing an account
of the mode of treatment of epidemic cholera. June, 1832. New-
York, Pr. for the society [1832]
16 p. DLC; MHi; NjR; OClM;
PU.   13225

Kater, Henry, 1777-1835.
A treatise on mechanics. By
Capt. Henry Kater... and the Rev.
Dionysius Lardner... Philadelphia,
Carey & Lea, 1832. 287, 2 p.
CU; ICJ; MB; NjR; RNR. 13226

Kay, James.
Twenty questions to Trinitar-
ians with answers from Scripture
by James Kay. Boston, Gray &
Brown, 1832. 18 p. DLC; MB;
MH; MMeT-Hi; TxDaM.   13227

Keepsake Americaine. New York
[etc.] C. DeBehr, 1832. [et Phil-
adelphie, 1832, all in French]
362 p. DLC; MB; NN; TU.
                                       13228
Keightley, Thomas, 1789-1872.
Outlines of universal history
embracing a concise history of
the world, from the earliest period to the present time... to
which are added tabular views of

royal dynasties, etc. Ed. by
John Frost. Philadelphia, Key,
Mielkes, 1832. 66 p. MB;
MiDSH; MiDU; NW; PPM. 13229

Keith, Alexander, 1791-1880.
...Evidence of the truth of the
Christian religion, derived from
the literal fulfilment of prophecy;
particularly as illustrated by the
history of the Jews, and by the
discoveries of recent travellers.
By the Rev. Alexander Keith...
From the 6th Edinburgh ed....
New York, J. & J. Harper, 1832.
284 p. CU; LNB; MdBD; NcU;
PPA; ScCoT.   13230

---- The signs of the times, as
denoted by the fulfilment of historical predictions traced down
from the Babylonian captivity to
the present time. 2 vol. New
York, Johnathan Leavitt; Boston,
Crocker & Brewster, 1832. 2 vol.
CtY; GHi; InCW; NjR; ViRU.
                               13231
Keith, Thomas, 1759-1824.
A new treatise on the use of
the globes; or, A philosophical
view of the earth and heavens...
preceded by an extensive selection of astronomical, and other
definitions; and illustrated by a
great variety of problems, questions for the examination of the
student, etc. etc. Designed for
the instruction of youth. By Thos.
Keith. Rev. and cor. by Rbt.
Adrian... New York, S. Wood &
sons, 1832. 334 p. CSt; DLC;
IEG; LNP; MH; NNC; PPL.
                               13232
Kelley, Hall Jackson, 1790-1874.
The Western spelling book,
designed for common schools.
Containing the elements of the
English language, lessons in
orthography and reading, with
the pronunciation of Walker's
Critical pronouncing dictionary...
By Hall J. Kelley... Cincinnati,
Hubbard & Edmands; Boston,

Lincoln and Edmands, 1832.
168 p. DLC.   13233

Kemble, Butler Frances Anne,
1809-1893.
Dramatic sketch. New York
Mirror...1832. PU.   13234

---- Francis the First; a tragedy
in five acts as performed at the
Theatre royal, Covent garden.
New York, Peabody, 1832. 63 p.
ICU; MWA; PU; RNR; ViU.
                               13235
---- ---- Philadelphia, W. Tur-
ner, 1832. 79, [1] p. CSt; MBAt;
MH; MWA; RPB.   13236

Kempis, Thomas A., 1340-1471.
The Imitation of Christ; in 3
books (in one). By Thos. A. Kempis. Rendered into English from
the original Latin by John Payne,
with an introductory essay by
Thomas Chalmers. A new ed.,
edited by Howard Malcom. Boston, Lincoln & Edmands, 1832.
228 p. IaDa; MB; MoS; ScNC.
                               13237
Kendall, Benjamin F., 1799-1854.
The doleful tragedy of the
raising of Jo Burnham or the
"cat let out of the bag." In five
acts, illustrated with engravings.
By Timothy Tickle. Woodstock,
Pr. by W. W. Prescott, 1832.
96 p. DLC; MH.   13238

Kennebec Association.
Minutes of the Kennebec As-
sociation. Third anniversary.
Augusta, W. Hastings, 1832. 8 p.
MiD-B.   13239

[Kennedy, Grace] 1782-1825.
Anna Ross; a story for chil-
dren. ...4th Amer. ed. Oxford,
N.Y., Pr. by Chapman & Flagler
for G. Hunt, 1832. 144 p. CSmH;
DLC.   13240

[Kennedy, John Pendleton] 1795-
1870.

Swallow barn, or A sojourn in
the Old Dominion... Philadelphia,
Carey & Lea, 1832. 2 v. CSmH;
LNT; MH; PPA; PU; ScC.   13241

[Kennedy, William]
An only son, a narrative by
the author of "My Early Days."
1st Amer. ed. Boston, L. C.
Bowles, etc. , 1832. 272 p. MB;
MH; NCats.   13242

Kenrick, Francis Patrick, 1797-
1863.
Substance of a sermon,
preached in St. Patrick's Church,
Pittsburgh, Pa. , on Sunday the
11th of November, 1832 the twenty second Sunday after Pentecost.
Pub. by request. Pittsburg, Pr.
by Conway & Phillips, 1832. 12 p.
NNF; OCHP; PHi.   13243

Kenrick, William, 1789-1872.
Annual catalogue of fruit and
hardy ornamental trees, shrubs
... Boston, New England farmer
office, 1832. 30 p. DLC. 13244

---- The new American orchard-
ist, or an account of the most
valuable varieties of fruit adapted
to cultivation in the climate of
the United States. Also a brief
description of the most ornamental forest trees, shrub, flowers,
etc. Boston, Carter, Hendee
[1832] 423 p. NIC.   13245

Kent, George, 1796-1884.
The characteristics and claims
of the age in which we live. An
oration, pronounced at Dartmouth
College, August 23, 1832, before
the New-Hampshire Alpha of the
Phi Beta Kappa Society. By Geo.
Kent. Pub. by request of the Society. Concord, Moses G. Atwood, 1832. 42 p. DLC; ICN;
KWiU; PHi; RPB.   13246

Kent, James, 1763-1847.
Commentaries on American

law. By James Kent... 2d ed.
New-York, O. Halsted, 1832.
4 v. DLC; ICP; NcD; TNP; VtU.
                          13247
Kentucky.
Acts passed at the first session of the fortieth General Assembly for the Commonwealth of
Kentucky, begun and held in the
town of Frankfort, on Monday the
7th day of November, in the year
1831, and of the Commonwealth
the fortieth.   Thos. Metcalfe,
Governor. Pub. by authority.
Frankfort, Ky. , Albert G. Hodges,
public pr. , 1832. 252 p. IaU-L;
Ky; KyHi; W; Wa-L.   13248

---- General Assembly.
House of Representatives. Se-
lect committee on nullification.
Kentucky legislature-nullification.
... Washington, Pr. by Duff Green,
1832. 8 p. DLC; RPB.   13249

---- Journal of the House of Representatives of the commonwealth
of Kentucky, begun and held in
the town of Frankfort, on Monday,
the third day of Dec. , in the year
of our Lord 1832, and of the commonwealth the forty first. Frankfort, Pr. by Albert G. Hodges,
for the state, 1832. InU; Ky;
KyU-L.   13250

---- Journal of the Senate of the
Commonwealth of Kentucky, begun and held in the town of Frankfort, on Monday the third day of
December, in the year of our
Lord 1832, and of the Commonwealth the Forty-First. Frankfort, Albert G. Hodges, Pr. for
the state, 1832. 424 p. Ky;
KyHi; KyU.   13251

Kenyon College. Gambier, Ohio.
Nu pi Kappa Society Library
Accession list... 1832-1839.
OGaK.   13252

Ketcham, John.

The devil's dream interpreted, and corruptions adversary: or Ketcham's exposition of Whitcomb's circular, and conduct, on the eve of the August election of 1830, with general remarks, to which is added a few biographical sketches of the aforesaid Whitcomb. Bloomington, M'Collough & Co., prs., 1832. 84 p. In.   13253

Kettner, Johann G.
    Anhang. Vortrefliche Hulfsmittel gegen die Cholera-Epidemie, herausgegeben von dem Hamburgischen Gesundheits-Rathe. Philadelphia, 1832. 12 p. PHi.   13254

Key, Francis Scott, 1780-1843.
    Speech of Francis S. Key, esq., counsel for Gen. Samuel Houston, on his trial before the House of Representatives for a breach of privilege. Washington, Globe Office, 1832. 16 p. ICN; NUtHi; NdU; OCHP; TxU.   13255

Kilbourn, John, 1787-1831.
    History of the canals. Public documents concerning the Ohio canals, which are to connect Lake Erie with the Ohio River... from their commencement down to the close of the session of the Legislature of 1831-32. Columbus, I. N. Whiting, 1832. 53 p. OCLaw; PPA.   13256

King, Alonzo, 1796-1835.
    An address delivered at Portland before the Cumber County Temperance Society, Feb. 9, 1832. By Rev. Alonzo King. Portland, Office of Zion's Advocate, 1832. 18 p. MH; MeHi; MeWaC.   13257

Kingsley, George.
    The Sunday School singing book; to which is added a few moral songs. By Geo. Kingsley. Approved by the Boston Sunday School Society. Boston, Charles Bowen, 1832. 120 p. MB; MH-AH; MHi; MPlyA; PMA.   13258

Kingston, Stephen.
    Seizure of the ship Cicero. Philadelphia, 1832. PPL.   13259

Kingston Academy, Kingston, R. I.
    Catalogue of the trustees, instructors, and students of Kingston Academy; containing the names of the instructors and students from 1819 to the term ending April 26, 1832. Kingston, J. J. Brenton, pr., 1832. RPB.   13260

Kinkade, William.
    The Bible doctrine of God, Jesus Christ, atonement, and faith; to which is prefixed, an essay on natural theology and the truth of revelation. By William Kinkade, A companion of all them that fear God and keep his commandments. Revised by Joseph Badges, Minister of the gospel at West Mendon. Rochester, N. Y., Marshall & Dean, 1832. 319 p. CBPac; IEG; IHi; NRHi; NRU.   13261

Kippis, Andrew, 1725-1795.
    A narrative of the voyages round the world, performed by Capt. James Cook. With an account of his life, during the previous and intervening periods. By A. Kippis. Boston, N. H. Whitaker, 1832. 2 v. in 1. CSt; MsCLiM; MsJMC; MoS; NAlf.   13262

Kirchliches Jahrbuch. Bericht von... der Tennessee Synode während ihrer elften Sitzung, gehalten in der Immanuels-Kirche, Greene Caunty, Tenn. vom 13ten bis 14ten September, 1830. Neu-Market... S. Henkel... 1832. 6 p. ViHarHi.   13263

Kirk, James Balderstone.

Practical observations of
cholera asphyxia,... by James B.
Kirk. Greeneck, R. B. Lusk
[etc., etc.] 1832. DLC; DNLM;
OClW-H; PPC; PU.   13264

---- ---- New York, Peter Hill,
Greeneck, R. B. Lusk, 1832.
73 p. CtY; DSG; MdBM; ScU;
WUM.   13265

Kirkham, Samuel.
English grammar in familiar
lectures, accompanied by a compendium; embracing a new systematic order of parsing, a new
system of punctuation, exercises
in false syntax...38th ed. Baltimore, Pr. by Sands and Neilson,
1832. 240 p. CtHT; MdHi; OOxM.
                          13266
---- ---- New York, M'Elrath
and Bangs, 1832. 228 p. MiD-B;
NRHi; TxD-T.   13267

---- ---- Rochester, Marshall
and Dean, 1832. CtHT; NRU.
                          13268
Kirtland, O. L.
Address delivered at the anniversary of the Greene County
Temperance Society, held at the
court house, in the village of
Catskill. Catskill, Messenger
office, 1832. 14 p. MB.   13269

Kitchiner, William, 1775?-1827.
The Cook's Oracle; and House-
keeper's Manual, New ed. Adapt-
ed to the American public by a
medical gentleman from the last
London ed. New York, J. & J.
Harper, 1832. 432 p. CtWatk;
MA; ScCliTO.   13270

Die Kleine Lieder-Sammlung, oder
Auszug aus dem Psalterspiel der
Kinder Zions, zum Dienst inniger
heilsuchender Seelen, insonderheit
aber der Bruderschaft der Taufer
...Neu-Berlin [Penna.], Gedruckt
und zu haben bey Geo. Miller,
1832. 216 p. NbHi; PReaAT.
                          13271

Knapp, Samuel Lorenzo, 1783-
1838.
Advice in the pursuits of literature; containing historical, biographical, and critical remarks;
by Samuel L. Knapp... 2d ed.
New-York, Porter, 1832. x, 7-
296 p. CtY; ICN; NBu; NNC;
OCY.   13272

---- Polish chiefs, an historical
romance. See under Thomas,
Frederick William.

Kneeland, Abner, 1774-1884.
National hymns, original and
selected; for the use of those who
are 'Slaves to no Sect.'"...Boston,
1832. 140 p. CtWatk; NNUT; RPB;
ViU.   13273

Knickerbocker's almanac for...
1833. New York, R. Bartlett and
S. Raynor [1832] 18 p. PHi.
                          13274
[Knight, Charles] 1791-1873.
...The rights of industry; addressed to the working-men of
the United Kingdom. By the author
of "The results of machinery."
...1st Amer. ed. Philadelphia,
Carey & Hart, [etc., etc.] 1832.
213 p. CtHT; ICarbs; MdBJ; OO;
RPB.   13275

Knight, Nehemiah Rice, 1780-
1854.
Gov. Knight's address to the
farmers of Rhode-Island. October
1832. Providence, Pr. by Cranston & Hammond [1832] 15 p. MH;
MBC; NjR; RPB.   13276

---- Remarks of Mr. Knight on
Mr. Clay's resolution in Senate,
February 14, 1832. n.p., n.d.
2 p. MHi; OClWHi.   13277

Knight's penny magazine. v. 1-9,
Mar. 31, 1832-Dec. 31, 1840;
v. 10-14 (new ser. [v. 1-5]) Jan.
2, 1841-Dec. 27, 1845; [v. 15-
16 (3d ser. v. 1-2) 1846. New

York, William Jackson, etc.,
[1832-1846] 16 v. AzU; CSt;
DLC; PPT; TNJ-P.   13278

[Knill, Richard] 1787-1857.
Memoir of John Knill; a little
boy who died of the cholera, in
St. Petersburg, July 1, 1831.
Boston, Peirce & Parker; New
York, H. C. Sleight, 1832. 36 p.
DLC; PPM; ViRut.   13279

Knowles, James Davis, 1798-
1838.
Importance of theological institutions. An address, delivered
before the trustees, students and
friends of the Newton theological
institution, Nov. 14, 1832. By
James D. Knowles...Boston,
Lincoln & Edmands, 1832. 24 p.
KyLoS; MBAt; NNC; OClWHi;
RHi; ViRu.   13280

---- Memoir of Mrs. Ann H.
Judson, late missionary to Bur-
mah, including a history of the
American Baptist mission in the
Burman empire, by James D.
Knowles, 5th ed. Boston, Lin-
coln & Edmands, 1832. 408 p.
CtY-D; MHa; NhRo; NjPT; ScSp.
                           13281
Knowles, James Sheridan, 1784-
1862.
The hunchback. A play in five
acts. By James Sheridan Knowles
...Baltimore, J. Robinson, 1832.
78 p. MWA; MdBJ; PU.   13282

---- ---- With the author's latest
corrections. Unmutilated ed. Boston, Walker H. Baker & Co.,
[1832] 72 p. OrPr.   13283

---- ---- New-York, Owen
Phelan [1832?] CtY; MH; NN;
TxU.   13284

---- ---- New York, Peabody &
Co., 1832. 76 p. DLC; MH;
MWA; NN; ScU.   13285

---- ---- Philadelphia, Turner
& Son, 1832. 70 p. MB; PPL.
                           13286
---- Virginius, a tragedy, in five
acts...as performed at the London and Baltimore theatres. Baltimore, J. Robinson, 1832. 72 p.
ICU.   13287

Knowlton, Joseph.
A short but comprehensive
grammar, designed for the use
of schools. By Joseph Knowlton.
2d ed. With alterations and improvements. Salem, Pr. by Foote
& Brown, 1832. 84 p. MH;
MPeHi; NNC.   13288

Koch, Christophe Guillaume de,
1737-1813.
History of the revolutions in
Europe, from the subversion of
the Roman empire in the west,
till the Congress of Vienna; from
the French of C. W. Koch; by
Andrew Crichton, rev. and cor.
by an American editor. Hartford,
D. F. Robinson & Co., 1832. 2
vols. in 1. Ct; ICMe; InGrD;
NcU; OHi-C.   13289

Krauth, Charles Philip, 1797-
1867.
Oration on the advantages arising to the American student from
his access to German literature
by means of the knowledge of the
German language... Gettysburg,
Press of the Theological Seminary, 1832. 24 p. DLC; MiU;
NCH; PHi; ScCoT.   13290

L

Ladd, Joseph Brown, 1764-1786.
The literary remains of Joseph
Brown Ladd, M.D. Collected by
his sister, Mrs. Elizabeth Haskins, of Rhode Island. To which
is prefixed, A sketch of the author's life, by W. B. Chittenden
...New York, H. C. Sleight,

1832. 228 p. CtSoP; DLC; MnU;
PU; TxU.   13291

[Ladd, William] 1778-1841.
A dissertation on a congress
of nations. By Philanthropos
[pseud.] Pub. by order of the
American Peace Society. [Boston?] Press of J. Loring, 1832.
28 p. DLC; ICMe; PPL; ScC;
WHi.   13292

---- ---- 2d ed. (Boston?) Loring, 1832. 28 p. MHi; MMeT-L;
MWA; NNC-L.   13293

---- The hero of Macedon, or
History of Alexander the Great,
viewed in the light of the gospel.
By William Ladd... Boston, J.
Loring, 1832. 108 p. DLC; ICBB;
MAub.   13294

The ladder of learning; to be ascended early in the morning.
New Haven, S. Babcock, Sidney's
press, 1832. 24 p. CSmH; ICN;
RPB.   13295

Ladies Repository.
The Universalist... Sebastian
Streeter, editor... Boston, Pr. by
G. U. Stacy, for B. B. Mussey,
1832. v. 1. 1832. MBilHi;
MMeT-Hi.   13296

Lady (pseud.)
Thunder storm. Dover, 1832.
14 p. Nh-Hi.   13297

The lady's cabinet album... New
York, Peabody, 1832. 348 p.
ICU; MB; NNC; RNR; WU. 13298

Laënnec, Meridaec.
A manual of percussion and
auscultation. Composed from the
French of Merie dec Laennec[!]
By James Birch Sharp... New
York, S. Wood & sons, 1832.
120 p. CtY; MA; PPCP; RPM;
ViU.   13299

Lamb, Charles, 1775-1834.
Tales from Shakespeare. Designed for the use of young persons. Ornamented with wood engravings, by Dr. Anderson. Boston, Munroe & Francis; New
York, C. S. Francis, 1832. MH;
MiU; NjP.   13300

Lancaster, Mass. Church of
Christ.
Records of the Church in the
case of Deacon James G. Carter
and a reply to the communication
made by him to the brethren, on
the day of his removal from office of Deacon. Lancaster, Mass.
Pr. by Carter, Andrews & Co.,
1832. 15 p. M; MB; MH; MWA.
                            13301

Lander, Richard Lemon, 1804-
1834.
...Journal of an expedition to
explore the course and termination of the Niger, with a narrative of a voyage down that river
to its termination, by Richard and
John Lander... New York, J. & J.
Harper, 1832. 2 v. DLC; Nh;
ORP; PPA; RNR; ViU.   13302

Landis, Robert W.
A plea for the Catholic doctrine of the trinity. By Robert
W. Landis... Philadelphia, n. p.,
1832. 227 p. GDecCT; IEG; MW;
PHi; OSW.   13303

Landon, Letitia Elizabeth, 1802-
1838.
Romance and reality. By L. E.
L., author of "The improvisatrics,"
"The Venetian bracelet" &c. New
York, J. & J. Harper, 1832. 2
vols. MH; MiD; NNS; PPA; PPL-
R; RPB.   13304

Lane Theological Seminary. Cincinnati, O.
Catalogue of the officers and
students of Cincinnati Lane Seminary; together with a brief view
of its present condition, advan-

tages, and prospects. August,
1832. Cincinnati, A. F. Robin-
son, 1832. 16 p. MBC; PPPrHi.
                              13305
---- Lane Seminary and Walnut
Hill School. Its character advan-
tages and prospects. Cincinnati,
Pr. by Robinson, 1832. 7 p.
PPPrHi.   13306

---- Laws of the Cincinnati Lane
Seminary. [Cincinnati, F. S. Benton, 1832?] 16 p. DLC.   13307

Langshaw, George, 1806-1843.
   The Hulsean Prize Essay for
the year 1831. Cambridge, T.
Stevenson, 1832. 104 p. CtY;
MB.   13308

Lankester, Edwin, 1814-1874.
   Vegetable substances used for
the food of man. Boston, Lilly
and Wait (late Wells and Lilly),
and Carter & Hendee (etc., etc.)
1832. 396 p. CSfA; MiDU; Nh;
OCIW; PPGI.   13309

Lanman, James, 1769-1841.
   A discourse, addressed to the
citizens of Norwich, on the centennial birthday of George Washington, 1832; by James Lanman.
Norwich [Conn.] W. Faulkner,
1832. 20 p. DLC; MeB; MiU-C.
                              13310
Lansing, Dirk Cornelius.
   Remedy for intemperance. A
sermon, delivered in the Bleeck-
er-Street Presbyterian Church,
in Utica,...July 15, 1832...
Utica, Pr. by Hastings & Tracy,
1832. 16 p. CSmH; DLC; MH-
AH; NNUT; PPPrHi.   13311

Lardner, Rev. Dionysius, 1793-
1859.
   The cabinet of biography conducted by the Rev. Dionysus
Lardner...assisted by eminent
literary and scientific men. Philadelphia, Carey & Lea, 1832.
280 p. MB; MdHi; NP; NjR;

OCX.   13312

---- The cabinet of history. Conducted by Rev. Dionysius Lardner,...History of Spain and Portugal. Philadelphia, Carey &
Lea, 1832. 295 p. MdHi; MeBa;
NRU; OmC.   13313

---- ---- History of Switzerland.
Philadelphia, Carey & Lea, 1832.
288 p. KyD; MoU; WU.   13314

---- The Cabinet of natural phi-
losophy. Conducted by the Rev.
Dionysius Lardner...Assisted by
eminent literary men. A treatise
on mechanics. By Capt. Henry
Kater and the Rev. Dionysius
Lardner. Philadelphia, Carey &
Lea, 1832. 287 p. PMA; OOxM.
                              13315
---- ...Hydrostatics and pneu-
matics. By the Rev. Dionysius
Lardner. With notes by the
American editor [Benjamin F.
Joslin] [1st Amer., from 1st
London ed.] Philadelphia, Carey
& Lea, 1832. 273 p. CU; DLC;
LNP; OOxM; TxU.   13316

---- A treatise on the origin,
progressive improvement, and
present state of the manufacture
of porcelain and glass. Philadelphia, Carey & Lea, 1832.
252 p. Ct; MiU; NjP; NRU; TxU.
                              13317
Larrabee, William Clark, 1802-
1859.
   Inaugural address of Rev. Wm.
C. Larrabee, A.M., delivered
November 10th, 1831, on being
inducted into office as principal
of the Oneida Conference Seminary, Gazenovia, N.Y. Gazenovia [1832] 27 p. CtMW; NN;
WHi.   13318

Larrey, Dominique Jean, baron,
1766-1842.
   Memoirs of military surgery,
tr. from the French by J. C.

Mercer, Philadelphia, 1832.
KyLx.   13319

---- Observations on wounds,
and their complications by erysi-
pelas, gangrene and tetanus...
Philadelphia, Key, Mielke & Biddle, 1832. 332 p. CtY; IaU; KyLo;
PU; WU-M.   13320

---- Surgical memoirs of the
campaigns of Russia, Germany
and France, by Baron D. J.
Larrey... Trans. from the French
by John C. Mercer... (Quot.)
Philadelphia, Carey & Lea, 1832.
293 p. CtY; IaU; KyLo; PU; RNR;
MsU.   13321

... The last day's debate, on the
Tariff, in the Senate of the United
States. Address to the People of
South-Carolina, by their Senators
and Representatives in Congress;
and Address and Resolutions
adopted by the State Rights and
Free Trade Party, at Charleston,
July 30, 1832. Also, Proceed-
ings of a Meeting held in Geor-
gia, &c. 1832. Charleston, Van
Brunt, 1832. 24 p. A-Ar; ICU;
MHi; NcD; ScU.   13322

The last hours of persons eminent for piety; of unhappy infidels,
and of converted infidels who
testified to the truth of Christianity. To which is Added, A whole
family in Heaven. Boston, J. Loring, 1832. 108 p. DLC; MBC.
                               13323
Lathrop, Joseph, 1731-1820.
    Christ's warning to the church-
es, to beware of false prophets...
in two discourses... From 11th
rev. ed. with an introductory essay to John W. Nevin. Pittsburgh, Loomis, 1832. 88 p. PPi;
PPiNs; PPPrHi.   13324

---- Discourse on the mode and
subjects of Christian baptism; or
An attempt to shew that pouring

or sprinkling is a scriptural
mode; and the infants of believers
are proper subjects of the baptism instituted by Christ; with an
examination of various objects,
particularly those contained in a
course of anonymous letters to
Bishop Hoadly. By Joseph Lathrop, D. D. pastor of the First
Church in West-Springfield...
Albany, Pr. by E. B. Child,
1832. 153 p. KyBC; PCC; VtRut.
                               13325
---- The Nature and design of
a Christian Church. By the late
Rev. Joseph Lathrop... 4th ed.
with remarks on the Lord's supper, by another hand. Boston,
Samuel G. Simpkins, 1832. 163 p.
CBPac; MH-AH; MNotn.   13326

Lathrop, Samuel.
    Letter of the Hon. Samuel La-
throp [addressed to the State Anti-
Masonic Committee of Massachu-
setts]. West Springfield, Aug. 20,
1832. Broadside. MHi.   13327

Latimer, Hugh, 1485?-1555.
    Select sermons; with account
of the author and his writings.
Boston, Mass., Hilliard G. & Co.,
1832. 288 p. CtMW; MH-AH;
NNC; RNPL; TNP.   13328

Latrobe, John Hazelhurst Bone-
val, 1803-1891.
    Picture of Baltimore, contain-
ing a description of all objects of
interest in the city; and embellished with views of the principal
public buildings. Baltimore, F.
Lucas, Jr. [1832] 249 p. DLC;
MWA; MdBJ; PPL.   13329

Laurens, Edward B.
    An address delivered in Charles-
ton, before the Agricultural Society of S. C., on Sept. 18th, 1832;
by Edward R. Laurens... Charleston, Pr. by A. E. Miller, 1832.
16 p. NcD; ScD.   13330

Laurinian School, Boston.
Laurinian System of mercan-
tile penmanship. At the request
of a number of gentlemen...
Boston, 1832. Broadside. MB.
                              13331
Laurins, James.
Sermons by the Rev. James
Laurins; tr. by Robert Robinson,
Henry Hunter, and Joseph Sut-
loffe. New ed. rev. lg. Samuel
Burden. Baltimore, Plaskett,
1832. 2 v. NcD.   13332

Laussat, Antony, 1806-1833.
Address on the death of
Charles Carroll of Carrollton,
delivered before the military di-
vision in the Arch st. theatre.
Philadelphia, 1832. 8 p. PHC;
PPAmP.   13333

Lavalette, Antoine Marie Cha-
mant Comte de, 1769-1830.
The memoirs of Count Laval-
lette. Written by himself. 1st
American, from 2d London ed.
Philadelphia, T. T. Ash, 1832.
243 p. Ct; IEG; MdBP; OCl;
PPA; PPL-R; WBeloC.   13334

Lavater, Johann Casper, 1741-
1801.
The pocket Lavater; or, The
science of physiognomy to which
is added an inquiry into the an-
alogy existing between brute and
human physiognomy, from the
Italian of Porta. Hartford, Andrus & Judd, [1832] 116 p. DLC;
DNLM; LNL; NcD; PLF; PPC;
RNR.   13335

Law, Thomas, 1756-1834.
Presented: a plan for one uniform circulating medium, to be
sufficient for our population, and
commensurate with our property
at all times; and to accelerate
improvements, and to lower interest; and to abolish usury and all
the miseries of our present financial system, now tottering.

[Washington? 1832?] 8 p. ICJ.
                              13336
Law, William, 1686-1761.
A serious call to a devout and
holy life: adapted to the state and
condition of all orders of Christians...19th ed. To which is added, some account of the author,
and three letters to a friend...
Philadelphia, L. Johnson, 1832.
276 p. CtY; KyLoP; PPPrHi;
RNR; ScDue.   13337

Lawrence, B.
The complete cattle-keeper, or
farmer's and grazier's guide in
the choice and management of
neat cattle and sheep...Philadel-
phia, E. L. Carey & A. Hart;
Boston, Carter & Hendee [etc.]
1832. 201 p. IU; MH; OClWHi;
TxHuT; ViU.   13338

Lawrence, John [1753-1839]
Moubray on breeding, rearing
and fattening all kinds of poultry,
cows, swine, and other domestic
animals. Boston, 1832. CtHWatk.
                              13339
---- A Treatise on breeding,
rearing and fattening all kinds of
poultry, cows, swine and other
domestic animals. By B. Moubray,
Esq. Repr. from 6th London ed.
Boston, Lilly & Wait; and Carter
& Hendee, 1832. 266 p. DLC;
ICJ; MeU; TxU; ViU.   13340

Lawrence, Myron, 1799-1852.
Address delivered before the
Hampshire, Franklin and Hampden Agricultural Society, at their
annual fair, holden at Northampton, October 24, 1832. By Myron
Lawrence...Northampton, J. Metcalf, 1832. 16 p. CSmH; MDeeP;
NN; NjPT; PP.   13341

Lawrence, William Beach, 1800-
1881.
Origin and nature of the representative and federative institutions of the United States of Amer-

ica, an anniversary discourse, delivered before the New York Historical Society, on the 19th of April, 1832. New York, G. & C. & H. Carvill, 1832. 44 p. InU; MWA; NjPT; PHi; WHi. 13342

---- Two lectures on political economy, delivered at Clinton hall, before the mercantile library association of the city of New York, on the 23d and 30th of December, 1831. By William Beach Lawrence. New York, G. & C. & H. Carvill, 1832. 72 p. CtY; LU; NjR; RPB; ScU. 13343

Lawrence and Lemay's North Carolina Almanack for 1833. Raleigh [1832] 20 p. MH; NcHiC; NcU. 13344

Laws and Constitution of the Scots Thistle Society of Philadelphia... (n. p.) Pr. by Adam Waldie, 1832. 66 p. Sabin. 13345

Laws of the Colonial and State Governments, relating to Indians and Indian Affairs from 1633 to 1831, inclusive. With an Appendix, containing the Proceedings of the Congress of the Confederation; and the Laws of Congress, from 1800 to 1830, on the same subject. Washington City, Thompson & Homans, 1832. 72 p. DLC; Ia; MnU; PU; ScU. 13346

Lawson, James, 1799-1880. Giordano. A tragedy. By James Lawson... New York, E. B. Clayton (etc.) 1832. 102 p. CSmH; MB; MiU; NhPoA; RPB. 13347

The Lay Missionary; or, The Way to Do Good. By Sallucia Abbott. Boston, Peirce & Parker; New York, H. C. Sleight, 1832. 81 p. DLC; GDecCT; MeB; PPeSchw. 13348

The lay of the last pilgrim. By the author of "The pilgrimage of Ormond. "... Charleston, Pr. by W. Riley, 1832. 48 p. CoCsC; DLC; LNH; MB; NN. 13349

Lea, Isaac, 1792-1886. Observations on the genius UNIO, together with descriptions of new genera and species. Philadelphia, Pr. by Kay, jun. & co., [etc.] 1832-74. 13 vols. A-GS; CtMW; KyU; MdBP; PU. 13350

Leavitt, Joshua, 1754-1873, comp. The Christian lyre; adapted for use in families, prayer meetings and revivals of religion; the music printed in patent notes. New York, Jonathan Leavitt, 1832. 216 p. Ct; NBuG; NRCR; PPPrHi. 13351

---- ---- 1st patent note ed.... New York, Jonathan Leavitt [etc., etc., 1832] 216 p. NNUT; ODW; RPB. 13352

---- ---- 3d patent-note ed. Cincinnati, Corey & Fairbank, 1832. 216 p. OClWHi. 13353

---- ---- The work complete, two volumes in one, with a supplement. 11th ed., rev. New York, J. Leavitt, 1832. 2 vols. LNH; MB; NNUT; NcC; PMA. 13354

---- Easy lessons in reading; for the use of the younger classes in common schools. By Joshua Leavitt. Boston, Keene, N. H., J. & J. W. Prentiss, 1832. 156 p. MGrot. 13355

---- ---- 3d ed. Watertown, Knowlton & Rice, 1832. 156 p. CSmH. 13356

Le Bas, Charles Webb, 1779-1861. ...The life of Wiclif. By Charles Webb Le Bas...New-York, J. & J. Harper, 1832.

395 p. CtY; DNC; NjR; PPA;
PPPrHi; ScU.　　　　　　13357

Leben der Mary Lothrop, ges-
torben in Boston, den 18. März
1831, in einem alter von seche
jahren und drei monaten. Aus
dem munde der Sauglinge hast du
dir lob bereiter. Aus dem Englischen uberfekt. Herausgegeben
von der Amerikanischen Tractat-
Gesellschaft. New York, Gedruckt bei D. Fanshaw [1832]
104 p. IU; MnS; OBerB.　　13358

Lee, Henry, 1782-1867.
　An exposition of evidence in
support of the memorial to Congress... prepared in pursuance
of instructions from the permanent committee appointed by the
free trade convention assembled
at Philadelphia to prepare the
memorial to Congress, by Henry
Lee, of Massachusetts. Boston,
Pr. at the Boston Press, 1832.
16 p. CtY; PPA.　　　　　13359

---- ---- Boston, Pr. at the
Boston press, 1832. [70] p. DLC;
MH-BA; MnHi; NN; NcU.　　13360

---- ---- Boston, Pr. at the
Boston press, 1832. 192 p. CU;
DLC; FU; NIC; ViU.　　　　13361

---- ---- Observations on the
writings of Thomas Jefferson, with
particular reference to the attack
they contain on the memory of the
late Gen. Henry Lee. In a series
of letters, by H. Lee, of Virginia.
New York, C. DeBehr, 1832.
237 p. CtHT; InHi; MdBF; NcD;
RNR; ViU.　　　　　　　　13362

Lee, N. K. M.
　The Cook's own book: being a
complete culinary encyclopedia:
comprising all valuable receipts
for cooking, meat, fish, fowl,
etc. ...with numerous original
receipes, and a complete system

of confectionary. By a Boston
housekeeper. Boston, 1832. 300p.
CtHWatk; ICU; MH; MBevHi;
MHi.　　　　　　　　　　13363

Lee, Samuel, 1803-1881.
　A Letter addressed to Rev.
Amos Clarke.... By Samuel Lee.
Boston, Pr. by Peirce & Parker,
1832. 28 p. CtY; ICN; MH-AH;
MWA; MeBat.　　　　　　　13364

---- A more excellent way. A
sermon, preached in the Evangelical Church in Sherburne...
1832... By Samuel Lee. Boston,
Pr. by Peirce & Parker, 1832.
24 p. CtY; ICN; MH; MeBat;
NjR.　　　　　　　　　　13365

---- A sermon preached in the
Evangelical Church in Sherburne
at the funeral of Miss Clarissa
Leland. Boston, Pr. by Peirce
& Parker, 1832. 22 p. CtHC;
MBAt; MH; PLT; RPB.　　13366

Lee, Thomas J., d. 1835.
　A spelling book, containing the
rudiments of the English language
... Boston, Munroe & Francis,
1832. 180 p. CtHWatk.　　13367

Lee, Mass. Congregational
Church.
　Manual, 1832. 23 p. MBC.
　　　　　　　　　　　　13368
Legendre, Adrien Marie, 1752-
1833.
　Elements of geometry and trigonometry; with notes. Tr. from
the French of A. M. Legendre...
by David Brewster... Rev. and
altered for the use of the Military
Academy at West Point. 3d ed.
New-York, N. & J. White; Collins & Hannay [etc.] 1832. 316 p.
CtHT; GU; OO; PHC; ViU. 13369

Lehigh Coal and Navigation Company.
　Report of the Board of Managers of the Lehigh Coal and

Navigation Co. to the stockholders January 9, 1832... Philadelphia, Pr. by Wm. F. Geddes, 1832. 16 p. NRom; P.　13370

---- To the committee... See White, Josiah.

Lehmanowsky, John Jacob, b.1773.
History of Napoleon, Emperor of the French, King of Italy, by J. J. Lehmanowsky. Washington, John A. W. Duncanson, 1832. 54 p. ICP; KyDC; OCHP; ScU; WHi.　13371

Leigh, Benjamin Watkin, 1781-1849.
The letter of Appomattox(!) to the people of Virginia: exhibiting a connected view of the recent proceedings in the House of delegates on the subject of the abolition of slavery; and a succinct account of the doctrines broached by the friends of abolition, in debate: and the mischievous tendency of those proceedings and doctrines. Richmond, Pr. by T. W. White, 1832. 47 p. CSmH; MB; NcU; PPAmP; ViL.　13372

Leighton, Robert, abp. of Glasgow, 1611-1684.
The select works of Archbishop Leighton. Prepared for the practical use of private Christians. With an introductory view of the life, character, and writings of the author. By George B. Cheever. Boston, Peirce & Parker; New York, H. C. Sleight, (etc., etc.) 1832. 569 p. CU; KyBC; MB; NNUT; PLT.　13373

Lempriere, John, 1765?-1824.
... Bibliotheca classica; or, A dictionary of all the principal names and terms relating to the geography, topography, history, literature, and mythology of antiquity and of the ancients; with a chronological table. by J.

Lempriere, D.D. Rev. and cor. and divided... into three parts... By Lorenzo L. Da Ponte and John D. Ogilby. 7th Amer. ed. New-York, Collins & Hannay, etc., 1832. 2 v. IU; MH; OHi; PHi.　13374

---- Classical dictionary for schools and academies, containing every name and all that is either important or useful in the original work. Philadelphia, Towar & Hogan; New York, Pendleton and Hill; Boston, Lord & Holbrook, 1832. CtMW; MBC; NPV; OMC; MWal; RPB. 13375

Leonard, George, 1802-1831.
Sermons on various subjects. To which is prefixed the Rev. Mr. Babcocks sermon, occasioned by the author's death, and including a sketch of his life and character. Compiled by Abigail C. Leonard. Portland, Pr. at the office of Zion's Advocate, 1832. 180 p. CSmH; LNH; MBC; MHi; NPV.　13376

Le Ray de Chaumont, James Donatien, 1760-1840.
... Addresses before the Jefferson Co. Agricultural Society by J. Le Ray de Chaumont... V. Le Ray de Chaumont... Edmund Kirby... Albany, 1832. PPL.　13377

Leslie, Charles, 1650-1722.
Short and easy methods with the deists. New York, Emory & Waugh, 1832. 226 p. IaDmD.　13378

Leslie, Eliza, 1787-1858.
Cards of Boston, comprising a variety of facts and descriptions relative to that city, in past and present times; so arranged as to form an instructive and amusing game for young people. [Boston, 1832] 59 cards. DLC; MB.13379

---- Domestic French cookery,

chiefly translated from Sulpice
Barue. By Miss Leslie, author
of "Seventy-five receipts," Philadelphia, Carey & Hart, 1832.
120 p. CtY; NjP; PPWa.   13380

---- Seventy-five receipts for
pastry, cakes and sweetmeats...
4th ed. Boston, Munroe & Francis, 1832. 104 p. MWA; NN;
RPB.   13381

---- 200 receipts for French
cookery. Philadelphia, 1832.
120 p. CU-S.   13382

---- Wonderful travels; being the
narratives of Munchausen, Gulliver, and Sinbad abridged from
the original works with numerous
alterations and original designs.
Boston, Munroe & Francis, etc.,
etc. 1832. MH.   13383

Leslie, John, 1766-1832.
  ...Narrative of discovery and
adventures in the polar seas and
regions...By Prof. Leslie, Prof.
Jameson, and Hugh Murray...
New York, Pr. by J. & J. Harp-
er, 1832. 373 p. DI-GS; ICJ;
MiD; NcD; ViU.   13384

Lessons for children. Consisting
of words of one and two syllables.
New York, Mahlon Day, 1832.
17 p. NN; OClWHi.   13385

Let not the Faith, nor the Laws
of the Commonwealth, be Violated. [n.p., 1832?] 30 p. DLC;
NNC; PHi; PPAmP.   13386

Letter from a young lady of Ca-
zanovia, N.Y. to her minister,
on Masonry. Boston, 1832. 8 p.
MBC.   13387

Letter on the relations of the
States and General Government.
n.p., n.p., 1832. 8 p. MWA.
                         13388
A letter to the Rev. John Butler,

containing a review of his Friendly Letters to a Lady together
with a general outline of the doctrine of the Free Will Baptist.
Limerick, Silas Curtis, 1832.
160 p. DLC; MWA; MeLewB.
                         13389
The Letter writer, containing a
great variety of letters on the
following subjects: relationship,
business, love, courtship, and
marriage, friendship, and miscellaneous letters, law forms,
etc.... selected from judicious
and eminent writers. Boston,
Charles Gaylord, 1832. 144 p.
MH; NN; NjP; RPB.   13390

Letters on Ecclesiastical history.
Written for the American Sunday-
School Union, and revised by the
committee of publication. Phila-
delphia, American Sunday-School
Union, 1832. 2 vols. GDecCT;
KyBC; MH; NN; OO.   13391

Letters, on the present State
and probable results of theological speculations in Connecticut
by an Edwardean. n.p., n.p.,
1832. 44 p. MWA.   13392

Letters to a brother, on practical subjects. By a clergyman.
Lowell, Brooks Shattuck & Co.,
1832. 106 p. CU; DLC; MHA;
NN; RPB.   13393

Letters to a young student, in the
first stage of a liberal education.
Boston, Perkins & Marvin, 1832.
174 p. ScCoT.   13394

Leverett, Frederick Percival,
1803-1836.
  A key to the new Latin tutor;
or, Exercises in etymology, syntax and prosody, by F. P. Leverett. Boston, Hilliard, Gray &
Co., 1832. 100 p. CtMW; MB;
NNC; NjR; OMC.   13395

---- The new Latin tutor; or,

Exercises in etymology, syntax and prosody, compiled chiefly from the best English works. By Frederick P. Leverett. Boston, Hillard, Gray & Co., 1832. 350 p. CtHWatk; GMilvC; MB; NN; PU; WGr.   13396

Levert, Henry S.
Letters addressed to the mayor of Mobile, on the subject of malignant cholera, by Henry S. Levert, M.D. Mobile, Pr. at the office of the Register and Patriot, 1832. 7 p. A-Ar; TxU.   13397

Levings, Noah.
Advice to young men; a sermon preached in the Methodist Episcopal Church in New-Haven, Conn., on the evening of Dec. 18, 1831, by Noah Levings,... New Haven, J. Barber's press, 1832. 22 p. CtSoP; NNMHi.   13398

Levizac, Jean Pons Victor Lecoutz de abbé, d. 1813.
A theoretical and practical grammar or the French Tongue; ... By M. DeLevizac. Rev. and corr. by Stephen Pasquier, M.A. 7th ed. New York, Pr. by W. E. Dean, etc., 1832. x, 444 p. GHi; MChiA; MH; OCoC; TNP.   13399

Lewis, Dixon Hall, 1802-1848.
Speech of Mr. Lewis of Alabama, on the bill proposing a reduction of the duties on imports. Delivered in the House of Representatives, June 15, 1832. Washington, Pr. by Duff Green, 1832. 20 p. DLC; NN; NNC; PPAmP; ScU.   13400

Lewis, Morgan, 1754-1844.
An oration delivered in the Middle Dutch Church, in the city of New York, before the Common Council and citizens, on the first centennial anniversary of the birth of George Washington. By Maj. Gen. Morgan Lewis....

New York, G. F. Hopkins & Son, 1832. 30 p. DLC; MB; NIC.   13401

Lexington, Kentucky.
Ordinances of the city of Lexington [Supplements to the Kentucky Reporter, February 8, 15, 22, 1832] 32 p.   13402

---- First Presbyterian Church.
Report to the Congregation of the First Presbyterian Church, Lexington, Ky. March 1832. ICU.   13403

Lexington, Mass.
Report of a committee appointed by a vote of the town to investigate the ministerial fund of Lexington. Concord, Herman Atwill, 1832. 36 p. ICN; MWA; NcD.   13404

Lhomond, Charles François, 1727-1794.
Epitome historiae sacre, auctoire [!] L'Homond. Quan. prosodiae signis, novaque vocum ominum interpretations. Ardonavit [!] Georgius Ironside, A.M. A new ed., in which the quantity of almost every syllable is marked. Improved and cor., by a gentleman of Princeton. New York, Collins & Hannay, 1832. 139 p. CtHWatk; DLC; MH.   13405

---- ...Epitome historiae sacrae, auctore L'Homond. Ed. nova. Quam prosodiae signis, novaque vocum omnium interpretatione, adornavit Georgius Ironside, A.M. ed. sex. Quam correxit et emedavit. Thomas S. Joy... Novi-Eboraci, G. Long, 1832. 156 p. MH; OO; RNHi; TxHR; ViU.   13406

---- Viri illustres urbis Romae, a Romulo ad Augustum. Auctore C. F. L'Homond...Editio Novi Eboraci, Emendata et stereotypa. To which is added, a dictionary of all the words which occur in

this book.... By James Hardie,
A. M. New York, George Long,
1832. 134 (110) p. DLC; IaHi;
NjR; OMC; PHi.   13407

The life and adventures of Peter
Wilkins. See Paltock, Robert,
1697-1767.

... Life and character of the late
Mr. Cornelius... [Boston, 1832]
250-264 p. NN.   13408

The life of Benjamin Franklin.
Illustrated by tales, sketches,
and anecdotes. Adapted for the
use of schools. With engravings.
New York, Collins & Hannay,
1832. 180 p. CSmH; DLC; IaDaM;
MB; MWA.   13409

The life of Christopher Columbus, illustrated by tales, sketches,
and anecdotes. Adapted to the use
of schools... New York, Collins
and Hannay, 1832. 187 p. DLC;
IP; NCatt; OClWHi; ViU.   13410

The Life of David, King of Israel. See Hooker, Mary Ann
Brown, 1796-1838.

The life of the Rev. Joseph Ben-
son. Abridged from authentic
sources. By a friend of Sabbath
Schools. New York, J. Emory
and B. Waugh, for the Methodist
Episcopal Church, 1832. 94 p.
MsNF; NcD; OCl.   13411

Lilly, Lambert. See Hawks,
Francis Lister.

Lillybridge, C.
   An appeal to the community
of Norfolk from aspersions in re-
gard to a correspondence between
Rev. H. W. Ducachet and C. Lil-
lybridge with that correspondence.
Norfolk, Va. , 1832. MB; NjPT.
                             13412
Lincoln, Ensign, 1779-1832.
   Aids to devotion; including

Walt's Guide to Prayer. 2d ed.
Boston, Lincoln & Edmands;
Philadelphia, Key & Meilke; Baltimore, Cushing & Sons & J. Jewett; Cincinnati, Hubbard & Edmands; New York, J. Leavitt,
1832. 324 p. GDecCT; IEG;
MBNEB; NhPet; PPP.   13413

---- The Sabbath School class
book. 3d ed. Boston, etc. 1832.
120 p. CSt; MH.   13414

Lincoln, Levi R.
   Tariff, or rates of duties, payable from and after the 3d of
March, 1833 on all goods, wares
and merchandise, imported into
the United States of America, in
American vessels; with a compendium of custom house regulations, and an abstract of the revenue laws, relating thereto...
Boston, S. Condon, pr. , 1832.
162 p. IEN; InU; MH; MnHi; PP.
                             13415
Lindley, Jacob.
   ... Account of a journey to at-
tend the Indian treaty, proposed
to be held at Sandusky, in the
year 1793, interspersed with various observations, remarks, and
circumstances, that occurred on
this interesting occasion. [Phila-
delphia, 1832] [49]-156 p. CtY;
OClWHi.   13416

Lindmark, John.
   The Vigilant Farmers: A
Western tale; and The Magic Stone:
An Eastern tale... New York, the
Author, 1832. 70 p. DLC. 13417

Lindsley, Philip, 1786-1855.
   An address delivered at Nashville, Ten. Feb. 22, 1832, at the
request of the Citizens of Nashville and its vicinity, on the occasion of the Centennial Birth Day
of George Washington. By Philip
Lindsley, D. D. President of the
University of Nashville. Nashville, Pr. by Hunt, Tardiff &

Co., 1832. 36 p. CSmH; DLC; MBAt; PPAmP; RPB.　13418

---- Baccalaureate address, delivered on the fourth anniversary commencement of the University of Nashville, October 7, 1829. 2d ed. Nashville, Pr. by Hunt, Tardiff & Co., 1832. 47 p. CSansS; ICP; MHi; NjPT; PHi.　13419

---- Bacculaureate address, pronounced on the fourth anniversary commencement of the University of Nashville, October 5, 1831 (sic) Nashville, Pr. at the Herald office, 1832. 36 p. MdU-M.　13420

---- Baccalaureate address, pronounced on the seventh anniversary commencement of the University of Nashville, October 3, 1832. By Philip Lindsley. Nashville, Pr. by Hunt, Tardiff & Co., 1832. 20 p. CSansS; IAlS; NjP; PU; TNP.　13421

---- The cause of education in Tennessee. An address delivered to the young gentlemen admitted to the degree of bachelor of arts, at the first commencement of the University of Nashville, October 4, 1826. By Philip Lindsley, D. D. President of the University. New ed. Nashville, Hunt, Tardiff & co., prs., 1832. 39 p. NN; P; TNL.　13422

The lion's den. Philadelphia, W. Johnson, Mead Alley, 1832. 13 p. CSmH; DLC; NNC.　13423

[Lister, Thomas Henry] 1800-1842.
Arlington, a novel by the author of Granby...New York, Harper, 1832. 2 vols. CtHT; KyLxT; NBuG; PPL-R; ViU.　13424

Litchfield, Francis.
Three years' results of the Farthinghoe Clothing Society, with a few remarks on the policy of encouraging provident habits among the working classes. Northampton, J. Freeman, 1832. 22 p. MH-BA; NN.　13425

The little book of songs. Being a choice patriotick, Yankee, English and Irish collection...Watertown, New York, Knowlton & Rice, 1832. 72 p. N.　13426

The little deceiver reclaimed... Philadelphia, American Sunday School Union, 1832. 69 p. DLC.　13427

Little Frank's almanack, to show little boys and girls their play days. Concord, J. W. Moore & Co., 1832. 8 p. [6] p. DLC.　13428

The little month of the Holy Infancy; or, The first mysteries of the life of Our Lord Jesus Christ, proposed to the imitation of youth; tr. from the French of the Abbe Letourneur...and dedicated to the members of the Society of the Holy Childhood. New York, P. O'Shea, 1832. 348 p. MoSJ; OClUC.　13429

The little present for a good child. Wendell, Mass., John Metcalf, 1832. 8 l. MA; PP. 13430

The Little reader; a progressive step to knowledge... Boston, Carter, Hendee & Co., 1832. 199 p. MNBedf. NIDHi.　13431

Little rhymes for little readers. Wendell, J. Metcalf, 1832. 16 p. MH; NNC.　13432

Little Susan and her lamb. Philadelphia, American Sunday School Union, 1832. 864 p. BrMus.　13433

The little wanderers. Founded upon fact. By the author of "The gold thimble," "Jane Courtney,"

"The Contrast," "The Adventures of a bodkin," "The Flower
girl," "Edwin," "Contentment,"
etc. Boston, Cottons & Barnard,
1832. 16 p. MB; MiU-C. 13434

Lives of the apostles & early
martyrs of the church, designed
for Sunday reading: by the author
of "The trial of skill." New York,
J. & J. Harper, 1832. 204 p.
CtMW; ICN; NcWsS; ScCMu.
                              13435

Livingston, John Henry, 1746-
1825.
    Analysis of a system of the-
ology composed chiefly from lectures delivered by the late John
H. Livingston, D. D. S. T. P. ...
by the Rev. Ava Neal, A. M.
New York, J. F. Sebell, 1832.
332 p. CSansS; GDecCT; IEG;
PCC; ViRut.   13436

---- A sermon, delivered before
the New York Missionary Society,
at their annual meeting, April 3,
1804. To which is added an appendix. 3d ed. Providence, Marshall, 1832. 48 p. ICM; MH-
AH; NjR; PPPrHi; RPB.   13437

Livius, Titus.
    Titi Livii Patavini historiar-
um. Liber primus et selecta qua-
dam capita. Curavit notulisque
instruxit Cardus Folsom, A. M.
Editio stereotypa. Cantabrigiae
(Mass.), Sumptibus Hilliard et
Brown, 1832. 287 p. IaHi; ICU;
MeHi; OO.   13438

Lloyd, David.
    Economy of agriculture: being
a series of compendious essays
on different branches of farming.
By David Lloyd. Germantown,
Pa., Pr. by P. R. Freas & Co.,
1832. 120 p. ICBB; MiU-C; NjR;
PPL; PU.   13439

Lobenstein, Johann Friedrich
Daniel, 1777-1840.

Remarks on the pernicious ef-
fects and fatal consequences of
blood-letting;...By J. F. Daniel
Lobenstein. New York, Pr. by
W. Mitchell, 1832. 16 p. CtY-
M; DLC; DSG; MB; MBAt; NNC.
                              13440

Locke, John, 1632-1704.
    A treatise on the conduct of
the understanding. Also, a
sketch of His Life. Boston, C.
D. Strong, 1832. 132 p. ICM;
MB; MBNMHi; MeU.   13441

Lockhart, John Gibson, 1794-
1854.
    ...The history of Napoleon
Buonaparte. New York, J. & J.
Harper, 1832. 2 vols. CtHC;
LNH; MWA; OrP; ViU.   13442

Lockwood, Thomas P.
    A geography of S. C. adapted
to the use of Schools and families...interspersed with historical anecdotes. A general view of
the State...with a sketch of its
Agricultural, commercial and
natural history. By Thos. P.
Lockwood, with a new map of the
State. Charleston, J. S. Burges,
1832. 135 [1] p. DLC; GHi; ICN;
NN; ScU.   13443

Longfellow, Henry Wadsworth,
1807-1882.
    Manuel de proverbes drama-
tiques...Seconde Edition. Boston, Gray & Bowen, 1832. 346 p.
CtY; ICU; KyBC; MnU; NjP.
                              13444
---- Saggi de' novillieri italiani
d'ogni secolo; tratti du' piu cel-
ebri scrittori; con brevi notizie
intorno alla vita di ciascheduno.
Da H. W. Longfellow...Boston,
Presso Gray e Bowen [Cam-
bridge, Dai torchi de E. W. Metcalf e compagno], 1832. 168 p.
CSt; DLC; OrU; TxU; ViU.
                              13445
---- Syllabus de la grammaire
italienne. Par H. W. Longfellow

...A l'usage de ceux qui possed-
ent la langue française. Boston,
Gray et Bowen, 1832. 104 p.
DLC; ICT; MH; NjP; TxU; ViU.
13446

Longinus, Cassius.
A new literal translation of
Longinus On the sublime; for the
use of schools, colleges, and uni-
versities: illustrated with notes,
original and select. By a graduate of Trinity college, Dublin...
New York, C. S. Francis, 1832.
70 p. CtHT; MeBaT; RPB; ViU;
WU. 13447

Longstreet, Augustus Baldwin,
1790-1870.
Oration on the centennial
birthday of Geo. Washington.
Augusta [Ga.], Lawson, 1832.
23 p. CSmH; GEU; GU; ViU.
13448

Longworth's American almanac,
New York register, and City di-
rectory, for the 57th year of
American Independence... New
York, Thos. Longworth, 1832.
750 p. NNA; NNS; NNMuCN;
NjR; RNHi. 13449

Loomis' Calendar, or, The New
York and Vermont Almanack. By
a successor to Andrew Beers.
Albany, Clark & Hosford, 1832.
MWA. 13450

Loomis' magazine almanac for
1833. Pittsburgh, Pa., Cramer & Spear, 30th No. [1832]
36 p. MWA. 13451

Lorain County Temperance Society.
An appeal to patriots, philan-
thropists, and Christians, in behalf of our endangered republic,
and its suffering members; by
the Lorain county temperance
society... Elyria, Ohio, Park &
Burrell, prs., 1832. 16 p. OO.
13452

Lothian, John.

Bible atlas, containing a plate
of the family descent of Christ
from Adam. Also a historical
notice of the Bible. From 3d London ed., to which is added a
brief history of Palestine, an
improved ed. Hartford, Newton
Case, Folsom & Hurlburt, prs.,
1832. 48 p. CtY; MBC; MH;
MWA; OO: RPB. 13453

Louisiana.
An act to incorporate the subscribers to an association for the
pressing of cotton and other purposes, and by-laws adopted at a
general meeting of the stock
holders of the Levee Steam Cotton
Press Company... New Orleans,
Tribune Office, 1832. 15 p. NcD.
13454
---- Acts passed at the third session of the Tenth Legislature, of
the state of Louisiana, begun and
held in the city of New-Orleans,
on Monday the second day of
January, in the year of our Lord,
one thousand eight hundred and
thirty-two, and of the independence of the United States of America, the fifty-sixth. Pub. by authority. New-Orleans, Stroud &
Pew, state prs., 1832. 204 p.
A-SC; IaU-L; MdBB; PU; T.
13455
Louisiana and Mississippi Almanac for 1833. New Orleans,
Hotchkiss and Company [1832]
18 p. DLC. 13456

Louisville Association for the Improvement of the Breed of Horses.
Constitution of the Association.
Rules and regulations for the government of the course. Louisville,
Ky., Pr. by W. W. Worsley,
1832. (2) 12 p. KyLoF. 13457

Louisville Directory. See Collins, Gabriel.

Lowrie, W. F.
Toxicologia, or a Treatise on

Internal Poisons, in their relation to Medical Jurisprudence,
physiology, and the practice of
Physic, by W. F. Lowrie, M.D.
New York, W. Stodart, 1832.
82 p. ArCH; CSt-L; MBM; NNN;
NRAM.   13458

Lubbock, John.
   The Origin of civilization, and
the primitive condition of man.
4th ed., with additions. New
York, 1832. MNan.   13459

Lumpkin, Jack.
   A sermon preached on the education of ministers; preached
before the Baptist Convention of
Georgia, at Powelton on April
8th, 1832. Augusta [Ga.] W. Lawson, 1832. GU; PCA.   13460

Lusk, William, 1802-1879.
   Discourses on the covenant of
works; the fall of man and original sin. By William Lusk. Troy,
N.Y., Pr. by N. Tuttle, 1832.
225 p. MWA; MiU; NjPT; PCC;
PPA; PPL.   13461

Luther, Martin, 1483-1546.
   Smaller Catechism; translated
from the original. Pub. by the
General Synod of the Lutheran
Church. 3d ed. Gettysburg, Lu-
cas & Deaver, 1832. 72 p. CoD;
CtY; N; NN; PPLT.   13462

Luther, Seth.
   An address to the working men
of New England, on the state of
education, and on the condition of
the producing classes in Europe
and America. By Seth Luther.
Boston, n.p., 1832. 39 p. DLC;
IaU; MHi; PHi; WHi.   13463

Lynchburg, Va. Ordinances etc.
   Revised ordinances of the cor-
poration of Lynchburg, preceded
by the acts of incorporation...
Pub. by order of the Common
Council, July, 1832. Revised by

G. Ward. Lynchburg, Fletcher
& Toler, 1832. 62 p. Vi.   13464

The Lynn directory and Town
register for 1832...By C. F.
Lummus. Lynn, Geo. Lummus,
1832. 72 p. MB; NN.   13465

Lyon, Chittenden, 1786-1842.
   To the citizens of Todd, Chris-
tian, Trigg and other counties in
Ky. A letter on the proceedings
of the first session of the 22nd
Congress. [Washington, 1832] 8 p.
DLC.   13466

[Lytton, Edward George Earle
Lytton Bulwer-Lytton], 1st baron,
1803-1873.
   Conversations with an ambiti-
ous student in ill health: with
other pieces. By the author of
"Pelham," "Eugene Aram," &c.
New York, J. & J. Harper, 1832.
205 p. IEN-M; KyLoS; MB; NNC;
TNP.   13467

---- Devereux, a tale. New York,
The Mershon co., [1832] 824 p.
GAl; OKEn.   13468

---- The disowned. By Edward
Bulwer-Lytton. New York, Hurst
& co., [1832] 417 p. CtMW;
GSAJC; NBUSM; OClW; OO.
                              13469
---- Eugene Aram. A tale. By
the author of "Pelham," "The
Disowned," "Devereux," etc. New
York, J. & J. Harper, 1832. 2
vols. CU; DLC; MnU; NjP; PPA;
ViU.   13470

---- Paul Clifford. By Edward
Lytton Bulwer. New York, Pr.
by J. & J. Harper, 1832. 2 vols.
AU; KyU; MeU; NcD.   13471

---- Pelham; or, The Adventures
of a Gentleman. From 2d London
ed., rev. and cor. by author. In
2 vols. New York, Pr. by J. & J.
Harper, 1832. 213 p. MeU;

NCasti. 13472

M

McAllister, A.
A dissertation on the medical properties and injurious effects of the habitual use of tobacco: read, according to appointment, before the Medical society of the county of Oneida, at their semi-annual meeting, January 5, 1830. By A. McAllister, M. D. 2d ed., imp. and enl., with an introductory preface, by Moses Stuart. Boston, Peirce & Parker; New York, H. C. Sleight, 1832. 36 p. IEN-M; MH; PPPrHi; TxU; VtU. 13473

McCaffrey, John, 1806-1882.
Eulogy on Charles Carroll of Carrolton, delivered before the Academy Society of Mt. St. Mary's College, December 20, 1832. Baltimore, Wm. R. Lucas, 1832. 32 p. DLC; Md; MdW. 13474

M'Calla, William Latta, 1788-1859.
A discourse of Christian baptism as to its subjects, its mode, its history and its effect upon civil and religious society in opposition to the views of Alexander Campbell, Rev. John Walker, Mr. Robinson and other baptist authors. Philadelphia, George M'-Glaughlin, 1832. 396 p. MiD; NHC-S; NRAB; NRCR; PWmpDS. 13475

M'Carter's Almanac for 1833. Charleston, S. C. Charleston Press [1832] 18 p. MWA. 13476

M'Carter's Country Almanac for 1833. By David Young. Charleston, J. J. M'Carter [1832] 18 p. CtY. 13477

McClung, John Alexander, 1804-1859.

Sketches of western adventure: containing an account of the most interesting incidents connected with the settlement of the West, from 1755 to 1794; together with an appendix. By John A. M'Clung. Maysville, Ky., L. Collin's, 1832. 360 p. ICU; KHi; OClWHi; PPM; WHi. 13478

---- ---- Philadelphia, Grigg and Elliot [Maysville, Ky., Pr. by L. Collins, 1832. CtY; IdU; MWA; NNC; TKL. 13479

McClure, Alexander Wilson.
Lectures on ultra-Universalism. Boston, Peirce & Parker, 1832. 59 p. CtHC; MBC; MeBat; OO; PPPrHi. 13480

McConaughy, David, 1775-1852.
An address delivered before the Temperance Society of Washington county, at their quarterly meeting, held in the court house, Washington, Pa. December 24th, 1832. [Washington, Pa.?] Pr. by Wm. Somple [1832] 16 p. MiU-C. 13481
---- Inaugural address, delivered May 9, 1832, on induction to the office of president of Washington College. Washington, Pa., Grayson, 1832. 16 p. DLC; MiU-C; PPPrHi; PHi. 13482

M'Coy, Alexander.
Two letters, Second and Third, addressed to the Rev. Samuel Findley, editor of the "Religious Examiner," by... minister of the Reformed Dissenting Presbyterian Church. West Union, O., Pr. by Crapsey, 1832. MiU; PPPrHi. 13483

McCoy, Isaac, 1784-1846.
Country for Indians west of the Mississippi. Letter from the Secretary of War, transmitting a copy of the report made by Isaac McCoy on the subject of the coun-

try reserved for the indians
west of the Mississippi, March
16, 1832, read & laid upon the
table. [Washington, 1832?] 15 p.
CoU.   13484

M'Coy, Rice.
Circular letter... for the annual meeting of the Lost-river Association of 1832. But was rejected in toto by a majority of
said association... [Indiana?
1832?] 2 p. In.   13485

MacDill, David.
A discourse originally prepared for the Associate Reformed Congregation, of Hamilton & Rosaville. Hamilton, Pr.
by Woods, 1832. PPPrHi. 13486

[McDowall, John Robert] 1801-
1836.
Magdalen facts... New York,
Pr. for the author, 1832- DLC;
ICP; MnU; NjR; PHi.   13487

[McDowell, J. R.]
Henry Wallace: or The victim
of lottery gambling. A moral
tale. By a friend to American
youth... New York, Wilson &
Swain, 1832. 108 p. DLC; MWA;
NjP; OMC; PPL-R.   13488

McDowell, James, 1796-1851.
Speech of James M'Dowell, jr.
(of Rockbridge,) in the House of
delegates of Virginia, on the
slave question: delivered Saturday
January 21, 1832. 2d ed. Richmond, Pr. by T. W. White, 1832.
33 p. DLC; MH; NjP; PU. 13489

McDowell, Joseph Nash.
An introductory lecture... on
anatomy and surgery. Pub. by
his class. Cincinnati, Pr. at the
office of the Cincinnati Chronicle, 1832. 16 p. CSmH; InU;
MH-M; OClWHi.   13490

McDuffie, George, 1790-1851.

Defence of a liberal construction of the powers of Congress,
as regards internal improvement,
etc., with a complete refutation
of the ultra doctrines respecting
consolidation and state sovereignty. Written by the Hon. George
M'Duffie, in the year 1821, over
the signature of "One of the people. " To which are prefixed, an
encomiastic advertisement of the
work, by Major (now Governor)
Hamilton, and a preface by the
Philadelphia editor. 2d Philadelphia ed. Philadelphia, W. F.
Geddes, 1832. 24 p. DLC; ICU;
MB; PU; ScU.   13491

---- Speech of Mr. McDuffie, of
South Carolina, on the bill proposing a reduction of the duties
on imports. Delivered in the
House of Representatives May 28,
1832. Washington, Duff Green,
1832. 48 p. ICN; MB; PHi; ScU;
TxU.   13492

---- ---- June 1832. Washington, Pr. by Duff Green, 1832.
24 p. DLC; MHi; MiD-B; ScU;
TxU.   13493

---- Speech of Mr. McDuffie, on
the third reading of the Tariff
bill--Delivered in the House of
Representatives on the 28th of
June, 1832. Charleston, Pr. by
A. E. Miller, 1832. 16 p. MBAt;
MHi; NN; NcD.   13494

M'Ewen, William.
Grace and truth, or The fulness of the Redeemer displayed:
in an attempt to explain, illustrate, and enforce the most remarkable types, figures, and al-
legories of the Old Testament;
to which is added thoughts on various subjects. By Wm. McEwen,
Philadelphia, Towar & Hogan,
1832. 359 p. GDecCT; IaBo; InU;
OWoC.   13495

Macfarlane, Charles, 1799-1858.
The Romance of History. Itly. By Charles Macfarlane, New York, J. & J. Harper, 1832. 2 vols. AzU; CSmH; NcD; RP; ViPet. 13496

MacGowan, John, 1726-1780.
The dialogues of devils on the many vices which abound in the civil and religious world. By the Rev. John Macgowan... Philadelphia, Key & Biddle, 1832. 284 p. NNUT; TxH. 13497

---- Infernal conference; or Dialogues of devils. By the listener. Pittsburgh, Johnston & Stockton, 1832. 297 p. CLSU; DLC; MH; NjPT; PPi. 13498

Machpelah Cemetery Society of Philadelphia.
Charter and by-laws of the Machpelah Cemetery... of Philadelphia. Instituted in 1830. Philadelphia, 1832. 14 p. PHi. 13499

McIlvaine, Charles Pettit, 1799-1873.
The evidence of Christianity: in their external division, exhibited in a course of lectures delivered in Clinton hall, in the Winter of 1831-2, under the appointment of the University of the city of New York. By Charles P. M'Ilvaine. New York, G. & C. & H. Carvill, 1832. 565 p. IaDm; LPL; MH; NNS; RNR; WaPS. 13500

M'Kenney, D.
A brief statement of facts, shewing the rise, progress and necessity of African colonization; addressed to those citizens of the state of Virginia... [Richmond? T. White, 1832] 8 p. CSmH; NcD; OClWHi. 13501

Mackintosh, James, 1765-1832.
A general view of the prog-

ress of ethical philosophy, chiefly during the seventeenth and eighteenth centuries. By the Rt. Honourable Sir James Mackintosh... Philadelphia, Carey & Lea, 1832. 304 p. GHi; MdBP; PHi; PPA; RNR; VtU. 13502

Mackray, William.
Effect of the reformation on civil society. By William Mackray. New York, Robert Nesbit, 1832. 143 p. ICBB; MWA; NBuG; NGlo; PPPrHi. 13503

McLellan, Isaac, jr., 1806-1895.
The year with other poems. By the author of The fall of the Indian, &c. A new year's gift. Boston, Carter & Hendee, 1832. 60 p. CtHWatk; DLC; MB; MH; RPB. 13504

Maclure, William, 1763-1840.
Essay on the formation of rocks; or, An inquiry into the probable origin of their present form and structure. By William Maclure... New-Harmony, Ind., Pr. for the author, 1832. 53 p. CSt; In; MH; NN; OU; WHi. 13505

---- Observations on the geology of the West India Islands, from Barbadoes to Santa Cruz, inclusive. By Wm. Maclure. New Harmony, Ind., Pr. for the author, 1832. 17 p. CtY; LNH; MH; NjR; Vi. 13506

MacMahon, Bernard.
The American gardener's calendar, adapted to the climates and seasons of the U. S. ... for every month in the year... together with a copius index to the body of the work. 8th ed. imp. Philadelphia, 1832. 618 p. PHC. 13507

McMaster, Gilbert, 1778-1854.
Ministerial work and sufficiency; a sermon, Jan. 26, 1832 at the ordination and installation of

John McMaster in the Reformed
Presbyterian church, Schenect-
ady. Albany, Little & Cumming;
Schenectady, J. C. Magoffin,
1832. 40 p. CSmH; MBC; NjPT;
PPPrHi; RPB.   13508

---- The moral character of
civil government, considered with
reference to the political institutions of the United States, in
four letters. By Gilbert McMaster... Albany, W. C. Little;
Schenectady, J. C. Magoffin,
1832. 72 p. CSmH; MBC; NBuG;
NN; OClWHi; PPL; PPPrHi;
RPB.   13509

McNemar, Richard, 1770-1839.
     Principles, & regulations of
the United Society of Believers
called Shakers. See under
Shakers.

---- A series of lectures on
orthodoxy and heterodoxy, in al-
lusion to the testimony of
Christ's second appearing. Introduced by A reply to sundry de-
famatory letters written by A. M.
Bolton... Designed for the edifi-
cation of young believers. By E.
W. [pseud.] Dayton, O., 1832.
12 p. NN; OClWHi.   13510

McVickar, John, 1787-1868.
     A biographical memoir of the
Rev. Edmund D. Griffin... New
York, Pr. at the Protestant
Episcopal Press, 1832. 117 p.
CtHT; MH; NGH; NNC; WHi.
                               13511
Maddock, Henry, d. 1824.
     A treatise on the principles
and practice of the High court of
chancery, under the following
heads: I. Common law jurisdiction. II. Equity jurisdiction. III.
Statutory jurisdiction. IV. Spe-
cially delegated jurisdiction. By
Henry Maddock... 4th Amer. from
the last London ed.: with references to the principal American

decisions... Philadelphia, Key,
Mielke & Biddle, 1832. 2 v. CoU;
DLC; InCW; OO; TU.   13512

Maddy, Watkin, d. 1857.
     Elements of the theory of as-
tronomy. A new ed., rev. and
greatly enl. by J. Hymers. Cambridge, J. & J. J. Daighton,
1832. DN-Ob; OClW; OKU;
PPeSchw.   13513

Madison, Indianapolis and Lafayette Railroad Company.
     An act to incorporate the Mad-
ison, Indianapolis and Lafayette
Rail-Road company, passed at the
sixteenth session of the General
Assembly of the state of Indiana,
and approved, February 2, 1832.
Madison, Pr. by Arion & Lodge,
1832. 12 p. MWA.   13514

Maffitt, John Newland, 1794-1850.
     Literary and religious sketches.
By Rev. John Newland Maffitt.
New York, Press of T. Harries,
1832. 240 p. CtHC; IU; LNH;
NjMD; RPB.   13515

---- An oration delivered June,
1832 at Ashgrove, Washington
county, N. Y. over the grave of
Philip Embury the earliest Minister in the American Methodist
church by Rev. John Newland Maf-
fatt of the Methodist Episcopal
church. New York, Press of
Pierey & co., 1832. 16 p.
MBNMHi; TxDaM-L.   13516

Magill, John.
     The pioneer to the Kentucky
emigrant a brief topographical
and historical description of the
state of Kentucky. Frankfort, Ky.,
Marshall, 1832. KyLoF; PPPrHi;
PPiU.   13517

Maguire, Thomas.
     Trial of the Rev. Mr. Maguire
for seduction, in the court of Ex-
chequer, Dublin, on the 13th and

Maine

14th December, 1827. New York, J. M'Loughlin, 1832. 45 p. ICU; MB; MWH. 13518

Maine.

Additional resolves respecting the northeastern boundry. Passed January 23, 1832. Augusta, I. Berry & co., 1832. 4 p. MH; MBAt; MHi; MeBa; PPL. 13519

---- Documents relating to the northeastern boundary communicated by the Governor of Maine to both branches of the legislature. January, 1832. Pr. by order of the Senate. Augusta, I. Berry and co., 1832. 35 p. NN. 13520

---- Joint select committee on the tariff and internal improvements communication from the governor of Maine to Executive of Maryland, enclosing a report and resolutions of the Legislature of that state on the tariff and internal improvements. Annapolis, Jeremiah Hughes, 1832. 14 p. MdBE. 13521

---- Private and special acts of the state of Maine, passed by the 12th Legislature, at its session commencing January 4, 1832. Pub. agreeably to the resolve of June 20, 1820. Augusta, I. Berry and co., 1832. 340-461 p. A-SC; IaU-L; InSC; MeU; Nj. 13522

---- Public acts of the state of Maine, passed by the twelfth Legislature, at its session, held in January, 1832... Augusta, I. Berry and co., 1832. (3), 49, (7) p. IaU-L; In-SC; MeU; Nv; TxU-L. 13523

---- ---- 50 p. IaU-L; MeBa; MeU; Nj; NNLI. 13524

---- Report of the Committee on Literature and Literary Institutions, and resolve in favor of

Waterville College. Submitted to the Legislature of Maine, February 23, 1832. August, I. Berry and Co., 1832. 7 p. MeB. 13525

---- Report of the Joint Select Committee of the Legislature of Maine, on so much of the governor's message as relates to the northeastern boundry. Augusta, I. Berry & Co., 1832. 8 p. DLC; MH; MHi; MeBa; MiOC. 13526

---- Reports of the cases argued and determined in the Supreme Judicial Court of the state of Maine. By Simon Greenleaf, counselor-at-law. Hallowell, Pr. by Goodale, Glazier & co., 1832. vol. 7. 13527

---- Resolutions of the Legislature of the state of Maine respecting the advice of the king of the Netherlands in relation to the northeastern boundry. Portland, T. Todd, 1832. 8 p. DLC; MH-L; MeHi; PPAmP; WHi. 13528

---- Resolves of the twelfth Legislature of the state of Maine passed at the session which commenced on the fourth day of January, and ended on the ninth day of March, 1832. Augusta, I. Berry & Co., 1832. 296 p. IaU-L; Ky; MeU; Nj; R. 13529

---- Rules and orders to be observed in the state of Maine during the continuance of the twelfth Legislature, 1832. Augusta, I. Berry and Co., 1832. 22 p. MH-L; MeHi. 13530

---- State tax. Tax for the year 1832. State of Maine. Augusta, I. Berry and Co., 1832. 16 p. ICJ. 13531

Maine family almanack. Boston, Allen and Co. [1832] MWA. 13532

The Maine farmers' almanac for

the year of our Lord 1833. By
Daniel Robinson. Augusta, Dole
and Redington, 1832. 48 p. MWA;
MeB.   13533

---- Hallowell, Glazier, Masters
and co. [1832] MWA.   13534

---- Portland, Gershom Hyde &
Co., 1832. 48 p. MWA; MeHi.
                              13535
The Maine Register and United
States calendar, for the year of
our Lord, 1832. Portland, G.
Hyde and Co., 1832. 112 (2) p.
MeBat; MeHi; MeLewB; MeU.
                              13536
Maine Wesleyan Seminary,
Kent's Hill.
    Catalogue of the officers and
students of Maine Wesleyan Semi-
nary, Readfield, fall term, 1832.
Hallowell, Glazier, Masters &
Co., 1832. 12 p. MBAt; MeHi.
                              13537
Malcolm, Howard.
    The extent and efficacy of the
atonement. A discourse delivered
by appointment before the Boston
Baptist Association met at Newton,
Mass. Sept. 19, 1832. Boston,
Allen & Ticknor, 1832. 70 p.
MHC-S; OCX.   13538

Malin, William Gunn.
    Some account of the Pennsyl-
vania hospital; its origin, objects
and present state. Philadelphia,
T. Kite & Co., 1832. 3-46 p.
DLC; MB; MWA; NBuG; PPL.
                              13539
Mallary, Charles D.
    Memoirs of Elder Edmund
Botsford. By Charles D. Mallary.
Charleston, W. Riley, 1832.
CtHWatk; DLC; GMM; PPPrHi;
ScCliTO.   13540

Maltby, Erastus, 1796-1883.
    Paul's belief; a sermon
preached at the installation of the
Rev. Elbridge G. Howe, as pastor of the Congregational Church

and Society in Halifax, Massachusetts, November 15, 1832. Taunton, F. Dunbar, 1832. 26 p.
CSmH; DLC; IEG; MWA; RPB.
                              13541
Malte-Brun, Conrad, 1775-1826.
    A new general atlas, exhibiting
the five great divisions of the
globe, Europe, Asia, Africa,
America and Oceana...drawn and
engraved particularly to illustrate
the universal geography, by M.
Malte-Brun. Philadelphia, Grigg
& Elliot, 1832. 6 vols. AU; DLC;
GDecCT; ICU; WaPS.   13542

---- Universal geography, or a
description of all parts of the
world, on a new plan...By M.
Malte-Brun. Philadelphia, John
Laval, 1832. 5 vol. CtHC; GHi;
MLaw; OCN; PHi.   13543

Manchester, William C., b. 1794.
    Songs of Zion, or, Conference
hymns selected and original; to
which is added a brief sketch of
the author's life and experience.
2d ed. Providence, H. H. Brown,
1832. 224 p. RPB.   13544

[Mancinelli, Filippo]
    A collection of colloquial
phrases, on every topic necessary
to maintain conversation, the whole
so disposed as considerably to facilitate the acquisition of the Italian language. By an Italian gentleman [Pseud.] Philadelphia, Carey
& Lea, 1832. 148 p. DLC; MH;
MdBP; PU-Penn; ViU.   13545

---- Dialoghi disposti per facili-
tare lo studio della lingua Itali-
ana. Philadelphia, 1832. PPL.
                              13546
Manesca, John, 1774-1837?
    Strictures on phenological doc-
trines upon a humans intellect,
in a letter addressed to Dr. Spur-
gheim by John Manesca. New
York, Butts & Anstice, 1832.
28 p. DSG; MB; NN; PPAmP;

OMC. 13547

Mangum, Willis Person, 1792-1861.
Speech on the tariff: delivered in the Senate of the U.S. Feb. 7 & 8, 1832 on Mr. Clay's resolution...Washington, Jonathan Elliot, 1832. 28 p. DLC; Mi; NbU; PHi; ScC. 13548

Manley, J. K.
Special medical council (N.Y.) New York, 1832. MB. 13549

Manley, James R.
Letters addressed to the Board of Health and to Richard Riker, on the subject of his agency in constituting a special medical council. New York, P. Van Pelt, 1832. 27 p. DSG; MBC; MB; MH; NBMS. 13550

Mann, Joel, 1789-1884.
A sermon, preached in Greenwich, Connecticut, August 5, 1832. By Joel Mann, Pastor of the Second Congregational Church. New York, Pr. by Sleight & Robinson, 1832. 16 p. Ct; ICT; MBC; MiD-B; PPM. 13551

Manning, Robert.
Moral entertainments, on the most important practical truths on the Christian religion. In two vol. by the Rev. Robert Manning. Baltimore, Fielding Lucas, Jr., 1832. 2 v. IaDuMtC; MBBC; MdW; OCX; PLor; WOccR. 13552

Map of woodstock. Drawn by a committee from the Woodstock Institute-1832. Boston, Pendleton's Lithography [1832] VtU. 13553

Marcet, Jane (Haldimand), 1769-1855.
Conversations on natural philosophy in which the elements of that science are familiarly explained...with corrections, improvements, and considerable additions in the body of the work; appropriate questions, and a glossary; by Dr. Thomas P. Jones. Philadelphia, Grigg & Elliot, 1832. 220 p. CtSoP; ICU; NjR; OCl; PPAmP; TNT. 13554

Maria. Written for the American Sunday-School Union [anon.] Philadelphia, American Sunday School Union, 1832. 15 p. DLC. 13555

Marine seizures: or, A vindication of the right of jury trial in the Federal Courts, in cases of seizures, made upon the waters, under the laws of import, navigation and trade of the United States. New York, B. G. Jansen, Bookseller, 1832. 28 p. MiU-L; PPL. 13556

Mariner's Church, Boston, Mass.
Articles of faith and covenant of the Mariner's Church, Boston. Boston, Perkins & Marvin, 1832. 11 p. ScCC. 13557

---- History, articles of faith... of the Mariner's Church. Boston, 1832. 11 p. 13558

Marks, F.
A brief survey of the moral state of the world...Extracted from the writings of Thomas Dick, and others. By F. Marks. Geneva, N.Y., J. Bogart, 1832. GEU; MH. 13559

Marsh, Christopher Columbus.
The art of single-entry bookkeeping improved by the introduction of proof or trial balance... By C. C. Marsh, accountant... Baltimore, George McDowell & Son, 1832. 118 p. DLC; IU; MB; NNC; OS. 13560

Marsh, John, 1788-1868.
An epitome of general ecclesiastical history, from the earliest

period to the present time... 3d
ed. By John Marsh, A. M. New
York, Pr. by W. E. Dean, 1832.
449 p. CSmH; NN.   13561

Marshall, Humphrey, 1760-1841.
   Biography of Henry Clay... By
Geo. D. Prentice. Reviewed and
revised by Humphrey Marshall,
in relation to himself and the
late Col. J. H. Daviess... (Maysville, Ky. , Pr. at the Monitor
office) [1832] 24 p. ICU; PPL;
WHi.   13562

---- Humanity; being essays on
the mind of man, and other constitutional properties of the human race. Frankfort, Kentuckian
Commentator Office, 1832. 159 p.
PPPrHi.   13563

Marshall, John, 1755-1835.
   Atlas to Marshall's life of...
Philadelphia, J. Crissy, 1832.
1 p. DLC.   13564

---- The life of George Washington, commander in chief of the
American forces, during the war
which established the independence of his country, and first
president of the United States.
Comp. under the inspection of
the Honourable Bushrod Washington, from original papers... By
John Marshall. 2d ed. rev. and
cor. by the author... Philadelphia,
J. Crissy [1832] 2 v. Ct; LNB;
OHi; PPA; Tx; WaPS.   13565

Marshall, Thomas.
   The speech of Thomas Marshall, in the House of delegates
of Virginia, on the abolition of
slavery. Delivered Friday, January 20, 1832. Richmond, Pr. by
Thos. W. White, 1832. 12 p.
InU; MB; PHi; NN; PPAmP;
ScCC; Vi.   13566

---- ---- 2d ed. Richmond,
Thos. W. White, 1832. 12 p.

MB; NC; NjP; PHi; Vi.   13567

Martineau, Harriet, 1802-1876.
   ... Brooke and Brooke farm,
a tale... Boston, L. C. Bowles,
1832. 200 p. CtHT; MB-FA; MH;
MCon; NRU.   13568

---- Demerara, a tale. Boston,
L. C. Bowles, 1832. DLC; MH;
MNan.   13569

---- Ella of Garveloch; a tale.
Boston, L. C. Bowles, 1832.
206 p. MCon; MH; MNan. 13570

---- Five years of youth; of
sense and sentiment. By Harriet
Martineau. 1st Amer. ed. Bos-
ton, Leonard C. Bowles, and B.
H. Greene, 1832. 258 p. CLU;
ICN; NN; MBAU; PMA; RPB.
                             13571
---- ... The hill and valley. A
tale. By Harriet Martineau... Bos-
ton, L. C. Bowles, 1832. 216 p.
MB-FA; MH; MdBJ.   13572

---- Illustrations of political
economy. By Harriet Martineau.
Boston, Leonard C. Bowles,
1832-1835. 19 vols. ICJ; KPea;
MPiB; NN; ViU; WU.   13573

---- ---- Philadelphia, E. Littel,
1832-1835. 19 vols. CtHT; ICJ;
MdBS; NNS; WHi.   13574

---- Life in the Wilds. A tale.
Illustrations of political economy.
No. 1. Boston, Leonard C.
Bowles, 1832. 116 p. MB-FA;
MH.   13575

---- ---- Philadelphia, Littell,
1832. 116 p. PU.   13576

---- The times of our Savior.
By Harriet Martineau. Reprinted,
after revision, from the English
edition. 2d ed. Boston, L. C.
Bowles and B. H. Greene, 1832.
139 p. MB; MH; Nh; RPB. 13577

The Martyrs of Lyons and Vi-
enne, in France. Written for the
American... Philadelphia, American Sunday School Union, 1832.
35 p. AmSSchU; DLC.   13578

Mary and her lamb. New Haven,
1832. 8 p. MWA.   13579

Mary Carter... Written for the
American Sunday School Union,
and revised by the Committee of
Publication. Philadelphia, American Sunday School Union, 1832.
33 p. DLC; IAlS; MoSpD. 13580

Maryland.
An act further to amend the
act incorporating the Chespeake
and Ohio Canal Company, April
25, 1832. [Washington, 1832] 3 p.
ViU.   13581

---- Board of Managers for removing the free people of color.
Colonization of the free colored
population of Maryland, and of
such slaves as may hereafter become free. Statement of facts,
for the use of those who have not
yet reflected on this important
subject. Baltimore, Pub. by the
managers appointed by the State
of Maryland, 1832. 16 p. CSmH;
MA; MBAt; MiU; PPL.   13582

---- ---- News from Africa. A
collection of facts relating to the
colony in Liberia, for the information of the free people of Col-
or in Maryland. Pub. by the Colonization managers appointed by
the state of Maryland. Baltimore,
Pr. by J. D. Toy, 1832. 36 p.
DLC; MH; MdHi; RP; WHi.
                          13583
---- Catalogue of Law books belonging to the State Library.
Annapolis, Pr. by J. Green,
1832. 18 p. PHi.   13584

---- Index to the laws and resolutions of Maryland, from the

year 1825 to the year 1831, in-
clusively. Prepared and pub. by
authority. Annapolis, Wm. M'-
Neir, 1832. [344] p. MiU-L;
NcD-L.   13585

---- Index to the laws and resolutions of Maryland, from the
year 1826 to the year 1831, in-
clusively. Prepared and pub. by
authority. Annapolis, Pr. by Wm.
M'Neir, 1832. 350 p. Md; MdHi;
Nj; TxU; WaU.   13586

---- Journal of the proceedings
of the House of Delegates of...
Maryland, December session,
1831. Dec. 26th, 1831 to March
14, 1832. Pub. by authority.
Annapolis, Pr. by Jeremiah
Hughes, 1832. 720 p. MdHi.
                          13587
---- Journal of the proceedings
of the Senate of the State of
Maryland, December session,
1831. Dec. 26th, 1831 to March
14th, 1832. Pub. by authority.
Annapolis, Pr. by Wm. M'Neir,
1832. 376 p. MdBB; MdHi.
                          13588
---- Laws made and passed by
the General Assembly of the State
of Maryland, at a session begun
and held at Annapolis, on Monday the 26th Day of December,
1831 and ended on Wednesday,
the 14th day of March, 1832.
Pub. by authority. Annapolis, Pr.
by J. Hughes, 1832. 650 p.
MdHi; Nj; Nv; W.   13589

---- Message from the executive
to the Legislature of Maryland,
December session 1832. Annapolis, J. Hughes, 1832. 11 p. DLC;
MiU-T; NN.   13590

---- Report. L. D. Teackle,
Chairman on the part of the
House of Delegates. By the House
of Delegates, February 20, 1832.
Read the first time and ordered
to lie on the table, and be print-

ed. Annapolis, J. Hughes, 1832.
19 p. DLC; MdBP; MdHi; MH.
13591
---- Report and resolutions relative to the Southern and Western
limits of this State. Annapolis,
Pr. by Wm. M'Neir, 1832. 52 p.
DLC; MdHi; RPB; TxU.   13592

---- Report of the Committee on
Grievances and Courts of Justice,
of the House of Delegates, relative to the colored population of
Maryland. H. Brawner, chairman. Annapolis, Pr. by Jeremiah Hughes, 1832. 10 p. MB;
PPL.   13593

---- Report of the Committee on
Internal Improvement to the Legislature of Maryland, W. C.
Johnson, Chairman, Annapolis,
Pr. by Jeremiah Hughes, 1832.
32 p. MdHi; MiU-T; NN; PPL.
13594
---- Report of the Committee on
Ways and Means, in obedience
to an order of the House of Delegates, instructing that committee
to report its opinion upon the sufficiency of the existing revenue
to sustain the several propositions,
involving charges upon the Treasury... L. D. Teackle, chairman.
Annapolis, Pr. by Jeremiah
Hughes, 1832. 16 p. DLC; MBC;
MdHi; PHi; PPL.   13595

---- Report of the Committee of
Ways and Means upon the petitions for the establishment of a
financial institution. Baltimore,
J. Lucas and E. K. Deaver, 1832.
16 p. MBC; MdHi.   13596

---- Report of the directors of
the Maryland Penitentiary made
to the executive and communicated by his excellency, Governor
Howard, to the Legislature, at
December session, 1832. Baltimore, Pr. by Sands and Neilson,
1832. 18 p. MdHi.   13597

---- Report relative to the State
Library, made by the Committee
appointed on that subject. L. D.
Teackle, Chairman. Annapolis,
Pr. by Jeremiah Hughes, 1832.
8 p. MdHi.   13598

---- Reports of cases argued
and determined in the Court of
Appeals of Maryland, by Richard
W. Gill, attorney at law, and
John Johnson, clerk of the Court
of Appeals, containing cases in
1830-31-32. Baltimore, William & Joseph Neal, 1832.
539 p. Az; G; P; Vi-L; W.
13599

Maryland Savings Institution. Baltimore.
    Reports of the board of public
examiners of the Maryland Savings Institutions made in conformity to its charter, by authority of
the General Assembly of Maryland. Baltimore, James Lucas and
E. K. Deaver, 1832. 38 p. DLC;
MdBLC; PHi.   13600

Maryland State Colonization So-
ciety. See Maryland Board of
Managers for Removing the Free
People of Color.

Maryland State Temperance Society.
    First annual report of the
Maryland State Temperance Society, presented at the meeting in
Annapolis, January, 1832. Annapolis, Pr. by Jeremiah Hughes,
1832. 22 p. DLC; MdBE; MdHi.
13601
Mary's book of hymns. Concord,
M. G. Atwood, 1832. 16 p. RPB.
13602
Mary's book of sports. With beautiful pictures. Sidney's press.
New Haven, S. Babcock, 1832.
8 p. CtNwchA; CtY.   13603

Mary's childhood. Boston, Massachusetts Sabbath School Co.,

1832. 32 p. DLC.   13604

Mary's primer. Sidney's press.
New Haven, S. Babcock, 1832.
8 p. CtY.   13605

Mason, John, 1706-1763.
Self-knowledge. A treatise
showing the nature and benefit of
that important science, and the
way to attain it. Baltimore, Jos.
N. Lewis, 1832. 218 p. CtHT;
PSC-Hi.   13606

---- A treatise on self knowledge;
showing the nature and benefit of
that important science, and the
way to attain it. By John Mason,
A. M. With questions adapted for
the use of schools. Revised
stereotype ed. Boston, James
Loring, 1832. 143 p. MB; TNP.
                        13607
Mason, John Mitchell, 1770-1829.
The writings of the late John
M. Mason, D.D., consisting of
sermons, essays, and miscellanies, selected and arranged by
the Rev. Ebenezer Mason. New
York, Ebenezer Mason, 1832. 4
vol. CtHT; GDecCT; KyLoP;
MBC; NjPT; ViRut.   13608

Mason, Lowell, 1792-1872.
The Boston Glee Book. Boston,
J. H. Wilkins and R. B. Carter,
and Jenks & Palmer, 1832. 261 p.
MBrigStJ.   13609

---- The choir: or Union collection of church music. Arranged
and harmonized by Lowell Mason.
Boston, Carter, Hendee & Co.,
1832. 358 p. CtHWatk; DLC; ICU;
MB; NNUT.   13610

---- Church psalmody: A collection of psalms and hymns, adapted to public worship, selected
from Dr. Watts and other authors.
(By Lowell Mason and David
Greene). Boston, Perkins &
Marvin, 1832. 576 p. DLC; MH-

AH; PPPrHi; TNF; WGr.   13611

---- Juvenile Lyre; or, Hymns
and songs, religious, moral, and
cheerful. Set to appropriate music,
for the use of primary and common schools. Boston, Richardson,
Lord & Holbrook; Hartford, H. &
F. J. Huntington, 1832. 72 p.
CU-S; DLC; MB; MPeHi; NN.
                        13612
---- Lyra sacra: consisting of
anthems, notes, sentences, chants,
etc... Boston, Richardson, Lord
& Holbrook, 1832. 383 p. CtMW;
ICN; MB; NNUT; OO.   13613

---- Manual of Christian psalmody: a collection of psalms and
hymns, for public worship. Boston, Perkins & Marvin; Philadelphia, French & Perkins, 1832.
[37]-588 p. DLC; MB; NPV; RPB;
WNaH.   13614

---- The sacred harp: or Eclectic harmony. A collection of
church music consisting of psalms
and hymn tunes... harmonized and
arranged by Lowell Mason and T.
B. Mason... New ed. Cincinnati,
Truman and Smith (1832?] 232 p.
IEN.   13615

Mason, Thomas, 1769-1851.
Zion's songster; or, A collection of hymns and spiritual songs,
usually sung at camp-meetings,
and also in revivals of religion.
7th ed. New York, Wiggins &
Arthur, 1832. 348 p. MBU-T;
NcWsW.   13616

Masonic oaths, with notes to
which are added practical proofs
of the character and tendency of
Free Masonry. Montpelier, Pr.
by Knapp & Jewett, 1832. 108 p.
PPFM.   13617

Massachusetts.
Abstracts of the returns from
the banks & from the institution

for savings in Mass. Boston, 1832. IU; MB; MH.   13618

---- An act for apportioning and assessing a tax of three hundred and three thousand six hundred and thirty four pounds and six pence. Boston, Pr. by Benjamin Edes & Sons, Prs. to the Commonwealth of Massachusetts [1832] 10 p. MHi.   13619

---- [An act for the due regulation of licensed houses, and to repeal all former laws on the subject. Boston] 1832. 15 p. MH.   13620

---- An act in addition to an Act to provide for the inspection of Hops for exportation. [Boston, 1832] 2 p. MH.   13621

---- Acts regulating Banks & Banking, passed in 1829, 1831, and 1832. 3d ed. Boston, 1832. 39 p. MHi.   13622

---- Amendment of the constitution on choosing Representatives. 1832. 5 p. MBC.   13623

---- By His Excellency, Levi Lincoln, a proclamation: The people of this Commonwealth... by united observing Thursday, the fifth day of April next...[Boston, 1 March 1832] Bdsd. MHi. 13624

---- By His Excellency, Levi Lincoln, Governor of the Commonwealth of Massachusetts. A Proclamation for a day of public Thanksgiving and praise... Boston, 19th Oct. 1832. Bdsd. Matt; MBB.   13625

---- A charge delivered to the grand jury for the county of Essex, at the Supreme judicial court, held at Ipswich. May term, 1832. Pub. at their request. By Lemuel Shaw, C.J. Boston, Steam power press office, 1832.

16 p. DLC.   13626

---- Decision of the Supreme Judicial Court of Massachusetts, in a case relating to the sacramental furniture of a church in Brookfield, with the entire arguments of Hon. Samuel Hoar, Jr., for the plaintiff and of Hon. Lewis Strong for the defendant. Boston, Peirce & Parker, 1832. 48 p. MH; MoU; MWA; NjR; PHi.   13627

---- Digest of Probate laws of Massachusetts, relative to the power and duty of executors, administrators, guardians, heirs, etc. Also an appendix containing all the additional laws... to and including the winter and June sessions of the Legislature, A. D. 1831. Worcester, 1832. 216 p. MB; MH-L; MWA.   13628

---- Documents... including reports of inspectors, warden... 1831/2-48/9. [Boston, 1832-49] 18 v. in 2. MH; MnU.   13629

---- The General laws of Massachusetts. From June 1822, to June 1831. Edited by Theron Metcalf, esq. Boston, Hilliard Gray, Little, and Wilkins, 1832. 3 vols. M; MH-L; NNLI.   13630

---- General orders. ("Carrying the sentence (in the trial of Lieut. Col. G. T. Winthrop, commanding officer of the independent company of cadets, on charges exhibited against him by Adjutant Gen. W. H. Sumner) into effect, dissolving the court, and discharging Lieut. Col. Winthrop from arrest." Boston, 1832.) 12 p. MB; MH.   13631

---- Geological map of Massachusetts by Edward Hitchcock. Boston, 1832. MB.   13632

---- Journal of the Convention for framing a constitution of government for the state of Massachusetts Bay... Boston, Dutton & Wentworth, prs. to the state, 1832. 264 p. Ct; DLC; Ia; NcD; PU; WHi.   13633

---- Laws of the Commonwealth of Massachusetts, passed by the General Court, at their session which commenced on Wednesday, the fourth of January, and ended on Saturday, the twenty-fourth of March, one thousand eight hundred and thirty-two. Pub. agreeably to a resolve of the sixteenth January, 1812. Boston, Dutton & Wentworth, prs. to the State, 1832. 320 p. A-SC; M; Nj; Nv; R.   13634

---- List of the House of Representatives, 1832. [Boston] Dutton & Wentworth, prs. to the state [1832] broadside. NN.   13635

---- Memorials, Washington. Celebration of the Centennial Anniversary of the birthday of George Washington, by the Legislature of Massachusetts. (Feb. 22, 1832.) [Boston] broadside. MHi.   13636

---- A Message to the Legislature, Jan. 9, 1832. Boston, 1832. 31 p. MB; MBC; MHi.   13637

---- ...Report of commissioners appointed to prepare and report a revision of the laws concerning the form of bank bills, and the plates from which they shall hereafter be impressed, &c. [Boston, 1832] 20 p. DLC.13638

---- Report of Commissioners Appointed under a resolve of the Legislature of Massachusetts, to Superintend the Erection of a Lunatic Hospital at Worcester, and to report a system of discipline and government for the same. Made January 4th, 1832. Boston,

Dutton & Wentworth, prs. to the state, 1832. 32 p. Ct; CtY-M; MBC; MH; NN.   13639

---- Report of the Attorney General. 1832- Boston, 1832- DLC; KU; NcD; TxU; WaU-L.   13640
---- Report of the committee on public lands, on the subject of the North Eastern Boundary. Boston, Dutton & Wentworth, state prs., 1832. 24 p. CtY; DLC; MeB; NN; PPAmP.   13641

---- Report of the committee on the petition of the President and fellows of Harvard college (for a fire-proof building for the library). Boston, 1832. 15 p. MBAt; PPAmP; RPB.   13642

---- [Report of the Committee to whom was referred a Report on the punishment of death]...[Boston, 1832] 8 p. M.   13643

---- ... Report [of the Committee, to whom was referred the subject of a general vaccination. Boston, 1832] 3 p. DLC. 13644

---- [Report of the joint special committee on the petition of the president and fellows of Harvard University, for a grant to enable them to erect a building in their library. With the petition of the corporation. B. 1832] 15 p. MH.   13645
---- Report of the state valuation committee, Jan. 3, 1832. Boston, Dutton & Wentworth, 1832. DLC; M; MA; MHi; WHi.   13646

---- Report relating to the enclosure of Cambridge common. [Boston, 1832] 11 p. MH. 13647

---- Report to the committee of both houses to whom was referred the message of the Governor communicating certain resolutions of

the General Assembly of the
state of Rhode Island relating to
the southern boundary of Massachusetts. Boston, 1832. 15 p.
M; MH-L; MiD-B.   13648

---- Reports of cases argued
and determined in the Supreme
judicial court of the commonwealth of Massachusetts, containing the cases for the year 1814...
Boston, Hilliard, Gray & co.;
Cambridge, Brown, Shattuck &
Co., 1832. 576 p. In-SC; M;
MdBB; W.   13649

---- Resolves of the General
Court of the Commonwealth of
Massachusetts, passed at their
session, which commenced on
Wednesday, 4th of Jan. and ended
on Saturday, 24th of March, 1832.
Pub. agreeably to a resolve of
the 15th of Jan. 1812. Boston,
Dutton & Wentworth, prs. to the
State, 1832. 234 p. IaU-L; NNLI;
R; W.   13650

---- Rules and Orders. House of
Representatives, Mass. Boston,
Dutton & Wentworth, State prs.,
1832. 45 p. M.   13651

---- Rules and Orders. Senate.
Mass. Boston, Dutton & Wentworth, State prs., 1832. 38 p.
32 p. M.   13652

---- Rules and Regulations for
the Government of the Massachusetts State Prison. Boston, 1832.
M.   13653

---- Special message of Governor Lincoln, to the Legislature
of Massachusetts, Mar. 17, 1832.
And correspondence between him
and the governor of Maine, in
relation to a negotiation for the
territory north east of the St.
John. Boston, Pr. by Dutton &
Wentworth, 1832. 8 p. DLC; MB;
MH; MeHi; Nh-Hi.   13654

---- Statement of donations made
by the Commonwealth of Massachusetts to the literary institutions
(except Academies). 1832. 19 p.
MBC.   13655

Massachusetts Ancient & Honor-
able Artillery Co.
   Annual record. Boston, 1832.
Mi.   13656

Massachusetts Anti Masonic State
Convention.
   Third Anti Masonic State Convention of Massachusetts, Worcester Sept. 5-6, 1832, for the
nomination of candidates for electors of President and Vice President of the United States and for
Governor and Lt. Governor of
Massachusetts, proceedings, resolutions, address to the people.
Boston, Pr. by Perkins & Marvin, 1832. 55 p. M; MB; PPFM.
                           13657
Massachusetts Anti-Slavery Society.
   ...Annual report of the board
of managers of the Massachusetts
anti-slavery society with some account of the annual meeting...
Boston, Isaac Knapp, 1832- Tx.
                           13658
---- Constitution of the New-England anti-slavery society: with an
address to the public. Boston,
Pr. by Garrison & Knapp, 1832.
16 p. CSmH; MB; MiU; MnU;
NcWfC; OO.   13659

Massachusetts Charitable Fire
Society.
   Act of incorporation... Boston,
1832. 27 p. DLC.   13660

Massachusetts Colonization Soci-
ety.
   ...American colonization soci-
ety, and the colony at Liberia.
Pub. by the Massachusetts Col-
onization Society. Boston, Pr. by
Perkins & Marvin, 1832. 16 p.
DLC; IU; MHi; NcD; OO. 13661

---- [Circular letter, Boston, June, 1832 to ministers of churches, asking for contributions.] (2) p. MHi.   13662

---- Statement of Facts relating to Slavery, by the Massachusetts Colonization Society. Boston, 1832.   13663

Massachusetts Medical Society.
Acts of incorporations and acts regulating the practice of physic and surgery, with the by-laws and orders... Massachusetts Medical Society. Boston, W. L. Lewis, 1832. 88 p. DLC; MiDw-M; NNN; PU.   13664

---- Circular of the committee on accounts. Boston, 1832. MBAt.   13665

---- Library of practical medicine of the Massachusetts Medical Society. Boston, Stimpson & Clapp, 1832. 16 vols. MdBM; MH-M; MNF; P.   13666

---- A report on spasmodic cholera, prepared by a committee under the direction of the counselors of the Massachusetts Medical Society. Boston, Pub. by Carter & Hendee, 1832. 190 p. MB; MoS; NIC; PU; ViU.   13667

Massachusetts Sabbath School Society. Committee of Publication.
The reformation;... Boston, 1832. DLC.   13668

Massachusetts Society for Promoting Christian Knowledge.
Annual report of the directors ... Boston, 1832. DLC.   13669

The Massachusetts Family Almanac, or the Merchants & Farmers Calendar... for the year of our Lord 1833. Calculated for the State of Massachusetts, but will answer for Connecticut, R. Island, N. Hampshire, Maine and Vermont... Boston, Proprietors of the copy-right. Allen & Co., [1832] (36) p. MH; MWA; NjR; RPB; WHi.   13670

The Massachusetts Register and United States calendar, for 1833, also city officers in Boston, and other useful information. Boston, James Loring [1832] 252 p. ICN; KWiU; MHa; MeHi; RPB.   13671

Massey, John M.
Remarks on the subject of electing judges by the people. Addressed to the delegates of the state convention at Jackson, Sept. 1832.   13672

Match-making, and other tales. By Miss Mitford, Mrs. S. C. Hall, Leitch Ritchie, L. E. L., Mrs. Opie, Derwent Conway, &c. &c. Philadelphia, E. L. Carey & A. Hart, 1832- 2 vols. DLC; MBL; MdBP; PPA; WaS.   13673

Mathematical tables: Difference of latitude and departure; logarithims... artificial sines, tangents and secants. Stereotyped ed., carefuly rev. and cor. Philadelphia, Kimber & Sharpless, [1832] 152 p. IaDaM; PBL. 13674

Mather, Benjamin.
Plan of the Town of Lowell and Belvidere Village... Boston, 1832. MB; NIC.   13675

Matthews, Alinos.
An address delivered before Constellation Lodge no. 103, in the Masonic hall, Mayfield, N. Y. December 27th, A. L. 5831. By Alinos Matthews, P. M. of said lodge... New York, Constellation Lodge no. 103, Mayfield, Montgomery Co., 1832. 16 p. MNFM.   13676

Matthias, John J.
Sabbath school teachers' second

book; containing a harmony of the
four gospels; and questions on
the history, miracles, discourses,
and parables of our Lord... By
The Rev. J. J. Matthias. New
York, B. Waugh and T. Mason,
1832. 234 p. CtMW; MoS;
NNMHi; NSyU; Vi.   13677

Maunder, Samuel, 1785-1849.
    Treasury of knowledge, and
Library of reference. Parts 1-2-
3. 1st ed. New York, James
Conner, 1832. 3 v. ICU; GAGT;
MB; NFred.   13678

Mauran, Joseph, 1796-1873.
    Remarks on the Cholera, em-
bracing facts and observations
collected at New York, during a
visit to the city expressly for
that purpose. Providence, Pr. by
W. Marshall & Co., 1832. 34 p.
DLC; MB; MH; NNNAM; RPB.
                          13679
---- ---- 3d ed. Providence, Pr.
by W. Marshall & Co., 1832.
32 p. NNU-M; RPB.   13680

Maxwell, William.
    An oration commemorative of
the late Rev. John Holt Rice, D. D.
spoken before the literary and
philosophical society of Hampden
Sydney College, at their anniversary meeting, on Thursday the
27th of September, A.D. 1832.
By William Maxwell. Pub. by request. Richmond, Robert I. Smith,
1832. 33 p. CSmH; DLC; ICU;
MH-AH; NcD; PHi; PPPrHi; ViW.
                          13681
May, Frederick, 1773?-1847?
    The argument submitted to the
committee of the Senate on the
Washington bridge... Washington?
1832? 8 p. DLC.   13682

May, Samuel Joseph, 1797-1871.
    A discourse on slavery in the
United States, delivered in Brooklyn, July 3, 1831... Boston, Garrison & Knapp, 1832. 29 p.

CBPSR; ICMe; NjP; OClWHi; RP;
WHi.   13683

Mayes, Daniel, 1792-1861.
    An address delivered on the
first anniversary of Van Doren's
Collegiate Institute for Young
Ladies, in the city of Lexington,
Ky. on the last Thursday of July,
1832. By the Hon. Daniel Mayes,
to which is added a prospectus
of the institute. Lexington, N. L.
Finnell & J. F. Herndon, 1832.
14 p. DLC; KyLoF; MHi; MWA;
NjPT.   13684

---- An introductory lecture, delivered to the law class of Transylvania University... Nov. 5th,
1832; with prospectus of the law
department. By Daniel Mayes.
Lexington, Ky., H. Savory & Co.,
1832. 32, 4 p. CSmH; DLC;
KyDC; NNF; NjPT; OCGHM.
                          13685
Maygrier, Jacques Pierre, 1771-
1835.
    The anatomists manual; or, A
treatise on the manner of preparing all the parts of anatomy, followed by a complete description
of these parts... By J. P. Maygrier... Tr. from the 4th French
ed. by Gunning S. Bedford...
New York, Collins & Co., 1832.
2 v. in 1. CSt-L; PU; OClM;
RPM; VtU.   13686

Maynard, William [Hale] 1786-
1832.
    Speech delivered in the Senate
of New York... Feb. 1832; on the
resolution against renewing the
charter of the Bank of U. S. Albany, Packard, 1832. 38 p. InHi;
MBC; MH; NjR; OClWHi. 13687

---- The speech of the Hon. Wm.
Maynard, in the Senate of New
York, delivered in committee of
the whole, on the bill introduced
by Mr. Bronson, chairman of the
committee on finance, for impos-

ing a direct tax; and upon the substitute offered by Mr. Maynard. Utica, Wm. Williams, 1832. 16 p. ICU; IU; NBNMHi; NCH; NNC. 13688

[Mead, Asa] 1792-1831.
Memoir of John Mooney Mead, who died at East Hartford, Conn., April 8, 1831, aged 4 years, 11 months, and 4 days. New York, American Tract Society, 1832. 118 p. AU; CtHC; IEG; MH; OM; TNT. 13689

---- ---- 2d ed. Boston, Peirce, 1832. 108 p. CtHT; MWA; MnM; NhD; OClW. 13690

---- ---- 3d ed. Boston, Peirce & Parker; New York, H.C. Sleight, Clinton Hall, 1832. 108 p. MWA. 13691

Mead, Matthew, 1630?-1699.
The Almost Christian Discovered; or, The False Professor Tried and Cast. 2d. ed. Philadelphia, George & Latimer, 1832. 204 p. MWA; OMC; ScCliTO. 13692

Mealy, Stephen Albion.
A funeral sermon, occasioned by the death of the Rev. Christopher F. Bergman, pastor of the Evangelical Lutheran Church at Ebenezer, Georgia, delivered in that church on Sunday, May 6, 1832. Savannah, Ga., Pr. by Purse & Stiles, 1832. 24 p. GHi; PPLT. 13693

Mease, James, 1771-1846.
...On some of the vegetable materials from which cordage, twine and thread, are made. By James Mease... [New Haven? 1832?] 14 p. DLC; PPAmP. 13694

---- On the causes, cure, and prevention of the sick headache. By James Mease...4th ed. Philadelphia, H. H. Porter, 1832.

52 p. CSt; ICJ; MeB; NBMS; OClM. 13695

Meckel, Johann Friedrich, 1781-1833.
Manual of general, descriptive, and pathological anatomy, by J. F. Meckel...Tr. from the German into French, with additions and notes, by A. J. L. Jourdan... and G. Breschet...Tr. from the French, with notes by A. Sidney Doane...Philadelphia, Carey & Lea, 1832. 3 vols. DLC; ICJ; MdBJ; OU; TxU. 13696

Medical Society of Maine.
Address to the community on the necessity of legalizing the study of anatomy, by order of the Medical Society of Maine. Brunswick, Jos. Griffin, 1832. 22 p. MHi. 13697

Medical Society of the County of Cayuga, Auburn, N.Y.
Transactions of the Medical Society of the County of Cayuga for 1832. Auburn, Pub. by the Society, 1832. 38 p. DHU; DNLM; NAuT. 13698

Medical Society of the County of New York.
By-laws of the Medical Society of the County of New-York. Rev. and adopted for 1832-33. New-York, Pr. by Ludwig & Tolefree, 1832. 15 p. NNNAM. 13699

---- Report of a committee on applications to the next Legislature... New-York, Pr. by Ludwig & Tolefree, 1832. 8 p. NNNAM. 13700

Medico-Chirurgical Society of Baltimore.
A system of medical ethics, adopted by the Medico-Chirurgical Society of Baltimore; being the report of the Committee on ethics, and published by order of the so-

ciety. Baltimore, Pr. by James Lucas & E. K. Deaver, 1832. 23 p. MBAt; MdBE; MH-M; NNNAM. 13701

Meeker, Eli.
The infantile instructor: being a series of questions and answers, intended to facilitate instruction in infant schools...Rev. and enl. By the Rev. Eli Meeker. New York, J. & W. Day, 1832. 166 p. LNB; MiU. 13702

Meikle, James, 1730-1799.
Solitude sweetened; miscellaneous meditations on various religious subjects, written in distant parts of the world. By James Meikle late surgeon at Carnwath... Cincinnati, Roff & Young, 1832. 286 p. InUpT; PPM. 13703
---- The traveller, or, Meditations on various subjects written on board a man of war. To which is added Converse with the world unseen to which is prefixed the life of the author. New York, J. H. Turney, 1832. 246 p. CtMW; NPtjerHi; PCC. 13704

Meineke, Carl, ca.1783-1845?
Summers gone. Ballad. The words by Mrs. Norton, the music by C. Meineke. Baltimore, Geo. Willig, Jr. [1832?] 3 p. ViU. 13705

Melish, John.
Map of Pennsylvania, from the county surveys authorized by the State, & other original documents by John Melish. Philadelphia, 1832. PPL. 13706

Mellin, W. G.
Pennsylvania Hospital. Some account of the Pennsylvania Hospital. Philadelphia, T. Kite, 1832. WHi. 13707

Melvill, Henry, 1798-1871.
Bible thoughts. New York,

American Tract Society [1832] 354 p. CtHC; FMU; ViU. 13708

Memes, John Smythe.
Memoirs of the Empress Josephine. New York, J. & J. Harper, 1832. 396 p. Ia; MB-FA; PPA; ScC; ViU. 13709

Memoir of Addison Pinneo, who died in Hanover, N. H., Sept. 17, 1831...2d ed. Boston, Perkins & Marvin, 1832. 79 p. NhM. 13710
Memoir of Florence Kidder, who died in Medford, (Mass.) April, 1832, aged eleven years. See under [Warner, Aaron]

Memoir of John Arch, a Cherokee Young Man, compiled from Communications of Missionaries in the Cherokee Nation. Rev. by the publishing committee. 2d ed. Boston, Massachusetts Sabbath School Union, 1832. 33 p. ICP. 13711
Memoir of Mary Lathrop who died in Boston, March 18, 1831, aged six years and three months. New York, American Tract Society, 1832. 108 p. DLC; MeB; OcLWHi; RPB; WaS. 13712

---- ---- 2d ed. Boston, Perkins & Marvin, etc., 1832. MH. 13713
Memoir of Mrs. Chloe Spear, a native of Africa, who was enslaved in childhood and died in Boston, Jan. 3, 1815...By a lady of Boston... Boston, J. Loring, 1832. 108 p. AU; ICN; MB; OCIWHi; TNF. 13714

Memoir of the Life and Ministry of Mr. William Bramwell, lately an itinerant Methodist Preacher: also, extracts from his correspondence. 4th Amer. ed. New York, Pr. by J. Collard, 1832. 243 p. MBNMHi. 13715

Memoir of William P. Hutchinson, who died at Bethlehem, N. H., April 12th, 1832. Aged four years, seven months and twenty days. Rev. by the Publishing committee. Boston, Massachusetts Sabbath School Society, 1832. 34 p. DLC; Nh.   13716

Memoirs of Andrew Jackson. See Eaton, John Henry, 1790-1856.

Memorial against the Masonic incorporations of Connecticut; together with the report and some of the debates in the General Assembly, May session, 1832. [Hartford? 1832?] 8 p. PPFM.
                                 13717
The memorial of the hardware merchants of the City of New York [to the Honorable the Senate and House of Representatives of the United States.] n. p., n. p., 1832. 14 p. MWA.   13718

Mercadante, Saverio, 1795-1870.
   Eliza and Claudio, or Love protected by friendship; a melodrama. As performed at the Richmond-Hill theatre. New York, L. Da Ponte, 1832. 77 p. ICU; MH; NN; PU; RPB.   13719

Merrill, Daniel, 1765-1833.
   Autobiography of Daniel Merrill. Philadelphia, Baptist General Tract Society [1832] 12 p. MH.
                                 13720
---- ---- Sedgwick, Me., 1832. 12 p. MHi.   13721

Merritt, Timothy, 1775-1845.
   The Christian's Manual, a treatise on Christian perfection; with directions for outlining that State. Compiled principally from the works of the Rev. John Wesley. By the Rev. T. Merritt. New York, B. Waugh & T. Mason, 1832. 144 p. KyBvU. 13722

---- A discussion on universal salvation; in three lectures and five answers against that doctrine. By Rev. Timothy Merritt. To which are added two discourses on same subject by Rev. Wilbur Fisk, A. M. New York, B. Waugh & T. Mason, 1832. 240 p. GDecCT; IaHoL; MB; TxDaM; Vt.   13723

The Messenger of the German Reformed Church. York, Pa., Pr. by May & Glossbrenner, 1832-   MoWgT.   13724

Metamorphosis: or, A transformation of pictures representing, 1. Gen. Washington, 2. An Indian waylaying an officer, 3. Burning a captive. 4. A centaur. 5. An alligator pursuing a man. 7. Man sleeping. 8. A tiger on the springing upon a man. 11. Doctor and patient. 12. An emblem of death. New Haven, Conn., 1832. 1 sheet to be folded in various ways. CSmH; CtY; DLC.
                                 13725
[Metcalf, David] 1795-1884.
   Letters addressed to Rev. Wilbur Fisk, D. D. in reply to a sermon on predestination & election. Springfield, Pr. by G. & C. Merriam, 1832. CtHC; MB; MH-AH; PPPrHi; RPB.   13726

Methodist Episcopal Church.
   A collection of hymns, for the use of Methodist Episcopal Church, principally from the collection of the Rev. John Wesley, M. A. Rev. and cor. with the titles of appropriate tunes, and the corresponding page of the harmonist, prefixed to each hymn. New-York, J. Emory & B. Waugh, for the Methodist Episcopal Church at the conference office, 1832. 543 p. CBB; FOA; IEG; MBC; MiHi.
                                 13727
---- ---- New York, Waugh & Mason, 1832. 550 p. CtMW;

InFtwL; MH; NNUT; TxD-T.
13728

---- The Doctrines and Discipline of the Methodist Episcopal Church. New York, B. Waugh & T. Mason, for the Methodist Episcopal Church, at the Conference Office, 1832. 196 p. CoDI; GEU; LNB; MBC; TNP.   13729

---- Minutes of the annual conferences of the Methodist Episcopal Church, for the year 1832. New York, B. Waugh & T. Mason, for the Methodist Episcopal Church, at the conference office, 1832. 48 p. CoDI; NbHi.   13730

---- Selection of hymns for the Sunday School Union. New York, Waugh & Mason, 1832. 149 p. MBU-T; NNUT; NPV.   13731

---- Conference.
A collection of interesting tracts explaining several important points of scripture doctrine. See under title.

Mexico.
The Constitution of the Republic of Mexico, and of the state of Counuila & Texas. Containing also an abridgement of the laws of the general and state governments, relating to colonization... With a description of the soil, climate, production, local and commercial advantages of that interesting country. New York, Pr. by Ludwig & Tolefree, 1832. 113 p. CU-B; KyDC; MB; PHi; ScU.   13732

Miami University, Oxford, Ohio.
Catalogue of the officers and students of Miami University. Oxford, Ohio, Pr. by W. W. Bishop, 1832. OOxM.   13733

---- Report of the trustees, Jan. 1, 1832. 5 p. OCIW.   13734

Michigan.

Acts passed at the first session of the fifth legislative council of the Territory of Michigan, begun and held at the council chamber, in the City of Detroit, on Tuesday, the first day of May, in the year of our Lord one thousand eight hundred and thirty two. Detroit, Pr. by Sheldon M'Knight, 1832. 96 p. DLC; IaU-L; MH-L; Mi; WHi.   13735

---- Fifth council. First session. June 11, 1832. Read the first time and laid on the table. A bill, to incorporate Kalamazoo Academy. [Detroit, 1832] broadsheet. MiD-B.   13736

---- Fifth council. First session. June 19, 1832. Read the first time and laid on the table. A bill to amend the several acts to provide for the assessment and collection of county and township taxes. [Detroit, 1832] broadsheet. MiD-B; WHi.   13737

---- Journal of the legislative council of Michigan; being the first session of the fifth council, begun and held at the City of Detroit, May 1, 1832. Detroit, Pr. by Geo. L. Whitney, 1832. 226 p. DLC; M; Mi; MiU; WHi.   13738

---- Legislative council of the Territory of Michigan. Fifth council. First session. Detroit, Sheldon M'Knight, pr., 1832. 12 p. WHi.   13739

---- To the electors of the Territory of Michigan. Fellow Citizens--The undersigned having been designated as a committee to address you on the subject of the approaching Territorial election for Delegate to the ensuing Congress of the United States... [Detroit? 1832?] broadside. WHi.
13740

Middlebrook's Almanac for 1833.

By Elijah Middlebrook. New
Haven, Conn., S. Babcock
[1832] MWA; NN.   13741

Middlebury College. Middlebury
Vermont.
   Catalogue of books belonging
to the library of the Philomathe-
sian Society. Middlebury, Pr. by
H. H. Houghton, 1832. 12 p.
VtMidSm; VtMiS.   13742

---- Catalogue of the corporation, officers, and students of
Middlebury College. October,
1832. [n.p., 1832] 16 p. VtU.
                               13743
---- Catalogus senatus academici; et eorum qui munera et officia academica gesserunt, quique alioujus gradus laurea exor-
nati fuerunt, in Collegio Medio-
buriensi in Republica viridimon-
tana. Medioburiae, 1832. 15 p.
DLC; MH; NN; PHi.   13744

---- The laws of Middlebury College. Middlebury, Pr. by E. D.
Barber, 1832. 16 p. NN. 13745

Middleton, Mass., Church of
Christ.
   Confession of faith and covenant adopted by the Church of
Christ in Middleton. Salem, Pr.
by Warwick & Palfray, Jr., 1832.
7 p. NjR.   13746

Millard, David.
   The unity of God and the son-
ship of Jesus Christ; sermon in
the Methodist Chapel, West
Bloomfield, New York July 19,
1832 (with) an appendix on a sermon by Wilber Houg. Rochester,
Marshal H. Dean, 1832. 75 p.
MH; NRU; ODefC; RPB.   13747

Miller, J. R.
   The history of Great Britain
from the death of George II to
the Coronation of George IV, designed as a continuation of Hume

and Smollet. By J. R. Miller.
Philadelphia, M'Carty and Davis,
1832. 724 p. GDecCT; KyLxT;
NbOM; TNP; ViU.   13748

Miller, Samuel, 1769-1850.
   An essay on the warrant, nature and duties of the office of
the ruling elder, in the Presbyterian church. Philadelphia, Presbyterian Board of Publication
[1832] 339 p. CoD; InU; MH;
PPPrHi; ViRut.   13749

---- ---- 2d. ed. New York,
Jonathan Leavitt; Boston, Crocker
& Brewster, 1832. 322 p. CSt;
GDecCT; MBC; PU; ScCoT.
                             13750
---- The importance of the Gos-
pel truth. Pittsburgh, 1832. NjP;
NjR.   13751

---- Letter on the observance of
the monthly concert in prayer.
By Samuel Miller. Pub. by Presbyterian Board of Publication,
1832. 106 p. ArBaA.   13752

---- Spruce Street Lectures. On
ecclesiastical polity. Philadelphia,
Russell, 1832. PPPrHi.   13753

Miller, Stephen Decatur, 1787-
1838.
   Speech... on the tariff, delivered in the Senate of the United
States, on the 21st & 23d of Feb.
1832 on Mr. Clay's resolution in
relation to the tariff. Washington,
1832. 37 p. A-Ar; MdHi; PU;
ScU; TxDaM.   13754

Miller's Planters' & Merchants'
Almanac for 1833. Charleston,
S.C., A. E. Miller [1832] MWA.
                             13755
---- Second ed. Charleston, A.
E. Miller, [1832] 24 p. MWA;
ScC.   13756

Mills, Robert, 1781-1855.
   The American pharos, or,

Light-house guide: founded on official reports received at the
Treasury Dept. also a general
view of the coast, from the St.
Lawrence to the Sabine. Washington, Thompson & Homans, 1832.
184 p. DLC; MiU; PPA.   13757

---- Atlas of the State of South
Carolina, made under the authority of the Legislature, prefaced
with a geographical, statistical
and historical map of the State.
Philadelphia, 1832. ScC.   13758

Milman, Henry Hart, 1791-1868.
   Fazio; or, The Italian wife; a
tragedy in five acts... New York,
Samuel French [1832?] 60 p. OCl.
                            13759
---- The history of the Jews,
from the earliest period to the
present time. By the Rev. H. H.
Milman. Harper's stereotyped ed.
New-York, J. & J. Harper, 1832.
3 v. DeWi; FU; GHi; NcGA; ViU;
WvW.   13760

Milton, John, 1608-1674.
   Paradise Lost; a poem in (12)
books. New York, John H. Turney, 1832. 321 p. MoS; NCH;
PPL; RPB.   13761

---- Paradise regained and other
poems. By John Milton. New
York, J. H. Turney, 1832. 215 p.
CtMW; ICartC; MFiHi; MiMars;
PPL.   13762

---- Poetical works, consisting
of Paradise Lost, Paradise Regained, Mask of Comus, Samson
Agonistes, and Poems on several occasions, &c. &c. Together
with the life of the author. New
York, J. H. Turney, 1832. 2 v.
in 1. CtY; IU; MH; NjP; PPA;
WaS.   13763

---- ---- Philadelphia, John
Grigg, 1832. 5 v. in 1. CtMW;
KyDC; LNT; OTU; ViRut. 13764

Mina, Caroline Estradas de. See
Estradas de Mina, Caroline Al-
malic, 1809-1832.

Miner, Charles, 1780-1865.
   Extract from a speech delivered in the House of Representatives of the United States in 1829,
on the subject of slavery and the
slave trade in the District of Columbia, with notes. Bethania,
Pa., Reuben Chambers, 1832.
18 p. DeWi; MAbD.   13765

Ming's Hutchins' Improved Alman-
ac and Ephemeris...for...1833.
New York, Alexander Ming
[1832] 18 p. M; MWA; NHi; NjR.
                            13766
Miniature Almanac for 1833.
Boston, Allen & Co.; New York,
William Minns & Co. [1832] 16 ll.
MB; MHi; MnU; MWA.   13767

---- Concord, N.H., M'Farland
and Ela... [1832] 22 p. NhHi.
                            13768
Miniature Almanack. Boston,
Carter, Hendee & Co. [1832]
InU; MWA; MHi; NN.   13769

Ministry at large for the Poor of
Cities. New York, 1832. See
Tuckerman, Joseph.

Mirick, Benjamin L.
   The history of Haverhill, Mas-
sachusetts...Haverhill, A. W.
Thayer, 1832. 227 p. ICN; MnU;
NN; OCY; WHi.   13770

A mirror for the young; or, The
good rewarded and the vicious
punished. Greenfield, A. Phelps,
1832. NPV.   13771

Miscellaneous thoughts on several subjects of divinity, much con-
troverted world. By a Cumberland Presbyterian. Repub. by T.
W. Haynes. Pittsburgh, Pr. by
D. & M. Maclean, 1832. 72 p.
T.   13772

---- Princeton, Ky. , Brock,
1832. 80 p. KyDC; NN; PPPrHi.
                                13773
Missionary gazetteer. See Edwards, Bela Bates.

A Missionary hymn recommended
to be sung at the anniversary
celebrations of all the missionary;
Bible, tract and Sunday school societies in the United States...
2d ed. Philadelphia, 1832. 8 p.
NIC.   13774

Missionary museum; or An account of missionary enterprises, in
conversation between a mother and
her children. 1st series. India
and Africa. Vol. I-II. New Haven,
Jeremy L. Cross, 1832. 2 v.
CtY; DLC; ICBB; MH-AH; NNMR.
                                13775
Mississippi.
    The constitution of the state of
Mississippi. As revised in convention, on the twenty-sixth day
of October, A. D. 1832. Jackson
P. Isler, 1832. 27 p. DLC; L;
Ms-Ar; NN; OCLaw.   13776

---- Journal of the Convention of
the state of Mississippi, held in
the town of Jackson. Pub. by authority. Jackson, Pr. by P. Isler, 1832. 304 p. L; Mi-L; NN;
OCLaw; TMeB.   13777

---- A proclamation... (Jackson,
1832). Broadside. Ms-Ar. 13778

---- Report of Committee on Ex-
ecutive Department. [Jackson,
Peter Isler, 1832] 3 p. Ms-Ar.
                              13778a
---- Report of the Committee on
General Provisions. [Jackson,
Peter Isler, 1832] broadside.
Ms-Ar.   13779

---- Report of the Committee on
the Bill of Rights. [Jackson,
Peter Isler, 1832] broadside.
Ms-Ar.   13780

---- Report of the Committee on
the Judicial Department. Jackson,
Peter Isler, 1832. Ms-Ar. 13781

---- Report of the Committee on
the Legislative Department. Jackson, Peter Isler, 1832. Ms-Ar.
                                13782
---- Resolutions submitted by Mr.
Williams [Jackson, Peter Isler,
1832] broadside. Ms-Ar.   13783

---- Rules and standing orders,
for conducting business in the
Convention of the State of Mississippi. Jackson, Pr. by Peter Isler, 1832. 8 p. Ms-Ar.   13784

---- Secretary of State's Office
... I have the honor to state that,
inobedience to a resolution adopted
on yesterday...requesting the Secretary of State to "prepare and
furnish the Convention with a tabular statement, shewing (sic) the
free white population in each
county of this State...[Jackson,
Peter Isler, 1832] Ms-Ar. 13785

---- Secretary of State's Office,
Jackson, 25th Sept. 1832. The
Honorable P. R. Pray, President of the Convention. Sir: in
conformity to a resolution adopted
by the Convention...I have the
honor to hand you...a tabular
statement of the votes given for
Governor in the year 1831...
[Jackson, Peter Isler, 1832]
Ms-Ar.   13786

---- The undersigned being a minority of the committee to whom
was referred so much of the present Constitution as relates to the
Judicial Department...[Jackson,
Peter Isler, 1832] broadside.
Ms-Ar.   13787

---- The undersigned, one of the
committee to whom was referred
the Judicial Department of the
Government, though concurring

in much of the report, as submitted... [Jackson, Peter Isler, 1832] broadside. Ms-Ar.   13788

Mississippi State Colonization Society.
First annual report of the Mississippi State Colonization Society, auxiliary to the American Colonization Society, for colonizing the free people of colour of the United States. Natchez, Pr. at the Natchez Office, 1832. 11 p. NcU.   13789

Missouri.
Laws of the State of Missouri, passed at the first session of the seventh General Assembly, begun and held at the city of Jefferson, on Monday, the nineteenth day of November, in the year of our Lord, one thousand eight hundred and thirty two. (n.p., 1832?) 157 p. ICLaw; MB; Mo; MoHi.   13790

Mister Van Buren and the war. [Albany, 1832?] 9 p. DLC; PPL; WHi.   13791

Mitchell, Samuel Augustus, 1792-1868.
Map of Louisiana, Mississippi and Alabama, constructed from the latest authorities. Philadelphia, Mitchell, 1832. MB; OC.   13792

---- Map of North and South Carolina and Georgia constructed from the latest authorities. Philadelphia, 1832. MdBP.   13793

---- Map of Pennsylvania, New Jersey & Delaware. By S. Augustus Mitchell. Philadelphia, 1832. 1 p. PHi.   13794

---- Map of the states of Ohio, Indiana, and Illinois and part of the Michigan Territory. Compiled from the latest authorities. Philadelphia, S. A. Mitchell, 1832. OOxM.   13795

---- Mitchell's traveller's guide through the United States; a map of the roads, distances, steam boat & canal routes by J. H. Young. Philadelphia, S. A. Mitchell, 1832. Ct; MB; MH; OCl; OO.   13796

Mitchell, Thomas Duché, 1791-1865.
Elements of chemical philosophy: Elements of Chemical philosophy, on the basis of Reid, comprising The rudiments of that science and the requisite experimental illustrations with plates & diagrams. By Thos. D. Mitchell, M.D. Cincinnati, Carey & Fairbanks; New York, Jonathan Leavitt, 1832. 553 p. DSG; KyLxT; MoS; OCHP; PP; TxU.   13797

---- Hints on the connexion of labour with study as a preventive of diseases peculiar to students ...to which is appended, the substance of an introductory lecture on medical education, delivered on October, 1831... Cincinnati, Corey, Fairbank & Co.; New York, Jonathan Leavitt, 1832. 85 p. DLC; IaU; OClWHi; PU; WNaE.   13798

Mitchell, William R.
The speech of Mr. Mitchell, of South Carolina, before the committee of the whole, on the tariff bill, of the committee of manufactures; and the amendment of Mr. Stewart, of Pennsylvania. Delivered in the House of Representatives, on the 6th day of June, 1832. Washington, Jonathan Elliot, 1832. 20 p. A-Ar; ScCC. 13799

---- Speech... on the resolution for a select committee to inquire into the management of the Bank of the United States, delivered in the House of Representatives, March 1, 1832. Washington, Gales and Seaton, 1832. 11 p.

A-Ar; PU.   13800

Mitford, Mary Russell, 1787-
1855.
   Our village. Philadelphia, The
Rogers Co. 1832(?). 348 p.
IaDm; TxH.   13801

Möhler, Johann Adam, 1786-
1838.
   Symbolism: or, Exposition of
the doctrinal differences between
Catholics and Protestants, as
evidenced by their symbolical
writings; tr. from the German,
with a memoir of the author,
preceded by an historical sketch
of the state of Protestantism and
Catholicism in Germany for the
last hundred years, by James
Burton Robertson. 3d ed. New
York,   Catholic Pub. House
[1832] 504 p. IaDuC.   13802

The monthly class book: devoted
to cotemporary (sic) history, literature, and miscellany...Vol. 1.
from August 1831 to January,
1832, inclusive. New York, J. W.
Seymour, at his school book establishment, 1832. 216 p. NNC.
                             13803
The monthly journal of medical
literature, and American medical
students' gazette, by E. Bartlett,
M.D. no. 1, January, 1832.
Boston, Carter & Hendee, 1832.
3 nos. 32 p. DLC; MHi; NNNAM.
                             13804
Montpelier, Vermont. First Congregational Church.
   Confession of faith, covenant,
and rules of church government,
adopted by the First Congregational Church in Montpelier,
March 1832. Montpelier, Pr. by
E. P. Walton, 1832. 11 p. 13805

[Moody, Richard]
   Otiska. An Indian tale. Ro-
chester, 1832. 123 p. CSmH;
NRU; WHi.   13806

Moody, Robert.
   An address, delivered before
the Williston Temperance Society,
March 8, 1832. Pub. by request
of the Society. Burlington, Chauncey Goodrich, 1832. 24 p. VtHi.
                             13807
Moore, Alfred, 1783-1837.
   Address delivered before the
North Carolina institute of education of their annual meeting, June
19th, 1832. Newbern, J. I. Pasteur, 1832. 16 p. NcD; NcU;
NN.   13808

Moore, Gabriel, 1785-1845.
   Letter from Gabriel Moore,
one of the Senators in Congress
from the state of Alabama, in reply to the resolutions adopted by
a part of his constituents at a
meeting held at Courtland. [Wash-
ington, 1832?] 24 p. AB; DU;
NcD; NNC; ScU.   13809

---- Remarks in support of his
proposition, submitted in favor
of the amendment to the bank
charter, securing to the states
the right of taxation [etc. Also
remarks on public lands, n.p.
1832] 8 p. DLC.   13810

---- Speech of Mr. Moore, of
Alabama, on the subject of Mr.
Clay's resolutions providing for
a reduction of the duties on imports. Delivered in the Senate of
the United States, March 15,
1832. Washington, 1832. 7 p.
DLC; ICN; NNC.   13811

Moore, Henry, 1751-1844.
   The Life of Mrs. Mary Flet-
cher, consort...of the Rev. John
Fletcher, vicar of Madeley, Salop
...New York, B. Waugh & T.
Mason, 1832. 319 p. ArPb;
CtHC; ICU; MBC; NNMHi. 13812

Moore, Jeremiah.
   The doctrines of universal salvation examined. Wincester, Va.,

Davis, 1832. NcWfC.   13813

Moore, Thomas, 1779-1852.
Come, rest in this bosom.
Written by Thos. Moore, esq.
Boston, C. H. Keith, 1832.
4 p. KU.   13814

---- Memoirs of Richard Brins-
ley Sheridan. By Thos. Moore.
Philadelphia, H. C. Carey & I.
Lea, 1832. 602 p. MdBP. 13815

---- The poetical works of Thos.
Moore, including... complete in
one volume. Philadelphia, J.
Crissy and J. Grigg, 1832. 419 p.
KyLo; LNT; MAm; TBri. 13816

Moravian Church. Liturgy and
ritual.
A collection of hymns, for the
use of the Protestant church of
the united brethren... new and
rev. ed. Philadelphia, Pr. by I.
Ashmead & co., 1832. 326, (46)
p. ArBaA; CtHT; ICBB; NNUT;
PPL-R.   13817

More, Hannah, 1745-1833.
The book of private devotion,
a series of prayers and meditations with an introductory essay
on prayer chiefly from the writings of Hannah More. Rev. and
enl. New York, Daniel Appleton,
1832. 256 p. CtHC; IEG; MB;
RPB; WGrNM.   13818

---- Complete Works of Hannah
More. First complete ed. New
York, Harper & Bros., 1832.
587 p. KyDC.   13819

---- The works of Hannah More,
with a sketch of her life. Philadelphia, J. J. Woodward, 1832.
2 v. ArLP; CtHT; NjN; TNP;
ViL.   13820

Morison, John, 1791-1859.
Counsels on matrimony; or,
Friendly suggestions to husbands
and wives: and a remembrance
for life. With an appendix, containing extracts on the subject of
marriage, from the writings of
several Christian divines. By
John Morison. Brookfield, E.
Merrian & Co., 1832. 128 p.
N; NStc.   13821

The morning ramble; or, The
mountain top. New Haven, Sidney's press, S. Babcock, 1832.
CtY; MNS.   13822

The morning ride. Philadelphia,
American Sunday School Union,
1832. 16 p. DLC; MFiHi; MH.
                            13823
Morrell, Abby Jane (Wood),
b. 1809.
Narrative of a voyage to the
Ethiopic and south Atlantic ocean,
Indian ocean, Chinese sea, north
and south Pacific ocean, in the
years 1829, 1830, 1831. New
York, 1832. 230 p. OCHP.
                            13824
Morrell, Benjamin, 1795-1839.
A narrative of four voyages to
the South Sea, north and south
Pacific Ocean, Chinese Sea, Ethi-
opic and southern Atlantic ocean,
Indian and Antarctic ocean. From
the year 1822 to 1831... By Capt.
Benjamin Morrell, jr. New York,
J. & J. Harper, 1832. 492 p.
CSt; GHi; MBAt; PPA. ScC; WHi.
                            13825
Morris, John Gottlieb, 1803-1895.
Catechetical exercises; or, A
familiar illustration of the five
principal articles of Luther's
Smaller catechism. Baltimore,
Joel Wright, 1832. 72 p. PPLT.
                            13826
---- The catechumen's and com-
municant's companion; designed
for the use of young persons of
the Lutheran church... By a Pas-
tor. [2d ed.] Baltimore, Joel
Wright, 1832. 245 p. MdHi;
PPLT.   13827

Morris Canal and Banking Company.

Report of a joint committee of the directors and stockholders ... New York, Pr. by Clayton & Van Norden, 1832. 13 p. MH-BA.   13828

Morrison, John.

An oration... in commemoration of the birthday of Thomas Paine: ...New York, Pr. by Evans & Brooks, 1832. 32 p. CU; NjR; RPB.   13829

Morse, Sidney Edward, 1794-1871.

A geographical view of Greece and an historical sketch of the recent revolution in that country accompanied with a map. New Haven, N. & S. Jocelyn, 1832. 24p. MBAt.   13830

Morse, Thomas.

A brief account of the singular circumstances attending the death of Joseph Morse, of East-Haverhill, Mass., as related by his brother. Haverhill, Pr. at the Iris office, 1832. 7 p. MH; MHaHi; Nh-Hi.   13831

Morse, William.

Address delivered just previous to the raising of the new universalist meeting house, at Quincy, Mass., July 16, 1832. Boston, Hiram Tupper, pr., 1832. 11 p. NCaS; NNC.   13832

Morton and Smith's western farmer's almanac for 1833. Louisville, Morton and Smith [1832] KyBgW; KyHi.   13833

Mosheim, Johann Lorenz, 1694?-1755.

An ecclesiastical history, ancient and modern;...By the late learned John Laurence Mosheim ...Tr. from the original Latin, and illustrated with notes, chronological tables, and an appendix,

by Archibald Maclaine, D.D. a new ed. ...continued to the present time by Charles Coote, LL.D. also, a dissertation on the state of the primitive Church. By the Rt. Rev. Dr. George Gleig... Baltimore, J. J. Harrod, 1832. 2 vols. CtY; KyWA; MnM; ScCoT; ViU.   13834

---- ---- Baltimore, P. N. Wood & Co., 1832. 2 v. CSmH; In; NNG; PPA; TJaU; ViU.   13835

---- Institutes of ecclesiastical history; ancient and modern in four books, much corrected, enl. and improved, from the primary authorities. By John Lawrence Von Mosheim. A new and literal transl. from the original Latin. By James Murdock. New Haven, A. Maltby, 1832. 3 vols. GMM; IaPeC; MBC; NhD; ScCC. 13836

Mount Auburn Cemetery.

Catalogue of lot owners in the cemetery...1832. Boston, Buckingham [etc., 1832-] MB; MH; MHi; MiD-B.   13837

Mount Hope College. Baltimore.

Laws of Mount Hope College. [Baltimore, n.p., 1832] 14 p. MH; NN.   13838

Mount Pleasant Military Academy, Ossining, N.Y.

Catalogue. Mount Pleasant Academy. Circular. Mount Pleasant Academy. (Catalogue) Mount Pleasant military academy. (Catalogue) Mount Pleasant Academy. (1832) MH.   13839

Mount Vernon Female Seminary.

Catalogue containing the names of the trustees, instructors, and pupils, 1832. Boston, 1832. AU; MB; MBAt.   13840

Mudge, Enoch, 1776-1850.

The parables of our Lord

Jesus Christ: illustrated in a
concise and perspicuous manner.
Boston, Kane & Co., 1832.
140 p. MBNMHi; MH-AH.   13841

Mudie, Robert, 1777-1842.
A popular guide to the obser-
vation of nature... By Robert
Mudie. New York, J. & J. Harper, 1832. 343 p. IP; UU.   13842

Müller, Johannes von, 1752-
1809.
An Universal history, in twen-
ty-four books. Tr. from the
German of John von Müller.
Boston, Stimpson & Clapp, 1832.
4 vols. LShC; MNBedf; OMC;
TNP; VtWinds.   13843

Mulkey, William.
A primary book for children:
arranged for the purpose of aiding the pupil to find a particular
page, table, or word without a
knowledge of numbers. By Wm.
Mulkey. [Philadelphia] Stereotyped
by J. Howe [1832] [48] p. DLC;
PHi.   13844

Munchausen.
Guilliver Redivivus, or The
celebrated and entertaining travels and adventures, of the re-
nowned baron Munchausen, by sea
and land; including a tour to the
United States of America, in the
year 1803. Philadelphia, Key &
Mielke, 1832. 162 p. DLC; MH;
PHi.   13845

Munroe, Francis.
Catalogue of English books.
Philadelphia, 1832. 50 p. MHi.
                        13846
Murray, Hugh, 1779-1846.
Historical and descriptive ac-
count of British India, from the
most remote period to the pres-
ent time. New York, J. & J.
Harper, 1832. 3 v. CtHT; GEU;
MnU; PPA; TU; WvW.   13847

Murray, John, 1741-1815.
The life of Rev. John Murray
...Written by himself. The records contain anecdotes of the
writers' [!] infancy, and are extended to some years after the
commencement of his public la-
bors in America. To which is
added a brief continuation to the
closing scene... Stereotype ed.,
with notes and remarks, by Rev.
L. S. Everett. Boston, Marsh,
Capen and Lyon, 1832. 270 p.
CtY; CU; MH.   13848

Murray, Lindley, 1745-1826.
Abridgment of Murray's English grammar... Designed for the
younger classes of learners...
Rev., prepared, and adapted to
the use of the "English exercises."
By Israel Alger, Jun., Boston,
Lincoln & Edmands, etc., etc.,
1832. KyBgW; MH.   13849

---- English exercises adapted
to Murray's English grammar...
Designed for the benefit of private learners, as well as for the
use of schools... Stereotyped
from the last English ed. by H.
& H. Wallis, New York. New
York, Collins & Co., 1832. 180 p.
AzU.   13850

---- English Grammar adapted to
the different classes of learners;
with an appendix containing rules
and observations for assisting the
more advanced student to write
with perspicuity and accuracy. By
Lindley Murray. New York, Collins & Co., 1832. 232 p. INormN;
MiU; NcA-S.   13851

---- ---- Philadelphia, Key,
Mielke & Biddle, 1832. 210 p.
AzU; MH; MiU; PHi; TNT. 13852

---- ---- 46th ed. York, Pr. by
T. Wilson, 1832. MH.   13853

---- An English Grammar com-

prehending, the principles and
rules of the language, illustrated
by appropriate exercises, and a
key to the exercises. By Lindley
Murray... 7th Amer. from the
last English ed. , cor. and much
enl. New York, Collins & Co. ,
1832. 2 v. in 1. IGK; NWM;
OUrC; PMA; TxU-T; ViRU.
                                          13854
---- English grammar, rev. ,
simplified, and adapted to
the inductive and explanatory
mode of instruction. By H. T. N.
Benedict... Frankfort, Ky. , Pr.
by A. G. Hodges, 1832. 192 p.
DLC; ICU; KyHi; KyU; MH.
                                          13855
---- The English reader, or
Pieces in prose and poetry, selected from the best writers.
With a few preliminary observations on the principles of good
reading. Cincinnati, N. & G.
Guilford, 1832. MH.   13856

---- ----Elizabethtown, N.J. ,
T. O. Sayre, 1832. NjP; PPeSchw.
                                          13857
---- ---- Hamilton [N. Y.] Wil-
liams, Orton & Co. , 1832. 250 p.
CMoroSM; NSyHi; WHi.   13858

---- ---- New York, Collins,
1832. 252 p. CtY; DcU; In; MB;
MH; PHC.   13859

---- ---- Philadelphia, Jos. M'-
Dowell, 1832. 263 p. PLFM.
                                          13860
---- ---- Philadelphia, L. John-
son, 1832. 252 p. InRchE; MH.
                                          13861
---- ---- Philadelphia, M. Fith-
ian, 1832. 252 p. OClWHi. 13862

---- ---- Philadelphia, S. Probasco, 1832. 252 p. KyBgW;
MH; P.   13863

---- ---- Utica, Wm. Williams,
1832. 250 p. NN; NUtHi. 13864

---- ---- Imp. by the addition of
a concordant and synonymising vocabulary, by Jeremiah Goodrich,
Providence, Hutchens & Shepard,
1832. 304 p. MB; MH; RHi.
                                          13865
---- Introduction to the English
reader; or, A selection of pieces
in prose and poetry... to which is
added rules and observations for
assisting children to read with
propriety. By Lindley Murray...
Philadelphia, L. Johnson, 1832.
162 p. NjR; OHi.   13866

---- Key to the exercise adapted
to Murray's English grammar.
Calculated to enable private learners to become their own instructors, in grammar and composition. By Murray. Philadelphia,
John Grigg, 1832. 168 p. MH;
MOCgSV; NjP; OOxM.   13867

---- Questions adapted to Murray's grammar. By a teacher.
Baltimore, J. N. Lewis, 1832.
36 p. DLC; MdHi.   13868

Musical Carcanet: A choice collection of the most admired popular songs, arranged for the voice,
flute, and violin. New York, Collins & Hannay, 1832. 144 p.
CtHWatk; ICN; MB; MH; RPB.
                                          13869
Mutual Fire Society.
     Constitution, articles of asso-
ciation, Mutual Fire Society. Worcester, Pr. by Moses W. Grout,
1832. 13 p. MWHi; NN.   13870

My brother, a poem... New-
York, Mahlon Day, 1832. 17 p.
DLC.   13871

My Father, a poem. New York,
Pr. by Mahlon Day, 1832. 13 p.
DLC; MLex.   13872

My own history. By the author of
"the gold thimble. " Boston, Cottons & Barnard, 1832. 20 p. MB.
                                          13873

My Own Hymn Book. Sidney's
Press. New-Haven, S. Babcock,
1832. MB.   13874

Myers, Peter D.
    The Zion songsters: a collec-
tion of hymns and spiritual songs,
generally sung at camp and
prayer meetings, and in revivals
of religion. Compiled by Peter
D. Myers...10th ed., enl. and
imp. New York, M'Elrath &
Bangs, 1832. 352 p. CtMW;
GAGTh; NNUT; ODW.   13875

Mylius, William Frederick.
    An abridged history of Eng-
land, for the use of schools; to
which is added an abstract of the
Constitution and a geographical
treatise. Baltimore, Fielding
Lucas, Jr., 1832? 364 p. DLC;
MoU; OClJC.   13876

N

Narrative of the capture and providential escape of Misses Frances
and Almira Hall... Likewise is
added, the interesting narrative
of the captivity and sufferings of
Philip Brigdon, a Kentuckian...
Communicated by persons of respectability living in the neigh-
borhood of the captives. [New
York, 1832] 24 p. ICN; MB; NN;
OClWHi; ViU.   13877

Narrative of the suffering and adventures of the Brethren Eber-
hard Gutsleff, Francis H. Helt-
erhof, John Gattlob Fritsche, and
David Siegmund Krugelstin, who
for the Gospels sake suffered a
twelve years imprisonment at
Petersburg in Russia. Philadelphia, American Sunday School
Union, 1832. 107 p. GDecCT;
NcU; NcWsM.   13878

Narrative of the sufferings of
William Moore, John Philly and

Richard Seller in the inquisition
of Hungary. Philadelphia, 1832.
26 p. PHi; PPPrHi; PSC-Hi.
                             13879

Nathan ben-Saddi, 1703-1764,
pseud.
    The chronicles of the kings of
England, from the reign of William the conqueror, first King of
England, down to His present
Majesty George the third. By the
late Dr. B. Franklin. New-Harmony, Ind., J. D. Wattles, 1832.
84 p. CtY.   13880

The national calendar and annals
of the United States for 1832.
Washington City, P. Force, 1832.
300, 60 p. CtHWatk; MiD; NPV;
PLFM; RNR.   13881

National circular on temperance.
12 p. Boston, np. n.p., 1832.
MWA.   13882

National Republican Party. Connecticut. Convention of Young
Men, 1832.
    Proceedings of the state Con-
vention of National Republican
Young Men, holden at Hartford,
on Wednesday, October 17, 1832.
Hartford, Hammer & Comstock
[1832?] 16 p. CtY; ICN; IU;
MWA; NNC.   13883

---- Maryland. Baltimore.
    An address to the people of
Maryland, by the National Republican Central Committee of Baltimore, shewing (sic) the necessity
of a vigorous and united action,
to preserve the constitution and
laws, rights and liberties of the
people of the United States. Baltimore, Sands and Neilson, 1832.
27 p. DLC; MB; MWA; NN.
                             13884
---- ---- ---- An address, to
the people of Maryland, from
their delegates in the late National Republican Convention made in
obedience to a resolution of that

body. Baltimore, Pr. by Sands & Neilson, 1832. 62 p. DLC; ICN; MWA; ScU; WHi.   13885

---- ---- ---- The Central Committee of the National Republicans of the city of Baltimore, to the people of Maryland. [Baltimore, Sands & Neilson, 1832] 18 p. DLC; MB; MdU; MiU-C; WHi.   13886

---- Massachusetts. Convention, 1832.
Journal of the proceedings of the National Republican Convention, held at Worcester, October 11, 1832. Boston, Stimpson & Clapp, 1832. 75 p. DLC; IU; MnU; TxU; WHi.   13887

---- New York.
Summary of the proceedings of a convention of republican delegates. Albany, Packard & van Benthuysen, 1832. 24 p. MWA.   13888

---- ---- Cayuga County.
National Republican nomination. For president, Henry Clay, of Kentucky. For vice-president, John Sergeant, of Penn. [Auburn, 1832] 4 p. NAuHi.   13889

---- ---- Oneida County.
Forgery or treachery...[Utica, 1832] broadside. NBuHi.   13890

---- ---- ---- Republican Young Men's Convention. The convention of Republican young men of the county of Oneida convened at the court house in Whitesboro', Sept. 26th, 1832...[Utica? 1832] Broadside. NBuHi.   13891

---- Pennsylvania.
Proceedings of the National Republican Convention of Pennsylvania, which assembled at Harrisburg, on the twenty-ninth day of May, 1832, for the nomination of an electoral ticket. Pub. by order of the convention, Harris-

burg, Pr. at the Intelligencer office [1832] 32 p. DLC; P; WHi.   13892

---- ---- Proceedings... with address and appendix. Easton, Pa., Hetrich, [1832?] 18 p. PHi.   13893

---- Vermont.
An address to the Freemen of Vermont, by their delegation to the National Republican Convention, holden at Baltimore, Maryland, in December, 1831. Middlebury, Pr. by H. H. Houghton [1832?] 16 p. CSmH; Vt; VtMiM; VtU.   13894

---- Virginia. Convention, 1832.
Proceedings... which convened at Staunton on the 16th of July, 1832. Pub. by order of the convention. Lynchburg, Fletcher & Toler, 1832. 24 p. NcD; NcU.   13895

---- Washington, D. C.
Proceedings of the National Republican Convention of Young Men, which assembled in the city of Washington May 7, 1832. Washington, Pr. by Gales & Seaton, 1832. 24 p. IaU; LU; OClWHi; PU; ScU; WHi.   13896

National Republican Young Men's Committee of the City of New-York.
Address... to the Young Men of the United States. New-York, 1832. 12 p. MWA; NN.   13897

Natural history of insects. 1st series. New York, J. & J. Harper, 1832. 292 p. LNH; MWhB; OWervO; ScSoh; WvW.   13898

The nature of the Lord Jesus Christ, and the personality and deity of the Holy Spirit. Selected from J. G. Pike's Guide to Young Disciple. Limerick, D. Marks, book-agent for the Free Will Baptist Convention, 1832. 24 p. MWA; MeLewB.   13899

Neal, C. , firm, bookseller,
Philadelphia.
A catalogue of plays, farces,
&c. for sale by C. Neal, at the
Dramatic repository and circu-
lating library... Philadelphia.
[New-York, Pr. by Clayton &
Van Norden,] 1832. 24 p. DLC.
13900

Neue Americanische Landwirth-
schafts Calender, 1833. Von Carl
Friedrich Egelmann. Reading,
Pa. , Johann Ritter und comp.
[1832] MWA; NN; PHi; PPL.
13901

Neuer Calender für Bauern und
Handwerker, 1833. Von Carl
Egelmann. Philadelphia, Pa. ,
Geo. W. Mentz und Sohn [1832]
CtY; InU; MWA; NjP; PHi. 13902

Neuer gemeinnutziger Pennsyl-
vanischer Calender. Lancaster,
Johann Bar [1832] CtY; MWA; P;
PPG; PHi.   13903

Neuman, Henry.
Neuman and Baretti's dictionary of the Spanish and English
language. Stereotype ed. Boston,
Hilliard, Gray, Little & Wilkins,
1832. 2 vols. MdBD; NAnge;
Nh; OCX; POx.   13904

---- A Pocket dictionary of the
Spanish and English languages.
Compiled from the last improved
editions of Neuman and Baretti...
Philadelphia, Carey & Lea, 1832.
714 p. ArLSJ; MdBD; MdBS; NjP;
P.   13905

Nevin, John Williamson, 1803-
1886.
The scourge of God, a sermon
preached in the first Presbyterian
Church, July 6, 1832, on the occasion of a city fast, observed in
reference to the approach of the
Asiatic cholera. Pittsburgh, Johnston & Stockton, 1832. 24 p.
OClWHi. PLERC-Hi.   13906

---- A summary of Biblical antiquities; compiled for the use of
Sunday-school teachers, and for
the benefit of families. By John
W. Nevin, late assistant teacher
in the Theological Seminary of
Princeton. Vol. II. Rev. and cor.
by the author for the American
Sunday School Union. Philadelphia,
American Sunday School Union,
1832. 252 p. (2 v.) NcCJ; PAtM.
13907

---- The trinitarian and unitarian
doctrines concerning Jesus Christ.
Pittsburgh, 1832. NjR.   13908

New Bedford, Massachusetts.
Report of the selectmen, for
the expences of the town of New
Bedford, as paid by them for the
year ending March 23, 1832.
New-Bedford, B. T. Congdon,
1832. broadside. MNBedf. 13909

---- North Sabbath School Society.
First semi-annual report of the
executive board of the North Sabbath School Society, together with
the consitution and by-laws of the
society. Presented and adopted
October 6, 1832. New-Bedford,
Pr. by Benjamin T. Congdon,
1832. 12 p. MNBedf.   13910

New Brunswick (N. J.) Almanack
for 1833. New Brunswick, Joseph
C. Griggs, 18 l. MWA; N; NjHi;
NjP.   13911

New clerk's magazine; containing
all the most useful forms, which
occur in business transactions between man and man. Comprising
many valuable forms not before
given in any one collection. Calculated for the use of the citizens
of the United States, and made
conformable to law. By a member
of the Massachusetts bar. Boston,
Lilly & Wait, [etc.] 1832. 327 p.
DLC; KWiU; MB; MH; PPi.
13912

The New England almanac for...

1833... by Anson Allen. Hartford, Andrus & Judd, [1832] 36 p. CtHi; In; MBC; NNA; RNHI.   13913

The New England almanack and farmer's friend, for the year of our Lord Christ, 1833:... Fitted to the meridian of New-London, ... The astronomical calculations performed by Nathan Daboll. New-London, Samuel Green [1832] (32) p. InU; MWA; PHi; RWe; WHi.   13914

New England Almanack for 1833. By Nathan Daboll. New London, Conn. , Samuel Green [1832] MWA.   13915

New England anti-masonic almanac. No. 5, 1833. Boston, Wm. Souther, John March & Co. , pr. , 1832. 43 p. IaCrM; MH; MWA; MMal; NjR.   13916

New England Anti Slavery Society. See Massachusetts Anti-Slavery Society.

New England artisan and laboring man's repository. v. 1, no. 8- Feb. 23, 1832-Pawtucket, 1832- MH-BA.   13917

The New England farmer, and Horticultural Journal, containing essays, original and selected, relating to agriculture and domestic economy; with engravings and the prices of country produce. By Thos. G. Fessenden. Boston, John B. Russell, 1832. 416 p. RNR.   13918

... The New England farmers' almanac, for the year 1833, by Thomas G. Fessenden... Boston, Pr. by I. R. Butts, for Carter, Hendee & Co. [1832] 20 p. 45, 46, & 18 p. (Various paging) ICMcHi; MWA; MeHi; NjR; WHi.
                              13919

The New England farmer's almanack, with an ephemeris for the year of the Christian era, 1833. By Truman W. Abell. Windsor, Simeon Ide, etc. [1832] 22 l. DLC; MH; MWA; NhHi; VtU.   13920

The New-England farmer's and scholar's almanac. By Dudley Leavitt. Concord, Horatio Hill & Co. , [1832] MWA.   13921

New England preacher.
   A series of sermons in monthly numbers. Providence, Wm. Marshall & Co. [1832] 24 p. MB; MWA; RHi; RPB.   13922

New England primer. To which is added the shorter catechism. Pittsburgh, Johnston & Stockton, 1832. 48 p. CLCM; PSew. 13923

The New England Sunday School hymn book, prepared by the Board of Managers of the Hartford County Union. 2d ed. Hartford, D. F. Robinson & Co. , 1832. 110 p. MAtt; MBC. 13924

New Hampshire Annual Register and United States Calendar for 1833. By John Farmer. Concord, Marsh, Capen & Lyon [1832] 144 p. CtY; ICN; KyU; MWA; NhHi.   13925

New Hampshire Family almanac. The, or Merchants and Farmer's Calendar; calculated on a new, useful and improved plan, for the year of our Lord 1833. Boston, Allen & Co. [1832] 18 l. MB; NhHi.   13926

New-Hampshire pocket register. By N. J. T. George. Concord, Horatio Hill & Co. [1832] InU; MWA; Nh; NhHi; NhKe.   13927

New Haven. First Church of Christ.

Catalogue of the members of
the First Church in New Haven,
from March 1st, 1758 to Oct.
20th, 1832. To which are prefixed the profession of faith,
covenant & articles of practice.
New Haven, Nathan Whiting,
1832. 46 p. Ct; MB; MiD-B.
                                    13928
New hymns, songs and verses,
for little children. Springfield,
Mass., G. & C. Merriam, 1832.
64 p. DLC.   13929

New Jersey.
    Acts of the fifty-sixth General
Assembly of the State of New Jersey. At a session begun at Trenton, on the twenty-fifth day of
October, one thousand eight hundred and thirty-one. Being the
first sitting. Trenton (N.J.), Pr.
by Jos. Justice, 1832. 224 p.
IaU-L; InSC; MdBB; NjR; T.
                                    13930
---- Acts relative to the Delaware and Raritan Canal Company
and Camden and Perth Amboy
Railroad and Transportation Co.,
Princeton, N.J., Robt. E. Horner, 1832. 30 p. CtY; MH-BA;
NNE; Nj; PHi.   13931

---- Governor's message. By
Peter D. Vroom. [Trenton, n.p.,
1832] 7 p. NJR.   13932

---- Journal of the proceedings
of the Legislative Council convened... twenty-fifth day of October, Anno Domini, one thousand
eight hundred and thirty-one...
being the first sitting of the fifty-
sixth session. Woodbury, N.J.,
Pr. by Jos. Sailer, 1832. 191 p.
NN.   13933

---- Rules for the government of
the Legislative Council... Trenton, 1832. NN.   13934

New Jersey almanac for 1833.
By David Young. Newark, Benja-

min Olds [1832] CtY; DLC; MH;
MWA; NjR; P.   13935

New Jersey Railroad and Transportation Company.
    An act to incorporate the New-
Jersey Railroad and Transportation Company... Newark, Pr. at
the Eagle office, 1832. 16 p.
DLC; NN; NNE.   13936

A new selection of hymns and
spiritual songs, designed for
prayer, conference and camp
meetings. By a brother in the
ministry. Woodstock, N. Haskell,
1832. 144 p. CSmH; MB; NN.
                                    13937
New York (City).
    Celebration of the centennial
anniversary of the birth of George
Washington. New-York, February
22, 1832. [New-York, 1832] 11 p.
DLC; ICHi; NHi; OCHP; PPL.
                                    13938
---- Proceedings relating to the
centennial anniversary of the birth
of George Washington. [New York,
1832] 32 p. NIC.   13939

---- Board of Aldermen. Committee on Fire and Water.
    Report [of the Committee on
Fire and Water of the Board of
Aldermen, December 28, 1831]
relative to introducing into New
York a supply of pure and wholesome water. [New York, 1832]
75 p. DNLM; ICC; MB; MH;
WHi.   13940

---- ---- Committee on Police.
    The Police committee to whom
was referred that part of the
mayor's message relating to a
more efficient code of police regulations presented the following
report together with a law which
was read and directed to be
printed for the use of the members. n.p. [1832] 8 p. MH.
                                    13941
---- ---- Committee on Streets.

The committees on streets, roads and canals, on the petition of the New-York and Harlaem Canal Company, for permission to extend their rails to Prince-street, and through such other streets as the Corporation will permit in conformity to their amended Charter, presented the following report, which was read, laid on the table--the Street Commissioner to advertise for objections--and directed to be printed for the use of the members. April 23, 1832. [New York, 1832] 4 p. MB; MH; NN. 13942

---- Board of Assistant Aldermen.
...Board of assistants July 2, 1832. The committee on police, watchman, and prisons, to whom was referred the resolution on the law regulating hackney coaches and carriages, and stage coaches, and revising the same. New York, 1832-[1834] NjR.
13943

---- Board of Health.
Report of the commissioners employed to investigate the origin and nature of the epidemic cholera of Canada. New York, 1832. 68 p. DNLM; MB; MBM. 13944

---- Charter.
The charter of the City of New-York. Pub. pursuant to an order of the common council. New-York, Gould, Banks & Co., 1832. 114 p. MB; Mi; NjP; NNC.
13945

---- Citizens.
The proceedings of divers inhabitants of the city of New-York, on the subject of a rail road from the city of New-York to the city of Albany... The memorial of the president, directors and company of the Highland turnpike... [New York, 1832] 3 p. NN. 13946

---- Commissioners.
Commissioners to establish a permanent regulation of the streets and avenues south of Thirty-fourth street. Reports and documents relative to the Stuyvesant Meadows, from the year 1825 to 1831, inclusive. New York, Pr. by Geo. Robertson, 1832. 50 p. NNUT. 13947

---- Common Council.
Proceedings relating to the Centennial anniversary of the birth of George Washington. [New York, 1832] 32 p. MH. 13948

---- Comptroller.
Annual report of the comptroller with the accounts of the corporation of the City of New-York, for the year ending with the 31st day of December, 1831. Also the account current of the commissioners of the sinking fund, for the same period. New-York, Pr. by Peter Van Pelt, 1832. 56 p. DNA. 13949

---- ---- Ferry leases now in force; printed under the direction of the comptroller; ordered by the resolution of the Board of assistant aldermen, of October 22, 1832. [1832?] 57 p. MB; MiU; NB. 13950

---- Dept. of Finance.
A list of real estate belonging to the corporation of the city of New York, prepared by the comptroller, and presented to the common council, November 19, 1832. New York, Pr. by Peter Van Pelt, 1832. 20 p. NNMuCN; NjR.
13951

---- Ordinances.
A law to regulate the public markets. New York, 1832. DLC.
13952

---- University.
The statutes of the University of the City of New York. New York, Pr. by Wm. A. Mercein, 1832. 15 p. DHEW; DLC;

NNNAM; NjR.   13953

New York (State) Adjutant-general's office.
...Report of the adjutant-general, in obedience to two several resolutions of the Senate, of the 21st and 23d of April last. [Albany, 1832] 64 p. DLC; MB; NbU; WHi.   13954

---- Canal Board.
Rates of toll, canal regulations and distances on the New York State canals; as established by the canal board, the commissioners of the canal fund, and the canal commissioners, and in force on said canals on the 16th February, 1832. Albany, Pr. by Croswell, Van Benthuysen & Burt, 1832. 39 p. NRom; NbU.
                               13955
---- Commissioners of the Canal Fund.
...Annual report of the Commissioners of the canal fund, respecting the tolls collected, and the property transported on the canals... with other statistical information. Albany, 1832-48. DLC; NN; NNC.   13956

---- Dept. of Public Instruction.
Report of the superintendent of common schools, in relation to the instruction to the deaf and dumb. Made to the Legislature, April 16, 1832. Albany, Pr. by Croswell, Van Benthuysen and Burt, 1832. 24 p. NbU; NjR.
                               13957
---- Governor.
In Senate, March 27, 1832, Message from the Governor, relative to the adulteration of potash. Albany, 1832. 8, 10 p. NjR.   13958

---- Laws, Statutes, etc.
An Act directing the manner of choosing Electors of President and Vice-President, passed April

15, 1829; with forms for carrying the same into effect, prepared by the Secretary of State, in obedience to Chapter 249, of the Session Laws of 1832: together with the Act to divide the State into Congressional Districts, passed June 29, 1832. Albany, Pr. by Croswell, Van Benthuysen & Burt, 1832. 15 p. CSmH; NbU.   13959

---- ---- An act relative to the county loans, passed April 13, 1832; together with the comptroller's circular to the commissioners of loans and loan officers. Albany, Croswell, Van Benthuysen & Burt, 1832. 3, 8-15 p. NN.
                               13960
---- ---- An act to abolish imprisonment for debt, and to punish fraudulent debtors. Passed by the Legislature of the state of New-York, April 26, 1831; and takes effect March 1, 1832. Albany, Webster & Skinners, 1832. 12 p. CSmH.   13961

---- ---- An act to abolish imprisonment for debt, and to punish fraudulent debtors. Passed April 26, 1831. Also, A synopsis of the same by S. M. Stilwell. 2d ed. New York, Elliott & Palmer, 1832. 24 p. NN; NjR.
                               13962
---- ---- Laws of the state of New York, passed at the fifty-fifth session of the Legislature, begun and held at the city of Albany, the third day of January, 1832. Albany, Pr. by E. Croswell, prs. to the state, 1832. 639 p. IaU-L; MH-L; N; Nj; WaL.   13963

---- ---- The Poor Laws of the State of New-York, containing the first six titles of Chapter XX of the first part of the Revised Statutes, and such subsequent acts as relate to the support and

management of the poor; together with suitable forms, and an
exposition of the said titles,
prepared by the Secretary of
State, in obedience to Section 2,
of Chapter 114, of the Session
Laws of 1832. Albany, Croswell,
Van Benthuysen & Burt, 1832.
DLC; MB; NN; NbU; WHi. 13964

---- Legislature.
   The constitutions of the United
States and state of New York,
and Articles of Confederation;
together with the rules and orders,
standing committees, list of members of the Senate and Assembly
for 1832, list of counties, etc.
Albany, N.Y., Croswell, 1832.
222 p. NIC; NP; NRHi.   13965

---- ---- Assembly.
   Documents of the Assembly of
the state of New York, fifty-fifth
session, 1832. Albany, Pr. by
E. Croswell, pr. to the state,
1832. 4 v. IU; MB; NNLI. 13966

---- ---- ---- Journal of the
Assembly of the state of New-
York, at their fifty-fifth session,
begun and held at the capitol, in
the city of Albany, the 3rd day
of January, 1832. Albany, Pr.
by E. Croswell, pr. to the state,
1832. 963 p. NNLI; PPL-R.
                        13967
---- ---- ---- Committee
on Canals and Internal Improvements.
   ...Report of the Committee
on canals and improvements, on
the subject of the Chenango canal...[Albany?] 1832. 5 p. 13968

---- ---- ---- Committee on
Railroads.
   ...Report of the Committee
on rail-roads, on so much of
the governor's message as relates to the subject. [Albany,
1832] 20 p. CtY; DBRE; MiU-T;
MWA; NN.   13969

---- ---- ---- Select Committee
on Memorial of Jacob Trumpbour
and Holmes Hutchinson.
   ...Report of the select committee to which was referred the
memorial of Jacob Trumpbour
and Holmes Hutchinson...[Albany,
1832] 71 p. DLC.   13970

---- ---- ---- Select Committee
on the practicability on introducing the manufacture of silk and
the propriety of giving a bounty
upon the cultivation of the mulberry tree.
   Report. [Albany] 1832. 8 p.
N.   13971

---- ---- ---- Select Committee
to examine into the state of prisons at Mt. Pleasant and Auburn.
   ...Report... [Albany? 1832]
39 p. CU.   13972

---- ---- ---- Select Committee
to inquire into the expediency of
a total abolition of capital punishment.
   The report of the honorable
S. M. Stillwell, Chairman of a
select committee appointed by a
resolution...Albany, Pr. by
Packard, Hoffman and White,
1832. 19 p. DLC; MWA; Md;
NjR; WHi.   13973

---- ---- Senate.
   Documents of the Senate of
New-York, fifty-fifth session.
1832. Albany, Pr. by E. Cros-
well, pr. to the state, 1832. 2 v.
MnU; NNLI.   13974

---- ---- ---- Journal of the
Senate of the state of New-York,
at their fifty-fifth session, begun
and held at the capitol in the
city of Albany, the 3d day of
January, 1832. Albany, Pr. by
E. Croswell, pr. to the state,
1832. 450 p. CHi; N; NNLI.
                        13975
---- ---- ---- Committee on

Finance.

Report of the committee relative to the rates of interest. [1832] 24 p. NNC.   13976

---- ---- ---- ---- Report ... on so much of the governor's message as relates to the finances of the state, and the report of the comptroller, relative to the loans [1832]   20 p. NNC.   13977

---- Militia. 10th Infantry Brigade. Light Infantry Battalion.

Regulations for the separate battalion of light infantry, attached to the Tenth Brigade New York State Infantry. President's Guards. New-York, Pr. by Clayton & Van Norden, 1832. 22 p. NbU.   13978

---- Secretary of State.

...Report of the Secretary of State, giving the census of the several congressional districts in 1820, 1825, and 1830, in compliance with a resolution of the Senate of the 23d of February, 1832. Albany, 1832. 12 p. NN.
13979

---- Supreme Court.

Reports of cases argued and determined in the Supreme Court of judicature, and in the Court for the trial of impeachments and the correction of errors of the state of New York. [1828-41] by John L. Wendell. Albany, Gould, Banks & Co. [etc., etc.] 1832-1854. 26 v. CU; LNT-L; Nc-S; P; W.   13980

---- University. College of Physicians and Surgeons.

Catalogue of the regents of the University, and of the trustees, faculty, fellows, graduates and students, of the College of Physicians and Surgeons, in the city of New York, 1831-'32. Pub. by the class. New York, Pr. by

Thos. P. Evans, 1832. 12 p. NNC.   13981

New York. Brick Presbyterian Church.

Catalogue of the officers and members of the Brick Presbyterian Church in the City of New-York. New-York, Pr. by John T. West, Feb. 1832. 29 p. NUtHi.   13982

New York almanac for 1833. By David Young. New York, Benjamin Olds, 1832. MH; MWA.
13983

---- New York, J. C. Totten, 1832. MH; MWA.   13984

New York and Albany Railroad Company.

Facts and suggestions relating to the New-York and Albany railroad. With the act of incorporation. New-York, Ludwig & Tolefree, prs., 1832. 32 p. CSt; DLC; MBC; MH-BA; PPFrankI.
13985

New York and Erie Railroad Co.

Charter, by-laws, reports, etc. 1832-1844. New York, 1832?- 1844. NN; PPFrankI; ViU. 13986

New York and Schuylkill Coal Company.

Description of the coal lands of the N.Y. and Schuylkill Coal Co. situated in Schuylkill County Pennsylvania. New York, Pr. by W. A. Mercein, 1832. 19 p. DLC; DI-GS; NN; PHC; PHi.
13987

New York and Stonington Railroad Company.

An act to incorporate the New York and Stonington Railroad Company. Passed May, 1832. [New York, Pr. by J. M. Eliott, 1832] 9 p. CSt; DBRE; MBAt; NN; RPB.   13988

The New-York Annual Register for the year of our Lord 1832.

Containing an almanac; civil and judicial list; with political, statistical, and other information, respecting the State of New-York and the United States. By Edwin Williams. New-York, Pr. by J. Seymour, 1832. 396 p. CoCsC; MiD-B; NNLI; NNNG; NUtHi; PPA.   13989

New York Bible Association of Friends.
First report of the New York Bible Association of Friends. New York, Pr. by Mahlon Day, 1832. 8 p. InRchE.   13990

The New-York Christian messenger, and Philadelphia Universalist; devoted to the doctrine of universal benevolence--the defence of liberal principles generally in religion, and miscellaneous reading of chaste and moral tendency. Ed. by T. J. Sawyer, A. C. Thomas and P. Price. V. 1-4; Oct. 29, 1831-Oct. 24, 1835. New-York, P. Price, 1832-35. 4 v. DLC; ICN; MB; MH-BA; PPL.   13991

The New-York cries, in rhyme. New-York, Mahlon Day, 1832. 23 p. MiU-C; NBuG; OCIWHi.   13992
The New-York Farmer's Almanack for 1833 by Thomas Spofford. New York, David Felt [1832] 18 p. M; MB; MWA; NN; PHi; ViHi.   13993

New York Free Presbyterian Church.
Church manual, No. 11, for the communicants of the Free Presbyterian Church, City of New York; containing their names, with the names and addresses of the officers, also the form of admission, together with the notices of the stated meetings of the church and congregation, also, the plan of

benevolence, etc. New York, 1832. 48 p. NIC.   13994

New York Life Insurance and Trust Company.
In Chancery, before the Chancellor, in the matter of the New-York Life Insurance and Trust Company. Order, answer, and report. April, 1832. New York, Clayton & Van Norden, 1832. 68 p. DLC; MB; MBC; NN; N-L.   13995

New York Protestant Episcopal City Mission Society.
The first annual report of the managers of the New York Protestant Episcopal City Mission Society... New York, Protestant Episcopal Press, 1832. 16 p. MdBD; NjR.   13996

New York, Providence and Boston Railroad Company.
An act to incorporate the New York, Providence, and Boston Railroad Company. Passed June, 1832. [Boston? 1832] 12 p. CSt; DBRE; NN; RHi; RPB.   13997

---- Some remarks showing the advantages of the proposed railroad from Providence to Stonington. [New York, 1832?] 14 p. RPB.   13998

New York State Agricultural Convention, Albany.
Proceedings of the State Agricultural Convention, held at the Capitol in the city of Albany, on the 14th, 15th and 16th February, 1832: with the constitution a State Agricultural Society, agreed to and adopted, by the said Convention. Albany, Pr. by Webster & Skinners, 1832. 43 p. ICJ; MBC; MH; MWA; MiU-C; NjR.   13999
New York Truth Teller. At a meeting of friends... The following resolutions were carried unan-

imously: Resolved--That we consider the New York Truth Teller, to be a pure Democratic, Republican Jackson Paper, devoted to the interests of Ireland. . . Thos. S. Brady, Chairman, Christopher C. Rice, Vice. , Daniel M'Grath, Secretary. [1832] DNA.   14000

New York Young Men's Colonization Society.
    Constitution. . . with an abstract of the proceedings of the meeting at which it was adopted: March 15, 1832. New York, W. Osborn & Co. , 1832. 15 p. PHi.   14001

New York Young Men's Society.
    First annual report, with the constitution, by-laws, and standing rules. . . New York, J. T. West & Co. , 1832. 25 p. MiD-B; ScCC.   14002

Newburyport, Mass. First Religious Society.
    Constitution Sunday School Association, etc. Newburyport, 1832. MB.   14003

---- School Committee.
    Regulations for the public schools of the town of Newburyport, adopted by the School committee Oct. 1831. [Newburyport] J. H. Buckingham, 1832. 18 p. M; MH.   14004

---- Second Congregational Church.
    The Confession of Faith and Covenant of the Second Church of Christ in Newbury, Mass. Adopted in the year of our Lord 1808. Revised, and adopted Feb. 1832. Newburyport, Pr. by W. & J. Gilman, 1832. 12 p. MBC; MNe.
                              14005
[Newcomb, Harvey, 1803-1862]
    Scenes of intemperance, exhibited in familiar conversations, between a mother and her children. Philadelphia, American Sunday School Union [1832] 47 p.

AmSSchU; MB; MH; MMedHi; MPeHi.   14006

Newell, Fanny, 1793-1824.
    Memoirs, with corrections and improvements. By Mrs. Fanny Newell. 2d ed. Springfield, Pr. by Merriam, Little & co. , 1832. 216 p. ICBB; ICN; MSHi; Nh.
                              14007
Newell, Harriet [Atwood] 1793-1812.
    The life and writings of Mrs. Harriet Newell. Rev. by the Committee of Publication of the American Sunday School Union. Philadelphia, American Sunday School Union, 1832. 267 p. CSansS; MH; NcGu; PCA; ViU.   14008

Newman, Samuel Phillips, 1797-1842.
    A practical system of rhetoric . . . By Samuel P. Newman. 3d ed. enl. & imp. Boston, Wm. Hyde & Co. , 1832. 262 p. ILM; MB; MH; OMC.   14009

Newnham, William, 1790-1865.
    A tribute of sympathy, addressed to mourners. By W. Newnham, esq. 1st Amer. from 6th London ed. New York, Swords, Stanford & Co. , 1832. 228 p. CtHT; GDecCT; MH; OMC; TxU.
                              14010
Newport, Rhode Island.
    A list of persons assessed in the Town-Tax of six thousand eight hundred and thirty-four dollars, voted by the freemen of Newport, June, 1832. With the amount of the valuation and tax of each. Newport, Pr. by Wm. Marshall & Co. , 1832. 18 p. RHi; RNH.   14011

Newton, Sereno.
    Engineers', millwrights', and machinists' tables; containing a table of the proportional radii of wheels, from ten to four hundred teeth; together with other tables

and rules, applicable to the construction of millwork and other machinery. By Sereno Newton. New York, G. & C. & H. Carvill, 1832. 25 p. DLC; PPF; PPFrankI.   14012

Newton, Thomas, 1704-1782.
Dissertation on the prophecies, which have remarkably been fulfilled and at this time are fulfilling in the world... Rev. by the Rev. W. S. Dobson... London, J. F. Dove; Repr. by J. J. Woodward, Philadelphia, 1832. 649 p. CtHC; KyLxT; MiD; PLT; TJaU.   14013

Newton, Mass. Baptist Church of Christ.
Articles of Christian doctrine and Church Covenant, adopted by the church Oct. 14, 1832. Boston, Lincoln and Edmands, 1832. 7 p. MH; MNtCA.   14014

Nicholson, Peter.
The mechanic's companion; or, The elements and practice of carpentry, joinery, bricklaying, masonry, slating, plastering, painting, smithing, and turning... By Peter Nicholson. Philadelphia, James Locken, 1832. 333, 1 p. ICMS; MA; MH; NjR; PU.
                                         14015

Nickerson, C. V.
Flowers of Wit,... See under title.

---- Nickerson's Humorous, sentimental and naval songster; or, Museum of mirth! [5th ed.] Baltimore, C. V. Nickerson, 1832. RPB.   14016

Nicklin, P. H. and T. Johnson (firm).
Catalogue of law books, for sale by P. H. Nicklin and T. Johnson, Law Booksellers. Philadelphia, Pr. by John Bioren, [1832] 15 p. IaU-L.   14017

[Niles, William Woodruff?]
Ought I to become a missionary to the heathen? An essay, read before the "Society of Inquiry" in the Literary and Theological Institution, at South Hanover, Indiana. Accompanying the First Annual Report of the "Committee on Foreign Missions."
By a Student. Cincinnati, Pr. by M'Millan & Clopper, 1832. 15 p. In; OCHP.   14018

Noble, Mason, 1809-1881.
A sermon delivered in the Fourth Presbyterian Church in the city of Washington, on the day of Thanksgiving (Nov. 22, 1832) for the departure of the cholera from that city. Washington, Pub. at the request of the congregation, Pr. by J. Gideon, 1832. 19 p. DLC; RPB.   14019

North-American Calendar, or the Columbian Almanac for 1833. Wilmington, Del., P. B. Porter [1832] 36 p. DLC; DeHi; MWA; NjR.   14020

North American Mining Company.
An act to incorporate the North American Mining Company. [New York? 1832] 21 p. MH-BA; NN.   14021

North Carolina.
Acts passed by the General Assembly of the state of North Carolina, at the session of 1831-32. Raleigh, Lawrence & Lemay, prs. to the state, 1832. 148, 20, 4 (1) p. Ar-SC; IaU-L; L; Nb; W.   14022

---- Debate in the Legislature on a proposed appropriation for rebuilding the capitol and on the convention question, in the months of Dec. and Jan. 1831-32. Raleigh, 1832. 126, 73 p. ICU; MH-L; NcD; NcU.   14023

---- Journals of the Senate and House of Commons of the General Assembly of the State of North Carolina at the session of 1831-32. Raleigh, Pr. by Lawrence & Lemay, 1832. 255 p. Nc; NcWfC.   14024

---- Report and counter report of the Joint Select Committee on the subject of convention. Raleigh, Ramsey, 1832. 8 p. NcU. 14025

---- Report on the situation of the Cape Fear Navigation Company. Raleigh, Lawrence, 1832. 8 p. Nc; NcD; NcU.   14026

---- Reports of cases adjudged in the Superior Courts of law and equity of the State of North Carolina. By John Haywood. Raleigh, Pr. by Jas. Gales & Son, 1832. 605 p. MH-L; Md; Mn-U; NV; PU-L.   14027

---- University.
University of North-Carolina. A ball, complimentary to the graduates...Chapel Hill, March 10, 1832. Hillsborough, Pr. by D. Heartt [1832] 1 p. NcU. 14028

North Eastern boundary of United States. Boston, 1832. See under Daveis, Charles Stewart, 1788-1865.

North Haven, Connecticut.
Church of Christ.
A confession of faith & covenant, with the names of the members belonging to the Church of Christ in North Haven, August, 1832. New-Haven, Peck & Newton, [1832] 12 p. Ct.   14029

North Sabbath School Society.
First semi-annual report of the Executive Board of the North Sabbath School Society, together with the constitution and by-laws of the society. Presented and adopted

October 6, 1832. New Bedford, B. T. Congdon, 1832. 12 p. MNBedf.   14030

Northampton, Mass. First Parish.
First church in Northampton, Mass. Confession of faith and catalogue of members, Jan. 1, 1832. Northampton, T. W. Shepard, pr., 1832. 40 p. MNHi; OO; WHi.   14031

Northern Liberties & Penn Township Rail Road.
An act to incorporate a company to make a rail road through the northern section of the county of Philadelphia from the river Delaware to Schuylkill, or to terminate at a junction with the Columbia & Philadelphia Rail Road to be called the Northern Liberties & Penn Township Rail Road. Philadelphia, Alexander, 1832. 11 p. IU; NN; PHi.   14032

Northern Liberties' Fuel Savings Society, Philadelphia.
Constitution. Instituted March 22, 1832. Philadelphia, 1832. 12 p. IU.   14033

Northern regions: or, Uncle Richard's relation of Capt. Parry's voyages for discovery of a northwest passage. (Added) Franklin's and Cochranes's overland journeys... New York, Burgess, 1832. 228 p. CtY; DLC; MWA. 14034

Norwood, Abraham, Jr.
Religious prescriptions for opinions sake, containing an account of the dealings of the First Congregational Church in Beddeford with the author. And also some of the prominent features of orthodoxy. Copyright secured according to law. Saco, William Condon, 1832. 80 p. MBC; MMet; NNUT.   14035

Notice of Mr. Adams' eulogium on

the life and character of James Monroe. See under [Armstrong, John] 1758-1843.

Nott, Samuel, 1754-1852.
Ministers of the gospel are ...then vessels; sermon at Lisbon, at the funeral of Andrew Lee. Norwich, J. Dunham, 1832. 12 p. Ct; MBC; PPL-R; RPB.
14036
---- Reasons for ministerial fidelity. A half century sermon: preached at Franklin, March 13, 1832... Norwich, J. Dunham, 1832. 28 p. IaHA; MBC; PPPrHi; RPB; WHi.   14037

---- Telescope; or, Sacred Views of Things Past, Present, and to Come. Boston, Perkins & Marvin, 1832. ICBB; MBC; MeBat; Nh-Pet; OMC.   14038

Noyes, George Rapall, 1798-1868.
The Gospel exhibited in a Unitarian ministers preaching. By George R. Noyes. Boston, Gray & Bowen, 1832. 36 p. ICMe; GEU-T; MB; MeB; PPWe. 14039

---- A review of a discourse, delivered before the Second Congregational Society in Brookfield, Nov. 7, 1831, by George R. Noyes... Brookfield, Merriam, 1832. 24 p. CBPac; MBC; MBrof; OClWHi.   14040

---- A sermon upon Isaiah, IX. 6, also, an explanation of John, 1. By George R. Noyes. Pr. for the Worcester West Association. Brookfield, Pr. by E. Merriam & Co., 1832. 24 p. ICN; MB; MNe; N; RPB.   14041

Nuttall, Thomas, 1786-1859.
A manual of the ornithology of the United States and of Canada. By Thomas Nuttall... The land birds. Cambridge [Mass.] Hilli-

ard and Brown, 1832. 683 p. CSt; ICJ; MH; OO; PPA; Vi.
14042
---- ---- Cambridge, Hilliard and Brown; Boston, Hilliard and Gray, 1832-34. 4 v. DeU; ICF-A; MH; NcA-S; PPC.   14043

Nutting, Rufus, 1793-1878.
Memoirs of Mrs. Emily Egerton. Boston, Pr. by Perkins & Marvin, 1832. 180 p. DLC; GDecCT; MWA; OClW.   14044

O

O'Bryan, William.
On the millennium, a sermon on Revelation XX. 6, by William O'Bryan, minister of the gospel. 3d ed. corr. [quotation] New York, Pr. by S. Hoyt & Co. for the author, 1832. 29 p. ICP.
14045
The ocean; a description of wonders and important products of the sea... New York, Carlton & Porter [1832?] 112 p.   14046

Odd Fellows, Independent Order of. Maryland Grand Lodge.
Constitution of the Grand Lodge of Maryland of the Order of Independent Odd Fellows. Adopted July 30, 1832. Baltimore, Lucas and Deaver, 1832. 20 p. PPL.   14047

The Odd Volume: a collection of odds and ends in prose and verse. Collected and arranged by an Odd Fellow. New York, Peabody & Co., 1832. 144 p. DLC; NBuG; PPL; RP; TxU.   14048

Offley, David.
Correspondence (about the treaty with Turkey: 1828, 1829). Washington, 1832. 27 p. PHi.
14049
Ogilby, John David, 1810-1851.
First anniversary address be-

fore the associate society of the city of New York for the promotion of literature, science, and the arts. Jan. 16, 1832. MSbri.
14050

Oglethorpe, pseud.
The doctrine of nullification examined: an essay first published in the Georgia constitutionalist, under the signature of Oglethorpe. To which is annexed, the proceedings of the meeting of the union & state rights party of Charleston, June 12, 1832. Charleston, Pr. by J. S. Burges, 1832. 24 p. DLC; MH; NN; ScC; ViU.   14051

---- Georgia and the Supreme Court. An examination of the opinion of the Supreme Court of the United States, at January time, 1832. Delivered by Mr. Chief Justice Marshall, in the case of Samuel A. Worcester, plaintiff in error, Versus the State of Georgia... Augusta (Ga.), 1832. 22 p. CtY; GU-De; MH; OKHi; Vi.
14052

Ohio. Convention, Columbus, 1832.
Address and proceedings of the Ohio State Convention which met at Columbus, O., January 9, 1832, to nominate a governor and a ticket for electors favorable to the re-election of Andrew Jackson as president of the United States. Columbus, Pr. at the office of the "Sentinel," 1832. 24 p. OCHP.   14053

The Ohio antimasonic almanack for 1833. By William Brown. Columbus, Jenkins and Glover [1832] 48 p. OMC.   14054

Ohio Baptist Education Society.
Periodical, No. 1 annual meeting of the Ohio Baptist Education Society, and of the Trustees of the Granville Literary and Theological Institution. October 6th,

1832. Cincinnati, Pr. by Whetstone and Johnson, 1832-1837. 6 v. OCIWHi.   14055

Der Ohio Bauern calender auf 1833. By Samuel Burr. Lancaster, N. and G. Guilford, [1832] 18 ll. OCIWHi.   14056

The Ohio Farmers' Almanack, for the year 1833: Being the first year after bissextile, or leap year, and after the fourth of July, the fifty-eighth year of American independence. Calculated for the meridian of Columbus. Washington [D. C.] By William Brown. Columbus, Jenkins & Glover, 1832. [16] p. OFH; MWA. 14057

Ohio Historical and Philosophical Society.
Circular... See Cincinnati Historical Society.

The Ohio officer's guide. And clerk's companion. Containing a summary view of the principal provisions of the statutes, as revised in 1830-'31. Relating to the duties of justices of the peace, and all other township officers; with appropriate forms: also a collection of useful forms of deeds, articles of agreements, powers of attorney, bonds, wills, &c. &c.. By a member of the bar. Steubenville, J. & B. Turnbull, 1832. 308 p. C-L; NjR; OCHP; OCLaw; OCIWHi.   14058

O'Leary, Arthur, 1729-1802.
Essays and tracts, in which is introduced his correspondence with Rev. John Wesley, Lewistown, Charles Bell & Sons, 1832. 165 p. DGU; IaDmDC; MdW; NNC; PLatS.   14059

Oliver, Benjamin Lynde, 1788-1843.
The rights of an American citizen; with a commentary on state

rights, and on the Constitution and policy of the United States. By Benjamin L. Oliver... Boston, Marsh, Capen & Lyon; Philadelphia, P. N. Nicklin & T. Johnson, 1832. 411 p. CU; LU; MBAt; PEal; WHi.   14060

Oliver, Daniel, 1787-1842.
An address delivered before the Temperance Society of the medical class in Dartmouth College, October 31, 1832. Windsor, Chronicle Press [1832] 16 p. MB; MBAt; MH; Nh; Vt.   14061

Olmsted, Denison, 1791-1859.
An introduction to natural philosophy; designed as a text book for the use of the students in Yale College. Compiled by Denison Olmsted, A. M. ... New Haven, Hezekiah Howe & Co, 1832. 2 v. MH; MeB; OMC; PPAmP. 14062

Olney, Jesse, 1798-1872.
A new and improved school atlas to accompany The practical system of modern geography. Hartford, D. F. Robinson & Co., 1832. MH; NRMA; PHC. 14063

---- A practical system of modern geography; or, A view of the present state of the world. Simplified and adapted to the capacity of youth; containing numerous tables, exhibiting the divisions, settlements, population, extent, lakes, canals, and the various institutions of the United States and Europe, the different forms of government, prevailing religions, the latitude and longitude of the principal places on the globe. Embellished with numerous engravings of manners, customs, etc. Accompanied by a new and improved atlas. By J. Olney. 10th ed. Hartford, D. F. Robinson & Co., 1832. 283 p. CtY; MBevHi; MH; NNC; NBuT.   14064

---- ---- 11th ed. Hartford, D. F. Robinson & Co., 1832. 288 p. CtY; DLC; MB; NNC; OKEnP; ViU.   14065

The omnibus, or Universal newsteller and wonderful intelligencer. Not by Sir Walter Scott & J. Fenimore Cooper. New-York, P. Body, 1832. 59 p. CtY; MH.
                                     14066
On the best precautions necessary to be taken in these serious and pestilential times; a discourse delivered during the prevalence of the cholera in London, by a lady of the rotunda. New York, Matsell, 1832. 23 p. NB.   14067

On the Holy Scriptures, and the observance of the first day of the week. Philadelphia, Tract Association of Friends, 1832. 12 p. OClWHi; PSC-Hi.   14068

On the nature and efficacy of the cross of Christ. Philadelphia, Tract Association of Friends, 1832. 16 p. InRchE; OClWHi.
                                     14069
On the practical importance of faith in the divinity of Christ. Philadelphia, To be had of Wm. Salter, 1832. 20 p. InRchE.
                                     14070
[Onderdonk, Benjamin Tredwell] 1791-1861.
A form of prayer and thanksgiving; to be used in the Diocese of New York. 4 p. NNG. 14071

---- A form of prayer to be used on the Fourth of July, 1832. [New York, 1832] 4 p. NNG.
                                     14072
Onderdonk, Henry Ustick, 1789-1858.
Regeneration by H. U. O. From the Protestant Episcopalian for May and June, 1832. By Henry Ustick Onderdonk, bp. of Pennsylvania. n. p. [1832] 33 p. CtY; IaHi; MH; NNG; NcU.   14073

---- A sermon preached at the opening of the general convention of the Protestant Episcopal Church in the United States, in St. Paul's Chapel, New York, October 17, 1832. By the Rt. Rev. Henry U. Onderdonk, D. D. Pub. in accordance with a standing resolution of the convention. New-York, Pr. at the Protestant Episcopal Press, 1832. 18 p. CtHT; InID; MB; PHi; RPB.
14074

---- A sermon preached in St. Paul's Chapel, New York, on the occasion of the consecration of the Rt. Rev. John H. Hopkins ...Rt. Rev. Benjamin B. Smith ...Rt. Rev. Charles P. McIlvaine ...and the Rt. Rev. George W. Doane... New York, Protestant Episcopal press, 1832. DeU; MWA; N; NjP; OO.   14075

The one hundred and nineteenth psalm. American Sunday School Union, Philadelphia, 1832. 60 p. MNBedf.   14076

Opie, Amelia [Alderson] 1769-1853.
Illustrations of Lying in all its branches. By Amelia Opie. Exeter, N. H., J. C. Gerrish, 1832. 224 p. CU; ICP; MBC; MH; MiU.   14077

Oration delivered at the Mariner's Baptise Bethel, Philadelphia, on the centennial anniversary of the illustrious Washington Feb. 22, 1832, by an old sailor. Philadelphia, 1832. 17 p. PHi.   14078

[Orme, William] 1787-1830.
Memoirs of John Urquhart. Compiled for the American Sunday School Union, and revised by the Committee of Publication. Philadelphia, American Sunday School Union, 1832. 174 p. CLSU; DLC.   14079

Orr, Isaac, 1793-1844.
Strictures on Lee's... See Hambden, pseud.

Ostrander, Tobias.
The mathematical expositor; containing rules, theorems, lemmae, and explanations, of various parts of the mathematical science, in a series of lectures, calculated for the use of teachers and students of schools and academies in the United States. By Tobias Ostrander, teacher of mathematics...2d ed., rev. and cor., to which is added a key to the miscellaneous questions of the "Elements of numbers, or Easy instructor," by the author. Palmyra [N. Y.], E. B. Grandin, Strong, 1832. 168 p. CSmH; DAU; MiU; NBU; RPB.   14080

---- The Planetarium and Astronomical Calculator etc., etc. By Tobias Ostrander, teacher of mathematics and author of the "Elements of Numbers," etc., etc. Lyons, [N. Y.] Pr. at the office of the Western Argus, 1832. 262 p. FDb; MH; NCH; OUrC; TxU.   14081

Otis, Oran G.
Oration delivered on the Centennial Anniversary of the birthday of Washington, in the city of Albany, on the twenty-second of February, 1832, by the Hon. Oran G. Otis, of the Assembly, on the appointment of the Legislature of New York. Albany, Pr. by Croswell, Van Benthuysen & Burt, 1832. 16 p. MB; MdBD; NCH; Nh-Hi; TxH.   14082

Ouseley, Sir William Gore, 1797-1866.
Remarks on the statistics and political institutions of the United States, with some observations on the ecclesiastical system of America, her sources of revenue,

&c. To which are added statistical tables, &c. By Wm. G. Ouseley... Philadelphia, Carey & Lea, 1832. 226 p. CtHC; IaU; LNP; PPA; PU; ScC; TNF.
14083

The outline of a public debate, held in the Court-House at Edenton, on the 28th and 29th May, 1832. Edenton, N. C., Pr. at the Miscellany Press [1832] 8 p. MMeT.
14084

Owen, John, 1616-1683.
The death of death in the death of Christ; A treatise of the redemption and reconciliation that is in the blood of Christ [etc.] Philadelphia, Green & McLaughlin, 1832. 392 p. NNUT; NbOP; PPM.
14085

---- The grace and duty of being spiritually minded, declared and practically improved... Carefully corrected from the author's ed. New York, R. Carter, 1832[?] 385 p. CtY.
14086

---- On temptation: on the dominion of sin and grace; and on the grace and duty of being spiritually minded. By John Owen, D.D. A new ed., edited by the Rev. C. Bradley. Philadelphia, Manning & Son, 1832. 431 p. IaPeC.
14087

P

Packard, Hannah James, 1815-1831.
The choice: a tragedy, with other miscellaneous poems. By Hannah J. Packard. Boston, Leonard C. Bowles, 1832. 142 p. ICN; MnU; NjR; PU; RPB. 14088

Page, William, d. 1856.
A discourse, on the subject of truth, as connected with regeneration. Delivered to the First

Presbyterian Church and congregation in Ithaca, March 4, 1832. By Rev. William Page. Ithaca, N.Y., Pr. by D. D. & A. Spencer, 1832. 20 p. CSmH; NAuT; PPPrHi; VtMidbC.
14089

Paine, Martyn, 1794-1877.
Lecture on the improvement of medical education in the United States; introductory to a course of lectures in the University of New York... New York, 1832. DLC; DNLM; KyU; MB.
14090

---- Letters on the cholera asphyxia, as it has appeared in the city of New York; addressed to John C. Warren, M. D. of Boston, and originally published in that city, together with other letters, not before published, by Martyn Paine... New York, Collins & Hannay, 1832. 160 p. CtHT; LNT-M; NhD; PU; RPM; ViU.
14091

Paine, Thomas, 1737-1809.
Age of reason, in two parts. Wilmington, Del., Delaware Free Press Office, 1832. 68 p. DeWi.
14092

---- The theological works of Thomas Paine. To which are added the Profession of faith of a Savoyard vicar, by J. J. Rousseau; ...Boston, Pr. for the advocates of common sense, 1832. FOA; MiU.
14093

Paley, William, 1743-1805.
Moral and Political Philosophy...by Wm. Paley. Boston, N. H. Whitaker. Stereotyped by David Hills, 1832. 247 p. NvGa.
14094

---- ... The principles of moral and political philosophy. By Wm. Paley, D.D. Adapted to the use of female seminaries. With questions for the examination of students. By John Frost... Boston, N. H. Whitaker, 1832. 2 vols. AU; DLC; IGK; MBBC; PPM.
14095

[Palfrey, Cazneau]
A sermon on making good resolutions delivered in the Unitarian church, Washington City, Jan.
1, 1832. Washington, Gales,
1832. 16 p. DLC; MBAt; PPAmP.
14096
Palfrey, John Gorhan, 1796-1881.
A discourse delivered in the
church in Brattle Square, Boston,
August 9, 1832, the day appointed
for fasting and prayer in Massachusetts, on account of the approach of cholera. Boston, Gray
& Bowen, 1832. 26 p. CtSoP;
ICMe; MH-AH; NCH; WHi. 14097

---- ---- 2d ed. Boston, Gray &
Bowen, 1832. 26 p. MB; MH;
MeB; OClWHi; RPB.   14098

[Palmer, Ray] 1808-1887.
Memoirs and select remains,
of Charles Pond, late member of
the sophomore class in Yale college. Compiled by a classmate
...Rev. by the publishing committee. 3d ed. Boston, Massachusetts Sabbath School Society,
1832. 140 p. NNUT.   14099

Palmer's New England Almanac
for 1833. By J. N. Palmer. New
Haven, Conn., Durrie & Peck
[1832] CtB; CtY; InU; MWA; OrP.
14100
Paltock, Robert, 1697-1767.
The life and adventures of
Peter Wilkins, containing an account of his visit to the flying is-
landers. Taken from his own
mouth, in his passage to England, from off Cape Horn, in
America, in the ship Hector. By
R. S., a passenger in the Hector.
Boston, 1832. 186 p. MHi.
14101
[Panizzi, Anthony] 1797-1879.
Stories from Italian writers,
with a literal interlinear translation, on Locke's plan of classical
instruction...1st Amer. from the
last London ed. ...Philadelphia,

Carey & Lea, 1832. 169 p. CtMW;
MH; PPL; ViU; WGr.   14102

Parent's assistant for the Sabbath
evening instruction of his children... Schenectady, Magoffin,
1832. PPPrHi.   14103

Parker, Joel.
Lectures on Universalism, by
Joel Parker. 2d ed. New York, J.
Leavitt, 1832. 148 p. CtSoP;
GDecCT; IaMp; NPV; TWcW.
14104
Parker, John R.
The United States telegraph vocabulary; being an appendix to El-
ford's marine telegraph signal
book...By John R. Parker. Boston, Pr. by W. L. Lewis, from
the Steam Power Press Office,
1832. 132 p. ICJ; MBAt; MHi;
MdAN; MSaP.   14105

Parker, Richard Green, 1798-
1869.
Progressive exercise in English composition. By R. G. Parker...(1st ed.) Boston, Lincoln &
Edmands, 1832. (5)-107, (1) p.
DLC; MH; PP; PPL; PHi. 14106

---- ---- 2d ed. Boston, Lincoln
& Edmands; Cincinnati, Hubbard
& Edmonds, 1832. [5]-108 p. MB;
MH; NN; ViU.   14107

Parker, Zechariah.
A sketch of the arbitrary proceedings of the Baptist church, in
Ludlow, Vt. relative to the ex-
communication of Zechariah Parker, Jun. To which is added, brief
remarks on baptism and close
communion. Keene, N.H., Pr.
for the author, 1832. 16 p. MH.
14108
Parker's Miniature Almanac for
1833. Boston, Mass., Pr. by
Jonathan How, for Amos B. Parker, [1832] MWA.   14109

Parkes, Frances [Byerley]

Domestic duties; or, Instructions to young married ladies, on the management of their households, and the regulations of their conduct in the various relations and duties of married life. 3d Amer. from 3d London ed. , with notes and alterations adapted to the American reader. New York, J. & J. Harper, 1832. 408 p. MFmT; MPiB; MWinchrHi. 14110

Parkhurst, John Luke, 1789-1850.
Elements of moral philosophy. By John L. Parkhurst. 2d ed. , rev. and imp. Boston, Perkins and Marvin, 1832. 213 p. CtMW; InCW; MBC; PLT; ScCoT. 14111

---- Latin Lessons for Children on the inductive method of instruction. Boston, W. Hyde, 1832. 36 p. DLC; BrMus. 14112

Parkinson, William, 1774-1848.
The funeral sermon of Elder Elkanah Holmes, preached in the meeting house of the First Baptist Church, in the city of New York, Lord's Day, Feb. 26, 1832. New York, G. F. Bunce, 1832. 42 p. MNtcA; NHC-S; OCIWHi. 14113

Parrish, Isaac.
Remarks on spinal imitation as connected with nervous diseases, with cases. Extracted from the American Journal of the Medical Science, for Aug. 1832. Philadelphia, 1832. 24 p. CSt-L; MBM; NNNAM; PHi; PaHosp. 14114

The Parthenon and Academian's Magazine. Pub. by undergraduates of Union College. v. 1-2; Nov. 1832-July 1834. Schenectady, N. Y. , Pr. by S. S. Riggs, 1832-1834. 2 V. Ct; DLC; NjR; NSchHi; OO; PPPrHi. 14115

Pattison, Granville Sharp,

1791-1851.
A discourse delivered on commencing the lectures in Jefferson Medical College. . . By Granville Sharp Pattison, M. D. . . . Philadelphia, French & Perkins, 1832. 39 p. CtHWatk; DLC; MB; NNNAM; OO; PAMPH; PPM. 14116

---- Introductory Lectures in Jefferson Medical College, 1832. Philadelphia, 1832. 39 p. Jeff MedC; PHi; PU. 14117

---- Letter on cholera, from Professor Pattison, to Dr. Carmichael, of Virginia. Originally published in the Washington Telegraph. Philadelphia, Wm. F. Geddes, 1832. 16 p. NNNAM; P; ViU. 14118

Patton, William.
A review of the constitution and discipline of the Methodist Protestant Church: by C. Also a review of "an address delivered at the laying of the corner stone, of the Methodist Protestant Church of Abingdon, Va. by Lewis F. Cosby. " By the Rev. Wm. Patton. . . Jonesborough, Tenn. , Pr. by J. Howard, 1832. 85 p. MoS. 14119

Paulding, James Kirke, 1778-1860.
Westward Ho! a tale. By James Kirke Paulding. . . New York, J. & J. Harper, 1832. 2 vols. DLC; MB; NjP; PPA; RPB; WaU. 14120

Paulison, Christian Zabriskie, 1805-1851.
An address to the friends of true Godliness, yet in connection with the true Reformed Dutch Church. . . By Christian Z. Paulison. . . New York, Anderson & Smith, 1832. 61 p. NjMo; NjNbs. 14121

---- Difficulties between the classis of Hackensack and. . . New

York, 1832. PPL.   14122

No entry.   14123

Pawtucket Anti Slavery Society.
   Constitution, etc. of Pawtucket Anti-Slavery Society
[1832]   4 p.   14124

Pawtucket Congregational
Church.
   Confession and covenant of the
Congregational Church, Paw-
tucket... Boston, Pr. by Perkins
and Marvin, 1832. 23 p. M.
                                14125

Paxton, James, 1786-1860.
   An introduction to the study of
human anatomy. By James Paxton... 1st Amer. ed., with additions, by Winslow Lewis, Jr. ...
Boston, Carter & Hendee, 1832-
1834. 2 v. GEU-M; KyLxT;
MeB; OrUM; PPiU.   14126

Paxton, Mass. Congregational
Church.
   Articles of faith, and form of
covenant, adopted by the Congregational Church in Paxton, Oct.
11, 1832. Moses Winch, pastor.
Worcester, Pr. by S. H. Colton
& Co., at the Spy Office, 1832.
8 p. MPax; MWA.   14127

Payne, John Howard, 1792-1852.
   Clari; or, The maid of Milan:
a drama, in three acts... and a
memoir of W. H. (Sedley) Smith.
24 p. New York, London, Samuel
French [1832] OCl.   14128

Payson, Edward, 1783-1827.
   Sermons for Christian Family,
on the most important relative
duties. By the late Rev. Edward
Payson, D.D... Boston, Crocker
& Brewster; New York, Jonathan
Leavitt, 1832. 284 p. CtMW;
GAU; MH; Nh-Hi; RPB.   14129

Peabody, Elizabeth Palmer.
   First steps to the study of
history. Being part first of a
key to history. By Elizabeth P.
Peabody. Boston, Hilliard, Gray
& Co., 1832. 89 p. MHi;
MNBedf; MS; NIC; TNP.   14130

Peabody, William Bourne Oliver,
1799-1847.
   The Loss of Children. A sermon (on 2 Kings i v. 26) delivered Jan. 22, 1832. [Springfield,
Mass., Samuel Bowles, 1832]
8 p. CSmH; DLC.   14131

Peak, John, 1761-1842.
   Memoir of Elder John Peak,
written by himself... Boston, Pr.
by J. Howe, 1832. 203 p. CtSoP;
ICN; MnHi; NjP; OCHP.   14132

---- ---- 2d ed. Rev. and enl.
Boston, Pr. by J. Horne, 1832.
253 p. MHi; Nh-Hi; OO; RPB;
WHi.   14133

---- Sermon on sanctification to
which is added a memoir of Mrs.
Gale and a memoir of Mrs. Es-
ther Peak... Boston, Pr. by J.
Howe, 1832. 89 p. MB; MH-AH;
MiD-B.   14134

Pearce, Dutee Jerauld, 1779-1849.
   Speech... delivered in the
House of Representatives, on the
5th, 6th, and 7th days of April,
on the resolution of the Judiciary
committee, relative to the collector of Wiscasset. Washington, Pr.
by Jonathan Elliot, 1832. 34 p.
MBAt; MH; RHi-RP; RPB; RNHi.
                                14135

The Pearl; or Affections gift; a
Christmas and New Years present. Philadelphia, Thos. T. Ash,
1832. 223 p. CtHWatk; ICU; MA;
PP; TxElp.   14136

Pearson, Abel.
   An analysis of the principles
of the divine government, in a
series of conversations... between
A. P. and N. P. and a dissertation

on the prophecies in reference to the rise and fall of the beast... together with a calculation showing the exact time of the death of Christ... Athens, Tenn., Thos. A. Anderson, 1832-'33. 419 p. CSmH; ICP; MoS; ScCpW; TxU. 14137

Pearson, John, 1758-1826.
Principles of surgery. Boston, Stimpson & Clap, 1832. 263 p. DLC; ICJ; MWA; PLFM; WU. 14138

Peck, John Mason.
The design and influence of Sunday schools promotive of the best interests of our country. Addressed to the people of Illinois, by one of their fellow citizens. [Rock Spring? Ill.] 1832. 16 p. 14139

Peculiarities of the Shakers... See under [Silliman, Benjamin] 1779-1864.

Peep amongst the workmen for children. Watertown, N.Y., Pr. by Benjamin Cory, 1832. 16 p. DLC. 14140

[Peirce, Isaac]
The Narraganset Chief; or, The Adventures of a Wanderer. Written by Himself... (anon.) New York, J. K. Porter, 1832. 195 p. CtY; DLC; IUC; MB; OC; RPB. 14141

Pell, Alfred & brothers.
A specimen of their printing types, from their type & stereotype foundry... New York, Van Norden, 1832. PPAmP. 14142

Pendleton, Edmund Henry, 1788-1862.
The crisis. (Letters) To the Honourable Josiah S. Johnston, U.S. Senator, n.p. 1832. 35 p. DLC; MB; NjR; PPL; Vi. 14143

---- Speech on presenting a petition from Duchess County, New York, relative to the missionaries,

Worcester & Butlet, imprisoned under a judgment of a state court in Ga. Washington, J. Elliot, 1832. 19 p. MB; NN; NNC; PPAmP; PPi. 14144

Pennsylvania.
An act for establishing a health office, and to secure the city and Port of Philadelphia from the introduction of pestilential and contagious diseases; and for other purposes. Passed January 29, 1818, with its supplements passed from 1821 to 1832. Philadelphia, L. R. Bailey, 1832. 56+ p. DNLM; WU-M. 14145

---- An act incorporating the Schuylkill Valley Navigation Company passed the 20th of March 1827 together with the supplements. Pottsville, Benjamin, 1832. 16 p.? MWA. 14146

---- An act to enable the mayor, aldermen, and citizens of Philadelphia to carry into effect certain improvements, and execute certain trusts. Philadelphia, J. Bioren, 1832. 7 p. PPAmP. 14147

---- An act to incorporate the Pennsylvania Coke & Iron Co. Harrisburg, Clark and Raser, 1832. 8 p. PHC. 14148

---- Census of the Eastern and Western Districts of Pennsylvania, 1830. Pr. by order of the House of Representatives. Harrisburg, Pr. by Henry Welsh, 1832. 18 p. MiD-B; NIC-A; PHi. 14149

---- Committee of vice and immorality. Report of the committee of vice and to whomever referred the message of the governor and sundry memorials relating to the abolition of lotteries. Read in the Senate, February 21, 1832, Mr. Fullerton, Chairman. Philadelphia, 1832. 15 p. NcD. 14150

254 Pennsylvania

---- Communication from the auditor general to the Pennsylvania Legislature accompanied with a statement of certain banks, read in the House of Representatives, January 10, 1832. Harrisburg, Henry Welsh, 1832. 32 p. MB; NNC; P; PPL. 14151

---- Counter report of the minority of the committee to whom was referred the memorials... praying that the same rates of toll may be charged on the Delaware division of the Pennsylvania canal as are charged by the Lehigh Coal & Navigation Co. for the use of the Lehigh canal... read Feb. 25, 1832. Harrisburg, H. Welsh, 1832. 12 p. MH-BA; PHi; PPAmP. 14152

---- A digest of the acts of assembly, and the ordinances of the commissioners and inhabitants of the Kensington district of the Northern Liberties... Philadelphia, Joseph Rakestraw, 1832. 3 v. PPL; PU. 14153

---- In the Supreme Court for the Eastern District of Pennsylvania, in equity. Charles J. Wolbest vs. The City of Philadelphia. Bill and Exhibits. Philadelphia, Pr. by Crissy & Markley [1832?] 12 p. PPB. 14154

---- Laws of the General Assembly of the State of Pennsylvania, passed at the session 1831-32, in the fifty-sixth year of independence. Pub. by authority. Harrisburg, Pr. by Henry Welsh, 1832. 649 p. PL; Nv; T; TxU-L; Wa-L. 14155

---- Pennsylvania bank reports. 1832. n.p., n.p., 1832? 451-508 p. NjR. 14156

---- Report of the Board of Inspectors of Eastern Pennsylvania to the Legislature. Read in Senate, January 20, 1832. Harrisburg (Pa.), Henry Welsh, 1832. 12 p. CU; IaHi. 14157

---- Report of the Canal Commissioners relative to amount paid for repairs upon the Pennsylvania Canal and Rail Road. ...Harrisburg, 1832. 8 p. 14158

---- Report of the committee of the House of Representatives, to whom were referred the message of the Governor and sundry memorials relating to the abolition of lotteries. Philadelphia, 1832. 32 p. MBC. 14159

---- Report of the Committee of Vice & Immorality of the Senate ...to whom were referred the message of the Governor & sundry memorials relating to the abolition of lotteries, read in the Senate, Feb. 21, 1832. Harrisburg, Welsh, 1832. 15 p. PHi; PPAmP; PPL; PPL-R; TxHuT. 14160

---- Report of the Committee on Education to the House... Harrisburg, 1832. 6 p. Sabin. 14161

---- Report of the committee on lotteries. Philadelphia, Pr. by S. C. Atkinson, 1832. 32 p. IaHi; MnU; PPL. 14162

---- Report of the committee on the militia system. Harrisburg, 1832. PHi. 14163

---- Report of the committee to whom were referred the message of the Governor & sundry memorials relating to the abolition of lotteries; read Feb. 10, 1832. Harrisburg, Welsh, 1832. 37 p. MH-BA; PHi; PPAmP; PU. 14164

---- Report of the State Treasurer on the Finances...December 7, 1832. Harrisburg, 1832. 22 p. 14165

---- Report of the State Treasurer shewing the receipts and expenditures at the Treasury of Pennsylvania... Harrisburg, 1832-37. 4 v. PPA.   14166

---- Report relative to the superintendents, engineers, and c. in the employment of the state upon the Pennsylvania canal and railroad, read in the House of Representatives, Mar. 9, 1832. Harrisburg, Welsh, 1832. 16 p. PHi; PPAmP; PU.   14167

---- Reports of cases adjudged in the Supreme Court of Pennsylvania. By Charles B. Penrose, and Frederick Watts, Counsellors at law. Volume II. Carlisle, Pr. by Geo. Fleming, 1832. 586 p. Ia; Ms; NNU; P; PPL.   14168

---- Reports of committees (in German) on cholera, banks, agriculture, &c. Harrisburg, 1832. PPL-R.   14169

---- Resolutions of the House of Nullifications. Harrisburg, 1832. PPL.   14170

---- Resolutions relative to protective duties, and the Bank of the United States, which unanimously passed both houses of the Legislature of Pennsylvania. Pr. by order of the House of Representatives. Harrisburg, Pr. by Henry Welsh, 1832. 4 p. P.   14171

---- Rules for the government of the House of Representatives of Pennsylvania; with Constitution of the United States and of Pennsylvania. Harrisburg, 1832. 72 p. PHi.   14172

---- Second report of the commissioners appointed to revise the code of Pennsylvania. Read in the House of Representatives, March 7, 1832. Harrisburg (Pa.),

Pr. by Henry Welsh, 1832. 62 p. IaU-L; MiD-B.   14173

---- Second Report of the Commissioners appointed to revise the Civil Code of Pennsylvania. Read in the Senate March 7, 1832. Harrisburg, Pr. by Henry Welsh, 1832. In-SC.   14174

Pennsylvania Almanac for 1833. Calculated by John Ward. Philadelphia, Pa., M'Carty & Davis [1832] CtY; MWA; PHi.   14175

Pennsylvania and Ohio Railroad.
   Report of the engineer appointed to examine the route of the Pennsylvania and Ohio Railroad. 1832? 6 p. OCIW.   14176

Pennsylvania Company for Insurances on Lives & Granting Annuities.
   [Philadelphia, 1832] 3 p. PHi.   14177
Pennsylvania Historical Society.
   Constitution, by-laws, etc. Philadelphia, 1832. 7 p. PPAmP.   14178
Pennsylvania Hospital.
   Contributor's certificate in the name of Wm. E. Horner, M.D., dated Mar. 16, 1832. PaHosp.   14179
Pennsylvania Prison Society.
   Annual report of the acting committee. 1832- PP; PPAmP; PPL-R; PU.   14180

Pennsylvania Society for Discouraging the Use of Ardent Spirits.
   ...To innkeepers, and the friends of order and economy, in the state of Pennsylvania. Philadelphia, Kite, 1832. PHi; PPPrHi.   14181

Pennsylvania University.
   Catalogue of the officers and students of the University of Pennsylvania. Philadelphia, Skerrett, 1832. 26 p. TNP.   14182

256 Pennsylvanische

---- Laws for the government of
the collegiate dept. revised &
amended to 1832. Philadelphia,
Skerrett, 1832. 8 p. PHi; PP;
PPL; PU.   14183

Pennsylvanische Anti-Freimaurer
Calender. Lancaster, Samuel
Wagner [1832] CtY; DeWint;
MWA; PP; PYHi.   14184

The Penny Magazine of the Society for the diffusion of useful
knowledge.   See Knight's penny
magazine.

Pepper, George.
    Kathleen O'Neil; or, A picture
of feudal times in Ireland, (a national melo-drama of the fourteenth century).   In three acts.
By George Pepper... Philadelphia,
Pr. by T. Town, 1832. 84 p.
CU; MH; RPB.   14185

The Percy anecdotes. A revised
ed. to which is added a valuable
collection of American anecdotes,
original and select. New York,
J. & J. Harper, 1832. 2 v. in 1.
AMob; GDecCT; MB; RPB; ViU.
                           14186
Perkins, William S.
    A discourse preached before
the Legislature of Vermont, on
the Day of General Election, October 11, 1882 (sic). Pub. at the
request of the Legislature. Montpelier, Knapp & Jewett, 1832.
19 p. CtHT; MBC; OCHP; Vt;
VtHi.   14187

Perkins School for the Blind,
Watertown, Mass.
    Perkins institution & Mass.
school for the blind.   Annual report. All dates from 1832-1936.
IU.   14188

Perkiomen Railroad Company.
    An Act to Incorporate the Nor-
ristown Parks and Lehigh Railroad Co. Philadelphia, Jos. Rake-

straw, 1832. PPeSchw.   14189

Perrin, Jean Baptiste, fl. 1786.
    Elements of French & English
conversation... Rev. & cor. by
C. Preudhamme. Philadelphia,
A. Towar, etc., 1832. 216 p.
ICMcHi; MH; OClWHi; PPL;
VtU.   14190

---- Fables amusantes avec une
table generale et particuliere.
Des Mots et de leur signification
en anglais selon L'ordre des
fables, pour entendre la traduc-
tion plus facile à Lecolier. Par
M. Perrin. Edition revue et corrigée par un maître de langue
Française. Philadelphia, Alexander Towar, 1832. 180 p. DCU;
GHi;   IaDuMtC; MH; MdBP;
OCX.   14191

---- A grammar of the French
tongue; grounded upon the deci-
sions of the French Academy...
By John Perrin. ...New-York,
Samuel Wood & Sons, 1832. 334 p.
CtY; DLC; MB; NjR; OO. 14192

---- A selection of one hundred
of Perrin's fables, accompanied
with a key... By A. Bolmar...
Philadelphia, Carey & Lea, 1832.
22, 61, 181 p. DLC; ICP; NjR;
PPA; RNR.   14193

Perry, Marshall Sears, d. 1859.
    First book of the fine and use-
ful arts, for the use of schools
and lyceums... Boston, Carter &
Hendee, 1832. 126 p. CtHWatk;
MB; MHi; PPAmP; PU; TxU-T.
                           14194
Perry, William.
    ...The orthoepical guide to the
English tongue, being Perry's
spelling-book rev. and corr., with
Walker's pronunciation precisely
applied on a new scheme. Containing also, moral lessons,
fables, and much useful matter
for the instruction of youth. By

Israel Alger... Boston, Richardson, Lord & Holbrook, 1832. 168 p. MB.   14195

Persy, N.
Elementary treatise on the forms of cannon & various systems of artillery, translated for the use of the cadets of the U.S. Military academy from the French Military academy. West Point, 1832. 60 p. DN; ICJ; NN; OCl; PPAmP.   14196

[Pettis, Samuel]
Boston and its environs; as they appear from the cupola of the State house; a poem. ...Boston, L. C. Bowles, 1832. 47 p. DLC; MBNEH; MWA; RPB.   14197

Phelps, A. R.
To the public. At the town meeting held in Shrewsbury... in November, 1831, I was arrested on a writ, A. Eaton of Boston, against myself, etc. (On a question of debt.) [Shrewsbury, Mass.] 1832. 7 p. BrMus.   14198

Phelps, Almira (Hart) Lincoln, 1793-1884.
Familiar lectures on botany, including practical and elementary botany, with generic and specific descriptions of the most common native and foreign plants and a vocabulary of botanical terms, for the use of higher schools and academies; by Mrs. Almira H. Lincoln, vice-principal of Troy Female Seminary. 3d ed. Hartford, F. J. Huntington [Pr. at the secretary office by P. Canfield] 1832. 440 p. A-GS; KyDC; LU; MsU; RPB.
                                 14199
Phelps, Dudley, 1798-1849.
The making of a new heart a reasonable duty; a discourse delivered in the First parish meeting house...Dec. 11, 1831. Haverhill, Pr. at the Iris office, 1832. 39 p. CBPSR; MBC; MIIa; MHi. 14200

Phelps, Humphrey.
Map of the City of New York, with the latest improvements. New York, 1832. 1 p. IU; MB; NBU; NBuG; PHi.   14201

Phi Beta Kappa. Alpha of N. Y.
Catalogue of the fraternity of the New York Alpha of the BK. Schenectady, Riggs, 1832. PPPrHi.   14202

---- New Haven Alpha. Yale University.
Catalogues of the Connecticut Alpha of the Phi Beta Kappa... 1832. New Haven, 1832. 35 p. Ct; NBLiHi.   14203

Philadelphia (City).
Accounts of Receipts and Payments at the City Treasury: Jan. 15, 1830-Jan. 1, 1832. Philadelphia [1832] 30 p. PHi.   14204

---- Accounts of the Receipts and Payments of the Mayor and Aldermen in trust for the Girard Fund. Philadelphia, 1832. PHi. 14205

---- An act for establishing a Health Office... Philadelphia, 1832. PPL.   14206

---- Address of the Mayor to the high constables... Philadelphia, 1832. PPL-R.   14207

---- Agreements of June 3, 1819, July 20, 1820, & Jun 14, 1824 between the mayor, aldermen & citizens of Philadelphia; and the Schuylkill Navigation Company, relative to the water power, &c. at Fair Mount. Philadelphia, L. R. Bailey, 1832. 31 p. ICJ; MWA.
                                 14208
---- Correspondence submitted to councils by the chairman of the Watering Committee, at their meeting on December 13, 1832. n. t. -p. [Philadelphia, 1832] 3 p. NN.
                                 14209

---- Market ordinances... en-
acted January, A.D., 1832.
Philadelphia, 1832. 16 p.
PPAmP.　　　　　　　14210

---- On cholera. [Philadelphia,
1832] 12 p. DLC; NN; ScU.
　　　　　　　　　　14211
---- Report of the Commission
appointed by the Sanitary Board
of the City Councils, to visit
Canada for the investigation of
the epidemic cholera, prevailing
in Montreal and Quebec. Philadelphia, Pr. by Mifflin & Parry,
1832. 37 p. CtY; ICJ; MiD-B;
MnU-B; NN.　　　　　14212

---- Report of the committee of
the select and common councils of
Philadelphia, on the navigation of
the river Schuylkill. [Philadelphia]
L. R. Bailey, 1832. 28 p. MWA;
MiU-C; N; NN; PPFrankI. 14213

---- Report of the Watering committee, to the select and common
councils. Read January 12, 1832.
Pub. by order of the councils.
Philadelphia, Pr. by Lydia R.
Bailey, 1832. 44 p. PPL-R; THi.
　　　　　　　　　　14214
---- Rules, for the government of
the Select and Common councils of
the city of Philadelphia; and also
for regulating the intercourse and
business between them. To which
is appended a Schedule of the real
estate owned by the city corporation. Nov. 22, 1832. Philadelphia,
Pr. by Lydia R. Bailey, 1832.
24 p. CSmH; MiD-B; PHi; PPL.
　　　　　　　　　　14215
---- Schedule of the Real Estate
owned by the Corporation of...
Philadelphia, Nov. 22, 1832.
Philadelphia, 1832. PPL. 14216

---- Schuylkill river crossing at
Market Street commemorating the
construction of the bridge & sub-
way tunnel Nov. 18, 1832.
PPFHi.　　　　　　　14217

---- Statement of devises, bequests, & grants, to the corporation of the city of Philadelphia
in trust. Including Girard's will.
Pub. by order of Councils. Philadelphia, Pr. by Lydia R. Bailey,
1832. 34 p. CtY; ICU; LNH; MB;
PHi.　　　　　　　　14218

---- Christ Church.
　Charter of Christ Church, in
the City of Philadelphia, and St.
Peter's Church... Philadelphia,
as established by an act of the
Legislature...1832...Philadelphia,
C. Alexander, 1832. 26 p. MiU-
C; NNG; PPAmP; PU.　　14219

---- Citizens of Colour.
　The memorial of the subscribers, free people of colour, residing in the county of Philadelphia. [Philadelphia? 1832?] 12 p.
NIC.　　　　　　　　14220

---- ---- Memorial to the honourable the Senate and House of
Representatives of the Commonwealth of Pennsylvania: the memorial of the people of Colour of the
city of Philadelphia and its vicinity, respectfully sheweth: That
they have learned with deep re-
gret that two resolutions have
passed the House of Representatives of this Commonwealth, directing the committee on the judiciary to inquire... [Philadelphia,
1832] 8 p. NHi; PHi.　　14221

---- Eleventh Presbyterian Church.
　Charter and by-laws... Philadelphia, Martin, 1832. PPPrHi.
　　　　　　　　　　14222
---- First Presbyterian Church.
　Constitution and articles of incorporation... in Penn Township.
Philadelphia, 1832. 6 p. PPPrHi.
　　　　　　　　　　14223
---- St. Peters Church.
　Rules, statutes, and ordinances
of St. Peter's Church, in the city
of Philadelphia; enacted on the

second day of July...1832. Phil-
adelphia, Pr. at the office of the
Daily Chronicle, 1832. 14 p.
NBuDD; NjR; PHi; PU.   14224

---- Second Presbyterian
Church.
Report of a special committee of the Second Presbyterian
Church of Philadelphia exhibiting
a general view of the financial
concerns of the church, its congregational school, the burial
ground; the asylum, etc. Adopted
by the Board, Apr. 12, 1832.
Philadelphia, Allen, 1832.
PPPrHi.   14225

---- ---- Rules, etc. adopted by
the association of Elders of the
Second Presbytery of Philadelphia.
Philadelphia, 1832. 14 p. PHi;
PPPrHi.   14226

---- Tenth Presbyterian Church.
Class book of the Sabbath
School. Philadelphia, 1832.
PPPrHi.   14227

Philadelphia and Trenton Railroad
Company.
An act...to incorporate the
Philadelphia & Trenton Railroad
Co. [Harrisburg, 1832] 1 p.
DLC; NN.   14228

Philadelphia Association for Cele-
brating the 4th of July.
Addresses, orations, etc. In-
gersoll, C. J. 1832. PPAmP.
                            14229
Philadelphia Association of
Friends for the Instruction of
Poor Children.
The origin and proceedings...
Philadelphia, J. Rakestraw, 1832.
11 p. PHi.   14230

Philadelphia, Germantown and
Norristown Rail Road Company.
An act supplementary to an
act entitled an act to incorporate
the Philadelphia, Germantown and

Norristown Rail Road Company.
Philadelphia, 1832. 4 p. NN.
                            14231
Philadelphia liberalist, a weekly.
V.1- June 9, 1832- Philadelphia
[Pr. by J. Richards] 1832- DLC;
MnU; PHi; PPC; WHi.   14232

Philadelphia Lying-in Charity
Hospital.
Address of the Philadelphia
Lying-in Charity, to the humane
and liberal minded of their fel-
low citizens. [1832] 16 p.
PPM.   14233

---- Constitution and charter.
Philadelphia Lying-In Charity.
Philadelphia, 1832. 20 p. PHi.
                            14234
Philadelphia Medical Society.
Report of the committee of the
Medical Society of Philadelphia,
on epidemic cholera... Philadel-
phia, Pr. by Lydia R. Bailey,
1832. 17 p. DLC; IEN-M;
NNNAM; OCHP; PPM.   14235

Philadelphia Morals and Manners:
1832. The Young Man's Own
Book. Philadelphia, 1832. 307 p.
PHi.   14236

Philadelphia Synod, 1832.
Acta synodi Diocesanae Phila-
delphiensis primae habitae...
Philadelphiae, Eugenius Cummiskey edidit, Ex typis F. Pierson,
1832. 14 p. MBtS; MdW; PPiD;
PPPrHi.   14237

---- Constituiones in synodo dioe-
cesana Philadelphienis prima la-
tae ot promulgatae, die 15a Maji,
1832. [Philadelphia? 1832?] [3]-
6 p. MBtS.   14238

Philadelphia Western Bank.
Act of incorporation; with oth-
er acts of assembly, and by-laws.
Philadelphia, 1832. 33 p. PHi.
                            14239
Philanthropos See Ladd, Wil-

liam, 1778-1841.

Philips, Charles.
   The speeches of the celebrated
Irish orators, Phillips, Curran
and Grattan, to which is added
the powerful appeal of Robert Emmett, at the close of his trial
for high treason. By Charles
Philips. Philadelphia, Key,
Mielke & Biddle, 1832. 370 p.
KyLoS; MNBedf; MB; MNF.
                              14240
Phillips, Richard, 1767-1840.
   An easy grammar of natural
and experimental philosophy, for
the use of schools. By David
Blair [pseud.] 2d ed., rev. and
enl. by Benjamin Hallowell. Philadelphia, Kimber & Sharpless,
1832. 249 p. IaDuMtC; NN; P.
                              14241
---- A geographical view of the
world embracing the manners,
customs and pursuits of every
nation, founded on the best authorities; by Rev. J. Goldsmith,
author of Grammar of geography,
Grammar of British geography,
etc. 2d Amer. ed., rev., cor.,
and imp. by James G. Percival.
Illustrated by eight copperplate
views. Hartford, D. F. Robinson
& Co., 1832. 406, 46 p. ICBB;
IObB.   14242

[Phillips, Stephen Clarenden]
1801-1857.
   Practical Infidelity briefly considered in reference to the present times. 2d ed. Pr. for the
American Unitarian Association.
Boston, Gray & Bowen, 1832.
20 p. CBPac; ICMe; MB-FA;
MB-HP; MMeT-Hi.   14243

Phillips Exeter Academy.
   A catalogue of the officers and
students of Phillips Exeter Academy, July, 1832. Exeter, News-
Letter Office, L. F. Shepard, pr.,
1832. (5), 12 p. MBC; MHaHi.
                              14244

Philo, Pseud.
   Ministry at large for the poor
of cities. See Tuckerman,
Joseph.

Philo Biblicus, pseud.
   A candid examination of the
principal passages of Scripture,
which are supposed to have a
bearing upon the question when
does the Sabbath begin?... Hartford, H. Benton, 1832. 18 p.
NN.   14245

Philo-Paidos [pseud.]
   Common incidents recommend-
ed by the book committee of the
Maine Sabbath School Union.
Portland, G. Hyde, 1832. 108 p.
NNC; RPB.   14246

---- My teachers. By Philo Pai-
dos, author of "Common incidents." [pseud. on] Boston,
Massachusetts Sabbath School Society, 1832. 53 p. DLC.   14247

The Philological museum, v. 1-2.
Cambridge, Pr. by J. Smith for
Deightons, 1832-1833. 2 vols.
ICU; LNH; MH; OU; RPA. 14248

Philom, Ammah, pseud. See
Ammah Philom, pseud.

Phinneys' Calendar or, Western
Almanac, for the year of our
Lord, 1832. Calculated for the
meridian of Otsego. By Edwin E.
Prentiss. Containing as usual, a
great variety of interesting mat-
ter. Cooperstown, Pr. by H. &
E. Phinney and Co., Utica, J. C.
Smith & Co., Little Falls, L.
Todd, Hartwick-Levi Bladeslee;
New Berlin, and George Hunt,
Oxford [1832] NCH; NHtHi. 14249

Phoenix Fire Society, Exeter
(N. H.)
   Constitution. Exeter, Exeter
News-letter office, 1832. 8 p.
NN; Nh-Hi.   14250

Pickering, David, 1788-1859.
Golden calf; a sermon delivered in Providence. Boston, Edwin M. Stone, 1832. 8 p. RPB. 14251

---- Psalms and hymns, for social and private worship, carefully selected from the best authors. 2d ed. Providence, Marshall & Brown, 1832. 405 p. DLC; RPB. 14252

Pickering, John, 1777-1846.
A Greek and English lexicon; adapted to the authors read in the colleges and schools of the United States...3d ed. Boston, Hilliard, Gray, Little, and Wilkins, 1832. GEU-M. 14253

Picket, Albert, 1771-1850.
The juvenile instructor, an American school book being a natural grammar and reader... New York, R. Bartlett & S. Raynor, 1832. 214 p. ICBB. 14254

---- The juvenile mentor, or select readings; being American school class-book no. 3... Last revised ed. Cincinnati, John W. Picket, 1832. 254, 31 p. CaBVaU; OCIWHi. 14255

---- ---- New York, R. Bartlett & S. Raynor, 1832. 247 p. OCIWHi. 14256

The picture primer; intended as a first book for children, and as an introduction to the Picture reading book. By a friend to youth. New Haven, S. Babcock, 1832. 36 p. CtY. 14257

The Pictured A, B, C. book. Wendell, Mass., J. Metcalf, 1832. DLC; MH. 14258

Pictures of animals. Wendell, Mass., J. Metcalf, 1832. CtY; ICU. 14259

Pictures of the Country. Philadelphia, 1832. DLC. 14260

Pierpont, John, 1785-1866.
The American first class book; or, Exercises in reading and recitation. Selected principally from modern authors of Great Britain and America, and designed for the use of the highest class in publick and private schools. Boston, Carter, Hendee, 1832. 480 p. IU; KAS; MB; NN; WU. 14261

---- ---- Boston, Hilliard, Gray, Little and Wilkins & Richardson, Lord & Holbrook, 1832. 480 p. IaHi; MH; PU; OMC; ViU. 14262

---- Introduction to the national reader; a selection of easy lessons. Designed to fill the same place in the common schools of the United States that is held by Murray's Introduction, and the compilations of Guy, Mylius, and Pinnock, in those of Great Britain. Boston, Carter, Hendee & Co., 1832. 168 p. MH; MWeyHi; NN; VtMidbC. 14263

---- The national reader; a selection of exercises in reading and speaking. Boston, Richardson, Lord & Holbrook, etc., 1832. 276 p. ArU; CtMW; MH; OC; VtNofN. 14264

---- On Substitutes for Religion. By John Pierpont. Boston, Gray & Bowen, 1832. 23 p. ICMe; MH; MPeHi; MeB; RP. 14265

---- ---- 2d ed. 1st series. No. 56. Boston, Gray & Bowen, 1832. ICMe; MB-Fa; MHi; MMeT-Hi; MeBat. 14266

---- On the moral influences of physical science...delivered before the American Institute of Instruction. Boston, 1832. MDeeP. 14267

---- The young reader; to go
with the spelling book. Boston,
Carter, Hendee, 1832. 162 p.
CU-S; CtY; InGrD; MH.   14268

Pike, John Gregory, 1784-1854.
   A guide for young disciples of
the Holy Saviour, in their way to
immortality: forming a sequel to
persuasives to early piety. By J.
G. Pike. 1st Amer. from 3d London ed. New York, J. Leavitt;
Boston, Crocker & Brewster,
1832. 383 p. MH-AH; NAnge;
OMC; PCA; VtMidSM.   14269

Pike, Nicholas, 1743-1819.
   Pike's system of arithmetick,
abridged & a short system of
bookkeeping by Dudley Leavitt.
Pittsburgh, R. Patterson, 1832.
228 p. ICU; PPine.   14270

Pinckney, Henry Laurens, 1794-
1863.
   An oration delivered at the Cathedral of St. Finbar before the
St. Patrick Benevolent Society,
and the Irish volunteers on the
17th March, 1832. Charleston,
1832. 38 p. NIC-L; PPAmP;
ScC.   14271

The pious minstrel, a collection
of sacred poetry, J. T. compiler.
From London ed. Boston, William
Hyde & Co.; New York, J. P.
Haven, 1832. 15, 304 p. CtHC;
DLC; IEN; NNG; PPL.   14272

---- Philadelphia, Towar & Hogan, 1832. 390 p. IEG; MBC;
NjR; PPL; RPB.   14273

The pious remembrancer... Philadelphia, Nathan Kite, 1832. 96 p.
CtSoP; PHC.   14274

Pirsson, Joseph P.
   The discarded daughter; a com-
edy in five acts. New York, W.
Stodart, 1832. 64 p. MH; NN;
NNC; RPB.   14275

Pirtle, Henry, 1798-1880.
   A digest of the decisions of the
Court of Appeals of Kentucky. By
Henry Pirtle. Pub. under the
patronage of the Legislature.
Louisville, Pr. by S. Penn, Jr.,
1832. 2 v. In-SC; KyU; MH-L;
NcD; TMeB.   14276

Pise, Charles Constantine, 1802-
1866.
   Discourse delivered in St.
Mary's Church, Philadelphia,
May 6th, 1832. Philadelphia, Pr.
by Mifflin & Parry, 1832. 18 p.
ICMe; MWo; PHi; PPAmP;
MBrigStJ.   14277

---- Oration in honour of the late
Charles Carroll of Carrollton, de-
livered before the Philodemic So-
ciety of Georgetown College...
Georgetown, D. C., Pr. by Joshua
N. Rind, 1832. 24 p. MdHi; NIC-
L; PPL; ScU; WHi.   14278

Pitman, John, 1785-1864.
   An oration, delivered on the
centennial anniversary of the birth
of Washington. Feb. 22, 1832. By
John Pitman. Providence, Pr. by
Weeden & Knowles, 1832. 36 p.
CtHC; ICN; MH-AH; Nh-Hi; RPB.
                                  14279
Pittsburgh. Citizens.
   Address of a committee ap-
pointed by the citizens of Pitts-
burgh, July 20, 1831, on the sub-
ject of a railroad, from the west-
ern termination of the Pennsyl-
vania canal to the Ohio canal.
Pittsburgh, Pr. by Johnston &
Stockton, 1832. 24 p. CtY; DLC;
NNE; PPi; ScU.   14280

---- University.
   Catalogue of the officers and
students of the Western Univer-
sity of Pennsylvania. Pittsburgh,
J. B. Butler, 1832. 12 p. PPL.
                                  14281
---- Western Collegiate Institute.
   The Western Collegiate Insti-

tute. for young ladies. July 4, 1832. n. p. 1832. 3 p. OCIWHi. 14282

A Plain Guide to Baptism; being a short treatise upon the subjects and mode. By a servant of Jesus Christ. Boston, Press of Peirce & Parker, 1832. 28 p. ICU; LNB; MBC; MBrZ; MWA; RPB. 14283

A plain statement of the misrepresentations concerning the Rev. L. Skidmore. "Eli Ball, editor Ball & Sands publishers" Richmond, Pr. by Samuel Shepherd & Co., 1832. 20 p. TxDaM. 14284

Plan of Philadelphia, or, The stranger's guide to the public building, places of amusement, streets, alleys, roads, avenues, courts wharves, principal hotels, steamboat landings, stage offices etc. of Philadelphia and adjoining districts. Philadelphia, E. L. Carey & A. Hart, 1832. 54 p. GMW; MH; PHi; PPL. 14285

Planter's Almanac for 1833. Mobile, Odiorne and Smith [1832] NcD. 14286

Planter's Bank of Mississippi.
The charter and amendments thereto... Natchez, Pr. by Wm. Du Val, 1832. 67 p. MH-BA; NNS. 14287

Playfair, John.
Elements of Geometry: Containing the first six books of Euclid, with a supplement on the Quadration of the circle and the Geometry of solids. By John Playfair, F. R. S. From the last London edition enl. Philadelphia, A. Walker, agent, 1832. (v)-xvi, (17)-333 p. KyU; LU-E; MdBS; OSW; PHi. 14288

Pleas for the Heathen; or, Heathenism Ancient and Modern. Boston, Sabbath School Society Press, 1832. MB; MH-AH; OMC; ViRut. 14289

Pleasants, James A.
Treatise on the functions, disorders and treatment of the teeth, designed for the use of individuals and private families. New York, Elliott, 1832. 48 p. PPCP; PU. 14290

Plummer, Franklin E., d. 1802.
Speech of Franklin E. Plummer, of Mississippi, in defence of the administration, on the report of the Judiciary committee, in the case of the collector of Wiscasset. Delivered in the House of Representatives of the United States, April, 1832. Washington [D. C.] Jonathan Elliot, 1832. 36 p. MdHi; TxU. 14291

Plumptre, Robert.
Hints respecting some of the University officers: its jurisdiction, its revenues, &c. By Robt. Plumptre... Cambridge, Pr. by F. Archdeacon, 1832. 28 p. NjR. 14292

Plutarchus, ca. 50-120.
Plutarch's lives; translated from the original Greek: with notes, critical and historical; and a life of Plutarch, by John Langhorne and William Langhorne. Baltimore, Pub. by Wm. & Jos. Neal, 1832. 748 p. IaWel; NBCP; PLor; TCh; TMeT. 14293

---- ---- New York, W. C. Borradaile, 1832. 432 p. CLSU; GU; KyLoP; MH; MHarw; RLa. 14294

---- ---- Philadelphia, Hickman & Hazzard, 1832. 4 vol. MoKSV. 14295

Poe, Edgar Allan, 1809-1849.
Poems. To which is added a full and impartial memoir of the poet. New York, Hurst & Co. [1832?] 194 p. IaLeo. 14296

The poet Cowper and his brother.

Philadelphia, Tract Association of
Friends, 1832. 12 p. InRchE;
MntcA.   14297

The poetical works of Milton,
Young, Gray, Beattie, and Collins. Complete in one volume.
Philadelphia, J. Grigg, 1832.
530 p. IU; MB; NN; OCX; ViU.
                              14298
The poetical works of Rogers,
Campbell, J. Montgomery, Lamb,
and Kirke White. Complete in one
volume. Philadelphia, J. Grigg,
1832. 496 p. ICU; LNT; MNan;
NjR; OCIW; ScNC.   14299

Poinsett, Joel Roberts.
   Address of the Washington Society to the people of South Carolina. Charleston, n.p. , 1832.
8 p. PHi.   14300

---- Substance of a speech, delivered by the Hon. Joel R.
Poinsett, at a public meeting
held at Seyle's, 5th October,
1832. Pub. by request. Charleston, Pr. by J. S. Burges, 1832.
16 p. A-Ar; MBAt; NN; TxU.
                              14301
A political balance dedicated to
those Citizens who would not sac-
rifice 25 Dollars in 1828 and
1832 to preserve the Union. Philadelphia, 1832. 4 p. MdHi; N.
                              14302
The Political register. Washington, D. Green, 1832. Dec. 24,
1832-May 29, 1835. CU; CtY;
MB; MH; MiU.   14303

Polk, James Knox.
   Speech of Mr. Polk, of Tennessee, delivered in the House of
Representatives, May 9th, 1832,
the case of Gov. Houston being
under consideration, on the power
of the House to punish for a contempt or breach of privilege.
[Washington] Globe office, 1832.
16 p. DLC; In; TxU.   14304

Pollok, Robert.
   The course of time, a poem
in ten books, with a memoir of
the author. 14th ed. New York,
M'Elrath and Bangs, 1832. 32,
240 p. CtHWatk; GEU; IU; LNH;
RPB.   14305

Pomeroy, Samuel Wyllys.
   A memorial, on the subject of
a revision of the patent laws, by
Samuel Wyllys Pomeroy. Gallipolis, O. , Pr. by J. J. Coombs,
at the 'Phoenix' office, 1832. 8 p.
MdHi; OCHP.   14306

Pomey, Francois Antoine, 1618-
1673.
   Tooke's pantheon of the heath-
en gods and illustrious heroes.
Revised for a classical course of
education and adapted for the use
of students of every age and either sex. Illustrated with engravings from new and original designs. Baltimore, Wm. & Joseph
Neal, 1832. 305 p. KyLoHoS.
                              14307
Pomfret, Conn. First Congregational Church.
   The confession of faith & form
of covenant of the First Church
in Pomfret, adopted February 8th,
1832, with a catalogue of the
members... Brooklyn, Conn. ,
People's press off. , 1832. 16 p.
Ct.   14308

Poor Richard's Almanac, for
1833. Cincinnati, O. , Roff &
Young [1832] MWA.   14309

---- Rochester, C. & M. Morse,
[1832] 12 p. MWA.   14310

---- Rochester, Marshall & Dean
[1832] 12 p. MWA; NRU; RHi.
                              14311
Poor Richard's almanack, for the
year of our Lord, 1833... astronomical calculations by the successor of Oliver Loud... Utica,
Geo. Tracy [1832] 24 p. MS; N;

NutHi; WHi.   14312

Poor Robin's almanac for 1833.
By Joshua Sharp. Philadelphia,
Griggs & Dickinson, [1832]
DLC; MWA; PHi.   14313

Poor Will's almanac, for the year
1833...by William Collom. Philadelphia, Joseph M'Dowell [1832]
34 p. CLU; MWA; InU; NjR; P.
                              14314
Poor Will's Pocket almanac.
Philadelphia, Uriah Hunt [1832]
DLC; InU; MWA; MnU; PP.
                              14315
Pope, Alexander, 1688-1744.
   An essay on man; in four
epistles to H. St. John, Lord Bo-
lingbroke. Hartford, Silas Andrus,
1832. 67 p. CtY; InGr   14316

---- ---- Portland, Hyde & Co.,
1832. 72 p. MWA.   14317

Pope, Richard Thomas Pembroke.
   The authentic report of the
controversial discussion between
the Rev. Richard T. P. Pope,
and the Rev. T. Maguire, held at
the lecture room of the Dublin
institution...1827. New York, J.
M'Laughlin, 1832. 332 p. ICU;
MB; MWAH; MdCatS; PRosC.
                              14318
Porter, Anna Maria, 1780-1832.
   The Hungarian brothers...By
Miss Ann Maria Porter...Exeter,
N.H., J. C. Gerrish, 1832-1836.
2 vols. CSfCW; LNT; MPlyA;
NHem; Nh-Hi.   14319

Porter, Ebenezer, 1772-1834.
   Letters on revivals of religion.
Pub. by the revival association in
the Theological Seminary [And-
over, Mass., 1832-1833] 92 p.
MA; MH; MH-AH; MWA; PPPrHi.
                              14320
---- Letters on the religious revivals which prevailed about the
beginning of the present century
by the Rev. Dr. Porter. Andover,

Revival Association in the Theological Seminary, 1832. 1-8, 19-
47 p. MNtcA; OO.   14321

---- The rhetorical reader, consisting of instructions for regulating the voice, with a rhetorical
notation, illustrating inflection,
emphasis and modulation, and a
course of rhetorical exercises.
Designed for the use of academies
and high schools. By Ebenezer
Porter, D. D. Principal of the
Theological Seminary, Andover.
4th ed. with an appendix. Andover, Flagg and Gould; New York,
J. Leavitt, 1832. 304 p. CSt;
MiSH; NBuG.   14322

[Porter, George Richardson]
1792-1852.
   A treatise on the origin, progressive improvement, and present state of the manufacture of
porcelain and glass. See under
Lardner, Dionysius, 1793-1859.
                             14322a
Porter, Henry H.
   An account of the origin, symptoms, and cure of the influenza
or epidemic catarrh; with some
hints respecting common colds
and incipient pulmonary consumption. Philadelphia, Henry Porter
1832. 80 p. NcU-H.   14323

---- Catechism of health; or,
Plain and simple rules for the
preservation of the health and
vigour of the constitution from infancy to old age, for the use of
schools. Philadelphia, Office of
the Journal of Health, 1832. PP;
PU.   14324

Porter, James Madison, 1793-
1862.
   An address, delivered before
the Literary Societies of Lafa-
yette College, at Easton, Pa.,
July 4, 1832. By James Madison
Porter, Easton, Pr. by J. P.
Hetrich, 1832. 16 p. PHi;

PLERC-Hi; PP; TxU.   14325

Porter, Jane, 1776-1850.
The Scottish chiefs. Hartford,
Silas Andrus, 1832. 2 v. NGH.
                            14326
---- Scottish chiefs; romance.
Hartford, Silas Andrus, 1832.
5 v. in 3. InE; InEv.   14327

---- Thaddeus of Warsaw... By
Miss Porter... Exeter, N.H.,
J. C. Gerrish, 1832. 218 p.
CSfA; NNF.   14328

Porter, William Augustus.
Memoir of W. A. Porter, with
selections from his writings.
Boston, Privately printed, 1832.
115 p. CtHC; RPB.   14329

Porter, William Smith.
The musical cyclopedia: or,
The principles of music considered as a science and an act;
embracing a complete musical
dictionary, and the outlines of a
musical grammar, and of the theory of sounds and laws of harmony; with directions for the
practice of vocal and instrumen-
tal music, and a description of
musical instruments. Boston, J.
Loring, 1832. 432 p. LNP.
                            14330
Porter's health almanac for 1832;
calculated generally for all parts
of the U.S. ...the calculations by
Wm. Collom. Philadelphia, Henry H. Porter, 1832. 80 p. MWA;
MeHi; PP; PHi.   14331

...A portion of the citizens of
this county, deeply impressed
with the alarming crisis that has
arrived in our affairs... Conceive
it to be the duty of all... to unite
in the adoption of those measures
which are calculated to defeat that
object... [Montgomery, Ala.?
1832?] Broadside. NcU.   14332

Porteus, Beilby, 1731-1808.

A summary of the principal
evidences for the truth and divine
origin of the Christian revelation.
Designed chiefly for the use of
young persons. By Beilby Porteus,
D.D. ...with notes and questions.
By Robt. Emory. New York, J.
Emory and B. Waugh, for the
Methodist Episcopal Church, 1832.
82 p. CtMW; MsAb; NSgU.   14333

Portland, Maine.
The charter, joint rules and
orders of the common council and
standing committees, together
with a list of the city officers.
Portland, J. & W. E. Edwards,
1832. 24 p. MB; MH; MeHi.
                            14334
---- Athenaeum.
Catalogue of the books in the
Portland Athenaeum, with the library regulations. Portland, T.
Todd, 1832. 42 p. MeHi; NN.
                            14335
---- Congregational Church of
Christ.
Articles of faith and covenant
adopted by the Third Congregational Church of Christ in Portland. Together with rules and
regulations for its government
and discipline. Organized Sept.
9, 1825. Portland, Arthur Shirley, 1832. 38 p. MeHi.   14336

---- School Committee.
Report of the school commit-
tee, for 1832. Report signed by
Oliver Gerrish, Chairman. Port-
land, March 21, 1832. 8 p.
MMeT-Hi.   14337

---- Young Ladies' High school.
Adverisement of the young ladies high school, Portland, with a
sketch of some of the branches to
be studied in the course of an education. Portland, Todd, 1832. MH.
                            14338
A portrait of Masonry and Anti-
masonry, as drawn by Richard
Rush, John Quincy Adams, Wil-

liam Wirt, &c. Providence, Pr. at the office of the Daily Advertiser, 1832. 60 p. IaCrM; MH; MWA; RNHi; RP.   14339

Portsmouth, Virginia. Citizens.
A meeting of the citizens of Portsmouth... to take into consideration the expedience of constructing a railroad from Portsmouth to some point near the town of Weldon on the Roanoke River... [1832] 1 p. Vi.   14340

A postscript to the "Second Letter" addressed to Mr. Howell. By an Episcopalian. Norfolk, Pr. by T. G. Broughton, 1832. 20 p. DLC; MWA; MdBD; NcU; PHi.
                               14341

Powell, Robert.
An appeal to the Christian public, on the subject of speculative free masonry; in which the author vindicates himself, and other seceders, from the unprincipled slanders of adhering masons, and editors of papers under their control. By Robert Powell, Pastor of the Baptist church in Palmyra, N. Y. Rochester, Pr. by E. Shepard, 1832. 48 p. NHC-S.   14342

Power, John, 1792-1849.
The Catholic's Manual. New York, James Ryan, 1832. 449 p. DCU; NRSB; NYStJ.   14343

Power, Thomas, 1786-1868.
Secrecy: a poem, pronounced at the installation of the officers of the Boston encampment of Knights templars, Feb. 28, 1832. ...Boston, Moore & Sevey, 1832. 24 p. IaCrM; MH; NNFM; NjR; WHi.   14344

---- ---- 2d ed. Boston, Moore & Sevey, 1832. 31, [1] p. DLC; ICU; MH; OCHP; TxU.   14345

Poynter, William.
Christianity; or the evidences

and characters of the Christian religion by Bishop Poynter. Baltimore, Fielding Lucas, Jr., 1832. 236 p. KyLoSL; MdBLC; NNF; OCX; PV.   14346

Practical directions and forms, for proceedings under the "Act to abolish imprisonment for debt, and to punish fraudulent debtors," passed April 26, 1831, with an appendix containing the act and references. Canandaigua, Morse & Harvey, 1832. 39, 8 p. MH-L; NCH; NCanHi.   14347

Practical gardener; containing directions for cultivating a great variety of garden vegetables and fruits. [Cincinnati] 1832. 119 p. NIC.   14348

Practical proofs of the soundness of the Hygeian System of Physiology. 3d ed. New York, 1832. 202 p. MBC; MBM; MWA. 14349

Prentice, George Denison, 1802-1870.
Biography of Henry Clay; by George D. Prentice. Hartford, Samuel Hanmer, Jr., and John Jay Phelps, 1832. 304 p. ICU; MBAt; PPL; WHi.   14350

Presbyterian Church in the U. S. A. Board of Education.
Annual of the Board of education of the General Assembly of the Presbyterian Church in the U. S., ed. by John Breckenridge, Philadelphia, Russell & Martien, 1832-47. CtHC; GDecCT; KyDC; NNUT; PPPrHi.   14351

---- ---- Constitution & laws of the Presbyterian Board of Education. Philadelphia, 1832. 12 p. PHi.   14352

---- ---- Education papers, by the Board of Education of the General Assembly of the Presbyterian church. Philadelphia, Russel, 1832. 24 p. CSansS; GDC; PPPrHi.   14353

---- General Assembly.
Minutes to the General Assembly of the Presbyterian church in the United States of America: with an appendix. Philadelphia, Pr. by Wm. F. Geddes, for the Stated Clerk of the Assembly, 1832. [3]-310-466 p. GDecCT; InU; MsJS; ViRut; WHi.   14354

---- Presbytery of Cleveland.
A summary confession of faith, covenant and articles of practice, recommended by the presbytery of Cleveland to the Churches under their care, to be used in the admission of members. New York, Sleight and Robinson, prs., 1832. 12 p. ICN; NNUT; OClWHi; OO. 14355

---- Presbytery of Geneva.
A narrative of the late revivals of religion, within the bounds of Geneva Presbytery. Geneva, Pub. by order of the presbytery, 1832. 30 p. CtY; DLC; ICN; MH; NBuG.   14356

---- Presbytery of Mississippi.
Extracts from the records of the Mississippi Presbytery. From October 1829 to January 1832. Natchez, Pr. by R. Semple, 1832. 66 p. CSmH; NcMHi.
                                 14357
---- Synod of New York.
Circular to all Presbyterians in these United States praying them to take... into serious consideration, the question "Is baptism by a Roman Catholic priest valid?" New York, March, 1832. PPPrHi.   14358

---- ---- Psalms and hymns.
New York, 1832. PPL.   14359

Presbyterian Educational Society. Indiana branch.
First annual report etc... Madison, Arion & Lodge, 1832. 16 p. OCHP.   14360

The Presbyterian preacher v.1-5, 1832-May, 1837. Pittsburgh, 1832-37. 5 v. CSmH; MB; MoWgT; NjR; OClWHi.   14361

Prescott, Edward Goldsborough, 1804-1844.
An oration: delivered before the officers of the militia, and members of the volunteer companies of Boston and the vicinity ... Boston, Pr. by J. H. Eastburn, 1832. 30 p. ICMe; MB; MH; NNC; PPL.   14362

Pressly, John Taylor.
An address to the students of the theological seminary of the associate reformed synod of the west, at the opening of the session, tenth December, 1832. Pittsburgh, Johnston & Stockton, 1832. 14 p. OClWHi; PPPrHi.
                                 14363
---- The Sabbath. A sermon preached before the auxiliary Sabbath union society of Pittsburgh, on Sabbath evening, 24th June, 1832. 12 p. OClWHi.
                                 14364
Preston, John.
The saint's daily exercise. A treatise, unfolding the whole duty of prayer; in five sermons upon I. Thes. V. 17. By John Preston. Xenia, Pr. by J. H. Purdy, 1832. 124 p. OClWHi; OCo; TWcW.   14365

Preston, Lyman.
Preston's treatise on bookkeeping: or, Arbitrary rules made plain: in two parts... The first part being designed for the use of mechanics of all classes; the second... showing the method

of keeping accounts by double entry... By Lyman Preston... New
York, Pr. by Sleight & Robinson,
1832. 174 p. MH.   14366

Preston, William B.
    The speech of William B.
Preston, (of Montgomery) in the
House of Delegates of Virginia, on
the policy of the State in relation
to her colored population: deliv-
ered Jan. 16, 1832. Richmond,
Thomas White, pr., 1832. 12 p.
MB.   14367

Preston's Wallet Reckoner and Almanac for 1833. By Lyman Preston. New York, N.Y., R. & G. S.
Wood [1832] 18 l. MWA; NRMA.
                                14368
Prince, Thomas, 1687-1758.
    An account of the revival of
religion in Boston, in the years
1740-1-2-3. Repr. Boston, 1832.
55 p. WHi.   14369

Prince, William.
    ... Annual catalogue of fruit
and ornamental trees and plants,
cultivated at the Linnaean botanic
garden and nurseries, 1832-33.
Providence, Wm. Marshall & Co.,
1832. KyDC; RP.   14370

Prince, William Robert, 1795-
1869.
    The pomological manual; or,
A treatise on fruits; containing
descriptions of a great number...
for the orchard and garden. By
Wm. Robert Prince... aided by
Wm. Prince... Part I. 2d ed. New
York, T. & J. Swords, 1832. 2 v.
in 1. ArU; MdU; MoU; NjR;
RNR.   14371

Princeton Theological Seminary.
    Catalogue of the officers and
students of the Theological Seminary, Princeton, N.J. ... Princeton, N.J., Pr. by D'Hart & Connolly, 1832. 7 p. MB; Nh; NjP;
NjR.   14372

---- General catalogue... Princeton, N.J. Princeton, N.J., Pr.
by D'Hart & Connolly, 1832. 19 p.
MB; MBC; NjR.   14373

Princeton University.
    Laws of the College of New
Jersey; revised, amended and
adopted by the Board of Trustees,
April, 1832. Princeton, N.J., Pr.
by D'Hart & Connolly, 1832. 27 p.
DLC; PHi.   14374

Prindle's Almanac for 1833. By
Charles Prindle. New Haven,
Conn., A. H. Maltby & Co.
[1832] CtHi; MWA; NN; OMC.
                                14375
Proceedings & address, of the
committee of the anti-Jackson men
of Franklin County, Pennsylvania.
[Chambersburg? Pr. by Geo. K.
Harper, 1832?] 48 p. PPA.
                                14376
Proceedings and speeches at a
meeting held in the Capitol at
Washington, Jan. 13, 1832, for
the promotion of temperance in
the United States. [Washington,
D.C.? 1832?] 12 p. MB; PPL;
NN; NcD; ViU.   14377

Proceedings at the dinner to
Isaac Hill, at the Eagle Coffee
House, Concord, N.H., Aug. 8,
1832. [Concord? 1832?] 16 p.
MH.   14378

Proceedings of the convention of
South Carolina upon the subject
of nullification. See under South
Carolina. Convention.

Proceedings of the military convention which assembled at Harrisburg, Pa. Monday, Jan. 2,
1832. Pr. by order of the Convention. Harrisburg, Pr. by Henry
Welsh, 1832. 24 p. DLC; NbU;
PHi; PPi.   14379

Proceedings of the state agricultural convention held at the capitol

city of Albany... See under
New York State Agricultural Convention, Albany.

Proceedings of the tariff meeting
held at Easton, Pa. June 9, 1832
with the address delivered on that
occasion by James Madison Porter. Easton, Pa., J. P. Hetrich
[1832?] 18 p. PHi.   14380

Proposals and rates of the United
States Insurance Company of Bal-
timore, South Street, Baltimore.
Washington, 1832. 14 p. DLC;
MdHi; PPL.   14381

Prospectus of the Georgia Medi-
cal Reporter. By John G. Slappey,
M. D. Nov. 29, 1832. 1 sheet.
NcU.   14382

Protestant Episcopal Church in
the U.S.A.
    The book of common prayer,
and administration of the sacraments and other rites and ceremonies of the church, according
to the use of the Protestant Episcopal church in the United States
of America, together with the
psalter or Psalms of David.
Baltimore, J. N. Lewis [1832?]
360 p. MdBE.   14383

---- ---- Hartford, Andrus,
1832. 545, 124 p. DLC; MB;
WHi.   14384

---- ---- New-York, New-York
Bible and Common Prayer Book
Society, Pr. at the Protestant
Episcopal Press, 1832. 480 p.
CtHWatk; CtMW; MB; MBD; TNM.
                            14385
---- Canons for the government
of the Protestant Episcopal church
in the United States of America
...to which are annexed the constitution of the church, and the
course of ecclesiastical studies,
established by the House of Bishops...New York, Pr. at the Prot-

estant Episcopal press, 1832.
42 p. CtY; MB; NjR; PHi;
TxDaM.   14386

---- The Catechism of the Protestant Episcopal Church, in the
United States of America; with
scripture proofs, and poetical illustrations. Compiled by Andrew
Fowler, A. M. formerly rector of
St. Bartholomew's Parish, South
Carolina. Boston, J. R. Butts,
1832. 36 p. ScHi.   14387

---- ---- Philadelphia, L. Johnson [1832] 16 p. DLC.   14388

---- Constitution and canons for
the government of the... of America. [n. p.] Pr. for the convention, 1832- CU; MiU; NNG.
                            14389
---- First annual report of the
board of managers. New-York,
Protestant Episcopal Press, 1832.
39 p. CBCDS.   14390

---- Alabama Diocese.
    Journal of the proceedings of
the second Annual Convention of
the clergy and laity of the Prot-
estant Episcopal Church in the
Diocese of Alabama held in
Christ Church, Tuscaloosa on
Monday Jan 2, Tuesday Jan. 3,
and Thursday Jan. 5, 1832. Tus-
caloosa, Pr. by Order of the
Convention by Wiley, M'Guire &
Henry, 1832. 16 p. ABCA; MBD;
NN NBuDD; TxU.   14391

---- Domestic and Foreign Mis-
sionary.
    Proceedings of the Board of
Directors of the Domestic and
Foreign Missionary Society of the
Protestant Episcopal Church.
Philadelphia, Pr. by Wm. Stave-
ly, 1832. 88 p. MBD; MnHi;
WHi.   14392

---- Eastern Diocese.
    Journal of the Proceedings of

the annual convention of the
Protestant Episcopal Church in
the Eastern Diocese, Trinity
Church, Boston. Lowell, E. C.
Purdy, Journal Press, 1832.
17 p. MBD; NN.   14393

---- General Convention.
   Hymns of the Protestant Episcopal Church in the United States
of America, set forth in general
conventions of said church, in
the year of our Lord, 1789,
1808, and 1826. Hartford, 1832.
124 p. MiD; NNG; PPLT; WHi.
                              14394
---- ---- ---- [New York,
1832?] 48 p. MB; NNUT. 14395

---- ---- A pastoral letter, to
the clergy and members of the
Protestant Episcopal Church in
the United States of America,
from the bishops of the same, assembled in General Convention,
in the city of New-York, October
1832. New York, Pr. at the
Protestant Episcopal Press,
1832. 24 p. CtHT; IEG; MBD;
MHi; RPB.   14396

---- General Theological Semi-
nary.
   The Act of Incorporation, Con-
stitution, and Statutes... New
York, 1832. 22 p. MBD; MH;
MHi; PHi.   14397

---- Georgia Diocese.
   Journal of the proceedings of
the Tenth Annual Convention of
the Protestant Episcopal Church
in the diocese of Georgia. Held
in Macon on the 7, 8 & 9th of
May, together with the convention
sermon, preached at the opening
of the same, on Sunday morning,
May 6, 1832. By the Rev. T. B.
Bartow, Rector of Christ Church,
St. Simon's Island. Pub. at the
request of the Convention. Savannah, W. T. Williams, 1832. 28 p.
NBuDD.   14398

---- Kentucky Diocese.
   Journal of the proceedings of
the fourth convention... in Hop-
kinsville...June, 1832. Danville,
Ky. , Pr. by J. J. Polk, 1832.
19 p. NN.   14399

---- Maryland Diocese.
   Constitution of the Missionary
Society of the Protestant Episco-
pal Church in the Diocese of
Maryland...Baltimore, J. Robin-
son, 1832. 7 p. MdBD.   14400

---- ---- Journal of a convention
of the Protestant Episcopal Church
of Maryland, held in St. Paul's
Church, Baltimore, Wednesday,
May 30th; Thursday, May 31st;
and Friday, June 1st, 1832. Baltimore, Pr. by J. Robinson,
1832. 44 p. MBD; MdBD; NBuDD;
ViRU.   14401

---- Massachusetts Diocese.
   Journal of the proceedings of
the annual convention... Boston,
June 20 & 21, 1832. Boston,
Stimpson & Clapp, 1832. 46 p.
MBD; MiD-B; MiD-MCh. 14402

---- New York Diocese. Educa-
tion Missionary Society.
   The constitution and by-laws
of the Education and Missionary
Society of the Protestant Episco-
pal Church in the state of New
York... New York, Protestant
Episcopal Press, 1832. 23 p.
CtHT; NNG.   14403

---- ---- ---- First annual report of the Board of managers;
read before the society at the
anniversary meeting in St. John's
chapel, Oct. 4, 1832. Together
with the reports of the missionaries of the diocese, and the proceedings of the late convention...
New-York, Protestant Episcopal
Press, 1832. 40 p. MdBD; NNC.
                              14404
---- ---- 47th Convention, 1832.

Journal of the proceedings of the Forty-seventh convention of the Protestant Episcopal Church in the state of New York... New York, Protestant Episcopal Press, 1832. 88 p. MBD; NBuDD; NGH; NjR.   14405

---- North Carolina Diocese.
Journal of the Proceedings of the Sixteenth Annual Convention of the Protestant Episcopal Church in the State of North Carolina... 1832. Fayetteville, Pr. by Edward J. Hale, 1832. 48 p. MBD; NBuDD.   14406

---- Ohio Diocese.
An address to the Churchman of the United States, on the Difficulties in the Diocese of Ohio. 1832. 19 p. Ohi.   14407

---- ---- Journal of the Proceedings of the Fifteenth Annual Convention of the Protestant Episcopal Church in the Diocese of Ohio, 1832. Gambier, Ohio. Acland Press, Pr. by Geo. W. Myers, 1832. 26 p. MBD; NN.
                                        14408
---- Pennsylvania Diocese.
Journal of the Proceedings of the Forty-eighth Convention of the Protestant Episcopal Church in the State of Pennsylvania. Held in St. James' Church, in the City of Philadelphia, on Tuesday, May 15, Wednesday, May 16, and Thursday, May 17, 1832. Philadelphia, Pr. by Jesper Harding, for Order of the Convention, 1832. 60 p. ICU; MBD; NBuDD.
                                        14409
---- South Carolina Diocese.
Journal of the proceedings of the 44th annual convention... in St. Michael's Church, Charleston ... 1832. Charleston, Pr. by A. E. Miller, 1832. 39 p. MBD; NN; NBuDD.   14410

---- Tennessee Diocese.

Journal of the proceedings of the fourth convention of the clergy & laity of the Protestant Episcopal church in the state of Tennessee, held in Christ Church, Nashville, on the 28th, 29th and 30th days of June, 1832. Nashville, Pub. by order of the convention, Pr. by Hunt, Tardiff & Co., 1832. 17, [1] p. NBuDD; NN; T. 14411

---- Vermont Diocese.
Journal of the proceedings of the Convention of the Protestant Episcopal Church in the State of Vermont, 1832. Woodstock, Pr. by David Watson, 1832. 23 p. MB; MBD; MHi.   14412

Protestant Episcopal Theological Seminary. Virginia.
Catalogue of the officers and students of the Protestant Episcopal Theological Seminary, Fairfax County, Virginia. January 1832. Washington, Pr. by P. Force, 1832. 7 p. NNC; NNG.
                                        14413
Proudfit, Alexander.
The universal extension of Messiah's kingdom; a sermon... Boston, 1832. MSaE.   14414

Providence, Rhode Island.
Charter of the City of Providence, and the act of the General Assembly for organizing the government under the same, passed at October Session, 1831. Together with a list of the City Officers for the year 1832. Also, The Mayor's Address to the City Council, delivered at the organization of the City Government, June 4th, 1832. Pr. by order of the City Council. Providence, Wm. Marshall & Co., prs., 1832. 36 p. IU; MH; NN; RHi.   14415

---- A list of freeman with the city officers of Providence. Providence, Pr. by H. H. Brown, 1832. 24 p. RHi; RPB.   14416

---- Proxies for voting (Lists of candidates for elections) (Providence, 1832?) Broadside. RPB.
14417

---- First Baptist Church.
A list of members of the First Baptist Church in Providence, with biographical sketches of the pastors. Providence, H. H. Brown, 1832. 48 p. NHC-C; PCA; RHi; RPB.   14418

---- M. Robinson's Circulating Library.
Catalogue of additions for 1832. [Providence? 1832?] 8 p. RPB.
14419

---- School Committee.
Regulations established for the government of the public schools, in the city of Providence, June 13, 1832. Providence, Pr. by J. Knowles, 1832. 12 p. MWA; MiD-B; RNHi.   14420

Providence Association for the Promotion of Temperance.
Report of the board of managers. Presented and read at their annual meeting held in Mechanics Hall, Monday evening, Oct. 22, 1832. Providence, W. Marshall & Co., [1832] 12 p. DLC; MBC; NN; RHi.   14421

Providence Auxiliary Unitarian Association.
First Semi-annual report. Providence, T. Doyle, [1832] 16 p. MWA; RHi.   14422

The Providence Directory, containing names of the inhabitants, their occupations, places of business, and dwelling-houses; With lists of the Streets, Lanes, Wharves, etc. Also, Banks, Insurance offices, and other public institutions; The whole carefully collected and arranged. Providence, H. H. Brown, 1832. 144 p. DLC; RHi; RP.   14423

Providence Society for the Encouragement of Faithful Domestic Servants.
Annual report, 1st. Providence, Pr. by H. H. Brown, 1832. 16 p. RHi; RPB.   14424

Provo, Peter.
Aphorisms of wisdom; or, A collection of nine hundred maxims & observations. Boston, Allen & Goddard, 1832. 222 p. OUrC; PBa.   14425

Putnam, Daniel.
A summary declaration of the faith and practice of the First Baptist Church, Clinton... By Daniel Putnam, Pastor of the Church. Utica, From the press of Bennett & Bright, 1832. 12 p. PScrHi.
14426

Putnam, George Palmer, ed.
Putnam's home cyclopedia. Hand-book of chronology and history. The world's progress, a dictionary of dates...6th ed. New York, G. P. Putnam, 1832. 692 + 48 p. OClWHi.   14427

Putnam, Samuel.
...The analytical reader, containing lessons in simultaneous reading and defining, with spelling from the same. To which are added, questions, and references to an appendix, containing sketches of characters, persons, and places, alluded to in the work. By Samuel Putnam... Philadelphia, French & Perkins, 1832. 228 p. DLC; MH; MeHi; PPM.   14428

---- Sequel to the analytical reader: in which the original design is extended, so as to embrace an explanation of phrases and figurative language, by Samuel Putnam. Stereotype ed. Dover, E. French; Boston, Perkins & Marvin, 1832. 300 p. CtHT-W; MB; MH; Nh-Hi; PHi.   14429

Pye, S.
Essay on negro emancipation.
Originally published in the Long
Island Star, under the signature
of S. Pye. Also an essay on the
phenomena of dreams, by the
same. Brooklyn, Pr. by A.
Spooner, 1832. 35 p. NBLiHi;
PPPrHi; RP.   14430

Q

Queens County (N. Y.) Lyceum.
Constitution and by laws...
adopted...1831. Hempstead, L. I.,
1832. 7 p. NBLiHi.   14431

Quevedo y Villegas, Francisco
Gomez de, 1580-1645.
The visions of Quevedo. Tr.
from the Spanish, by Wm. El-
liot, esq. Philadelphia, Henry H.
Porter, 1832. 216 p. CU; DLC;
GDecCT; MiDSH; NNH; PPA.
                               14432
Quincy, Josiah, 1772-1864.
An address delivered at the
dedication of Dane law college in
Harvard University, Oct. 23, 1832.
By Josiah Quincy...Cambridge,
E. W. Metcalf & Co., prs. to the
University, 1832. (4) 27 p. CtHC;
ICMe; MdHi; OCHP; RNR. 14433

---- An oration delivered July 4,
1832, before the City Council and
inhabitants of Boston. By Josiah
Quincy, Jr. Boston, John H.
Eastburn, City pr., 1832. (3) 21
p. CtSoP; ICMe; MH; NCH; RPB.
                               14434
Quincy Lyceum.
Constitution and by-laws of the
Quincy Lyceum. Adopted Dec. 31,
1830. Boston, Pr. by Perkins &
Marvin, 1832. 12 p. ICMe; MQ.
                               14435

R

Radcliffe, Ann (Ward) 1764-1823.

The romance of the forest.
Interspersed with some pieces of
poetry. By Mrs. Radcliffe, authoress of A Sicilian romance,
etc. In two volumes. Woodstock,
R. Colton, 1832. 2 vols. MB;
MWA; NSchHi.   14436

Raffles, Thomas, 1788-1863.
Hints for those who are en-
gaged in Sabbath schools, by the
Rev. Thomas Raffles. New Haven,
Whitmore & Minor, 1832. 62 p.
GDecCT; MBC.   14437

Rafinesque, Constantine Samuel,
1783-1840.
Alsographia Americana; or,
An American grove of trees and
shrubs by C. S. Rafinesque. Phil-
adelphia, 1832. 76 p. PHi.
                               14438
---- American florist, containing
36 figures of beautiful or curious
American and garden flowers,
plants, trees, shrubs and vines.
Philadelphia, 1832. 36 p. DLC;
NIC.   14439

---- Atlantic Journal and Friend
of knowledge in eight numbers.
Samuel Constantine Rafinesque,
ed. Philadelphia, 1832-1833.
212 p. CU; ICN; LNH; NjR; PHi.
                               14440
---- Eighteen figures of handsome
American garden flowers by C. S.
Rafinesque. Philadelphia, 1832.
N; PPAN.   14441

---- A monograph of the fluvia-
tile bivalve shells of the river
Ohio, containing twelve genera &
sixty-eight species... Philadelphia,
J. Dobson, 1832. 72 p. ICJ; MH;
OU; PPAmP; PPi; WHi.   14442

---- Statements respecting a six
per cent savings bank, or institution, to be established in the city
of Philadelphia. [Philadelphia
1832] 4 p. MH-A.   14443

---- Tabular view of the compared Atlantic alphabets &
glyphs of Africa and America.
Philadelphia, 1832. 1 p.
PPAmP.   14444

Raikes, Robert.
    Address at the celebration of
the Sunday School Jubilee, or the
fiftieth year from the institution
of Sunday Schools, by Robert
Raikes: delivered at Charlestown,
S. C. on Wednesday, 14th of September, 1831. By Thos. Grimke.
American Sunday School Union,
1832. 20 p. KyLoS.   14445

Railway locomotives and cars.
Philadelphia, etc. January 1832-
ICJ; In; NN; PPL; V.   14446

Railway-mechanical engineer. See
Railway locomotives and cars.

Ramsey, David, 1749-1815.
    The life of George Washington,
Commander-in-chief of the Armies
of the United States of America,
throughout the war which established their independence, and
first President of the United
States, by David Ramsey, M.D.
Revised and enl. by Wm. Grimshaw... Baltimore (Md.), Cushing
& Sons, and Joseph Jewett, 1832.
252 p. DLC; IaPeC; MiU; PHi;
ViR.   14447

Rand, Asa, 1783-1871.
    The new divinity tried; an ex-
amination of a sermon by Rev.
C. G. Finney, on making a new
heart. Boston, Lyceum Press,
Light & Harris, 1832. 16 p.
CtHWatk; RPB.   14448

---- On teaching grammar and
composition... delivered before the
American Institute of Instruction,
Boston, 1832. MDeeP.   14449

---- The teacher's manual for
instructing in English grammar.

By Asa Rand. Re-pub. from the
Education Reporter, with amendments and additions. Boston,
Richardson, Lord & Holbrook,
1832. 89, [1] p. MH; NNC.
                               14450
---- A vindication of "The new
divinity tried," in reply to a review of the same. Boston, Peirce,
1832. 40 p. MBC; MH-AH;
PPPrHi.   14451

Randolph, Thomas Jefferson,
1792-1875.
    The speech of Thomas J. Ran-
dolph, (of Albemarle) in the
House of Delegates of Virginia,
on the abolition of slavery: delivered... Jan. 21, 1832. 2d ed.
Richmond, Pr. by Thos. W.
White, 1832. 22 p. IaU; MH;
OCIWHi; PPL; ViU.   14452

Randolph, Thomson.
    The practical teacher, being
an easy and rational introduction
to arithmetic. Designed for beginners, of every age, adapted to
every mode of instruction and
particularly the monitorial. By
Thomson Randolph. 3d ed., carefully rev. and cor. Philadelphia,
Uriah Hunt, 1832. 192 p. OOxM.
                               14453
Rantoul, Robert, Jr., 1805-1852.
    An oration, delivered before
the inhabitants of the town of
South Reading and its vicinity, on
the Fourth of July, 1832. By
Robert Rantoul, Jr., Pub. by request. Salem, Press of Foote &
Brown, 1832. 36 p. CtHWatk;
MBAt; MH; NjR; RPB.   14454

---- Speech of Hon. Robert Rantoul, Jr., at the Democratic District Convention, held at Salem,
July 5, 1832. Lynn, Pr. at the
Bay State office, L. Josselyn,
1832. 7 p. MBevHi.   14455

Rapp, Adam William.
    A complete system of scien-

tific penmanship (without ruling)
and penmaking by which method
any number of pens may be made
to correspond with each other:
containing six elegant engravings
illustrating the whole system, together with all the explanations
of the same, and also two fac-
similes of improvement. Philadelphia, Pithian, 1832. 31 p.
MB; MBAt; NRHi; PHi; WHi.
                                14456
Rasles, Sebastien.
    Prospectus of a Dictionary of
the Abnaki Language of North
America. Pub. from the Author's
Manuscript in the Library of Harvard (College). Cambridge, 1832.
3 p. MHi.   14457

A rational view of the spasmod-
ic cholera, ... By a physician.
Boston, Clapp & Hull, [1832] 36 p.
MB; MH-M; MWA; NNNAM; NRU-
M.   11458

[Ravenel, Edmund] 1797-1870.
    An address to the people on
the subject of renewing the
charter of the United States Bank,
with a list of foreign stockholders,
and notes. Charleston, Pr. by A.
E. Miller, 1832. 39 p. ScU.
                                11459
Rawle, William.
    Discourse on study of law; a
discourse on the nature and study
of law, delivered before the Law
academy of Philadelphia, by Wm.
Rawle, LL. D. ... Philadelphia, Pr.
by Thos. Kite, for F. H. Nicklin
and T. Johnson, 1832. 26 [2] p.
MB; NIC-L; OCLaw; PHi;
WWauHi.   11460

Rawlings, Augustus.
    Eulogy on Daniel Webster be-
fore students and friends of Albany Medical College Oct. 28,
1832. Albany, 1832. 25 p. PHi.
                                11461
Rayner, B. L.
    Sketches of the life, writings,

and opinions. . . with selections of
the most valuable portions of his
voluminous and unrivaled private
correspondence. By B. L. Raynor.
New York, A. Francis & W.
Boardman, 1832. 556 p. CtHT;
GDecCT; NBuG; MnHi; PPi; WHi.
                                14462
Rayner, Menzies, 1770-1850.
    A review of Dr. Tyler's Mis-
sionary Sermon by Menziers Rayner, Pastor of the First Universalist Society in Portland, Me.
Portland, M. Rayner, Jr., 1832.
28 p. MMeT; MMeT-Hi; MWA.
                                14463
Raynham Debating Society.
    Constitution of the Raynham
Debating Society. [Taunton, Pr.
by E. Anthony, 1832?] MiD-B.
                                14464
Reading, Mass. Second Congregational Church.
    A statement of proceedings
against Mrs. Emily Richardson,
in the Second Congregational
Church in Reading. Charlestown,
W. W. Wheildon, 1832. 38 p.
ICU; ICN; MBC; MWA; RPB.
                                14465
The Reasoner, or Anti-clerical
politics, consisting of select and
original communications in opposition to a union of church and
state, the conjunction of Christianity with politics and the
abuses of religion. Columbia,
S. C. , Pr. by Spencer J. M.
Morris, 1832. 86 p. ScU. 14466

Reasons for embracing the Catholic religion. Boston, 1832. 47 p.
MBC.   14467

Rede, Leman Thomas.
    The art of money getting;
showing the means by which an
individual may obtain and retain
health, wealth, and happiness, by
Leman Thomas Rede. Boston,
Richardson, 1832. 144 p. MH-BA;
NNC.   14468

[Reed, Anna C.]

The life of George Washington. Written for the American Sunday School Union, and revised by the committee of publication. Philadelphia, American Sunday School Union, [1832] 268 p. CU; DLC; MdBP; NNU; PHi.   14469

Reed, John.

On prayer. A sermon preached ... on occasion of a public fast observed in consequence of the prevailing epidemic. By John Reed, D. D. New York, W. Van Norden, 1832. 12 p. NNG. 14470

Reese, David Meredith.

Plain and practical treatise on the epidemic cholera, as it prevailed in the city of New York, in the summer of 1832... To which is added by way of appendix, a brief essay on the medical use of ardent spirits. New York, 1832. MdBP.   14471

Reese, W. I.

The Catechumen's Guide; or Scriptural Questions and Answers, ... 2d ed. Boston, 1832. 56 p. MHi.   14472

Reformed Church in America.

The acts and proceedings of the general synod of the Reformed Dutch Church in North America, at New York, in June, and Albany in October, 1832. New York, Pr. for General Synod, 1832. 133 p. IaPeC; NjR.   14473

---- The acts and proceedings of the general synod of the True Reformed Dutch Church, in the United States of America, at New York, June, 1832. New York, Pr. by Anderson & Smith, 1832. 15 p. IaDuU-Sem.   14474

---- Additional hymns, adopted by the general synod of the Reformed Dutch church in North America, at their session, June, 1831, and authorized to be used in the churches under their care. 3d ed. New York, Wm. A. Mercein, 1832. 96 p. NjR; TxU.   14475

---- The constitution of the German Reformed Church, in the United States of North America, approved by the classes and adopted by the Synod, at Mifflinsburgh, Pa. , 1828. York, Pr. by May & Glossbrenner, 1832. 19 p. PLERC-Hi.   14476

---- Constitution of the German Reformed Synod of Ohio. Lancaster, Pr. by Ohio Eagle, 1832. 24 p. MoWgT.   14477

---- The psalms and hymns, with catechism, confession of faith and liturgy of the Reformed Dutch church of North America, by John H. Livingston, D. D. S. T. P. , Mercein's stereotyped ed. , to which are added additional hymns and the canon of the synod of Dordrecht. 3d ed. New York, Rutger's Press, Wm. A. Mercein, 1832. 77 p. IU; PLT; PPPrHi; RPB.   14478

---- Verhandlungen einer allgemeinen Synode der Hochdeutschen Reformirten Kirche. In dem vereinigten staaten von Nord America Gehalten in Friedrichstadt Md. vom 16ten dis 21sten September, 1832. York, Pa. , 1832. 64 p. MoWgT; PLERCHi.   14479

Reformed Dutch Church in America. See Reformed Church in America.

Reformed medical journal. (Reformed medical Society of the United States) New York V 1-12, January-December 1832. DSG; MWA; MdBM; N; NNN.   14480

Regeneration. A discussion of the Scripture doctrine of regen-

eration. Dover, John Mann, 1832.
36 p. MWA.   14481

Reid, Robert, 1773-1865.
An address to the people on
the subject of renewing the charter of the United States Bank...
Charleston, A. E. Miller, 1832.
39 p. DLC; ScU.   14482

Reid, Thomas.
Treatise on clock and watch
making, theoretical and practical, by Thomas Reid. Philadelphia, Carey & Lea, 1832. 476 p.
IU; MiD; NcU; OC; OMI.   14483

Reinhard, Francis Volkmar,
1753-1812.
Memoirs and confessions of
Francis Volkmar Reinhard,
S. T. D. ...from the German, by
Oliver A. Taylor. Boston,
Peirce & Parker, 1832. MA;
MB.   14484

---- ---- New York, H. C.
Sleight, 1832. 164 p. IaB; MoS;
PPLT; PU; WU.   14485

The Religious souvenir; a Christ-
mas, New Year's and birthday
present. Philadelphia, Key,
Mielke & Biddle [1832] 287 p.
CtHWatk; ICN; LNH; OClWHi;
WU.   14486

Remarks on propagated depravity
and sin as the necessary means
of the greatest good. New Haven,
Baldwin & Treadway, 1832. 40 p.
MWA.   14487

Remarks on the cholera, embracing facts and observations collected at New-York...2d ed. Providence, W. Marshall & Co., 1832.
34 p. MWA.   14488

---- 3d ed. Providence, Pr. by
W. Marshall & Co., 1832. 34 p.
MWA.   14489

Remarks respecting the Sodus
Canal, and its probable immedi-
ate, and prospective Revenue.
New York, Pr. by Elliott &
Palmer, 1832. 24 p. M; NN; NHi.
                              14490
Remington, James.
A sermon, preached at the fu-
neral of Deacon Asa Field; who
died at Cayuga Creek; Erie Coun-
ty, N. Y. Dec. 6, 1831. Aged 74.
Buffalo, Pr. by Steele & Faxon,
1832. 14 p. MB; MBAt.   14491

A remonstrance against the proceedings of a meeting, held Nov.
23d, 1831, at Upton's, in Dock
Street, Philadelphia. Philadelphia,
1832. 8 p. PHi.   14492

[Rennie, James] 1787-1867.
...Insect miscellanies. Boston,
Lilly and Wait; (late Wells & Lilly)
and Carter & Hendee, 1832. 426 p.
CtMW; IU; MB; NhPet; WU.
                              14493
---- ... The menageries. Quad-
rupeds, described and drawn
from living subjects... Boston,
Lilly and Wait, Carter and Hen-
dee [etc., etc.] 1832. 396 p.
KyDC; MnBedf; OU.   14494

Renshaw, James.
To the officers of the Navy of
the U. S. [Washington, 1832]
MBAt.   14495

Renwick, James, 1790-1863.
The elements of mechanics.
By James Renwick, LL. D., pro-
fessor of natural experimental
philosophy and chemistry, in
Columbia College, New York.
Philadelphia, Carey & Lea, 1832.
508 p. GU; MdW; NjR; PPi;
RNR; ViU.   14496

Reply concerning piece of poetry
issued about the Shakers of Kentucky. New Lebanon, 1832. 12 p.
OClWHi.   14497

Reply to Rev. Mr. Rand's vindication of "The new divinity tried. "
Pub. as an appendix to the 2d ed.
of a "Review" of the same. Boston, Peirce & Parker, 1832. 12 p.
CtHC; MBC; MWA; PPPrHi.
                              14498
Report of deaths of cholera, that
have occurred in Cincinnati, from
the 24, of September, to the 14,
of November. Alphabetically arranged, by an attentive observer.
Cincinnati, Pr. by Wood & Stratton, 1832. 18 p. OCHP.   14499

Reports and documents relative to
the Stuyvesant Meadows, from the
year 1825 to 1831 inclusive. New
York, George Robertson, 1832.
50 p. MWA.   14500

Representation of the heart of man
in its depraved state by nature,
and the changes which it experiences under the influence of the
spirit of God operating upon it.
10th ed. New York, Nafis and
Cornish, 1832. CtmmHi; PPL-R.
                              14501
Resolutions of Virginia and Kentucky, penned by Madison and Jefferson, in relation to the Alien
and sedition laws: and debates in
the House of Delegates of Virginia, in December, 1798, on the
same. Richmond, R. I. Smith,
1832. 72, 183 p. DLC; ICJ; MnU;
NcAS; NcD; ViPet.   14502

Result of an Ex-parte council convened in Providence, June 19,
1832. Providence, H. H. Brown,
1832. 24 p. MWA.   14503

A retrospect of Andrew Johnson's
Administration. n. p. , 1832.
19 p. MWA.   14504

Revere, John.
  A discourse introductory to the
course of lectures on the theory
and practice of physic,...by John
Revere, M. D. , Philadelphia,

French & Perkins, 1832. 24 p.
JeffMedC; MB; NNNAM; PPM;
RNR.   14505

Review of the veto. Containing an
examination of the principles of
the President's message, and his
objections to the bill...recharter-
ing the Bank of the United States.
[Washington? 1832?] 32 p. MWA;
MiD-B; NNC; NcD; ScU.   14506

Rhode Island.
  At the General Assembly of the
state of Rhode Island and Providence Plantations, begun and hold-
en by adjournment at Providence
within and for said state, on the
second Monday of January, in the
year of Our Lord one thousand
eight hundred and thirty-two, and
of Independence the fifty-sixth.
Providence, Pr. by W. Marshall,
1832. 56 p. DLC; MdBB; RNCH.
                              14507
---- At the General Assembly of
the state of Rhode Island and
Providence Plantations, begun and
holden at Newport, within and for
said state, on the first Wednesday
of May in the year of Our Lord
one thousand eight hundred and
thirty-two, and of Independence
the fifty-sixth. Providence, Pr.
by W. Marshall, 1832. 18 p.
DLC; Ia; MdBB; RNCH.   14508

---- At the General Assembly of
the state of Rhode Island and
Providence Plantations, begun and
holden at Newport, within and for
said state, on the third Monday of
June in the year of our Lord one
thousand eight hundred and thirty-
two, and of Independence the fifty-
sixth. Providence, W. Marshall,
state pr. , 1832. 92 p. DLC; Ia;
MiL; R; RNCH.   14509

---- At the General Assembly of
Rhode Island and Providence Plantations, held at Newport, August
1832. 18 p. MdBB.   14510

---- At the General Assembly of the state of Rhode Island and Providence Plantations, begun and holden at Providence within and for said State, on the last Monday of October, in the year of Our Lord, one thousand eight hundred and thirty-two, and of Independence the fifth seventh (sic) Providence, W. Marshall, state pr., 1832. 48 p. DLC; Ia; MdBB; RNCH.   14511

---- Documents relating to the boundary question, Rhode Island vs. Massachusetts. Message from Gov. Levi Lincoln of Massachusetts; Resolutions of the General Assembly of Rhode Island, etc. [Providence? 1832?] 4 p. RHi; RPB.   14512

---- An official report, by Wm. Sprague, Jr., one of the Committee of the House of Representatives of Rhode Island, upon subject of Masonry. Providence, Pr. at the Office of Daily Advertiser, 1832. 12 p. DLC; IaCrM; MB; PHi; WHi.   14513

---- Report of the committee appointed by the General Assembly of the State of Rhode Island and Providence Plantations, to investigate the charges in circulation against Free-Masonry and Masons in said state: Together with all the official documents and testimony relating to the subject. Providence, Pub. by order of the General Assembly, Superintended by the Committee. Wm. Marshall, state pr., 1832. 72, 143 p. DLC; Nh; PHi; PPFM; RP.   14514

The Rhode-Island Almanack, enlarged and improved for the year 1833: By R. T. Paine. Calculated for the City of Providence, in lat. 71°25'56" West... Providence, H. H. Brown, [1832] 24 p. ICU; MWA; NBuG; OMC; RPE. 14515

Rhode Island State Temperance Society.
   Proceedings of the Rhode Island State Temperance Society at its Second Annual Meeting, held in... Providence, ... Oct. 22, 1832. Providence, Wm. Marshall & Co., 1832. 24 p. RPE. 14516

Rice, Christopher Carleton.
   The oration, as delivered, on the fourth of July, 1832, 56th. anniversary of American Independence, by Dr. Christopher Carleton Rice, Orator of the Day. Honorary member of the "Painters" Association;" in the Bethel Baptist Church, before the several Civic Societies in New-York. New-York, Pr. by E. Conrad, 1832. 18 p. DLC; MdBLC.   14517

Rice, Daniel T.
   An eulogium, on the sublime virtues of the illustrious hero and philanthropist, Gen Lafayette; with sketches of the American and French revolutions. By Daniel T. Rice... Enfield, J. Howe, 1832. RPB.   14518

Rice, John Holt, 1777-1831.
   Historical and philosophical considerations on religion; addressed to James Madison, esq., late President of the United States. By Rev. John H. Rice, D.D. Richmond, Pr. by J. Macfarlan, 1832. 110 p. CSmH; MH-AH; PPPrHi; TxU.   14519

---- Memoir of James Brainard Taylor. By John Holt Rice, D.D. and Benjamin Holt Rice, D.D. 2d stereotype ed. Rev. under the sanction of the surviving compiler. New York, American Tract Society, [1832] 528 p. NcSalL.
                                14520

Richards, James, 1767-1843.
   Lectures on the prayer of faith: read before the theological students of Auburn, N.Y. ...

New York, J. Leavitt, 1832.
38 p. CtHC; MiU; OClWHi;
OCHP; PPPrHi.   14521

Richards, Jonathan.
Lectures on the prayer of
Faith, read before the Theological Students at Auburn, N. Y. ,
and pub. at their request. New
York, Jonathan Leavitt, 1832.
38 p. MA.   14522

Richards, Samuel.
Sketches of Farmington, Connecticut, from its first settlement
to the present time. By an in-
habitant. Windsor, Pr. at the
Chronicle Press, 1832. 16 p. Ct;
CtHC; CtHT-W; MB.   14523

Richardson, James, 1791-1875.
An address to the Massachusetts Society for Promoting Agriculture. Delivered at their request, Oct. 17, 1832. By James
Richardson, Esq. Boston, Christian Register Office, 1832. 20 p.
DLC; MBHo; MLei; MNBedf;
MWA.   14524

Richland School.
Catalogue of the Officers and
Students, and Regulations...De-
cember 1831. Columbia, 1832.
12 p. MHi.   14525

Richmond, Legh, 1722-1827.
The African servant. An authentic narrative. New York
[1832?] 16 p. NN.   14526

Richmond Athenaem and Young
Men's Institute. Prospectus,
1832. [3] p. Vi.   14527

Riggs, Elias, 1810-1901.
Manual of the Chaldee language,
containing a Chaldee grammar
chiefly from the German of G. B.
Winer...By Elias Riggs. Boston,
Perkins & Marvin; Philadelphia,
French and Perkins, 1832. CU;
GDC; NNF; RPB; ScCC.   14528

Ringan Gilhaize; or The Coven-
anters. By the author of "Annals
of the Parish," "Sir Andrew Wylie," "The Entail," &c. &c. New-
York, Pr. by J. & J. Harper,
1832. 2 v. MdHi.   14529

Rio, Andres Manuel del, 1765-
1849.
Elementos De Orictognosia,
Del Conocimiento De Los Fosiles,
Segun El Sistema De Bercelio, Y
Segun Los Principios De Abraham
Gottloe Werner. Con La Sinonim-
ia Inglesa, Alemana Y Francesa,
Para Uso Del Seminario Nacional
De Mineria De Mexico. For el C.
Andres Del Rio... Parte Practica
--Segunda Edicion. Filadelfia,
Imprenta De Juan F. Hurtel, 1832.
683 p. DLC; MsU; PPAmP; TxU.
                            14530
Ripley, H. J.
Hints on the promotion of piety
in ministers of the gospel: read
before the Conference of Baptist
Ministers in Massachusetts, at
their annual meeting in Boston.
May 29, 1832. By H. J. Ripley,
Professor of biblical literature
and pastoral duties in the Newton
Theological Institution. Boston,
Lincoln and Edmands, 1832. 12 p.
DLC; MNtCA; MWA; NHCS; PCA.
                            14531
Ripley, Thomas Baldwin, 1795-
1876.
A discourse delivered in the
Baptist meeting-house in Packman,
September 12, 1832, before the
Penobscot Association, by Ripley,
pastor of the Baptist church in
Bangor. Bangor, Burton & Carters,
1832. 20 p. MW; PHi.   14532

Ritchie, Leitch, 1800?-1865.
Traveling sketches in the North
of Italy, the Tyrol, and on the
Rhine, with twenty-six engravings.
From drawing by Clarkson Stan-
ford (being Heath's picturesque
Annual for 1832). Philadelphia,
Thos. Wandle, 1832. 256 p. Ia;
                            14533

Robbins, Asher, 1757-1845.

Speech of the Hon. Asher Robbins of Rhode Island, in defense of the system for the protection of American industry. Delivered in the Senate of the United States, March 2, 1832. Washington, Pr. by Gales & Seaton, 1832. 14 p. LU; MWA; NNC; RHi; VtU. 14534

---- A statement of some leading principles and measures adopted by General Jackson, in his administration of the national government;... Addressed to the citizens of Rhode-Island, Providence, Pr. by W. Marshall & Co., 1832. 12 p DLC; MBC; MWA; WHi; RHi. 14535

[Robbins, Eliza] 1786-1853.

Sequel to American popular lessons, intended for the use of schools, by the author of American popular lessons... New York, Collins & Hannay, 1832. 376 p. ICU; IEG; MdB; NRNHi. 14536

---- Tales from American history (2d series, chiefly relating to the conquest of Mexico and Peru, by Hernando Cortez & Francisco Pizarro;... By the author of "American popular lessons." New York, W. Burges, 1832. 247, 18 p. DLC; RPB. 14537

Robbins, Royal, 1788-1861.

The world displayed in its history and geography embracing a history of the world from the creation to the present day... By the Rev. Royal Robbins. New York, W. W. Reed & Co., 1832. 2 vols. DLC; InCW; IU; OCl; ScDuE. 14538

Roberts, Daniel, 1658-1727.

Some account of the persecutions and sufferings of the people called Quakers, in the 16th century, exemplified in the memoirs of the life of John Roberts, 1665. To which are added several epistles, essays, &c. New York, D. Cool-

edge, 1832. 256 p. InRchE; MH; MNan; PHC; PSC-Hi. 14539

Robertson, William, 1721-1793.

... The history of the discovery and settlement of America... Complete in one volume. New York, Harper & Bros., 1832. 570 p. CtMW; KHi; MBC; NcWfC; ScDuE. 14540

Robinson, Charles.

An address delivered before the Woonsocket Falls Temperance Society, January 15, 1832, by Rev. C. Robinson. Pawtucket, Pr. by S. M. Fowler, 1832. 14 p. MHi; RHi; RPB. 14541

Robinson, Conway, 1805-1884.

The practice in the courts of law and equity in Virginia. By Conway Robinson. Richmond, S. Shepherd & Co., 1832-1839. 3 v. C; DLC; MH-L; MdBB; Nb; ViU. 14542

Robinson, Frederick.

A letter to the Hon. Rufus Choate containing a brief exposure of law craft... (Marblehead, Mass.) Pr. for the purchaser, 1832. 19 p. MB; OCLaw; RP. 14543

Robinson, Samuel.

A course of fifteen lectures, on medical botany, denominated Thomson's new theory of medical practice; in which the various theories that have preceded it are reviewed and compared. Delivered in Cincinnati, Ohio, by Samuel Robinson. With introductory remarks by the proprietor. Columbus, Pub. by Pike, Platt and Co., 1832. 206 p. GU-M; KyLxJ; MoS; RPM; ScSp. 14544

---- A lecture, introductory to a course, on the science of life, organization, etc. Bound with-Howard-An improved system of botanic medicine. Columbus, 1832. 24 p. RPM. 14545

Roche, Martin.

Compendious rules for book-keeping... By Martin Roche... Philadelphia, Pr. by Garden & Thompson, 1832. 9, (3) p. DLC; NNC.   14546

Rogers, Ammi.
Memoirs of Ammi Rogers, a clergyman of the Episcopal church ...4th ed. Concord, Fisk, 1832. 264 p. MA; MBD.   14547

Rogers, Hester Ann, 1756-1794.
Account of the experience of Hester Ann Rogers and her funeral sermon. By Rev. T. Coke, LL. D. To which is added her spiritual letters. New York, B. Waugh & T. Mason, 1832. 243 p. IC; ICU; LNH; MH; ODaB.   14548

Rogers, John G.
Specimen of printing types from the Boston type & stereotype foundry, nos. 37 & 39 Congress Street. Boston, S. N. Dickinson, 1832. ICN; MH; NNC-Atf.
                                       14549

Rogers, William.
Roger's Arithmetick, with questions and answers. A new system of arithmetick in which the rules are familiarly demonstrated, and the principles on the science clearly and fully explained... 2d ed. By Wm. Rogers, A. B., Watertown, N. Y., Knowlton & Rice, Booksellers, 1832. 264 p. NWattJHi.   14550

Rollin, Charles, 1661-1741.
The ancient history of the Egyptians, Carthaginians, Assyrians, Macedonians & Grecians... Baltimore, Geo. McDowell & Son, 1832. 2 vols. KPea; MiD-B; NBuG; PU; ViRut.   14551

---- History of Egypt, abridged from Rollins with additional observations by a friend of Sunday schools; revised by the editors. New York, B. Waugh and T. Ma-

son, for the Sunday School Union of the Methodist Episcopal Church at the Conference place, 1832. 214 p. NcGC.   14552

Romaine, Benjamin.
State sovereignty, and a certain dissolution of the union, by Benjamin Romaine, An old citizen of New York. To the honorable John C. Calhoun, now vice president of the United States. New York, Pr. by J. Kennaday, 1832. 54 p. CU; ICU; NbU; PHi; TxU.
                                       14553

Romani, Felice, 1788-1865.
The pirate (Libretto) See Bellini, Vincenzo, 1801-1835.

[Ronaldson, Richard]
Banks and a paper currency; their effects upon society. By a friend of the people. Philadelphia, 1832. 12 p. ICU; MH.   14554

[Roosevelt, Clinton] 1804-1898.
Proposition of a new system of Political Economy; and a party to prevent the threatened civil war between the North and South. New-York, O. Holsted, 1832. 8 p. DLC; MBAt.   14555

Root, Erastus, 1773-1846.
The speeches on the resolution of Mr. Clayton, of Georgia, proposing a committee of visitation to the Bank of the U. S., delivered to the 7th, 8th and 14th days of March, 1832, in the House of Representatives. [Washington? 1832] 24 p. DLC; MHi; NN; OCIWHi; PHi; TxDaM.   14556

Roscoe, Henry, 1800-1836.
A digest of the law of evidence on the trial of actions at nisi prius... 1st Amer. from 2d London ed. ... Philadelphia, P. H. Nicklin & T. Johnson, 1832. 607 [1] p. DLC; Ia; LNB; PP; TxU-L.
                                       14557

Rose, John.

A key to the fifth edition of
the United States Arithmetician.
Philadelphia, Thos. Sutton &
John Rose, 1832. 196 p. DAU.
                              14558
---- The United States arithmetician or the science of arithmetic simplified... By John Rose.
5th stereotyped ed., cor. Philadelphia, G. W. Mentz & Son,
1832. 180 p. DLC; MoInRC;
OClWHi; PU.   14559

The Rose bud. Mar. 1832-Feb.
1834. Vol. 1-2. Lowell, Oliver
Sheple, 1832-1833. DLC; MB;
MiD-B; NjR.   14560

Rosecrucius, pseud.
    The occasional Olla Podrida,
written against idleness, and between times... Baltimore, J.
Robinson, 1832. 36 p. DLC;
MdHi.   14561

[Rossini, Gioachino Antonio]
    The Italian in Algiers, as per-
formed at the Richmond-Hill
Theatre. New York, L. Da Ponte,
1832. 71 p. MH; NCaS.   14562

---- Moses in Egypt, a sacred
oratorio, to be sung at the Richmond Hill Theatre in New York.
[New York?] L. Da Ponte, 1832.
40 p. MB; MH; PPL; PU. 14563

Rowbotham, John, 1793?-1846.
    A practical grammar of the
French language. With alterations
and additions by F. M. J. Surault.
2d ed. Boston, Hilliard, Gray,
& Co., etc., etc., 1832. 324 p.
CtHWatk; MB; MH; MDeeP; MeBa.
                              14564
Rowe, Elizabeth.
    Devotional exercises of the
heart in meditation, soliloquy,
prayer and praise. Baltimore,
John J. Harrod, 1832. 220 p.
AmSSchU; CtHC; MB; PPAmS.
                              14565
Rowland, Henry Augustus, 1804-

1859.
    The real glory of a church. A
dedication sermon preached in
Fayetteville, N. C., at the opening of the Presbyterian Church,
which was destroyed by fire in the
conflagration of the town on the
29th of May 1831, and rebuilt and
dedicated August 12th 1832. By
Henry A. Rowland, pastor of the
church. New York, J. Leavitt
and J. P. Haven, 1832. 34 p.
DLC; MBC; MH-AH; NcU; PPPrHi.
                              14566
Rowlatham, J.
    Grammar of the French lan-
guage. By J. Rowlatham. Boston,
1832. UU.   14567

Rowson, Susanna (Haswell), 1762-
1824.
    Charlotte Temple, a tale of
truth... Cincinnati, U. P. James,
1832. 139 p. NN.   14568

---- ---- Hartford; Hallowell
(Me.), U. C. J. Wilson, 1832.
136 p. CtY.   14569

---- ---- New York, John Lomax, 1832.   14570

Rudd, John Churchill, 1779-1848.
    The temple destroyed, or The
parish in affliction. A sermon,
preached in the court house, Auburn, Cayuga county, N. Y. The
sixth Sunday after Epiphany, Feb.
12, 1832, being the Sunday following the destruction of St. Peter's
church by fire. By J. C. Rudd...
Auburn [N. Y.] Pr. by H. B. Ten
Eyck, 1832. 16 p. CSmH; MB;
NGH; NN; RPB.   14571

Ruffin, Edmund, 1794-1865.
    An essay on calcareous ma-
nures. By Edmund Ruffin. Petersburg, Campbell, 1832. 242 p.
DLC; NGeno; NcWfC.   14572

Ruger, William.
    Ruger's Arithmetick. A new

system of arithmetick. 2d ed.
Watertown, N.Y., Knowlton &
Rice, 1832. 264 p. DAU; MH;
NIC; NICLA.   14573

Ruschenberger, Mrs.
Henry and Eleanora; a tragedy
founded on events, during the
American Revolution. Philadelphia,
Pr. for the author by F. Turner,
1832. 51 p. MH.   14574

Russell, Michael, bp. of Glas-
gow and Galloway, 1781-1848.
...Palestine; or, The Holy
Land. From the earliest period
to the present time. By the Rev.
Michael Russell...New York, J.
& J. Harper, 1832. 330, [10] p.
ArCH; CtMW; IaU; NmU; PPP;
ViU.   14575

Russell, Philemon R.
More than two hundred rea-
sons for being a restorationist...
By Philemon R. Russell. Boston,
Press of the Independent Mes-
senger, 1832. 52 p. MBC; MHi;
MMeT-Hi; Nh.   14576

Russell, William, 1741-1793.
History of modern Europe;
with a view of the progress of
society from the rise of the modern kingdoms to the peace of Paris in 1763...New York, J. & J.
Harper, 1832. 3 vols. In; FOA;
MoS; OCY; ViU.   14577

Rutherforth, Thomas, 1712-1771.
Institutis of natural laws; being the substance of a course of
lectures on Gratius De jure belli
et pacis, read in St. John's College, Cambridge. By T. Rutherforth...2d Amer. ed., carefully
rev. and cor. Baltimore, W. & J.
Neal, 1832. 596 p. DLC; Ia; NcU;
PU; ViU.   14578

Ryan, John.
Intolerance: or civil rights
denied, on account of religious

belief: in the case of John Ryan,
of Quebec...Lower Canada. Boston, 1832. 16 p. MHi.   14579

Ryan, Michael, 1793-1840.
A Manual of medical jurisprudence compiled from the best
medical and legal works: being an
analysis of a course of lectures
on forensic medicine annually delivered in London. 1st Amer. ed.,
with notes and additions by R.
Eglesfeld Griffith. Philadelphia,
Casey, 1832. 327 p. ICJ; MB;
NNN; PPCP; ScNC.   14580

Ryland, Dr.
Daily provision; or, A brief
directory for Christians in general, and more particularly ministers; selected by Dr. Ryland.
Hartford, 1832. MBC.   14581

S

The Sabbath. A sermon... See
Pressley, John Taylor.

The Sabbath School Library...
Vol. 1. Boston, Perkins & Marvin, Pr. by A. W. Thayer, 1832.
224 p. ICBB.   14582

Sacred vocalist, or pocket collec-
tion of select and original tunes.
New York, Burnett & Smith,1832.
LNH; MB; MBC; NN.   14583

Saddle horse; a complete guide
for riding and training. New York,
Judd, 1832. 95 p. PU-V. 14584

St. Clair, Henry.
The United States criminal
calendar: or an awful warning to
the youth of America;...by Henry
St. Clair. Boston, Charles Gaylord, 1832. 355 p. MAbD; MB;
MHi.   14585

St. John, James Augustus, 1801-
1875.

The Lives of celebrated travellers. By James Augustus St. John... New York, J. & J. Harper, 1832. 3 vols. GEU; LNB; NjR; TNP; WaU.   14586

St. Louis College.
The third annual examination of the students attached to this institution, will take place on Monday, the 30th, instant... P. J. Verhaegen, President. July 28, 1832. Broadside. MoSU.   14587

Salem, Mass. Committee to examine into the concerns of the Salem almshouse.
Documents on the subject of the ... reported by a committee of the town... Salem, Foote & Brown, 1832. 12 p. DLC; M.   14588

---- First Church.
Correspondence between the First Church and The Tabernacle Church in Salem, in which the duties of the church is discussed. ...Salem, Press of Foote & Brown, 1832. 176 p. CSmH; ICMe; MWA; NNUT; WHi. 14589

---- Independent Congregational Church.
Order of services at the installation of Rev. James W. Thompson, as Pastor of the Independent Congregational Church in Barton Square, Salem on Wednesday, March 7, 1832. Pr. by W. & L. B. Ives, Observer Office [1832] broadside. MHi.   14590

Sales, Francis.
Colmena española, o, piezas escogido de varios autores españoles, murales, instructinas y divertidas. ...Segunda edición. Boston, S. Burdett, 1832. 216 p. DLC; MH; NjP; PPM; OMC.
        14591
Sallustius Crispus, C.
Opera omnia quae extant, interpretatione et notis illustravit

Daniel Crispinus in usum serenissimi Delphini; in hac secunda ed. Americana pleraque Londiniens errata, diligentissime animadversa, corriguntur. Philadelphia, M'-Carty and Davis, 1832. 256 p. CtHT; DLC; ICP; MdW.   14592

Sam Patch. Philadelphia, W. Johnson, Mead Alley, 1832. 15 p. DLC; NNC.   14593

Sampson, Ezra.
The Youth's Companion; or, a Historical Dictionary... originally compiled by Ezra Sampson... carefully rev. and abridged by John B. Longgley... St. Clairsville, O., Pr. by Horton J. Howard for the compiler, 1832. 300 p. DLC; NN; OClWHi; OMC; PPM.   14594

Sandford, Peter P.
Christian baptism. A discourse on Acts II, 38, 39. In which an attempt is made to investigate the nature and perpetuity, the subjects, and the mode of Christian baptism. 2d ed. New York, J. Collord, 1832. 33 p. KSalW; NHCS; NjR; OO; PMA.   14595

---- The Christian Sabbath; or, The universal and perpetual obligation of the Sabbath... being a discourse on Matthew XII, 8. By Rev. P. P. Sanford. 2d ed., rev. by the author. New York, B. Waugh & T. Mason, for the Methodist Episcopal Church, 1832. 24 p. MBC; NNMHi; PPPrHi.
        14596
Sandham, Elizabeth.
Providential care: a tale founded on facts by the author of the Twin Sisters, Boy's School, School fellows &c. 2d Amer. ed. New York, Wm. Burgess, Juvenile Emporium, 1832. 108 p. NAnge.   14597

Sanford, Enoch.
The history of the first church

and society in Raynham, in two discourses, delivered January 1, 1832. Taunton, Edward Anthony, 1832. 24 p. CBPSR; MB; MiD-B; PHi; RPB. 14598

Sanitary precepts, in relation to epidemic cholera morlus, published by the Hamburg Council of Health. Trans. and repub. with an appendix. By John G. Kettner. Philadelphia, 1832. 9 p. PReaHi. 14599

Saratoga and Fort Edward Railroad Company.
Act incorporating... estimates and costs... Saratoga Springs, Pr. by Bennett and Lord, 1832. 11 p. CSmH; DLC; MH-BA. 14600

Sargent, John, 1780-1833.
An address delivered at the request of the managers of the apprentices' Library Co. of Philadelphia, 23rd November. By John Sargent, LL.D. Pres. of the institution. Philadelphia, Pr. by James Kay, Jun & Co., 1832. 37 p. DLC; MB; PU; WHi; ViAl. 14601
---- A memoir of the Rev. Henry Martyn, B.D. ...By the Rev. John Sargent, M.A.... From the 10th London ed., cor. and enl. 2d ed. Boston, Perkins & Marvin; Philadelphia, French & Perkins, 1832. 467 p. CBPSR; ICP; MH; NbOP. 14602

[Saunders, James M.]
Ode. (At Phillips Exeter Academy, August 23, 1832.) broadside. MHi. 14603

Saurin, James, 1677-1730.
Sermons of the Rev. James Saurin, late pastor of the French Church at The Hague. From the French by the Rev. Robert Robinson, Henry Hunter and Joseph Sutcliff. Rev. and corr. by Samuel Burder. Baltimore, Plaskitt & Co., 1832. 2 vols. CtMW; InU;

MdHi; NjP; ScDuE. 14604

Savage, James, 1784-1873.
Constitution of Massachusetts. Address delivered before the Massachusetts Lyceum, January 26, 1832. By James Savage. 12 p. Ct; DLC; MB; MHi; MdBJ. 14605

Say, Jean Baptiste.
A treatise on political economy; or, The production, distribution and consumption of wealth. By Jean Baptiste Say. Tr. from the 4th ed. of the French by C. R. Prinsep, M.A. With notes by the translator. 5th Amer. ed. Philadelphia, Grigg & Elliott, 1832. 1832. 455 p. CSmH; IaB; MnHi; OCY; ScCC. 14606

Say, Thomas, 1787-1834.
American conchology... Part IV. New-Harmony, Ind., Pr. at the School Press, 1832. DLC; In; NbU; OU; P. 14607
---- ---- Part V. New-Harmony, Ind., Pr. at the School Press, 1832. ICJ; NbU; MB; PHi. 14608
---- A glossary of Say's Conchology. New Harmony, Ind., Pr. by Richard Beck and James Bennett, 1832. 25 p. CoU; DLC; InHi; OU; P. 14609
---- New species of North American insects, found by Joseph Barabino, chiefly in Louisiana. By Thos. Say. New Harmony, Pr. at the School Press, 1832. 16 p. MBM. 14610

Saying and doing, or, Frank and Harry. New York, Mahlon Day, 1832. 16 p. DLC. 14611

Schauffler, William Gottlieb, 1790-1883.
Essay upon the right use of property. By the Rev. Wm. G. Schauffler, Missionary to the

Jews of Turkey. Boston, Pr. by
Crocker & Brewster, 1832. 12 p.
Ct; MBAt; NjR; OCHP; ViRut;
WHi.   14612

Schipper, Benedict J.
    A concise and comprehensive
practical grammar of the Latin
tongue, with an appendix illustrating many peculiarities and
difficulties met with the classics,
to which is annexed a vocabulary
for the exercises, quotations,
and mythology... Philadelphia, Pr.
by Mifflin for the author, 1832.
275 p. CtMW; DLC; MB; MdBS;
NjP; PAtM.   14613

[Schmid, Christoph von], 1768-
1854.
    Geneveva; a tale of antiquity,
translated from the German,
by Frederick D. Tschiffely.
Washington, Thompson & Homans, 1832. 147 p. CtY; MdBG;
MdBP; MdHi; PPL.   14614

Schoene Geistliche Ausserlesene
und Einfaltige Raetzel- Stueck-
lein, Aus Gottes Wort Zusamm-
em gezogen. Trenton, Butler
County, Ohio, zu finden Bei
Peter Schertz [1832] Broadside.
InGo.   14615

Scholefield, James.
    Hints for an improved transla-
tion of the New Testament. Cambridge, J. Smith, 1832. 98 p.
MBC.   14616

School children at noon... Philadelphia, American Sunday-School
Union, 1832. 16 p. DLC. 14617

Schoolcraft, Henry Rowe.
    An address delivered before
the Chippewa County Temperance
Society, on the influence of ardent spirits, on the condition of
the North American Indians. Detroit, Pr. by Geo. L. Whitney,
1832. 13 p. CSmH; MB; MWA;

OCX; PPAmP.   14618

Schrevel, Cornelis.
    ... Lexicon Manuale graeco-
latinum et latino-graecum: studio
atque opera Joseph Hill, Joannis
Entick, Gulielmi Bowyer, nec non
Jacobi Smith adactum... Hanc
editionem XXII curavit et auctorem
fecit Petrus Steele... New York,
Collins & Hannay, 1832. 531 p.
DLC; IU; MdBS; TxU; ViU.14619

Schuylkill Navigation Company.
    Agreements of June 3, 1819,
July 20th and June 14, 1824, between the Mayor, Alderman and
citizens of Philadelphia, and the
Schuylkill Navigation Company,
relative to the water power at
Fairmount. Philadelphia, Bailey,
1832. 31 p. DLC; PPFrankI.
                                  14620
Scientific tracts & family lyceum:
designed for instruction & entertainment & adopted to schools,
lyceums & families. Boston, Allen & Ticknor, 1832-35. 5 vols.
PPins; PPFrankI; PU.   14621

Scott, David.
    Calm examination of Dr. Mc-
Master's letters on civil government. Newburgh, C. U. Cushman, 1832. 44 p. CSmH; MH;
NcMHi; PPPrHi.   14622

Scott, Job.
    The power of religion exempli-
fied in the life, sickness, and
death of... Philadelphia, n.p.,
1832. PHC.   14623

Scott, John.
    Narratives of two families ex-
posed to the great plague of London, A.D. 1665. With conversations on religious preparation for
pestilence. By John Scott. 1st
Amer. ed. New York, Edward
J. Swords, 1832. 179 p. CtHT;
GDecCT; NjR; OrPD; PPiD.
                                  14624

Scott, Orange.
New and improved camp meeting hymn book. . . a choice selection of hymns. . . designed to aid in the public and private devotion of Christians. 3d ed. Brookfield, Mass. , Merriam, 1832. 192 p. CtWatk; PPLT.   14625

Scott, Walter, 1771-1832.
The abbot; being the sequel to the monastery. Parker's ed. , rev. and cor. with a general preface. . . and notes, historical and illustrative, by the author. Boston, Parker, 1832. 2 vols. NCH; NjR.   14626

---- The antiquary. Parker's ed. rev. and cor. with a general preface. . . and notes historical and illustrative, by the author. Boston, Parker, 1832. 2 vols. NCH.   14627

---- . . . The betrothed--The talisman. From the last rev. ed. , containing the author's final corrections, notes, etc. Parker's ed. Boston, Bazin & Ellsworth, [1832] DLC; MCan.   14628

---- The fortunes of Nigel. Boston, Parker, 1832. 2 vols. MB-FA.   14629

---- Letters on demonology and witchcraft, addressed to J. G. Lockhart Esq. by Sir Walter Scott, Bart. New York, J. & J. Harper, 1832. 338 p. MDeeP; OO; OrPD.   14630

---- The life of Napoleon Buonaparte [sic], emperor of the French. With a preliminary view of the French revolution. By the author of "Waverley," &c. . . . Exeter [N. H.] J. & B. Williams, 1832. 2 vols. MH; OClWHi; PLFM; TNP.   14631

---- Peveril of the Peak. Boston,

Parker, 1832. 2 vols. MB-FA.   14632

---- The poetical works of Sir Walter Scott. With life, by Wm. Chambers, LL. D. New York, Hurst & Co. , 1832. 536 p. KyLoP.   14633

---- . . . Quentin Durward; a romance. Parker's ed. . . ; Boston, Samuel H. Parker, 1832. 2 vols. GHi; MB; MeBa.   14634

---- Red gauntlet; a tale of the eighteenth century. . . Boston, Bazin and Ellsworth [1832?] DLC; NCH.   14635

---- . . . St. Roman's well. . . From the last rev. ed. , containing the author's final corrections, notes, etc. Parker's ed. Boston, Bazin and Ellsworth [1832] CFrT; DLC; MB-FA; NN.   14636

---- Tales of my landlord, the heart of mid-lothian. In two vols. Vol. 1, Parker's ed. rev. and cor. , with a general preface, an introduction to each novel, and notes, historical and illustrative, by the author. Boston, Samuel H. Parker, 1832. 2 vols. RPB; WM.   14637

---- ---- Philadelphia, Carey & Lea, 1832. 3 v. LU; PPiU; RPB.   14638

---- The Talisman. A tale of the crusaders and the chronicles of the cannongate by Sir Walter Scott, Bart. The Diamond of the Desert. Boston, DeWolfe, Fiske & Co. , 1832? 513 p. FTaA; NcAT; NcRSA.   14639

---- . . . Woodstock; or the cavalier. From the last rev. ed. containing the author's final corrections, notes. . . Parker's ed. Boston, Bazin & Ellsworth, [1832] 2 v. in 1. DLC; IaDm.   14640

Scott, William.
   The border exploits...2d ed.
Carlisle, C. Thurman, 1832.
379 p. NN.   14641

Scott, William K.
   An address delivered at Union
Village, December 7, 1831, before the Washington Co. Temperance Society; by Dr. Wm. K.
Scott. Pub. by order of the society. Sandy-Hill, N.Y., Pr. at
the Temperance Advocate Office,
1832. 19 p. CtWatk; MWA.14642

Scougal, Henry, 1650-1678.
   The life of God in the soul of
man; or, The nature and excel-
lency of the Christian religion.
By Henry Scougal, M.A. some
time professor of divinity in the
University of Aberdeen... Boston,
Lincoln & Edmands, 1832. 80 p.
TNP.   14643

Scoutetten, Raul Henri Joseph,
1799-1871.
   A medical and topographical
history of the cholera morbus,
including the mode of prevention
and treatment...With a report
read at the Royal academy of
medicine, at Paris, September
17, 1831. Transl. from the
French by A. Sidney Doane. Boston, Carter & Hendee, 1832. 100
p. ICU-R; MdBJ; NNUT; PPA;
VtU.   14644

Searle, Moses C.
   The importance of continued
revivals. A farewell discourse,
delivered at Grafton, Mass., on
Sabbath, April 1, 1832. Boston,
Peirce & Parker, 1832. 27 p.
ICN; MWA; OClWHi; RPB. 14645

Sears, James H.
   Standard Spelling book. New-
ark, N.J., n.p., 1832. MDeeP.
                                  14646
Seavy, Joseph.
   A treatise on the Asiatic chol-

era, giving an account of it's rise
and progress; character and na-
ture; symptoms; preventions and
method of treatment. By Doctor
Joseph Seavy. New York, Pr. by
Elliott & Palmer, 1832. 28 p.
MnU; MoSU-M; NBMS; NNN;
NNNAM.   14647

A second letter to Mr. Howell
being a short answer to his Letter
to Dr. Ducachet, in reply to an
"Examination" of his "Review" of
"The office of sponsors" etc. By
an Episcopalian. Norfolk, T. G.
Broughton, 1832. 22 p. MdBD;
NjPT.   14648

Secrest, John.
   A selection of psalms, hymns,
and spiritual songs, carefully examined and improved. St. Clairsville, Pr. by Horton J. Howard,
for the compiler, 1832. 128 p.
OClWHi.   14649

Sedgwick, Catherine Maria, 1789-
1867.
   Mary Hollis; an original tale.
New York, The New York Uni-
tarian Book Society, 1832. 22 p.
MeB.   14650

---- Tales of Glauber-Spa See
under Bryant, William Cullen,
1794-1878, ed.

Sedgwick, Elizabeth (Dwight).
   The beatitudes. 2d ed. Boston,
Bowles, 1832. 106 p. MBSi.
                                  14651
Seeger, C. L.
   A lecture on the epidemic cholera, delivered in Springfield on
the 2nd of August, and in Northampton on the 9th of August, and
published at the request of a number of inhabitants of both places.
Boston, Carter & Hendee, 1832.
26 p. DSG; MB; MiU; MBM;
NNNAM.   14652

Seidenstuecker, J. H. P.

Elementary practical books for learning...the French language... Trans. by Mrs. B. O. Addicks. Philadelphia, for translorator, 1832. DLC; IU; MH; NNC; PPL-R.   14653

Seixas, Joshua.
[A manual Hebrew grammar for the use of beginners.] [Andover, 1832?] MB.   14654

Select circulating library. Oct. 1, 1832-April 1842. Philadelphia, Waldie, 1832-1842. 17 vols. TNP.
                                                    14655
Self Examination; or the Churchman on a sick bed. With prayers for the use of the sick. Charleston, S. C. ? A. E. Miller, Pr. to the Society, 1832. 15 p. NcU.
                                                    14655a
Seller, Richard.
Narratives of the sufferings of R. S. a member of the religious Society of Friends, in support of their testimony against war: and of William Moore, and John Philly, members of the same society in the inquisition of Hungary. Philadelphia, U. Hunt, 1832. 26 p. MdBP; MU; NN; PHC.   14656

The senator unmasks, being a letter to Daniel Webster on his speech in the Senate of U. S. on bill to continue Charter of Bank of U. S.   Philadelphia, 1832. 25 p. PHi.   14657

Sergeant, John, 1779-1852.
Eulogy on Charles Carroll of Carrollton. Delivered at the request of the select and common councils of the City of Philadelphia, Dec. 1832. PPB; PPL.
                                                    14658
---- Orations. Philadelphia, 1832. MdAS.   14659

---- Select speeches of John Sergeant, of Pennsylvania [1818-1828] Philadelphia, E. L. Carey

& A. Hart, 1832. 367 p. CtHT; DLC; MH; NjR; PPA; RPA.
                                                    14660
A series of numbers upon three theological points, enforced from various pulpits in the city of New York. By Investigation. New York, O. Halstead, 1832. 396 p. ViRut.
                                                    14661
A sermon on Contentment. Delivered in Philadelphia, December 10, 1832. Pr. by John C. Clark [1832] 8 p. KyLx.   14662

Sermon on the day of public humiliation recommended by the Mayor. New York, n. p. , 1832. PPL.   14663

Sermon on the manner and nature of an acceptable fast. Boston, J. Howe, 1832. 11 p. MWA.
                                                    14664
Seventh-Day Baptist General Conference.
An Apology for the practice of a strict communion. Addressed to a Pedo-Baptist Clergyman. New York, Pub. under direction of the Publishing Committee appointed by the Seventh-Day Baptist General Conference, 1832. 12 (2) p. RHi.   14665

Severance, Moses.
American Manual, or, New English reader...to which are added...history of the colonies ...Declaration of Independence... constitution of the U. S. and of... New York. Geneva, N. Y. , R. Robbins & Co. , 1832. 295 p. CSmH; MiD-B; NPV; NRMA; OrCa.   14666

[Sewall, Charles C.]
The Rich and Poor meet together: The Lord is the maker of them all. A sermon preached in the First Unitarian Church, Danvers, Mass. By the minister of that church. Brooklyn, Pr. by C. Webber, 1832. 12 p. MWA.
                                                    14667

[Sewall, Henry Devereux]
A collection of psalms and hymns, for social and private worship. 3d ed. Boston, Gray & Bowen, 1832. 422 p. CBPac; IEG; MB-FA; OCoC; PMA. 14668

Sewall, Thomas, 1786-1845.
Memoir of Dr. Godman: being an introductory lecture delivered Nov. 1, 1830, by Thos. Sewall, M.D. New York, R. Waugh & T. Mason, 1832. 24 p. CtHT; InHi; MB; PU; VtU. 14669

Seward, William Henry.
Speech of... on the resolution against renewing the charter of the United States bank, in the Senate of New York. Albany, Pr. by Packard, Hoffman & White, 1832. 16 p. MBC; MH-BA.
14670

Sewell, William, 1654-1720.
History of the rise, increase, and progress of the Christian people called Quakers. Philadelphia, Uriah Hunt, 1832. 2 vols. DeWi; MiU-C; PPF; OO; RLa.
14671

Seymour, Thomas Hart, 1807-1868.
An oration on education, delivered at Norwich, Vt., Sept. 5, 1831, on the eleventh anniversary of the American Literary, Scientific & Military Academy... Norwich, Vt., 1832. 16 p. Ct; DLC; MH; MWA. 14672

Shakers.
A brief exposition of the established principles, and regulations of the United society of believers called Shakers. Pr. at Albany, in the year 1830; and now repr. with sundry improvements... Watervliet, O., 1832. 36 p. ICU; MdBD; NN; OO; WHi.
14673

Shakespeare, William, 1564-1616.
The dramatic works of William Shakespeare, accurately printed from the text of the corrected copy left by the late Geo. Stevens. With a glossary, and notes, and a sketch of the life of Shakespeare, in two vols. Hartford, Silas Andrus, 1832. 2 vols. KTW; MoS; MoWgW; NNS. 14674

---- ---- New York, James Conner, 1832. 844 p. InEvC; NNC; NcAS; NcD; SdMit. 14675

---- King John, a historical play; with prefatory remarks. Boston, Wells & Lilly, etc., etc., 1832. 88 p. MH. 14676

Sharp, Daniel, 1783-1853.
Apostolic mode of preaching. A sermon delivered in Boston, before the Conference of Baptist ministers, May 29, 1832. By Daniel Sharp, pastor of Charles-street Baptist church. Boston, Lincoln & Edmands [1832?] 16 p. CBPSR; MB; MH; MW; NHC-S.
14677

---- Tribute of respect to the character and memory of Mr. Ensign Lincoln, who died Dec. 2, 1832. Boston, Lincoln & Edmands, 1832. 16 p. CtSoP; MB; MH-AH; MNtCA; NHC-S. 14678

Sharpless, John T.
...Description of the American wild swan, proving it to be a new species. Cygnus Americanus. By John T. Sharpless, M.D., of Philadelphia. Read before the Academy of National Sciences of Philadelphia, Feb. 7th, 1832. 8 p. NNM. 14679

Shaw, Edward.
Civil architecture: or, A complete theoretical and practical system of building. Containing the fundamental principles of the art, with the five orders of architecture. Also a great variety of ex-

amples, selected from Vitruvius, Stuart, Chambers, and Nicholson. 2d ed. rev. & enl. Boston, Marsh, Capen & Lyon, 1832. 192, 97 p. IU; MH; NhD; RP; USI.   14680

---- Operative Masonry; or, A theoretical and practical treatise on building; containing a scientific account of stones, clays, bricks, mortars, cement, etc. Boston, Capen & Lyon, 1832. 140 p. DLC; NNE; PP; RP; ViU.
14681

Shaw, Lemuel, 1781-1861.
A charge delivered to the grand jury for the county of Essex, at the supreme judicial court held at Ipswick, May term, 1832. Pub. at their request. Boston, 1832. 16 p. CtWatk; DLC; MBAt; MH; OO.   14682

Shaw, Oliver A.
A description of the visible numerator, with instructions for its use; illustrated with plates. Designed to impart to learners a clear and an adequate knowledge of the principles of arithmetic, and to accompany the apparatus. By Oliver A. Shaw. Boston, T. R. Marvin, 1832. CtWatk; MiU; NNC; PP; TxU-T.   14683

---- A series of illustrative plates... By Oliver A. Shaw. Boston, n. p., 1832. DLC; MWC.
14684

Shearman, Sylvester Gardner, 1820-1868.
An address delivered by Sylvester G. Shearman, Esq. before the North Kingstown Temperance Society, on the 4th day of November, 1832, at the Baptist Meeting House in Wickford, R. I. Providence, Wm. Simons, Jr, pr., 1832. 16 p. RPB.   14685

Shecut, John Lewis Edward Whitridge.

Strictures on certain select passages in Doctor Adam Clarke's commentary, particularly on those of the New Testament... By J. L. E. W. Shecut. Charleston, 1832. 53 p. MMeT-Hi; ScC; ScCC; TxU.
14686

Sheffield, F. U.
Strictures on Elder Robert Powell's appeal "To the Christian public," on the subject of speculative free-masonry... Palmyra, Pr. by Strong & Grandin, for the author, 1832. 45 p. CSmH; NN.   14687

Shelburne, Mass. Congregational Church.
Congregational Church in Shelburne, Mass., March 12, 1832. Greenfield, Mass., Phelps & Ingersoll, 1832. 11 p. MH. 14688

Shepard, Charles Upham, 1804-1886.
Treatise on mineralogy. New Haven, Hezekiah Howe, 1832-1835. 3 vols. in 1. Ct; DLC; MB; MH; VtU.   14689

Shepard, Thomas, 1605-1649.
The autobiography of Thomas Shepard, the celebrated minister of Cambridge, N. E. With additional notices of his life and character, by Nehemiah Adams... Boston, Peirce & Parker, 1832. 129 p. CtHC; ICT; MH-AH; NNUT; OCIWHi.   14690

The Sheperd Boy; Wendell, Mass., J. Metcalf, 1832. 18 p. MA; MH; MWA.   14691

Shepherd, William, 1768-1847.
A history of American Revolution published in London under the superintendence of the Society for the diffusion of useful knowledge. 1st Amer. ed. with notes and cuts. Boston, Stimpson & Clapp, 1832. 202 p. Ct; ICN; MBB; MdHi; OCY; P.   14692

Sherman, Alpheus.
Speech against the joint resolution offered in the Senate of...
New York, "instructing our Senators and requesting our representatives in Congress to vote
against renewing the charter of
the bank of the United States.
Albany, 1832. 8 p. NNC. 14693

Sherman, Eleazer, b. 1795.
Conference Hymns, selected
and original. By E. Sherman.
"Let the inhabitants of the rock
sing." 2d ed. Providence, Pr. by
H. H. Brown, 1832. 156, 63 p.
RHi; RPB.   14694

---- The narrative of Eleazer
Sherman, giving an account of his
life, experience, call to the ministry of the gospel, and travels as
such to the present time. Providence, H. H. Brown, 1832. 3 vol.
in 1. CtWatk; LNB; MBC; OClWHi;
RPB; TxU.   14695

Sherman, Roger Minott, 1773-
1844.
To the Hon. Elisha Phelps,
controller of public accounts,
Hartford, Conn... New Haven
[1832] CtY.   14696

[Sherman, Thomas]
Divine breathings; or, A pious
soul thirsting after Christ...
Philadelphia, G. Latimer & Co.,
1832. 110 p. KyHi; NNG. 14697

Sherrill, Hunting.
An essay on epidemics, as
they appeared in Dutchess county,
from 1809 to 1825: also, a paper
on diseases of the jaw-bones:
with an appendix, containing an
account of the epidemic cholera,
as it appeared in Poughkeepsie
in 1832. By Hunting Sherrill.
New York, Pr. by Booth & Smith,
1832. CtMW; MH; OO; PPCP;
RPM.   14698

Sherwood, Mary Martha [Butt]
1755-1851.
The hedge of thorns, by Mrs.
Sherwood,... New York, Samuel
Wood & sons and Samuel S.
Wood & Co. [1832] 87 p. NNC.
                             14699
---- History of little Henry and
his bearer... Philadelphia, 1832.
AmSSchu; BrMus.   14700

---- Little Robert and the owl;
by Mrs. Sherwood. New-York,
Mahlon Day, 1832. 23 p. MH.
                            14700a
---- ... Roxobel. By Mrs. Sherwood, author of "The lady of the
manor," "Little Henry and his
bearer," &c. &c. New-York, J.
& J. Harper, 1832. 3 vols.
TNP.   14701

---- Scripture prints, with explanations in the form of familiar
dialogues... New-York, Pendleton
and Hill, 1832. 254 p. DLC;
MPeaHi; MPiB.   14702

Short, Charles Wilkins, 1794-
1863.
A biographical memoir of H.
Hulbert Eaton... by Charles W.
Short... (delivered Nov. 10th, as
an introductory address to the
medical class, at the opening of
the session of 1832-3.) [Lexing-
ton? Ky. 1832-3] 15 p. KyLoF;
KyLxT; N; NN; NNC.   14703

A short account of the Blue Coat
Charity School in St. Philip's
church yard, Birmingham, from
its institution in 1724 to 1830.
Birmingham, Pr. for H. C. Lang-
bridge, 1832. 86 p. MH. 14704

A shot from a backwoodsman.
Relating to the Lehigh Navigation
Company. Philadelphia, 1832.
PPL.   14705

The Show of animals. Philadelphia, American Sunday School

Union, Philadelphia, 1832. 14706

[Shreve, Joseph]
Poems on the conclusion of the winter schools at Salem, at the close of the winters, 1831 and 1832. By the teacher. New Lisbon, Pub. by the pupils, John Watt, 1832. 21 p. NN; OClWHi.
14707

The Shrine. Conducted by a number of undergraduates in Amherst college... v. 1-2; May 1832-July 1833. Amherst, J. S. & C. Adams; Boston, Cottons & Barnard, 1832-33. 2 vols. DLC; MB; MH; MBC; MS.   14708

Shuttleworth, Philip Nicholas, 1782-1842.
The consistency of the whole scheme of revelation with itself and with human reason, by Philip Nicholas Shuttleworth. New York, J. & J. Harper, 1832. 267 p. MBC; NhD; OC; PPLT; ViAl.
14709

[Silliman, Benjamin] 1779-1864.
Peculiarities of the Shakers, described in a series of letters from Lebanon Springs, in the year 1832, containing an account of the origin, worship & doctrines of the Shakers' society, by a visiter. New York, J. K. Porter, 1832. 116 p. ICN; MH; NBuG; ViU; WHi.   14710

---- Some of the causes of national anxiety, an address delivered in the Centre Church in New-Haven, July 4, 1832. n. p. [1832] 27 p. CtY; MH.   14711

Simeon, Charles.
The offices of the holy spirit. Four sermons preached before the University of Cambridge, November, 1831. 1st Amer. from 2d London ed. New-York, Swords, Stanford & Co., 1832. 103 p. CtHC; GDecCT; ICU; NNG; WNaE.
14712

[Simms, William Gilmore] 1806-1870.
Atlanti's. A story of the sea; in three parts... New-York, J. & J. Harper, 1832. 80 p. A-Ar; MiU-C; PPi; RPB; ScC.   14713

---- Pelayo; A story of the Goth. Harper, 1832. 2 vols. ScDuE.
14714

Simond de Sismondi, Jean Charles Léonard, 1773-1842.
A history of the Italian republics. Being a view of the origin, progress, and fall of Italian freedom. Not an abridgement but an entirely new history. Philadelphia, Carey & Lea, 1832. 23-300 p. CU; GU; IaU; MiDU; OCY. 14715

---- ---- New ed. New York, Harper & Bros., [1832] 23-300 p. GEU; MnS; PPA; RWoH; WJan.
14716

Simple rhymes for little children. Written for the American Sunday-School Union, and revised by the committee of publication. Philadelphia, American Sunday-School Union, 1832. 17 (3) p. DLC; NjR.
14717

Simple Scripture biographies: or, The third part of a conversation between Mary and her mother. Prepared for the American Sunday School Union by Rev. Thos. H. Gallaudet... Philadelphia, American Sunday School Union, 1832. 162 p. DLC.   14718

Simpson, Stephen, 1789-1854.
Biography of Stephen Girard, with his will affixed; comprising an account of his private life, habits, genius, and manners; together with a detailed history of his banking and financial operations for the last twenty years. ...Embellished with a handsome portrait. Philadelphia, Thos. L. Bonsal, 1832. 281, 35 p. IU; KyU; MH; NIC; PPA.   14719

Sinclair, John.
Dumbarton's Bonnie Dell. Ballad. Sung with great applause by Mr. Sinclair, at the Park & Chestnut St. Theatres. Poetry by C. M. Westmoicott Esq. Composed by John Sinclair. Philadelphia, J. Edgar, 1832. 5 p. MB; ViU.　14720

The singer's own book, a well selected collection of the most popular, sentimental, amatory, patriotic, naval and comic songs. New ed. Philadelphia, Key, Mielke & Biddle [c1832] 320 p. MB; MH; MW; TxU.　14721

The singular and extraordinary adventures of poor little bewildered Henry, who was shut up in an old abbey for three weeks. A story founded on fact. By the author of "Nothing at all" &c. New-York, Mahlon Day, 1832. 21 p. OCIWHi.　14722

Siret, Charles Joseph Christopher, 1760-1830.
Epitome Historiae Graecae. New Haven, 1832. 155 p. MWA.　14723

Skinner, Otis Ainsworth.
Sermons on the doctrines of universal salvation. Baltimore, Md., 1832. 18 p. GEU-T; MdHi.　14724

Skinner, Thomas Harvey, 1791-1871.
Disbelieving the atonement, a rejection of the gospel. A sermon, preached in the chapel of the theological seminary, Andover, Sept. 8, 1833... By Thos. H. Skinner... Andover, Flagg, Gould & Newman, 1833. 37 (1) p. NNUT.　14725

---- Doctrinal preaching. An address, delivered before Porter rhetorical society, in the Theological seminary, Andover, Sept. 11, 1832. By Thos. H. Skinner.

Boston, Pr. by Peirce & Parker, 1832. 28 p. IEG; MeBat; NjR; OO; PHi; WHi.　14726

---- Hints designed to aid Christians in their efforts to convert men to God. Boston, Cong. Pub. Society [1832] 38 p. OO.　14727

---- ---- Cincinnati, A. R. T. & B. Soc., 1832. 31 p. OO. 14728

---- ---- Hartford, J. W. Judd & Co., 1832. 50 p. MH; MtU.　14729

---- ---- 2d ed. Philadelphia, French & Perkins, 1832. 36 p. MWA; NbOP; RPB.　14730

---- ---- 3d ed., enl. Philadelphia, French & Perkins, 1832. 64, [6] p. IEG; GDecCT; MBC; NNUT; OO.　14731

Slade, William, 1786-1859.
Speech of Mr. Slade, of Vermont, on the Resolution relative to the Collector of Wiscasset. Delivered in the House of Representatives, May, 1832. Washington, Pr. at the office of Jonathan Elliot, 1832. 52 p. CtHWatk; MWA; MiD-B; MBAt; PPL-R.　14732

Sly, Costard, pseud.
Sayings and doings at the Tremont House, in 1832. Ed. by Zachary Philemon Vangrifter. Boston, 1832. 2 vols. MdBP.　14733

Smedley, Edward, 1788-1836.
Sketches from Venetian History. By Edward Smedley. New York, J. & J. Harper, 1832. 2 vols. DLC; MiU; NGH; RNR; ScU.　14734

Smellie, William, 1740-1795.
The philosophy of natural history, by William Smellie... with an introduction and various additions and alterations... By John Ware, M. D. 4th ed. Boston,

Hilliard, Gray, Little & Wilkins, 1832. 327 p. CtMW; MB; NhPet; GMM; PU.   14735

Smiley, Thomas T.
Easy introduction to the study of geography, on an improved plan, compiled for the use of schools, with a view to render the acquisition of geographical science easy and pleasant to the student...16th ed. Philadelphia, Harding, 1832. 256 p. PPAN; PPL; PU.   14736

---- The new federal calculator ... Philadelphia, Grigg & Elliot, 1832. 180 p. OClWHi.   14737

Smith, Asa Dodge, 1804-1877.
Letters to a Young Student in the First Stage of a Liberal Education. Boston, Perkins & Marvin, 1832. 174 p. CtHT; ICP; MeB; OMC; TNP.   14738

Smith, Ashbel, 1806-1886.
The cholera spasmodica, as observed in Paris in 1832: comprising its symptoms, pathology, and treatment... New York, P. Hill, 1832. 80 p. CtHWatk; NNN; OCHP; PPAmP; RNR; WU.   14739

Smith, Eli, 1801-1857.
Trials of missionaries. An address delivered in Park Street Church, Boston... Oct. 24, 1832, to the Rev. Elias Riggs (et al) about to embark as missionaries to the Mediterranean. Boston, Pr. by Crocker & Brewster, 1832. 18 p. CtSoP; MH-AH; NjR; OO; PPPrHi.   14740

Smith, Elias, 1796-1846.
The American physician, and family assistant: in four parts. 3d ed. Boston, H. Bowen's Print, 1832. 198 p. MB; MBC; MBM; VtNofN; WaPS.   14741

Smith, Emma.
A selection of hymns. [Independence, Mo., 1832]   14742

Smith, Frederick, 1747-1823.
The infidel reclaimed; being an extraordinary instance of the goodness and the power of omnipotence, to one of his benighted children, related by Frederick Smith, a minister of the Society of Friends, in London, in a letter to John Murray, of New-York. Pr. for the trustees of Obadiah Brown's Benevolent Fund. Providence, Pr. by H. H. Brown, 1832. 12 p. MH.   14743

Smith, George.
Henry Martyn, saint and scholar, first modern missionary to the Mohammedans, by Geo. Smith, New York, Rewell, 1832. 580 p. ICP.   14744

Smith, Horance.
Tales of the early ages. By Horance Smith, esq. New York, J. & J. Harper, 1832. 2 vols. KTW; LNH; MFiT; NNS; PPA; RJa.   14745

Smith, James.
Miscellaneous thoughts... See under title.

Smith, James H.
An oration delivered by appointment before the Union & state rights party, on the 4th of July, 1832, at the Second Presbyterian Church, by James H. Smith, esq., and published at the request of the Washington society and Union and state rights party. Charleston, Wm. S. Blain, 1832. 28 p. A-Ar; MBAt; NIC; ScC; ScU.   14746

Smith, John.
The curiosities of common water; on the advantage thereof in curing cholera, intemperance,

and other maladies... by John
Smith, O. M. 5th ed. Salem,
Whipple & Lawrence, 1832. 54 p.
MB; MH-Z; NIC; NNNAM; MWA.
                              14747
Smith, Matthew Hale.
  Compendium of Christian du-
ties, a sermon delivered in Hart-
ford, by M. H. Smith. Hartford,
Pr. by G. W. Kappel's, 1832.
6 p. NNUT.   14748

---- The end of the world, a lecture sermon delivered before the
first Universalist Society in Hartford, on the evening of the first
Sunday in April, 1832. Hartford,
Pr. by G. W. Kappel, 1832. 16 p.
MMeT; MMeT-Hi; NNUT. 14749

Smith, Nathan Ryno, 1797-1877.
  Surgical anatomy of the arter-
ies, with plates and illustrations.
By Nathan R. Smith, M.D....
Baltimore, J. N. Toy & W. R.
Lucas, 1832. 104 p. IaU; KyLxT;
MbU-M; MdUM; WU.   14750

Smith, Roswell Chamberlain,
1797-1875.
  English grammar on the pro-
ductive system. A method of instruction recently adopted in Germany and Switzerland. Designed
for schools and academies. By
Roswell C. Smith... Boston, Perkins & Marvin, 1832. 192 p. MH;
MdBS; NRHi.   14751

---- Intellectual and practical
grammar in a series of inductive
questions, connected with exercises in composition. New York,
Lockwood, 1832. 123 p. CtHWatk;
IP; MB; NNC; RPB.   14752

---- The little federal calculator.
Boston, 1832. MH.   14753

---- Practical and mental arithmetic, on a new plan, ... A complete system for all practical
purposes; being in dollars and

cents. Stereotype ed., rev. and
enl., with exercises for the slate.
To which is added, a practical
system of bookkeeping. By Roswell C. Smith. Boston, Carter,
Hendee & Co., Brattleboro' power-
press office [1832] 268 p. MBC;
NN; PU.   14754

---- Practical Grammar. Boston
and New York, Perkins & Marvin,
1832. MAm.   14755

Smith, Samuel, 1752-1839.
  Speech in Senate of the United
States on the resolution proposing
to purchase sixty copies of the
History of the bank of the United
States. Washington, 1832. 8 p.
MdHi; NN; NNC; PPAmP; WHi.
                              14756
---- Speech in the Senate of the
United States on the subject of the
resolution in relation to the tariff,
which were offered by Mr. Clay.
Washington, Blair, 1832. 7 p.
[pamphlet] MdHi; Mid-B; PHi;
PPAmP; WHi.   14757

---- Speech of the Hon. Samuel
Smith, in the Senate of the United
States, on the renewal of the
charter bank of the United States,
Washington, Gales & Seaton, 1832.
6 p. LNH; MdHi; MiD-B; MWA;
PPL.   14758

---- Speech of Mr. Smith, of
Maryland, on the nomination of
Mr. Van Buren. Washington, 1832.
4 p. WHi.   14759

Smith, Stephen Renssalaer, 1788-
1850.
  Sermon; "for whom the Lord
loveth, he chasteneth and scourg-
eth every son whom he received."
[Hartford] 1832. 8 p. CtSoP.
                              14760
[Smith, Thomas] accountant, of
London.
  An essay on currency and bank-
ing. Being an attempt to show

their true nature, and to explain the difficulties that have occurred in discussing them. With an application to the currency of this country. Philadelphia, J. Harding, 1832. 4, 76 p. MH.   14761

Smith, Thomas, 1775?-1830.
The origin and history of missions... comp. from authentic documents; forming a complete missionary repository, illustrated by numerous engravings, from original drawings made expressly for this work... by the Rev. Thos. Smith... and Rev. John O. Choules... Boston, S. Walker, and Lincoln & Edmands, 1832. 2 vols. CU-B; DLC; ICU; NjP; TNS.
                                           14762
Smith, Thomas, 1808-1873.
The design and duty of a church, a sermon delivered in the Second Presbyterian Church in Charleston, S. C., on Sabbath morning, April 1, 1832, being the 21 anniversary of the dedication of that Church. Charleston, Observer Office Press, 1832. 25 p. GDecCT; PPPrHi; ScC.
                                           14763
Smith, William.
Bible dictionary, comprising its antiquities, geography, and biography. By Wm. Smith. New York, Alden, 1832. 703 p. GBar.
                                           14764
Smith, William.
Speech of the Hon. William Smith, delivered on Monday, Aug. 1, 1831, at a meeting of the citizens of Spartanburg district against the doctrine of nullification. Columbia, S. C., Pr. at the office of the Hive, 1832. 43 p. A-Ar; MB; MdHi.   14765

Smith, William G.
An inaugural dissertation on opium... by Wm. G. Smith... [New York,] 1832. 23 p. DSG; NNC; NNNAM.   14766

Smith, William Loughton, 1758-1812.
A comparative view of the constitutions of the several states with each other, and with that of the United States .. City of Washington, Thompson & Homand, 1832. 135 p. NcD; PPB; PPL; ScSp; ScU.   14767

Smith & Wooster's Mississippi & Louisiana Almanac, for the year 1833... calculated for the meridian of Natchez, Mississippi... astronomical calculations by John S. Stephens. Natchez, Smith & Wooster [1832] [36] p. MWA; Ms-Ar; MsJS.   14768

[Smollet, Tobias George] 1721-1771.
The history of England, from the revolution in 1688 to the death of George the Second... Philadelphia, McCarty & Davis, 1832. 967 p. CtMW; CLSU; MB; NbOM; TNP.   14769

---- Select works; with memoir of the author by Sir Walter Scott. Philadelphia, Carey & Son, 1832. 539 p. RPB.   14770

Snell, James.
A practical guide to operations on the teeth. To which is prefixed a historical sketch of the rise and progress of dental surgery. By James Snell... Philadelphia, Carey & Lea, 1832. 207 p. CU-M; ICJ; NbOM; PPHa; TxHAM; ViU.   14771

Snelling, William Joseph, 1804-1848.
Truth, a gift for scribblers. 2d ed., with additions and emendations by Wm. J. Snelling. Boston, B. B. Mussey, 1832. 72 p. GEU; MB; OO; TxU; WHi. 14772

Snow, Josiah.
An oration... at the young

men's celebration of the fifty
sixth anniversary of American
independence... Southbridge, Jos-
lin & Tiffany, 1832. 20 p. MiD-
B; MSbri.   14773

Snowden, Richard.
    The history of North and South
America, from its discovery to
the death of General Washington.
By Richard Snowden, esq. Rev.,
cor., and imp. and the history
of North America brought down to
the cession of Florida in 1821,
and of South America to the battle of Carobobo in the same year.
By Chas. W. Bazeley... Philadelphia, M'Carty & Davis, 1832.
348 p. CU-B; ICBB; MH; NT;
OClWHi.   14774

Society for Promoting Theological Education.
    Address of the directors of the
Society for promoting theological
education with the act of incorporation, by laws, and a list of
the members of the society. Boston, Pr. by W. L. Lewis at
Steam power press office, 1832.
16 p. CBPac; MWA; NCH; NjR;
WHi.   14775

Society for Propagating the Gospel Among the Indians and Others in North America.
    Report of the select committee
of the Society for propagating the
Gospel among the Indians and
others in North America. Read
and accepted Nov. 1, 1832. Boston, Pub. by order of the society, Press of Putnam & Damrell,
1832. 28 p. KHi; MeB; NbHi;
PHi; WHi.   14776

Society for the Prevention of
Pauperism in the City of New
York.
    Report on the penitentiary sys-
tem in the United States. New
York, Mahlon Day, 1832. 107 p.
LNT.   14777

Society for the Reformation of
Juvenile Delinquents in the City
of New York.
    Documents relative to the
House of Refuge, instituted by the
Society for the Reformation of
Juvenile Delinquents in the City
of New York, in 1824... By Na-
thaniel C. Hart, Supt. New York,
Pr. by Mahlon Day, 1832. 311 p.
CtMW; IU; Nh; OClWHi; PPL-R.
                             14778
Society of the New York Hospi-
tal.
    By-laws and regulations of the
New York Hospital, and Bloom-
ingdale Lunatic Asylum... Rev.
and passed Dec. 4th, 1832. New
York, Pr. by R. & G. S. Wood,
1832. 64 p. NNNAM.   14779

Some account of J. S. extracted
from a letter, written by him in
Jamaica, to a citizen of Philadelphia. Philadelphia, 1832. 8 p.
MBC.   14780

Somerville, C.
    Mechanism of the Heavens.
By C. Somerville. Philadelphia,
1832. NPV.   14781

Somerville, Mary [Fairfax]
    A preliminary dissertation on
the mechanism of the heavens.
By Mary F. Somerville. Philadelphia, Carey & Lea, 1832. CtMW;
MdHi; NNC; P; RKi.   14782

Sophia Alden: or The evening
Sabbath school... Boston, Massachusetts Sunday School Union,
1832. 72 p. DLC.   14783

The sorrows of a rover contrasted with the agreeable history of
a dutiful and pious youth. By the
author of Jacob Newman... Nicol
Gray, &c. Boston, James Loring, General Sabbath School Depository, 1832. 108 p. DLC; ICHi;
MMedHi.   14784

South Carolina.
Acts and resolutions of the
General Assembly, of the State
of South Carolina, passed in
December, 1832. Columbia, Pr.
by Miller & Branthwaite, state
prs., 1832. 67, 2 p. Mi-L; Mo;
Nj; R; Sc.   14785

---- Proclamation by the Governor of South Carolina. The Governor's answer to President
Jackson's proclamation. Columbia, The Columbia Telescope,
1832. DLC; DNA; NcD.   14786

---- Report of the President of
the Banks of the State of South
Carolina, for 1832. Columbia,
Pr. by A. S. Johnston, pr. to
the House of Representatives,
1832. 6 p. A-Ar.   14787

---- State of South Carolina.
Governor Hayne's message. Pr.
by A. S. Johnston [1832] 12 p.
MdHi.   14788

---- Convention.
Documents ordered by the convention of the people of South
Carolina on the subject of the
several acts of Congress, imposing duties for the protection of
domestic manufacturers... Columbia, S. C., A. S. Johnson, 1832.
24 p. NN; Nj; PHi.   14789

---- ---- Proceedings of Convention of South Carolina on subject of nullification with remarks
of Gov. Hamilton on taking the
President's Chair. Ordinance
nullifying tariff laws. Boston,
1832. 52 p. ICU; MWA; OO;
PHi; PU.   14790

---- ---- The report, ordinance
and addresses of the Convention
of the people of South Carolina
adopted Nov. 24th, 1832. Columbia, Pr. by A. S. Johnston, pr.
to the Convention, 1832. 28, 15,

16 p. DLC; MB; PHi; RP; ScHi;
WHi.   14791

South Carolina Canal and Rail
Road Company.
By-laws of the South Carolina
Canal and Rail Road Company,
adopted by the stockholders, May
13, 1828. Together with the act
of incorporation, granted by the
state Legislature. Charleston,
Pr. by James S. Burges, 1832.
16 p. ScHi.   14792

---- Report of H. Allen, Chief
Engineer, to the board of directors, February 6, 1832. [Charles-
ton?] [1832] 8 p. DLC; ScHi;
WU.   14793

South Reading, Mass. South Bap-
tist Church.
Ecclesiastical record of the
South Baptist Church, in South
Reading, Mass. Boston, Pr. by
Jonathan Howe, 1832. 24 p. CtY;
MBC; MWA; MNtCA.   14794

Southard, Samuel Lewis, 1787-
1842.
An address delivered before
the Alumni association of Nas-
sau-hall, on the day of the annual commencement of the college,
September 26, 1832. By Samuel
L. Southard, LL.D. Pub. by request of the Association. Princeton, N.J., Pr. by D'Hart & Connolly, 1832. 30 p. CtY; MB; OC;
PPAmP; ScU.   14795

---- Centennial address. By Sam-
uel L. Southard. Delivered at
Trenton, N.J., Feb. 22, 1832.
[Trenton, Pr. by P. J. Gray,
1832] 24 p. MB; OClWHi; PHC;
TxU; WHi.   14796

---- An eulogium upon the Hon.
Charles Ewing, late chief justice
of New Jersey. By Samuel L.
Southard. Trenton, D. Fenton,
1832. 38 p. CtY; Nh; PU; TxU;
Vi.   14797

The Southern Pioneer, and Gospel
Visitor. Edited by an association
of gentlemen. Vol. I. Pub. simul-
taneously in Baltimore, Md. and
Richmond, Va. Baltimore, Pr.
by Wm. Wooddy, 1832. 284 p.
DLC; MBUPH; N; PPL; Vi.
						14798
Southern rose. V.1-7 Aug. 11,
1832-Aug. 17, 1839. Charleston,
W. Estill, for the editor, 1832-
1839. DLC; NjP.			14799

Southey, Robert, 1774-1843.
	Southey's life of Nelson. A new
edition, complete in one vol. New
York, J. & J. Harper, 1832.
309 p. LNH.				14800

Southwick, Solomon, 1773-1839.
	A view of the origin, powerful
influence and pernicious effects
of intemperance, supported by
scriptural authority... address delivered before the first ward temperance society of the city of Albany... Feb. 17, 1832. Albany,
1832. 38 p. CSmH; KyLx; MB;
PPPrHi; WHi.			14801

Sparks, Jared, 1789-1866.
	The life of Gouverneur Morris,
with selections from his correspondence and miscellaneous papers; detailing events in the American revolution, the French revolution, and in the political history
of the United States. By Jared
Sparks... Boston, Gray & Bowen,
1832. 3 vols. DLC; GU; NbU;
PPA; WHi.				14802

---- Proposals for public works
of George Washington. Boston,
1832. MB.				14803

Sparrow, William, 1801-1874.
	A reply to the charges and ac-
cusations of the Rt. Rev. Philander Chase, D.D., by Rev. Wm.
Sparrow. Gambier, O., Pr. at
the office of the Observer, 1832.
35 p. CtHT; MiD-B; NNG;

OClWHi; OGaK.			14804

The spectator; with notes and a
general index; from the London
stereotype ed. Philadelphia, J. J.
Woodward, 1832. 2 v. in 1.
CtHC; KyLx; OCl; NJam; WRac.
						14805
The Spectator with sketches of
the lives of the authors, an index, and explanatory notes. In
12 vols. Philadelphia, James
Crissy, 1832. 12 vols. ArVb;
IaCrM; NCH; RPA; TxU.	14806

Speece, Frederick.
	My native land, and other po-
ems. Philadelphia, Pr. by Lydia
R. Bailey, for Augustine Left-
wich, Lynchburg, Va., 1832.
156 p. MPlyA; NcElon; Vi.
						14807
Speeches and other proceedings
at the public dinner in honor of
the centennial anniversary of
Washington, to which is added
Washington's farewell address,
City of Washington, Pr. at the
office of Jonathan Elliot, 1832.
32 p. CU; ICN; MBC; MWA; Nh;
PPFM; ScC.			14808

Speeches made in the Senate of
the United States on the rejection
of Martin Van Buren, as Minister
to the Court of St. James. Albany, M. M'Pherson, 1832. 46 p.
MH; NN.				14809

Speight, Jesse.
	To the freemen of the counties
of Johnson, Wayne, Green, Lenoir,
Jones, Craven, and Carteret, com-
posing the 4th Congressional District of North Carolina. [Washing-
ton, 1832] 8 p. MWA.	14810

Spencer, John Canfield.
	A portrait of freemasonry.
[Washington, 1832] 8 p. MB; RP.
						14811
Spencer, Thomas, 1793-1857.
	... Practical observations on

epidemic diarrhoea, known as the epidemic cholera, spasmodic cholera, &c. &c., with a brief outline of its treatment, founded on the pathology of the disease. By Thos. Spencer. Utica, Pr. by E. A. Maynard, 1832. 7 p. CSmH; MB; MWA; NNNAM; OU. 14812

Spirit of practical godliness. v. 1- no. 1- New York, 1832. PPPrHi; WHi. 14813

The Spiritual Mirror; or, Looking-Glass: exhibiting the human heart as being either the temple of God, or habitation of Devils, exemplified by a series of ten engravings; intended to aid in a better understanding of man's fallen nature. By Peter Bauder. 4th Amer. ed. Newburyport, Charles Whipple, 1832. 80 p. MBAt; MNe; NNC; RPB. 14814

The Spiritual Voyage. Performed in the Ship Convert, under the command of Capt. Godly-fear, from the port of repentance-unto-life, to the haven of felicity on the continent of glory, an allegory. New York, Pr. by S. Marks & Son, 1832. 72 p. NBuG. 14815

Sprague, Peleg, 1793-1880.
Speech of Mr. Sprague of Maine upon the arrangement of the Colonial trade with Great Britain, delivered in the Senate of the United States on the 3d day of April, 1832. Washington, Pr. by Jonathan Elliott, 1832. 23 p. MHi; MeBaT; NvHi; OClWHi; WHi. 14816

---- Speech of Peleg Sprague, (of Maine), on the tariff. Delivered in the Senate of the United States, on the 22d of March, 1832, on Mr. Clay's resolution in relation to the tariff. Washington, Jonathan Elliot, 1832. 20 p. Ct; MBAt; NjR; OCHP; WHi. 14817

Sprague, William Buell, 1795-1876.
The God of the Christian, and the God of the infidel. Sermon CXXXIV. By Wm. B. Sprague, D. D., Albany, N. Y. New York, The American National Preacher, 1832. 97-112 p. MB; MPiB. 14818

---- Lectures on revivals of religion, by William B. Sprague, D. D. with an introductory essay by Leonard Woods, D. D. also an appendix consisting of letters... Albany, Webster & Skinners, O. Steele and C. Little, 1832. 287, 165 p. CSansS; DLC; KyLoP; MiD; PPL. 14819

---- An official report by... one of the committee of the House of Representatives of Rhode Island upon the subject of masonry. Providence, Office of the Daily Advertiser, 1832. 23 p. MnHi. 14820

---- Review of Dickinson's prize letters. New Haven, Baldwin & Treadway, 1832. 21 p. MI. 14821

Spring, Gardiner, 1785-1873.
A sermon preached Aug. 3, 1832, a day set apart in the city of New York, for public fasting, humiliation, and prayer on account of malignant cholera, by Gardiner Spring, D. D. New York, Jonathan Leavitt, 1832. 5 p. CtSoP; GDecCT; MBC; NjR; PHi. 14822

Spring, Samuel, 1792-1877.
The only safe expedient, a discourse delivered before the Hartford Temperance Society; by Samuel Spring, pastor of the North Church in Hartford. Hartford, Pr. [by G. F. Olmsted] for James W. Judd & Co., 1832. 31 p. CtY; MBC; MH; NNUT; NjR; PPPrHi. 14823

Springer, Cornelius.
A review of the late decision of Supreme Court of Ohio, which

has went [sic] virtually to incorporate the Methodist Episcopal
Church in the U S. ...The whole
giving a developement of the
Principles of the Government of
the M. E. Church showing that
the creation of such a corporation, holding such a vast amount
of property, is a dangerous engine in a free government. By C.
Springer. Cincinnati, 1832. 71 p.
                                  14824
Springer, Moses, 1796-1870.
    Songs of Zion: being a collec-
tion of hymns, for the use of the
pious of all denominations. 7th
ed. Hallowell, Glazier, Masters
& Co., 1832. 160 p.   14825

Springwater, Dr., pseud.
    The cold-water-man; or, A
pocket companion for the temper-
ate. By Doctor Springwater, of
North America... Albany, Pr. by
Packard and Van Benthuysen,
1832. 216 p. MH; MiD; NIC; NT.
                                  14826
Spurzheim, Johann Gaspar, 1776-
1832.
    Outlines of Phrenology; being
also a manual of reference for
the marked bust. Boston, Marsh,
Capen and Lyon, 1832. 96 p.
MHi; NB; OMC; PHC; RPB.
                                  14827
---- Philosophical catechism of
the natural laws of man. 2d ed.
imp. Boston, Marsh, Capen &
Lyon, 1832. 171 p. ICN; MH;
NBu; OMC; PPL-R.   14828

---- ---- 3d ed. imp. Boston,
Marsh, Capen & Lyon, 1832.
171 p. MBM; NBu.   14829

---- Phrenology; or, The doctrine of the mental phenomena;
1st Amer. ed., greatly imp. by
the author, from 3d London ed.
Boston, Marsh, 1832. 2 vols.
CSfCMS; ICU; MBM; NBMS;
PPA.   14830

---- A view of the elementary
principles of education... 1st
Amer. ed., rev. and imp. by the
author, from 3d London ed. Boston, Marsh, Capen & Lyon, 1832.
318 p. CtHC; ICU; MH-AH; PPA;
RPB; TxU.   14831

Stanhope, Louisa Sidney.
    Bandit's bride, or, The maid
of Saxony; a romance. Exeter, J.
C. Gerrish, 1832. 3 vols. in 2.
DLC; KyHi; NRivHi; PPL. 14832

Stanhope, Philip Henry Stanhope,
5th earl, 1805-1875.
    The life of Belisarius. By
Lord Mahon, Philadelphia, Carey
& Lea, 1832. 473, (1) p. DLC;
MdBE; NNF.   14833

Starkie, Thomas, 1782-1849.
    A practical treatise on the law
of evidence, and digest of proofs,
in civil and criminal proceedings.
...4th Amer. ed. Philadelphia,
P. H. Nicklin & T. Johnson, 1832.
3 vols. C; InHuP; Ky; MsU;NcD;
OCIW.   14834

---- Treatise on the law of slander, libel scandalum magnatum &
false rumours... with notes, &
references to American decisions
by Thos. Huntington. New York,
Collins and Hannay, 1832. 456 p.
IaMp; Ky; NjP; PP; WaU. 14835

Starling, Thomas.
    Family cabinet atlas. 1st
Amer. ed. rev. cor. and enl.
Philadelphia, Carey & Lea, 1832.
11, [2] p. KyBC; MdBJ; NPV;
RPB; ViU.   14836

The State Rights and Free Trade
Almanac... 1833... pub. by the
State Rights and Free Trade As-
sociation... Charleston, Pr. by
A. E. Miller [1832] [84] p. DLC;
MWA; MHi; PHi; WHi.   14837

State Rights and Free Trade Association.

...Address by the Free Trade
and State Rights Association, to
the people of South Carolina...
Columbia [S. C.] 1832. 16 p.
ICN; NcD; ScU.   14838

---- ...An appeal to the people
on the question, what shall we do
next...Columbia, Pub. by the
Association, 1832. 12 p. MHi;
ScU; WHi.   14839

---- Free trade and American
system, a dialogue between merchant and planter. Pub. by the
State Rights and Free Trade Assoc. Columbia, 1832. 12 p. ICU;
MHi; NcD; RP; ScU; WHi. 14840

---- The Last Day's Debate on
the Tariff, in the Senate of the
United States. Address to the
people of South-Carolina, by their
Senators and Representatives in
Congress; and Address and Resolutions adopted by the State Rights
and Free Trade Party, at Charleston, July 30, 1832. Also, Proceedings of a Meeting held in
Georgia, &c. Charleston, Pr. by
E. J. Van Brunt, for the Association, 1832. 24 p. RP.   14841

---- Proceedings of the State
Rights & Free Trade Convention,
held in Charleston (S. C.) on the
22nd and 25th February, 1832?
Charleston, 1832? 16 p. MHi.
                                  14842
---- A view of the remedies pro-
posed for existing evils. Colum-
bia, State Rights & Free Trade
Association, 1832. ICU; MHi;
NcD; WHi.   14843

Stearns, John G.
    The primitive church; its or-
ganization and government.
Churches of different denominations examined and compared with
it. Remarks on councils, associations, ministerial titles and oth-

er subjects. By John G. Stearns.
Utica, Press of Bennett & Bright,
1832. 108 p. PCA.   14844

Stedman, James S.
    The fatal effects of vicious
company, being an authentic narrative of the life of James S. Stedman. Also, an extract from the
memoirs of Stephen B. Stedman.
Washington, O. , Pr. for Samuel
F. Yeoman, at A. Crihfield's
book and job office, 1832. 298,
[2] p. OClWHi.   14845

Steele, Oliver Gray.
    The Traveller's Directory. See
under title.

Steele and Faxon's Buffalo almanac for the year of our lord 1832:
Being bissextile or leap year; and
(till July 4th) the 56th of American independence. Calculated for
the Horizon and meridian of Buffalo, Erie Co. , (N. Y.), but will
serve for any of the adjoining
counties of this state... Buffalo,
Steel & Faxon [1832] NHi. 14846

Steele's Albany Almanac for...
1833...by a successor of the
late Andrew Beers. Albany, O.
Steele [1832] 18 p. N; NHi.
                                  14847
Steele's Buffalo almanac for 1833.
Buffalo, O. G. Steele [1832] 12 ll.
NHi.   14848

Stephens, John L.
    Incidents of travel in Yucatan.
New York, Harper & bros. , 1832.
2 vols. ScU.   14849

[Stevens, Alexander H.]
    A synopsis of a course of lec-
tures on surgery. New-York,
George P. Scott, prs. , 1832.
21 p. NNNAM.   14850

Stevens, Charles.
    Consitutional arguments indi-
cating the rights and policy of the

southern states. By Charles
Stevens. Charleston, Pr. by J.
S. Burges, 1832. 24 p. DLC;
MBAt; MHi; PU; ScU.   14851

Stevens, William, 1786-1868.
    (Dr. Stevens's) treatise on the
cholera, extracted from his work
entitled "Observations on the
healthy and diseased properties
of the blood. New York, G. & C.
& H. Carvill, 1832. 63 p. CSt-L;
MB; RNR; ScU; WU-M.   14852

Stevenson, George.
    A dissertation on the atone-
ment, in three parts, by George
Stevenson. 1st Amer. from 2d
Edinburgh ed. Philadelphia, Tow-
ar, J. & D. Hogan, 1832. 193 p.
GDecCT; NNUT; NjR; OWoC;
PPiW.   14853

Stewart, Andrew, 1792-1872.
    Speech...in support of an ap-
propriation for the preservation
and repair of the Cumberland
road. Delivered in the H.R., May
18, 1832. Washington, 1832.
8 p. DLC.   14854

---- Speech of Mr. Stewart, of
Pennsylvania, in support of the
tariff policy, and in reply to Mr.
M'Duffie. Delivered in the House
of Representatives. Washington,
June 5, 1832. New York, Pr. by
Flagg & Gould, 1832. 15 p. Ct;
MHi; MBAt; NdU; PPM; WHi.
                             14855

Stewart, Henry.
    The planter's guide; or, A
practical essay of the best method of giving effect to wood by the
removal by large trees and underwood...interspersed with ob-
servation on general planting...
1st Amer. from 2d London &
Edinburgh ed. New York, G.
Thorburn & sons, 1832. 122 p.
MH; NjP; O; P; PPM.   14856

Stewart, Marie W.

Meditations; from the pen of
Mrs. Marie W. Stewart. Pre-
sented to the First African Bap-
tist Church and Society in the
City of Boston. Boston, Pr. by
Garrison & Knapp, 1832. 24 p.
MB; MsJS.   14857

Stimpson, Charles.
    Plan of the city of Boston.
Boston, 1832. MBAt; Nh-Hi.
                             14858
Stimpson's Boston directory: containing the names of the inhabitants, their occupations, places of
business, and dwelling houses,
and the city register, with lists
of the streets, lanes and wharves
etc. ...Boston, Stimpson & Clapp,
1832. 348 p. MMal; WHi. 14859

Stockton, Joseph, 1779-1832.
    The western calculator, or A
new and compendious system of
practical arithmetic; containing the
elementary principles and rules of
calculation, in which, mixed, and
decimal numbers, arranged, de-
fined, and illustrated, in a plain
and natural order; adapted to the
use of schools, throughout the
western country and present commerce of the United States. In
eight parts. By J. Stockton, A.M.
Pittsburgh, Johnston & Stockton,
1832. DLC; IaDmD; OClWHi;
PBa; PSt.   14860

Stoddard, John.
    Perseverance of the saints. A
sermon delivered in Peru, March
11, 1832. By John Stoddard, Minister of the Gospel. Plattsburgh,
Pr. by E. P. Allen, 1832. 15 p.
ScCoB.   14861

Stoddard's diary; or the Columbia Almanack for...1833...by
Edwin E. Prentiss. Hudson, Ash-
bell Stoddard [1832] 18 p. M;
MWA; PHi.   14862

Stoddart, Isabella (Wellwood),

d. 1846.

Arthur Monteith, a moral tale, founded on an historical fact; calculated to improve the minds of young people, being a continuation of "The Scottish Orphans," to which is added the Young West Indian: 3d Amer. ed. Mrs. Martha Blackford, New York, W. Burgess, 1832. 137 p. MBSi; MnS; OCIWHi.   14863

---- The Scottish orphans, a moral tale founded on an historical fact and calculated to improve the minds of young people. 3d Amer. ed. New York, Wm. Burgess, 1832. 139 p. DLC; MnS; NN.   14864

Stokes, Robert, 1783-1859?

In memory of the noble act of Mr. Charles Ridgely, late Governor of Maryland: with my address to all those who may disbelieve. Baltimore, Pr. for the author, 1832. 19 p. MB; MdToN.
                                                14865

Stone, William Leete, 1792-1844.

Letters on Masonry and anti-Masonry, addressed to Hon. John Quincy Adams... New-York, J. Halsted, 1832. 566, 7 p. CtHC; ICP; MBC; NNP; RNR; Vi. 14866

Stories for Emma. New Haven, Sidney's Press, S. Babcock, 1832. CtY.   14867

Stories for little girls; or, A present from mother. New Haven, S. Babcock, 1832. 22 p. CtY.
                                                14868

Stories of common life. Boston, Carter & Hendee, 1832. 127 p. MiD-B.   14869

Stories of the second and third centuries. Compiled for the American Sunday School Union and revised by the committee of publication. Philadelphia, American Sunday School Union, 1832. 192 p.

ICPNA.   14870

Story, Joseph, 1779-1845.

Commentaries on the constitution of the United States... Boston, Hilliard, Gray & Co., 1832. OCIW.   14871

---- Commentaries on the law of bailments, with illustrations from the civil and foreign law. By Joseph Story, LL. D. Cambridge, Hilliard & Brown, 1832. 411 p. Ct; IaU-L; NcU; OC; ViU. 14872

---- The Law of Bailments, with illustrations from Civil and Foreign Law, 1832 ed. Cambridge, Hilliard & Brown, 1832. 411 p. Ia; MH-L; MWCL; OCoSc. 14873

The story of the kind little boy. Philadelphia, American Sunday-School Union, 1832. 16 p. MiHi.
                                                14874

Stow, Baron.

Memoir of Harriet Dow, of Newport, N. H., who became a Christian at the age of eight years. In ten letters to a niece. By Baron Stow... Boston, J. Loring (etc.) 1832. 107 p. DLC; MH; MWA; Nh; Nh-Hi.   14875

[Strachan, John]

A letter to the Rev. Thomas Chalmers... on the life and character of the Rt. Rev. Dr. Hobart ...New-York, Swords, Stanford & Co., 1832. 56 p. MB; MdBD; NNG; PHi.   14876

Streeter, Russell.

Latest news from three worlds, Heaven, Earth, and Hell... in letters to eight Calvinistic ministers. By Russell Streeter... Boston, B. B. Mussey, 1832. 102 p. MMet-Hi; NN.   14877

Streeter, S.

Consolatory views of death. A sermon delivered in the Univer-

salist Chapel in Lowell, on the
morning of Sept. 9, 1832. Being
the Sabbath following the death of
Mrs. Mary Gardner, wife of Rev.
Calvin Gardner. By S. Streeter,
pastor of the First Universalist
Society in Boston. Boston, Pr.
at the office of the Universalist,
1832. 16 p. MMeT; MMeT-Hi;
RPB.   14878

Streeter, Sebastian, 1723-1867.
    The new hymn book, designed
for Universalist Societies: compiled from approved authors, with
variations and additions. By Sebastian and Russell Streeter...
Stereotyped at the Boston Type
and Stereotype Foundry. 5th ed.
Boston, Marsh, Capen & Lyon,
1832. 408 p. MB; MoSpD. 14879

Strictures on a sermon by Edward D. Griffin, president of
Williams College. Pub. in the
National Preacher, for Feb.
1832. The design of which are to
exhibit and defend what is mis-
called "New Divinity." By a
friend to revivals. New York, J.
Leavitt; Auburn, H. Ivison & Co.,
[Utica] 1832. 39 p. CSmH; MB;
MH; NAuT; OO; PLT.   14880

Strong, Solomon.
    A charge delivered to the
grand jury of the county of Wor-
cester, at March term of the C.
C. Pleas, 1832. By Hon. Solo-
mon Strong...Worcester, Pr. by
S. H. Colton & Co., 1832. 12 p.
MBC; MH; NN; OClWHi; RPB.
                              14881
[Strong, Titus] 1787-1855.
    The Deerfield captive: an In-
dian story, being a narrative of
facts for the instruction of the
young. Greenfield (Mass.), A.
Phelps, 1832. 68 p. MDeeP;
MNF; MWA; MWinchrHi; NN.
                              14882
Stuart, Moses, 1780-1852.
    A commentary on the Epistle

to the Romans, with a translation and various excursus. Andover, Flagg & Gould, 1832. 576
p. CtSoP; GDecCT; ICU; NBuG;
ScNC; ViRut; CBPSR.   14883

---- A Hebrew Chrestomathy...
By Moses Stuart...Andover, Flagg
& Gould; New York, J. Leavitt,
1832. 219 p. ICP; MCom;
NcMHi; NNF; NjP.   14884

---- ---- 2d ed. Andover, Flagg
& Gould; New York, J. Leavitt,
1832. 231 p. CBPSR; LN; MdBD;
NNG; PPP; TSewU.   14885

Sturm, Christoph Christian, 1740-
1786.
    Sturm's reflections on the
works of God, and His providence
throughout all nature...Philadel-
phia, J. J. Woodward, 1832.
486 p. ILM; MiU; NjP; PSal;
TNP; ViU.   14886

Sturtevant, Peleg.
    Examination of the opinions of
Astronomers relative to the Com-
et, which is to appear in 1832.
Harrisburg, 1832. 22 p. PHi.
                              14887
Stuyvesant Meadows, New York
City.
    Reports and documents rela-
tive to the Stuyvesant Meadows
from the year 1825 to 1831, in-
clusive. New-York, Pr. by Geo.
Robertson, 1832. 50 p. NHi.
                              14888
Suggestions concerning a national
bank. [Philadelphia, 1832] 8 p.
MH.   14889

Suggestions to those who believe
they have souls, respecting the
guides they follow. Newburyport,
Charles Whipple, 1832. 11 p.
CtHC; MWA; MLow.   14890

[Sullivan, John L.]
    ...To the mechanics of New-
York, on the subject of supplying

the city with pure water. [New York, 1832] 23 p. WHi.   14891

Sullivan, William, 1774-1839.
A discourse delivered before the Boston mercantile association, and others, assembled on their invitation on Tues. eve., Feb. 7, 1832. Boston, Carter & Hendee, 1832. 36 p. DLC; MHi; MiD-B; NCH; PPL.   14892

---- A discourse delivered before the Massachusetts Society for the Suppression of Intemperance, May 23, 1832. By Wm. Sullivan. Pub. at the request of the society. Boston, Richardson, Lord & Holbrook, 1832. 64 p. CBPSR; ICU; MHi; WHi; RPB.   14893

---- The political class book... By Wm. Sullivan... with an appendix upon studies for practical men; with notices of books suited to their use. By George B. Emerson. Boston, Richardson, Lord & Holbrook, 1832. 148 p. KU; MBC; MH; OMC; PLFM.   14894

---- Specimen of the political class book; intended to instruct the higher classes in schools in the origin, nature, and use of political power. With an appendix upon studies for practical men; with notices of books suited to their use. By Geo. B. Emerson. New ed., with amendments and additions. Boston, Richardson, Lord & Holbrook, 1832. 116 p. MH; MHi; MiD-B; NN.   14895

Sumner, John Bird.
A practical exposition of the Gospel of St. Luke, in the form of lectures... by John Bird Sumner, D.D. 1st Amer. ed. New York, Protestant press, 1832. 327 p. CtHT; GHi; InID; MdBD; NNUT.   14896

Sumner, William Hyslop.

Sketch of Adjutant General Sumner's address to the Charlestown Artillery Company, upon delivering their field pieces, November 23, 1831. Charlestown, W. W. Wheildon, 1832. 22 p. MH; MWat; NbU.   14897

The Supremacy of St. Peter and his lawful successors. Hartford, U.S. Catholic Press, 1832. 15 p. MdBL.   14898

Surtees, Robert Smith.
The horseman's manual: Being a treatise on soundness... and generally on the laws relating to horses. By R. S. Surtees, gent. New-York, W. R. H. Treadway, 1832. 132 p. NNN; NjP; OC; RPB.   14899

Susquehanna and Delaware Canal and Railroad Company.
Report on the survey of a route for the proposed Susquehanna and Delaware Railroad... with an estimate of its cost, by Ephraim Beach, with preliminary observations... and additional statements and remarks by the Pennsylvania commissioners. New York, Bliss, 1832. 38 p. CSt; MA; NN; PPAmP.   14900

Sutcliffe, Joseph, 1762-1856.
An introduction to Christianity ... By Joseph Sutcliffe, rev. by the American editor... New York, B. Waugh & T. Mason, 1832. 282 p. KyLo; MoSpD; OSW.   14901

Swain, William.
A collection of cases illustrating the restorative and sanative properties of Swain's panacea, in a variety of diseases... Philadelphia, 1832. MdBJ-W.   14902

Swedenborg, Emanuel, 1688-1872.
Treatise on the worship and love of God... original Latin of Emanuel Swedenborg. 1st Amer. and 2d London ed. Boston, John

Allen, 1832. 213 p. CtHT; MiU; NjR; OUrC; PU.   14903

Sword's pocket almanack, church-man's calendar, and ecclesiasti-cal register, for the year of our Lord 1833; from the creation of the world 5837: Being the first after Bissextile or leap year, and, until July 4, the 57th of the in-dependence of the United States. Fitted to the meridian of New York... New York, Swords, Stan-ford, & Co. [1832] (15), 112 p. MBAt; MWA; NNS; NRHi; PU.
14904

Syme, James, 1799-1870.
    The principles of surgery. By James Syme, F.R.S.E. fellow of the Royal Colleges of Surgeons in London and Edinburgh, Surgeon to the Edinburgh Surgical Hospi-tal, and lecturer on surgery in Edinburgh. Philadelphia, Carey & Lea, 1832. (29), 375 p. GU-M; MBM; MH; Nh; TxU-M.   14905

T

A table of logarithms, of loga-rithmic lines, and a traverse table. New York, J. & J. Harper, 1832. 91 p. MNBedf; NTEW; P; PAnL; PPFrankl.   14906

Tacitus, Cornelius.
    The historical annals of Cor-nelius Tacitus: with supplements by Arthur Murphy...3d Amer. from last London ed. Philadelphia, L. Johnson, 1832. 3 vols. CtHWatk; CU; GMilvC; PPWe.
14907

Tackett, Ignatius H.
    A review of a pamphlet by Mr. Oliver Barr, entitled 'Truth Triumphant.' By Ignatius H. Tac-kett. Pittsburgh, The author, 1832. 22 p. MoS.   14908

Tahiti, receiving the Gospel. Philadelphia, American Sunday

School Union, 1832? 195 p. ICN; InThE; MA; NjP.   14909

Tallmadge, Nathaniel Pitcher, 1795-1864.
    Speech delivered in the Senate of the state of New York, Febru-ary, 1832, on the resolution against renewing the charter of the bank of the United States. Albany, Packard, 1832. 37 p. InU; MB; MH; MWA; NjR; PPL-R.   14910

Tanner, Henry Schenck, 1786-1858.
    A geographical and statistical account of the epidemic cholera, from its commencement in India to its entrance into the United States. Philadelphia, the author, 1832. 35 p. DSG; NN; PPAmP; PPCP; PaHosp.   14911

---- Map of the United States of America. By Henry S. Tanner. Philadelphia, Tanner, 1832. CL; DLC.   14912

[Tappan, Henry Philip] 1805-1881.
    A letter to the Rev. Joel Hawes, D.D. on Dr. Taylor's theological views, from "Views in theology," No. X, for May 1832. New-York, John P. Haven, 1832. 49 p. GDecCT; ICN; MAnP; NIC.
14913

Tatem, Henry.
    ...Rev. H. Tatem's reply to the summons of the R. I. Royal arch chapter. [Providence? 1832] 8 p. DLC; MB; MH; NjP; WHi.
14914

The Tatler, complete in one vol-ume. With notes and a general in-dex. Philadelphia, Woodward, 1832. 444 p. DLC; P.   14915

Taunton, Mass. Trinitarian Con-gregational Church.
    The confession of faith and form of covenant. Taunton, 1832. 8 p. MBC.   14916

Tayler, Charles Benjamin, 1797-1875.

A fireside book or, The account of a Christmas spent at Old Court. By the author of May you like it. 1st Amer. ed. Boston, Stimpson & Clapp, 1832. 207 p. DLC; ViU.   14917

---- The records of a good man's life. By the Rev. Charles B. Tayler...1st Amer. ed. New York, W. Van Norden, 1832. 247 p. DLC; MB; MH; NNG; PPL-R.   14918

Taylor, Ann (Hinton).
Correspondence between a mother and her daughter at school. From 7th London ed. Boston, Perkins & Marvin, 1832. 125 p. MH.   14919

Taylor, C. B.
A universal history of the United States of America, embracing the whole period, from the earliest discoveries, down to the present time...In three parts. By C. B. Taylor. New York, Ezra Strong, 1832. 498 p. CoPu; TxGR.   14920

[Taylor, Isaac] 1787-1865.
Essay on the application of abstract reasoning to the Christian doctrines: Originally published as an introduction to Edwards on the Will. By the Author of Natural history of Enthusiasm. 1st Amer. ed. Boston, Crocker & Brewster; New-York, Jonathan Leavitt, 1832. 163 p. CU; ICU; KyLoP; MoS; NNUT; PLT.   14921

---- Saturday evening. By the author of Natural history of enthusiasm. From the London ed. Boston, Crocker & Brewster; New York, J. Leavitt, 1832. 340 p. CU; KyLoS; NjP; OO; ViU.   14922

---- ---- New-York, John P. Haven, 1832. 426 p. MWiW; PPA.   14923

---- Scenes in Europe for the amusement and instruction of little tarry-at home-travellers. By the Rev. Isaac Taylor. 4th Amer. ed. Philadelphia, U. Hunt, 1832. 96 p. MBE; MdBJ; RPB. 14924

Taylor, Jane, 1783-1824.
The Contributions of Q. Q. By Jane Taylor. Boston, Perkins & Marvin, 1832. 5 vols. MVh.
                           14925
---- Essays in rhyme on morals and manners. By the late Jane Taylor. Boston, Perkins & Marvin, 1832. 108 p. AMob; LNH; PCA.   14926

---- Memoirs, correspondence & poetical remains; ed. by Isaac Taylor. Boston, Perkins & Marvin, 1832. 346 p. MB; MWA; Nh; PHC.   14927

---- Select rhymes for the nursery. New York, Mahlon Day, 1832. PP.   14928

---- A walk to Weller's woods; or, The old apple-man... New York, Pr. by Mahlon Day, 1832. 23 p. MiD-B.   14929

---- The writings of Jane Taylor... Boston, Perkins, 1832. 5 vols. DLC; CtMW; InThE; LNH; MDeeP; VtU.   14930

Taylor, Jefferys, 1792-1853.
The forest; or, Rambles in the woodland, by Jefferys Taylor ... New York, Betts & Anstice, 1832. 208 p. IaDmD; MoSB; NUt; NjN; OU.   14931

Taylor, Jeremy, 1613-1667.
The life of our blessed Lord and Saviour, Jesus Christ. Philadelphia, Key, Mielke, 1832.

243 p. CtMW; ICBB; KU; NcRSh; OkU.   14932

Taylor, Nathaniel William, 1786-1858.
    Correspondence between Rev. Dr. Taylor and Rev. Dr. Hawes. From the Connecticut Observer. [Hartford, 1832] 8 p. CBPac; CtY; DLC; IaDuU-S; OO.   14933

---- Remarks on propagated depravity and sin as the necessary means of the greatest good. New Haven, Pr. by Baldwin & Treadway, 1832. 40 p. Ct; CtHC; CtW; MBC; MH-AH.   14934

---- Reply to Dr. Tyler's examination. Boston, Pr. by Peirce & Parker, 1832. 24 p. CU; ICT; MBC; MdBJ; OCHP.   14935

Taylor, Oliver A.
    [Memoirs and Confessions of Francis Volkmar Reinhard, S. T. D. Court preacher of Dresden.] See Reinhard, Franz Volkmar, 1753-1812.

Taylor, Robert, 1784-1844.
    The devil's pulpit... New York, 1832. 2 vols. DLC.   14936

---- The diegesis; being a discovery of the origin, evidences, and early history of Christianity, never yet before or elsewhere so fully and faithfully set forth. By the Rev. Robert Taylor... Boston, J. Gilbert, 1832. 440 p. ICP; KyDC; MB; NCaS; ScC.
                                14937
The teacher's gift, to an industrious scholar. New Haven, S. Babcock, Sidney's press, 1832. 23 p. CtY.   14938

Telemachus.
    The beauties of Reform; or, The munificent message of the Great Reformation, by Telemachus. New Brunswick [N.J.?]

1832. 16 p. PHi.   14939

Temperance almanac, for the year of our Lord 1832... Containing besides the astronomical matter, many useful hints, friendly admonitions, and solemn warnings, on the subject of intemperance. Rochester, Hoyt, Porter & Co., 1832. 36 p. MWA.   14940

Temperance Almanac for 1833. Albany, N. Y., Oliver Steele [1832] M; MB; MWA; NbO. 14941

---- New Haven, Conn., Durrie & Peck [1832] 13 l. CtY; InU; MWA; N.   14942

---- Rochester, Hoyt, Porter & Co. [1832] 16 l. NRMA; NRU.
                                14943
Temperance Calendar. Sandy Hill, N. Y., Temperance Advocate, 1832. MWA; NN.   14944

---- Utica, Gardiner Tracy [1832] 16 l. NUt.   14945

Temperance. National circular, addressed to the head of each family in the United States. 1832. 12 p. MBC.   14946

Temperance recorder. [Devoted exclusively to the cause of temperance] v. 1-2; Mar. 6, 1832-Feb. 4, 1834. Albany, N. Y. Executive committee of the New York State Temperance Society, 1832-34. DLC; MH; NN; PHi.
                                14947
Templeman, George.
    Statement of congressional documents, journals, registers, of debates, &c. & catalogue of all other books for sale by him. Washington, D. C., Greer, 1832. 11 p. DLC; MHi; PPAmP. 14948

Tennessee.
    An act to charter the Union Bank of the State of Tennessee.

Passed eighteenth October, 1832. Nashville, Pr. by Hunt, Tardiff & Co., 1832. 15 p. CSmH; MH; PPL; T; THi.   14949

---- An argument against capital punishments, reported by order of the judiciary committee, in support of a bill abolishing such punishments as to all free persons in the State of Tennessee. Prepared by A. V. Brown, Chairman. Nashville, Allen A. Hall, pr. to the House, 1832. 56 p. PPAmP.   14950

---- Journal of the House of Representatives at the called session of the Nineteenth General Assembly of the State of Tennessee held at Nashville, 1832. Nashville, Allen A. Hall and F. S. Heiskell, 1832. 153 p. T; TKL-Mc; TMeC; TNV; TU.   14951

---- Journal of the Senate, at the called session of the Nineteenth General Assembly of the State of Tennessee held at Nashville, 1832. Nashville, Allen A. Hall and F. S. Heiskell, 1832. 150 p. TKL-Mc; TMeC; TNV; TU.   14952

---- Opinions of the Hon. John Carton, J. Peck and R. White, and the dissenting opinion of the Hon. Nathan Green in the case of James Campbell and others, against Micah Taul and others. At August Term, 1832. of the Supreme Court at Sparta. Sparta, Tenn., M. A. Long, pr., 1832. 23 p. TKL-Mc.   14953

---- Private acts passed at the called session of the Nineteenth General Assembly of the State of Tennessee. Held at Nashville, 1832. Nashville, Allen A. Hall, and F. S. Heiskell, State prs., 1832. 138 p. IU; MdBB; Mi-L; T; TU.   14954

---- Private acts passed at the stated session of the Nineteenth General Assembly of the State of Tennessee. 1831. Nashville, Allen A. Hall and F. S. Heiskell, 1832. 268 p. IU; M; Mi-L; OCLaw; T.   14955

---- Public acts passed at the called session of the Nineteenth General Assembly of the State of Tennessee, 1832. Nashville, Pr. by Allen A. Hall & F. S. Heiskell, prs. to the state, 1832. 72 p. IU; IaU-L; Nj; T; TU.   14956

---- Public acts passed at the stated session of the Nineteenth General Assembly of the State of Tennessee, 1831. Nashville, Allen A. Hall and F. S. Heiskell, prs. to the State, 1832. 170 p. DLC; Mi-L; Nj; T; TU.   14957

---- Report of the Committee on Internal Improvements in the Senate of Tennessee: to which is annexed a report of the Board of Internal Improvements in East Tennessee; comprising also a report on the improvement of Holston and Tennessee Rivers by Lt. Col. S. H. Long of the U.S. Topographical Engineers, and Memorandum of a contract for making certain Improvements in Tennessee River. Nashville, Pr. by Hunt, Tardiff & Co., 1832. 79 p. THi; TMeC.   14958

---- Report of the Committee on the Penitentiary in the House of Representatives, October 17, 1832. Nashville, Allen A. Hall, 1832. 7 p. THi.   14959

---- Reports of cases argued and determined in the Supreme Court of Tennessee [1818-1837] By Geo. S. Yerger, reporter to the state...Nashville, Pr. at the Republican and Gazette office [Hall & Heiskell, state prs., 1832-

1838]. 10 vols. Ar-SC; L; MH-
L; OCLaw; T.   14960

---- Reports of cases argued and
determined in the Supreme Court
of Tennessee (1825-1828) by John
H. Martin and Geo. S. Yerger,
Nashville, Hunt, 1832. 444 p. No
more published. Az; Ct; KyU-L;
MsU; T.   14961

Tennessee State Medical Society.
Minutes of the proceedings of
the medical society of Tennessee
at the third annual meeting held
in Nashville, May, 1832. Nashville, Pr. by Hunt, Tardiff &
Co., 1832. 15 p. T.   14962

Tenney, Caleb Jewett, 1780-1847.
A sermon preached at Wethers-
field, January 1st, 1832 on the
death of the Rev. Alfred Mitchell
of Norwich City, by Caleb J.
Tenney, pastor of the First
Church in Wethersfield. Hartford,
Pr. by Geo. F. Olmsted, 1832.
24 p. Ct; CtHT; MBC; MHi; MiD-
B; RPB.   14963

Tests of true Religion. Boston,
Pr. by Gray & Bowen, 1832.
20 p. MMeT.   14964

Texas.
Proceedings of the general
convention of delegates representing the citizens and inhabitants of
Texas: held at the town of San
Felipe, in Austin's colony, the
first week of October, one thousand, eight hundred and thirty-
two... Brazoria, Tex., D. W.
Anthony, 1832. 35 p. CtY; Ia;
NNC; OCLaw; TxU.   14965

Thacher, James, 1754-1844.
History of the town of Ply-
mouth; from its first settlement
in 1620, to the year 1832. By
James Thacher. Boston, Marsh,
Capen and Lyon, 1832. 382 p.
DLC; ICU; MBC; OCY; WBeloC.
                          14966

Thacher, Moses, 1795-1878.
An address delivered before
the members of Anti-masonic
state convention; assembled at
Augusta, Maine, July 4, 1832.
Boston, J. B. Chapman & Co.,
1832. 20 p. DLC; IaCrM; MHi.
                          14967
---- ---- Hallowell, Herrick &
Farewell, 1832. 32 p. DLC; MB;
NjP; PHi; WHi.   14968

Thacher, Peter Oxenbridge,
1776-1843.
Charge to the grand jury of the
county of Suffolk for the commonwealth of Massachusetts, at the
opening of the municipal court of
the city of Boston, on the first
Monday of December, A. D. 1831.
Boston, Stimpson & Clapp, 1832.
20 p. CtSoP; MB; NIC; PHi;
WHi.   14969

Thatcher, Benjamin Bussey,
1809-1840.
Indian biography: or, An historical account of those individuals
who have been distinguished among
North American natives as orators,
warriors, statesmen, and other
remarkable characters. By B. B.
Thatcher, esq. New York, J. &
J. Harper, 1832. 2 v. CoD; DLC;
GHi; MHi; ViU.   14970

---- Tales of the Indians; being
prominent passages of the history
of the North American natives.
Taken from authentic sources...
Boston, Waitt & Dow, 1832.
253 p. OFH.   14971

Thayer, Caroline Matilda.
Religion recommended to youth,
in a series of letters addressed
to a young lady... by Caroline M.
Thayer. New York, B. Waugh and
T. Mason, 1832. 187 p. TxD-T.
                          14972
Thayer, Christopher Toppan.
A discourse delivered in the
First Church, Beverly... August

9, 1832. By Christopher Thayer, Minister of the First Parish in Beverly. Salem, Press of Foote & Brown, 1832. 16 p. IaHi; MH; N; PHi; RPB.   14973

Thayer, John, 1758-1815.
An account of the conversion of the Rev. John Thayer, formerly a Protestant minister of Boston, written by himself. To which is added a letter to his brother and his controversial writings. Hartford, By the editors of the U.S. Catholic Press, 1832. 38 p. CtY; DLC; MH; MoFloSS; MoSU.   14974

Thayer, Nathaniel, 1769-1840.
Records of the Church in the case of Deacon James G. Carter. See under Lancaster, Mass., Church of Christ.

Theal, William Y.
A grammar of the French language; or modern French rendered into English on a new and easy system, by William Y. Theal, New York, Peabody & Co., 1832. 176 p. MH; NCaS; NPV.   14975

Thelwall, Algernon Sydney.
Thoughts in affliction. 1st Amer. ed., rev. and enl. To which is added, Bereaved parents consoled, by John Thornton. Also, Sacred poetry, selected by a clergyman. New York, D. Appleton, etc., etc., 1832. 320 p. MH; MdBD; NBuU; NSyU; NjP.   14976

Therapeutic Institute of Philadelphia.
Program... of instruction by William Barton. Philadelphia, 1832. MH.   14977

Things as they have been, are, and ought to be. Addressed to the people, upon the subject of the coming election for governor of the Commonwealth of Pennsyl-

vania, n.p., n.p., 1832. 16 p. PHi; MWA.   14978

Third District Medical Society of Ohio.
Proceedings and correspondence of the Third District Medical Society of the state of Ohio, in reference to the Medical College of Ohio. Pub. by order of the Committee charged with that subject. [Xenia, O.] 1832. 39 p. DSG; ICACS; ICJ; PPPrHi.14979

The third general epistle of Peter to the rulers of the visible church. Baltimore, Pr. for the publisher, 1832. 11 p. DLC; MdHi.   14980

Thomas, F. W.
Farmer and mechanic; an address delivered before the Hamilton county agricultural society, at their annual exhibition, Sept. 27, 1832. Cincinnati, 1832. 26 p. WU-A.   14981

Thomas, Frederick William.
The Polish chiefs; an historical romance, by the author of Sketches of character... New York, J. K. Porter, 1832. 2 v. in 1. DLC; MH; MeBa; PFal; RPB.   14982

Thomas, John.
The origin and course of intemperance, a poem, in five cantos. By John Thomas. New York, Burnett & Smith, 1832. 59 p. CtMW; ICBB; NBuG; OMC; RPB.   14983

Thompson, David.
History of the late war between Great Britain and the United States of America. Niagara, Pr. by T. Sewell, 1832. 300 p. MnHi.   14984

Thompson, James W., 1805-1881.
A sermon, delivered by request of the Female Charitable Society, in Salem, at their anniversary,

June 24, 1832. Salem, Mass.,
1832. 15 p. DLC; IaHi; MBC;
RPB; WHi.   14985

Thompson, Zadock, 1796-1856.
  The youth's assistant in theo-
retic and practical arithmetic.
Designed for the use of the
schools in the United States. 4th
ed. Burlington, Chauncey Goodrich, 1832. 168 p. MH; OClWHi;
VtU.   14986

---- ---- 6th ed. Burlington, E.
Smith, 1832. MH; MeBat; MiU.
                             14987
Thompson and Homans.
  Catalogue of books on sale by
Thompson & Homans. Washing-
ton, Force, 1832. 136 p. KyDC;
PPAmP.   14988

Thomson, Andrew Mitchell,
1779-1831.
  Sermons and sacramental ex-
hortations. By the late Andrew
Thomson, D.D., minister of St.
George's church, Edinburgh. 1st
Amer. ed. Boston, Crocker &
Brewster; New York, J. Leavitt,
1832. 447 p. CtHC; DLC; IEG;
MBC; NbOP; ViRut.   14989

Thomson, James, 1700-1748.
  The seasons; to which is pre-
fixed the life of the author, by
P. Murdock. Hartford, Silas
Andrus, 1832. 192 p. CtY; MB;
MBC; MiHi.   14990

Thomson, John.
  Curtius on the seizure and ab-
duction of American Citizens
from Madawasica. n.p., 1832?
                             14991
Thomson, Samuel, 1769-1843.
  A narrative of the life and
medical discoveries of Samuel
Thomson: containing an account
of his system of practice, and
the manner of curing disease
with vegetable medicine upon a
plan entirely new... Columbus,

O., Pike, Platt & Co., 1832.
290, (5) p. MH; OClWHi. 14992

---- New guide to health; or,
"Botanic family physician. Containing a complete system of practice on a plan entirely new: with
a description of the vegetables
made use of, and directions for
preparing and administering them,
to cure disease... By Samuel
Thomson. 3d ed. Boston, Pr. by
J. Howe, for the author, 1832.
2 vols. in 1. CU; MB; OC; TNV;
ViU.   14993

---- ---- 8th ed. by Samuel
Thomson. Columbus, O., Pike,
Platt & Co., 1832. 208 p. ArCH;
ICHi; KyLxT; OCGHM; TxD-T.
                             14994
---- The Thomsonian recorder;
or, Impartial advocate of botanic
medicine and the principles which
govern the Thomsonian practice.
By Dr. Samuel Thomson. Thos.
Hershey, senior editor. 1832
[-1833] Pr. at the Ohio Register
Office, for the proprietors.
MsCliM.   14995

Thorn, William.
  ... Dipping not baptizing. By
Rev. W. Thorn... New York, Nel-
son & Phillips [1832?] 51 p.
NNUT.   14996

Thornton, John.
  Bereaved parents, or, An affectionate address to those who
are mourning the loss of children, especially such as have
died in infancy. By John Thornton. With an introduction by an
American clergyman. Richmond,
Va., Robt. I. Smith, 1832. 130 p.
MoBolS.   14997

Thoughts on the importance of
religion. Philadelphia, Tract Association of Friends of Philadelphia, 1832. 8 p. InRchE;
OClWHi; PHi.   14998

Three short stories, for good
little boys. Sidney's Press, New
Haven, 1832. 8 p. DLC.   14999

Tidd, Jacob.
A discourse, containing remarks upon the primitive and
present state of man, with his
future destiny, in which some of
the most prominent doctrinial
questions...By Jacob Tidd. Boston, Pr. for the Author, 1832.
28 p. CBPac; ICMe; MMeT-Hi;
MWA; NCH.   15000

Tilton, J.
Bill of mortality for Exeter,
N.H., 1830. Exeter, 1832. Brd-
sd. MBM.   15001

Timbs, John, 1801-1875.
Knowledge for the people: or,
The plain why and because. Fa-
miliarizing subject of useful curi-
osity and amusing research. By
John Timbs. Boston, Lily & Wait
and Carter & Hendee; New York,
E. Bliss; Philadelphia, Carey &
Lea; New Orleans, M. Carroll;
Portland, S. Coleman, 1832. 68 p.
DLC; ICP; LNH; MH; MiD-B; P.
15002
[Tipton, John B.]
[Address] To the public. A re-
ply to a snapping and kicking
blunderbuss that has emanated
from the quiver of the Rev. Mr.
Birdwell. [Maryville, 1832] 12 p.
T.   15003

Tissot, Samuel Auguste Andre
David.
A treatise on the diseases produced by onanism. Tr. from a
new ed. of the French, with notes
and an appendix. New York, Collins & Hannay, 1832. 132 p. ICJ;
NNN; OCGHM; RPM; ScCMe.
15004
To the citizens of New Haven.
It is generally known that during
the late year a plan was formed
and put into operation, to raise

by private donation, an adequate
fund for Yale College...[New
Haven? 1832?] broadside. 15005

To the citizens of the State of
Pennsylvania. [Philadelphia, Pr.
by Thos. Town, 1832] 15 p.
MdBJ; P.   15006

To the honourable the Senate and
House of Representatives of the
Commonwealth of Pennsylvania.
The memorial of the people of
color of the city of Philadelphia,
and its vicinity. n.p., n.p.,
1832. 8 p. MWA.   15007

To the people of Maine. The
conduct of the administration. The
Indians and the missionaries. A
campaign broadside in behalf of
Henry Clay and John Sergeant,
denouncing the wholesale spoila-
tion of the Cherokees. Portland,
1832. broadside. NN.   15008

To the people of Maryland. Address of the Republican delegates
in favor of Clay and Sergeant.
Baltimore, 1832. 82 p. PPL.
15009
Tocqueville, Alexis Charles Henri Maurice Clerel de.
Democracy in America. By
Alexis de Tocqueville...Trans.
by Henry Reeve, esq. With an
original preface and notes by
John C. Spencer...4th ed. rev.
and cor. from 8th Paris ed.
Boston, Allyn, 1832. 2 vols.
LNP.   15010

The Tocsin: A solemn warning
against the dangerous doctrine of
nullification...See Carey, Matthew.

[Todd, Charles W.]
Woodville; or, the anchoret
reclaimed. A descriptive tale.
Knoxville, T., Pr. by F. S.
Heiskell, for the author, 1832.
278 p. DLC; MoS; NcAS; T;

TKL-Mc.   15011

The token; or, Affection's gift,
a Christmas and New Year's
present. Edited by S. G. Goodrich. Boston, Gray & Bowen,
1832. 392 p. MHi; MNF; OC;
PU; WU.   15012

Tom Thumb. Philadelphia, W.
Johnson, 1832. 15 p. DLC; NNC.
                           15013
Tommy Tucker; or, The lovely
boy. New Haven, Sidney's press,
S. Babcock, 1832. CtY.   15014

Tompkins County [New York]
Bank.
    Facts relative to the trade,
commerce, population and resources of the County of Tompkins, submitted to the Legislature
of the State of New York, by the
applicants for the incorporation of
the Tompkins County Bank.
Ithaca, 1832. 8 p. NIC; NN.
                           15015
Toplady, Augustus Montague,
1740-1778.
    Free-will and merit fairly ex-
amined; or, Men not their own
saviours. A discourse preached
in the parish church of St. Anne,
Blackpriars, London, on Wednesday, May 25, 1774. (By Aug.
Montague Toplady.) Pittsburgh,
J(ohn) Wallace, 1832. 24 p. MH.
                           15016
Topsfield, Mass. Congregational
Church.
    The confession of faith and
covenant... Andover, 1832. 8 p.
MBC.   15017

Torrey, Jesse, fl. 1787-1834.
    A dissertation on the causes,
preventatives and remedies of
plague, yellow fever, cholera,
dysentery, and other pestilential,
epidemic, or contagious diseases.
Philadelphia, J. Grigg, 1832.
80 p. KyLoJM; MBM; PHi;
PPCP; TNV.   15018

---- The primary spelling book;
introductory to the 'Familiar
spelling book, ' comprising easy
elementary lessons, for teaching
English pronunciation, spelling,
and reading. By Jesse Torrey...
Philadelphia, Grigg & Elliot, 1832.
[36] p. DLC.   15019

The Touch stone; or, prejudice
unveiled; being an exposition of
facts etc. Philadelphia, 1832.
24 p. PHi.   15020

A tour through college... The
easy means of acquiring a liberal education without the cost &
hardship of the present academic
course. In two parts. By A. M.
Esq.... Boston, Marsh, Capen,
& Lyon, 1832. 129 p. MBBC;
MH.   15021

Towar, Alexander.
    Der Amerikan pferdearet, ent-
haltind eine an weifung Zur erzie-
hung und haltung der pferde, so
wie auch eine beschreibung aller
der Krankheiten, welchensie unter
worten find, und den bewahrtes-
ten und besten arzneymitteln
dagegen... Philadelphia, Towar,
1832. MeLewB; PPeSchw; ScNC.
                           15022
Tower, David.
    Four lectures on the Thom-
sonian practice of medicine. By
David Tower, physician at Avon
mineral springs... Canandaigua
[N. Y.] Pr. by Bemis, Morse &
Ward (for the author) 1828;
Poughkeepsie [N. Y.] Repr. by
Thos. S. Ranney, by a resolution
of the Dutchess Botanic Medical
Society, 1832. 71 p. CSmH.
                           15023
Towle, Nancy, 1796-
    Vicissitudes illustrated, in the
experience of Nancy Towle, in
Europe and America. Written by
herself. With an appendix of let-
ters, &c. An engraving and
preface by Lorenzo Dow. (The

profites, will be devoted to charitable purposes.)... Chaleston, Pr. by James L. Burges, for the authoress, 1832. 294 p. MAtt; MiD-B; NNMHi; OClWHi; TxDaM.   15024

Town and Country Almanac. By Nathan Bassett. Baltimore, Cushing & Sons, [1832] MWA; MdBE.
15025

Towndrow, Thomas, 1810-1898.
A complete guide to stenography, or An entire new system of writing short hand...By T. Towndrow...2d ed. New Haven, H. Howe; New York, Jocelyn, Darling & Co., 1832. 32 p. CtY; MH; NNG; TxU.   15026

Townley, James.
An introduction to the literary history of the Bible. By Rev. James Townley...1st Amer. ed. New York, F. S. Wiggins, 1832. 274 p. MH-AH; MoWgT; OO.
15027
The township officer's and young clerk's assistant, comprising the duties of justices of the peace, and all other township officers in the state of Ohio,...By a citizen of Ohio. 3d ed. enl. and imp. Columbus, T. Johnson, 1832. DLC; OHi; OO.   15028

Transylvania University, Lexington, Kentucky.
A catalogue of the officers and students of the medical and law departments. Lexington, Ky., Pr. by J. F. Herndone Co., 1832. KyU; PPAmP.   15029

Trattle, Marmaduke.
A catalogue of the unique collection of coins and medals, in gold, silver, and copper, of... Marmaduke Trattle...which will be sold at auction by Mr. Sothby and son...1832. 204 p. PPAmP; PPM.   15030

The Traveller's Directory, and Emigrant's Guide; containing general descriptions of different routes through the states of New-York, Ohio, Indiana, Illinois, and the Territory of Michigan, with short descriptions of the climate, soil, productions, prospects, &c. Buffalo, Steele & Faxon, 1832. 82, 2 p. DLC; NBuHi; IHi.   15031

Treasury of knowledge and library of reference: with various other useful information. 6th ed. enl. and cor. New York, Conner & Cooke, 1832. 448 p. LNStM; OMC.   15032

A treatise on intercessory prayer. New Haven, Baldwin & Treadway, 1832. 29 p. CSmH; MWA. 15033

Treatment of the premonitory symptoms of the cholera, by a citizen of New York. New York, Morgan & Burger, 1832. 20 p. MB; NNNAM.   15034

[Trelawny, Edward John] 1792-1881.
Adventures of a younger son ... New-York, J. & J. Harper, 1832. 2 vols. CtMW; GAuY; MBL; ScCMu; ViPet.   15035

Trench, R. C.
On the study of words... New York, 1832. PPL-R.   15036

Trench, Richard Chenevix, 1807-1886.
Memoirs of the life, character, and labours of the Rev. John Smith, late of Sheffield. By Sir Richard Chenevix Trench...New York, Harper, 1832. 178 p. CtY-D; NjMD.   15037

The trials of a school girl. By the author of 'Days of childhood', &c. Boston, Leonard C. Bowles, and B. H. Greene, 1832. 134 p. DLC; MB; MFiHi; WHi.   15038

Trimmer, Mary.
  A Natural history of the most
remarkable quadrupeds, birds,
fishes, serpents, reptiles and insects. By Mrs. Mary Trimmer.
... Particularly designed for youth
in the United States, and suited to
the use of schools. Boston, Hilliard, Gray, Little & Wilkins,
1832. 233 p. MByDA; RPB.
                                  15039
Trinity College, Hartford, Conn.
  Catalogue of books in the library of Washington College.
Hartford, 1832. 24 p. Ct; CtHT-
W; DLC; M; NjR; RPB.   15040

Trollope, Frances (Milton),
1780-1863.
  Domestic manners of the Americans. By Mrs. Trollope. Complete in one volume. New York,
Whittaker, Treacher & Co., 1832.
325 p. CtHT; DLC; ICU; RPB;
Vi.   15041

Trott, Samuel.
  The image of the beast illus-
trated and the signs of the times,
set forth in seven letters. New
York, Beebe, 1832. 26 p. IEG;
PPPrHi.   15042

Truair, John.
  Gold, silver, precious stones,
wood, hay, stubble; a discourse
delivered at Conway, 1832. Northampton, Pr. by John Metcalf,
1832. 34 p. MNF.   15043

---- The validity of creeds, articles of faith, &c. as laws for
the church, examined... Northampton, Pr. by Metcalf [1832]
28 p. MH; MWA.   15044

Trumbull, Henry.
  History of the discovery of
America, of the landing of our
forefathers at Plymouth, and of
their most remarkable engage-
ments with the Indians, 1620-79.
Boston, George Clark, 1832.

Ct; KyLo; MBC; PPAmP; RPJCB.
                                  15045
Trumbull, John, 1756-1843.
  Catalogue of paintings, by Col.
Trumbull; including eight subjects
of the American revolution, with
near two hundred and fifty portraits, of persons distinguished in
that important period. Painted by
him from the life. Now exhibiting
in the gallery of Yale college,
New Haven... New Haven, Pr. by
E. Howe & Co., 1832. 35 p.
CtY.   15046

Tuck, David G.
  An essay upon the curing,
management, and cultivation of tobacco; by D. G. Tuck. Washington, Gales & Seaton, 1832. 60 p.
DLC.   15047

Tuckerman, Joseph.
  Ministry at large for the poor
of cities. [New York, Pr. by
Philip French, 1832] 16 p. MBAt;
NNUT; PPAmP.   15048

Tudor, William, 1779-1830.
  The life of James Otis, of
Massachusetts: containing also,
notices of some contemporary
characters and events, from the
year 1760 to 1775. By Wm. Tudor. Boston, Wells & Lilly, 1832.
508 p. DLC; ViU.   15049

Tuffnell, F.
  The Gentleman's Pocket-Far-
rier: shewing (sic) how to use
your horse on a journey, and
what remedies are proper for
common accidents that may befall
him on the road. By F. Tuffnell,
Veterinary surgeon. Boston,
Carter, Hendee & Co., 1832. 34 p.
MA; MWA; NIC.   15050

Turnbull, Robert James, 1775-
1833.
  An oration delivered in the city
of Charleston, before the State
Rights & Free Trade Party... on the

4th of July, 1832... Charleston, A. E. Miller, 1832. 45 p. DLC; ICU; MBAt; ScHi; WHi.   15051

Turner, Edward, 1798-1837.
A discourse, delivered before the Female Benevolent Society in Charlestown... Nov. 5, 1823. By Edward Turner... Boston, Pr. by Jonathan Howe, 1832. 12 p. MeBat.   15052

---- Elements of chemistry, including the recent discoveries and doctrines of the science. By Edward Turner... 4th Amer. from 3d London ed.... Philadelphia, Grigg & Elliott, 1832. 622 p. DSG; KyLxT; MH; NjP; WaPS.
15053

Turner, Nat.
The confessions of Nat Turner, the leader of the late insurrection in Southampton, Va., a... made to Thos. R. Gray, in the prison where he was confined and acknowledged by him to be such when read before the court of Southampton... convened at Jerusalem, Nov. 5, 1831, for his trial. Also an authentic account of the whole insurrection, with lists of the whites who were murdered... &c. Richmond, 1832. 24 p. DLC; ICN; PHi; Vi.   15054

Turner, Samuel Hulbeart.
... On occasion of the matriculation of a new class, in November 1828... a sermon, by the Rev. Samuel H. Turner... [New York? 1832] 171-186 p. NNG.   15055

Turner, Sharon, 1768-1847.
... The sacred history of the world, as displayed in the creation and subsequent events to the deluge. Attempted to be philosophically considered in a series of letters to a son. New York, Harper, 1832.   428 p. CBPSR; DLC; ICP; OCl; PPA; RPB; VtU.
15056

Tuttle, George, 1804-1872.
Stories about whale catching. By the author of stories about elephants, with cuts by Anderson. New Haven, S. Babcock, Sidney's Press, 1832. 111 p. Ct; MBAt; NN.   15057

[Tuttle, Sarah]
The African traveller, or prospective missions in Central Africa... Boston, Massachusetts Sabbath School Society, 1832. 150 p. DLC; ICN; ICP; MH-AH; TNF.   15058

---- Hugh Clifford; or, prospective missions on the Northwest coast, and at the Washington islands. By the author of Conversations on the Sandwich islands mission [etc.] ... Revised by the Publishing committee. Boston, Massachusetts Sabbath School Union, 1832. DLC.   15059

---- The widow of monmouth; or, Family instruction, by the author of conversations on the Sandwich Islands mission - the naval chaplain-Malvina Ashton - claims of the Africans, etc. etc. Revised by the Publishing committee. Boston, Massachusetts Sabbath School Society, 1832. 150 p. DLC; ICBB; OMC.   15060

Twenty-eight sermons on doctrinal and practical subjects. Contributed by different ministers of the Methodist Episcopal Church. Boston, C. D. Strong, 1832. 391 p. NNMHi.   15061

Tyerman, Daniel, 1773-1828.
Journal of voyages and travels by the Rev. Daniel Tyerman and George Bennet, esq., Boston, Crocker & Brewster; New York, J. Leavitt, 1832. 3 vols. CU; KyLoS; MBC; PPA; ViU.   15062

Tyler, Bennet, 1783-1858.

Dr. Tyler's Examination of the Theological Views of Dr. Taylor., By Bennet Tyler, D.D., Boston, Pr. by Peirce & Parker, 1832. 12 p. ICT.   15063

---- ...Human and divine, agency united in the salvation of the soul. New York, 1832. 48 p. NNUT.   15064

---- [The Prospects of the Heathen without the Gospel; a sermon preached in Portland, on Sabbath evening, Feb. 26, 1832, by Bennet Tyler, D.D. Pastor of the Second Congregational Church in Portland, Me. Portland, A. Shirley, 1832] 22 p. CSmH; MeB; Nh; OCHP; RPB.   15065

---- Remarks on Rev. Dr. Taylor's letter to Dr. Howes. By Bennet Tyler, D.D. Boston, Pr. by Peirce & Parker, 1832. 12 p. MB; MeB; MeBat; MoSpD; NIC.
                             15066
Tyler, John, 1790-1862.
  Speech of Mr. Tyler, of Virginia, on the subject of Mr. Clay's resolutions providing for a reduction of the duties on imports. Delivered in the Senate of the United States, Feb. 9, 1832. Washington, Pr. by Duff Green, 1832. 36 p. Ct; PHi; ScC; TxU; Vi.   15067

Tyng, Stephen Higginson, 1800-1885.
  The Christian's own book. Meditations drawn from the piety of former ages. With an introductory essay by Stephen H. Tyng, A.M. ...Philadelphia, Geo. Latimer & Co., etc., etc. 1832. 288 p. Baltimore, Armstrong & Plaskitt, 1832. 288 p. CtSoP; GDecCT; MH; PPM; ViAl. 15068

---- The young man's glory and the duty of a young disciple, by Stephen H. Tyng... Philadelphia,

George Latimer & Co., 1832. 68 p. MB; NNG.   15069

U

Uncle Sam's almanack for 1833. By Joseph Cramer. Philadelphia, Grigg's and Dickinson, for Denny and Walker [1832] InU; MWA; NjR.   15070

Uncle Sam's Large Almanack for 1833. Philadelphia, Pa., Denny & Walker [1832] 35, [1] p. MWA; WHi.   15071

Underwood [Joseph C.]
  Address before the Colonization Society Bowling Green. July 4, 1832. Frankfort? 1832. KyDC; OCHP; OClWHi.   15072

Union and State Rights Party.
  Remonstrance & protest of the Union and State Rights Party. [Columbia, 1832] Broadside. MH.
                             15073
---- The report of the committee of the convention of the Union and State Rights Party, assembled at Columbia, 10th December, 1832, with their remonstrance & protest. 16 p. A-Ar; MBAt; MWA; ViL.   15074

---- The Unionist, extra. Charleston, S.C., Dec. 22, 1832. broadside. MH; PU; ScU.   15075

Union Bank of Louisiana, New Orleans.
  Act to incorporate the subscribers of the Union Bank of Louisiana, approved April 2, 1832 ...New Orleans, 1832. 16 p. M.
                             15076
---- ---- With the rules and regulations of the company. New York, Clayton & Van Norden, 1832. 29 p. NN.   15077

---- Acte pour incorporer les

souscripturs a la Banque Del'-
Union de La Louisiane... Nouvelle-
Orleans, n. pub. de l'imprimérie
de J. Bayon. 1832. 15 p. NjR.
15078

Union Benevolent Association.
First annual report of the executive board of the Union Benevolent Association. Philadelphia,
Pr. by J. Harding by order of
the Association, 1832. 12 p.
MdBD; P; PPAmP.   15079

Union College. Adelphic Society.
Catalogue of books belonging
to the Library of the Adelphic
Society, in Union College, 1832.
Schenectady, 1832. 36 p. MH;
MHi; MWA.   15080

United States.
... Abstract of the returns of
the fifth census, showing the
number of free people, the number of Slaves, the federal or
representative number; and the
aggregate of each county of each
state of the United States. Prepared from the corrected returns of the Secretary of State to
Congress. By the Clerk of the
House of Representatives. Washington, D. C., Pr. by Duff Green,
1832. 51 p. (22d Congress, 1st
Sess.), (H. R. 263). MB; MiD;
PPL-R; ScU.   15081

---- An act concerning invalid
pensions. July 12, 1832. Received.
[Washington, 1832] 2 p. (H. R.
271) DNA; MB.   15082

---- An act concerning patents for
useful inventions. May 21, 1832.
Read, and passed to a second
reading. [Washington, 1832] 3 p.
(H. R. 551) DNA; MB.   15083

---- An act defining the qualifications of voters in the territory
of Arkansas. February 27, 1832.
Read, and passed to a second
reading. February 29, 1832. Read

the second time, and referred to
the Committee on the Judiciary.
[Washington, 1832] 1 p. (H. R.
364) DNA; MB.   15084

---- An act for giving effect to
a commercial arrangement between the United States and the
Republic of Colombia. January
31, 1832. Received. February
1, 1832. Read, and passed to a
second reading. [Washington,
1832] 2 p. (H. R. 320) DNA; MB.
15085
---- An act for quieting possessions, enrolling conveyances,
and securing the estates of purchasers within the District of
Columbia. April 13, 1832. Received. [Washington, 1832] 3 p.
(H. R. 322) DNA; MB.   15086

---- An act for the adjustment
and settlement of the claims of
the state of South Carolina against
the United States. February 20,
1832. Read twice, and referred
to the Committee on Military
Affairs. [Washington, 1832] 3 p.
(H. R. 4) DNA; MB.   15087

---- An act for the apportionment of Representatives among
the several states according to
the fifth census. February 16,
1832. Read, and passed to a second reading. [Washington, 1832]
2 p. (H. R. 206) DNA. MB.
15088
---- An act for the discharge of
sundry judgements against the
former marshal of the Eastern
District of Pennsylvania. July 12,
1832. Received. [Washington,
1832] 1 p. (H. R. 590) DNA. MB.
15089
---- An act for the improvement
of certain harbors, and the navigation of certain rivers. June 6,
1832. Read twice, and referred
to the Committee on Commerce.
[Washington, 1832] 5 p. (H. R.
516) DNA. MB.   15090

---- An act for the re-appropri-
ation of certain unexpended balances of former appropriations.
May 26, 1832. Read twice, and
referred to the Committee on Finance. [Washington, 1832] 3 p.
(H.R. 525) DNA; MB.   15091

---- An act for the relief of
Archibald Watt. December 25,
1832. Read twice, and referred
to the Committee of Claims.
[Washington, 1832] 2 p. (H.R.
239) DNA; MB.   15092

---- An act for the relief of cer-
tain pensioners therein named.
December 28, 1832. Read twice,
and referred to the Committee on
Pensions. [Washington, 1832]
4 p. (H.R. 626) DNA; MB.
                             15093
---- An act for the relief of Ed-
mund Brooke. April 10, 1832.
Received. [Washington, 1832]
2 p. (H.R. 291) DNA; MB.
                             15094
---- An act for the relief of
Gates Hoit. April 10, 1832. Re-
ceived. [Washington, 1832] 1 p.
(H.R. 146) DNA; MB.   15095

---- An act for the relief of
John Knight. March 28, 1832.
Received. [Washington, 1832] 1 p.
(H.R. 130) DNA; MB.   15096

---- An act for the relief of
John Roberts, late major of infantry in the war of the revolution. February 8, 1832. Received. February 9, 1832. Read
twice, and referred to the Committee of Claims. [Washington,
1832] 1 p. (H.R. 94) DNA; MB.
                             15097
---- An act for the relief of
Peter McCormick. December 28,
1832. Read twice, and referred
to the Committee on Private
Land Claims. [Washington, 1832]
2 p. (H.R. 250) DNA; MB.
                             15098

---- An act for the relief of Robert Jones and William A. Fleming. January 5, 1832. Read twice,
and referred to the Committee
on the Public Lands. [Washing-
ton, 1832] 2 p. (H.R. 45) DNA;
MB.   15099

---- An act for the relief of the
heirs and residuary legatees of
William Carter, late of the state
of Virginia, deceased. February
21, 1832. Read, and passed to
a second reading. [Washington,
1832] 1 p. (H.R. 107) DNA; MB.
                             15100
---- An act for the relief of the
heirs of Nicholas Hart, deceased. December 28, 1832.
Read twice, and referred to the
Committee on Revolutionary
Claims. [Washington, 1832] 2 p.
(H.R. 232) DNA; MB.   15101

---- An act for the relief of the
heirs of William Vawters. February 8, 1832. Received. February 9, 1832. Read twice, and referred to the Committee of
Claims. [Washington, 1832] 1 p.
(H.R. 93) DNA; MB.   15102

---- An act for the relief of the
Invalid Pensioners of the United
States. July 5, 1832. Received.
[Washington, 1832] 1 p. (H.R.
225) DNA; MB.   15103

---- An act for the relief of the
legal representatives of Nimrod
Farrow and of Richard Harris.
May 26, 1832. Read twice, and
referred to the Committee of
Claims. [Washington, 1832] 1 p.
(H.R. 277) DNA; MB.   15104

---- An act for the relief of the
representatives of David Dardin,
deceased. February 3, 1832. Received. February 7, 1832. Read
twice, and referred to the Committee of Claims. [Washington,
1832] 1 p. (H.R. 92) DNA; MB.
                             15105

---- An act for the relief of the representatives of William P. Gibbs, executor of Benjamin Gibbs, of Kentucky. February 21, 1832. Read, and passed to a second reading. [Washington, 1832] 1 p. (H. R. 191) DNA; MB. 15106

---- An act in addition to an act, entitled "An act to provide for certain persons engaged in the land and naval service of the United States in the revolutionary war," approved March 18, 1818. May 2, 1832. Received. [Washington, 1832] 6 p. (H. R. 157) DNA; MB. 15107

---- An act in addition to the "Act for the gradual improvement of the navy of the United States." February 16, 1832. [Washington, 1832] 2 p. (H. R. 622) DNA; MB. 15108

---- An act making appropriations for a custom-house in the city of New York, and for other purposes. July 5, 1832. Received. [Washington, 1832] 2 p. (H. R. 490) DNA; MB. 15109

---- An act making appropriations for fortifications for the year one thousand eight hundred and thirty-two. February 20, 1832. Read twice, and referred to the Committee of Finance. [Washington, 1832] 2 p. (H. R. 174) DNA; MB. 15110

---- An act making appropriations for the Indian Department for the year one thousand eight hundred and thirty-two. April 4, 1832. Received. April 5, 1832. Read twice, and referred to the Committee on Indian Affairs. [Washington, 1832] 3 p. (H. R. 173) DNA; MB. 15111

---- An act making appropriations for the Indian Department for the year one thousand eight hundred and thirty-three. February 16, 1832. [Washington, 1832] 4 p. (H. R. 630) DNA; MB. 15112

---- An act making appropriations for the Naval Service for the year one thousand eight hundred and thirty-two. February 20, 1832. Read twice, and referred to the Committee on Finance. [Washington, 1832] 4 p. (H. R. 223) DNA; MB. 15113

---- An act making appropriations for the support of government for the year one thousand eight hundred and thirty-two. March 20, 1832. Received. March 21, 1832. Read twice, and referred to the Committee on Finance. [Washington, 1832] 19 p. (H. R. 116) DNA; MB. 15114

---- An act making appropriations for the support of the army for the year one thousand eight hundred and thirty-two. March 20, 1832. Received. March 20, 1832. Read twice, and committed to the Committee on Finance. [Washington, 1832] 5 p. (H. R. 164) DNA; MB. 15115

---- An act making appropriations in conformity with the stipulations of certain treaties with the Creeks, Shawnees, Ottoways, Senecas, Wyandots, Cherokees, and Choctaws. May 24, 1832. Read twice, and referred to the Committee on Indian Affairs. [Washington, 1832] 5 p. (H. R. 566) DNA; MB. 15116

---- An act making appropriations, in part, for the support of government for the year one thousand eight hundred and thirty-three, and for certain expenditures of the year one thousand eight hundred and thirty-two. January 4, 1832. Read twice, and referred to the Committee on Finance. [Washington, 1832] 2 p. (H. R. 621) DNA; MB. 15117

---- An act making provision for
the sale and disposition of the
public grounds in the cities of St.
Augustine and Pensacola, and to
reserve certain lots and buildings
for public purposes, and to provide for their repair and preservation. May 24, 1832. Read twice,
and referred to the Committee on
Public Lands. [Washington, 1832]
3 p. (H.R. 405) DNA; MB. 15118

---- Act of the legislative council
of Florida. Feb. 11, 1832. Act
for the protection of the fisheries in the Territory of Florida.
House Ex. Docs., No. 201, 22d
Cong., 1st sess. Vol. V. [Wash-
ington, 1832] 11 p. MB.   15119

---- An act providing for the
postponement of the trial of certain cases now pending in the Superior Courts of Arkansas Territory, and for withholding from
sale or entry certain lands in
said territory. April 10, 1832.
Received. [Washington, 1832]
DNA; MB.   15120

---- Act relative to the Chesapeake and Ohio Canal. March 23,
1832. Act of the General Assembly of Maryland to amend the act
incorporating the Chesapeake and
Ohio Canal Company. House Ex.
Docs., No. 217, 22d Cong., 1st
sess., Vol. V. [Washington,
1832] 3 p. MB.   15121

---- An act supplementary to the
several acts making appropriation for the civil and military service during the year one thousand
eight hundred and thirty-two.
July 5, 1832. Received. [Washing-
ton, 1832] 4 p. (H.R. 601) DNA;
MB.   15122

---- An act to alter and amend
the several acts imposing duties
on imports. June 29, 1832. Read
twice, and referred to the Com-

mittee on Manufactures. [Washing-
ton, 1832] 20 p. (H.R. 584) MB.
                           15123
---- An act to alter and amend
the several acts imposing duties
on imports. July 7, 1832. Ordered, that the following bill as
amended in Senate be printed.
[Washington, 1832] 22 p. (H.R.
584) MB.   15124

---- An act to amend an act, entitled "An act to alter and amend
an act to set apart and dispose
of certain public lands for the
encouragement of the cultivation
of the vine and olive," approved
nineteenth February, one thousand eight hundred and thirty-one.
December 24, 1832. Received.
[Washington, 1832] 2 p. (H.R.
350) DNA; MB.   15125

---- An act to amend an act, entitled "An act to enlarge the powers of the several corporations
of the District of Columbia," April
13, 1832. Received. [Washington,
1832] 2 p. (H.R. 357) DNA; MB.
                           15126
---- An act to authorize the disposition of the fund arising from
the sale of a quarter section of
land, reserved for the use of
schools, in Florida. June 25,
1832. Read twice, and referred
to the Committee on Public Lands.
[Washington, 1832] 2 p. (H.R.
259) DNA; MB.   15127

---- An act to authorize the sur-
veying and laying out a road from
Detroit, to the mouth of Grand
River of Lake Michigan, in the
Michigan Territory, and for the
survey of canal routes in the ter-
ritory of Florida. June 25, 1832.
Read twice, and referred to the
Committee on Roads and Canals.
[Washington, 1832] 2 p. (H.R.
158) DNA; MB.   15128

---- An act to carry into effect

certain Indian treaties. July 5, 1832. Received. [Washington, 1832] 2 p. (H.R. 575) DNA; MB. 15129

---- An act to carry into effect the convention between the United States and His Majesty the King of the French, concluded at Paris on the fourth of July, one thousand eight hundred and thirty-one. June 29, 1832. Read twice, and referred to the Committee on Finance. [Washington, 1832] 5 p. (H.R. 415) DNA; MB. 15130

---- An act to change the time of holding the United States' district court at Staunton, in the western district of Virginia. February 21, 1832. Read twice, and referred to the Committee on the Judiciary. [Washington, 1832] 1 p. (H.R. 263) DNA; MB. 15131

---- An act to establish a land office in the territory of Michigan. December 24, 1832. Received. [Washington, 1832] 1 p. (H.R. 102) DNA; MB. 15132

---- An act to explain an act entitled "An act to reduce the duties on coffee, tea, and cocoa," passed the twentieth of May, one thousand eight hundred and thirty. December 24, 1832. Received. [Washington, 1832] 2 p. (H.R. 63) DNA; MB. 15133

---- An act to extend the time of issuing military land warrants to officers and soldiers of the revolutionary army. June 6, 1832. Read, and passed to a second reading. June 7, 1832. Read a second time, and referred to the committee on Military Affairs. June 18, 1832. Reported with an amendment, to wit, to add a new section. [Washington, 1832] 2 p. (H.R. 594) MB. 15134

---- An act to oblige vessels coming from foreign ports or places, or ports or places within the United States, to the District of Columbia, to perform quarantine. July 5, 1832. Received. [Washington, 1832] 9 p. (H.R. 606) DNA; MB. 15135

---- An act to provide for paying certain arrearages for surveys made by naval officers, and for other purposes. June 27, 1832. Read twice, and referred to the Committee on Naval Affairs. [Washington, 1832] 2 p. (H.R. 91) DNA; MB. 15136

---- An act to provide for the appointment of three Commissioners to treat with the indians, and for other purposes. July 12, 1832. Received. [Washington, 1832] 2 p. (H.R. 484) DNA; MB. 15137

---- An act to provide for the extinguishment of the Indian title to lands lying in the states of Missouri and Illinois. July 5, 1832. [Washington, 1832] 1 p. (H.R. 597) DNA; MB. 15138

---- An act to provide iron tanks for the use of the Navy of the United States. June 27, 1832. Read twice, and referred to the Committee on Naval Affairs. [Washington, 1832] 1 p. (H.R. 88) DNA; MB. 15139

---- An act to provide the means of extending the benefits of vaccination, as a preventive of the small pox, to the Indian tribes, and thereby, as far as possible, to save them from the destructive ravages of that disease. April 10, 1832. Received. [Washington, 1832] 2 p. (H.R. 526) DNA; MB. 15140

---- An act to refund a fine imposed on the late Matthew Lyon, under the sedition law, to his heirs and representatives. February 13, 1832. Read twice, and referred to the Committee on the Judiciary. [Washington, 1832] 1 p. (H. R. 290) DNA; MB. 15141

---- An act to remove the land office from Mount Salus to Jackson, in the state of Mississippi, and to remove the land office from Franklin to Fayette, in the state of Missouri. March 29, 1832. (sic) [Washington, 1832] MB.   15142

---- An act to secure to mechanics and others payment for labor done and materials furnished in the erection of buildings in Washington city. December 20. Read twice and referred to the Committee on the District of Columbia. [Washington, 1832] 4 p. (H. R. 497) DNA; MB.   15143

---- An act vesting in the corporation of Washington city, all the rights of the Washington Canal Company, and for other purposes... April 13, 1832. Received. [Washington, 1832] 11 p. (H. R. 492) DNA; MB.   15144

---- Acts of Congress relative to United States Bank. Feb. 20, 1832. Act incorporating the United States Bank; Act amendatory thereto; Charter of bank. House Ex. Docs., No. 128, 22d Cong., 1st sess., Vol. IV. [Washington, 1832] 26 p. MB.
                                    15145
---- Amendment. January 16, 1832. Read, and committed to the Committee on the Whole House, to which the said bills are committed. Mr. Wickliffe submitted the following, which, when the bills (H. R. No. 54) supplementary to the several laws for the sale of public lands, and the bill from the Senate (No. 22) of the same title, shall be taken up for con-

sideration, he will move as an amendment. [Washington, 1832] 1 p. (H. R. 54) DNA; MB. 15146

---- ---- February 8, 1832. Read, and committed to the Committee of the Whole House on the state of the Union, to which the said bill is committed, Mr. Binton submitted the following, which, when the bill making appropriations for certain internal improvements shall be taken up for consideration, he will move as an amendment. [Washington, 1832] 1 p. (H. R. 267) DNA; MB.
                                    15147
---- ---- February 13, 1832. Read, and committed to the Committee of the Whole House to which the said bill is committed. Mr. Verplanck submitted the following, which, when the bill (H. R. No. 267) making appropriations for certain internal improvements for the year one thousand eight hundred and thirty-two, shall be taken up for consideration, he will move as an amendment. [Washington, 1832] 3 p. (H. R. 267) DNA; MB.   15148

---- ---- February 20, 1832. Committed to the Committee of the Whole House to which the said bill is committed. Mr. Irvin submitted the following, which, when the bill (H. R. No. 267) making appropriations for certain improvements, for the year one thousand eight hundred and thirty [sic] shall be taken up for consideration, he will move as an amendment. [Washington, 1832] 1 p. (H. R. 267) DNA; MB.
                                    15149
---- ---- February 28, 1832. Read, and committed to the Committee of the Whole House on the state of the Union, to which the said bill is committed. Mr. Root, submitted the following; which, when the bill (H. R. No. 365) to

renew and modify the charter of the Bank of the United States, shall be taken up for consideration, he will move as an amendment. [Washington, 1832] 2 p. (H. R. 365) DNA; MB.   15150

---- ---- March 3, 1832. Read, and committed to the Committee of the Whole House to which the said bill is committed. Mr. Mardis submitted the following: which, when the bill (H. R. No. 177,) "to appropriate certain lands within the State of Alabama for the purposes of improving the navigation of the Tennessee and Coosa rivers, and connecting their waters by a canal or railroad," shall be taken up for consideration, he will move as an amendment. [Washington, 1832] 3 p. (H. R. 177) DNA; MB.
                                15151
---- ---- March 3, 1832. Read, and committed to the Committee of the Whole House to which the said bill is committed. Mr. Wickliffe submitted the following; which, when the bill (H. R. No. 157) in addition to an act, entitled "An act to provide for certain persons engaged in the land and naval service of the United States in the revolutionary war," approved March 18, 1818, shall be taken up for consideration, he will move as an amendment. [Washington, 1832] 1 p. (H. R. 157) DNA; MB.   15152

---- ---- March 6, 1832. The bill from the House of Representatives, entitled "An act for an apportionment of Representatives among the several states, according to the fifth census," being under consideration, Mr. Webster proposed thereto the following amendment. [Washington, 1832] 2 p. (H. R. 208) DNA; MB. 15153

---- ---- March 14, 1832. The

bill from the House of Representatives (No. 208) "For the apportionment of Representatives among the several states according to the fifth census," having been read the third time, Mr. Webster moved to re-commit the bill to a select committee, with instructions to amend the same by striking out all after the enacting clause, and inserting the following amendment. [Washington, 1832] 2 p. (H. R. 208) DNA; MB.
                                15154
---- ---- March 23, 1832. Mr. Smith, from the Committee on Finance, to which was recommitted the bill to exempt merchandise imported under certain circumstances from the operation of the act of the nineteenth of May, eighteen hundred and twenty-eight, entitled "An act in alteration of the several acts imposing duties on imports," reported the same with the following: [Washington, 1832] 1 p. (S. 69) DNA; MB.
                                15155
---- ---- April 5, 1832. Mr. Webster, from the select committee, to whom was referred the bill from the House of Representatives among the several states according to the fifth census, reported the same with the following amendment. [Washington, 1832] 2 p. (H. R. 208) DNA; MB.
                                15156
---- ---- April 13, 1832. Read, and committed to the Committee of the Whole House on the state of the Union, to which the said bill is committed. Mr. Appleton submitted the following: which, when the bill (H. R. No. 365) to renew and modify the charter of the bank of the United States, shall be taken up for consideration, he will move as an amendment. [Washington, 1832] 2 p. (H. R. 365) DNA; MB.   15157

---- ---- April 23, 1832. Read,

and committed to the Committee of the Whole House to which the said bill is committed. Mr. Davis, of Massachusetts, submitted the following; which, when the bill H. R. No. 361, to reduce and equalize the duties on imports, shall be taken up for consideration, he will move as an amendment. [Washington, 1832] 3 p. (H. R. 361) DNA; MB.
15158

---- ---- May 1, 1832. Mr. McKennan submitted the following: which, when the bill (H. R. No. 267) making appropriations for certain internal improvements for the year one thousand eight hundred and thirty-two, shall be taken up for consideration, he will move as an amendment. [Washington, 1832] 1 p. (H. R. 267) DNA; MB.   15159

---- ---- May 2, 1832. Committed to the Committee of the Whole House on said bill No. 340. Mr. Doddridge submitted the following: which, when the bill (H. R. No. 340) entitled "An act declaring the assent of Congress to the acts of the General Assemblies of Maryland and Pennsylvania," hereinafter recited, shall be taken up, he will move as an amendment. [Washington, 1832] 12 p. (H. R. 340). DNA; MB.
15160

---- ---- May 7, 1832. Amendment of the Senate's amendment, submitted by Mr. E. Everett, from the Select Committee to which the apportionment bill, with the amendment of the Senate, was referred. [Washington, 1832] 2 p. (H. R. 208) DNA; MB.   15161

---- ---- May 9, 1832. Mr. Silsbee offered the following amendment to the bill for the relief of John F. Lewis: [Washington, 1832] 2 p. (S. 84) DNA; MB.
15162

---- ---- May 10, 1832. Read, and committed to the Committee of the Whole House to which the said bill is committed. Mr. Mardis submitted the following; which, when the bill (H. R. 361) to reduce and equalize the duties on imports, shall be taken up for consideration, he will move as an amendment. [Washington, 1832] 1 p. (H. R. 361) DNA; MB.
15163

---- ---- May 14, 1832. Amendment of the Senate's amendment, submitted by Mr. E. Everett, from the Select Committee to which the apportionment bill, with the amendment of the Senate, was referred. [Washington, 1832] 2 p. (H. R. 208) DNA; MB.   15164

---- ---- May 26, 1832. The following amendment was proposed by Mr. Webster, to be added to the "bill to modify and continue the charter of the Bank of the United States." [Washington, 1832] 1 p. (S. 147) DNA; MB.   15165

---- ---- May 26, 1832. To be proposed by Mr. Moore to the bill to modify and continue the charter of the Bank of the United States. [Washington, 1832] 1 p. (S. 147) DNA; MB.   15166

---- ---- June 2, 1832. Read, and committed to the Committee of the Whole House to which the said bill is committed. Mr. Doubleday submitted the following; which, when the bill (H. R. No. 584) to alter and amend the several acts imposing duties on imports, shall be taken up for consideration, he will move as an amendment. [Washington, 1832] 2 p. (H. R. 584) DNA; MB.
15167

---- ---- June 2, 1832. Read twice, and committed to the Committee of the Whole House on the

state of the Union, to which the said bill is committed. Mr. Stewart submitted the following; which, when the bill (No. 584) to alter and amend the several acts imposing duties on imports, shall be taken up for consideration, he will move as an amendment. [Washington, 1832] 9 p. (H.R. 584) DNA; MB.
15168

---- ---- June 5, 1832. Read, and committed to the Committee of the Whole House to which the said bill is committed. Mr. Sutherland submitted the following, as amendments to the bill (H.R. No. 584) to alter and amend the several acts imposing duties on imports. [Washington, 1832] 1 p. (H.R. 584) DNA; MB.
15169

---- ---- June 7, 1832. Mr. Davis, of Massachusetts, moved the following amendment to the bill (No. 584) further to amend the several acts imposing duties on imports. [Washington, 1832] 1 p. (H.R. 584) MB.
15170

---- ---- June 11, 1832. Amendment intended to be proposed by Mr. Tanzewell to the "bill to repeal, in part, the duties on imports," viz. Strike out all after the enacting clause, and insert the following: [Washington, 1832] 14 p. (S. 167) DNA; MB.
15171

---- ---- June 11, 1832. Mr. Dickerson proposed that the "bill to repeal, in part, the duties on imports," be amended as follows, viz. [Washington, 1832] 4 p. (S. 167) DNA; MB.
15172

---- ---- June 11, 1832. Read, and committed to the Committee of the Whole House to which the said bill is committed. Mr.

Crawford submitted the following, as amendments to the bill (H.R. No. 584) to alter and amend the several acts imposing duties on imports. [Washington, 1832] 2 p. (H.R. 584) DNA; MB.
15173

---- ---- June 16, 1832. Mr. John Davis, of Massachusetts, submitted the following, which, when the bill (H.R. No. 584) to alter and amend the several acts imposing duties on imports, shall be taken up, he will move as an amendment. [Washington, 1832] 3 p. (H.R. 584) MB.
15174

---- ---- June 23, 1832. Mr. John Q. Adams submitted the following amendment in lieu of the second and third sections of the bill reported by the Committee on Manufactures to amend the several acts laying duties on imports. [Washington, 1832] 3 p. (H.R. 584) MB.   15175

---- ---- June 26, 1832. Mr. Forsyth, from the Committee on Commerce, to whom was referred the bill from the House of Representatives, entitled "An act for the improvement of certain harbors, and the navigation of certain rivers," reported the same with the following amendment. [Washington, 1832] 2 p. (H.R. 516) DNA; MB.   15176

---- ---- June 26, 1832. Mr. King, from the Committee on Public Lands, to whom was recommitted the "Bill for the appointment of a Recorder of the General Land Office, and prescribing the mode by which patents for public lands shall be executed, granted, and issued," with the amendment made thereto in Senate, reported that the said amendment as follows in [brackets] be stricken out, and that which follows in italics be inserted in lieu thereof. [Washington, 1832] 1 p. (S. 83) DNA; MB.   15177

---- ---- December 28, 1832. Mr. Mercer, from the Committee on Roads and Canals, to which was recommitted the bill (H.R. No. 560) to incorporate the St. Francis Road Company of the Territory of Arkansas, reported the following amendment; [Washington, 1832] 1 p. (H.R. 560) MB.   15178

---- ---- December 28, 1832. Read, and committed to the Committee of the Whole House on the state of the Union, to which the said bill is committed. Mr. Clay, from the Committee on the Public Lands, submitted the following, as an amendment of the bill (H.R. No. 402) to reduce and graduate the price of the public lands. [Washington, 1832] 2 p. (H.R. 402) DNA; MB.   15179

---- ---- December 28, 1832. Read, and committed to the Committee of the Whole House on the state of the Union, to which the said bill is committed. Mr. Wickliffe, from the minority of the Committee on the Public Lands, reported the following amendment to the bill (H.R. No. 402) to reduce and graduate the price of the public lands. [Washington, 1832] 3 p. (H.R. 402) DNA; MB.   15180

---- ---- After the enacting words, strike out the residue of the bill, and insert the following: June 30, 1832. Read, and committed to the Committee of the Whole House to which the said bill is committed. Mr. Watmough submitted the following: which, when the bill (H.R.

249) to reorganize the navy of the United States shall be taken up for consideration, he will move as an amendment. [Washington, 1832] 3 p. (H.R. 249) DNA; MB.   15181

No entry.   15182

---- ---- After the enacting words, strike out the residue of the bill, and insert the following: December 27, 1832. Mr. Watmough, from the Committee on Naval Affairs, submitted the following bill (No. 249) "to reorganize the Navy of the United States" shall be considered, will be moved as an amendment. [Washington, 1832] 6 p. (H.R. 249) DNA; MB.   15183

---- Amendment intended to be proposed by Mr. Webster, to the bill from the House of Representatives, entitled "An act for the apportionment of Representatives among the several states, according to the fifth census." February 27, 1832. [Washington, 1832] 2 p. (H.R. 208) DNA; MB.   15184

---- Amendment to bill (H.R. 635)--being "A bill to create new land offices in the Choctaw purchase, and for the more convenient organization of the land districts in the states of Mississippi." February 12, 1832. Mr. Clay, of Alabama, from the Committee on Public Lands, reported the following amendment. [Washington, 1832] 2 p. (H.R. 635) DNA; MB.   15185

---- Amendment to the bill, to re-organize the Navy of the United States. January 20, 1832. Read, and referred to the Committee of the Whole House to which the said bill is committed.

Mr. Watmough submitted the
following, which, when the bill
(H.R. No. 249) to re-organize
the Navy of the United States,
shall be taken up for consideration, he will move as an
amendment. [Washington, 1832]
1 p. (H.R. 249) DNA; MB.
15186

---- Amendment to the resolution of the twenty-eighth of
April last. July 9, 1832. Mr.
Whittlesey, from the committee
to which the subject had been
referred, reported the following
joint resolution respecting the
Biennial Register. Read twice,
and ordered to be engrossed, and
read the third time to-morrow.
[Washington, 1832] 2 p. (H.R.
13) DNA; MB.   15187

---- Amendments. March 22,
1832. The Committee on Finance, to which was referred
the bill from the House of Representatives, entitled "An act
making appropriations for the
support of the Army for the year
(1832)," report the same with
the following: [Washington,
1832] 1 p. (H.R. 164) DNA;
MB.   15188

---- Amendments. March 26,
1832. The Committee on Finance,
to which was referred the bill
from the House of Representatives, entitled "An act making appropriations for the support of
government for the year one thousand eight hundred and thirty-
two," report the same with the
following amendments. [Washing-
ton, 1832] 3 p. (H.R. 116) DNA;
MB.   15189

---- ---- March 28, 1832. Mr.
Smith, from the Committee on Finance, reported the following
amendments to the bill from the
House of Representatives, entitled

"An act making appropriation for
the support of government for
the year one thousand eight hundred and thirty-two: [Washington,
1832] 2 p. (H.R. 116) DNA; MB.
15190

---- ---- April 9, 1832. Read,
and committed to the Committee
of the Whole House on the state
of the Union to which the said
bill is committed. Mr. Clay submitted the following, which, when
the bill (H.R. No. 365) to renew
and modify the charter of the
Bank of the United States, shall
be taken up for consideration, he
intends moving as amendments.
[Washington, 1832] MB.   15191

---- ---- April 10, 1832. The
Committee on the Post Office and
Post Roads, to whom was referred
the bill, entitled "An act to establish certain post roads, and to
discontinue others, and for other
purposes," report the same with
the following amendments. [Wash-
ington, 1832] 3 p. (H.R. 343)
DNA; MB.   15192

---- ---- May 24, 1832. Mr. Irvin submitted the following: which,
when the bill (H.R. No. 365) to
renew and modify the charter of
the Bank of the United States,
shall be taken up for consideration, he will move as amendments.
[Washington, 1832] 1 p. (H.R. 365)
DNA; MB.   15195

---- ---- June 1, 1832. Mr. Forsyth, from the Committee on Commerce, to whom was referred the
bill from the House of Representatives, entitled "An act making appropriations for certain internal
improvements for the year one
thousand eight hundred and thirty-
two," reported the same with the
following amendments. [Washing-
ton, 1832] 2 p. (H.R. 267) DNA;
MB.   15194

---- ---- June 1, 1832. The bill to modify and continue the act, entitled "An act to incorporate the subscribers to the Bank of the United States," being under consideration, Mr. Benton proposed thereto the following: [Washington, 1832] 2 p. (S. 147) DNA; MB.   15195

---- ---- June 13, 1832. Mr. Stewart submitted the following as amendments to the bill (H. R. No. 584) to alter and amend the several acts imposing duties on imports. [Washington, 1832] 14 p. (H. R. 584) MB.   15196

---- ---- June 20, 1832. The bill to appropriate, for a limited time, the proceeds of the sales of the public lands of the United States, being under consideration, Mr. Poindexter gave notice that he would, when the amendment reported to the bill should be disposed of, propose to add to the bill the following sections: [Washington, 1832] 2 p. (S. 179) MB.
15197

---- ---- July 3, 1832. Mr. Dickerson, from the Committee on Manufactures, to whom was referred the bill from the House of Representatives, entitled "An act to alter and amend the several acts imposing duties on imports," reported the same with the following amendments. [Washington, 1832] 7 p. (H. R. 584) MB.   15198

---- Amendments to the bill "authorizing the location of Virginia military land warrants on a portion of the public lands." Mr. Doddridge, when the above bill shall come under consideration, will offer the following amendments. [Washington, 1832] 1 p. (H. R. 335) DNA; MB.   15199

---- Amendments to the pension bill. April 17, 1832. Read and committed to the Committee of the Whole House to which the said bill is committed. Mr. L. Condict submitted the following, as amendments to the bill (H. R. No. 157) in addition to an act entitled "An act to provide for certain persons engaged in the land and naval service of the United States in the revolutionary war," approved March 18, 1818, [Washington, 1832] 2 p. (H. R. 157) DNA; MB.   15200

---- American state papers. Documents, legislative and executive, of the Congress of the United States... Selected and edited under the authority of Congress... Washington, Gales & Seaton, 1832-61. 38 vols. DLC; Ia; In-SC; L; MB; MH-L; P.   15201

---- Annual message, with documents. President Andrew Jackson. Dec. 4, 1832. Ex. Docs., No. 2, 22d Cong., 2d sess., Vol. I. Condition of the country; Foreign affairs; Northeastern boundary; Finances; Removal and preservation of the Indians; Opposition of South Carolina to the revenue laws; United States Bank; Public lands; Internal improvements; Judicial system. [Washington, 1832] 240 p. MB.   15202

---- Army-Enlistment of Minors, etc., Dec. 17, 1832. Pr. by order of the House of Representatives. Washington, Duff Green, pr., 1832. 6 p. 22d Congress, 2d sess. MB.   15203

---- Articles of Agreement for the Coast Survey. Aug. 6, 1832. Library of the Coast Survey. Between Louis McLane, Secretary of the Treasury, and F. R. Hassler, relative to the survey of the coast of the United States. [Washington, 1832] 2 p. MB.
15204

---- Biennial Register. Secretary of State. 1832. Compiled by order of Congress. Register of all officers and agents, civil, military, and naval, in the service of the United States. [Washington, D. C.] Pr. by Wm. A. Davis [1832] 407 p. MB.   15205

---- A bill allowing office rent to the Registers and Receivers of the several land offices. February 14, 1832. Mr. King, from the Committee on Public Lands, reported the following bill; which was read, and passed to a second reading: [Washington, 1832] 1 p. (S. 113) DNA; MB.   15206

---- A bill amendatory to an act entitled "An act for the relief of Robert C. Jennings, and of the executors of James Roddy, deceased." Dec. 19, 1832. Read, and postponed until Friday next. Mr. E. Whittlesey, from the Committee of Claims, reported the following bill: [Washington, 1832] 1 p. (H. R. 629) DNA; MB.   15207

---- A bill authorizing a subscription of stock in the Baltimore and Ohio Railroad Company. Feb. 2, 1832. Agreeably to notice, Mr. Smith asked and obtained leave to bring in the following bill; which was read, and passed to a second reading: Feb. 3, 1832. Read the second time, and referred to the Committee on Roads and Canals. Feb. 14, 1832. Reported with an amendment; to wit: Add section three, in italics. [Washington, 1832] 2 p. (S. 93) DNA; MB.   15208

---- A bill authorizing certain persons therein named to prosecute suits against the United States. Jan. 25, 1832. Read twice, and committed to a Committee of the Whole House tomorrow. Mr. Bullard, from the

Committee on Private Land Claims, reported the following bill: [Washington, 1832] 4 p. (H. R. 311) DNA; MB.   15209

---- A bill authorizing the appointment of an agent to reside among the Choctaw Indians west of the Mississippi, in pursuance of the thirteenth article of the treaty concluded with the Choctaws on the twenty-seventh September, one thousand eight hundred and thirty. Mar. 17, 1832. Read twice, and committed to a Committee of the Whole House to-morrow. Mr. Bell, from the Committee on Indian Affairs, reported the following bill: [Washington, 1832] 1 p. (H. R. 482) DNA; MB.   15210

---- A bill authorizing the Commissioner of the General Land Office to issue patents to persons therein named. Jan. 16, 1832. Read twice, and committed to a Committee of the Whole House tomorrow. Mr. Carr, from the Committee on Private Land Claims, reported the following bill: [Washington, 1832] 2 p. (H. R. 275) DNA; MB.   15211

---- A bill authorizing the construction of a building for the use of the customs, and for other government purposes, at Pensacola, in Florida. Dec. 29, 1832. Read twice, and committed to a Committee of the Whole House on the state of the Union. Mr. Cambreleng, from the Committee on Commerce, reported the following bill: [Washington, 1832] 1 p. (H. R. 649) DNA; MB.   15212

---- A bill authorizing the entry of vessels and merchandise arriving from the Cape of Good Hope, or beyond the same, at the port of Edgartown, in Massachusetts. May 23, 1832. Read twice, and ordered to be engrossed, and read the third time to-morrow. Mr. Cambreleng, from the Committee on Commerce, reported the following bill: [Washington, 1832] 1 p. (H.R. 585) DNA; MB.   15213

---- A bill authorizing the Governor of the territory of Arkansas to lease the Salt Springs, in said territory, and for other purposes. Jan. 16, 1832. Read twice, and ordered to be engrossed, and read the third time to-morrow. Mr. Irwin, from the Committee on the Public Lands, reported the following bill: [Washington, 1832] 2 p. (H.R. 274) DNA; MB.   15214

---- A bill authorizing the location of Virginia military land warrants on a portion of the public lands. Jan. 31, 1832. Read twice, and committed to a Committee of the Whole House to-morrow. Mr. Irwin, from the Committee on the Public Lands, reported the following bill: [Washington, 1832] 2 p. (H.R. 335) DNA; MB.   15215

---- A bill authorizing the President of the United States to cause a road to be opened from Helena to the mouth of Cache river, in the territory of Arkansas. April 12, 1832. Reported without amendment. [Washington, 1832] 1 p. (S. 174) DNA; MB.   15216
---- A bill authorizing the Register and Receiver of the St. Helena land district, in Louisiana, to receive evidence respecting the claim of Josiah Barker, assignee of Madam Hindson, to a tract of land therein mentioned. Jan. 13, 1832. Read twice, and committed to a Committee of the Whole House to-morrow. Mr. Carr, from the Committee on Private Land Claims, reported

the following bill. [Washington, 1832] 2 p. (H.R. 265). DNA; MB.   15217

---- A bill authorizing the revision of the rules and regulations of the naval service. Jan. 24, 1832. Mr. Watmough, from the Committee on Naval Affairs, reported the following bill: [Washington, 1832] 1 p. (H.R. 306) DNA; MB.   15218

---- A bill authorizing the Secretary of the Treasury to permit a wharf to be built near the site of the light-house, on Stratford Point, in the state of Connecticut. May 7, 1832. Read twice, and ordered to be engrossed, and read the third time to-morrow. Mr. Cambreleng, from the Committee on Commerce, reported the following bill: [Washington, 1832] 1 p. (H.R. 564) DNA; MB.   15219

---- A bill changing the times of holding the Courts in the District of Columbia. April 18, 1832. Read twice, and committed to a Committee of the Whole House to-morrow. Mr. Washington, from the Committee for the District of Columbia, reported the following bill: [Washington, 1832] 1 p. (H.R. 550) DNA; MB.   15220

---- A bill concerning certain officers of the Marine Corps. Mar. 13, 1832. Mr. Hayne, from the Committee on Naval Affairs, reported the following bill; which was read, and passed to a second reading: [Washington, 1832] 1 p. (S. 151) DNA; MB.   15221

---- A bill concerning Navy Agents. Jan. 3, 1832. Mr. Hayne, from the Committee on Naval Affairs, reported the following bill; which was read, and passed to a second reading: [Washington,

1832] 2 p. (S. 36) DNA; MB.
15222
---- A bill concerning patents for
useful inventions. Apr. 18, 1832.
Read the first time, and ordered
that it be read the second time on
Wednesday, 25th of April, instant.
Mr. Taylor, from the Select Committee upon the Patent Laws, reported the following bill: [Wash-
ington, 1832] 3 p. (H.R. 551)
DNA; MB.   15223

---- A bill concerning the gold
and silver coins of the United
States, and for other purposes.
June 30, 1832. Read twice, and
committed to the Committee of the
Whole House on the state of the
Union. Mr. Campbell P. White,
from the Select Committee on
Coins, reported the following bill:
[Washington, 1832] 4 p. (H.R. 603)
MB.   15224

---- A bill concerning the gold
coins of the United States. Mar.
17, 1832. Read twice, and committed to the Committee of the
Whole House on the state of the
Union. Mr. C. P. White, from the
Select Committee on Coins, reported the following bill: [Wash-
ington, 1832] 2 p. (H.R. 487)
DNA; MB.   15225

---- A bill concerning the issuing
of patents to aliens, for useful
discoveries and inventions. Jan.
6, 1832. Read the first and second
time, and ordered to be engrossed,
and read the third time on Monday
next. Mr. Taylor, from the Select
Committee on the subject of Patent
Laws, reported the following bill:
[Washington, 1832] 1 p. (H.R. 222)
DNA; MB.   15226

---- A bill concerning tonnage duty
on Spanish vessels. June 30, 1832.
Mr. Smith, from the Committee on
Finance, reported the following
bill; which was read, and passed

to a second reading: [Washington,
1832] 2 p. (S. 211) DNA; MB.
15227
---- A bill conferring rank upon
the officers of the pay department of the army of the United
States. Dec. 28, 1832. Read
twice, and committed to a Committee of the Whole House on the
state of the Union. Mr. Richard
M. Johnson, from the Committee
on Military Affairs, reported the
following bill: [Washington, 1832]
1 p. (H.R. 645) DNA; MB.
15228
---- A bill confirming an act of
the General Assembly of Virginia
relating to the Chesapeake and
Ohio Canal Company, which passed
Feb. twenty-seventh, one thousand
eight hundred and twenty-nine. May
28, 1832. Read twice, and committed to a Committee of the
Whole House to-morrow. Mr.
Doddridge, from the Committee
for the District of Columbia, reported the following bill: [Washing-
ton, 1832] 1 p. (H.R. 589) DNA;
MB.   15229

---- A bill confirming an act of
the legislature of Virginia relating to the Chesapeake and Ohio
Canal Company, passed Feb. thirteenth one thousand eight hundred
and thirty. May 25, 1832. Read
twice, and committed to the Committee of the Whole House on the
state of the Union. Mr. Craig,
from the Committee on Internal
Improvements, reported the following bill: [Washington, 1832]
1 p. (H.R. 587) DNA; MB.
15230
---- A bill confirming certain
land claims in the district of St.
Stephens, in Alabama. May 1,
1832. Mr. King, from the Committee on Public Lands, reported
the following bill; which was read,
and passed to a second reading:
[Washington, 1832] 1 p. (S. 191)
DNA; MB.   15231

---- A bill confirming the claim of Maria Holliday to a tract of land in Louisiana. Jan. 5, 1832. Mr. Kane, from the Committee on Private Land Claims, reported the following bill; which was read, and passed to a second reading: [Washington, 1832] 1 p. (S. 46) DNA; MB.   15232

---- A bill declaring the assent of Congress to the acts of the General Assemblies of Pennsylvania and Maryland, hereinafter received. Feb. 1, 1832. Read twice, and committed to a Committee of the Whole House to-morrow. Mr. Mercer, from the Committee on Internal Improvements, reported the following bill: [Washington, 1832] 19 p. (H.R. 340) DNA; MB.   15233

---- A bill declaring the assent of Congress to the acts of the General Assemblies of Pennsylvania and Maryland, hereinafter recited. Feb. 14, 1832. Mr. Hendricks, from the Committee on Roads and Canals, reported the following bill; which was read, and passed to a second reading: [Washington, 1832] 19 p. (S. 111) DNA; MB.   15234

---- A bill declaring the effect of judgments in the circuit and district courts of the United States, and for other purposes. Jan. 10, 1832. Read twice, and committed to a Committee of the Whole House to-morrow. Mr. Beardsley, from the Committee on the Judiciary, reported the following bill: [Washington, 1832] 2 p. (H.R. 238) DNA; MB.
15235

---- A bill defining the qualifications of voters in the territory of Arkansas. Feb. 9, 1832. Read twice, and postponed until Monday next, 13th instant. Mr. William B. Shepard, from the Committee

on the Territories, reported the following bill: [Washington, 1832] 1 p. (H R. 364) DNA; MB.
15236

---- A bill directing a code of laws, civil and criminal, for the District of Columbia, to be prepared and reported to Congress. Jan. 27, 1832. Read twice, and committed to a Committee of the Whole House to-morrow. Mr. Doddridge, from the Committee for the District of Columbia, reported the following bill: [Washington, 1832] 2 p. (H.R. 323) DNA; MB.   15237

---- A bill directing letters patent to be issued to Thomas Knowles, James Lang, and William Steel, respectively. Feb. 17, 1832. Read the first time, and ordered that it be read the second time on Thursday next. Mr. Taylor, from the Select Committee on the subject of the Patent Laws of the United States, reported the following bill: [Washington, 1832] 2 p. (H.R. 395) DNA; MB.   15238

---- A bill establishing land districts in the territory of Arkansas. April 10, 1832. Read twice, and committed to a Committee of the Whole House to-morrow. Mr. Clay, from the Committee on the Public Lands, reported the following bill: [Washington, 1832] 2 p. (H.R. 541) DNA; MB.
15239

---- A bill establishing the territorial government of Wisconsin, Jan. 6, 1832. Read twice, and committed to the Committee of the Whole House on the state of the Union. Dec. 17, 1832. Pr. by order of the House, as amended. [Washington, 1832] 12 p. (H.R. 220) DNA; MB.   15240

---- A bill establishing the territorial government of Wisconsin.

Jan. 6, 1832. Read twice, and committed to the Committee of the Whole House on the state of the Union. Mr. Kerr, from the Committee on the Territories, reported the following bill: [Washington, 1832] 12 p. (H. R. 220) DNA; MB.   15241

---- A bill extending further the right of debenture to the port of Key West, and altering the limits of the district of Key West. Feb. 28, 1832. Agreeably to notice given, Mr. Hayne asked and obtained leave to bring in the following bill; which was read twice, and referred to the Committee of Commerce. May 8, 1832. Reported without amendment. [Washington, 1832] 2 p. (S. 127) DNA; MB.   15242

---- A bill extending further the right of debenture to the port of Key West, and altering the limits of the district of Key West. May 24, 1832. Read twice, and ordered to be engrossed, and read the third time to-morrow. Mr. Cambreleng, from the Committee on Commerce, reported the following bill: [Washington, 1832] 1 p. (H. R. 586) MB.   15243

---- A bill for altering the time of holding the district court of the United States for the district of Indiana. April 10, 1832. Read twice, and ordered to be engrossed and read the third time this day. Mr. Davis, of South Carolina, from the Committee on the Judiciary, reported the following bill: [Washington, 1832] 1 p. (H. R. 539) DNA; MB.   15244

---- A bill for altering the time of holding the district court of the United States for the western district of Louisiana. Feb. 10, 1832. Read twice, and ordered to be engrossed, and read the third

time to-morrow. Mr. White, of Louisiana, from the Committee on the Judiciary reported the following bill: [Washington, 1832] 1 p. (H. R. 370) DNA; MB.
15245
---- A bill for changing the course of Tiber Creek, in the City of Washington, and for other purposes. May 2, 1832. Read twice, and committed to a Committee of the Whole House to-morrow. Mr. Doddridge, from the Committee for the District of Columbia, reported the following bill: [Washington, 1832] 1 p. (H. R. 559) DNA; MB.   15246

---- A bill for giving effect to a commercial arrangement between the United States and the Republic of Colombia. Jan. 26, 1832. Read twice, and ordered to be engrossed, and read the third time to-morrow. Mr. Archer, from the Committee on Foreign Affairs, reported the following bill: [Washington, 1832] 1 p. (H. R. 320) DNA; MB.   15247

---- A bill for granting further relief of Joel Byington. July 2, 1832. Read twice, and committed to a Committee of the Whole House to-morrow. Mr. Hogan, from the Committee of Claims, reported the following bill: [Washington, 1832] 1 p. (H. R. 604) DNA; MB.   15248

---- A bill for improving Pennsylvania Avenue, supplying the public buildings with water, and for paving the walk from the western gate to the Capitol with flagging. Feb. 15, 1832. Read twice, and committed to a Committee of the Whole House to-morrow. Mr. Washington, from the Committee for the District of Columbia, reported the following bill: [Washington, 1832] 2 p. (H. R. 376) DNA; MB.   15249

---- A bill for laying out and making a road to run southwardly from lower Sandusky to the boundary line established by the treaty of Greenville, in the state of Ohio, agreeably to the provisions of the treaty of Brownstown. April 13, 1832. Read twice, and committed to a Committee of the Whole House to-morrow. Mr. Leavitt, from the Committee on Internal Improvements, reported the following bill: [Washington, 1832] 3 p. (H.R. 547) DNA; MB. 15250

---- A bill for making Calais and Pembroke, in the state of Maine, ports of delivery. May 31, 1832. Read twice, and committed to a Committee of the Whole House to-morrow. Mr. Jarvis, from the Committee on Commerce, reported the following bill: [Washington, 1832] 1 p. (H.R. 591) DNA; MB. 15251

---- A bill for promoting the growth and manufacture of silk. Jan. 20, 1832. Read twice, and committed to a Committee of the Whole House to-morrow. Mr. Root, from the Committee on Agriculture, reported the following bill: [Washington, 1832] 8 p. (H.R. 294) DNA; MB. 15252

---- A bill for quieting possessions, enrolling conveyances, and securing the estates of purchasers within the District of Columbia. Jan. 27, 1832. Read twice, and committed to a Committee of the Whole House to-morrow. Mr. Doddridge, from the Committee for the District of Columbia, reported the following bill: [Washington, 1832] 3 p. (H.R. 322) DNA; MB. 15253

---- A bill for the apportionment of Representatives among the several states according to the fifth census. Jan. 4, 1832. Read twice, and committed to the Committee of the Whole House on the state of the Union. Mr. Polk, from the Select Committee, to which the subject had been referred, reported the following bill: [Washington, 1832] 2 p. (H.R. 208) DNA; MB. 15254

---- A bill for the benefit of Abram Forbes. Jan. 27, 1832. Read twice, and committed to a Committee of the Whole House to-morrow. Mr. Cave Johnson, from the Committee on Private Land Claims, reported the following bill: [Washington, 1832] 1 p. (H.R. 321) DNA; MB. 15255

---- A bill for the benefit of Isaac Thomas and William M. Wilson. March 16, 1832. Read twice, and committed to a Committee of the Whole House to-morrow. Mr. Marshall, from the Committee on Private Land Claims, reported the following bill: [Washington, 1832] 1 p. (H.R. 474) DNA; MB. 15256

---- A bill for the benefit of Joseph Dukes. Jan. 30, 1832. Read twice, and committed to a Committee of the Whole House to-morrow. Mr. Plummer, from the Committee on the Public Lands, reported the following bill: [Washington, 1832] 2 p. (H.R. 334) DNA; MB. 15257

---- A bill for the benefit of Robert Weatherhead. Feb. 7, 1832. Read twice, and committed to a Committee of the Whole House to-morrow. Mr. Cave Johnson, from the Committee on Private Land Claims, reported the following bill: [Washington, 1832] 1 p. (H.R. 355) DNA; MB. 15258

---- A bill for the benefit of Saint Vincent's Female Orphan Asylum of the city of Washington,

under the direction of the "Sisters of Charity." Mar. 13, 1832. Mr. Tyler, from the Committee on the District of Columbia, reported the following bill, which was read, and passed to a second reading: [Washington, 1832] 2 p. (S. 149) DNA; MB.
15259

---- A bill for the benefit of the legal representatives of William G. Christopher, deceased. Feb. 6, 1832. Read twice, and committed to a Committee of the Whole House to-morrow. Mr. Marshall, from the Committee on Private Land Claims, reported the following bill: [Washington, 1832] 1 p. (H.R. 349) DNA; MB.
15260

- A bill for the benefit of Wm. Marbury. Jan. 11, 1832. Read twice, and committed to a Committee of the Whole House to-morrow. Mr. Cave Johnson, from the Committee on Private Land Claims, reported the following bill: [Washington, 1832] 1 p. (H.R. 247) DNA; MB.   15261

---- A bill for the better organization of the United States' Corps of Marines. Feb. 24, 1832. Read twice, and committed to the Committee of the Whole House on the state of the Union. Mr. Watmough, from the Committee on Naval Affairs, reported the following bill: [Washington, 1832] 1 p. (H.R. 413) DNA; MB.
15262

---- A bill for the continuation of the Cumberland road in the states of Ohio, Indiana, and Illinois. Jan. 16, 1832. Mr. Hendricks, from the Committee on Roads and Canals, reported the following bill; which was read, and passed to a second reading: [Washington, 1832] 2 p. (S. 61) DNA; MB.   15263

---- A bill for the discharge of

sundry judgements against the former marshal of the Eastern District of Pennsylvania. May 29, 1832. Read twice, and committed to the Committee of the Whole House on the state of the Union. Mr. Verplanck, from the Committee of Ways and Means, reported the following bill: [Washington, 1832] 3 p. (H.R. 590) DNA; MB.   15264

---- A bill for the encouragement of Augusta College, in Kentucky. Feb. 29, 1832. Agreeably to notice given Mr. Clay asked and obtained leave to bring in the following bill; which was read twice, and referred to the Committee on Public Lands. Mar. 7, 1832. Reported without amendment. [Washington, 1832] 1 p. (S. 128) DNA; MB.   15265

---- A bill for the erection of a National Armory upon the western waters of the United States. Jan. 4, 1832. Read twice, and committed to the Whole House on the state of the Union. Mr. Drayton, from the Committee on Military Affairs, reported the following bill: [Washington, 1832] 1 p. (H.R. 195) DNA; MB.   15266

---- A bill for the erecting of barracks, quarters, and storehouses, and the purchase of a site, in the vicinity of New Orleans. Jan. 4, 1832. Mr. Benton, from the Committee on Military Affairs, reported the following bill; which was read, and passed to a second reading: [Washington, 1832] 1 p. (S. 43) DNA; MB.
15267

---- A bill for the establishment of a military board for the administration and government of the ordnance department. April 9, 1832. Read twice, and laid upon the table. Mr. Drayton, from the Committee on Military Affairs,

reported the following bill:
[Washington, 1832] 1 p. (H.R.
536) DNA; MB.   15268

---- A bill for the exchange of
certain public grounds at Prairie
du Chien, in the territory of
Michigan. April 13, 1832. Read
twice, and committed to a Committee of the Whole House to-
morrow. Mr. Hunt, from the
Committee on the Public Lands,
reported the following bill:
[Washington, 1832] 1 p. (H.R.
545) DNA; MB.   15269

---- A bill for the final adjust-
ment of private land claims in
Missouri. Feb. 15, 1832. Mr.
Kane, from the Committee on
Private Land Claims, reported
the following bill; which was read,
and passed to a second reading:
[Washington, 1832] 3 p. (S. 114)
DNA; MB.   15270

---- A bill for the final adjustment of private land claims in
Missouri. Mar. 6, 1832. Read
twice, and committed to the Committee of the Whole House on the
state of the Union. Mr. Wickliffe, from the Committee on the
Public Lands, reported the following bill: [Washington, 1832]
3 p. (H.R. 445) DNA; MB.
                                 15271
---- A bill for the final adjustment of the claims to lands in
the southeastern land district of
the state of Louisiana. Feb. 28,
1832. Read twice, and committed to a Committee of the Whole
House on Tuesday, the sixth of
March next. Mr. Wickliffe,
from the Committee on the Public Lands, reported the following
bill: [Washington, 1832] 3 p.
(H.R. 424) DNA; MB.   15272

---- A bill for the further improvement of Pennsylvania Avenue. December 20, 1832. Read

twice, and committed to the Committee of the Whole House on the
state of the Union. Mr. Washington, from the Committee for the
District of Columbia, reported the
following bill: [Washington, 1832]
2 p. (H.R. 631) DNA; MB.
                                 15273
---- A bill for the improvement
of certain harbors, and the navigation of certain rivers. Mar.
29, 1832. Read twice, and committed to the Committee of the
Whole House on the state of the
Union. Mr. Mercer, from the
Committee on Internal Improvements, reported the following
bill: [Washington, 1832] 4 p.
(H.R. 516) DNA; MB.   15274

---- A bill for the improvement
of Pennsylvania Avenue, in the
city of Washington. Mar. 13,
1832. Agreeably to notice given,
Mr. Chambers asked and obtained
leave to bring in the following
bill; which was read twice, and
referred to the Committee on the
District of Columbia. April 12,
1832. Reported without amendment. [Washington, 1832] 2 p.
(S. 148) DNA; MB.   15275

---- A bill for the improvement
of the mail road between Louisville and St. Louis. Mar. 23,
1832. Read, and passed to a second reading. Mar. 26, 1832.
Read a second time, and referred
to the Committee on Roads and
Canals. Apr. 3, 1832. Reported
without amendment. [Washington,
1832] 1 p. (S. 161) DNA; MB.
                                 15276
---- A bill for the improvement
of the mail road, between Louisville and St. Louis. Mar. 26,
1832. Read twice, and committed
to a Committee of the Whole
House to-morrow. Mr. McCarty,
from the Committee on Internal
Improvements, reported the following bill: [Washington, 1832]

DNA; MB.   15277

---- A bill for the more perfect
defence of the frontiers. Dec. 28,
1832. Read twice, and committed
to a Committee of the Whole
House on the state of the Union.
Mr. Richard M. Johnson, from
the Committee on Military Affairs, reported the following bill:
[Washington, 1832] 2 p. (H.R.
646) DNA; MB.   15278

---- A bill for the prevention of
frauds upon the revenue. Mar. 21,
1832. Read twice, and committed
to the Committee of the Whole
House on the state of the Union.
Mr. Adams, from the Committee
of Manufactures, reported the following bill: [Washington, 1832]
5 p. (H.R. 498) DNA; MB.
                           15279

---- A bill for the promotion of
learning within the District of
Columbia. Mar. 7, 1832. Read
twice, and committed to a Committee of the Whole House to-
morrow. Mr. T. Thomas, from
the Committee for the District of
Columbia, reported the following
bill: [Washington, 1832] 2 p.
(H.R. 452) DNA; MB.   15280

---- A bill for the purchase of
certain copies of Watterston and
Van Zandt's Statistical Tables, and
to authorize a subscription for the
continuation of the same. Feb. 27,
1832. Read twice, and committed to the Committee on the
Whole House on the state of the
Union. Mr. Edward Everett, from
the Committee of the Library,
reported the following bill: [Wash-
ington, 1832] 1 p. (H.R. 421)
DNA; MB.   15281

---- A bill for the re-appropria-
tion of certain unexpended balances of former appropriations.
April 3, 1832. Read twice, and
committed to the Committee of

the Whole House on the state of
the Union. Mr. Verplanck, from
the Committee of Ways and Means,
reported the following bill: [Wash-
ington, 1832] 2 p. (H.R. 525)
DNA; MB.   15282

---- A bill for the regulation of
the navy and privateer pension
and navy hospital funds. Feb. 17,
1832. Read twice, and committed
to the Committee of the Whole
House on the state of the Union.
Mr. Branch, from the Committee on Naval Affairs, reported
the following bill: [Washington,
1832] 3 p. (H.R. 387) DNA; MB.
                           15283
---- A bill for the relief of Abijah Crane. Feb. 2, 1832. Mr.
Sprague, from the Committee on
Pensions, reported the following
bill; which was read, and passed
to a second reading: [Washington,
1832] 1 p. (S. 95) DNA; MB.
                           15284
---- A bill for the relief of Abijah Fisk. Jan. 18, 1832. Read
twice, and committed to a Committee of the Whole House to-
morrow. Mr. Reed, of New York,
from the Committee on Invalid
Pensions, reported the following
bill: [Washington, 1832] 1 p.
(H.R. 287) DNA; MB.   15285

---- A bill for the relief of Abijah Warren, and others. Jan. 19,
1832. Mr. Marcy, from the Committee on Finance, reported the
following bill; which was read,
and passed to a second reading:
[Washington, 1832] 1 p. (S. 66)
DNA; MB.   15286

---- A bill for the relief of Abner Morgan and Edward Herndon.
Mar. 19, 1832. Read twice, and
committed to a Committee of the
Whole House to-morrow. Mr.
Pendleton, from the Committee
on Revolutionary Pensions, reported the following bill: [Wash-

ington, 1832] 1 p. (H.R. 495)
DNA; MB.   15287

---- A bill for the relief of Alexander Donelson. Jan. 16, 1832. Read twice, and committed to a Committee of the Whole House to-morrow. Mr. Whittlesey, from the Committee of Claims, reported the following bill: [Washington, 1832] 1 p. (H.R. 269) DNA; MB.   15288

---- A bill for the relief of Alexander Macomb. Dec. 18, 1832. Read twice, and committed to the Committee of the Whole House to which is committed the bill (H.R. No. 252) for the relief of Abraham A. Masias. Mr. Ward, from the Committee on Military Affairs, reported the following bill: [Washington, 1832] 1 p. (H.R. 624) DNA; MB.   15289

---- A bill for the relief of Alexander Naismisth. Mar. 14, 1832. Mr. Foot, from the Committee on Pensions, reported the following bill; which was read, and passed to a second reading: [Washington, 1832] 1 p. (S. 153) DNA; MB.   15290

---- A bill for the relief of Amos W. Brown, a Canadian volunteer. Feb. 1, 1832. Read twice, and committed to a Committee of the Whole House to-morrow. Mr. Carr, from the Committee on Private Land Claims, reported the following bill: [Washington, 1832] 1 p. (H.R. 339) DNA; MB.   15291

---- A bill for the relief of Andrew Cushman. Mar. 12, 1832. Mr. Sprague, from the Committee on Pensions, reported the following bill; which was read, and passed to a second reading: [Washington, 1832] 1 p. (S. 144) DNA; MB.   15291a

---- A bill for the relief of Andrew Moore. Jan. 16, 1832. Read twice, and committed to a Committee of the Whole House to-morrow. Mr. Whittlesey, from the Committee of Claims, reported the following bill: [Washington, 1832] 1 p. (H.R. 270) DNA; MB.   15292

---- A bill for the relief of Ann Mortimer Barron. Feb. 17, 1832. Read twice, and committed to a Committee of the Whole House to-morrow. Mr. Muhlenberg, from the Committee on Revolutionary Claims, reported the following bill: [Washington, 1832] 1 p. (H.R. 384) DNA; MB. 15293

---- A bill for the relief of Anthony Bollermann. Mar. 6, 1832. Read twice, and committed to a Committee of the Whole House to-morrow. Mr. Cambreleng, from the Committee on Commerce, reported the following bill: [Washington, 1832] 1 p. (H.R. 447) DNA; MB.   15294

---- A bill for the relief of Anthony M. Menter and John Brantley. Feb. 24, 1832. Mr. King, from the Committee on Public Lands, reported the following bill; which was read, and passed to a second reading: [Washington, 1832] 2 p. (S. 124) DNA; MB.   15295

---- A bill for the relief of Antoine Cruzat. Jan. 25, 1832. Read twice, and committed to a Committee of the Whole House to-morrow. Mr. Mardis, from the Committee on Private Land Claims, reported the following bill: [Washington, 1832] 1 p. (H.R. 314) DNA; MB.   15296

---- A bill for the relief of Antonio Segura and others. Mar. 16, 1832. Read twice, and committed to a Committee of the

Whole House to-morrow. Mr. Bullard, from the Committee on Private Land Claims, reported the following bill: [Washington, 1832] 1 p. (H.R. 475) DNA; MB. 15297

---- A bill for the relief of Archibald Gamble. Jan. 10, 1832. Read twice, and committed to a Committee of the Whole House to-morrow. Mr. C. Johnson, from the Committee on Private Land Claims, reported the following bill: [Washington, 1832] 1 p. (H.R. 231) DNA; MB. 15298

---- A bill for the relief of Archibald W. Hamilton. Apr. 12, 1832. Read twice, and committed to a Committee of the Whole House to-morrow. Mr. E. Whittlesey, from the Committee of Claims, reported the following bill: [Washington, 1832] 1 p. DNA; MB. 15299

---- A bill for the relief of Archibald Watt. Jan. 10, 1832. Read twice, and committed to a Committee of the Whole House to-morrow. Mr. Bouldin, from the Committee on Revolutionary Claims, reported the following bill: [Washington, 1832] 1 p. (H.R. 239) DNA; MB. 15300

---- A bill for the relief of Augustine Taney. Jan. 31, 1832, Mr. Naudain, from the Committee of Claims, reported the following bill; which was read, and passed to a second reading: [Washington, 1832] 1 p. (S. 91) DNA; MB. 15301

---- A bill for the relief of Bartholomew Shaumburgh. Jan. 25, 1832. Mr. Brown, from the Committee of Claims, reported the following bill; which was read, and passed to a second reading: [Washington, 1832] 1 p. (S. 77) DNA; MB. 15302

---- A bill for the relief of Benjamin Burlingame. Jan. 13, 1832. Read twice, and committed to a Committee of the Whole House to-morrow. Mr. Lansing, from the Committee on Invalid Pensions, reported the following bill: [Washington, 1832] 1 p. (H.R. 266) DNA; MB. 15303

---- A bill for the relief of Benjamin Gibbs, of Kentucky. Jan. 3, 1832. Read twice, and committed to a Committee of the Whole House, to which is committed bill No. 107. Mr. Nuckolls, from the Committee on Revolutionary Claims, reported the following bill: [Washington, 1832] 1 p. (H.R. 191) DNA; MB. 15304

---- A bill for the relief of Benjamin S. Smoot. Jan. 11, 1832. Agreeably to notice given, Mr. King asked and obtained leave to bring in the following bill; which was read twice, and referred to the Committee of Claims, April 18, 1832. Reported without amendment. [Washington, 1832] 2 p. (S. 58) DNA; MB. 15305

---- A bill for the relief of Benjamin Sherfey. Feb. 27, 1832. Read twice, and committed to a Committee of the Whole House to-morrow. Mr. E. Whittlesey, from the Committee of Claims, reported the following bill: [Washington, 1832] 1 p. (H.R. 420) DNA; MB. 15306

---- A bill for the relief of Bradford Steele. Feb. 27, 1832. Mr. Foot, from the Committee on Pensions, reported the following bill: which was read, and passed to a second reading: [Washington, 1832] 2 p. (S. 126) DNA; MB. 15307

---- A bill for the relief of certain applicants for pensions. Feb. 16, 1832. Mr. Foot, from the

Committee on Pensions, reported the following bill; which was read, and passed to a second reading: [Washington, 1832] 1 p. (S. 116) DNA; MB.   15308

---- A bill for the relief of certain inhabitants of East Florida. Jan. 20, 1832. Read twice, and committed to a Committee of the Whole House to-morrow. Mr. Archer, from the Committee on Foreign Affairs, reported the following bill: [Washington, 1832] 2 p. (H.R. 297) DNA; MB.
15309
---- A bill for the relief of certain invalid and other pensioners, therein named. Jan. 19, 1832. Read twice, and committed to a Committee of the Whole House to-morrow. Mr. Burges, from the Committee on Invalid Pensions, reported the following bill: [Washington, 1832] 5 p. (H.R. 288) DNA; MB.   15310

---- A bill for the relief of certain invalid pensioners. Apr. 3, 1832. Read twice, and committed to a Committee of the Whole House to-morrow. Mr. Lansing, from the Committee on Invalid Pensions, reported the following bill: [Washington, 1832] 2 p. (H.R. 528) DNA; MB.   15311

---- A bill for the relief of certain invalid pensioners therein named. May 14, 1832. Read twice, and committed to a Committee of the Whole House to-morrow. Mr. Lansing, from the Committee on Invalid Pensions, reported the following bill: [Washington, 1832] 2 p. (H.R. 576) DNA; MB.   15312

---- A bill for the relief of certain invalid pensioners, therein named. Dec. 19, 1832. Read twice, and committed to the Committee of the Whole House to

which is committed the bill (H.R. No. 237) for granting pensions to certain revolutionary soldiers. Mr. Burges, from the Committee on Invalid Pensions, reported the following bill: [Washington, 1832] 4 p. (H.R. 626) DNA; MB.
15313
---- A bill for the relief of certain officers and soldiers whose property was destroyed by fire at Fort Delaware. Feb. 18, 1832. Read twice, and committed to a Committee of the Whole House to-morrow. Mr. Drayton, from the Committee on Military Affairs, reported the following bill: [Washington, 1832] 1 p. (H.R. 396] DNA; MB.   15314

---- A bill for the relief of certain persons therein named. Mar. 19, 1832. Read twice, and committed to a Committee of the Whole House to-morrow. Mr. Pendleton, from the Committee on Revolutionary Pensions, reported the following bill: [Washington, 1832] 1 p. (H.R. 494) DNA; MB.
15315
---- A bill for the relief of Chastelain and Ponvert. Jan. 4, 1832. Read twice, and committed to a Committee of the Whole House to-morrow. Mr. Cambreleng, from the Committee of Commerce, reported the following bill: [Washington, 1832] 1 p. (H.R. 203) DNA; MB.   15316

---- A bill for the relief of Coleman Fisher. Jan. 31, 1832. Read twice, and committed to a Committee on the Whole House to-morrow. Mr. Cave Johnson, from the Committee on Private Land Claims, reported the following bill: [Washington, 1832] 2 p. (H.R. 336) DNA; MB.   15317

---- A bill for the relief of Crosby Arey. Jan. 12, 1832. Read twice, and committed to a Committee of the Whole House to-morrow. Mr. Jarvis, from the Committee on Commerce, reported the following bill: [Washington, 1832] 1 p. (H.R. 251) DNA; MB.   15318

---- A bill for the relief of Cyrenius Hall. Apr. 24, 1832. Read twice, and committed to a Committee of the Whole House to-morrow. Mr. Archer, from the Committee on Foreign Affairs, reported the following bill: [Washington, 1832] 1 p. (H.R. 553) DNA; MB.   15319

---- A bill for the relief of Daniel Burr. Mar. 2, 1832. Mr. Sprague, from the Committee on Pensions, reported the following bill; which was read, and passed to a second reading: [Washington, 1832] 1 p. (S. 134) DNA; MB.   15320

---- A bill for the relief of Daniel Goodwin, executor of Benjamin Goodwin, deceased. Jan. 10, 1832. Read twice, and committed to a Committee of the Whole House to-morrow. Mr. Muhlenburg, from the Committee on Revolutionary Claims, reported the following bill: [Washington, 1832] 1 p. (H.R. 228) DNA; MB.   15321

---- A bill for the relief of Daniel Haselton and William Palmer. Mar. 2, 1832. Read twice, and committed to a Committee of the Whole House to-morrow. Mr. McIntire, from the Committee of Claims, reported the following bill: [Washington, 1832] 1 p. (H.R. 441) DNA; MB.   15322

---- A bill for the relief of Daniel Johnson. Jan. 3, 1832. Read twice, and committed to a Committee of the Whole House to-morrow. Mr. Drayton, from the Committee on Military Affairs, reported the following bill:

[Washington, 1832] 1 p. (H.R. 180) DNA; MB.   15323

---- A bill for the relief of Daniel Wyman. Mar. 2, 1832. Mr. Sprague, from the Committee on Pensions, reported the following bill; which was read, and passed to a second reading: [Washington, 1832] 1 p. (S. 135) DNA; MB.   15324

---- A bill for the relief of David Beard. July 9, 1832. Mr. Marcy, from the Committee on the Judiciary, reported the following bill; which was read, and passed to a second reading: [Washington, 1832] 1 p. (S. 213) DNA; MB.   15325

---- A bill for the relief of David Brooks. Feb. 6, 1832. Read twice, and committed to the Committee of the Whole House to which is committed bill No. 110. Mr. Pendleton, from the Committee on Revolutionary Pensions, reported the following bill: [Washington, 1832] 1 p. (H.R. 351) DNA; MB.   15326

---- A bill for the relief of Edmund Brooke. Jan. 19, 1832. Read twice, and committed to a Committee of the Whole House to-morrow. Mr. Bates, of Massachusetts, from the Committee on Revolutionary Claims, reported the following bill: [Washington, 1832] 2 p. (H.R. 291) DNA; MB.   15327

---- A bill for the relief of Edward Lewis. Jan. 30, 1832. Mr. Moore, from the Committee of Claims, reported the following bill; which was read, and passed to a second reading: [Washington, 1832] 1 p. (S. 87) DNA; MB.   15328

---- A bill for the relief of Elgira Debrill and Sophy Hancock. Feb. 7, 1832. Mr. King, from the Committee on Public Lands,

reported the following bill;
which was read, and passed to a
second reading: [Washington,
1832] 1 p. (S. 102) DNA; MB.
                                    15329
---- A bill for the relief of Elias Rector. Feb. 6, 1832. Mr.
King, from the Committee on
Public Lands, reported the following bill; which was read, and
passed to a second reading:
[Washington, 1832] 1 p. (S. 98)
DNA; MB.   15330

---- A bill for the relief of Elihu Hall Bay, and others, confirming grants to lands in the
district west of Pearl river, derived from the British Government of West Florida, and not
subsequently granted by Spain or
the United States. Jan. 25, 1832.
Agreeably to notice given, Mr.
Hayne asked and obtained leave
to bring in the following bill;
which was read twice, and referred to the Committee on Private Land Claims. Mar. 30,
1832. Reported without amendment. [Washington, 1832] 2 p.
(S. 78) DNA; MB.   15331

---- A bill for the relief of Elizabeth Magruder, of Mississippi.
Jan. 12, 1832. Agreeably to notice given, Mr. Ellis asked and
obtained leave, to bring in the
following bill; which was read
twice, and referred to the Committee on Private Land Claims.
Jan. 19, 1832. Reported without
amendment. [Washington, 1832]
1 p. (S. 59) DNA; MB.   15332

---- A bill for the relief of
Elizabeth Scott, assignee of Alexander Scott, junior. Feb. 24,
1832. Mr. Forsyth, from the
Committee on Commerce, reported the following bill; which was
read, and passed to a second
reading: [Washington, 1832] 1 p.
(S. 121) DNA; MB.   15333

---- A bill for the relief of
Elizabeth Scott, daughter of the
late Capt. William Blackwell.
Apr. 13, 1832. Mr. Benton,
from the Committee on Military
Affairs, reported the following
bill; which was read, and passed
to a second reading: [Washington,
1832] 1 p. (S. 177) DNA; MB.
                                    15334
---- A bill for the relief of
Elizabeth Scott, only surviving
child, and heir at law, of Capt.
William Blackwell, deceased.
Feb. 13, 1832. Mr. Naudain,
from the Committee on Private
Land Claims, reported the following bill; which was read, and
passed to a second reading:
[Washington, 1832] 1 p. (S. 110)
DNA; MB.   15335

---- A bill for the relief of Eze-
kiel Foster and Company, of
Eastport, state of Maine. Feb.
16, 1832. Read twice, and com-
mitted to a Committee of the
Whole House to-morrow. Mr.
Jarvis, from the Committee on
Commerce, reported the follow-
ing bill: [Washington, 1832] 1 p.
(H. R. 379) DNA; MB.   15336

---- A bill for the relief of Far-
ish Carter. Apr. 11, 1832. Mr.
Brown, from the Committee of
Claims, reported the following
bill; which was read and passed
to a second reading: [Washington,
1832] 1 p. (S. 171) DNA; MB.
                                    15337
---- A bill for the relief of
Francis Barnes. May 17, 1832.
Read twice, and committed to a
Committee of the Whole House
to-morrow. Mr. McIntire, from
the Committee of Claims, reported the following bill: [Wash-
ington, 1832] 1 p. (H. R. 577)
DNA; MB.   15338

---- A bill for the relief of
Francis Ducoing. Jan. 10, 1832.

Read twice, and committed to a Committee of the Whole House to-morrow. Mr. Evans, of Maine, from the Committee on Invalid Pensions, reported the following bill: [Washington, 1832] 1 p. (H. R. 236) DNA; MB.   15339

---- A bill for the relief of Frederick Raymer. Jan. 3, 1832. Read twice, and committed to a Committee of the Whole House to-morrow. Mr. Muhlenburg, from the Committee on Revolutionary Claims, reported the following bill: [Washington, 1832] 1 p. (H. R. 183) DNA; MB.   15340

---- A bill for the relief of Gabriel Godfroy and Jean Baptiste Beaugraud. Jan. 4, 1832. Read twice, and committed to a Committee of the Whole House to-morrow. Mr. McIntire, from the Committee of Claims, reported the following bill: [Washington, 1832] 1 p. (H. R. 199) DNA; MB.   15341

---- A bill for the relief of George Bowen. Mar. 8, 1832. Read twice, and committed to a Committee of the Whole House to-morrow. Mr. Conner, from the Committee on the Post Office and Post Roads, reported the following bill: [Washington, 1832] 1 p. (H. R. 453) DNA; MB.   15342

---- A bill for the relief of George Chinn. Feb. 17, 1832. Read twice, and committed to a Committee of the Whole House to-morrow. Mr. Whittlesey, from the Committee of Claims, reported the following bill: [Washington, 1832] 1 p. (H. R. 383) DNA; MB.   15343

---- A bill for the relief of George Davenport. Jan. 31, 1832. Read twice, and committed to a Committee of the Whole House to-

morrow. Mr. Duncan, from the Committee on the Public Lands, reported the following bill: [Washington, 1832] 1 p. (H. R. 337) DNA; MB.   15344

---- A bill for the relief of George E. Tingle. Jan. 3, 1832. Agreeably to notice given, Mr. Bibb asked and obtained leave to bring in the following bill; which was read twice, and referred to the Committee on the Judiciary. Feb. 28, 1832. Reported without amendment. [Washington, 1832] 1 p. (S. 38) DNA; MB.   15345

---- A bill for the relief of George Gordon, representative of Mathew Ramey, deceased. April 5, 1832. Read twice, and committed to a Committee of the Whole House to-morrow. Mr. Carr, from the Committee on Private Land Claims, reported the following bill: [Washington, 1832] 1 p. (H. R. 529) DNA; MB.   15346

---- A bill for the relief of George H. Jennings. Mar. 26, 1832. Read twice, and committed to a Committee of the Whole House to-morrow. Mr. E. Whittlesey, from the Committee of Claims, reported the following bill: [Washington, 1832] 1 p. (H. R. 508) DNA; MB.   15347

---- A bill for the relief of George Mayfield. Jan. 12, 1832. Read twice, and committed to a Committee of the Whole House tomorrow. Mr. Clay, from the Committee on the Public Lands, reported the following bill: [Washington, 1832] 1 p. (H. R. 258) DNA; MB.   15348

---- A bill for the relief of George W. Howard. Apr. 16, 1832. Mr. Buckner, from the Committee on Pensions, reported the following bill; which was read,

and passed to a second reading:
[Washington, 1832] 1 p. (S. 180)
DNA; MB.   15349

---- A bill for the relief of Gertrude Gates. Mar. 26, 1832.
Agreeably to notice given, Mr.
Dudley asked and obtained leave
to bring in the following bill;
which was read, and passed to a
second reading. Mar. 28, 1832.
Read the second time, and referred to the Committee of
Claims. Mar. 30, 1832. Reported
without amendment. [Washington,
1832] 2 p. (S. 162) DNA; MB.
                            15350

---- A bill for the relief of
Glover Broughton, of Marblehead, late owner of the fishing
schooner Union; and, also, for
the relief of the crew of said
vessel. Dec. 21, 1832. Read
twice, and committed to the
Committee of the Whole House to
which is committed the bill
(H.R. No. 346) for the relief of
Phineas Sprage et al. Mr. Davis,
of Massachusetts, from the Committee on Commerce, reported
the following bill: [Washington,
1832] 1 p. (H.R. 634) MB.
                            15351

---- A bill for the relief of
Grieve Drummond. Jan. 10,
1832. Read twice, and committed to a Committee of the Whole
House to-morrow. Mr. Evans,
of Maine, from the Committee
on Invalid Pensions, reported the
following bill: [Washington, 1832]
1 p. (H.R. 233) DNA; MB.
                            15352

---- A bill for the relief of Guy
W. Smith, Jan. 31, 1832. Mr.
Ruggles, from the Committee
of Claims, reported the following
bill; which was read, and passed
to a second reading: [Washing-
ton, 1832] 1 p. (S. 92) DNA; MB.
                            15353

---- A bill for the relief of Heman Allen. Jan. 4, 1832. Mr.

Ruggles, from the Committee of
Claims, reported the following
bill; which was read, and passed
to a second reading: [Washington,
1832] 1 p. (S. 41) DNA; MB.
                            15354

---- A bill for the relief of Henry Darling. Mar. 12, 1832. Read
twice, and committed to a Committee of the Whole House to-
morrow. Mr. Jarvis, from the
Committee on Commerce, reported the following bill: [Washing-
ton, 1832] 1 p. (H.R. 461) DNA;
MB.   15355

---- A bill for the relief of Henry Waller. Mar. 9, 1832. Mr.
Naudain, from the Committee of
Claims, reported the following
bill; which was read, and passed
to a second reading: [Washington,
1832] 1 p. (S. 141) DNA; MB.
                            15356

---- A bill for the relief of Horatio Gates Spafford. Mar. 6, 1832.
Read the first time, and ordered
for the second reading on Monday
next. Mr. Taylor, from the select committee on the subject of
the Patent Laws, reported the
following bill: [Washington, 1832]
1 p. (H.R. 449) DNA; MB.
                            15357

---- A bill for the relief of Hugh
Beard. Jan. 24, 1832. Read
twice, and committed to a Committee of the Whole House to-
morrow. Mr. Cave Johnson,
from the Committee on Private
Land Claims, reported the following bill: [Washington, 1832] 1 p.
(H.R. 307) DNA; MB.   15358

---- A bill for the relief of J.
and W. Lippincott and company.
Apr. 11, 1832. Mr. Forsyth,
from the Committee on Commerce, reported the following
bill; which was read, and passed
to a second reading: [Washington,
1832] 1 p. (S. 172) DNA; MB.
                            15359

---- A bill for the relief of Jacob C. Jordan. Apr. 12, 1832. Mr. King, from the Committee on Public Lands, reported the following bill; which was read, and passed to a second reading: [Washington, 1832] 1 p. (S. 175) DNA; MB. 15360

---- A bill for the relief of Jacob Remf, otherwise called Jacob Kemf. Mar. 2, 1832. Read twice, and ordered to be engrossed, and read the third time tomorrow. Mr. Irvin, from the Committee on Private Land Claims, reported the following bill: [Washington, 1832] 1 p. (H.R. 438) DNA; MB. 15361

---- A bill for the relief of James Bradford, of Louisiana. Feb. 6, 1832. Read twice, and committed to a Committee of the Whole House to-morrow. Mr. Mardis, from the Committee on Private Land Claims, reported the following bill: [Washington, 1832] 1 p. (H.R. 352) DNA; MB. 15362

---- A bill for the relief of James Brownlee. Jan. 6, 1832. Read twice, and committed to a Committee of the Whole House to-morrow. Mr. Muhlenburg, from the Committee on Revolutionary Claims, reported the following bill: [Washington, 1832] 1 p. (H.R. 216) DNA; MB. 15363

---- A bill for the relief of James Caulfield. Feb. 28, 1832. Read twice, and committed to a Committee of the Whole House to-morrow. Mr. Mardis, from the Committee on Private Land Claims, reported the following bill: [Washington, 1832] 1 p. (H.R. 429) DNA; MB. 15364

---- A bill for the relief of James Clark. Mar. 12, 1832. Mr. Sprague, from the Committee on Pensions, reported the following bill; which was read, and passed to a second reading: [Washington, 1832] 1 p. (S. 145) DNA; MB. 15365

---- A bill for the relief of James H. Brewer. Mar. 26, 1832. Read twice, and committed to the Committee of the Whole House to which is committed the bill (H.R. No. 508) for the relief of George H. Jennings. Mr. E. Whittlesey, from the Committee of Claims, reported the following bill: [Washington, 1832] 1 p. (H.R. 509) DNA; MB. 15366

---- A bill for the relief of James L. Stokes, and for other purposes. Jan. 20, 1832. Mr. Bullard, from the Committee on Private Land Claims, reported the following bill: [Washington, 1832] 1 p. (H.R. 300) DNA; MB. 15367

---- A bill for the relief of James Marsh. July 7, 1832. Read twice, and committed to a Committee of the Whole House to-morrow. Mr. Sutherland, from the Committee on Commerce, reported the following bill: [Washington, 1832] 1 p. (H.R. 611) DNA; MB. 15368

---- A bill for the relief of James Rodgers, a western Cherokee. May 5, 1832. Read twice, and committed to a Committee of the Whole House to-morrow. Mr. Thompson, of Georgia, from the Committee on Indian Affairs, reported the following bill: [Washington, 1832] 1 p. (H.R. 561) DNA; MB. 15369

---- A bill for the relief of James Selby. Apr. 3, 1832. Read twice, and committed to a Committee of the Whole House to-morrow. Mr. Sutherland, from the Committee on Commerce, reported the following bill: [Wash-

ington, 1832] 1 p. (H.R. 527)
DNA; MB.   15370

---- A bill for the relief of
James Taylor, of Kentucky. May
1, 1832. Mr. Ruggles from the
Committee of Claims, reported
the following bill: which was read,
and passed to a second reading:
[Washington, 1832] 1 p. (S. 189)
DNA; MB.   15371

---- A bill for the relief of
James Tilford. Feb. 17, 1832.
Read twice, and committed to a
Committee of the Whole House to-
morrow. Mr. Hogan, from the
Committee of Claims, reported
the following bill: [Washington,
1832] 1 p. (H.R. 388) DNA; MB.
                            15372
---- A bill for the relief of
James Vanderburgh and John Bonny. Mar. 15, 1832. Read twice,
and committed to a Committee of
the Whole House to-morrow. Mr.
Pendleton, from the Committee
on Revolutionary Pensions, reported the following bill: [Wash-
ington, 1832] 1 p. (H.R. 469)
DNA; MB.   15373

---- A bill for the relief of
James W. Hill, Elijah Hill, and
Philip Barnes. Feb. 7, 1832.
Read twice, and ordered to be
engrossed, and read the third
time to-morrow. Mr. Clay, from
the Committee on the Public
Lands, reported the following
bill: [Washington, 1832] 1 p.
(H.R. 354) DNA; MB.   15374

---- A bill for the relief of
James W. Zachary. Jan. 5, 1832.
Mr. Johnston, from the Commit-
tee on Finance, reported the fol-
lowing bill: which was read, and
passed to a second reading:
[Washington, 1832] 1 p. (S. 51)
DNA; MB.   15375

---- A bill for the relief of Jane

Dauphin, administratrix of John
Dauphin. Jan. 5, 1832. Read
twice, and commmitted to a Committee of the Whole House to-
morrow. Mr. Archer, from the
Committee on Foreign Affairs,
reported the following bill:
[Washington, 1832] 1 p. (H.R.
211) DNA; MB.   15376

---- A bill for the relief of Jared E. Groce, of the state of Alabama. Jan. 20, 1832. Read twice,
and committed to a Committee of
the Whole House to-morrow. Mr.
Clay, from the Committee on Public Lands, reported the following
bill: [Washington, 1832] 1 p.
(H.R. 298) DNA; MB.   15377

---- A bill for the relief of Jean
Francois Hertzog. Dec. 22, 1832.
Read twice, and committed to a
Committee of the Whole House to-
morrow. Mr. Ashley, from the
Committee on Private Land
Claims, reported the following
bill: [Washington, 1832] 1 p.
(H.R. 638) DNA; MB.   15378

---- A bill for the relief of Jef-
ferson College, in the State of
Mississippi. Jan. 5, 1832. Mr.
Ellis, from the Committee on
Public Lands, reported the fol-
lowing bill; which was read, and
passed to a second reading:
[Washington, 1832] 1 p. (S. 47)
DNA; MB.   15379

---- A bill for the relief of Jeremiah Adams and John Kidd. Mar.
17, 1832. Read twice, and committed to a Committee of the
Whole House to-morrow. Mr.
Pendleton, from the Committee
on Revolutionary Pensions, reported the following bill: [Wash-
ington, 1832] 1 p. (H.R. 486)
DNA; MB.   15380

---- A bill for the relief of
Jesse Bell. Mar. 17, 1832. Read

twice, and committed to the Committee of the Whole House to which is committed the bill from the Senate (No. 27) for the relief of Hartwell Vick, of the state of Mississippi. Mr. Plummer, from the Committee on the Public Lands, reported the following bill: [Washington, 1832] 1 p. (H. R. 480) DNA; MB.   15381

---- A bill for the relief of Joel Thomas. January 10, 1832. Read twice and committed to a Committee of the Whole House tomorrow. Mr. Stanberry, from the Committee on Private Land Claims, reported the following bill: [Washington, 1832] 2 p. (H. R. 227) DNA; MB.   15382

---- A bill for the relief of Joel Wright. Jan. 3, 1832. Read twice, and committed to a Committee of the Whole House to-morrow. Mr. Davis, of South Carolina, from the Committee on the Judiciary, reported the following bill: [Washington, 1832] 1 p. (H. R. 185) DNA; MB.   15383

---- A bill for the relief of John and Benjamin Welles. Feb. 3, 1832. Mr. Silsbee, from the Committee on Finance, reported the following bill; which was read, and passed to a second reading: [Washington, 1832] 1 p. (S. 97) DNA; MB.   15384

---- A bill for the relief of John Anderson, assignee of Jean B. Jerome and George McDougall. Apr. 10, 1832. Read twice, and ordered to be engrossed, and read the third time to-morrow. Mr. Wickliffe, from the Committee on the Public Lands, reported the following bill: [Washington, 1832] 3 p. (H. R. 540) DNA; MB.15385

---- A bill for the relief of John Bills. Feb. 29, 1832. Read twice, and committed to a Committee of the Whole House to-morrow. Mr. Carr, from the Committee on Private Land Claims, reported the following bill: [Washington, 1832] 1 p. (H. R. 432) MB.   15386

---- A bill for the relief of John Blake. Mar. 1, 1832. Mr. Sprague, from the Committee on Pensions, reported the following bill; which was read, and passed to a second reading: [Washington, 1832] 1 p. (S. 129) DNA; MB.   15387

---- A bill for the relief of John Brahan and John Read. Jan. 5, 1832. Mr. King, from the Committee on Public Lands, reported the following bill; which was read, and passed to a second reading: [Washington, 1832] 2 p. (S. 50) DNA; MB.   15388

---- A bill for the relief of John Bruce, administrator of Philip Bush, deceased. Jan. 10, 1832. Read twice, and committed to a Committee of the Whole House to-morrow. Mr. Crane, from the Committee on Revolutionary Claims, reported the following bill: [Washington, 1832] 2 p. (H. R. 229) DNA; MB.   15389

---- A bill for the relief of John Brunson. Jan. 16, 1832. Mr. Ruggles, from the Committee of Claims reported the following bill; which was read, and passed to a second reading: [Washington, 1832] 1 p. (S. 62) DNA; MB.   15390

---- A bill for the relief of John Caldwell, of Nicholas Scammon, administrator of Scammon, deceased, and of the legal representatives of Thomas Gordon, deceased. Feb. 17, 1832. Read twice, and committed to a Committee of the Whole House to-morrow. Mr. Crane, from the Committee on Revolutionary Claims, reported the following bill: [Washington, 1832] 2 p. (H.R. 390) MB.   15391

---- A bill for the relief of John D. Sloat. May 14, 1832. Read twice, and committed to a Committee of the Whole House to-morrow. Mr. Archer, from the Committee of Foreign Affairs, reported the following bill: [Washington, 1832] 1 p. (H.R. 572) DNA; MB.   15392

---- A bill for the relief of John F. Girod, of Louisiana. Mar. 2, 1832. Mr. Kane, from the Committee on Private Land Claims, reported the following bill; which was read, and passed to a second reading: [Washington, 1832] 2 p. (S. 132) DNA; MB.   15393

---- A bill for the relief of John F. Lewis. Jan. 30, 1832. Mr. Marcy, from the Committee on Finance, reported the following bill; which was read, and passed to a second reading: [Washington, 1832] 1 p. (S. 84) DNA; MB.   15394

---- A bill for the relief of John Hughes. Mar. 1, 1832. Read twice, and committed to the Committee of the Whole House, to which is committed the bill (H.R. No. 117,) for the relief of Benedict Joseph Flaget. Mr. Verplanck, from the Committee of Ways and Means, reported the following bill: [Washington, 1832] 1 p. (H.R. 435) DNA; MB.   15395

---- A bill for the relief of John L. Lobdell, Feb. 23, 1832. Read twice, and committed to a Committee of the Whole House to-morrow. Mr. Bullard, from the Committee on Private Land Claims, reported the following bill: [Washington, 1832] 1 p. (H.R. 407) DNA; MB.   15396

---- A bill for the relief of John Lacy. Jan. 5, 1832. Read twice, and committed to a Committee of the Whole House to-morrow. Mr. Milligan, from the Committee on Naval Affairs, reported the following bill: [Washington, 1832] 1 p. (H.R. 213) DNA; MB.   15397

---- A bill for the relief of John Peck. Mar. 9, 1832. Read twice, and committed to a Committee of the Whole House to-morrow. Mr. Crane, from the Committee on Revolutionary Claims, reported the following bill: [Washington, 1832] 2 p. (H.R. 455) DNA; MB.   15398

---- A bill for the relief of John Polhemus. Feb. 7, 1832. Read twice, and committed to a Committee of the Whole House to-morrow. Mr. Muhlenberg, from the Committee on Revolutionary Claims, reported the following bill: [Washington, 1832] 1 p. (H.R. 353) DNA; MB.   15399

---- A bill for the relief of John S. Devlin. Jan. 17, 1832. Read twice, and committed to a Committee of the Whole House to-morrow. Mr. Carson, from the Committee on Naval Affairs, reported the following bill: [Washington, 1832] 1 p. (H.R. 280) DNA; MB.   15400

---- A bill for the relief of John S. Flemming, administrator de bonis non of John Syme, deceased. Jan. 16, 1832. Read twice, and committed to a Committee of the Whole House to-morrow. Mr. Bouldin, from the Committee on Revolutionary Claims, made the following report: [Washington, 1832] 1 p. (H.R. 272) DNA; MB.   15401

---- A bill for the relief of John Sloughbough. Feb. 21, 1832. Read

twice, and committed to a Committee of the Whole House tomorrow. Mr. Cave Johnson, from the Committee on Private Land Claims, reported the following bill: [Washington, 1832] 1 p. (H.R. 404) DNA; MB.
15402

---- A bill for the relief of John T. Harlan. Feb. 24, 1832. Read twice, and committed to the Committee of the Whole House, to which is committed the bill H.R. No. 334, for the benefit of Joseph Dukes. Mr. Plummer, from the Committee on Public Lands, reported the following bill: [Washington, 1832] 1 p. (H.R. 411) DNA; MB.
15403

---- A bill for the relief of John Thomas and of Peter Foster. Jan. 4, 1832. Read twice, and committed to a Committee of the Whole House to-morrow. Mr. Bouldin, from the Committee on Revolutionary Claims, reported the following bill: [Washington, 1832] 1 p. (H.R. 200) DNA; MB.
15404

---- A bill for the relief of John Thompson. Dec. 14, 1832. Read twice, and committed to a Committee of the whole House to-morrow. Mr. E. Whittlesey, from the Committee of Claims, reported the following bill: [Washington, 1832] 1 p. (H.R. 617) DNA; MB.
15405

---- A bill for the relief of John W. Flowers, Nicholas Miller, William Drew, and Joseph Rodgers. May 10, 1832. Read twice, and committed to the Committee of the Whole House to which is committed the bill (H.R. No. 391) for the relief of the legal representatives of Joseph Brown. Mr. Mason, from the Committee on Indian Affairs, reported the following bill: [Washington, 1832] 1 p. (H.R. 570) DNA; MB.
15406

---- A bill for the relief of John Webber. Apr. 9, 1832. Read twice, and committed to a Committee of the Whole House tomorrow. Mr. E. Whittlesey, from the Committee of Claims, reported the following bill: [Washington, 1832] 1 p. (H.R. 535) DNA; MB.
15407

---- A bill for the relief of Jonathan Bean. January 12, 1832. Read twice, and committed to a Committee of the Whole House tomorrow. Mr. Burges, from the Committee on Invalid Pensions, reported the following bill: [Washington, 1832] 1 p. (H.R. 253) DNA; MB.
15408

---- A bill for the relief of Jonathan Fogg. Jan. 3, 1832. Read twice, and committed to a Committee of the Whole House tomorrow. Mr. Hubbard, from the Committee on Revolutionary Pensions, reported the following bill: [Washington, 1832] 1 p. (H.R. 192) DNA; MB.
15409

---- A bill for the relief of Jonathan Walton and John J. Degraff. Mar. 19, 1832. Read twice, and committed to a Committee of the Whole House to-morrow. Mr. Verplanck, from the Committee of Ways and Means, reported the following bill: [Washington, 1832] 2 p. (H.R. 493) DNA; MB.
15410

---- A bill for the relief of Joseph du Commun. Jan. 4, 1832. Read twice, and committed to a Committee of the Whole House tomorrow. Mr. Drayton, from the Committee on Military Affairs, reported the following bill: [Washington, 1832] 1 p. (H.R. 196) DNA; MB.
15411

---- A bill for the relief of Joseph du Commun. Apr. 17, 1832. Mr. Dallas, from the Committee

on Military Affairs, reported the
following bill; which was read,
and passed to a second reading:
[Washington, 1832] 1 p. (S. 181)
DNA; MB.   15412

---- A bill for the relief of Joseph Eaton, an assistant surgeon
in the Army of the United States.
Jan. 3, 1832. Read twice, and
committed to a Committee of the
Whole House to-morrow. Mr.
Drayton, from the Committee on
Military Affairs, reported the
following bill: [Washington, 1832]
1 p. (H.R. 181) DNA; MB.
                           15413
---- A bill for the relief of Joseph Elliott. Jan. 24, 1832. Mr.
King, from the Committee on Public Lands, reported the following
bill; which was read, and passed
to a second reading: [Washington,
1832] 1 p. (S. 76) DNA; MB.
                           15414
---- A bill for the relief of Joseph Guedry, Edward Lambert,
Michel Leboeuf, and Jean Vavas-
seur. Dec. 29, 1832. Read twice,
and committed to a Committee of
the Whole House to-morrow. Mr.
C. Johnson, from the Committee
on Private Land Claims, reported
the following bill: [Washington,
1832] 1 p. (H.R. 648) MB.
                           15415
---- A bill for the relief of Joseph M. Harper. Feb. 3, 1832.
Read twice, and committed to a
Committee of the Whole House to-
morrow. Mr. Hogan, from the
Committee of Claims, reported
the following bill: [Washington,
1832] 1 p. (H.R. 345) DNA; MB.
                           15416
---- A bill for the relief of Joseph Nourse. May 19, 1832. Mr.
Frelinghuysen, from the Committee on Judiciary, reported the
following bill; which was read,
and passed to a second reading:
[Washington, 1832] 1 p. (S. 202)
DNA; MB.   15417

---- A bill for the relief of Joseph V. Garnier, Mar. 2, 1832.
Read twice, and committed to a
Committee of the Whole House to-
morrow. Mr. White, of Louisiana, from the Committee on the
Judiciary, reported the following
bill: [Washington, 1832] 1 p.
(H.R. 443) DNA; MB.   15418

---- A bill for the relief of Joseph Watson. Jan. 24, 1832. Mr.
Ruggles, from the Committee of
Claims, reported the following
bill; which was read, and passed
to a second reading: [Washington,
1832] 1 p. (S. 74) DNA; MB.
                           15419
---- A bill for the relief of Joshua
P. Frothingham, and the heirs of
Thomas Hopping, deceased. Dec.
20, 1832. Read twice, and committed to the Committee of the
Whole House to which is committed the bill (H.R. No. 228) for
the relief of Daniel Goodwin, executor of Benjamin Goodwin, deceased. Mr. Bates, of Massachusetts, from the Committee on
Revolutionary Claims, reported
the following bill: [Washington,
1832] 1 p. (H.R. 632) DNA; MB.
                           15420
---- A bill for the relief of Josiah Barker. Mar. 16, 1832. Read
twice, and committed to a Committee of the Whole House to-morrow. Mr. Bullard, from the Committee on Private Land Claims,
reported the following bill: [Wash-
ington, 1832] 1 p. (H.R. 476)
DNA; MB.   15421

---- A bill for the relief of Josiah
Hedges. Feb. 17, 1832. Read
twice, and committed to a Committee of the Whole House to-
morrow. Mr. Hunt, from the
Committee on the Public Lands,
reported the following bill: [Wash-
ington, 1832] 1 p. (H.R. 381)
DNA; MB.   15422

United States 357

---- A bill for the relief of Josiah P. Creesy and others. Jan. 4, 1832. Read twice, and committed to a Committee of the Whole House to-morrow. Mr. Davis, of Massachusetts, from the Committee of Commerce, reported the following bill: [Washington, 1832] 1 p. (H.R. 198) DNA; MB. 15423

---- A bill for the relief of Judith Thomas. Jan. 10, 1832. Read twice, and committed to a Committee of the Whole House to-morrow. Mr. Evans, of Maine, from the Committee on Invalid Pensions, reported the following bill: [Washington, 1832] 1 p. (H.R. 235) DNA; MB. 15424

---- ---- Dec. 19, 1832. Read twice, and committed to a Committee of the Whole House to-morrow. Mr. Burges, from the Committee on Invalid Pensions, reported the following bill: [Washington, 1832] 1 p. (H.R. 628) DNA; MB. 15425

---- A bill for the relief of Lieut. George D. Ramsay, of the army of the United States. Dec. 29, 1832. Read twice, and ordered to be engrossed, and read the third time on the 4th day of January next. Mr. Vance, from the Committee on Military Affairs, reported the following bill: [Washington, 1832] 1 p. (H.R. 647) DNA; MB. 15426

---- A bill for the relief of Lieut. Harvey Brown. Jan. 21, 1832. Read twice, and committed to a Committee of the Whole House to-morrow. Mr. Drayton, from the Committee on Military Affairs, reported the following bill: [Washington, 1832] 1 p. (H.R. 302) DNA; MB. 15427

---- A bill for the relief of Lieut. John McDowel. Feb. 14, 1832. Read twice, and committed to a Committee of the Whole House to-morrow. Mr. Muhlenberg, from the Committee on Revolutionary Claims, reported the following bill: [Washington, 1832] 1 p. (H.R. 371) DNA; MB. 15428

---- A bill for the relief of Lieut. Robert Willmott. Mar. 8, 1832. Read twice, and committed to a Committee of the Whole House to-morrow. Mr. Muhlenberg, from the Committee on Revolutionary Claims, reported the following bill: [Washington, 1832] 1 p. (H.R. 454) DNA; MB. 15429

---- A bill for the relief of Luther L. Smith. Feb. 2, 1832. Read twice, and committed to a Committee of the Whole House to-morrow. Mr. Bullard, from the Committee on Private Land Claims, reported the following bill: [Washington, 1832] (H.R. 342) DNA; MB. 15430

---- A bill for the relief of Major Abraham A. Masias. Jan. 12, 1832. Read twice, and committed to a Committee of the Whole House to-morrow. Mr. Ward, from the Committee on Military Affairs, reported the following bill: [Washington, 1832] 1 p. (H.R. 252) DNA; MB. 15431

---- A bill for the relief of Marcus Quincy and William Gorham, of Portland. Dec. 26, 1832. Read twice, and committed to a Committee of the Whole House to-morrow. Mr. Cambreleng, from the Committee on Commerce, reported the following bill: [Washington, 1832] 1 p. (H.R. 640) DNA; MB. 15432

---- A bill for the relief of Maria Mallam Brooks, and the other heirs at law of Daniel Neil, deceased. Feb. 17, 1832. Read twice, and committed to a Committee of the Whole House to-mor-

row. Mr. Crane, from the Committee on Revolutionary Claims,
reported the following bill:
[Washington, 1832] 1 p. (H.R. 389)
DNA; MB.   15433

---- A bill for the relief of Martha Bailey, and others. May 5,
1832. Read twice, and committed
to a Committee of the Whole
House to-morrow. Mr. Hogan,
from the Committee of Claims,
reported the following bill: [Wash-
ington, 1832] 2 p. (H.R. 562)
DNA; MB.   15434

---- A bill for the relief of Mary
Daws, Robert Bont, James Pat-
ridge, and John G. Smith. Jan.
3, 1832. Read twice, and committed to a Committee of the
Whole House to-morrow. Mr. Irvin, from the Committee on the
Public Lands, reported the following bill: [Washington, 1832] 2 p.
(H.R. 184) DNA; MB.   15435

----A bill for the relief of Matthews Flournoy and R. J. Ward,
of the State of Mississippi, Jan.
10, 1832. Read twice, and committed to a Committee of the
Whole House to-morrow. Mr.
Clay, from the Committee on the
Public Lands, reported the following bill: [Washington, 1832]
1 p. (H.R. 230) DNA; MB.
                           15436
---- A bill for the relief of Mitchell Robertson. July 3, 1832.
Read twice, and committed to a
Committee of the Whole House
to-morrow. Mr. Nuckolls, from
the Committee on Revolutionary
Claims, reported the following
bill: [Washington, 1832] 1 p.
(H.R. 607) DNA; MB.   15437

---- A bill for the relief of N.
and L. Dana and Company. Feb.
24, 1832. Read twice, and committed to a Committee of the
Whole House to-morrow. Mr. Ver-

planck, from the Committee of
Ways and Means, reported the
following bill: [Washington, 1832]
1 p. (H.R. 409) DNA; MB.
                           15438
---- A bill for the relief of N.
Towson, Paymaster General of
the Army of the United States.
Jan. 6, 1832. Read twice, and
ordered to be engrossed, and
read the third time to-morrow,
Mr. Vance, from the Committee
on Military Affairs, reported the
following bill: [Washington, 1832]
1 p. (H.R. 217) DNA; MB.
                           15439
---- A bill for the relief of Nathan Carver. Mar. 2, 1832. Read
twice, and committed to a Committee of the Whole House to-
morrow. Mr. E. Whittlesey, from
the Committee of Claims, reported
the following bill: [Washington,
1832] 1 p. (H.R. 439) DNA; MB.
                           15440
---- A bill for the relief of Nathaniel Blake. Dec. 27, 1832.
Read twice, and committed to a
Committee of the Whole House to-
morrow. Mr. Verplanck, from
the Committee on Ways and Means,
reported the following bill: [Wash-
ington, 1832] 1 p. (H.R. 643)
DNA; MB.   15441

---- A bill for the relief of Nathaniel Patten. Feb. 28, 1832.
Read twice, and committed to a
Committee of the Whole House to-
morrow. Mr. Davis, of South Carolina, from the Committee on the
Judiciary, reported the following
bill: [Washington, 1832] 1 p. (H.R.
426) DNA; MB.   15442

---- A bill for the relief of Patrick Green. Jan. 12, 1832. Read
twice, and committed to a Committee of the Whole House to-
morrow. Mr. R. M. Johnson, from
the Committee on the Post Office
and Post Roads, reported the following bill: [Washington, 1832]

1 p. (H.R. 255) DNA; MB.
15443
---- A bill for the relief of Peregrine Gardner. Dec. 28, 1832. Read twice, and committed to a Committee of the Whole House to-morrow. Mr. Whittlesey, from the Committee of Claims, reported the following bill: [Washington, 1832] 1 p. (H.R. 644) DNA; MB.
15444
---- A bill for the relief of Peter Bargy, jr., Stephen Norton, and Hiram Wolverton. Jan. 25, 1832. Read twice, and committed to a Committee of the Whole House to-morrow. Mr. Whittlesey, from the Committee of Claims, reported the following bill: [Washington, 1832] 1 p. (H.R. 309) DNA; MB.
15445
---- A bill for the relief of Peter McCormock [sic]. Jan. 12, 1832. Read twice, and committed to a Committee of the Whole House to-morrow. Mr. Cave Johnson, from the Committee on Private Land Claims, reported the following bill: [Washington, 1832] 1 p. (H.R. 250) DNA; MB.   15446

---- A bill for the relief of Philip and Eliphalet Greerly. Feb. 24, 1832. Read twice, and committed to the Committee of the Whole House, to which is committed bill No. 409, for the relief of N. L. Dana and Company. Mr. Verplanck, from the Committee of Ways and Means, reported the following bill: [Washington, 1832] 1 p. (H.R. 410) DNA; MB.
15447
---- A bill for the relief of Philip Hicky. Feb. 29, 1832. Read twice, and committed to a Committee of the Whole House to-morrow. Mr. E. Whittlesey, from the Committee of Claims, reported the following bill: [Washington, 1832] 1 p. (H.R. 430) DNA; MB.
15448
---- A bill for the relief of Phil-ip Slaughter. Feb. 21, 1832. Read twice, and committed to a Committee of the Whole House to-morrow. Mr. Nuckolls, from the Committee on Revolutionary Claims, reported the following bill: [Washington, 1832] 1 p. (H.R. 403) DNA; MB.   15449

---- A bill for the relief of Phineas Sprague and others, late owners of the schooner Two Brothers; and, also, for the relief of Daniel Kiff, late owner of the boat Juno. Feb. 3, 1832. Read twice, and committed to a Committee on Commerce, reported the following bill: [Washington, 1832] 1 p. (H.R. 346) DNA; MB.
15450
---- A bill for the relief of Pierre Leglize. Feb. 15, 1832. Mr. Kane, from the Committee on Private Land Claims, reported the following bill; which was read and passed to a second reading: [Washington, 1832] 1 p. (S. 115) DNA; MB.   15451

---- A bill for the relief of Randall Allis, Timothy Twitchell, and John Lee Williams. Jan. 30, 1832. Read twice, and committed to a Committee of the Whole House to-morrow. Mr. Rencher, from the Committee of Claims, reported the following bill: [Washington, 1832] 1 p. (H.R. 328) DNA; MB.
15452
---- A bill for the relief of Ransom Mix. Jan. 26, 1832. Mr. Foot, from the Committee on Pensions, reported the following bill; which was read, and passed to a second reading: [Washington, 1832] 1 p. (S. 80) DNA; MB.
15453
---- A bill for the relief of Rebecca Blodget, widow of Samuel Blodget, deceased. May 4, 1832. Mr. Frelinghuysen, from the Committee on the Judiciary, reported the following bill; which was read,

and passed to a second reading: [Washington, 1832] 1 p. (S. 195) DNA; MB.   15454

---- A bill for the relief of Richard Bagnall, executor of James B. Vaughan. Dec. 14, 1832. Read twice, and committed to a Committee of the Whole House to-morrow. Mr. E. Whittlesey, from the Committee of Claims, reported the following bill: [Washington, 1832] 1 p. (H.R. 618) DNA; MB.   15455

---- A bill for the relief of Richard G. Morris. Jan. 23, 1832. Mr. Ruggles, from the Committee of Claims, reported the following bill; which was read, and passed to a second reading: [Washington, 1832] 1 p. (S. 70) DNA; MB.   15456

---- A bill for the relief of Richard Hardesty. Apr. 30, 1832. Read twice, and committed to a Committee of the Whole House to-morrow. Mr. Hogan, from the Committee of Claims, reported the following bill: [Washington, 1832] 1 p. (H.R. 558) DNA; MB.   15457

---- A bill for the relief of Richard Hargrave Lee. Mar. 28, 1832. Read twice, and committed to a Committee of the Whole House to-morrow. Mr. Verplanck, from the Committee of Ways and Means, reported the following bill: [Washington, 1832] 1 p. (H.R. 515) DNA; MB.   15458

---- A bill for the relief of Richard Wall. Feb. 14, 1832. Read twice, and committed to a Committee of the Whole House to-morrow. Mr. Bates, of Massachusetts, from the Committee on Revolutionary Claims, reported the following bill: [Washington, 1832] 1 p. (H.R. 372) DNA; MB.   15459

---- A bill for the relief of Riddle, Becktill, and Headington. Jan. 4, 1832. Read twice, and committed to a Committee of the Whole House to-morrow. Mr. Whittlesey, of Ohio, from the Committee of Claims, reported the following bill: [Washington, 1832] 1 p. (H.R. 204) DNA; MB.   15460

---- A bill for the relief of Robert Eaton. Jan. 4, 1832. Read twice, and committed to a Committee of the Whole House to-morrow. Mr. Gilbmore, from the Committee of Ways and Means, reported the following bill: [Washington, 1832] 1 p. (H.R. 205) DNA; MB.   15461

---- A bill for the relief of Robert Kane. Jan. 17, 1832. Read twice, and committed to a Committee of the Whole House to-morrow. Mr. Rencher, from the Committee of Claims, reported the following bill: [Washington, 1832] 1 p. (H.R. 278) DNA; MB.   15462

---- A bill for the relief of Robert Reynolds. Mar. 21, 1832. Read twice, and committed to a Committee of the Whole House to which is committed the bill (H.R. No. 318) for the relief of Jeremiah Adams and John Kidd. Mr. Pendleton, from the Committee on Revolutionary Pensions reported the following bill: [Washington, 1832] 1 p. (H.R. 500) DNA; MB.   15463

---- A bill for the relief of Russell Hotchkiss and others, owners of the brig Stranger. Jan. 4, 1832. Read twice, and committed to a Committee on Commerce, reported the following bill: [Washington, 1832] 1 p. (H.R. 197) DNA; MB.   15464

---- A bill for the relief of Samuel Andrews. Mar. 7, 1832. Mr. Sprague, from the Committee on

Pensions, reported the following bill; which was read, and passed to a second reading: [Washington, 1832] 1 p. (S. 140) DNA; MB. 15465

---- A bill for the relief of Samuel Dubose, administrator of Elias D. Dick, deceased. January 16, 1832. Read twice, and committed to a Committee of the Whole House to-morrow. Mr. McIntire, from the Committee of Claims, reported the following bill: [Washington, 1832] 2 p. (H.R. 273) DNA; MB. 15466

---- A bill for the relief of Samuel Eastforth. Mar. 15, 1832. Read twice, and committed to a Committee of the Whole House to-morrow. Mr. Pendleton, from the Committee on Revolutionary Pensions, reported the following bill: [Washington, 1832] 1 p. (H.R. 470) DNA; MB. 15467

---- A bill for the relief of Samuel May. Feb. 7, 1832. Mr. Bell, from the Committee of Claims, reported the following bill; which was read, and passed to a second reading: [Washington, 1832] 1 p. (S. 100) DNA; MB. 15468

---- A bill for the relief of Samuel Smith, Lynn Mac Ghee, and Semoier, Creek Indians. Apr. 27, 1832. Mr. King, from the Committee on Public Lands, reported the following bill; which was read, and passed to a second reading: [Washington, 1832] 1 p. (S. 187) DNA; MB. 15469

---- A bill for the relief of Samuel Thompson. Feb. 17, 1832. Read twice, and committed to a Committee of the Whole House to-morrow. Mr. Whittlesey, from the Committee of Claims, reported the following bill: [Washington, 1832] 1 p. (H.R. 382) DNA; MB. 15470

---- A bill for the relief of Silvia Posner. Jan. 23, 1832. Mr. Ruggles, from the Committee of Claims, reported the following bill; which was read, and passed to a second reading: [Washington, 1832] 1 p. (S. 72) DNA; MB. 15471

---- A bill for the relief of Sinclair D. Gervais. Mar. 17, 1832. Read twice, and committed to the Committee of the Whole House to which is committed the "Bill (H.R. No. 281) to amend the act for the relief of purchasers of the public lands that have reverted for the non-payment of the purchase money," passed 23d day of May, 1828. Mr. Plummer, from the Committee on the Public Lands, reported the following bill: [Washington, 1832] 1 p. (H.R. 479) DNA; MB. 15472

---- A bill for the relief of Stephen G. Peabody. Mar. 12, 1832. Mr. Sprague, from the Committee on Pensions, reported the following bill; which was read, and passed to a second reading: [Washington, 1832] 1 p. (S. 146) DNA; MB. 15473

---- A bill for the relief of Stephen Pleasonton, late Agent of the Treasury. Jan. 24, 1832. Mr. Grundy, from the Committee on the Judiciary, reported the following bill; which was read, and passed to a second reading: [Washington, 1832] 1 p. (S. 75) DNA; MB. 15474

---- A bill for the relief of sundry citizens of the United States who have lost property by the depradations of certain Indian tribes. July 14, 1832. Read twice, and committed to a Committee of the Whole House to-morrow. Mr. Mason, from the Committee on Indian Affairs, reported the following bill: [Washington, 1832] 2 p.

(H.R. 614) DNA; MB.   15475

---- A bill for the relief of Su-
san Marlow. May 2, 1832. Mr.
King, from the Committee on
Public Lands, reported the fol-
lowing bill; which was read, and
passed to a second reading:
[Washington, 1832] 1 p. (S. 192)
DNA; MB.   15476

---- A bill for the relief of Sylvester Havens. Apr. 23, 1832.
Read Twice, and committed to
the Committee of the Whole House
to which is committed the bill
from the Senate (No. 18) "to
amend an act entitled an act for
the relief of John Johnson,"
passed second March, one thousand eight hundred and thirty-one.
Mr. E. Whittlesey, from the
Committee of Claims, reported
the following bill: [Washington,
1832] 1 p. (H.R. 552) DNA; MB.
                             15477
---- A bill for the relief of
Thadeus Phelps and company.
Jan. 25, 1832. Read twice, and
committed to the Committee of
the Whole House, to which is
committed the bill H.R. No. 301,
for the relief of William Osborn,
Mr. Verplanck, from the Committee of Ways and Means, reported the following bill: [Wash-
ington, 1832] 1 p. (H.R. 316)
DNA; MB.   15478

---- A bill for the relief of the
administratrix of Capt. Paschal
Hickman. Apr. 4, 1832. Mr. Benton, from the Committee on Military Affairs, reported the following bill: which was read, and
passed to a second reading:
[Washington, 1832] 1 p. (S. 170)
DNA; MB.   15479

---- A bill for the relief of the
children of Charles Comb and
Marguerite Laviolet, his wife.
Jan. 4, 1832. Read twice, and

committed to a Committee of the
Whole House to-morrow. Mr. Bullard, from the Committee on Private Land Claims, reported the
following bill: [Washington, 1832]
1 p. (H.R. 201) DNA; MB.
                             15480
---- A bill for the relief of the
children of Henry Field. Mar. 10,
1832. Read twice, and committed
to a Committee of the Whole
House to-morrow. Mr. Hammons,
from the Committee on Revolutionary Claims, reported the following bill: [Washington, 1832]
1 p. (H.R. 458) DNA; MB.15481

---- A bill for the relief of the
executors of James Roddey, deceased. Feb. 2, 1832. Mr. Grundy, from the Committee on the
Judiciary, reported the following
bill; which was read, and passed
to a second reading: [Washington,
1832] 1 p. (S. 96) DNA; MB.
                             15482
---- A bill for the relief of the
heirs and executors of Thomas
Worthington, deceased. Jan. 12,
1832. Read twice, and committed
to a Committee of the Whole
House to-morrow. Mr. Foster,
from the Committee on the Judiciary, reported the following bill:
[Washington, 1832] 1 p. (H.R.
256) DNA; MB.   15483

---- A bill for the relief of the
heirs and legal representatives
of Alexander Garden, deceased.
Apr. 6, 1832. Read twice, and
committed to a Committee of the
Whole House to-morrow. Mr.
Muhlenberg, from the Committee
on Revolutionary Claims, reported
the following bill: [Washington,
1832] 1 p. (H.R. 530) DNA; MB.
                             15484
---- A bill for the relief of the
heirs and legal representatives
of Capt. Presley Thornton, deceased. May 14, 1832. Read
twice, and committed to a Com-

mittee of the Whole House to-morrow. Mr. Muhlenberg, from the Committee on Revolutionary Claims, reported the following bill: [Washington, 1832] 1 p. (H. R. 571) DNA; MB.   15485

---- A bill for the relief of the heirs and legal representatives of Dr. Samuel J. Axson, deceased. Apr. 7, 1832. Read twice, and committed to the Committee of the Whole House to which is commit-ted the bill (H. R. No. 154) for the relief of Ann D. Baylor. Mr. Muhlenberg, from the Committee on Revolutionary Claims, report-ed the following bill: [Washington, 1832] 1 p. (H. R. 531) DNA; MB.   15486

---- A bill for the relief of the heirs and legal representatives of Edward Barry, deceased. Feb. 8, 1832. Mr. Naudain, from the Committee of Claims, reported the following bill; which was read, and passed to a second reading: [Washington, 1832] 1 p. (S. 103) DNA; MB.   15487

---- A bill for the relief of the heirs and legal representatives of Frances Barham, deceased, and her husband, Fielding Barham. Jan. 17, 1832. Read twice, and committed to a Committee of the Whole House to-morrow. Mr. Mardis, from the Committee on Private Land Claims, reported the following bill: [Washington, 1832] 2 p. (H. R. 283) DNA; MB.   15488

---- A bill for the relief of the heirs and representatives of John Campbell, late of the city of New York, deceased. Jan. 20, 1832. Read twice, and committed to a Committee of the Whole House to-morrow. Mr. Muhlenberg, from the Committee on Revolutionary Claims, reported the following bill: [Washington, 1832] 1 p. (H. R. 292) DNA; MB.   15489

---- A bill for the relief of the heirs and legal representatives of John M. Gregory. Apr. 3, 1832. Read twice, and committed to a Committee of the Whole House to-morrow. Mr. Muhlenberg, from the Committee on Revolutionary Claims, reported the following bill: [Washington, 1832] 1 p. (H. R. 521) DNA; MB.   15490

---- A bill for the relief of the heirs and legal representatives of Lewis Miller, deceased. May 23, 1832. Agreeably to notice given, Mr. Chambers asked and obtained leave to bring in the fol-lowing bill; which was read twice, and referred to the Committee on Military Affairs, June 7, 1832. Reported without amendment. [Washington, 1832] 1 p. (S. 203) DNA; MB.   15491

---- A bill for the relief of the heirs and legal representatives of the late Capt. John Winston, deceased. Mar. 23, 1832. Read twice, and committed to a Com-mittee of the Whole House to-morrow. Mr. Muhlenberg, from the Committee on Revolutionary Claims, reported the following bill: [Washington, 1832] 1 p. (H. R. 507) DNA; MB.   15492

---- A bill for the relief of the heirs and representatives of the late Gen. William Macpherson, of the revolutionary army. Apr. 26, 1832. Mr. Dallas, from the Committee on Military Affairs, reported the following bill; which was read, and passed to a second reading: [Washington, 1832] 1 p. (S. 186) DNA; MB.   15493

---- A bill for the relief of the heirs at law of Richard Living-ston, a Canadian refugee, de-ceased. Feb. 24, 1832. Read twice, and committed to a Committee of the Whole House to-morrow. Mr. Crane, from the Committee on Revolutionary Claims, reported the following bill: [Washington, 1832] 1 p. (H.R. 412) DNA; MB.   15494

---- A bill for the relief of the heirs of Alexander Boyd, deceased. Jan. 6, 1832. Read twice, and committed to a Committee of the Whole House to-morrow. Mr. Carr from the Committee on Private Land Claims, reported the following bill: [Washington, 1832] 1 p. (H.R. 219) DNA; MB.   15495

---- A bill for the relief of the heirs of Andrew Nelson, and the heirs of Purnell Boyce. Feb. 24, 1832. Read twice, and committed to a Committee of the Whole House to-morrow. Mr. Hogan, from the Committee of Claims, reported the following bill: [Washington, 1832] 1 p. (H.R. 414) DNA; MB.   15496

---- A bill for the relief of the heirs of Jean Charles Boudrean. Mar. 16, 1832. Read twice, and committed to a Committee of the Whole House to-morrow. Mr. Bullard, from the Committee on Private Land Claims, reported the following bill: [Washington, 1832] 1 p. (H.R. 477) DNA; MB.   15497

---- A bill for the relief of the heirs of John Pettigrew and James Pettigrew, and the legatees of Alexander McKnight. Dec. 21, 1832. Read twice, and committed to a Committee of the Whole House to-morrow. Mr. Thompson, of Georgia, from the Committee on Indian Affairs, reported the following bill: [Washington, 1832] 1 p. (H.R. 636) DNA; MB.   15498

---- A bill for the relief of the heirs of John Wilson, deceased.

Jan. 13, 1832. Read twice, and committed to a Committee of the Whole House to-morrow. Mr. Crane, from the Committee on Revolutionary Claims, reported the following bill: [Washington, 1832] 1 p. (H.R. 260) DNA; MB.   15499

---- A bill for the relief of the heirs of Louis Pellerin. Feb. 10, 1832. Read twice, and committed to a Committee of the Whole House to-morrow. Mr. Bullard, from the Committee on Private Land Claims, reported the following bill: [Washington, 1832] 1 p. (H.R. 369) DNA; MB.   15500

---- A bill for the relief of the heirs of Nicholas Hart, deceased. Jan. 10, 1832. Read twice, and committed to a Committee of the Whole House to-morrow. Mr. Clay, from the Committee on Public Lands, reported the following bill: [Washington, 1832] 1 p. (H.R. 232) DNA; MB.   15501

---- A bill for the relief of the heirs of Thomas Davenport. Apr. 2, 1832. Mr. Bell, from the Committee of Claims, reported the following bill; which was read, and passed to a second reading: [Washington, 1832] 1 p. (S. 168) DNA; MB.   15502

---- A bill for the relief of the heirs of Thomas Wallace, deceased. Feb. 23, 1832. Read twice, and committed to a Committee of the Whole House to-morrow. Mr. Crane, from the Committee on Revolutionary Claims, reported the following bill: [Washington, 1832] 1 p. (H.R. 408) DNA; MB.   15503

---- A bill for the relief of the heirs of Thomas Wishart. July 13, 1832. Read twice and commited to a Committee of the Whole House to-morrow. Mr.

Crane, from the Committee on Revolutionary Claims, reported the following bill: [Washington, 1832] 1 p. (H. R. 613) DNA; MB.   15504

---- A bill for the relief of the heirs of Widow Robert Avart. Feb. 29, 1832. Read twice, and committed to a Committee of the Whole House to-morrow. Mr. E. Whittlesey, from the Committee of Claims, reported the following bill: [Washington, 1832] 1 p. (H. R. 431) DNA; MB.   15505

---- A bill for the relief of the heirs of William Pollard. Feb. 15, 1832. Read twice, and committed to a Committee of the Whole House to-morrow. Mr. Mardis, from the Committee on Private Land Claims, reported the following bill: [Washington, 1832] 1 p. (H. R. 378) DNA; MB.   15506

---- A bill for the relief of the Invalid Pensioners of the United States. Jan. 10, 1832. Read twice, and committed to a Committee of the Whole House to-morrow. Mr. Burges, from the Committee on Invalid Pensions, reported the following bill: [Washington, 1832] 1 p. (H. R. 225) DNA; MB.   15507

---- A bill for the relief of the legal heirs of Alexander Dick, deceased. Mar. 9, 1832. Mr. Hammons, from the Committee on Revolutionary Claims, reported the following bill: [Washington, 1832] 1 p. (H. R. 456) DNA; MB.   15508

---- A bill for the relief of the legal representative of James Morrison, deceased. July 9, 1832. Read twice, and committed to a Committee of the Whole House to-morrow. Mr. Whittlesey, from the Committee of Claims, to which was referred the petition of Henry Clay, executor of James

Morrison, deceased, reported the following bill: [Washington, 1832] 1 p. (H. R. 612) DNA; MB.   15509

---- A bill for the relief of the legal representative of John Miller, deceased. Jan. 12, 1832. Read twice, and committed to a Committee of the Whole House to-morrow. Mr. William B. Shepard, from the Committee on the Territories, reported the following bill: [Washington, 1832] 1 p. (H. R. 257) DNA; MB.   15510

---- A bill for the relief of the legal representatives of Arnold Henry Dohrman, deceased. Jan. 30, 1832. Mr. Ruggles, from the Committee on Private Land Claims, reported the following bill; which was read, and passed to a second reading: [Washington, 1832] 1 p. (S. 90) DNA; MB.   15511

---- A bill for the relief of the legal representatives of Christian Ish, deceased. Feb. 15, 1832. Read twice, and committed to a Committee of the Whole House to-morrow. Mr. Muhlenberg, from the Committee on Revolutionary Claims, reported the following bill: [Washington, 1832] 1 p. (H. R. 374) DNA; MB.   15512

---- A bill for the relief of the legal representatives of Col. John Laurens. Feb. 17, 1832. Read twice, and committed to a Committee of the Whole House to-morrow. Mr. Bates, of Massachusetts, from the Committee on Revolutionary Claims, reported the following bill: [Washington, 1832] 3 p. (H. R. 386) DNA; MB.   15513

---- A bill for the relief of the legal representatives of Daniel Wicks, deceased. March 2, 1832. Read twice, and committed to a Committee of the Whole House to-morrow. Mr. Standifer, from

the Committee on Revolutionary
Claims, reported the following
bill: [Washington, 1832] 1 p.
(H.R. 440) DNA; MB.   15514

---- A bill for the relief of the
legal representatives of Everard
Meade, deceased. July 7, 1832.
Read twice, and committed to a
Committee of the Whole House to-
morrow. Mr. Crane, from the
Committee on Revolutionary
Claims, reported the following
bill: [Washington, 1832] 1 p.
(H.R. 610) DNA; MB.   15515

---- A bill for the relief of the
legal representatives of J. B.
Vallery. Feb. 23, 1832. Read
twice, and committed to a Committee of the Whole House to-
morrow. Mr. Bullard, from the
Committee on Private Land
Claims, reported the following
bill: [Washington, 1832] 1 p.
(H.R. 406) DNA; MB.   15516

---- A bill for the relief of the
legal representatives of James
Brown. Feb. 17, 1832. Read
twice, and committed to a Committee of the Whole House to-
morrow. Mr. Bell, from the
Committee on Indian Affairs, reported the following bill: [Wash-
ington, 1832] 1 p. (H.R. 391)
DNA; MB.   15517

---- A bill for the relief of the
legal representatives of John
Coleman, deceased. Feb. 20,
1832. Read twice, and committed
to a Committee of the Whole
House to-morrow. Mr. Campbell
P. White, from the Committee
on Naval Affairs, reported the
following bill: [Washington, 1832]
1 p. (H.R. 400) DNA; MB.
                             15518
---- A bill for the relief of the
legal representatives of John P.
Cox. May 7, 1832. Read twice,
and committed to a Committee

of the Whole House to-morrow.
Mr. Rencher, from the Committee of Claims, reported the following bill: [Washington, 1832]
2 p. (H.R. 565) DNA; MB.
                             15519
---- A bill for the relief of the
legal representatives of John
Peter Wagnon, deceased. Jan.
18, 1832. Read twice, and committed to the Committee of the
Whole House, to which is committed the bill (H.R. No. 186,)
for the relief of Thomas Triplett.
Mr. Muhlenberg, from the Committee on Revolutionary Claims,
reported the following bill:
[Washington, 1832] 1 p. (H.R.
285) DNA; MB.   15520

---- A bill for the relief of the
legal representatives of John Pettigrew and James Pettigrew, and
the legatees of Alexander Mc-
Knight. Mar. 22, 1832. Read
twice, and committed to the Committee of the Whole House to
which is committed the bill (H.R.
No. 391) for the relief of the
legal representatives of Joseph
Brown. Mr. Lewis, from the
Committee on Indian Affairs, reported the following bill: [Wash-
ington, 1832] 1 p. (H.R. 504)
DNA; MB.   15521

---- A bill for the relief of the
legal representatives of Joseph
Knight. Jan. 10, 1832. Read
twice, and committed to a Committee of the Whole House to-
morrow. Mr. Evans, of Maine,
from the Committee on Invalid
Pensions, reported the following
bill: [Washington, 1832] 1 p.
(H.R. 246) DNA; MB.   15522

---- A bill for the relief of the
legal representatives of Joseph
Rowe, deceased. May 17, 1832.
Read twice, and committed to the
Committee of the Whole House to
which is committed the bill (No.

400) for the relief of John Coleman. Mr. Watmough, from the Committee on Naval Affairs, reported the following bill: [Washington, 1832] 1 p. (H.R. 579) DNA; MB.   15523

---- A bill for the relief of the legal representatives of Lathrop Allen, deceased. July 2, 1832. Read twice, and committed to a Committee of the Whole House to-morrow. Mr. Crane, from the Committee on Revolutionary Claims, reported the following bill: [Washington, 1832] 1 p. (H.R. 605) DNA; MB.   15524

---- A bill for the relief of the legal representatives of Laurence Milligan, deceased. May 30, 1832. Mr. Kane, from the Committee on Private Land Claims, reported the following bill; which was read, and passed to a second reading: [Washington, 1832] 1 p. (S. 205) DNA; MB.   15525

---- A bill for the relief of the legal representatives of Leonard Holly, deceased. April 3, 1832. Read twice, and committed to a Committee of the Whole House to-morrow. Mr. Drayton, from the Committee on Military Affairs, reported the following bill: [Washington, 1832] 1 p. (H.R. 523) DNA; MB.   15526

---- A bill for the relief of the legal representatives of Nimrod Farrow and of Richard Harris, Jan. 17, 1832. Read twice, and committed to a Committee of the Whole House to-morrow. Mr. Whittlesey, from the Committee of Claims, reported the following bill: [Washington, 1832] 1 p. (H.R. 277) DNA; MB.   15527

---- A bill for the relief of the legal representatives of Peter, Catharine, and Charles Surget.

Jan. 5, 1832. Mr. Ellis, from the Committee on Public Lands, reported the following bill; which was read, and passed to a second reading: [Washington, 1832] 2 p. (S. 45) DNA; MB.   15528

---- A bill for the relief of the legal representatives of Peter Celestino Walker and John Peter Walker, deceased, and of Joseph Walker, of the state of Mississippi. Mar. 2, 1832. Mr. Kane, from the Committee on Private Land Claims, reported the following bill; which was read, and passed to a second reading: [Washington, 1832] 2 p. (S. 133) DNA; MB.   15529

---- A bill for the relief of the legal representatives of Richard W. Meade. Feb. 10, 1832. Read twice, and committed to a Committee of the Whole House to-morrow. Mr. Archer, from the Committee on Foreign Affairs, reported the following bill: [Washington, 1832] 2 p. (H.R. 366) DNA; MB.   15530

---- A bill for the relief of the legal representatives of Rignald, alias Reynold, Hillary. Jan. 3, 1832. Read twice, and committed to the Committee of the Whole House, to which is committed bill No. 107. Mr. Nuckolls, from the Committee on Revolutionary Claims, reported the following bill: [Washington, 1832] 1 p. (H.R. 187) MB.   15531

---- A bill for the relief of the legal representatives of the late Col. John Thornton, deceased. Jan. 6, 1832. Read twice, and committed to a Committee of the Whole House to-morrow. Mr. Nuckolls, from the Committee on Revolutionary Claims, reported the following bill: [Washington, 1832] 1 p. (H.R. 218) DNA; MB.   15532

---- A bill for the relief of the legal representatives of the late Thomas Chapman, formerly Collector of the port of Georgetown, South Carolina. Apr. 24, 1832. Mr. Hayne, from the Committee on the Judiciary, reported the following bill; which was read, and passed to a second reading: [Washington, 1832] 1 p. (S. 184) DNA; MB.   15533

---- A bill for the relief of the legal representatives of Theodore Brightwell, June 7, 1832. Mr. Marcy, from the Committee on the Judiciary, reported the following bill; which was read, and passed to a second reading: [Washington, 1832] 1 p. (S. 206) DNA; MB.   15534

---- A bill for the relief of the legal representatives of Thornton Taylor, deceased. June 26, 1832. Read twice, and committed to a Committee of the Whole House to-morrow. Mr. Crane, from the Committee on Revolutionary Claims, reported the following bill: [Washington, 1832] 1 p. (H. R. 600) DNA; MB.   15535

---- A bill for the relief of the legal representatives of Walter Livingston, deceased. Feb. 2, 1832. Read twice, and committed to a Committee of the Whole House to-morrow. Mr. Hammons, from the Committee on Revolutionary Claims, reported the following bill: [Washington, 1832] 1 p. (H. R. 341) DNA; MB.
                                    15536
---- A bill for the relief of the legal representatives of William Young. Mar. 17, 1832. Read twice, and committed to a Committee of the Whole House to-morrow. Mr. Bell, from the Committee on Indian Affairs, reported the following bill: [Washington, 1832] 1 p. (H. R. 481)

DNA; MB.   15537

---- A bill for the relief of the officers and soldiers of Fort Delaware. Jan. 23, 1832. Mr. Dallas, from the Committee on Military Affairs, reported the following bill; which was read, and passed to a second reading: [Washington, 1832] 1 p. DNA; MB.   15538

---- A bill for the relief of the owners of the schooner Admiral. Mar. 22, 1832. Read twice, and committed to a Committee of the Whole House to-morrow. Mr. Jarvis, from the Committee on Commerce, reported the following bill: [Washington, 1832] 1 p. (H. R. 501) DNA; MB.   15539

---- A bill for the relief of the owners of the schooner Three Sisters, of Saybrook. Apr. 7, 1832. Read twice, and committed to a Committee of the Whole House to-morrow. Mr. Davis, of Massachusetts, from the Committee on Commerce, reported the following bill: [Washington, 1832] 1 p. (H. R. 532) DNA; MB.   15540

---- A bill for the relief of the personal representatives of Col. John Laurens. Jan. 4, 1832. Mr. Kane, from the Committee on Military Affairs, reported the following bill; which was read, and passed to a second reading: [Washington, 1832] 2 p. (S. 40) DNA; MB.   15541

---- A bill for the relief of the representatives of Elias Earle, deceased. Jan. 5, 1832. Agreeably to notice given, Mr. Hayne asked and obtained leave, to bring in the following bill, which was read twice, and referred to the Committee on the Judiciary. Jan. 10, 1832. Reported without amendment. [Washington, 1832] 1 p.

(S. 49) DNA; MB.   15542

---- A bill for the relief of the sureties of Amos Edwards. Jan. 3, 1832. Agreeably to notice given, Mr. Bibb asked and obtained leave, to bring in the following bill; which was read twice, and referred to the Committee of the Judiciary, Jan. 23, 1832. Reported without amendment. [Washington, 1832] 1 p. (S. 37) DNA; MB.   15543

---- A bill for the relief of the sureties of George Brown, deceased, late collector of internal duties and direct tax for the first district in the state of Maryland. Jan. 26, 1832. Agreeably to notice given, Mr. Chambers asked and obtained leave to bring in the following bill; which was read, and passed to a second reading: Jan. 31, 1832. Read the second time, and referred to the Committee on the Judiciary. Feb. 17, 1832. Reported without amendment. [Washington, 1832] 2 p. (S. 82) DNA; MB.   15544

---- A bill for the relief of the sureties of George Wheeler and Caleb Morrison. July 14, 1832. Read twice, and committed to a Committee of the Whole House to-morrow. Mr. Davis, of South Carolina, from the Committee on the Judiciary, reported the following bill: [Washington, 1832] 1 p. (H. R. 616) DNA; MB.
          15545
---- A bill for the relief of the widow of Joseph Knight. Dec. 19, 1832. Read twice, and committed to the Committee of the Whole House to which is committed the bill (H. R. No. 237) granting pensions to certain revolutionary soldiers. Mr. Burges, from the Committee on Invalid Pensions, reported the following bill: [Washington, 1832] 1 p. (H. R.

627) DNA; MB.   15546

---- A bill for the relief of Theodore Owens. Jan. 30, 1832. Read twice, and committed to a Committee of the Whole House to-morrow. Mr. Davis, of South Carolina, from the Committee on the Judiciary, reported the following bill: [Washington, 1832] 1 p. (H. R. 333) MB.   15547

---- A bill for the relief of thirty-one inhabitants of the old mines, in the state of Missouri. Feb. 17, 1832. Read twice, and committed to a Committee of the Whole House to-morrow. Mr. Cave Johnson, from the Committee on Private Land Claims, reported the following bill: [Washington, 1832] 2 p. (H. R. 380) DNA; MB.   15548

---- A bill for the relief of Thos. and James Massengail. Feb. 4, 1832. Read twice, and ordered to be engrossed, and read the third time to-morrow. Mr. Wickliffe, from the Committee on the Public Lands, reported the following bill: [Washington, 1832] 1 p. (H. R. 347) DNA; MB.   15549

---- A bill for the relief of Thos. Buford, Apr. 3, 1832. Read twice, and committed to a Committee of the Whole House to-morrow. Mr. Drayton, from the Committee on Military Affairs, reported the following bill: [Washington, 1832] 1 p. (H. R. 522) DNA; MB.
          15550
---- A bill for the relief of Thos. Chapman, executor of Thos. Chapman, deceased. June 30, 1832. Read twice, and committed to a Committee of the Whole House to-morrow. Mr. Foster, from the Committee on the Judiciary, reported the following bill: [Washington, 1832] 1 p. (H. R. 602) DNA; MB.   15551

---- A bill for the relief of
Thos. Cooper. Jan. 30, 1832.
Read twice, and committed to a
Committee of the Whole House
to-morrow. Mr. Davis, of South
Carolina, from the Committee on
the Judiciary, reported the follow-
ing bill: [Washington, 1832] 1 p.
(H. R. 332) DNA; MB.   15552

---- A bill for the relief of Thos.
D. Anderson, July 12, 1832. Mr.
Smith, from the Committee on
Finance, reported the following
bill; which was read, and passed
to a second reading: [Washington,
1832] 1 p. (S. 214) DNA; MB.
                                15553
---- A bill for the relief of Thos.
Dennis. Jan. 19, 1832. Mr. King,
from the Committee on Public
Lands, reported the following bill;
which was read, and passed to a
second reading: [Washington,
1832] 1 p. (S. 67) DNA; MB.
                                15554
---- A bill for the relief of Thos.
Holdup Stevens, and others. Mar.
13, 1832. Mr. Hayne, from the
Committee on Naval Affairs, reported the following bill; which
was read, and passed to a second
reading: [Washington, 1832] 1 p.
(S. 152) DNA; MB.   15555

---- A bill for the relief of Thos.
L. Winthrop and others, Direc-
tors of an association called the
New England Mississippi Land
Company. Jan. 18, 1832. Mr.
Hayne, from the Committee on the
Judiciary, reported the following
bill; which was read, and passed
to a second reading: [Washington,
1832] 1 p. (S. 63) DNA; MB.
                                15556
---- A bill for the relief of Thos.
Minor. July 6, 1832. Read twice,
and committed to a Committee on
Revolutionary Claims, reported
the following bill: [Washington,
1832] 1 p. (H. R. 608) DNA; MB.
                                15557

---- A bill for the relief of Thos.
Phillips. June 1, 1832. Read
twice, and committed to the Committee of the Whole House to
which is committed bills of the
Senate (No. 24) for the relief of
Joseph Chamberlain, and (No. 15)
for the relief of Edward S.
Meeder. Mr. E. C. Reed, from
the Committee on Invalid Pensions, reported the following bill:
[Washington, 1832] 1 p. (H. R.
593) DNA; MB.   15558

---- A bill for the relief of Thos.
Rhodes and Jeremiah Austill.
May 29, 1832. Mr. Grundy, from
the Committee on the Post Office
and Post Roads, reported the following bill; which was read, and
passed to a second reading:
[Washington, 1832] 1 p. (S. 204)
DNA; MB.   15559

---- A bill for the relief of Thos.
Richardson, Mar. 7, 1832. Read
twice, and committed to a Committee of the Whole House to-
morrow. Mr. E. Whittlesey,
from the Committee of Claims,
reported the following bill:
[Washington, 1832] 2 p. (H. R.
450) DNA; MB.   15560

---- A bill for the relief of Thos.
Triplett. Jan. 3, 1832. Read
twice, and committed to a Committee of the Whole House to-
morrow. Mr. Bouldin, from the
Committee on Revolutionary
Claims, reported the following
bill: [Washington, 1832] 1 p.
(H. R. 186) DNA; MB.   15561

---- A bill for the relief of Tim-
othy Risley. Feb. 24, 1832. Mr.
King, from the Committee on
Public Lands, reported the follow-
ing bill; which was read, and
passed to a second reading:
[Washington, 1832] 1 p. (S. 123)
DNA; MB.   15562

---- A bill for the relief of Walter Cockburn. Feb. 21, 1832. Mr. King, from the Committee on Public Lands, reported the following bill; which was read, and passed to a second reading: [Washington, 1832] 1 p. (S. 117) DNA; MB.
15563

---- A bill for the relief of Whitford Gill. Dec. 17, 1832. Read twice, and committed to a Committee of the Whole House to-morrow. Mr. E. Whittlesey, from the Committee of Claims, reported the following bill: [Washington, 1832] 1 p. (H. R. 620) DNA; MB.
15564

---- A bill for the relief of William A. Tennille, of Georgia. Jan. 13, 1832. Read twice, and committed to a Committee of the Whole House to-morrow. Mr. Ford, from the Committee on Invalid Pensions, reported the following bill: [Washington, 1832] 1 p. (H. R. 264) DNA; MB.
15565

---- A bill for the relief of William A. Tennille [of Georgia]. Feb. 23, 1832. Mr. Troup, from the Committee on Military Affairs, reported the following bill; which was read, and passed to a second reading: [Washington, 1832] 1 p. (S. 118) DNA; MB.
15566

---- A bill for the relief of Wm. B. Keene and John L. Martin, and for other purposes. Jan. 10, 1832. Read twice, and committed to a Committee of the Whole House to-morrow. Mr. Marshall, from the Committee on Private Land Claims, reported the following bill: [Washington, 1832] 1 p. (H. R. 243) DNA; MB.
15567

---- A bill for the relief of Wm. D. Acken. Apr. 13, 1832. Read twice, and committed to a Committee of the Whole House to-morrow. Mr. Hogan, from the Committee of Claims, reported the following bill: [Washington, 1832] 1 p. (H. R. 546) DNA; MB.
15568

---- A bill for the relief of Wm. Dickson. Feb. 24, 1832. Mr. Robinson, from the Committee on Public Lands, reported the following bill; which was read, and passed to a second reading: [Washington, 1832] 2 p. (S. 122) DNA; MB.
15569

---- A bill for the relief of Wm. Estis, late paymaster of the fourth regiment of Virginia troups, stationed at Norfolk. Feb. 10, 1832. Read twice, and committed to a Committee of the Whole House to-morrow. Mr. Davis, of South Carolina, from the Committee on the Judiciary, reported the following bill: [Washington, 1832] 1 p. (H. R. 367) DNA; MB.
15570

---- A bill for the relief of [William] Howze and George B. Dameron, of Mississippi. Feb. 9, 1832. Mr. Ellis, from the Committee on Public Lands, reported the following bill; which was read, and passed to a second reading: [Washington, 1832] 1 p. (S. 107) DNA; MB.
15571

---- A bill for the relief of Wm. Huntington. Mar. 15, 1832. Read twice, and committed to a Committee of the Whole House to-morrow. Mr. Pendleton, from the Committee on Revolutionary Pensions, reported the following bill: [Washington, 1832] 1 p. (H. R. 471) DNA; MB.
15572

---- A bill for the relief of Wm. McCormick. Mar. 21, 1832. Read twice, and ordered to be engrossed, and read the third time to-morrow. Mr. Wickliffe, from the Committee on the Public Lands, reported the following bill: [Washington, 1832] 1 p. (H. R. 499)

DNA; MB.   15573

---- A bill for the relief of Wm. Nelson, administrator of the estate of Andrew Nelson, deceased. Jan. 30, 1832. Mr. Hayne, from the Committee on Naval Affairs, reported the following bill; which was read, and passed to a second reading: [Washington, 1832] 1 p. (S. 85) DNA; MB.   15574

---- A bill for the relief of Wm. Osborn. Jan. 21, 1832. Read twice, and committed to a Committee of the Whole House tomorrow. Mr. Wilde, from the Committee of Ways and Means, reported the following bill: [Washington, 1832] 1 p. (H.R. 301) DNA; MB.   15575

---- A bill for the relief of Wm. R. Peckett. Feb. 17, 1832. Read twice, and ordered to be engrossed, and read the third time to-morrow. Mr. Wickliffe, from the Committee on the Public Lands, reported the following bill: [Washington, 1832] 2 p. (H.R. 385) DNA; MB.   15576

---- A bill for the relief of Wm. S. Anderson. Mar. 12, 1832. Read twice, and committed to a Committee of the Whole House to-morrow. Mr. E. Whittlesey, from the Committee of Claims, reported the following bill: [Washington, 1832] 1 p. (H.R. 459) DNA; MB.   15577

---- A bill for the relief of Wm. Saunders and Wm. R. Porter, sureties of Wm. Estis, late paymaster of the fourth regiment of Virginia troups, stationed at Norfolk during the late war. Jan. 25, 1832. Read twice, and committed to a Committee of the Whole House to-morrow. Mr. Davis, of South Carolina, from the Com-

mittee on the Judiciary, reported the following bill: [Washington, 1832] 1 p. (H.R. 319) DNA; MB.   15578

---- A bill for the relief of Wm. Smith. Apr. 30, 1832. Read twice, and committed to a Committee of the Whole House to-morrow. Mr. Rencher, from the Committee of Claims, reported the following bill: [Washington, 1832] 1 p. (H.R. 557) DNA; MB.   15579

---- A bill for the relief of Wm. Stewart. Jan. 24, 1832. Read twice, and committed to a Committee on the Public Lands, reported the following bill: [Washington, 1832] 1 p. (H.R. 303) DNA; MB.   15580

---- A bill for the relief of Wm. Wayne Wells, of the State of Indiana. Feb. 6, 1832. Mr. White, from the Committee on Indian Affairs, reported the following bill; which was read, and passed to a second reading: [Washington, 1832] 1 p. (S. 99) DNA; MB.   15581

---- A bill for the relief of Wm. Weedon. Mar. 6, 1832. Read twice, and committed to a Committee of the Whole House to-morrow. Mr. Clay, from the Committee on the Public Lands, reported the following bill: [Washington, 1832] 1 p. (H.R. 448) DNA; MB.   15582

---- A bill for the relief of [William] Williamson. Jan. 3, 1832. Read twice, and ordered to be engrossed, and read the third time to-morrow. Mr. Wickliffe, from the Committee on the Public Lands, reported the following bill: [Washington, 1832] 1 p. (H.R. 179) DNA; MB.   15583

---- A bill for the relief of Wyatt Singleton and James Andrews. Jan. 20, 1832. Read twice, and committed to a Committee of the Whole House to-morrow. Mr. Cave Johnson, from the Committee on Private Land Claims, reported the following bill: [Washington, 1832] 1 p. (H.R.293) DNA; MB.   15584

---- A bill for the relief of Zephaniah Halsey. Mar. 17, 1832. Read twice, and committed to a Committee of the Whole House to-morrow. Mr. Pendleton, from the Committee on Revolutionary Pensions, reported the following bill: [Washington, 1832] 1 p. (H.R. 485) DNA; MB.   15585

---- A bill for the sale of the unlocated lots in the fifty quarter townships in the United States' military district in the state of Ohio, reserved to satisfy warrants granted to individuals for their military services. Mar. 22, 1832. Read twice, and ordered to be engrossed, and read the third time to-morrow. Mr. Irvin, from the Committee on the Public Lands, reported the following bill: [Washington, 1832] 1 p. (H.R. 502) DNA; MB.   15586

---- A bill for the settlement of the claim of James Scrivener, a seaman in the service of the United States. Feb. 15, 1832. Read twice, and committed to a Committee of the Whole House to-morrow. Mr. Watmough, from the Committee on Naval Affairs, reported the following bill: [Washington, 1832] 1 p. (H.R. 375) DNA; MB.   15587

---- A bill for the settlement of the claim of the state of Connecticut against the United States for the services of her militia during the late war. Mar. 1, 1832. Read twice, and committed to the Committee of the Whole House on the state of the Union. Mr. Drayton,

from the Committee on Military Affairs, reported the following bill: [Washington, 1832] 2 p. (H.R. 433) DNA; MB.   15588

---- A bill further to amend the act, entitled "An act to incorporate the inhabitants of the city of Washington," &c., passed on the fifteenth day of May, one thousand eight hundred and twenty. Feb. 7, 1832. Read twice, and committed to a Committee of the Whole House to-morrow. Mr. Doddridge, from the Committee for the District of Columbia, reported the following bill: [Washington, 1832] 4 p. (H.R. 358) DNA; MB.   15589

---- A bill further to amend the several acts imposing duties on imports. May 1, 1832. Mr. Dickerson, from the Committee on Manufactures, reported the following bill; which was read, and passed to a second reading: [Washington, 1832] 7 p. (S. 190) DNA; MB.   15590

---- A bill further to extend the act, entitled "an act for further extending the powers of the judges of the superior court of the territory of Arkansas, under the act of the twenty-sixth day of May, one thousand eight hundred and twenty-four, and for other purposes." Feb. 28, 1832. Read twice, and committed to the Committee of the Whole House on the state of the Union. Mr. Davis, of South Carolina, from the Committee on the Judiciary, reported the following bill: [Washington, 1832] 2 p. (H.R. 427) DNA; MB.   15591

---- A bill further to extend pension heretofore granted to the widows of persons killed, or who died in the naval service. June 5, 1832. Read twice, and committed to the Committee of the Whole

House on the state of the Union. Mr. Watmough, from the Committee on Naval Affairs, reported the following bill: [Washington, 1832] 1 p. (H.R. 596) DNA; MB.
15592

---- A bill further to extend the time for entering certain donation claims to land in the territory of Arkansas. Dec. 26, 1832. Read twice, and ordered to be engrossed, and read the third time to-morrow. Mr. Wickliffe, from the Committee on the Public Lands, reported the following bill: [Washington, 1832] 2 p. (H.R. 639) MB.   15593

---- A bill giving the assent of Congress to an act of the legislature of North Carolina, entitled "An act to incorporate a company entitled the Roanoke Inlet Company, and for other purposes;" and also, to an act amendatory thereof, which passed in one thousand eight hundred and twenty-eight. Mar. 29, 1832. Read twice, and committed to the Committee of the Whole House on the state of the Union. Mr. Mercer, from the Committee on Internal Improvements, reported the following bill: [Washington, 1832] 1 p. (H.R. 517) DNA; MB.
15594

---- A bill giving the assent of the United States to an act of the General Assembly of Maryland, passed at their December session, in one thousand eight hundred and thirty-one, entitled "An act further to amend the act incorporating the Chesapeake and Ohio Canal Company." Apr. 25, 1832. Read twice, and committed to a Committee of the Whole House to-morrow. Mr. Doddridge, from the Committee for the District of Columbia, reported the following bill: [Washington, 1832] 1 p. (H.R. 554) DNA; MB.
15595

---- A bill granting a lot of ground to the town of Columbus, for the abutment of a bridge over the Chatahoochee river. Jan. 13, 1832. Mr. King, from the Committee on Public Lands, reported the following bill; which was read, and passed to a second reading: [Washington, 1832] 1 p. (S. 60) DNA; MB.   15596

---- A bill granting a pension to Alfred Baldwin. Feb. 8, 1832. Read twice, and committed to a Committee of the Whole House to-morrow. Mr. Evans, of Maine, from the Committee on Invalid Pensions, reported the following bill: [Washington, 1832] 1 p. (H.R. 360) DNA; MB.   15597

---- A bill granting a pension to Benjamin Dow. Jan. 25, 1832. Read twice, and committed to a Committee of the Whole House to-morrow. Mr. Evans, of Maine, from the Committee on Invalid Pensions, reported the following bill: [Washington, 1832] 1 p. (H.R. 310) DNA; MB.   15598

---- A bill granting a pension to Job Wood. Apr. 7, 1832. Read twice, and committed to a Committee of the Whole House to-morrow. Mr. E. C. Reed, from the Committee on Invalid Pensions, reported the following bill: [Washington, 1832] 1 p. (H.R. 533) DNA; MB.   15599

---- A bill granting a pension to Joseph Durfee. Mar. 13, 1832. Read twice, and committed to a Committee of the Whole House to-morrow. Mr. Denny, from the Committee on Revolutionary Pensions, reported the following bill: [Washington, 1832] 1 p. (H.R. 465) DNA; MB.   15600

---- A bill granting a pension to Noah Miller, an invalid Major of the militia. Jan. 10, 1832. Read twice, and committed to a Committee of the Whole House tomorrow. Mr. Evans, of Maine, from the Committee on Invalid Pensions, reported the following bill: [Washington, 1832] 1 p. (H. R. 234) DNA; MB.   15601

---- A bill granting a pension to Wm. Scott. Jan. 23, 1832. Mr. Buckner, from the Committee on Pensions, reported the following bill; which was read, and passed to a second reading: [Washington, 1832] 1 p. (S. 71) DNA; MB.
        15602
---- A bill granting a township of land to each of the states of Indiana, Illinois, Missouri, Mississippi, and Alabama. Mar. 26, 1832. Mr. King, from the Committee on Public Lands, reported the following bill; which was read, and passed to a second reading: [Washington, 1832] 1 p. (S. 163) DNA; MB.   15603

---- A bill granting a township of the public lands in aid of the Transylvania University, in Kentucky. Jan. 4, 1832. Read twice, and committed to a Committee of the Whole House to-morrow. Mr. Allan, from the Select Committee to which the subject had been referred, reported the following bill: [Washington, 1832] 1 p. (H. R. 209) DNA; MB.   15604

---- A bill granting certain city lots to the corporation of the Columbian College, for the purposes therein mentioned. Feb. 27, 1832. Read twice, and committed to a Committee of the Whole House to-morrow. Mr. Thomas, of Maryland, from the Committee for the District of Columbia, reported the following bill: [Washington, 1832] 2 p. (H. R. 422) DNA; MB.
        15605
---- A bill granting certain city

lots to the corporation of the Columbian College, for the purposes therein mentioned. Mar. 13, 1832. Mr. Chambers, from the Committee for the District of Columbia, reported the following bill; which was read, and passed to a second reading: [Washington, 1832] 2 p. (S. 150) DNA; MB.
        15606
---- A bill granting certain lots, and parts of lots, to the Washington City Orphan Asylum. May 3, 1832. Agreeably to notice given, Mr. Chambers asked and obtained leave to bring in the following bill; which was read, and passed to a second reading: May 4, 1832. Read a second time, and referred to the Committee on the District of Columbia. May 30, 1832. Reported with an amendment viz. Strike out all the first section, after the enacting clause, and insert what follows the same in italics. [Washington, 1832] 2 p. (S. 193) DNA; MB.   15607

---- A bill granting pensions to certain invalids therein mentioned. Mar. 2, 1832. Read twice, and committed to a Committee of the Whole House to-morrow. Mr. Lansing, from the Committee on Invalid Pensions, reported the following bill: [Washington, 1832] 2 p. (H. R. 444) DNA; MB.
        15608
---- A bill granting pensions to certain invalids therein named. Feb. 15, 1832. Read twice, and committed to a Committee of the Whole House to-morrow. Mr. Burges, from the Committee on Invalid Pensions, reported the following bill: [Washington, 1832] 2 p. (H. R. 377) DNA; MB.
        15609
---- A bill granting pensions to certain persons therein named. Mar. 13, 1832. Read twice, and committed to a Committee of the Whole House to-morrow. Mr.

Denny, from the Committee on Revolutionary Pensions, reported the following bill: [Washington, 1832] 1 p. (H.R. 464) DNA; MB.
15610

---- A bill granting pensions to certain persons therein named. Mar. 13, 1832. Read twice, and committed to the Committee of the Whole House to which is committed the bill (No. 110) granting a pension to John Bradshaw. Mr. Kavanagh, from the Committee on Revolutionary Pensions, reported the following bill: [Washington, 1832] 1 p. (H.R. 462) DNA; MB.
15611

---- A bill granting pensions to certain persons therein named. Mar. 13, 1832. Read twice, and committed to the Committee of the Whole House to which is committed the bill (H.R. No. 111) granting a pension to John Farrow. Mr. Doubleday, from the Committee on Revolutionary Pensions, reported the following bill: [Washington, 1832] 1 p. (H.R. 467) DNA; MB.   15612

---- A bill granting pensions to certain persons therein named. Mar. 15, 1832. Read twice, and committed to the Committee of the Whole House to which is committed the bill (H.R. No. 351) for the relief of David Brooks. Mr. Hubbard, from the Committee on Revolutionary Pensions, reported the following bill: [Washington, 1832] 1 p. (H.R. 472) DNA; MB.
15613

---- A bill granting pensions to certain persons therein named. Mar. 26, 1832. Read twice, and committed to a Committee of the Whole House to-morrow. Mr. Denny, from the Committee on Revolutionary Pensions, reported the following bill: [Washington, 1832] 1 p. (H.R. 510) DNA; MB.
15614

---- A bill granting pensions to certain persons therein named. Mar. 26, 1832. Read twice, and committed to a Committee of the Whole House to-morrow. Mr. Kavanagh, from the Committee on Revolutionary Pensions, reported the following bill: [Washington, 1832] 1 p. (H.R. 511) DNA; MB.
15615

---- A bill granting pensions to certain Revolutionary soldiers. Jan. 10, 1832. Read twice, and committed to a Committee of the Whole House to-morrow. Mr. Hubbard, from the Committee on Revolutionary Pensions, reported the following bill: [Washington, 1832] 1 p. (H.R. 237) DNA; MB.
15616

---- A bill granting pensions to Cornelius Lambert, Abraham Hitchcock, Elnathan Weed, Moses Higgins, Abijah Holmes, Wm. Johnson, Simeon Chase, and Richard Clarke. Jan. 3, 1832. Read twice, and committed to a Committee of the Whole House to-morrow. Mr. Hubbard, from the Committee on Revolutionary Pensions, reported the following bill: [Washington, 1832] 1 p. (H.R. 193) DNA; MB.
15617

---- A bill granting pensions to Daniel Felton and Samuel Frothingham. Read twice, and committed to a Committee of the Whole House to-morrow. Mr. Mitchell, (of South Carolina), from the Committee on Revolutionary Pensions, reported the following bill: [Washington, 1832] 1 p. (H.R. 188) DNA; MB.   15618

---- A bill granting pensions to James Richmond and Abner Smith. Jan. 4, 1832. Read twice, and committed to a Committee of the Whole House to-morrow. Mr. Denny, from the Committee on Revolutionary Pensions, reported the following bill: [Washington, 1832] 1 p. (H.R. 202) DNA; MB.
15619

---- A bill granting pensions to John Boone and Elisha Hammond. Mar. 13, 1832. Read twice, and committed to the Committee of the Whole House to which is committed the bill (H.R. No. 111,) granting a pension to John Farrow. Mr. Kavanagh, from the Committee on Revolutionary Pensions, reported the following bill: [Washington, 1832] 1 p. (H.R. 463) DNA; MB. 15620

---- A bill granting pensions to John Lowell, Jacob Hiler, Ephraim Hunt, Job Phillips, and Levi Tracy. Apr. 11, 1832. Read twice, and committed to a Committee of the Whole House tomorrow. Mr. Kavanagh, from the Committee on Revolutionary Pensions, reported the following bill: [Washington, 1832] 1 p. (H.R. 542) DNA; MB. 15621

---- A bill granting pensions to John Vinyard, Wm. Howell, Abner Peebles, Jabez Hawes, Jabez Winchester, and Rufus Gibbs. Jan. 3, 1832. Read twice, and committed to a Committee of the Whole House to-morrow. Mr. Mitchell, of South Carolina, from the Committee on Revolutionary Pensions, reported the following bill: [Washington, 1832] 1 p. (H.R. 190) DNA; MB. 15622

---- A bill granting pensions to Leonard Houston and John D. Howard. Jan. 3, 1832. Read twice, and committed to a Committee of the Whole House to-morrow. Mr. Mitchell, of South Carolina, from the Committee on Revolutionary Pensions, reported the following bill: [Washington, 1832] 1 p. H.R. 189) DNA; MB. 15623

---- A bill granting pensions to Martin Parker and Wm. Brackett. Apr. 3, 1832. Read twice, and committed to a Committee of the Whole House to-morrow. Mr. Evans, of Maine, from the Committee on Invalid Pensions, reported the following bill: [Washington, 1832] 1 p. (H.R. 524) DNA; MB. 15624

---- A bill granting pensions to persons therein named. Jan. 10, 1832. Read twice, and committed to a Committee of the Whole House to-morrow. Mr. Doubleday, from the Committee on Revolutionary Pensions, reported the following bill: [Washington, 1832] 1 p. (H.R. 244) DNA; MB. 15625

---- A bill granting pensions to Wm. Cole, David Parshall, and Samuel Clark, soldiers of the revolution. May 18, 1832. Read twice, and committed to a Committee of the Whole House to-morrow. Mr. Doubleday, from the Committee on Revolutionary Pensions, reported the following bill: [Washington, 1832] 1 p. (H.R. 580) DNA; MB. 15626

---- A bill granting pensions to Winthrop Davis, Simeon Bullock, Nelson Miller, James Mitchell, Oliver May, Jonathan Pearce, and Joshua Crosby. Jan. 3, 1832. Read twice, and committed to a Committee of the Whole House to-morrow. Mr. Hubbard, from the Committee on Revolutionary Pensions, reported the following bill: [Washington, 1832] 1 p. (H.R. 194) DNA; MB. 15627

---- A bill granting to John B. Chandonai a section of land. May 4, 1832. Mr. White, from the Committee on Indian Affairs, reported the following bill; which was read, and passed to a second reading: [Washington, 1832] 1 p. (S. 196) DNA; MB. 15628

---- A bill granting to Middleton McKay, a section of land in lieu of the reservation given him by the treaty of Dancing Rabbit Creek. Jan. 10, 1832. Mr. King, from the Committee on Public Lands, reported the following bill; which was read, and passed to a second reading: [Washington, 1832] 1 p. (S. 55) DNA; MB.   15629

---- A bill granting to the borough of Michillimakinac certain grounds for public purposes. July 6, 1832. Read twice, and committed to the Committee of the Whole House to which is committed the bill (H.R. No. 545) for the exchange of public grounds at Prairie du Chien, in the territory of Michigan. Mr. Irvin, from the Committee on Public Lands, reported the following bill: [Washington, 1832] 2 p. (H.R. 609) MB.   15630

---- A bill granting to the Territory of Arkansas, one thousand acres of land, for the erection of a court-house and jail at Little Rock. Jan. 10, 1832. Mr. King, from the Committee on Public Lands, reported the following bill; which was read, and passed to a second reading: [Washington, 1832] 1 p. (S. 54) DNA; MB.
15631

---- A bill in addition to an act, entitled "An act for the relief of certain insolvent debtors of the United States." Jan. 25, 1832. Read twice, and postponed until Monday next. Mr. Ellsworth, from the Committee on the Judiciary, reported the following bill: [Washington, 1832] 1 p. (H.R. 313) DNA; MB.   15632

---- A bill in addition to an act, entitled "An act to provide for certain persons engaged in the land and naval service of the United States in the revolutionary war," approved Mar. 18, 1818. As amended and reported from the Committee of the Whole House

on the 12th April, 1832. [Washington, 1832] 7 p. (H.R. 157) DNA; MB.   15633

---- A bill in addition to the "Act for the gradual improvement of the navy of the United States." Dec. 16, 1832. Read twice, and committed to a Committee of the Whole House on the state of the Union. Mr. Anderson, from the Committee on Naval Affairs, reported the following bill: [Washington, 1832] 2 p. (H.R. 622) DNA; MB.   15634

---- A bill in addition to the several acts regulating the intercourse with the Indian tribes. Mar. 17, 1832. Read twice, and committed to a committee of the Whole House to-morrow. Mr. Bell, from the Committee on Indian Affairs, reported the following bill: [Washington, 1832] 4 p. (H.R. 483) DNA; MB.   15635

---- A bill in aid of an act, entitled "An act for the relief of James Barnett." Jan. 6, 1832. Read twice, and committed to a Committee of the Whole House to-morrow. Mr. Standifer, from the Committee on Revolutionary Claims, reported the following bill: [Washington, 1832] 1 p. (H.R. 215) DNA; MB.   15636

---- A bill in relation to the Penitentiary for the District of Columbia. Mar. 30, 1832. Read twice, and committed to a Committee of the Whole House to-morrow. Mr. Washington, from the Committee for the District of Columbia, reported the following bill: [Washington, 1832] 1 p. (H.R. 519) DNA; MB.   15637

---- A bill increasing the pension of William McMillan, a Lieut. in the army of the revolution. Jan. 10, 1832. Read twice, and committed to a Committee of the Whole House to-morrow. Mr. Denny, from the Committee on Revolutionary Pensions, reported the following bill: [Washington, 1832] 1 p. (H.R. 226) DNA; MB. 15638

---- A bill making an additional appropriation for arming and equipping the whole body of the militia of the United States. Jan. 10, 1832. Read twice, and committed to a Committee of the Whole House to-morrow. Mr. Drayton, from the Committee on Military Affairs, reported the following bill: [Washington, 1832] 1 p. (H.R. 242) DNA; MB. 15639

---- A bill making an appropriation for a custom-house in the city of New York. Mar. 19, 1832. Read twice, and committed to the Committee of the Whole House on the state of the Union. Mr. Cambreleng, from the Committee on Commerce, reported the following bill: [Washington, 1832] 1 p. (H.R. 490) DNA; MB. 15640

---- A bill making an appropriation for a marine hospital at Portland, in Maine. May 7, 1832. Read twice, and committed to the Committee of the Whole House on the state of the Union. Mr. Cambreleng, from the Committee on Commerce, reported the following bill: [Washington, 1832] 1 p. (H.R. 563) DNA; MB. 15641

---- A bill making an appropriation for a marine hospital on Beacon Island, in North Carolina. Mar. 19, 1832. Read twice, and committed to the Committee of the Whole House on the state of the Union. Mr. Cambreleng, from the Committee on Commerce, reported the following bill: [Washington, 1832] 1 p. (H.R. 491) DNA; MB. 15642

---- A bill making an appropriation for carrying into effect the second article of the treaty of Fort Wilkinson. Jan. 30, 1832. Read twice, and committed to a Committee of the Whole House, to-morrow. Mr. Wilde, from the Committee of Ways and Means, reported the following bill: [Washington, 1832] 1 p. (H.R. 331) DNA; MB. 15643

---- A bill making an appropriation for the collection of American State Papers. Mar. 1, 1832. Read twice, and committed to the Committee of the Whole House on the state of the Union. Mr. Edward Everett, from the Committee on Foreign Affairs, reported the following bill: [Washington, 1832] 1 p. (H.R. 436) DNA; MB. 15644

---- A bill making an appropriation for the publication of certain diplomatic correspondence. Mar. 9, 1832. Read twice, and committed to the Committee of the Whole House on the state of the Union. Mr. Verplanck, from the Joint Library Committee, reported the following bill: [Washington, 1832] 1 p. (H.R. 457) DNA; MB. 15645

---- A bill making an appropriation to complete the new building for the mint establishment. May 26, 1832. Read twice, and committed to the Committee of the Whole House on the state of the Union. Mr. McDuffie, from the Committee of Ways and Means, reported the following bill: [Washington, 1832] 1 p. (H.R. 588) DNA; MB. 15646

---- A bill making an appropriation to complete the road leading from Fooy's opposite Memphis, in the state of Tennessee, to Little Rock, in the territory of Arkansas. Jan. 10, 1832. Read twice, and committed to the Committee

of the Whole House, to which is committed the bill No. 165, to authorize the surveying and making a road from La Plaisance Bay, in the territory of Michigan, to intersect the Chicago road. Mr. Letcher, from the Committee on Internal Improvements, reported the following bill: [Washington, 1832] 2 p. (H.R. 245) DNA; MB.
15647

---- A bill making an appropriation to procure copies of historical documents from the public offices in Great Britain. Jan. 25, 1832. Read twice, and committed to the Committee of the Whole House on the state of the Union. Mr. E. Everett, from the Committee on the Library, reported the following bill: [Washington, 1832] 1 p. (H.R. 317) DNA; MB.
15648

---- A bill making an appropriation towards the expense of laying out and opening a military road, from Fort Howard, at Green Bay, to Fort Crawford, on the Mississippi. Jan. 16, 1832. Read twice, and committed to a Committee of the Whole House tomorrow. Mr. Drayton, from the Committee on Military Affairs, reported the following bill: [Washington, 1832] 1 p. (H.R. 268) DNA; MB.
15649

---- A bill making appropriations for building light-houses, light-boats, beacons, and monuments, and placing buoys. May 9, 1832. Read twice, and committed to the Committee of the Whole House on the state of the Union. Mr. Newton, from the Committee on Commerce, reported the following bill: [Washington, 1832] 6 p. (H.R. 567) DNA; MB.
15650

---- A bill making appropriations for carrying on the fortifications of the United States during the year eighteen hundred and thirty-three. Dec. 18, 1832. Read twice, and committed to a Committee of the Whole House on the state of the Union. Mr. Verplanck, from the Committee of Ways and Means, reported the following bill: [Washington, 1832] 2 p. (H.R. 625) MB.
15651

---- A bill making appropriations for certain internal improvements for the year one thousand eight hundred and thirty-two. January 16, 1832. Read twice, and committed to the Committee of the Whole House on the state of the Union. Mr. McDuffie, from the Committee of Ways and Means, reported the following bill: [Washington, 1832] 2 p. (H.R. 267) DNA; MB.
15652

---- A bill making appropriations for certain internal improvements for the year one thousand eight hundred and thirty-two. May 3, 1832. The House having resolved itself into a Committee of the Whole House on the state of the Union, and having under consideration the bill making appropriations for certain internal improvements for the year one thousand eight hundred and thirty-two, Mr. Taylor reported the same with amendments. [Washington, 1832] 7 p. (H.R. 267) DNA; MB.
15653

---- A bill making appropriations for certain internal improvements for the year one thousand eight hundred and thirty-two. May 5, 1832. The House having resolved itself into a Committee of the Whole House on the state of the Union, and having under consideration the bill making appropriations for certain internal improvements for the year one thousand eight hundred and thirty-two, Mr. Taylor reported the same with amendments. [Washington, 1832] 6 p. (H.R. 267)

DNA; MB.   15654

---- A bill making appropriations
for Indian annuities, and other
similar objects, for the year one
thousand eight hundred and thirty-
two, Feb. 27, 1832. Read twice,
and committed to the Whole House
on the state of the Union. Mr.
McDuffie, from the Committee of
Ways and Means, reported the
following bill: [Washington, 1832]
6 p. (H.R. 417) DNA; MB.
15655

---- A bill making appropriations
for Indian annuities, and other
similar objects, for the year one
thousand eight hundred and thirty-
three. Dec. 22, 1832. Read
twice, and committed to a Committee of the Whole House on the
state of the Union. Mr. Verplanck, from the Committee of
Ways and Means, reported the
following bill: [Washington, 1832]
6 p. (H.R. 637) MB.   15656

---- A bill making appropriations
for the engineer and ordnance departments. Jan. 10, 1832. Read
twice, and committed to the Committee of the Whole House on the
state of the Union. Mr. Drayton,
from the Committee on Military
Affairs, reported the following
bill: [Washington, 1832] 3 p.
(H.R. 224) DNA; MB.   15657

---- A bill making appropriations
for the Indian department for the
year one thousand eight hundred
and thirty-three. Dec. 19, 1832.
Read twice, and committed to a
Committee of Ways and Means,
reported the following bill:
[Washington, 1832] 2 p. (H.R.
630) MB.   15658

---- A bill making appropriations
for the naval service for the year
one thousand eight hundred and
thirty-two. Jan. 6, 1832. Read
twice, and committed to the Com-

mittee of the Whole House on the
state of the Union. Mr. McDuffie, from the Committee of Ways
and Means, reported the following bill: [Washington, 1832] 4 p.
(H.R. 223) DNA; MB.   15659

---- A bill making appropriations
for the public buildings, and for
other purposes. Feb. 17, 1832.
Read twice, and committed to a
Committee of the Whole House to-
morrow. Mr. Jarvis, from the
Committee on the Public Buildings, reported the following bill:
[Washington, 1832] 1 p. (H.R.
394) DNA; MB.   15660

---- A bill making appropriations
for the revolutionary and other
pensioners of the United States,
for the year one thousand eight
hundred and thirty-three. Dec.
27, 1832. Read twice, and committed to a Committee of the
Whole House on the state of the
Union. Mr. Verplanck, from the
Committee of Ways and Means, reported the following bill: [Washing-
ton, 1832] 1 p. (H.R. 642) MB.
15661

---- A bill making appropriations
in conformity with the stipulations
of certain Indian treaties. Mar. 23,
1832. Read twice, and committed
to the Committee of the Whole House
on the state of the Union. Mr. Verplanck, from the Committee of
Ways and Means, reported the following bill: [Washington, 1832] 2 p.
(H.R. 505) DNA; MB.   15662

---- A bill making appropriations
in conformity with the stipulations
of certain treaties with the Creeks,
Shawnees, Ottoways, Senecas,
Wyandots, Cherokees, and Choctaws. May 9, 1832. Read twice,
and committed to the Committee
of the Whole House on the State of
the Union. Mr. Verplanck from
the Committee of Ways and Means,
reported the following bill: [Wash-

ington, 1832] 5 p. (H. R. 566)
DNA; MB.   15663

---- A bill making appropriations, in part, for the support of
government for the year one thousand eight hundred and thirty-
three, and for certain expenditures of the year one thousand
eight hundred and thirty-two.
Dec. 17, 1832. Read twice, and
committed to a Committee of the
Whole House on the state of the
Union. Mr. Verplanck, from the
Committee of Ways and Means,
reported the following bill: [Wash-
ington, 1832] 2 p. (H. R. 621)
MB.   15664

---- A bill making appropriations
to employ additional clerks in the
Surveyor General's Offices in
Mississippi and Missouri. Mar.
20, 1832. Mr. Ellis, from the
Committee on Public Lands, reported the following bill; which
was read, and passed to a second
reading: [Washington, 1832] 1 p.
(S. 156) DNA; MB.   15665

---- A bill making further provision for the Military Academy at
West Point. Jan. 5, 1832. Read
twice, and committed to the Committee of the Whole House on the
state of the Union. Mr. Drayton,
from the Committee on Military
Affairs, reported the following
bill: [Washington, 1832] 3 p. (H. R.
212) DNA; MB.   15666

---- A bill making provision for
inscribing the names of certain
persons on the invalid pension
roll. Feb. 2, 1832. Read twice,
and committed to a Committee of
the Whole House to-morrow. Mr.
Burges, from the Committee on
Invalid Pensions, reported the following bill: [Washington, 1832]
2 p. (H. R. 344) DNA; MB.
                                15667
---- A bill making provision for

the sale and disposition of the
public grounds in the cities of St.
Augustine and Pensacola, and to
reserve certain lots and buildings
for public purposes, and to provide for their repairs and preservation. Feb. 21, 1832. Read twice,
and committed to the Committee
of the Whole House on the state
of the Union. Mr. Wickliffe, from
the Committee on the Public
Lands, reported the following
bill: [Washington, 1832] 3 p.
(H. R. 405) DNA; MB.   15668

---- A bill providing for a deficit of appropriation therein mentioned. Apr. 9, 1832. Read twice,
and committed to the Committee
of the Whole House on the state
of the Union. Mr. Archer, from
the Committee on Foreign Affairs,
reported the following bill:
[Washington, 1832] 1 p. (H. R.
537) DNA; MB.   15669

---- A bill providing for the appointment of a recorder of the
General Land Office, and prescribing the mode by which patents for
public lands shall be executed,
granted, and issued. Jan. 27,
1832. Mr. King, from the Committee on Public Lands, reported
the following bill; which was read,
and passed to a second reading.
[Washington, 1832] 2 p. (S. 83)
DNA; MB.   15670

---- A bill providing for the establishment of a surveyor general's office in certain states and
territories. Mar. 16, 1832. Read
twice, and committed to the Committee of the Whole House on the
state of the Union. Mr. Duncan,
from the Committee on the Public
Lands, reported the following bill:
[Washington, 1832] 1 p. (H. R.
478) DNA; MB.   15671

---- A bill providing for the
more speedy administration of

justice within the District of Columbia. Jan. 27, 1832. Read twice, and committed to a Committee of the Whole House tomorrow. Mr. Doddridge, from the Committee for the District of Columbia, reported the following bill: [Washington, 1832] 31 p. (H. R. 325) DNA; MB. 15672

---- A bill providing for the postponement of the trial of certain cases now pending in the Superior Courts of Arkansas Territory, and for withholding from sale or entry certain lands in said territory. Mar. 30, 1832. Read the first and second time, and postponed until Monday next, Mr. Foster, from the committee on the Judiciary, reported the following bill: [Washington, 1832] 1 p. (H. R. 518) DNA; MB. 15673

---- A bill providing for the publication of a stereotype edition of the laws. Jan. 4, 1832. Read twice, and committed to a Committee of the Whole House to-morrow. Mr. White, of Louisiana, from the Committee on the Judiciary, reported the following bill: [Washington, 1832] 2 p. (H. R. 207) DNA; MB. 15674

---- A bill providing for the publication of a stereotype edition of the laws. Jan. 30, 1832. Mr. Robbins, from the Committee on the Library, reported the following bill; which was read, and passed to a second reading: [Washington, 1832] 1 p. (S. 86) DNA; MB. 15675

---- A bill providing for the purchase of one hundred copies of the American Annual Register. Jan. 19, 1832. Mr. Robbins, from the Committee on the Library of Congress, reported the following bill; which was read, and passed to a second reading: [Washington, 1832] 1 p. (S. 65) DNA; MB. 15676

---- A bill providing for the settlement of the accounts of certain diplomatic functionaries. Mar. 1, 1832. Read twice, and committed to the Committee of the Whole House on the state of the Union. Mr. Edward Everett, from the committee on Foreign Affairs, reported the following bill: [Washington, 1832] 2 p. (H. R. 437) DNA; MB. 15677

---- A bill regulating the commencement of invalid pensions. Jan. 19, 1832. Read twice, and committed to a Committee of the Whole House to-morrow. Mr. Burges, from the Committee on Invalid Pensions, reported the following bill: [Washington, 1832] 1 p. (H. R. 289) DNA; MB. 15678

---- A bill relating to the Orphans' Courts within the District of Columbia. Jan. 27, 1832. Read twice, and committed to a Committee of the Whole House to-morrow. Mr. Doddridge, from the Committee for the District of Columbia, reported the following bill: [Washington, 1832] 1 p. (H. R. 324) DNA; MB. 15679

---- A bill relative to naval schools. Jan. 24, 1832. Read twice, and committed to a Committee of the Whole House to-morrow. Mr. Watmough, from the Committee on Naval Affairs, reported the following bill: [Washington, 1832] 1 p. (H. R. 305) DNA; MB. 15680

---- A bill repealing a part of the fifth section of the act, entitled "An act to establish ports of delivery at Port Pontchartrain and Delaware city, and for other purposes." May 10, 1832. Read twice, and ordered to be engrossed, and read the third time to-morrow. Mr. Jarvis, from the Committee on Commerce, reported the follow-

ing bill: [Washington, 1832] 1 p.
(H. R. 569) DNA; MB.   15681

---- A bill restoring certain persons therein named to the list of
revolutionary pensioners. Mar.
12, 1832. Read twice, and committed to the Committee of the
Whole House to which is committed the bill (H. R. No. 110,)
granting a pension to John Bradshaw. Mr. Hubbard, from the
Committee on Revolutionary Pensions, reported the following bill:
[Washington, 1832] 1 p. (H. R.
460) DNA; MB.   15682

---- A bill restoring Lothario
Donaldson and Godman Noble, to
the list of revolutionary pensioners. Mar. 15, 1832. Read twice,
and committed to the Committee
of the Whole House to which is
committed the bill (H. R. No.
351) for the relief of David
Brooks. Mr. Hubbard, from the
Committee on Revolutionary Pensions, reported the following bill:
[Washington, 1832] 1 p. (H. R.
473) DNA; MB.   15683

---- A bill restoring the name of
Isaac Moore to the list of revolutionary pensioners. May 17,
1832. Read twice, and committed
to a Committee of the Whole
House to-morrow. Mr. Hubbard,
from the Committee on Revolutionary Pensions, reported the
following bill: [Washington, 1832]
1 p. (H. R. 578) DNA; MB.
                          15684
---- A bill restoring the names
of certain persons therein named
to the list of revolutionary pensioners. Mar. 26, 1832. Read
twice, and committed to a Committee of the Whole House to-
morrow. Mr. Kavanagh, from the
Committee on Revolutionary Pensions, reported the following bill:
[Washington, 1832] 1 p. (H. R.
512) DNA; MB.   15685

---- A bill restoring the names
of David Harsom, Hiram Huntington, and Eleazer Owen, to the
list of revolutionary pensioners.
Apr. 11, 1832. Read twice, and
committed to a Committee of the
Whole House to-morrow. Mr.
Kavanagh, from the Committee
on Revolutionary Pensions, reported the following bill: [Wash-
ington, 1832] 1 p. (H. R. 543)
DNA; MB.   15686

---- A bill restoring Thos. S.
Luther and John Eisler to the
list of revolutionary pensioners.
Mar. 26, 1832. Read twice, and
committed to a Committee of the
Whole House to-morrow. Mr.
Hubbard, from the Committee on
Revolutionary Pensions, reported
the following bill: [Washington,
1832] 1 p. (H. R. 513) DNA; MB.
                          15687
---- A bill restoring to the list
of revolutionary pensioners certain persons therein named. Mar.
13, 1832. Read twice, and committed to the Committee of the
Whole House, to which is committed the bill (H. R. No. 111) granting a pension to John Farrow.
Mr. Hubbard, from the Committee on Revolutionary Pensions,
reported the following bill:
[Washington, 1832] 1 p. (H. R.
466) DNA; MB.   15688

---- A bill restoring to the list
of revolutionary pensioners Jonas
Youmans, of New York. Mar. 19,
1832. Read twice, and committed
to a committee of the Whole
House to-morrow. Mr. Hubbard,
from the Committee on Revolutionary Pensions, reported the
following bill: [Washington, 1832]
1 p. (H. R. 496) DNA; MB.
                          15689
---- A bill restoring to the pension list Samuel Young and Solomon Mills, and granting a pension to Moses Sherwood. Feb. 18,

1832. Read twice, and committed to the Committee of the Whole House, to which is referred the bill H.R. No. 110, granting a pension to John Bradshaw. Mr. Hubbard, from the Committee on Revolutionary Pensions, reported the following bill: [Washington, 1832] 1 p. (H.R. 397) DNA; MB. 15690

---- A bill supplemental to the act "Granting certain relinquished and unappropriated lands to the state of Alabama, for the purpose of improving the navigation of the Tennessee, Coosa, Cahaba, and Black Warrior rivers," approved the twenty-third day of May, one thousand eight hundred and twenty-eight. May 18, 1832. Mr. Hendricks, from the Committee on Roads and Canals, reported the following bill; which was read, and passed to a second reading: [Washington, 1832] 1 p. (S. 201) DNA; MB. 15691

---- A bill supplemental to the act "Granting the right of preemption to settlers on the public lands," approved the twenty-ninth day of May, eighteen hundred and thirty. Jan. 10, 1832. Mr. King, from the Committee on Public Lands, reported the following bill; which was read, and passed to a second reading: [Washington, 1832] 2 p. (S. 56) DNA; MB. 15692

---- A bill supplementary to an act, entitled "An act for the relief of Garriques Flaujac, of Louisiana," approved on the twentieth May, one thousand eight hundred and twenty-six. Feb. 6, 1832. Read twice, and committed to a Committee on the Whole House to-morrow. Mr. Bullard, from the Committee on Private Land Claims, reported the following bill: [Washington, 1832] 1 p. (H.R. 348) DNA; MB. 15693

---- A bill supplementary to an act, entitled "An act more effectually to provide for the punishment of certain crimes against the United States, and for other purposes," passed on the third day of March, one thousand eight hundred and twenty-five. Apr. 18, 1832. Agreeably to notice given, Mr. Dallas asked and obtained leave to bring in the following bill; which was read twice, and referred to the Committee on the Judiciary. Apr. 27, 1832. Reported with the following amendment, viz. Strike out the first section, after the enacting clause, and insert what follows in italics. [Washington, 1832] 3 p. (S. 182) DNA; MB. 15694

---- A bill supplementary to "An act to incorporate the trustees of the Female Orphan Asylum of Georgetown, and the Washington City Asylum, in the District of Columbia. Apr. 9, 1832. Read twice, and committed to a Committee of the Whole House to-morrow. Mr. Washington, from the Committee for the District of Columbia, reported the following bill: [Washington, 1832] 3 p. (H.R. 538) DNA; MB. 15695

---- A bill supplementary to the act authorizing the territory of Florida to open canals between Chipola river and St. Andrew's Bay, and from Matanzas to Halifax river, in said territory, approved March second, one thousand eight hundred and thirty-two. Apr. 13, 1832. Agreeably to notice given, Mr. Johnson asked and obtained leave to bring in the following bill; which was read twice, and referred to the Committee on Roads and Canals. Apr. 24, 1832. Reported the following amendments ... [Washington, 1832] 3 p. (S. 176) DNA; MB. 15696

---- A bill supplementary to the act, entitled "An act to authorize the President of the United States to run and mark a line, dividing the Territory of Florida from the state of Georgia." Jan. 6, 1832. Read twice, and committed to a Committee of the Whole House to-morrow. Mr. Davis, of South Carolina, from the Committee on the Judiciary, reported the following bill: [Washington, 1832] 2 p. (H.R. 221) MB.   15697

---- A bill supplementary to the acts to promote the progress of the useful arts. Mar. 9, 1832. Mr. Marcy, from the Committee on the Judiciary, reported the following bill; which was read, and passed to a second reading: [Washington, 1832] 2 p. (S. 142) DNA; MB.   15698

---- A bill supplementary to the several acts making appropriation for the civil and military service during the year one thousand eight hundred and thirty-two. June 27, 1832. Read twice, and committed to the Committee of the Whole House on the state of the Union. Mr. Verplanck, from the Committee of Ways and Means, reported the following bill: [Washington, 1832] 3 p. (H.R. 601) DNA; MB.
                    15699
---- A bill to abolish imprisonment for debt. Jan. 17, 1832. Read twice, and committed to a Committee of the Whole House to-morrow. Mr. R. M. Johnson, from the Select Committee, to which the subject had been referred, reported the following bill: [Washington, 1832] 4 p. (H.R. 279) DNA; MB.   15700

---- A bill to add a part of the southern to the northern district of Alabama. Jan. 4, 1832. Read the first and second time, and ordered to be engrossed, and

read the third time to-morrow. Mr. Foster, from the Committee on the Judiciary, reported the following bill: [Washington, 1832] 1 p. (H.R. 206) DNA; MB.
                    15701
---- A bill to aid in the education of deaf and dumb persons. Feb. 17, 1832. Read twice, and committed to a Committee of the Whole House to-morrow. Mr. Irvin, from the Committee on the Public Lands, reported the following bill: [Washington, 1832] 1 p. (H.R. 392) DNA; MB.
                    15702
---- A bill to aid the vestry of Washington parish in the erection of a keeper's house, and the improvement and security of the ground, allotted for the interment of members of Congress, and other public officers. Feb. 7, 1832. Read twice, and committed to a Committee of the Whole House to-morrow. Mr. Washington from the Committee for the District of Columbia, reported the following bill: [Washington, 1832] 1 p. (H.R. 357) DNA; MB.   15703

---- A bill to alter and amend the several acts imposing duties on imports. May 23, 1832. Read twice, and committed to the Committee of the Whole House on the state of the Union. Mr. Adams, from the Committee on Manufactures, reported the following bill: [Washington, 1832] 19 p. (H.R. 584) DNA; MB.   15704

---- A bill to alter and amend the several acts imposing duties on imports. May 23, 1832. Reported by the Committee on Manufactures. June 21, 1832. Reported to the House with amendments, and ordered to be printed as amended. [Washington, 1832] 21 p. (H.R. 584) MB.   15705

---- A bill to alter and amend

the several acts imposing duties on imports. June 27, 1832. Printed, ordered to be engrossed, and read a third time to-morrow at 12 o'clock. [Washington, 1832] 20 p. (H.R. 584) MB. 15706

---- A bill to alter the place of holding the circuit and district courts of the United States for the Delaware district. May 14, 1832. Read twice, and ordered to be engrossed, and read the third time to-morrow. Mr. Ellsworth, from the Committee on the Judiciary, reported the following bill: [Washington, 1832] 1 p. (H.R. 573) DNA; MB. 15707

---- A bill to alter the times of holding the district court of the United States for the state of Illinois. Feb. 14, 1832. Mr. Marcy, from the Committee on the Judiciary, reported the following bill; which was read, and passed to a second reading: [Washington, 1832] 1 p. (S. 112) DNA; MB. 15708

---- A bill to amend an act entitled "An act fixing the compensation of public ministers, and of consuls residing on the coast of Barbary, and for other purposes." Feb. 27, 1832. Read twice, and committed to the Committee of the Whole House on the state of the Union. Mr. Archer, from the Committee on Foreign Affairs, reported the following bill: [Washington, 1832] 3 p. (H.R. 416) DNA; MB. 15709

---- A bill to amend an act entitled "An act for the better organization of the district courts of the United States within the state of Alabama," approved tenth March, eighteen hundred and twenty-four. June 8, 1832. Mr. Marcy, from the Committee on the Judiciary, reported the following bill; which was read, and

passed to a second reading: [Washington, 1832] 4 p. (S. 207) DNA; MB. 15710

---- A bill to amend an act, entitled "An act for the relief of purchasers of the public lands that have reverted for non-payment of the purchase money," passed twenty-third day of May, one thousand eight hundred and twenty-eight. [Washington, 1832] 3 p. (H.R. 281) DNA; MB. 15711

---- A bill to amend an act entitled "An act for the relief of purchasers of the public lands that have reverted for non-payment of the purchase money," passed twenty-third day of May, one thousand eight hundred and twenty-eight. Mar. 22, 1832. Mr. Tipton, from the Committee on Public Lands, reported the following bill; which was read, and passed to a second reading: [Washington, 1832] 3 p. (S. 158) DNA; MB. 15712

---- A bill to amend an act, entitled "An act to alter and amend an act to set apart and dispose of certain public lands for the encouragement of the cultivation of the vine and olive," approved nineteenth February, one thousand eight hundred and thirty-one. Feb. 6, 1832. Read twice, and committed to a Committee of the Whole House to-morrow. Mr. Mardis, from the Committee on Private Land Claims, reported the following bill: [Washington, 1832] 2 p. (H.R. 350) DNA; MB. 15713

---- A bill to amend an act, entitled "An act to authorize the state of Tennessee to issue grants and perfect titles to certain lands therein described, and to settle the claims to the vacant and unappropriated lands within the same," approved the eighteenth of April,

388 United States

one thousand eight hundred and
six. Jan. 24, 1832. Mr. Wickliffe, from the Committee on the
Public Lands, reported the following bill: [Washington, 1832]
2 p. (H.R. 308) DNA; MB.
15714
---- A bill to amend an act, entitled "An act to enlarge the
powers of the several Corporations of the District of Columbia." Feb. 7, 1832. Read twice,
and committed to a Committee of
the Whole House to-morrow, Mr.
McCoy, from the Committee for
the District of Columbia, reported the following bill: [Washington,
1832] 1 p. (H.R. 357) DNA; MB.
15715
---- A bill to amend an act, entitled "An act to grant a quantity
of land to the state of Illinois,
for the purpose of aiding in opening a canal to connect the waters
of the Illinois river with those of
Lake Michigan." Jan. 18, 1832.
Agreeably to notice given, Mr.
Robinson asked and obtained leave
to bring in the following bill;
which was read twice, and referred to the Committee on Roads
and Canals. Jan. 20, 1832. Reported without amendment. [Wash-
ington, 1832] 1 p. (S. 64). DNA;
MB.   15716

---- A bill to amend and consoli-
date the several acts of Congress
upon the subject of naturalization.
Feb. 9, 1832. Read twice and
committed to a Committee of the
Whole House to-morrow. Mr.
Davis, of South Carolina, from
the Committee on the Judiciary,
reported the following bill:
[Washington, 1832] 3 p. (H.R.
363) DNA; MB.   15717

---- A bill to amend the act entitled "An act to provide for miti-
gating or remitting the forfeitures,
penalties, and disabilities, accruing in certain cases therein men-

tioned." Mar. 2, 1832. Read
twice, and committed to a Committee of the Whole House to-
morrow. Mr. Beardsley, from
the Committee of the Judiciary,
reported the following bill:
[Washington, 1832] 2 p. (H.R.
442) DNA; MB.   15718

---- A bill to amend the act re-
linquishing the reversionary interest of the United States to certain
Indian reservations. Jan. 30,
1832. Read, and passed to a second reading. Jan. 31, 1832. Read
the second time, and referred to
the Committee on Public Lands.
Feb. 6, 1832. Reported without
amendment. [Washington, 1832]
1 p. (S. 89) DNA; MB.   15719

---- A bill to amend the charter
of Alexandria. Mar. 6, 1832.
Read twice, and committed to a
Committee of the Whole House
to-morrow. Mr. Washington,
from the Committee for the District of Columbia, reported the
following bill: [Washington, 1832]
2 p. (H.R. 446) DNA; MB.
15720
---- A bill to amend the several
acts establishing a territorial government in Florida. Jan. 10,
1832. Read the first and second
time, and ordered to be engrossed,
and read the third time to-morrow, Mr. Creighton, from the
Committee on the territories, reported the following bill: [Wash-
ington, 1832] 1 p. (H.R. 241)
DNA; MB.   15721

---- A bill to amend the several
acts for the establishment of a
territorial government in Florida.
May 18, 1832. Read twice, and
ordered to be engrossed, and
read the third time to-morrow.
Mr. Davis, of South Carolina,
from the Committee on the Judiciary, reported the following bill:
[Washington, 1832] 3 p. (H.R.

581) DNA; MB.   15722

---- A bill to appropriate, for a limited time, the proceeds of the sales of the Public Lands of the United States. Apr. 16, 1832. Mr. Clay, from the Committee of Manufactures, to whom the subject was referred by a resolution of the Senate of the twenty-second ultimo, reported the following bill; which was read, and laid on the table. [Washington, 1832] 3 p. (S. 179) DNA; MB.   15723

---- A bill to ascertain the losses at Detroit and the adjacent country during the late war. Mar. 17, 1832. Read twice, and committed to the Committee of the Whole House on the state of the Union. Mr. Johnson, of Kentucky, from the select committee to which the subject had been referred, reported the following bill: [Washington, 1832] 2 p. (H.R. 489) DNA; MB.   15724

---- A bill to authorize a court to be held at the Soult de St. Marie, in the territory of Michigan. Feb. 9, 1832. Read twice, and committed to a Committee of the Whole House to-morrow. Mr. Davis, of South Carolina, from the Committee on the Judiciary, reported the following bill: [Washington, 1832] 1 p. (H.R. 362) DNA; MB.
                                    15725
---- A bill to authorize a subscription to the stock of the Alexandria Canal Company. Mar. 30, 1832. Read twice, and committed to the Committee of the Whole House to which is committed the bill (No. 506) to erect a bridge and aqueduct over the Potomac river, at Georgetown. Mr. Mercer, from the Committee on Internal Improvements, reported the following bill: [Washington, 1832] 1 p. (H.R. 520) DNA; MB.
                                    15726
---- An act to authorize a sub-

scription to the stock of the Alexandrea Canal Company. May 26, 1832. Read twice, and referred to the Committee on the District of Columbia. [Washington, 1832] 1 p. (H.R. 520) DNA; MB.
                                    15727
---- A bill to authorize and empower the Secretary of War to enter into a compromise to secure to the United States a title, in fee simple, to an island in the state of Delaware, upon which Fort Delaware has been erected. Feb. 1, 1832. Read twice, and committed to the Committee of the Whole House on the state of the Union. Mr. Drayton, from the Committee on Military Affairs, reported the following bill: [Washington, 1832] 2 p. (H.R. 338) DNA; MB.
                                    15728
---- A bill to authorize and empower the Secretary of War to enter into a compromise to secure to the United States a title, in fee simple, to an island in the state of Delaware, upon which Fort Delaware has been erected. Mar. 1, 1832. Agreeably to notice given, Mr. Kane asked and obtained leave to bring in the following bill; which was read, and passed to a second reading. Mar. 2, 1832. Read the second time, and referred to the Committee on the Judiciary. Apr. 12, 1832. Reported without amendment. [Washington, 1832] 2 p. (S. 131) DNA; MB.   15729

---- A bill to authorize and require the proper accounting officers of the treasury to audit and settle the claims of citizens of Georgia founded upon depredations committed by the Creek tribe of Indians on the property of said citizens, between the years one thousand eight hundred and twenty-six and one thousand eight hundred and thirty. Feb. 20, 1832. Read twice, and committed to a

Committee of the Whole House
to-morrow. Mr. Thompson, of
Georgia, from the Committee on
Indian Affairs, reported the following bill: [Washington, 1832]
1 p. (H.R. 397) DNA; MB.
                                15730
---- A bill to authorize the county commissioners for the county
of Peoria, in the state of Illinois,
to enter a fractional quarter section of land for a seat of justice,
and for other purposes. Jan. 17,
1832. Read twice, and committed
to a Committee of the Whole
House to-morrow. Mr. Irvin,
from the Committee on Public
Lands, reported the following
bill: [Washington, 1832] 1 p.
(H.R. 282) DNA; MB.   15731

---- A bill to authorize the disposition of the fund arising from
the sale of a quarter section of
land, reserved for the use of
schools, in Florida. Jan. 13,
1832. Read twice, and committed
to a Committee of the Whole
House to-morrow. Mr. Clay,
from the Committee on the Public Lands, reported the following
bill: [Washington, 1832] 2 p.
(H.R. 259) DNA; MB.   15732

---- A bill to authorize the governor of the territory of Arkansas to select ten sections of land,
granted to said territory for the
purpose of building a legislative
house for said territory, and for
other purposes. Apr. 17, 1832.
Read twice, and ordered to be
engrossed, and read the third
time to-morrow. Mr. Duncan,
from the Committee on the Public
Lands, reported the following bill:
[Washington, 1832] 1 p. (H.R.
549) DNA; MB.   15733

---- A bill to authorize the issuing a warrant to Archibald Jackson, for the bounty land due to
James Gammons, a soldier in the

late war. Jan. 13, 1832. Read
twice, and committed to a Committee of the Whole House to-
morrow. Mr. Marshall, from the
Committee on Private Land
Claims, reported the following
bill: [Washington, 1832] 1 p.
(H.R. 261) DNA; MB.   15734

---- A bill to authorize the
judges of the courts of the United
States to take bail of the claimants of property seized, and perform other acts, in vacation. Jan.
25, 1832. Mr. Marcy, from the
Committee on the Judiciary, reported the following bill; which
was read, and passed to a second
reading: [Washington, 1832] 4 p.
(S. 79) DNA; MB.   15735

---- A bill to authorize the legal
representatives of the Marquis de
Maison Rouge, and those claiming
under him, to institute a suit
against the United States, and for
other purposes. Jan. 12, 1832.
Read twice, and committed to a
Committee of the Whole House to-
morrow. Mr. Bullard, from the
Committee on Private Land Claims,
reported the following bill: [Wash-
ington, 1832] 4 p. (H.R. 254)
DNA; MB.   15736

---- A bill to authorize the legislature of the state of Indiana, to
sell and convey certain lands
granted to said state, for the use
of the people thereof. Feb. 9,
1832. Mr. Tipton, from the Committee on Public Lands, reported
the following bill; which was read,
and passed to a second reading:
[Washington, 1832] (S. 105) DNA;
MB.   15737

---- A bill to authorize the payment of the five per centum of the
net proceeds of the sales of the
lands of the United States in the
state of Louisiana. Apr. 11, 1832.
Agreeably to notice given, Mr.

Johnson asked and obtained leave to bring in the following bill; which was read, and passed to a second reading. Apr. 12, 1832. Read a second time, and referred to the Committee on Public Lands. Apr. 19, 1832. Reported without amendment. [Washington, 1832] 1 p. (S. 173) DNA; MB.   15738

---- A bill to authorize the President of the United States to change the locations of the land offices in the United States. Jan. 6, 1832. Read twice, and committed to a Committee of the Whole House to-morrow. Mr. Wickliffe, from the Committee on the Public Lands, reported the following bill: [Washington, 1832] 1 p. (H. R. 214) DNA; MB.   15739

---- A bill to authorize the President of the United States to direct transfers of appropriations in the naval service, under certain circumstances. Jan. 25, 1832. Read, and postponed until Monday next. Mr. McDuffie, from the Committee of Ways and Means, reported the following bill: [Washington, 1832] 1 p. (H. R. 318) DNA; MB.   15740

---- A bill to authorize the sale of certain public lands in the state of Ohio. May 18, 1832. Read twice, and ordered to be engrossed, and read the third time to-morrow. Mr. Wickliffe, from the Committee on the Public Lands, reported the following bill: [Washington, 1832] 1 p. (H. R. 583) DNA; MB.   15741

---- A bill to authorize the sale of lands reserved from sale at Fort Jackson, in the state of Alabama, Feb. 9, 1832. Agreeably to notice given, Mr. King asked and obtained leave to bring in the following bill; which was read twice, and referred to the Com-

mittee on Public Lands. Feb. 14, 1832. Reported with an amendment; namely; Strike out [twenty-nine] in the second section, and insert thirty. [Washington, 1832] 1 p. (S. 108) DNA; MB.   15742

---- A bill to authorize the Secretary of the Treasury to compromise the claim of the United States on the Commercial Bank of Lake Erie. Jan. 18, 1832. Read twice, and ordered to be engrossed, and read the third time to-morrow. Mr. Ingersoll, from the Committee of Ways and Means, reported the following bill: [Washington, 1832] 1 p. (H. R. 286) DNA; MB.   15743

---- A bill to authorize the Secretary of the Treasury to compromise the claims of the United States on the German Bank of Wooster. May 14, 1832. Mr. Marcy, from the Committee on the Judiciary, reported the following bill; which was read, and passed to a second reading: [Washington, 1832] 1 p. (S. 198) DNA; MB.   15744

---- A bill to authorize the Secretary of the Treasury to compromise with the trustee of the late firm of Thos. H. Smith and Son, and their securities, the claims of the United States upon the said firm and their securities. Apr. 24, 1832. Agreeably to notice given, Mr. Frelinghuysen asked and obtained leave to bring in the following bill; which was read twice, and referred to the Committee on the Judiciary. May 1, 1832. Reported without amendment. [Washington, 1832] 1 p. (S. 183) DNA; MB.   15745

---- A bill to authorize the Secretary of War to adjust and pay to Benjamin Murphy, of Arkansas, the value of his corn, cattle, and hogs, taken by the Cherokee Indians in the month of December one thousand eight hundred and twenty-eight. [Washington, 1832] 1 p. (S. 138) DNA; MB.   15746

---- A bill to authorize the Secretary of War to release the title of the United States to the site of Fort Gansevoort, in the harbor of New York. Feb. 20, 1832. Read twice, and committed to a Committee of the Whole House to-morrow. Mr. Drayton, from the Committee on Military Affairs, reported the following bill: [Washington, 1832] 1 p. (H.R. 401) DNA; MB.   15747

---- A bill to authorize the State of Indiana to lay out and make certain roads through the public lands therein named, and for other purposes. Jan. 17, 1832. Read twice, and committed to a Committee of the Whole House to-morrow. Mr. McCarty, from the Committee on Internal Improvements, reported the following bill: [Washington, 1832] 2 p. (H.R. 284) DNA; MB.   15748

---- A bill to carry into effect certain Indian treaties. May 14, 1832. Read twice, and committed to the Committee of the Whole House on the state of the Union. Mr. Bell, from the Committee on Indian Affairs, reported the following bill: [Washington, 1832] 1 p. (H.R. 575) DNA; MB.
15749

---- A bill to carry into effect the convention between the United States and his Majesty the King of the French, concluded at Paris on the fourth of July, one thousand eight hundred and thirty-one. Feb. 27, 1832. Read twice, and committed to the Committee of the Whole House on the state of the Union. Mr. Archer, from the Committee on Foreign Affairs, reported the following bill:

[Washington, 1832] 4 p. (H.R. 415) DNA; MB.   15750

---- A bill to change the time of holding the United States' District Court, at Staunton, in the western district of Virginia. Jan. 13, 1832. Read twice, and committed to a Committee of the Whole House to-morrow. Mr. Davis, of South Carolina, from the Committee on the Judiciary, reported the following bill: [Washington, 1832] 1 p. (H.R. 263) DNA; MB.
15751

---- A bill to compensate Geo. E. Tingle, for certain services therein mentioned. Jan. 25, 1832. Read twice, and committed to a Committee of the Whole House to-morrow. Mr. Kerr, from the Committee on the Territories, reported the following bill: [Washington, 1832] 1 p. (H.R. 315) DNA; MB.   15752

---- A bill to confirm certain claims to land in the territory of Arkansas. Feb. 28, 1832. Read twice, and ordered to be engrossed, and read the third time to-morrow. Mr. Wickliffe, from the Committee on the Public Lands, reported the following bill: [Washington, 1832] 3 p. (H.R. 425) DNA; MB.   15753

---- A bill to construct a road from Zanesville, in Ohio, to Florence, in Alabama. Feb. 10, 1832. Read twice, and committed to a Committee of the Whole House to-morrow. Mr. Letcher, from the Committee on Internal Improvements, reported the following bill: [Washington, 1832] 4 p. (H.R. 368) DNA; MB.
15754

---- A bill to create new land offices in the late Choctaw purchase, and for the more convenient organization of the land districts in the state of Mississippi.

Apr. 2, 1832. Mr. Ellis, from the Committee on Public Lands, reported the following bill; which was read, and passed to a second reading: [Washington, 1832] 4 p. (S. 169) DNA; MB.   15755

---- A bill to create new land offices in the late Choctaw purchase, and for the more convenient organization of the land districts in the state of Mississippi. Dec. 21, 1832. Read twice, and postponed until Monday next, 24th instant. Mr. Wickliffe, from the Committee on the Public Lands, reported the following bill: [Washington, 1832] 4 p. (H. R. 635) MB.   15756

---- A bill to create the office of Surveyor of Public Lands for the Territory of Arkansas. Mar. 22, 1832. Mr. King, from the Committee on Public Lands, reported the following bill; which was read, and passed to a second reading: [Washington, 1832] 2 p. (S. 159) DNA; MB.   15757

---- A bill to empower the State of Illinois to surrender certain lands granted by the United States, and to provide more effectually for the construction of a canal from the river Illinois to Lake Michigan. Apr. 13, 1832. Read twice, and committed to a Committee of the Whole House tomorrow. Mr. Mercer, from the Committee on Internal Improvements, reported the following bill: [Washington, 1832] 5 p. (H. R. 548) DNA; MB.   15758

---- A bill to enable the heirs and legal representatives of Elisha Winter and Sons to institute proceedings to try the validity of their claims to certain lands. Mar. 22, 1832. Read twice, and committed to the Committee of the Whole House to which is commit-

ted the bill (No. 254) to authorize the legal representatives of the Marquis de Maison Rouge and others claiming under him to institute a suit against the United States, and for other purposes. Mr. Plummer, from the Committee on the Public Lands, reported the following bill: [Washington, 1832] 7 p. (H. R. 503) DNA; MB.   15759

---- ---- May 10, 1832. Agreeably to notice given, Mr. Waggman asked and obtained leave to bring in the following bill; which was read twice, and referred to the Committee on Private Land Claims. May 19, 1832. Reported without amendment. [Washington, 1832] 7 p. (S. 197) DNA; MB.   15760

---- A bill to enable the Secretary at War to release the title of the United States to Fort Gansevoort, in the harbor of New York. Feb. 10, 1832. Agreeably to notice given, Mr. Benton asked and obtained leave to bring in the following bill; which was read, and passed to a second reading. Feb. 14, 1832. Read a second time, and referred to the Committee on Military Affairs. Mar. 6, 1832. Reported without amendment. [Washington, 1832] 1 p. (S. 109) DNA; MB.   15761

---- A bill to encourage the introduction, and promote the cultivation, of tropical plants in the United States. Apr. 26, 1832. Read twice, and committed to a Committee of the Whole House tomorrow. Mr. Root, from the Committee on Agriculture, reported the following bill: [Washington, 1832] 2 p. (H. R. 555) DNA; MB.   15762

---- A bill to enforce quarantine regulations. Apr. 7, 1832. Read twice, and ordered to be engrossed, and read the third time to-morrow. Mr. Howard, from the Committee on Commerce, reported the folowing bill: [Washington, 1832] 2 p. (H.R. 534) DNA; MB.   15763

---- A bill to erect a bridge and aqueduct over the Potomac River, at Georgetown, in the District of Columbia. Mar. 23, 1832. Read twice, and committed to a Committee of the Whole House to-morrow. Mr. Doddridge, from the Committee for the District of Columbia, reported the following bill: [Washington, 1832] 5 p. (H.R. 506) DNA; MB.   15764

---- A bill to erect a bridge over the Ohio River, at the town of Wheeling. Jan. 27, 1832. Read twice, and committed to a Committee of the Whole House to-morrow. Mr. Mercer, from the Committee on Internal Improvements, reported the following bill: [Washington, 1832] 1 p. (H.R. 327) DNA; MB.   15765

---- A bill to erect a bridge over the Potomac River, at or near Georgetown, in the District of Columbia. June 28, 1832. Mr. Chambers, from the Committee on the District of Columbia, reported the following bill; which was read, and passed to a second reading; [Washington, 1832] 4 p. (S. 210) DNA; MB.   15766

---- A bill to establish a uniform rule for computing the mileage of members of Congress. Feb. 27, 1832. Read twice, and committed to a Committee of the Whole House to-morrow. Mr. Hall, of North Carolina, from the Committee on Public Expenditures, reported the following bill: [Washington, 1832] 1 p. (H.R. 419) DNA; MB.   15767

---- A bill to establish addition-

al land districts in the state of Alabama. Apr. 26, 1832. Read twice, and postponed until the 10th of May next. Mr. Clay from the Committee on Public Lands, reported the following bill: [Washington, 1832] 2 p. (H.R. 556) DNA; MB.   15768

---- A bill to establish certain post roads, and to alter and discontinue others, and for other purposes. Feb. 2, 1832. Read twice, and committed to a Committee of the Whole House to-morrow. Mr. Johnson, of Kentucky, from the Committee on the Post Office and Post Roads, reported the following bill: [Washington, 1832] 52 p. (H.R. 343) DNA; MB.   15769

---- A bill to establish the number of clerks, and fix their compensation, in the General Land Office. Feb. 2, 1832. Mr. King, from the Committee on Public Lands, reported the following bill; which was read, and passed to a second reading: [Washington, 1832] 2 p. (S. 94) DNA; MB.   15770

---- A bill to establish the office of Surgeon General of the Navy. Jan. 4, 1832. Mr. Hayne, from the Committee on Naval Affairs, reported the following bill; which was read, and passed to a second reading: [Washington, 1832] 2 p. (S. 42) DNA; MB.   15771

---- A bill to exempt merchandise imported under certain circumstances, from the operation of the act of the nineteenth of May, one thousand eight hundred and twenty-eight, entitled, "An act in alteration of the several acts imposing duties on imports." Jan. 23, 1832. Mr. Smith, from the Committee on Finance, reported the following bill; which was read, and passed to a second reading: [Washington, 1832] 2 p. (S. 69) DNA; MB.   15772

---- A bill to exempt merchandise imported under certain circumstances, from the operation of the act of the nineteenth of May, one thousand eight hundred and twenty-eight, entitled "An act in alteration of the several acts imposing duties on imports." Mar. 1, 1832. Read twice and committed to a Committee of the Whole House to-morrow. Mr. Mc-Duffie, from the Committee of Ways and Means, reported the following bill: [Washington, 1832] 2 p. (H.R. 434) DNA; MB.
15773

---- A bill to exempt merchandise imported under certain circumstances from the operation of the act of the nineteenth of May, one thousand eight hundred and twenty-eight, entitled "An act in alteration of the several acts imposing duties on imports." Dec. 14, 1832. Read twice, and committed to a Committee of the Whole House on the state of the Union. Mr. Verplanck, from the Committee of Ways and Means, reported the following bill: [Washington, 1832] 2 p. (H.R. 619) DNA; MB.   15774

---- A bill to exempt the vessels of Portugal from the payment of duties on tonnage. April 16, 1832. Mr. Forsyth, from the Committee on Foreign Relations, reported the following bill; which was read twice, and laid on the table: [Washington, 1832] 1 p. (S. 178) DNA; MB.   15775

---- A bill to explain and amend the eighteenth section of "An act to alter and amend the several acts imposing duties of imports," approved the fourteenth July, one thousand eight hundred and thirty-two. Dec. 21, 1832. Read, and

postponed until Wednesday, 26th instant. Mr. Cambreleng, from the Committee on Commerce, reported the following bill: [Washington, 1832] 4 p. (H.R. 633) DNA; MB.   15776

---- A bill to extend and confirm the limits of the state of Missouri. July 14, 1832. Read twice, and committed to the Committee of the Whole House on the state of the Union. Mr. Kerr, from the Committee on the Territories, reported the following bill: [Washington, 1832] 1 p. (H.R. 615) DNA; MB.   15777

---- A bill to extend the limits of Georgetown, in the District of Columbia. Jan. 20, 1832. Read twice, and committed to a Committee of the Whole House to-morrow. Mr. Chinn, from the Committee for the District of Columbia, reported the following bill: [Washington, 1832] 2 p. (H.R. 296) DNA; MB.   15778

---- A bill to extend the patent of Jethro Wood. Feb. 28, 1832. Read twice, and postponed until Tuesday next. Mr. Taylor, from the Select Committee on the subject of the Patent Laws, reported the following bill: [Washington, 1832] 1 p. (H.R. 428) DNA; MB.
15779

---- A bill to extend the period to which the charter of the Provident Association of Clerks was limited. Apr. 25, 1832. Mr. Chambers, from the Committee on the District of Columbia, reported the following bill; which was read, and passed to a second reading. [Washington, 1832] 1 p. (S. 185) DNA; MB.   15780

---- A bill to extend the provisions of the act, entitled "An act regulating commercial intercourse with the islands of Martinique and

Guadaloupe," approved the ninth of May, one thousand eight hundred and twenty-eight, and to refund the tonnage duties on the French ship Victorine. Jan. 11, 1832. Read twice, and committed to the Committee of the Whole House on the state of the Union. Mr. Cambreleng, from the Committee on Commerce, reported the following bill: [Washington, 1832] 1 p. (H. R. 248) DNA; MB. 15781

---- A bill to extend the provisions of the fifty-second section of an act passed the second Mar. one thousand seven hundred and ninety-nine, "To regulate the collection of duties on imports and tonnage. Mar. 7, 1832. Read twice, and committed to a Committee of the Whole House to-morrow. Mr. Cambreleng, from the Committee on Commerce, reported the following bill: [Washington, 1832] 2 p. (H. R. 451) DNA; MB. 15782

---- A bill to extend the right of pre-emption to the settlers of township five north, one west of the third principal meridian in Illinois. Feb. 8, 1832. Mr. Robinson, from the Committee on Public Lands, reported the following bill; which was read, and passed to a second reading: [Washington, 1832] 1 p. (S. 104) DNA; MB. 15783

---- A bill to extend the time allowed for the redemption of land sold for direct taxes, in certain cases. Jan. 13, 1832. Read twice, and committed to a Committee of the Whole House to-morrow. Mr. Davis, of South Carolina, from the Committee on the Judiciary, reported the following bill: [Washington, 1832] 1 p. (H. R. 262) DNA; MB. 15784

---- A bill to extend the time of issuing military land warrants to officers and soldiers of the revolutionary army. June 1, 1832. Read twice, and ordered to be engrossed, and read the third time to-morrow. Mr. Irvin, from the Committee of the Public Lands, reported the following bill: [Washington, 1832] 1 p. (H. R. 594) DNA; MB. 15785

---- A bill to grant a township of land to the French College of St. Louis, Jan. 9, 1832. Mr. King, from the Committee on Public Lands, reported the following bill; which was read, and passed to a second reading: [Washington, 1832] 1 p. (S. 53) DNA; MB. 15786

---- A bill to grant to the state of Missouri a certain quantity of land for purposes of internal improvement. Mar. 20, 1832. Agreeably to notice Mr. Benton asked and obtained leave to bring in the following bill; which was read, and passed to a second reading. Mar. 21, 1832. Read the second time, and referred to the Committee on Roads and Canals. Mar. 28, 1832. Reported with the following amendment, viz. After "Missouri," insert Mississippi and Louisiana. [Washington, 1832] 2 p. (S. 157) DNA; MB. 15787

---- A bill to grant to the state of Ohio certain lands for the support of schools, in the Connecticut Western Reserve. Jan. 10, 1832. Read twice, and committed to a Committee of the Whole House to-morrow. Mr. Irvin, from the Committee on the Public Lands, reported the following bill: [Washington, 1832] 1 p. (H. R. 240) DNA; MB. 15788

---- A bill to incorporate the St. Francis Road Company in the territory of Arkansas. May 2, 1832. Read twice, and committed to the Committee of the Whole House to

which is committed the bill (H.R. No. 468) to provide for opening a road in Arkansas Territory, from Villemont, in the county of Chicot, to Little Rock. Mr. Mercer, from the Committee on Internal Improvements, reported the following bill: [Washington, 1832] 8 p. (H.R. 260) DNA; MB.
15789

---- A bill to incorporate the trustees of the Methodist Protestant Church of Georgetown. Jan. 24, 1832. Read twice, and committed to a Committee of the Whole House to-morrow. Mr. Washington, from the Committee for the District of Columbia, reported the following bill: [Washington, 1832] 6 p. (H.R. 304) DNA; MB.
15790

---- A bill to increase and improve the Law Department of the Library of Congress. Jan. 20, 1832. Mr. Marcy, from the committee on the Judiciary, reported the following bill; which was read, and passed to a second reading: [Washington, 1832] 2 p. (S. 68) DNA; MB.
15791

---- A bill to increase and regulate the pay of the Medical Staff of the Army. Mar. 6, 1832. Mr. Benton, from the Committee on Military Affairs, reported the following bill; which was read, and passed to a second reading: [Washington, 1832] 2 p. (S. 139) DNA; MB.
15792

---- A bill to increase the number of surgeons and assistant surgeons in the army of the United States. Jan. 20, 1832. Read twice, and committed to the Committee of the Whole House on the State of the Union. Mr. Drayton, from the Committee on Military Affairs, reported the following bill: [Washington, 1832] 1 p. (H.R. 295) DNA; MB.
15793

---- ---- Feb. 23, 1832. Mr. Benton, from the Committee on Military Affairs, reported the following bill; which was read, and passed to a second reading: [Washington, 1832] 1 p. (S. 120) DNA; MB.
15794

---- A bill to increase the pay of the Master Armorers in the service of the United States. Jan. 3, 1832. Read twice, and committed to a Committee of the Whole House to-morrow. Mr. Drayton, from the Committee on Military Affairs, reported the following bill: [Washington, 1832] 1 p. (H.R. 182) DNA; MB.
15795

---- A bill to increase the salary of the governor, secretary, and judges of the territory of Arkansas. Jan. 30, 1832. Read twice, and committed to a Committee of the Whole House to-morrow. Mr. W. B. Shepard, from the Committee on the Territories, reported the following bill: [Washington, 1832] 1 p. (H.R. 330) DNA; MB.
15796

---- A bill to modify and continue the act, entitled "An act to incorporate the subscribers to the Bank of the United States." Mar. 13, 1832. Mr. Dallas, from the select committee appointed on the memorial of the Bank of the United States, praying a renewal of its charter, reported the following bill; which was read, and passed to a second reading: [Washington, 1832] 4 p. (S. 147) DNA; MB.
15797

---- A bill to oblige vessels coming from foreign ports or places, or ports or places within the United States, to the District of Columbia, to perform quarantine. July 2, 1832. Read twice, and committed to the Committee of the Whole House on the state of the Union. Mr. Doddridge, from the Committee for the District of Columbia, reported the following bill: [Washington, 1832] 9 p. (H.R. 606) DNA; MB.   15798

---- A bill to organize the Corps of Topographical Engineers. Mar. 5, 1832. Mr. Benton, from the Committee on Military Affairs, reported the following bill; which was read, and passed to a second reading: [Washington, 1832] 1 p. (S. 137) DNA; MB.   15799

---- A bill to organize the several fire companies of the District of Columbia. Jan. 27, 1832. Read twice, and committed to a Committee of the Whole House to-morrow. Mr. Doddridge, from the Committee for the District of Columbia, reported the following bill: [Washington, 1832] 5 p. (H.R. 325) DNA; MB.   15800

---- A bill to prevent and punish the making and transporting of counterfeit foreign coin. May 10, 1832. Read twice, and committed to the Committee of the Whole House on the state of the Union. Mr. Ellsworth, from the Committee on the Judiciary, reported the following bill: [Washington, 1832] 1 p. (H.R. 568) DNA; MB.   15801

---- A bill to prevent the confirmation of illegal and fraudulent French or Spanish grants to lands within the United States or territories thereof. June 12, 1832. Read the first time. Mr. Wickliffe, from the Committee on the Public Lands, reported the following bill: [Washington, 1832] 2 p. (H.R. 598) DNA; MB.   15802

---- A bill to prevent the separation of Captains, in the line of the Army, from their companies: for the better organization of the United States' Military Academy;

and for other purposes. Feb. 8, 1832. Read twice, and committed to the Committee of the Whole House on the state of the Union. Mr. Drayton, from the Committee on Military Affairs, reported the following bill: [Washington, 1832] 4 p. (H.R. 359) DNA; MB.   15803

---- A bill to provide for carrying into effect the treaty of limits between the United States of America and the United Mexican States. June 2, 1832. Read twice, and committed to the Committee of the Whole House on the state of the Union. Mr. Verplanck, from the Committee of Ways and Means, reported the following bill: [Washington, 1832] 2 p. (H.R. 595) DNA; MB.   15804

---- A bill to provide for constructing three steam batteries. Dec. 18, 1832. Read twice, and committed to a Committee of the Whole House on the state of the Union. Mr. Anderson, from the Committee on Naval Affairs, reported the following bill: [Washington, 1832] 1 p. (H.R. 623) DNA; MB.   15805

---- A bill to provide for erecting a building for a Patent Office. May 31, 1832. Read twice, and committed to a Committee of the Whole House to-morrow. Mr. Jarvis, from the Committee on the Public Buildings, reported the following bill: [Washington, 1832] 1 p. (H.R. 592) DNA; MB.   15806

---- A bill to provide for extending through the territory of Arkansas, the road from Washington to Jackson, in the said territory. Jan. 4, 1832. Read twice, and committed to a Committee of the Whole House to-morrow. Mr. Mercer, from the Committee on Internal Improvements, reported the following bill: [Washington,

1832] 1 p. (H.R. 210) DNA; MB.
15807
---- A bill to provide for laying
out and constructing a national
road from Portsmouth, in the
state of Ohio, to a point south of
the Lynnville Mountain, in North
Carolina. Feb. 17, 1832. Read
twice, and committed to a Committee of the Whole House to-
morrow. Mr. Blair, from the
Committee on Internal Improvements, reported the following bill:
[Washington, 1832] 4 p. (H.R.
393) DNA; MB.   15808

---- A bill to provide for liquidating and paying certain claims
of the Commonwealth of Virginia.
Jan. 16, 1832. Read twice, and
committed to the Committee of
the Whole House on the state of
the Union. Mr. J. S. Barbour,
from the Select Committee, to
which the sub[ject] had been referred, reported the following
bill: [Washington, 1832] 3 p.
(H.R. 276) DNA; MB.   15809

---- A bill to provide for
liquidating and paying certain
claims of the State of Virginia.
Jan. 30, 1832. Mr. Benton, from
the Committee on Military Affairs,
reported the following bill; which
was read, and passed to a second
reading: [Washington, 1832] 3 p.
(S. 88) DNA; MB.   15810

---- A bill to provide for opening
a road in Arkansas territory,
from Villemont, in the county of
Chicot, to Little Rock. March 14,
1832. Read twice, and committed
to the Committee of the Whole
House on the state of the Union.
Mr. Johnson, of Kentucky, from
the Committee on the Post Office
and Post Roads, reported the following bill: [Washington, 1832]
3 p. (H.R. 468) DNA; MB.
15811
---- A bill to provide for the ap-

pointment of a Commissioner on
Indian Affairs, and for other pur-
poses. Feb. 27, 1832. Mr.
White, from the Committee on
Indian Affairs, reported the fol-
lowing bill; which was read, and
passed to a second reading:
[Washington, 1832] 2 p. (S. 125)
DNA; MB.   15812

---- A bill to provide for the appointment of three Commissioners
to treat with the Indians, and for
other purposes. Mar. 17, 1832.
Read twice, and committed to the
Committee of the Whole House to-
morrow. Mr. Bell, from the Committee on Indian Affairs, reported
the following bill: [Washington,
1832] 3 p. (H.R. 484) DNA; MB.
15813
---- A bill to provide for the
better security of the lives of
passengers on board of vessels
propelled in whole or in part by
steam. May 18, 1832. Read twice,
and committed to the Committee
of the Whole House on the state
of the Union. Mr. Wickliffe, from
the Select Committee to which the
subject had been referred, reported the following bill: [Washington,
1832] 6 p. (H.R. 582) DNA; MB.
15814
---- A bill to provide for the distribution of the duties of the Commissioners of the Navy, and for
other purposes. Jan. 3, 1832.
Mr. Hayne, from the Committee
on Naval Affairs, reported the following bill; which was read, and
passed to a second reading:
[Washington, 1832] 4 p. (S. 35)
DNA; MB.   15815

---- A bill to provide for the extinguishment of the Indian title to
lands lying in the states of Missouri and Illinois. June 5, 1832.
Read twice, and committed to the
Committee of the Whole House on
the state of the Union. Mr. Bell,
from the Committee on Indian Af-

fairs, reported the following bill: [Washington, 1832] 1 p. (H.R. 597) DNA; MB.   15816

---- A bill to provide for the further compensation of the Marshal of the district of Delaware. Jan. 25, 1832. Read twice, and committed to a Committee of the Whole House to-morrow. Mr. Ellsworth, from the Committee on the Judiciary, reported the following bill: [Washington, 1832] 1 p. (H.R. 312) DNA; MB.
15817

---- A bill to provide for the payment of Joshua Kennedy, of Alabama, for the losses sustained by him by the destruction of his property, in the year one thousand eight hundred and thirteen, by the hostile Creek Indians, in consequence of its having been occupied as a fort or garrison by the troops of the United States. Jan. 10, 1832. Mr. White, from the Committee on Indian Affairs, reported the following bill, which was read, and passed to a second reading: [Washington, 1832] 1 p. (S. 57) DNA; MB.
15818

---- A bill to provide for the taking of certain observations preparatory to the adjustment of the northern boundary line of the state of Ohio. Mar. 20, 1832. Mr. Ewing, from the Select Committee appointed on the subject, reported the following bill; which was read, and passed to a second reading: [Washington, 1832] 1 p. (S. 155) DNA; MB.   15819

---- A bill to provide more effectually for the national defence, by organizing, arming, and establishing a uniform militia throughout the United States, and to provide for the discipline thereof. Feb. 27, 1832. Read twice, and committed to the Committee of the Whole House on the state of

the Union. Mr. Barringer, from the Committee on the Militia, reported the following bill: [Washington, 1832] 18 p. (H.R. 423) DNA; MB.   15820

---- A bill to provide the means of extending the benefits of vaccination, as a preventive of the small pox, to the Indian tribes, and thereby, as far as possible, to save them from the destructive ravages of that disease. Apr. 3, 1832. Read twice, and committed to the Committee of the Whole House on the state of the Union. Mr. Bell, from the Committee on Indian Affairs, reported the following bill: [Washington, 1832] 2 p. (H.R. 526) DNA; MB.
15821

---- A bill to re-appropriate the balance of an appropriation for the payment of the unsatisfied claims of the militia of the state of Georgia, for services rendered by them in the years seventeen hundred and ninety-two, seventeen hundred and ninety-three, seventeen hundred and ninety-four... Feb. 15, 1832. Read twice, and committed to a Committee of the Whole House to-morrow. Mr. Drayton, from the Committee on Military Affairs, reported the following bill: [Washington, 1832] 1 p. (H.R. 373) DNA; MB.
15822

---- A bill to reduce and equalize the duties upon imports. Feb. 8, 1832. Read twice, and committed to the Committee of the Whole House on the state of the Union. Mr. McDuffie, from the Committee of Ways and Means, reported the following bill: [Washington, 1832] 1 p. (H.R. 361) DNA; MB.   15823

---- A bill to reduce and graduate the price of the public lands. Feb. 21, 1832. Read twice, and committed to a Committee of the Whole House to-morrow. Mr.

Boon, from the Committee on the Public Lands, reported the following bill: [Washington, 1832] 1 p. (H.R. 402) DNA; MB. 15824

---- A bill to reduce and otherwise alter the duties on imports. Dec. 27, 1832. Read twice, and committed to the Committee of the Whole House on the state of the Union. Mr. Verplanck, from the Committee of Ways and Means, reported the following bill: [Washington, 1832] 12 p. (H.R. 641) MB. 15825

---- A bill to reduce the duties on Indian blankets, and certain other Indian goods. Jan. 4, 1832. Agreeably to notice given, Mr. Benton asked and obtained leave to bring in the following bill; which was read, and passed to a second reading. Jan. 5, 1832. Read a second time, and referred to the Committee on Manufactures. Feb. 7, 1832. Reported without amendment. [Washington, 1832] 1 p. (S. 44) DNA; MB. 15826

---- A bill to reduce the postage on periodicals and pamphlets, and for other purposes. Jan. 30, 1832. Referred to the Committee of the Whole House on the state of the Union. Mr. R. M. Johnson, from the Committee on the Post Office and Post Roads, reported the following bill: [Washington, 1832] 3 p. (H.R. 329) DNA; MB. 15827

---- A bill to refund a fine imposed on the Mathew Lyon, under the sedition law, to his heirs and representatives. Jan. 19, 1832. Read twice, and committed to a Committee of the Whole House to-morrow. Mr. Davis, of South Carolina, from the Committee on the Judiciary, reported the following bill: [Washington, 1832] 1 p. (H.R. 290) DNA; MB. 15828

---- The bill to release from duty, iron prepared for, and actually laid on railways or inclined planes, being under consideration, Mr. Hayne offered the following as an additional section: [Washington, 1832] 1 p. (S. 131) DNA; MB. 15829

---- A bill to remove the land office in the Choctaw district, in the state of Mississippi, from Mount Salus to Jackson. Feb. 27, 1832. Read the first and second time, and postponed until to-morrow. Mr. Plummer, from the Committee on the Public Lands, reported the following bill: [Washington, 1832] 1 p. (H.R. 418) DNA; MB. 15830

---- A bill to remove the Surveyor General's office south of Tennessee. Mar. 29, 1832. Mr. Ellis, from the Committee on Public Lands, reported the following bill; which was read, and passed to a second reading: [Washington, 1832] 1 p. (S. 166) DNA; MB. 15831

---- A bill to renew and modify the charter of the Bank of the United States. Feb. 10, 1832. Read twice, and committed to the Committee of the Whole House on the state of the Union. Mr. McDuffie, from the Committee of Ways and Means, reported the following bill: [Washington, 1832] 3 p. (H.R. 365) DNA; MB. 15832

---- A bill to re-organize the Navy of the United States. Jan. 11, 1832. Read twice, and committed to the Committee of the Whole House on the state of the Union. Mr. Branch, from Committee on Naval Affairs, reported the following bill: [Washington, 1832] 5 p. (H.R. 249) DNA; MB. 15833

---- A bill to repeal, in part, the duties on imports. Mar. 30, 1832. Mr. Dickerson, from the Committee on Manufactures, reported, in part, the following bill; which was read twice, and laid on the table: [Washington, 1832] 3 p. (S. 167) DNA; MB.
15834

---- A bill to repeal so much of the laws relative to Brevet Rank, as authorize the President to confer that rank on officers, and who shall have served ten years in any one grade. Feb. 23, 1832. Mr. Benton, from the Committee on Military Affairs, reported the following bill; which was read, and passed to a second reading: [Washington, 1832] 1 p. (S. 119) DNA; MB.   15835

---- A bill to repeal the postage on newspapers. May 15, 1832. Agreeably to notice given, Mr. Holmes asked and obtained leave to bring in the following bill; which was read twice, and referred to the Committee on Post Offices and Post Roads. May 19, 1832. Reported without amendment. [Washington, 1832] 1 p. (S. 199) DNA; MB.   15836

---- A bill to restore to the roll of revolutionary pensioners the names of John Fox, Jacob Fleisher, Michael Spartz, Adam Gramlin, and Calvin Pinkham, soldiers of the revolution. May 14, 1832. Read twice, and committed to a Committee of the Whole House to-morrow. Mr. Denny, from the Committee on Revolutionary Pensions, reported the following bill: [Washington, 1832] 1 p. (H.R. 574) DNA; MB.
15837
---- A bill to revive and continue in force, "An act authorizing the payment of certain certificates," approved seventh May, one thousand eight hundred and twenty-two.

Mar. 5, 1832. Mr. Smith, from the Committee on Finance, reported the following bill; which was read, and passed to a second reading: [Washington, 1832] 1 p. (S. 136) DNA; MB.   15838

---- A bill to revive and continue in force "An act for the relief of the representatives of John Donelson, Stephen Heard, and others." Jan. 20, 1832. Read twice, and ordered to be engrossed, and read the third time to-morrow. Mr. Clay, from the Committee on the Public Lands, reported the following bill: [Washington, 1832] 1 p. (H.R. 299) DNA; MB.
15839
---- A bill to secure to mechanics and others payment for labor done and materials furnished in the erection of buildings in Washington city. Mar. 20, 1832. Read twice, and committed to a Committee of the Whole House to-morrow. Mr. Doddridge, from the Committee for the District of Columbia, reported the following bill: [Washington, 1832] 3 p. (H.R. 497) DNA; MB.   15840

---- A bill to straighten F and G streets, in the city of Washington. Feb. 20, 1832. Read twice, and committed to a Committee of the Whole House to-morrow. Mr. Washington, from the Committee for the District of Columbia, reported the following bill: [Washington, 1832] 1 p. (H.R. 399) DNA; MB.   15841

---- A bill vesting in the corporation of Washington city, all the rights of the Washington Canal Company, and for other purposes ....Mar. 19, 1832. Read twice, and committed to a Committee of the Whole House to-morrow. Mr. Doddridge, from the Committee for the District of Columbia, reported the following bill: [Wash-

ington, 1832] 11 p. (H.R. 492)
DNA; MB.   15842

---- Brush Manufacturers, New
York, Philadelphia, Baltimore.
June 10, 1832. Referred to the
Committee of the Whole House on
the state of the Union. Pr. by
Duff Green, Washington, 1832.
1 p. 22d Cong., 1st sess. MB;
R.   15843

---- The case of Martha Bailey,
and others, May 5, 1832. Washington, Pr. by Duff Green, 1832.
4 p. 22d Cong., 1st sess. MB;
R.   15844

---- Circular Letter on the Coast
Survey. Secretary McLane. Aug.
9, 1832. Library of the Coast Survey. Requesting all owners
and occupiers of lands over which
Mr. Hassler and his assistants
may have occasion to pass in the
performance of their public duties
to permit them freely to pass over
and remain on the same as long
as may be necessary in executing the work of the survey of the
coast. [Washington, 1832] 1 p.
MB.   15845

---- Concerning Subdivision and
Surveys. May 8, 1832. Library
of the Interior Department. Circular to surveyors-general under
the act of Apr. 5, 1832, relating
to subdivision of sections and survey of fractional sections issued
by Secretary of the Treasury.
[Washington, 1832] 1 p. MB.
                                 15846
---- Congressional Directory,
Twenty-second Congress, 1st
sess. 1832. [Washington] Pr. by
Jonathan Elliot, 1832. 56 p. MB.
                                 15847
---- Congressional Directory,
Twenty-second Congress, Second
sess. [Washington] Duff Green,
1832. 15 p. MB.   15848

---- ---- [Washington] Jonathan
Elliot, 1832. 50 p. MB.   15849

---- ---- 1st. ed. [Washington]
Jonathan Elliot, 1832. 104 p.
MB.   15850

---- The Congressional Reporter.
1832. Political Pamphlets, Vol.
CXVI. Library of Congress. [This
appears to have been a reprint of
the report of the proceedings of
the House, made for a Washington
daily paper.] [Washington] 1832.
97 p. MB.   15851

---- Constitution of the United
States of America... Washington,
Pr. by D. Green, 1832. 60 p.
Ct; DLC; MB; MHi.   15852

---- Constitution of the U.S. of
America, the constitution of the
commonwealth of Pennsylvania,
and rules for the government of
the House of Representatives of
the said commonwealth. Harrisburg, Welsh, 1832. 11 p. MB;
PPAmP.   15853

---- Construction of Act concerning Reverted Lands. Oct. 24,
1832. Library of the Interior
Dept. Circular to registers and
receivers of credit system land
offices concerning the construction of the general provisions of
act of May 23, 1828, relieving
purchasers of lands which have
reverted for non-payment, and instructions thereunder. [Washing-
ton, 1832] 1 p. MB.   15854

---- Convention of United States
with France concerning French
Spoliations. Feb. 26, 1832. House
Ex. Docs., No. 126, 22d Cong.,
1st Sess., Vol. IV. [Washington,
1832] 4 p. MB.   15855

---- Correspondence relative to
Tariff. Secretary Louis McLane.
Feb. 14, 1832. Senate Docs.,

No. 64, 22d Cong. , 1st sess. ,
Vol. II. Copies of correspondence
with collectors of customs showing construction of acts regulating
duties on imports. [Washington,
1832] 184 p. MB.   15856

---- Debate in the Senate on the
nomination of Martin Van Buren,
to be Minister of the United
States to Great Britain. This debate took place mainly on the
24th and 25th of Jan. 1832, and
according to the rules of the Senate, in Secret Session. After the
question was decided, the injunction of secrecy was removed, by
a vote of the Senate, from the
debates as well as the proceedings in this case. In consequence
of which, the following proceeding and authentic sketches of
speeches delivered in that debate
were published in the National
Intelligencer and other papers,
etc. [Washington, 1832] 55 p. CU;
Ct; MB; MdHi; P; ScU.   15857

---- A digested index to the executive documents, and reports
of committees of the House of
Representatives, from the eighteenth to the twenty-first Congress, both included. . . Washington, Pr. by Duff Green, 1832.
152 p. ICU; MB; NWM; RPB.
                                   15858
---- Documents in Case of Sam
Houston. Apr. 18, 1832. House
Ex. Docs. , No. 210, 22d Cong. ,
1st sess. , Vol. V. Interroga-
tories by the Speaker to Sam
Houston in relation to his assault
upon Wm. Stanbery, a member of
the House of Representatives,
with his answers. [Washington,
1832] 2 p. MB.   15859

---- Documents in Case of Thos.
Worthington. Jan. 31, 1832.
House Ex. Docs. , No. 85, 22d
Cong. , 1st sess. , Vol. III. In re-
lation to the transfer of a judg-

ment in favor of the United States
against Thos. Worthington. [Wash-
ington, 1832] 7 p. MB.   15860

---- Documents laid on the table
by the chairman of the Committee
on Naval Affairs relating to Senate bill No. 44 "for the erection
of barracks, quarters, and storehouse, and the purchase of a site
in the vicinity of New Orleans"
Jan. 4, 1832 ordered to be printed. Washington, Pr. by Duff
Green, 1832. 22d Cong. , 1st
sess. MB; R.   15861

---- Documents on Apportionment
of Representatives. Senator Webster. Feb. 27, 1832. Senate Docs. ,
No. 75, 22d Cong. , 1st sess. ,
Vol. II. Statement showing number of Representatives under the
fifth census; Loss or gain of
representation of each State at the
ratio of one Representative for
47,000 persons. [Washington,
1832] 3 p. MB.   15862

---- Dcouments referring to Pay
of Navy Agents. Naval Committee.
Jan. 3, 1832. Senate Docs, No.
13, 22d Cong. , 1st sess. , Vol. I.
Relative to mode of paying extra
compensation to Navy agents.
[Washington, 1832] 2 p. MB.
                                   15863
---- Documents relative to Canals in Florida. Dec. 11, 1832.
Senate Docs. , No. 7, 22d Cong. ,
2d sess. , Vol. I. Documents to
accompany bill to authorize the
Territory of Florida to construct
canals between the Chipola River
and St. Andrew's Bay. [Washing-
ton, 1832] 45 p. MB.   15864

---- Documents relative to Imported Merchandise. Senator Silsbee. Mar. 16, 1832. Senate
Docs. , No. 104, 22d Cong. , 1st
sess. , Vol. II. Documents relative to exemption of merchandise
imported under certain circum-

stances from the operation of the act of May 19, 1828. [Washington, 1832] 21 p. MB. 15865

---- Documents relative to Manufactures in the United States. 1832. Ex. Docs., No. 308, 22d Cong., 1st sess, Vol. VII. Giving detailed information respecting all manufacturing establishments in the United States. [Washington, 1832] 1939 p. MB. 15866

---- Documents relative to Pay of Naval Officers. Dec. 27, 1832. Ex. Docs., No. 133, 22d Cong., 2d sess., Vol. III. Pay of naval officers as proposed by Commissioners of the Navy; Present pay and emoluments. [Washington, 1832] 13 p. MB. 15867

---- Documents relative to Pensions. June 28, 1832. Ex. Docs., No. 298, 22d Cong., 1st sess., Vol. VI. Pension act of 1832 and instructions of the War Dept. for carrying it into effect. [Washington, 1832] 7 p. MB. 15868

---- Documents relative to Representation Bill. May 11, 1832. House Ex. Docs., No. 234, 22d Cong., 1st sess., Vol. V. Opinions of the members of the Cabinet in 1792 on the representation bill, negatived in that year by the President. [Washington, 1832] 13 p. MB. 15869

---- Documents relative to United States Bank. N. Biddle, pres. Mar. 12, 1832. Senate Docs., No. 98, 22d Cong., 1st sess., Vol. II. Statements showing nature and amount of loans made by the bank and its branches; Notes of the bank on hand Feb. 1, 1832; Statement of real estate bought and sold; Cost and present value of banking-houses. [Washington, 1832] 50 p. MB. 15870

---- Documents to accompany Bill for Relief of Rev. John Hughes. Mar. 1, 1832. House Ex. Docs., No. 145, 22d Cong., 1st sess., Vol. IV. [Washington, 1832] 2 p. MB. 15871

---- Dress of the General Staff and Regimental Officers of the Army of the United States. Adjutant General's Office, Washington, 31st May, 1832. [Washington, 1832] 27 p. Half-title. No imprint. MB; NbU. 15872

---- Estimate of Appropriation. Secretary Louis McLane. Dec. 12, 1832. Ex. Docs., No. 10, 22d Cong., 2d sess., Vol. I. Transmitting estimates of appropriations required for the service of the Government for the year 1833. [Washington, 1832] 57 p. MB. 15873

---- Estimate of Funds for Engineer Department. Secretary Lewis Cass. Dec. 28, 1832. Ex. Docs., No. 29, 22d Cong., 2d sess., Vol. I. Transmitting additional estimates of funds required for the Engineer Department for the year 1833. [Washington, 1832] 2 p. MB. 15874

---- Estimates for Improvement of Tiber Creek. May 2, 1832. House Ex. Docs., No. 223, 22d Cong., 1st sess., Vol. V. Estimates for enclosing the public grounds situated in Washington between the circular road and Tiber Creek. [Washington, 1832] 1 p. MB. 15875

---- Executive documents printed by order of the House of Representatives at the 2d sess. of the 22d Congress, begun and held at the city of Washington, Dec. 3, 1832... In three vols. Vol. 1, containing documents from No. 1 to No. 45, inclusive. Washington,

Duff Green, 1832. 19 p. CoU;
MB; MW; Nj; R.   15876

---- Extracts from the Veto
message of Gen. Andrew Jackson,
and other documents, relating to
the United States Bank; respectfully recommended to the particular attention of the independent
electors of the City of New-York.
By a committee especially appointed for this purpose. New-
York, Pr. by C. N. Baldwin,
1832. 31 p. MB; NNC; P; PHi.
                          15877
---- Fifth census; or, Enumera-
tion of the inhabitants of the
United States. 1830. To which is
pre-fixed, a schedule of the
whole number of persons within
the several districts of the United
States, taken according to the
acts of 1790, 1800, 1810, 1820.
Pub. by authority of an act of
Congress. Washington, Pr. by
D. Green, 1832. 2 v. in 1. Ct;
DLC; MB; MnV; PU; TxU. 15878

---- History of Bank of United
States. M. St. C. Clarke and D.
A. Hall. Washington, 1832. Li-
brary of Congress. Legislative
and documentary history of the
Bank of the United States, includ-
ing the original Bank of North
America. [Washington, 1832]
MB.   15879

---- House Documents, 22d Cong.,
2d sess. From Dec. 3, 1832.
Vol. I. Docs. Nos. 1 to 45, inclusive; Vol. II, Docs. Nos. 46
to 109, inclusive; Vol. III, Docs.
Nos. 110 to 148 inclusive. [Wash-
ington] Pr. by Duff Green [1832]
MB.   15880

---- House Journal, 22d Cong.,
2d sess. Dec. 3, 1832. From
Dec. 3, 1832, to Mar. 2, 1833.
Speaker of the House, Andrew
Stevenson, of Virginia; Clerk of
the House, M. St. Clair Clarke,

of Pennsylvania. Washington, Pr.
by Duff Green [1832] 603 p. MB.
                          15881
---- House Reports, 22d Cong.,
2d sess. From Dec. 3, 1832.
Reports, Nos. 1 to 128, and
Resolutions 1, 2, and 3. [Wash-
ington] Pr. by Duff Green [1832]
MB.   15882

---- Information relative to Colonial Trade. Secretary Louis
McLane. Jan. 13, 1832. Senate
Docs., No. 28, 22d Cong., 1st
sess., Vol. I. Transmitting copies of instructions to collectors
of customs relative to trade with
the British colonies. [Washington,
1832] 18 p. MB.   15883

---- Information relative to
French Duties. Sec. Edward Livingston. Mar. 19, 1832. Senate
Docs., No. 106, 22d Cong., 1st
sess., Vol. II. Information that
the French committee on finance
has reported in favor of a tonnage duty on cotton, wool, and
raw sugar. [Washington, 1832]
1 p. MB.   15884

---- Instructions relative to Duties on Iron. Secretary Louis Mc-
Lane. Feb. 28, 1832. Senate
Docs., No. 131, 22d Cong., 1st
sess., Vol. III. Copies of instructions to collectors of customs since Apr. 20, 1818, concerning iron and manufactures of
iron. [Washington, 1832] 23 p.
MB.   15885

---- Joint resolution to authorize
the Secretary of the Navy to allow interest in certain cases.
Feb. 13, 1832. Mr. Smith, from
the Committee on Finance, reported the following resolution;
which was read, and passed to a
second reading: [Washington,
1832] 1 p.(S. 1) DNA; MB. 15886

---- Land Office Report. Library

of the Interior Dept. Dec. 3, 1832.
Annual report of the Commissioner
of the General Land Office for
fiscal year ending June 30, 1833.
[Washington, 1832] MB.   15887

---- Lands Offered and Unsold.
Mar. 10, 1832. Library of the
Interior Dept. Registers and receivers ordered to furnish statement of lands offered and which
remained unsold and subject to
entry on Dec. 31, 1831. [Wash-
ington, 1832] 1 p. MB.   15888

---- Laws of the United States,
22d Congress, 1st sess. 1832.
Law Library of Congress. Official edition, published under the
direction of the Secretary of
State. [Washington, 1832] 240 p.
MB.   15889

---- Laws on Indian Affairs. By
authority. 1832. Library of Congress. Laws of the colonial and
State governments relating to Indians and Indian affairs from 1633
to 1831, inclusive, with the proceedings of the Congress of the
Confederation and the laws of
Congress from 1800 to 1830 on
the same subject. [Washington,
1832] MB.   15890

---- Laws relating to Indians.
Law Library of Congress. Laws
of the colonial and State governments relating to the Indians and
Indian affairs from 1633 to [1832]
inclusive, with an appendix...
Washington, Thompson & Homans,
1832. 72 p. DNA; MB.   15891

---- Letter concerning the Army.
Gen. A. Macomb. Feb. 18, 1832.
Ex. Docs., No. 16, 22d Cong.,
2d sess., Vol. I. Transmitting
draft of bill proposed to improve
the condition of the rank and file
of the Army. [Washington, 1832]
6 p.   15892

---- ... Letter from the Secretary of State, transmitting the information required by a resolution of the House of Representatives, of the 26th of January,
inst., in relation to slaves returned in the 5th census, in
Maine, Massachusetts, and Ohio.
[Washington] Jan. 31, 1832. 2 p.
MB; TxFWTCU.   15893

---- Letter from the Secretary of
State, transmitting the information required by a resolution of
the House of Representatives of
the 24th Feb. last, in relation to
the number of cases tried, and
the number of days of session of
the Circuit Courts of the United
States for the States of Ohio,
Kentucky, and Tennessee, during
the last five years. Washington,
Pr. by Duff Green, 1832. MB; R.
    15894

---- Letter from the Secretary of
the Navy, transmitting an abstract
of the contingent expenses of the
navy, from the 1st of October to
the 30th September, 1832. Read,
and laid upon the table. Washington, Pr. by Duff Green, 1832.
13 p. MB; R.   15895

---- Letter from the Secretary of
the Treasury in reply to a resolution of the House, of the 20th
March last, requiring information
in relation to payments for lands
sold since 1st January, 1828, to
wit: whether in notes of the
Bank of the United States, notes
of State Banks, speci, or scrip.
May 9, 1832. Referred to the
Committee on Public Lands. Washington, Pr. by Duff Green, 1832.
MB; R.   15896

---- Letter from the Secretary of
the Treasury, transmitting a report of the commerce and navigation of the United States for the
year ending on the 30th September, 1831. [Washington, 1832]

301 p. MB; R.   15897

---- Letter from the Secretary of the Treasury, transmitting an abstract of the emoluments and expenditures of Officers of the Customs for the year 1831, April 20, 1832. Read, and laid on the table. Washington, Pr. by Duff Green, 1832. MB; R.   15898

---- Letter from the Secretary of the Treasury, transmitting the information required by a resolution of the House of Representatives, of the 11th inst., in relation to instructions given to the register and receiver of public money in Arkansas. Jan. 24, 1832. Referred to the Committee on the Public Lands. Washington, Pr. by Duff Green, 1832. MB; R. 15899

---- Letter from the Secretary of War, transmitting a statement of the expenditures made at the National Armories, and of the arms manufactured therein, during the year 1831. Mar. 15, 1832. Read, and laid upon the table. Washington, Pr. by Duff Green, 1832. MB; R.   15900

---- Letter from the Secretary of War, transmitting an abstract of the returns of the Militia of the United States for the year 1831. Feb. 7, 1832. Read, and laid upon the table. Washington, Pr. by Duff Green, 1832. MB; R. 15901

---- Letter on Claim of Harvey Brown. Quartermaster-General T. Cross. Jan. 17, 1832. House Ex. Docs., No. 65, 22d Cong., 1st sess., Vol. II. Transmitting papers in claim of Harvey Brown, lieutenant, for rent and quarters at Saint Augustine, Florida. [Washington, 1832] 4 p. MB.
                                 15902
---- Letter on Claims of Rhode Island Soldiers. Tristam Burgess.

May 24, 1832. House Ex. Docs., No. 246, 22d Cong., 1st sess., Vol. VI. Statement relative to claims of Rhode Island soldiers of the Revolutionary War for extra allowance on account of the depreciation of the currency in which they were paid. [Washington, 1832] 8 p. MB.   15903

---- Letter on Land Claims. Commissioner Elijah Hayward. Feb. 27, 1832. Ex. Docs., No. 297, 22d Cong., 1st sess., Vol. VI. Enclosing draft of proposed bill for relief of certain inhabitants of Missouri claiming land. [Washington, 1832] 2 p. MB.   15904

---- Letter on National Road. Secretary L. Case. Jan. 4, 1832. House Ex. Docs., No. 42, 22d Congress, 1st sess., Vol. II. Transmitting communication relative to a road between Green Bay and Prairie du Chien. [Washington, 1832] 4 p. MB.   15905

---- Letter on Road in Arkansas. J. C. Jones. Dec. 14, 1832. Ex. Docs., No. 39, 22d Cong., 2d sess., Vol. I. Transmitting map of southeastern portion of Arkansas to connection with statements concerning road from Little Rock to Villemont, Arkansas. [Washington, 1832] 5 p. MB.   15906

---- Letter on Spanish Land Claims. Secretary E. Livingston. June 12, 1832. House Ex. Docs., No. 274, 22d Cong., 1st sess., Vol. VI. Transmitting copy of bill proposed to satisfy claimants of land under Spanish grants. [Washington, 1832] 18 p. MB.   15907

---- Letter on the Coast Survey. Secretary McLane. Aug. 9, 1832. Library of the Coast Survey. Letter of the Secretary of the Treasury to F. R. Hassler, appointing him to make, under direction of the Treasury Dept., the survey of the coast as provided for by the acts of Feb. 19, 1807, and July 10, 1832. [Washington, 1832] 1 p. MB.   15908

---- Letter on the Culture of Silk. Peter S. Duponceau. May 8, 1832. House Ex. Docs., No. 232, 22d Cong., 1st sess., Vol. V. In relation to promoting the growth and manufacture of silk in the United States. [Washington, 1832] 5 p. MB; PPL.   15909

---- Letter on the relations of the States and General Government, Dec. 1832. [Washington, 1832] MB; MBAt.   15910

---- Letter on Treaty with Turkey. Secretary Edward Livingston. Jan. 18, 1832. Ex. Docs., No. 303, 22d Cong., 1st sess., Vol. VI. Requesting an appropriation for carrying into effect the treaty with the Sublime Porte. [Washington, 1832] 2 p. MB.   15911

---- Letter on Value of Coal. Benjamin Reeves. Feb. 6, 1832. House Ex. Docs., No. 100, 22d Cong., 1st sess., Vol. III. Statement showing the comparative value of Picton and Richmond coal. [Washington, 1832] 1 p. MB.   15912

---- Letter; Passenger arriving in the United States in 1831. Seamen in the ports of the United States 1831. 22 Cong., 1 sess., Ho. Doc. No. 293. [Washington] June 27, 1832. 40 p. MB; N.   15913

---- Letter referring to Barracks. Quartermaster-Gen. Thos. Jessup. March 31, 1832. House Ex. Docs., No. 204, 22d Cong., 1st sess., Vol. V. Recommends that the barracks at Prairie du Chien be transferred to the county of Crawford for county purposes. [Washington, 1832] 1 p. MB.   15914

---- Letter relative to Fort Griswold. Secretary Lewis Cass. Jan. 3, 1832. House Ex. Docs., No. 33, 22d Cong., 1st sess., Vol. II. Transmitting estimates for construction of fort projected for the site now occupied by Fort Griswold, near New London. [Washington, 1832] 6 p. MB.   15915

---- Letter relative to Ratio of Representation. E. H. Cummings. Jan. 3, 1832. Senate Docs., No. 17, 22d Cong., 1st sess., Vol. I. Transmitting tables showing the total Representation in Congress under any ratio of representation from 45,000 to 55,000 persons for each Representative. [Washington, 1832] 4 p. MB.   15916

---- Letter relative to Revolutionary Claims. Third Auditor P. Hagner. Feb. 27, 1832. Senate Docs., No. 94, 22d Cong., 1st sess., Vol. II. Statement relative to Revolutionary claims for half-pay for life or five years' full pay. [Washington, 1832] 5 p. MB.   15917

---- List of Reports to be made to the House. Dec. 3, 1832. Ex. Docs., No. 1, 22d Cong., 2d sess. Vol. I. List of reports to be made to the House of Representatives by the Executive Departments at the second session of the 22d Congress. [Washington, 1832] 14 p. MB.   15918

---- Massachusetts--Tariff. Resolutions of the wool growers and manufacturers of the County of Berkshire, Massachusetts. June 10, 1832. Referred to the Committee of the Whole House on the state of the Union. Washington, Pr. by Duff Green, 1832. 6 p. MB; R.   15919

---- Memorial against Erection of Bridge. Citizens of Pennsylvania. Mar. 15, 1832. House Ex.

Docs., No. 188, 22d Cong., 1st
sess.', Vol. V. Memorialists
protest against the erection of a
bridge at Wheeling, Virginia.
[Washington, 1832] 2 p. MB.
                              15920
---- Memorial against Nullification. Certain members of S. C.
Legislature, Jan. 23, 1832. House
Ex. Docs., No. 70, 22d Cong.,
1st sess., Vol. II. Memorialists
regard the doctrine of nullification as utterly hostile to the spirit of the Constitution. [Washington,
1832] 2 p. MB.   15921

---- Memorial against Recharter
of U.S. Bank. Citizens of Connecticut. Feb. 13, 1832. House
Ex. Docs., No. 107, 22d Cong.,
1st sess., Vol. IV. Memorialists
oppose the renewal of the charter
of the United States Bank. [Wash-
ington, 1832] 2 p. MB.   15922

---- ---- Citizens of Hartford,
Conn. Feb. 10, 1832. Senate
Docs., No. 56, 22d Cong., 1st
sess., Vol. II. Memorialists object to the renewal of the charter
of the Bank of the United States.
[Washington, 1832] 2 p. MB.
                              15923
---- ---- Citizens of Ohio. Mar.
29, 1832. Senate Docs., No. 115,
22d Cong., 1st sess., Vol. III.
Memorialists ask that the charter
of the United States Bank be not
renewed. [Washington, 1832] 2 p.
MB.   15924

---- ---- Citizens of Pennsylvania. Apr. 26, 1832. Senate
Docs., No. 135, 22d Cong., 1st
sess., Vol. III. Memorialists ask
that charter of the United States
Bank be not renewed. [Washington,
1832] 2 p. MB.   15925

---- ---- Citizens of South Carolina. May 14, 1832. House Ex.
Docs., No. 237, 22d Cong., 1st
sess., Vol. VI. Memorialists op-

pose the renewal of the charter
of the United States Bank. [Wash-
ington, 1832] 3 p. MB.   15926

---- Memorial against Reduction
of Duty on Slates. J. M. Porter.
May 12, 1832. Senate Docs., No.
149, 22d Cong., 1st sess., Vol.
III. Memorialist asks that the
duty on slates be not reduced.
[Washington, 1832] 2 p. MB.
                              15927
---- Memorial against Repeal of
Duties. Citizens of New Bedford.
Feb. 27, 1832. House Ex. Docs.,
No. 123, 22d Cong., 1st sess.,
Vol. IV. Memorialists pray that
the duties on imported tallow,
olive oil, and palm oil be not re-
pealed. [Washington, 1832] 3 p.
MB.   15928

---- Memorial against the Tariff.
Citizens of Pennsylvania. May 28,
1832. House Ex. Docs., No. 248,
22d Cong., 1st sess., Vol. VI.
Memorialists oppose the passage
of the tariff bill proposed by the
Secretary of the Treasury, and
ask that the duties on articles not
coming into competition with American products be repealed. [Wash-
ington, 1832] 2 p. MB.   15929

---- ---- ---- May 28, 1832.
Senate Docs., No. 153, 22d Cong.,
1st sess., Vol. III. Memorialists
protect against passage of bill
proposed by the Secretary of the
Treasury reducing the duty on imports. [Washington, 1832] 5 p.
MB.   15930

---- ---- Citizens of Vermont.
May 22, 1832. House Ex. Docs.,
No. 251, 22d Cong., 1st sess.,
Vol. VI. Memorialists are opposed to the passage of the tariff
bill proposed by the Secretary of
the Treasury. [Washington, 1832]
8 p. MB.   15931

---- Memorial concerning Brevet

Rank. Army officers. June 2, 1832. House Ex. Docs. , No. 253, 22d Cong. , 1st sess. , Vol. VI. Memorialists pray that the bill to abolish brevet rank in the Army may not be passed. [Washington, 1832] 3 p. MB.											15932

---- Memorial concerning Duties on silk. Citizens of New York. Mar. 26, 1832. Senate Docs. , No. 113, 22d Cong. , 1st sess. , Vol. III. Memorialists ask that a specific, instead of ad valorem, duty be imposed upon silk goods. [Washington, 1832] 2 p. MB.											15933

---- Memorial concerning the Tariff. Citizens of Philadelphia. Feb. 15, 1832. Senate Docs. , No. 87, 22d Cong. , 1st sess. , Vol. II. Memorialists ask that duties be estimated upon the actual cost of goods; That the rate of duty be equalized on all articles not now duty free. [Washington, 1832] 1 p. MB.											15934

---- Memorial for a Canal. Citizens of Pennsylvania. Dec. 11, 1832. Ex. Docs. , No. 12, 22d Cong. , 2d sess. , Vol. I. Asking an appropriation for the completion of the western section of the Chesapeake and Ohio Canal. [Washington, 1832] 1 p. MB.											15935

---- ---- Legislative Council of Florida. Apr. 27, 1832. Senate Docs. , No. 136, 22d Cong. , 1st sess. , Vol. III. Memorialists ask for grant of land in aid of the Chipola and St. Andrew's Canal Company. [Washington, 1832] 24 p. MB.											15936

---- Memorial for a Custom-House. Citizens of New York. June 1, 1832. House Ex. Docs. , No. 256, 22d Cong. , 1st sess. Vol. VI. Asking that an appropriation be made for the construction of a custom-house in New York

City. [Washington, 1832] 3 p. MB.											15937

---- Memorial for a National Hospital. Citizens of the Western States. Jan. 16, 1832. House Ex. Docs. , No. 66, 22d Cong. , 1st sess. , Vol. II. Memorialists ask for the establishment of a national hospital on the Ohio River. [Washington, 1832] 3 p. MB.											15938

---- Memorial for Abolition of Slavery. Citizens of Edgartown. Feb. 6, 1832. House Ex. Docs. , No. 96, 22d Cong. , 1st sess. , Vol. III. Memorialists ask that slavery be abolished in the District of Columbia. [Washington, 1832] 2 p. MB.											15939

---- Memorial for Additional Duties. Manufacturers of Baltimore. May 7, 1832. House Ex. Docs. , No. 229, 22d Cong. , 1st sess. , Vol. V. Memorialists ask that additional duties be imposed on the importation of musical instruments. [Washington, 1832] 3 p. MB.											15940

---- Memorial for Bank Charter. Citizens of Massachusetts. Feb. 6, 1832. House Ex. Docs. , No. 95, 22d Cong. , 1st sess. , Vol. III. Memorialists ask privilege of organizing a bank at the expiration of the charter of the United States Bank. [Washington, 1832] 4 p. MB.											15941

---- Memorial for Brevet Pay. Alexander Macomb. Dec. 11, 1832. Senate Docs. , No. 12, 22d Cong. , 2d sess. , Vol. I. Asking that he be allowed brevet pay as major-general, and that the amount be credited to him on his bond as surety for Lt. Chapman, paymaster. [Washington, 1832] 49 p. MB.											15942

---- Memorial for Bridge over

Potomac River. Corporation of
Georgetown. June 8, 1832. Senate Docs., No. 159, 22d Cong.,
1st sess., Vol. III. Memorialists ask that the bridge over the
Potomac River at Georgetown
may be so built as to preserve
the present depth of water.
[Washington, 1832] 3 p. MB.
                                15943
---- Memorial for Change in
Duty on Hardware. Jan. 31. 1832.
House Ex. Docs., No. 144, 22d
Cong., 1st sess., Vol. IV. New
York hardware merchants ask
that certain changes be made in
the duties on hardware. [Washing-
ton, 1832] 13 p. MB.   15944

---- Memorial for Charter for
Bank. Citizens of Massachusetts.
Jan. 26, 1832. Senate Docs.,
No. 37, 22d Cong., 1st sess.,
Vol. I. Memorialists ask to be
incorporated as a banking com-
pany, to take effect on the expira-
tion of the charter of the United
States Bank. [Washington, 1832]
4 p. MB.   15945

---- Memorial for Charter of U.S.
Bank. Officers Bank of Pennsylvania. Jan. 18, 1832. House Ex.
Docs., No. 64, 22d Cong., 1st
sess., Vol. II. Memorialists ask
that the charter of the United
States Bank be renewed. [Wash-
ington, 1832] 3 p. MB.   15946

---- Memorial for Compensation.
Capt. Isaac Hull. Dec. 29, 1832.
Ex. Docs., No. 27, 22d Cong.,
2d sess., Vol. I. Asking compensation for advances made and
services rendered as Navy agent
at the navy-yard at Washington,
District of Columbia. [Washing-
ton, 1832] 6 p. MB.   15947

---- ---- ---- Dec. 29, 1832.
Senate Docs. No. 18, 22d Cong.,
2d sess., Vol. I. Asking compensation for advances made and

services as Navy agent at the
navy-yard at Washington. [Wash-
ington, 1832] 6 p. MB.   15948

---- ---- Officers of the late
war. Jan. 3, 1832. House Ex.
Docs., No. 40, 22d Cong., 1st
sess., Vol. II. Memorialists
ask compensation for services
during the late war. [Washington,
1832] 2 p. MB.   15949

---- Memorial for Drawback on
Silks. Merchants of New York.
Jan. 18, 1832. House Ex. Docs.,
No. 72, 22d Cong., 1st sess.,
Vol. II. Memorialists ask that a
drawing be allowed on silks exported after being printed and
dyed in this country. [Washington,
1832] 2 p. MB.   15950

---- Memorial for Duty on Silks.
Citizens of Philadelphia. May 28,
1832. Senate Docs., No. 154,
22d Cong., 2d sess., Vol. III.
Memorialists ask equalization of
duties on silks. [Washington,
1832] 2 p. MB.   15951

---- Memorial for Free Canal.
Citizens of Pennsylvania. Dec.
17, 1832. Senate Docs., No. 11,
22d Cong., 2d sess., Vol. I.
Asking that the navigation of the
canal at the falls of the Ohio
River be made free. [Washington,
1832] 2 p. MB.   15952

---- ---- Citizens of St. Louis,
Missouri. Dec. 11, 1832. House
Ex. Docs., No. 5, 22d Cong.,
2d sess., Vol. I. Praying that
canal around the falls of the Ohio
be made free for navigation.
[Washington, 1832] 1 p. MB.
                                15953
---- Memorial for Improvement
of Harbor of Baltimore. Mar. 1,
1832. Senate Docs., No. 81, 22d
Cong., 1st sess., Vol. II. Corporation of Baltimore asks appropriation for improvement of the

harbor of Baltimore; Statement of amount expended on the harbor since 1798. [Washington, 1832] 3 p. MB.   15954

---- Memorial for Increase of Pay. Captains and masters commandant. Apr. 11, 1832. House Ex. Docs., No. 205, 22d Cong., 1st sess., Vol. V. Memorialists ask for an increase of pay and emoluments. [Washington, 1832] MB.   15955

---- Memorial for National Road. Legislature of Ohio. Feb. 12, 1832. House Ex. Docs., No. 148, 22d Cong., 1st sess., Vol. IV. Memorialists ask that Congress make an appropriation for the construction of a road from Zanesville, Ohio, to Florence, Alabama. [Washington, 1832] 4 p. MB.
                               15956
---- ---- ---- Feb. 11, 1832. Senate Docs., No. 69, 22d Cong., 1st sess., Vol. II. Memorialists ask that an appropriation be made to construct a national road from Zanesville, Ohio, to Florence, Alabama. [Washington, 1832] 4 p. MB.   15957

---- Memorial for Prevention of Cholera. New York Board of Health. Jan. 9, 1832. House Ex. Docs., No. 44, 22d Cong., 1st sess., Vol. II. Memorialists ask that Congress constitute a commission to investigate and report upon means for the prevention and cure of Asiatic cholera. [Washington, 1832] 2 p. MB.
                               15958
---- Memorial for Protection of Cherokee Indians. Citizens of Tenn. Mar. 12, 1832. House Ex. Docs., No. 163, 22d Cong., 1st sess., Vol. IV. Memorialists ask that the Cherokee Indians be protected against the usurpations of the State of Georgia. [Washington, 1832] 3 p. MB.   15959

---- Memorial for Protection of Indians. Citizens of Pennsylvania. Feb. 14, 1832. Senate Docs., No. 61, 22d Cong., 1st sess. Vol. II. Memorialists ask that Cherokee Indians be protected in their rights and the possession of their lands [Washington, 1832] 2 p. MB.   15960

---- Memorial for Quarantine. Corporations of the District of Columbia. June 30, 1832. House Ex. Docs., No. 295, 22d Cong., 1st sess., Vol. VI. Asking Congress to pass a law concerning quarantine for the protection of the District of Columbia. [Washington, 1832] 1 p. MB.   15961

---- Memorial for Recharter of Bank of United States. Feb. 9, 1832. Senate Docs., No. 68, 22d Cong., 1st sess., Vol. II. The officers of the Commercial Bank of Cincinnati ask that the charter of the Bank of the United States be renewed. [Washington, 1832] 4 p. MB.   15962

---- ---- Mar. 1, 1832. House Ex. Docs., No. 174, 22d Cong., 1st sess., Vol. IV. Charleston Chamber of Commerce asks that the charter of the United States Bank be renewed. [Washington, 1832] 1 p. MB.   15963

---- ---- Mar. 8, 1832. House Ex. Docs., No. 159, 22d Cong., 1st sess., Vol. IV. Merchants of New York ask that the charter of the United States Bank be renewed. [Washington, 1832] 2 p. MB.   15964

---- ---- Mar. 21, 1832. Senate Docs., No. 108, 22d Cong., 1st sess., Vol. II. New Orleans Canal and Banking Company asks for renewal of the charter of the United States Bank. [Washington, 1832] 2 p. MB.   15965

---- ---- Baltimore Marine Bank. Feb. 7, 1832. Senate Docs., No. 57, 22d Cong., 1st sess., Vol. II. Memorialists ask that the charter of the Bank of the United States be renewed. [Washington, 1832] 2 p. MB.   15966

---- ---- Bank of New Orleans. Mar. 7, 1832. House Ex. Docs., No. 184, 22d Cong., 1st sess., Vol. IV. Asking that the charter of the United States Bank be renewed. [Washington, 1832] 2 p. MB.   15967

---- ---- Bank of North America, Phila. Feb. 13, 1832. House Ex. Docs., No. 137, 22d Cong., 1st sess., Vol. IV. Memorialists ask that charter of United States Bank be renewed. [Washington, 1832] 4 p. MB.   15968

---- ---- Bank officers, Wyndham, Conn. Feb. 16, 1832. Senate Docs., No. 86, 22d Cong., 1st sess., Vol. II. Memorialists ask that charter of the United States Bank be renewed. [Washington, 1832] 1 p. MB.   15969

---- ---- Banks in Baltimore. Mar. 6, 1832. House Ex. Docs., No. 156, 22d Cong., 1st sess., Vol. IV. Asking that the charter of the United States bank be renewed. [Washington, 1832] 1 p. MB.   15970

---- ---- Banks in North Carolina. Mar. 1, 1832. House Ex. Docs., No. 106, 22d Cong., 1st sess., Vol. IV. Asking that the charter of the United States Bank be renewed. [Washington, 1832] 2 p. MB.   15971

---- ---- Chambersburg Bank. Feb. 16, 1832. House Ex. Docs., No. 138, 22d Cong., 1st sess., Vol. IV. Memorialists ask that charter of the United States Bank

be renewed. [Washington, 1832] 2 p. MB.   15972

---- ---- Citizens of Baltimore. Feb. 6, 1832. Senate Docs., No. 47, 22d Cong., 1st sess., Vol. I. Memorialists ask that charter of the United States Bank be renewed. [Washington, 1832] 3 p. MB.   15973

---- ---- Citizens of Boston. Jan. 6, 1832. Senate Docs., No. 48, 22d Cong., 1st sess., Vol. I. Memorialists ask that charter of Bank of the United States be renewed. [Washington, 1832] 2 p. MB.   15974

---- ---- ---- Jan. 18, 1832. House Ex. Docs., No. 92, 22d Cong., 1st sess., Vol. III. Memorialists ask that the charter of the United States Bank be renewed. [Washington, 1832] 2 p. MB.   15975

---- ---- Citizens of Connecticut. Feb. 13, 1832. House Ex. Docs, No. 108, 22d Cong., 1st sess., Vol. IV. In favor of the renewal of the charter of the United States Bank. [Washington, 1832] 6 p. MB.   15976

---- ---- Citizens of Danville. Mar. 6, 1832. House Ex. Docs., No. 158, 22d Cong., 1st sess., Vol. IV. Memorialists ask that the charter of the United States Bank be renewed. [Washington, 1832] 1 p. MB.   15977

---- ---- Citizens of Kentucky. Feb. 13, 1832. House Ex. Docs., No. 111, 22d Cong., 1st sess., Vol. IV. Favoring renewal of charter of the United States Bank. [Washington, 1832] 1 p. MB.   15978

---- ---- ---- Mar. 12, 1832. House Ex. Docs., No. 165, 22d Cong., 1st sess., Vol. IV. Memorialists ask that charter of the United States Bank be renewed. [Washington, 1832] 2 p. MB.   15979

---- ---- Citizens of Louisville. Jan. 27, 1832. House Ex. Docs., No. 142, 22d Cong., 1st sess., Vol. IV. Memorialists ask that the charter of the United States Bank be renewed. [Washington, 1832] 1 p. MB.   15980

---- ---- Citizens of Mass. Jan. 24, 1832. Senate Docs., No. 40, 22d Cong., 1st sess., Vol. I. Memorialists ask for bank charter to take effect at the expiration of the charter of the United States Bank. [Washington, 1832] 3 p. MB.   15981

---- ---- ---- June 18, 1832. House Ex. Docs., No. 284, 22d Cong., 1st sess., Vol. VI. In favor of renewal of charter of the United States Bank. [Washington, 1832] 3 p. MB.   15982

---- ---- Citizens of New York. Apr. 2, 1832. House Ex. Docs., No. 192, 22d Cong., 1st sess., Vol. V. Memorialists ask that charter of United States Bank be renewed. [Washington, 1832] 1 p. MB.   15983

---- ---- Citizens of Pittsburg. Mar. 7, 1832. House Ex. Docs., No. 150, 22d Cong., 1st sess., Vol. IV. Memorialists ask that charter of the United States Bank be renewed. [Washington, 1832] 2 p. MB.   15984

---- ---- Citizens of Vermont. Feb. 24, 1832. House Ex. Docs., No. 168, 22d Cong., 1st sess., Vol. IV. Memorialists ask that charter of the United States Bank be renewed. [Washington, 1832] MB.   15985

---- ---- ---- Mar. 6, 1832.

House Ex. Docs., No. 157, 22d Cong., 1st sess., Vol. IV. Memorialists ask that the charter of the United States Bank be renewed. [Washington, 1832] 1 p. MB.   15986

---- ---- Citizens of Virginia. Feb. 29, 1832. House Ex. Docs., No. 136, 22d Cong., 1st sess., Vol. IV. Memorialists ask that charter of United States Bank be renewed. [Washington, 1832] 1 p. MB.   15987

---- ---- Farmers' Bank, Amherst, Mass. Feb. 13, 1832. House Ex. Docs., No. 110, 22d Cong., 1st sess., Vol. IV. Favoring renewal of charter of United States Bank. [Washington, 1832] 5 p. MB.   15988

---- ---- Hartford Fire Insurance Co. Feb. 13, 1832. House Ex. Docs., No. 112, 22d Cong., 1st sess. Vol. IV. Memorialists ask that the charter of the United States Bank be renewed. [Washington, 1832] 1 p. MB.   15989

---- ---- Louisiana State Bank. Mar. 8, 1832. House Ex. Docs., No. 153, 22d Cong., 1st sess., Vol. IV. Memorialists ask that the charter of the United States Bank be renewed. [Washington, 1832] 3 p. MB; R.   15990

---- ---- Merchants of Albany. Feb. 27, 1832. House Ex. Docs., No. 139, 22d Cong., 1st sess., Vol. IV. Memorialists ask that charter of the United States Bank be renewed. [Washington, 1832] 2 p. MB.   15991

---- ---- Merchants of New York. Feb. 13, 1832. House Ex. Docs., No. 119, 22d Cong., 1st sess., Vol. IV. Memorialists ask that charter of the United States Bank be renewed. [Washington, 1832]

6 p. MB.   15992

---- ---- Officers Bank of North
America. Feb. 13, 1832. Senate
Docs., No. 74, 22d Cong., 1st
sess., Vol. II. Memorialists ask
that the charter of the Bank of
the United States be renewed.
[Washington, 1832] 4 p. MB.
                            15993
---- ---- Officers of Kensington
Bank. Feb. 13, 1832. House Ex.
Docs., No. 97, 22d Cong., 1st
sess., Vol. III. Memorialists ask
that charter of the United States
Bank be renewed. [Washington,
1832] 3 p. MB.   15994

---- Memorial for Reduction of
Duties on Paper-Hangings. July 2,
1832. Senate Docs., No. 177, 22d
Cong., 1st sess., Vol. III. Merchants of New York ask for reduction of duties on paper-hangings.
[Washington, 1832] 2 p. MB.
                            15995
---- Memorial for Reduction of
Newspaper Postage. Citizens of
Boston. Jan. 17, 1832. Senate
Docs., No. 59, 22d Cong., 1st
sess., Vol. II. Memorialists ask
for a reduction of postage on
newspapers and other periodical
publications. [Washington, 1832]
6 p. MB; R.   15996

---- Memorial for Reduction of
Postage. Citizens of Boston. Jan.
17, 1832. House Ex. Docs., No.
106, 22d Cong., 1st sess., Vol.
IV. Memorialists ask for reduction of postage on newspapers and
periodicals. [Washington, 1832]
6 p. MB.   15997

---- Memorial for Reduction of
the Tariff. Citizens of Pennsylvania. Feb. 15, 1832. House
Ex. Docs., No. 154, 22d Cong.,
1st sess., Vol. IV. Memorialists
ask for reduction of duties on imports. [Washington, 1832] 1 p.
MB.   15998

---- Memorial for Renewing
Charter of United States Bank.
Jan. 30, 1832. House Ex. Docs.,
No. 79, 22d Cong., 1st sess.,
Vol. II. Officers of the Bank of
Pennsylvania ask that the charter
of the United States Bank be re-
newed. [Washington, 1832] 1 p.
MB.   15999

---- Memorial for Repeal of Duties. Garsed Raines & Co. Philadelphia, Feb. 20, 1832. Senate
Docs., No. 82, 22d Cong., 1st
sess., Vol. II. Memorialists ask
repeal of duty on raw flax, and
increase of duty on thread and
twine made of flax. [Washington,
1832] 2 p. MB.   16000

---- Memorial for Repeal of the
Tariff. W. Harper and T. R. Dew.
Feb. 13, 1832. House Ex. Docs.,
No. 82, 22d Cong., 1st sess.,
Vol. II. Memorialists ask that the
present tariff laws be repealed.
[Washington, 1832] 11 p. MB.
                            16001
---- Memorial from Cherokee Indians. Jan. 5, 1832. House Ex.
Docs., No. 45, 22d Cong., 1st
sess., Vol. II. Memorialists refer Congress to former memorials relative to their removal
westward and to the spoliation of
their lands. [Washington, 1832]
5 p. MB.   16002

---- Memorial from the Cherokee Indians. Jan. 9, 1832. House
Ex. Docs., No. 56, 22d Cong.,
1st sess., Vol. II. Memorialists
oppose passage of the act to carry
into effect the fourth section of
treaty in relation to claims of
citizens of Georgia against Cherokee Indians. [Washington, 1832]
8 p. MB.   16003

---- Memorial from the Officers
and Soldiers of the Rhode Island
Brigade. Jan. 9, 1832. House
Ex. Docs., No. 77, 22d Cong.,

1st sess., Vol. II. Memorialists ask to be paid the difference between the value of specie and the depreciated paper in which they were paid for services in the Revolution. [Washington, 1832] 5 p. MB.   16004

---- Memorial of American Board of Foreign Missions. Boston, Mar. 24, 1832. House Ex. Docs., No. 194, 22d Cong., 1st sess., Vol. V. Memorialists ask Congress to take measures to ascertain the value of the buildings and improvements belonging to the board on the territory of the Choctaw Indians. [Washington, 1832] 17 p. MB.   16005

---- Memorial of Archibald Clark, Administrator of Robert Seagrove, deceased, for himself and other citizens of Georgia. Feb. 27, 1832. Referred to the Committee of the Whole House, to which is committed the bill H. R. No. 128. Washington, Duff Green, 1832. MB; R.   16006

---- Memorial of Captain Charles G. Ridgely. Dec. 19, 1832. Senate Docs., No. 13, 22d Cong., 2d sess., Vol. I. Asking to be allowed amount of expenses incurred in returning home from a distant station. [Washington, 1832] 2 p. MB.   16007

---- Memorial of Creek Indians. Feb. 15, 1832. Senate Docs., No. 65, 22d Cong., 1st sess., Vol. II. Memorialists ask indemnification for losses and injuries sustained at the hands of hostile Indians. [Washington, 1832] 4 p. MB.   16008

---- Memorial of Mary O'Sullivan, with Documents. Dec. 10, 1832. Ex. Docs., No. 88, 22d Cong., 2d sess., Vol. II. Claims indemnification for losses sustained by illegal seizure by United States authorities of vessel owned by her late husband, John O'Sullivan. [Washington, 1832] 28 p. MB.   16009

---- Memorial of Navy Chaplains for Compensation. Jan. 18, 1832. Senate Docs., No. 30, 22d Cong., 1st sess., Vol. I. Memorialists pray for passage of law to increase the compensation of chaplains in the Navy. [Washington, 1832] 2 p. MB.   16010

---- Memorial of Revolutionary Soldiers. Nov. 24, 1832. Ex. Docs., No. 14, 22d Cong., 2d sess., Vol. I. Asking such compensation as may be consonant with justice on account of the depreciation of the currency in which they received their pay. [Washington, 1832] 2 p. MB.   16011

---- Memorial of the Baltimore and Ohio Railroad Company. Feb. 14, 1832. Senate Docs., No. 63, 22d Cong., 1st sess., Vol. II. Memorialists ask national subscription to the stock of the company. [Washington, 1832] 6 p. MB.   16012

---- Memorial of the Creek Indians. Jan. 24, 1832. House Ex. Docs., No. 102, 22d Cong., 1st sess., Vol. III. Protest against their removal west of the Mississippi. [Washington, 1832] 5 p. MB.   16013

---- Memorial of the Provident Association of Clerks. Apr. 20, 1832. House Ex. Docs., No. 211, 22d Cong., 1st sess., Vol. V. Memorialists ask that the charter of the association be continued in the District of Columbia. [Washington, 1832] 3 p. MB.   16014

---- Memorial on Chesapeake and Ohio Canal. Howes Goldsborough. Jan. 14, 1832. House Ex. Docs.,

No. 67, 22d Cong., 1st sess.,
Vol. II. Asks to be protected
in his constitutional rights
against the encroachments of
the Chesapeake and Ohio Canal Company. [Washington,
1832] 2 p. MB.   16015

---- Memorial on Duty on Leather. Dealers in leather. May 21,
1832. Senate Docs., No. 148,
22d Cong., 1st sess., Vol. III.
Memorialists ask that the duty on
imported leather be not reduced.
[Washington, 1832] 2 p. MB.
                           16016
---- Memorial on Indian Depredations. Charles Clark. Feb. 27,
1832. House Ex. Docs., No. 148,
22d Cong., 1st sess., Vol. IV.
Memorialist prays that the bill
reported by the Committee on Indian Affairs to carry into effect
treaty with the Creek Indians relative to Indian depredations may be
passed. [Washington, 1832] 18 p.
MB.   16017

---- Memorial on Indian Treaties.
Citizens of New York. Mar. 5,
1832. House Ex. Docs., No. 175,
22d Cong., 1st sess., Vol. IV.
Memorialists ask Congress to
preserve inviolate the faith of
treaties with the Cherokee Indians. [Washington, 1832] 2 p.
MB.   16018

---- Memorial on National Road.
Legislature of Indiana. Dec. 26,
1832. Senate Docs., No. 28, 22d
Cong., 2d sess., Vol. I. Asking
for an appropriation to improve
the National Road from Louisville,
Kentucky, to St. Louis, Missouri.
[Washington, 1832] 1 p. MB.
                           16019
---- Memorial on Purchase of
Government Land. New York,
Apr. 12, 1832. Senate Docs., No.
123, 22d Cong., 1st sess., Vol.
III. Managers of the Society for
Reformation of Juvenile Delin-

quents ask passage of law releasing them from further payment to
the United States on land purchased for use of the institution.
[Washington, 1832] 3 p. MB.
                           16020
---- Memorial on Silk Culture.
New York State Agricultural College. Feb. 20, 1832. House Ex.
Docs., No. 162, 22d Cong., 1st
sess., Vol. IV. Asking passage
of bill now pending in the House
to promote the culture of silk.
[Washington, 1832] 2 p. MB.
                           16021
---- Memorial on the Macpherson
Claim. Apr. 27, 1832. Senate
Docs., No. 137, 22d Cong., 1st
sess., Vol. III. Memorialists ask
compensation for services of their
father, Gen. Wm. Macpherson,
in the Revolutionary War. [Wash-
ington, 1832] 11 p. MB.   16022

---- Memorial on the Tariff.
Citizens of Bardstown, Kentucky.
Apr. 9, 1832. House Ex. Docs.,
No. 221, 22d Cong., 1st sess.,
Vol. V. Memorialists ask that the
interests of the country may be
protected in the adjustment of the
tariff. [Washington, 1832] 3 p.
MB.   16023

---- ---- Citizens of Bedford.
June 18, 1832. House Ex. Docs.,
No. 290, 22d Cong., 1st sess.,
Vol. VI. Against the passage of
the tariff bill proposed by the
Secretary of the Treasury. [Wash-
ington, 1832] 2 p. MB.   16024

---- ---- Citizens of Bennington.
June 9, 1832. House Ex. Docs.,
No. 276, 22d Cong., 1st sess.,
Vol. VI. Against the passage of
the tariff bill proposed by the
Secretary of the Treasury. [Wash-
ington, 1832] 2 p. MB.   16025

---- ---- Citizens of Easton.
June 9, 1832. House Ex. Docs.,
No. 275, 22d Cong., 1st sess.,

Vol. VI. Against reduction of the tariff duties. [Washington, 1832] 2 p. MB.   16026

---- ---- Citizens of Kentucky. June 8, 1832. Senate Docs., No. 160, 22d Cong., 1st sess., Vol. III. Memorialists remonstrate against passage of bill proposed by the Secretary of the Treasury reducing the duties on imports. [Washington, 1832] 3 p. MB.
                              16027

---- ---- Citizens of Lynn. June 6, 1832. House Ex. Docs., No. 257, 22d Cong., 1st sess., Vol. VI. Against any reduction of the duty on leather and leather manufactures. [Washington, 1832] 2 p. MB.   16028

---- ---- Citizens of Massachusetts. June 4, 1832. House Ex. Docs., No. 261, 22d Cong., 1st sess., Vol. VI. Praying that any reduction of the present tariff duties be made on articles not coming into competition with American products. [Washington, 1832] 3 p. MB.   16029

---- ---- ---- June 6, 1832. House Ex. Docs., No. 258, 22d Cong., 1st sess., Vol. VI. Asking that the protection afforded by the present tariff to the manufacturers of wool may remain unimpaired. [Washington, 1832] 2 p. MB.   16030

---- ---- ---- July 2, 1832. Senate Docs., No. 181, 22d Cong. 1st sess., Vol. III. Memorialists ask Senate to strike out the clause in the tariff bill giving bounty to ships. [Washington, 1832.] 1 p. MB.   16031

---- ---- Citizens of Nantucket. May 14, 1832. House Ex. Docs., No. 235, 22d Cong., 1st sess., Vol. VI. Remonstrating against the repeal of the duties on imported tallow and olive and palm oils. [Washington, 1832] 3 p. MB.   16032

---- ---- Citizens of New Hampshire. June 18, 1832. House Ex. Docs., No. 277, 22d Cong., 1st sess., Vol. VI. Against the passage of the tariff bill proposed by the Secretary of the Treasury. [Washington, 1832] 2 p. MB.
                              16033
---- ---- Citizens of New Jersey. June 6, 1832. Senate Docs., No. 157, 22d Cong., 1st sess., Vol. III. Memorialists ask that there be no abandonment of the protective system. [Washington, 1832] 3 p. MB.   16034

---- ---- ---- June 14, 1832. House Ex. Docs., No. 287, 22d Cong., 1st sess., Vol. VI. Against any reduction of duties on articles coming into competition with American products. [Washington, 1832] 1 p. MB.   16035

---- ---- Citizens of Pennsylvania. June 16, 1832. Senate Docs., No. 167, 22d Cong., 1st sess., Vol. III. In favor of the protective system. [Washington, 1832] 1 p. MB.   16036

---- ---- ---- June 22, 1832. House Ex. Docs., No. 286, 22d Cong., 1st sess., Vol. VI. Against the reduction of duties on articles coming into competition with American products. [Washington, 1832] 1 p. MB.   16037

---- ---- Citizens of Philadelphia. May 29, 1832. House Ex. Docs., No. 255, 22d Cong., 1st sess., Vol. VI. Against any alteration in the tariff which shall lessen the protection now afforded agricultural products. [Washington, 1832] 5 p. MB.   16038

---- ---- Citizens of Schuylkill

County, Pa. June 22, 1832. House Ex. Docs., No. 289, 22d Cong., 1st sess., Vol. VI. Remonstrating against the passage of any bill reducing the tariff. [Washington, 1832] 4 p. MB.
16039

---- ---- Citizens of Trenton. June 4, 1832. House Ex. Docs., No. 271, 22d Cong., 1st sess., Vol. VI. Against any reduction of the duties on leather. [Washington, 1832] 2 p. MB.   16040

---- ---- Citizens of Vermont. June 18, 1832. House Ex. Docs., No. 283, 22d Cong., 1st sess., Vol. VI. Against any reduction of the duties on articles coming into competition with American products. [Washington, 1832] 2 p. MB.   16041

---- ---- Committee of free-trade convention. Jan. 23, 1832. Senate Docs., No. 55, 22d Cong., 1st sess., Vol. I. Memorialists set forth the evils of the existing tariff, and ask such a modification as shall be consistent with the needs of the revenue and equal in its operation. [Washington, 1832] 65 p. MB.   16042

---- ---- Dealers in leather. Philadelphia, May 21, 1832. House Ex. Docs., No. 240, 22d Cong., 1st sess., Vol. VI. Memorialists ask that the duty on imported leather be not reduced. [Washington, 1832] 2 p. MB.   16043

---- ---- Free-trade convention at Philadelphia. Jan. 23, 1832. House Ex. Docs., No. 82, 22d Cong., 1st sess., Vol. II. Memorialists ask that duties on imports be so reduced that the revenues of the country shall not exceed its necessary expenditures. [Washington, 1832] 55 p. MB.
16044

---- ---- Hat-makers at York.

June 12, 1832. House Ex. Docs., No. 273, 22d Cong., 1st sess., Vol. VI. Against any reduction of the duty on hats. [Washington, 1832] 1 p. MB.   16045

---- ---- Merchants of New York. June 12, 1832. House Ex. Docs., No. 278, 22d Cong., 1st sess., Vol. III. Asking for a reduction of the duty on linen. [Washington, 1832] 2 p. MB.   16046

---- ---- Philadelphia dealers in leather. June 2, 1832. House Ex. Docs., No. 252, 22d Cong., 1st sess., Vol. VI. Against any reduction in the present duties on leather and leather manufactures. [Washington, 1832] 2 p. MB.
16047

---- Memorial relative to Building Liens. Citizens of Dist. of Columbia. Mar. 20, 1832. House Ex. Docs., No. 193, 22d Cong., 1st sess., Vol. V. Memorialists ask Congress to make provisions to secure mechanics against imposition by contractors for building. [Washington, 1832] 2 p. MB.   16048

---- Memorial relative to Certain Duties. Manufacturers of Philadelphia. May 22, 1832. Senate Docs., No. 151, 22d Cong., 1st sess., Vol. III. Memorialists ask that the duties on bridle-bits, etc., be not reduced. [Washington, 1832] 1 p. MB.   16049

---- Memorial relative to Duties on Iron. Manufacturers of iron. July 2, 1832. Senate Docs., No. 176, 22d Cong., 1st sess., Vol. III. Memorialists pray for a reduction of the duties on iron. [Washington, 1832] 2 p. MB.
16050

---- Memorial relative to Duty on Hats. Manufacturers of hats. June 6, 1832. Senate Docs., No. 163, 22d Cong., 1st sess., Vol. III.

Memorialists ask that the duty on imported hats be not reduced. [Washington, 1832] 1 p. MB. 16051

---- ---- Manufacturers of Philadelphia. May 25, 1832. Senate Docs., No. 150, 22d Cong., 1st sess., Vol. III. Memorialists ask that the duty on hats be not reduced. [Washington, 1832] 1 p. MB. 16052

---- Memorial relative to French Spoliations. John Marrast. Jan. 7, 1832. Senate Docs., No. 14, 22d Cong., 1st sess., Vol. I. Asking indemnification for spoliations for spoliations by France prior to the year 1800. [Washington, 1832] 2 p. MB. 16053

---- Memorial relative to Mariner's Compass. Moses Smith. Jan. 3, 1832. House Ex. Docs., No. 32, 22d Cong., 1st sess., Vol. II. Memorialist prays compensation for improvement in mariner's and surveyor's compass. [Washington, 1832] 2 p. MB. 16054

---- Memorial relative to Tariff. Minority of South Carolina Legislature. Jan. 24, 1832. Senate Docs., No. 34, 22d Cong., 1st sess., Vol. I. Memorialists ask that the duties on imports be reduced to a scale commensurate with the necessary revenue of the United States. [Washington, 1832] 2 p. MB. 16055

---- Memorial relative to the tariff. Citizens of New York. June 5, 1832. House Ex. Docs., No. 254, 22d Cong., 1st sess., Vol. VI. Against the passage of any tariff law which shall take away from American manufacturers the protection now afforded them. [Washington, 1832] 3 p. MB. 16056

---- ---- Marble manufacturers. Philadelphia, May 23, 1832.

House Ex. Docs., No. 247, 22d Cong., 1st sess., Vol. VI. Memorialists ask that the duty on marble be not reduced. [Washington, 1832] 2 p. MB. 16057

---- Message concerning Fort Delaware. President A. Jackson. Jan. 20, 1832. House Ex. Docs., No. 68, 22d Cong., 1st sess., Vol. II. Transmitting documents relative to the propriety of compromising claim to the island on which Fort Delaware is situated. [Washington, 1832] 2 p. MB. 16058

---- Message from the President of the United States, to the Senate, returning the bank bill, with his objections, together with Judge White's speech, on the same subject. Knoxville, T., Pr. at the office of the "Knoxville Register." 1832. 31 p. MB; T; TKL-Mc. 16059

---- Message giving Expenditures on Breakwaters. President A. Jackson. Jan. 26, 1832. House Ex. Docs., No. 73, 22d Cong., 1st sess., Vol. II. Transmitting reports of expenditures on breakwaters since the year 1815. [Washington, 1832] 10 p. MB. 16060

---- Message on Bridge over Potomac River. President A. Jackson. Dec. 27, 1832. Ex. Docs., No. 22, 22d Cong., 2d sess., Vol. I. Transmitting reports of engineers on construction of bridge over the Potomac at Washington. [Washington, 1832] 17 p. MB. 16061

---- Message on Claim of Cyrenius Hull. President A. Jackson. Jan. 23, 1832. House Ex. Docs., No. 215, 22d Cong., 1st sess., Vol. V. Transmitting correspondence between the Secretary of State and the Minister to Great Britain relative to the claim of Cyrenius Hull for losses sustained

422 United States

in consequence of alleged illegal seizure of schooner by the collector of customs at Sandusky Bay. [Washington, 1832] 19 p. MB. 16062

---- Message on Colonial Trade. President Andrew Jackson. Apr. 4, 1832. Senate Docs., No. 118, 22d Cong., 1st sess., Vol. III. Copies of correspondence between the American Minister and the British Government relative to trade with the British colonies. [Washington, 1832] 27 p. MB. 16063

---- ---- ---- Apr. 20, 1832. Senate Docs., No. 132, 22d Cong., 1st sess., Vol. III. Transmitting correspondence relative to colonial and West Indian trade since April 20, 1818. [Washington, 1832] 36 p. MB. 16064

---- Message on Commerce with Colombia. President A. Jackson. Jan. 10, 1832. House Ex. Docs., No. 46, 22d Cong., 1st sess., Vol. II. Transmitting report on commercial arrangement with Republic of Colombia. [Washington, 1832] 12 p. MB. 16065

---- Message on Counterfeiting Foreign Coins. President A. Jackson. Apr. 23, 1832. House Ex. Docs., No. 214, 22d Cong., 1st sess., Vol. V. Transmitting a letter from the Secretary of State suggesting the propriety of passing a law for the punishment of uttering counterfeit foreign coins. [Washington, 1832] 2 p. MB. 16066

---- Message on Duties on Foreign Wines. President Andrew Jackson. Mar. 1, 1832. House Ex. Docs., No. 176, 22d Cong., 1st sess., Vol. IV. Transmitting information relative to the duties on red wines of Austria. [Washington, 1832] 5 p. MB. 16067

---- Message on Duty on Cotton.

President Andrew Jackson. Apr. 9, 1832. Senate Docs., No. 121, 22d Cong., 1st sess., Vol. III. Letters from Lord Aberdeen and Mr. McLane relative to proposed duty on cotton. [Washington, 1832] 5 p. MB. 16068

---- Message on Foreign Commerce. President Andrew Jackson. Feb. 29, 1832. Senate Docs., No. 80, 22d Cong., 1st sess., Vol. II. Statements relative to trade with the British colonies in America; Quantity of American and foreign tonnage entering into and departing from the United States to the British colonies from October 5, 1830, to September 30, 1831; Goods and merchandise imported into the United States during the same period. [Washington, 1832] 92 p. MB. 16069

---- Message on Imports and Exports. President A. Jackson. Apr. 18, 1832. Senate Docs., No. 130, 22d Cong., 1st sess., Vol. III. Transmitting statements showing value of imports from and exports to the British European ports during the year ending Sept. 30, 1831; Tonnage employed. [Washington, 1832] 2 p. MB. 16070

---- Message on Imprisonment of S. G. Howe. President A. Jackson. May 2, 1832. House Ex. Docs., No. 224, 22d Cong., 1st sess., Vol. V. Transmitting report from the Secretary of State stating that no information has been received at the Department of the imprisonment of Samuel G. Howe in the Kingdom of Prussia. [Washington, 1832] 1 p. MB. 16071

---- Message on Indian Agents. President Andrew Jackson. Mar. 12, 1832. Senate Docs., No. 101, 22d Cong., 1st sess., Vol. II. Transmitting report showing names and compensation of agents em-

ployed in the removal of the Choctaw and Cherokee Indians; Time employed; Money disbursed. [Washington, 1832] 20 p. MB.
16072

---- Message on Indian Annuities. President Andrew Jackson. Mar. 12, 1832. House Ex. Docs. , No. 161, 22d Cong. , 1st sess. , Vol. IV. Transmitting report of the Secretary of War relative to Indians who joined the enemy during the late war and are drawing annuities from the United States. [Washington, 1832] 1 p. MB.
16073

---- Message on Indian Lands. President Andrew Jackson. Jan. 24, 1832. House Ex. Docs. , No. 76, 22d Cong. , 1st sess. , Vol. II. Transmitting information relative to Choctaw reservations. [Washington, 1832] 7 p. MB.
16074

---- Message on Indian Treaties. President A. Jackson. Apr. 19, 1832. House Ex. Docs. , No. 210, 22d Cong. , 1st sess. , Vol. V. Transmitting copies of treaties concluded with Indian tribes. [Washington, 1832] 25 p. MB.
16075

---- Message on Internal Improvements. President A. Jackson. Dec. 6, 1832. Ex. Docs. , No. 17, 22d Cong. , 2d sess. , Vol. I. Returning with his objections the bill for the improvement of certain rivers and harbors. [Washington, 1832] 4 p. MB.   16076

---- Message on Public Lands. President A. Jackson. Apr. 23, 1832. Senate Docs. , No. 133, 22d Cong. , 1st sess. , Vol. III. Transmitting information relative to unsold public lands; Quantity granted to States. [Washington, 1832] 6 p. MB.   16077

---- Message on Removal of the Indians. President A. Jackson. Feb. 15, 1832. House Ex. Docs.

No. 116, 22d Cong. , 1st sess. , Vol. IV. Transmitting report from the Secretary of War relative to the removal westward of the Indians. [Washington, 1832] 17 p. MB.   16078

---- ---- ---- Mar. 12, 1832. House Ex. Docs. , No. 171, 22d Cong. , 1st sess. , Vol. IV. Transmitting statements showing amount of money expended in the removal of the Indians to the West. [Washington, 1832] 91 p. MB.   16079

---- Message on State Claims. President A. Jackson. Dec. 6, 1832. Senate Docs. , No. 3, 22d Cong. , 2d sess. , Vol. I. Returning with his objections the act providing for the final settlement of State claims for advances made to the General Government during the war. [Washington, 1832] 3 p. MB.   16080

---- Message on Support of the Patent Office. President A. Jackson. Apr. 4, 1832. House Ex. Docs. , No. 195, 22d Cong. , 1st sess. , Vol. V. Transmitting a letter from the Secretary of State as to the necessity of increased appropriations for the support of the Patent Office. [Washington, 1832] 2 p. MB.   16081

---- Message on Survey of River. President Jackson. Feb. 10, 1832. House Ex. Docs. , No. 104, 22d Cong. , 1st sess. , Vol. IV. Transmitting report of surveys of Savannah and Tennessee Rivers. [Washington, 1832] 23 p. MB.
16082

---- Message on the Fisheries. President Andrew Jackson. Feb. 6, 1832. House Ex. Docs. , No. 99, 22d Cong. , 1st sess. , Vol. III. Transmitting reports relative to the regulations of England, France, and the Netherlands respecting fisheries. [Washington, 1832] 279 p. MB. 16083

---- Message on the Fur Trade and Trade to Mexico. President Jackson. Feb. 8, 1832. Senate Docs., No. 90, 22d Cong., 1st sess., Vol. II. Statement of number of persons engaged in the fur trade and inland trade with Mexico; Capital employed. [Washington, 1832] 86 p. MB. 16084

---- Message on the Mint. President Andrew Jackson. Jan. 16, 1832. House Ex. Docs., No. 57, 22d Cong., 1st sess., Vol. II. Transmitting report on the United States Mint for the year 1831. [Washington, 1832] 3 p. MB. 16085

---- Message on the Republic of Colombia. President A. Jackson. Mar. 16, 1832. House Ex. Docs., No. 173, 22d Cong., 1st sess., Vol. IV. Transmitting a report from the Secretary of State relative to the Republic of Colombia and our diplomatic relations with it. [Washington, 1832] 18 p. MB. 16086

---- Message on Tonnage Duties. President Andrew Jackson. Apr. 13, 1832. House Ex. Docs., No. 206, 22d Cong., 1st sess., Vol. V. Transmitting letter from Secretary of State Relative to tonnage duties paid on vessels of Portugal in the ports of the United States. [Washington, 1832] 2 p. MB. 16087

---- Message on Trade with British Colonies. Pres. Andrew Jackson. Mar. 1, 1832. Senate Docs., No. 85, 22d Cong., 1st sess., Vol. II. Transmitting information relative to trade between the United States and the British colonies in America; Statement of duties payable upon merchandise not produced in Great Britain brought into the British colonies.

[Washington, 1832] 5 p. MB. 16088

---- Message on Treaties with Mexico. Pres. A. Jackson. May 1, 1832. House Ex. Docs., No. 225, 22d Cong., 1st sess., Vol. V. Transmitting copies of treaties concluded between the United States and Mexico. [Washington, 1832] 27 p. MB. 16089

---- Message on Treaty with Denmark. Pres. A. Jackson. May 28, 1832. House Ex. Docs., No. 249, 22d Cong., 1st sess., Vol. VI. Transmitting copy of instructions under which the treaty of indemnity with Denmark was negotiated. [Washington, 1832] 42 p. MB. 16090

---- Message on Treaty with Sublime Porte. Pres. A. Jackson. May 29, 1832. House Ex. Docs., No. 250, 22d Cong., 1st sess., Vol. VI. Transmitting copies of correspondence concerning the negotiation of treaty with Sublime Porte. [Washington, 1832] 27 p. MB. 16091

---- Message on Treaty with Turkey. Pres. A. Jackson. Feb. 7, 1832. Ex. Docs., No. 304, 22d Cong., 1st sess., Vol. VI. Transmitting copy of treaty of commerce and navigation concluded between the United States and the Sublime Porte. [Washington, 1832] 3 p. MB. 16092

---- Message on United States Bank. Pres. A. Jackson. July 10, 1832. Ex. Docs., No. 300, 22d Cong., 1st sess., Vol. VI. Returning with his objections the bill to renew and modify the charter of the United States Bank. [Washington, 1832] 14 p. MB. 16093

---- Message on United States Territory on Pacific Ocean. Pres. Jackson. Apr. 2, 1832. House Ex.

Docs., No. 191, 22d Cong., 1st sess., Vol. V. Transmitting information in response to resolution enquiring whether any United States territory on the Pacific Ocean has been taken possession of by any foreign power. [Washington, 1832] 2 p. MB. 16094

No entry. 16095

---- Message relative to United States Vessel at Peru. Pres. Jackson. Apr. 4, 1832. House Ex. Docs., No. 272, 22d Cong., 1st sess., Vol. VI. Transmitting report from the Secretary of State concerning the refuge afforded on the United States vessel St. Louis to the Vice-President of Peru and Gen. Miller. [Washington, 1832] 17 p. MB. 16096

---- Mint United States--assays--1831. Feb. 16, 1832. Read, and referred to the Select Committee appointed on the 15th of December last, on the subject of silver coins. Washington, Pr. by Duff Green, 1832. MB; R. 16097

---- Motion relative to the Tariff. Mr. Poindexter. Dec. 17, 1832. Senate Docs., No. 10, 22d Cong., 2d sess., Vol. I. Directing the Secretary of the Treasury to report to the Senate a list of articles of foreign growth or manufacture upon which in his opinion the duty ought to be reduced. [Washington, 1832] 1 p. MB. 16098

---- Naval Regulations. By command of the President. Washington, 1832. Library of Congress. Rules of the Navy Department regulating the civil administration of the Navy of the United States. [Washington,

1832] MB. 16099

---- Navigation of the Arkansas River. May 3, 1832, pr. by order of the House of Representatives. Washington, Pr. by Duff Green, 1832. MB; R; TrFwTCU. 16100

---- Navy Register. 1832. Pub. by the Navy Department. [Washington, 1832] 79 p. MB. 16101

---- New York--inhabitants of--Lien of judgements upon land. Feb. 21, 1832. Referred to the Committee of the Whole House to which is referred the bill (H.R. No. 238) declaring the effects of judgements in the Circuit and District Courts of the United States, and for other purposes. Feb. 24, 1832. Pr. by order of the House of Representatives. Washington, Duff Green, 1832. MB; R. 16102

---- Observations on the Manufacture of Salt. Feb. 16, 1832. Senate Docs., No. 66, 22d Cong., 1st sess., Vol. II. Manufacture of salt; Qualities of different kinds as manufactured by artificial heat or crystallized by solar evaporation. [Washington, 1832] 7 p. MB. 16103

---- Opinion of the Supreme Court of the United States at January term, 1832, delivered by Mr. Chief Justice Marshall ....in the case of Samuel A. Worcester...versus the state of Georgia... Pr. from authenticated copies. Washington, Pr. by Gales & Seaton, 1832. 39 p. Ct; MdHi; PHi; PP; WHi; NbHi. 16104

---- Petition against Reduction of Duty on Coal. Citizens of Philadelphia. Feb. 13, 1832. House Ex.

Docs., No. 117, 22d Cong., 1st sess., Vol. IV. Petitioners ask that no reduction be made in the duty on coal. [Washington, 1832] 2 p. MB.   16105

---- Petition for Banking Privilege. Citizens of Massachusetts. Feb. 13, 1832. House Ex. Docs., No. 109, 22d Cong., 1st sess., Vol. IV. Petitioners ask to be granted a privilege to organize a banking company. [Washington, 1832] 6 p. MB.   16106

---- Petition for Compensation for Services. John Conrad. Dec. 6, 1832. Senate Docs., No. 8, 22d Cong., 2d sess., Vol. I. Asks compensation for services as United States marshal of the eastern district of Pennsylvania in executing a writ against Edward Thompson. [Washington, 1832] 2 p. MB.   16107

---- Petition for Construction of a Road. Citizens of Arkansas. Mar. 6, 1832. House Ex. Docs., No. 151, 22d Cong., 1st sess., Vol. IV. Petitioners ask authority from Congress to raise money by lottery for the purpose of constructing a road from Memphis to Little Rock. [Washington, 1832] 2 p. MB.   16108

---- Petition for Increase of Pay. Officers of the Army. Jan. 30, 1832. House Ex. Docs., No. 90, 22d Cong., 1st sess., Vol. III. Petitioners ask for increase of pay to Army surgeons and assistant surgeons. [Washington, 1832] 2 p. MB.   16109

---- Petition for Pay for Recapture of Vessel. Heirs of naval officers. Jan. 9, 1832. House Ex. Docs., No. 62, 22d Cong., 1st sess., Vol. II. Petitioners ask for compensation on account of recapture of frigate Constitution.

[Washington, 1832] 2 p. MB.   16110

---- Petition for Recharter of United States Bank. Thames Bank, Conn. Mar. 2, 1832. House Ex. Docs., No. 164, 22d Cong., 1st sess., Vol. IV. Asking that the charter of the United States Bank be renewed. [Washington, 1832] 1 p. MB.   16111

---- Petition for Reduction of Duties on Woollen Goods. Journeymen tailors. Jan. 23, 1832. House Ex. Docs., No. 71, 22d Cong., 1st sess., Vol. II. Petitioners ask that the duties on imported woollen goods be reduced. [Washington, 1832] 4 p. MB.   16112

---- Petition for Reduction of Tariff on Woollens. Phila. journeymen tailors. Jan. 30, 1832. Senate Docs., No. 39, 22d Cong., 1st sess., Vol. I. Memorialists ask reduction of duties on woollen goods. [Washington, 1832] 4 p. MB.   16113

---- Petition for Uniform System of Liens. Citizens of New York. Feb. 24, 1832. House Ex. Docs., No. 122, 22d Cong., 1st sess., Vol. IV. Petitioners ask passage of law for a uniform system of liens on judgments. [Washington, 1832] 2 p. MB.   16114

---- Petition of the Managers of the Georgetown Female Orphan Asylum. Dec. 11, 1832. Ex. Docs. No. 31, 22d Cong., 2d sess., Vol. I. Asking Government aid for the institution. [Washington, 1832] 1 p. MB.   16115

---- Petition on the Tariff. Citizens of Pennsylvania. June 26, 1832. Senate Docs., No. 173, 22d Cong., 1st sess., Vol. III. Petitioners ask that the protective system be continued. [Washington, 1832] 2 p. MB.   16116

---- Petition relative to Auction
Sales. Merchants of New York.
June 18, 1832. House Ex. Docs.,
No. 280, 22d Cong., 1st sess.,
Vol. VI. Asking for the imposi-
tion of a duty on sales at auction.
[Washington, 1832] 1 p. MB.
16117

---- Petition relative to Duty on
Hair-Cloth. Manufacturers of New
York. May 26, 1832. Senate Docs.,
No. 152, 22d Cong., 1st sess.,
Vol. III. Petitioners ask that du-
ties on hair-cloth be not reduced.
[Washington, 1832] 2 p. MB.
16118

---- Petition relative to the Tariff. Brush manufacturers. May 20,
1832. House Ex. Docs., No. 268,
22d Cong., 1st sess., Vol. VI.
Asking that the duties on imported
bristles be repealed. [Washing-
ton, 1832] 1 p. MB.   16119

---- ---- Citizens of Pennsylvania. May 21, 1832. House Ex.
Docs., No. 241, 22d Cong., 1st
sess., Vol. VI. Petitioners ask
that no change in the duties on
wool be made at the present session of Congress. [Washington,
1832] 1 p. MB.   16120

---- Post-Office Laws. 1832. Law
Library of Congress. Laws relating to the Post-Office, with instructions and forms for postmas-
ters. Official edition. [Washing-
ton, 1832] 79 p. MB.   16121

---- Pre-emption Privileges to
Actual Settlers. May 8, 1832.
Library of the Interior Dept. Circular relating to pre-emption privileges to actual settlers being
housekeepers upon the public lands.
[Washington, 1832] 2 p. MB.
16122
---- Pre-emption Rights. July 28,
1832. Library of the Interior Dept.
Circular in relation to pre-emption
rights under act of May 29, 1830.
[Washington, 1832] 3 p. MB.
16123

---- Proclamation of Andrew
Jackson, president of the United
States, of the 10th Dec. 1832.
Pr. by order of the House of
Representatives. Harrisburg, Pr.
by H. Welsh, 1832, '33. 21 p.
A-Ar; DLC; OCHP; PPAmP; RP.
16124

---- Public Documents, printed
by order of the Senate of the
United States, 1st sess., 22d
Cong., begun and held at the city
of Washington, Dec. 7, 1831. In
3 vols. Washington, Pr. by Duff
Green, 1832. Nj; PScr; R;
TxFwTCU.   16125

---- Records of Cases in the Supreme Court. Library of the Supreme Court. [Washington, 1832]
MB.   16126

---- Regulations of the United
States military academy, at West
Point. New York, Pr. by J. & J.
Harper, 1832. 92, [6] p. PPAmP;
PU; TJoT; TxU.   16127

---- Report from the Commissioner of the General Land Office,
in compliance with a resolution
of the Senate on the subject of
unconfirmed land claims in the
State of Missouri, Jan. 3, 1832.
Read and ordered to be printed.
Washington, Pr. by Duff Green,
1832. 22d Cong., 1st sess. R.
16128
---- Report from the Secretary
of the Treasury, in compliance
with a resolution of the Senate,
relating to the affairs of the
Bank of the United States. Feb. 7,
1832. Read, Feb. 8--Mr. Dallas
moved to refer this report to the
Select Committee on the memorial of the Bank of the United States,
and that it be printed. Mr. Benton moved to refer it to the Committee on the Judiciary, and then
it was laid on the table. Feb. 29,
ordered to be printed. Washing-

ton, Pr. by Duff Green, 1832.
22d Cong., 1st sess. R.   16129

---- Report from the Secretary
of the Treasury, with monthly
statements of the Bank of the
United States for January and
February 1832, in compliance
with a resolution of the Senate.
Mar. 19, 1832. Read, and ordered to be printed. Washington,
Duff Green, pr., 1832. 22d Cong.,
1st sess. R.   16130

---- Report from the Secretary
of War, with drawings of certain
surveys made in Indiana, in compliance with a resolution of the
Senate, of 11th Jan. 1831. Dec.
19, 1832. Read, Jan. 5, 1832,
ordered to be pr. Washington,
Pr. by Duff Green, 1832. 22d
Cong., 1st sess. R.   16131

---- Report in Case of Bartholomew Delapierre. Com. on Military Pensions. Jan. 19, 1832.
Reports of Committees, No. 201,
22d Cong., 1st sess., Vol. I.
Reports bill for relief of petitioner. [Washington, 1832] 1 p. MB.
                         16132

---- Report of Canal Surveys.
Secretary of Lewis Cass. Feb.
10, 1832. House Ex. Docs., No.
113, 22d Cong., 1st sess., Vol.
IV. Transmitting report of surveys and estimates for the Farmington, Hampshire and Hampden
Canal. [Washington, 1832] 7 p.
MB.   16133

---- Report of Debates, Twenty-
Second Congress, Second Sess.
Dec. 3, 1832. Register of Debates
in Congress, by Gales & Seaton,
Vol. XIV. Proceedings, pp. 1-
1312. Vol. XV, Proceedings, pp.
1313-1940. [Washington, 1832]
MB.   16134

---- Report of Expedition to the
Indian Country. Secretary Lewis

Cass. Mar. 7, 1832. House Ex.
Docs., No. 152, 22d Cong., 1st
sess., Vol. IV. Transmitting an
account of an expedition made into the Indian country by Henry R.
Schoolcraft. [Washington, 1832]
20 p. MB.   16135

---- Report of the Secretary of
War [Lewis Cass] to the President of the United States. Dept.
of War, Nov. 25, 1832. [Wash-
ington, 1832] 17-42 p. ViL.
                         16136

---- Report on Abolition for Imprisonment for Debt. Select committee. Jan. 17, 1832. Reports
of Committees, No. 194, 22d
Cong., 1st sess., Vol. I. Recommends the abolition of imprisonment for debt; Bill reported.
[Washington, 1832] 11 p. MB.
                         16137

---- Report on Account of Na-
thaniel Mitchell. Auditor P. Hag-
ner. Dec. 26, 1832. Senate Docs.,
No. 16, 22d Cong., 2d sess.,
Vol. I. Review of the accounts of
Nathaniel Mitchell, major of the
Virginia line in the Revolutionary
War. [Washington, 1832] 4 p.
MB.   16138

---- Report on Action of Commissioner of General Land Office.
Apr. 20, 1832. Reports of Committees, No. 449, 22d Cong., 1st
sess., Vol. III. Committee on the
Judiciary reports that Commissioner was officially called upon
to designate the boundaries of the
land district in Michigan. [Wash-
ington, 1832] 20 p. MB. 16139

---- Report on an Indian Reservation. Committee on Public Lands.
June 6, 1832. Reports of Committees, No. 488, 22d Cong., 1st
sess., Vol. V. Committee is of
opinion that the title to a certain
Chickasaw Indian reservation has
reverted to the United States.
[Washington, 1832] 49 p. MB.
                         16140

---- Report on Apportionment of Representatives. Select committee. May 3, 1832. Reports of Committees, No. 463, 22d Cong., 1st sess., Vol. IV. Majority and minority reports on Senate bill relative to apportionment of Representatives under the fifth census. [Washington, 1832] 62 p. MB.
16141

---- Report on Bank of United States. Secretary Louis McLane. Feb. 29, 1832. Senate Docs., No. 79, 22d Cong., 1st sess., Vol. II. Statement of amount of paper currency in circulation; Amount of gold and silver coin and bullion annually remitted by each branch bank to the bank at Philadelphia. [Washington, 1832] 5 p. MB.
16142

---- Report on Biennial Register. Select committee. July 7, 1832. Reports of Committees, No. 506, 22d Cong., 1st sess., Vol. V. States the results of action taken by the committee under the resolution relative to the compilation and publication of the Biennial Register. [Washington, 1832] 20 p. MB.   16143

---- Report on Bill for Apportionment of Representatives. Select committee. Apr. 5, 1832. Senate Docs., No. 119, 22d Cong., 1st sess., Vol. III. Recommends substitute for bill. [Washington, 1832] 22 p. MB.   16144

---- Report on Bill for Relief of B. Schaumburgh. Committee on Claims. Apr. 6, 1832. Reports of Committees, No. 431, 22d Cong., 1st sess., Vol. III. Recommends passage of bill allowing petitioner, who was a paymaster in the Army, credit in his accounts for payments made to certain troops. [Washington, 1832] 1 p. MB.   16145

---- Report on Bill for Relief of Martha Randolph. Select committee. Mar. 20, 1832. Senate Docs., No. 107, 22d Cong., 1st sess., Vol. II. Recommends passage of bill granting public lands to Martha Randolph, only surviving child of Thomas Jefferson. [Washington, 1832] 5 p. MB.   16146

---- Report on Bill for Relief of Revolutionary Soldiers. Com. on Pensions. Jan. 24, 1832. Senate Docs., No. 33, 22d Cong., 1st sess., Vol. I. Recommends passage of bill granting annuities to surviving soldiers of the Revolution who have never received bounty or pension. [Washington, 1832] MB.   16147

---- Report on Bill to Abolish Duty on Alum Salt. Mar. 19, 1832. Senate Docs., No. 105, 22d Cong., 1st sess., Vol. II. Recommends that the bill be indefinitely postponed. [Washington, 1832] 11 p. MB.   16148

---- Report on Boiler Explosions. Select committee. May 18, 1832. Reports of Committees, No. 478, 22d Cong., 1st sess., Vol. V. Relative to the causes and mode of prevention of steamboat boiler explosions; Bill reported making regulations governing the matter. [Washington, 1832] 192 p. MB.
16149

---- Report on Breach of Privilege. Committee on Privileges. Apr. 17, 1832. Reports of Committees, No. 447, 22d Cong., 1st sess., Vol. III. Recommends course of proceedings in the case of the assault of Sam Houston on William Stanbery, a member of the House of Representatives. [Washington, 1832] 2 p. MB.
16150

---- Report on Bridge across Potomac River. Com. on District of Columbia. May 28, 1832. Reports of Committees, No. 484,

22d Cong., 1st sess., Vol. V. Recommends passage of bill, with amendments. [Washington, 1832] 3 p. MB.   16151

---- Report on Canal in Michigan. Secretary Lewis Cass. Jan. 24, 1832. House Ex. Docs., No. 78, 22d Cong., 1st sess., Vol. II. Transmitting estimates for construction of canal to connect La Plaisance Bay harbor, Michigan, with the River Raisin. [Washington, 1832] 4 p. MB.
16152

---- Report on Case of Cyrenius Hall. Committee on Foreign Affairs. Apr. 24, 1832. Reports of Committees, No. 453, 22d Cong., 1st sess., Vol. III. Recommends payment to petitioner for vessel seized by the United States; Bill reported. [Washington, 1832] 2 p. MB.   16153

---- Report on Case of Ephraim Shaler. Secretary Lewis Cass. Jan. 14, 1832. House Ex. Docs., No. 60, 22d Cong., 1st sess., Vol. II. Transmitting copies of papers in case of Ephraim Shaler, late lieutenant and adjutant 25th United States Infantry. [Washington, 1832] 3 p. MB.
16154

---- Report on Case of Hotchkiss & Forbes. Committee on Commerce. Jan. 4, 1832. Reports of Committees, No. 126, 22d Cong., 1st sess., Vol. I. Recommends refundment of tonnage duties paid by petitioners; Bill reported. [Washington, 1832] 2 p. MB.   16155

---- Report on Case of R. C. Jennings and Executors of J. Roddey. Dec. 19, 1832. Reports of Committees, No. 10, 22d Cong., 2d sess. The Committee on Claims reports bill extending time for carrying into effect an act for the relief of Robert C.

Jennings and of the executors of James Roddey. [Washington, 1832] 1 p. MB.   16156

---- Report on Case of Solomon Betton. Committee on Indian Affairs. Apr. 6, 1832. Reports of Committees, No. 430, 22d Cong., 1st sess., Vol. III. Recommends re-examination of accounts of Solomon Betton for compensation as commissioner in charge of cession of land to the Creek Indians. [Washington, 1832] 2 p. MB.   16157

---- Report on Cases in Circuit Courts. Secretary Edward Livingston. Apr. 12, 1832. House Ex. Docs., No. 207, 22d Cong., 1st sess., Vol. V. Transmitting information concerning cases tried in the circuit courts of Ohio, Kentucky, and Tennessee during the last five years. [Washington, 1832] 4 p. MB.   16158

---- Report on Celebration of Washington's Birthday. Joint committee. Feb. 13, 1832. Senate Docs., No. 62, 22d Cong., 1st sess., Vol. II. Recommends adjournment of Congress in commemoration of the one hundredth anniversary of the birthday of Washington, and that arrangements be made for its proper celebration. [Washington, 1832] 3 p. MB.   16159

---- Report on Cherokee Claims. Secretary Lewis Cass. Apr. 11, 1832. House Ex. Docs., No. 233, 22d Cong., 1st sess., Vol. V. Transmitting claims of certain Cherokee Indians on account of spoliation of stock and destruction of buildings. [Washington, 1832] 3 p. MB.   16160

---- Report on Claim of A. Jackson. Committee on Private Land Claims. Jan. 13, 1832. Reports

on Committees, No. 184, 22d
Cong., 1st sess., Vol. I. Recommends allowance of bounty
land to petitioner on account of
military services of James Gammons, his slave; Bill reported.
[Washington, 1832] 2 p. MB.
16161
---- Report on Claim of Alexander Donelson. Committee on
Claims. Jan. 16, 1832. Reports
of Committees, No. 188, 22d
Cong., 1st sess., Vol. I. Recommends allowance of claim of
petitioner as assignee of David
G. Howard for value of horse
and equipments lost in the United
States service; Bill reported.
[Washington, 1832] 2 p. MB.
16162
---- Report on Claim of Andrew
Boyle. Committee on Claims.
Jan. 30, 1832. Reports of Committees, No. 280, 22d Cong., 1st
sess., Vol. II. Adverse to granting compensation for horse lost
in the military service. [Wash-
ington, 1832] 1 p. MB.   16163

---- Report on Claim of Andrew
Moore. Committee on Claims.
Jan. 16, 1832. Reports of Committees, No. 189, 22d Cong., 1st
sess., Vol. I. Recommends allowance of claim of petitioner for
horse lost in the United States
Service; Bill reported. [Washing-
ton, 1832] 1 p. MB.   16164

---- Report on Claim of Antoine
Cruzat. Com. on Private Land
Claims. Jan. 25, 1832. Reports
of Committees, No. 234, 22d
Cong., 1st sess., Vol. II. Recommends allowance of claim of
petitioner to land in Louisiana;
Bill reported. [Washington,
1832] 1 p. MB.   16165

---- Report on Claim of Archibald Watt. Com. on Revolutionary
Claims. Jan. 10, 1832. Reports
of Committees, No. 165, 22d

Cong., 1st sess., Vol. I. Recommends allowance of claim of
petitioner for value of Revolutionary certificates, with interest;
Bill reported. [Washington, 1832]
1 p. MB.   16166

---- Report on Claim of B.
Gibbs. Committee on Revolutionary Claims. Jan. 3, 1832. Reports of Committees, No. 108,
22d Cong., 1st sess., Vol. I.
Recommends payment to petitioner of settlement certificate; Bill
reported. [Washington, 1832] 1 p.
MB.   16167

---- Report on Claim of Benjamin Sherfey. Committee on
Claims. Feb. 27, 1832. Reports
of Committees, No. 333, 22d
Cong., 1st sess., Vol. III. Recommends refundment to petitioner
of amount of fine paid for failure
to perform military duty; Bill reported. [Washington, 1832] 1 p.
MB.   16168

---- Report on Claim of Bernard
M. Patterson. Committee on
Claims. Jan. 30, 1832. Reports
of Committees, No. 248, 22d
Cong., 1st sess., Vol. II. Adverse to claim of petitioner for
refundment of amount of money
paid to settle his accounts as officer in the Army. [Washington,
1832] 2 p. MB.   16169

---- Report on Claim of Burns
& Manney. Committee on Claims.
Mar. 21, 1832. Reports of Committees, No. 402, 22d Cong., 1st
sess., Vol. III. Adverse to claim
of petitioners for damages on contract to furnish brick to Fort Macon. [Washington, 1832] 3 p. MB.
16170
---- Report on Claim of Charles
J. Catlett. Committee on Claims.
Mar. 26, 1832. Reports of Committees, No. 413, 22d Cong.,
1st sess., Vol. III. Adverse to

claim of memorialist for losses sustained by removal of tobacco by the enemy. [Washington, 1832] 4 p. MB.   16171

---- Report on Claim of Charles Moran. Committee on Claims. Mar. 28, 1832. Reports of Committees, No. 415, 22d Cong., 1st sess., Vol. III. Adverse to compensation of petitioner for injuries to his house while in the occupancy of United States troops. [Washington, 1832] 3 p. MB.
                                      16172

---- Report on Claim of Daniel Goodwin. Com. on Revolutionary Claims. Jan. 10, 1832. Reports of Committees, No. 149, 22d Cong., 1st sess., Vol. I. Recommends allowance of claim of petitioner for use of property occupied by the United States; Bill reported. [Washington, 1832] 1 p. MB.   16173

---- Report on Claim of David E. Twiggs. Committee on Claims. May 28, 1832. Reports of Committees, No. 485, 22d Cong., 1st sess., Vol. V. Adverse to claim of petitioner for expenses incurred in defending suits against him in his official capacity as an officer of the Army. [Washington, 1832] 5 p. MB.   16174

---- Report on Claim of Don Carlos Dehault Delassus. Com. on Claims. July 5, 1832. Reports of Committees, No. 500, 22d Cong., 1st sess., Vol. V. Reports, with amendment, bill reimbursing claimant for expenses in raising and equipping troops in aid of the United States forces during the Florida war. [Washington, 1832] 1 p. MB.   16175

---- Report on Claim of Ebenezer Cooley. Committee on Public Lands. Jan. 4, 1832. Reports of Committees, No. 146, 22d Cong.

1st sess., Vol. I. Adverse to allowance of claim of petitioner to land in Louisiana. [Washington, 1832] 4 p. MB.   16176

---- Report on Claim of Elizabeth Scott. Committee on Claims. Feb. 13, 1832. Senate Docs., No. 60, 22d Cong., 1st sess., Vol. II. Recommends allowance of claim of petitioner for land; Bill reported. [Washington, 1832] 1 p. MB.   16177

---- Report on Claim of Ephraim Howard. Committee on Commerce. Apr. 11, 1832. Reports of Committees, No. 449, 22d Cong., 1st sess., Vol. III. Adverse to claim of petitioner, as executor of Caleb Howard, for compensation for a brig owned by him and sold by the United States for salvage. [Washington, 1832] 2 p. MB.   16178

---- Report on Claim of Executors of James Roddey. Judiciary Committee. Feb. 2, 1832. Senate Docs., No. 44, 22d Cong., 1st sess., Vol. I. Recommends allowance of claim of petitioners for amount due for rations-furnishery the Army; Bill reported. [Washington, 1832] 30 p. MB.
                                      16179

---- Report on Claim of F. Raymer. Committee on Revolutionary Claims. Jan. 3, 1832. Reports of Committees, No. 93, 22d Cong., 1st sess., Vol. I. Recommends allowance of claim of petitioner for horse impressed into the Army; Bill reported. [Washington, 1832] 1 p. MB.
                                      16180

---- Report on Claim of Francis Barnes. Committee on Claims. Mar. 6, 1832. Reports of Committees, No. 352, 22d Cong., 1st sess., Vol. III. Petitioner prays to be allowed his expenses incurred in purchasing whiskey for the United States; Committee reports adversely. [Washington, 1832] 2 p. MB. 16181

---- ---- Secretary Levi Woodbury. Jan. 30, 1832. House Ex. Docs., No. 88, 22d Cong., 1st sess., Vol. III. Transmitting information relative to claim of Francis Barnes for losses on contract for furnishing whiskey to the Navy. [Washington, 1832] 13 p. MB. 16182

---- Report on Claim of G. Bowen. Com. on the Post-Office and Post-Roads. Mar. 8, 1832. Reports of Committees, No. 354, 22d Cong., 1st sess., Vol. III. Recommends that petitioner be paid additional amount claimed on contract with the Post-Office Dept.; Bill reported. [Washington, 1832] 1 p. MB. 16183

---- Report on Claim of George Mayfield. Committee on Public Lands. Jan. 13, 1832. Reports of Committees, No. 182, 22d Cong., 1st sess., Vol. I. Recommends allowance of claim for land patent; Bill reported. [Washington, 1832] 2 p. MB. 16184

---- Report on Claim of George Turnbull. Committee on Claims. Jan. 30, 1832. Reports of Committees, No. 247, 22d Cong., 1st sess., Vol. II. Adverse to claim of petitioner for building bridge on mail-route. [Washington, 1832] 2 p. MB. 16185

---- Report on Claim of Godfroy & Beaugrand. Committee on Claims. Jan. 4, 1832. Reports of Committees, No. 128, 22d Cong., 1st sess., Vol. I. Recommends allowance of claim of petitioners for value of buildings destroyed by the British and Indians; Bill reported. [Washington, 1832] 2 p. MB. 16186

---- Report on Claim of Heirs of Alex. Boyd. Com. on Private Land Claims. Jan. 6, 1832. Reports on Committees, No. 144, 22d Cong., 1st sess., Vol. I. Recommends that claimants be confirmed in title to land; Bill reported. [Washington, 1832] 2 p. MB. 16187

---- Report on Claim of Heirs of C. Comb. Com. on Private Land Claims. Jan. 4, 1832. Reports of Committees, No. 131, 22d Cong., 1st sess., Vol. I. Recommends that petitioners be confirmed in title to land in Louisiana; Bill reported. [Washington, 1832] 2 p. MB. 16188

---- Report on Claim of Heirs of Edward Barry. Committee on Claims. Feb. 8, 1832. Senate Docs., No. 53, 22d Cong., 1st sess., Vol. I. Recommends allowance of claim of petitioners for value of household property of Edward Barry, an officer in the navy-yard. [Washington, 1832] 2 p. MB. 16189

---- Report on Claim of Heirs of Robert Avart. Committee on Claims. Feb. 29, 1832. Reports of Committees, No. 339, 22d Cong., 1st sess., Vol. III. Recommends reference of claim of petitioners for value of property destroyed by the United States Army to the accounting officers of the Treasury; Bill reported. [Washington, 1832] 1 p. MB. 16190

---- Report on Claim of Heman Allen. Committee on Claims. Jan. 4, 1832. Senate Docs., No. 19, 22d Cong., 1st sess., Vol. I. Recommends allowance of claim of petitioner for compensation as United States marshal; Bill reported. [Washington, 1832] 1 p. MB. 16191

---- Report on Claim of Henry Clay. Committee on Claims. July 7, 1832. Reports of Committees, No. 505, 22d Cong., 1st sess., Vol. V. Recommends that claim of petitioner as executor of James Morrison be referred to the Secretary of the Treasury for settlement; Bill reported. [Washington, 1832] 1 p. MB.   16192

---- Report on Claim of Henry Waller. Committee on Claims. Mar. 9, 1832. Senate Docs., No. 97, 22d Cong., 1st sess., Vol. II. Recommends allowance of claim of petitioner for buildings destroyed by the British during the late war; Bill reported. [Washington, 1832] 2 p. MB.   16193

---- Report on Claim of Isaac Shannon. Committee on Indian Affairs. Apr. 28, 1832. Reports of Committees, No. 455, 22d Cong., 1st sess., Vol. III. Adverse to claim of petitioner for value of horse taken by the Osage Indians. [Washington, 1832] 1 p. MB.   16194

---- Report on Claim of Isidore Navarre. Committee on Claims. Mar. 28, 1832. Reports of Committees, No. 418, 22d Cong., 1st sess., Vol. III. Adverse to compensating memorialist for barn seized for the use of troops. [Washington, 1832] 8 p. MB.
16195
---- Report on Claim of J. L. Chisham. Committee on Claims. Feb. 8, 1832. Reports of Committees, No. 281, 22d Cong., 1st sess., Vol. II. Adverse to granting compensation for horse lost in the Army. [Washington, 1832] 2 p. MB.   16196

---- Report on Claim of J. M. Harper. Committee on Claims. Feb. 3, 1832. Reports of Committees, No. 267, 22d Cong.,

1st sess., Vol. II. Recommends allowance of claim of petitioner for expenses in defending suit brought against him for actions done in performance of his duty as an Army officer. [Washington, 1832] 1 p. MB.   16197

---- Report on Claim of James Brownlee. Com. on Revolutionary Claims. Jan. 6, 1832. Reports of Committees, No. 142, 22d Cong., 1st sess., Vol. I. Recommends allowance of claim of petitioner for seven years' half-pay on account of services of his brother; Bill reported. [Washington, 1832] 1 p. MB.   16198

---- Report on Claim of James Tilford. Committee on Claims. Feb. 17, 1832. Reports of Committees, No. 308, 22d Cong., 1st sess., Vol. II. Recommends allowance of claim of petitioner as assignee of certain soldiers; Bill reported. [Washington, 1832] MB.   16199

---- Report on Claim of Jane Dauphin. Com. on Foreign Affairs. Jan. 5, 1832. Reports of Committees, No. 140, 22d Cong., 1st sess., Vol. I. Recommends allowance of claim of petitioner for moiety of value of schooner owned by John Dauphin and libelled by the Government; Bill reported. [Washington, 1832] 4 p. MB.   16200

---- Report on Claim of Joel Byington. Committee on Claims. July 2, 1832. Reports of Committees, No. 497, 22d Cong., 1st sess., Vol. V. Recommends allowance of claim for destruction of house by United States troops; Bill reported. [Washington, 1832] 1 p. MB.   16201

---- Report on Claim of John Anderson. Committee on Claims. June 25, 1832. Reports of Committees, No. 492, 22d Cong., 1st sess., Vol. V. Adverse to claim of petitioner of compensation for house and store destroyed by the British. [Washington, 1832] 2 p. MB.   16202

---- Report on Claim of John Bruce. Com. on Revolutionary Claims. Jan. 10, 1832. Reports of Committees, No. 150, 22d Cong., 1st sess., Vol. I. Recommends allowance of claim of petitioner as administrator of Philip Bush for value of certificates issued during the Revolution; Bill reported. [Washington, 1832] 3 p. MB.   16203

---- Report on Claim of John Good. Committee on Claims. Jan. 27, 1832. Reports of Committees, No. 251, 22d Cong., 1st sess., Vol. II. Adverse to granting compensation to petitioner for damages to his farm by the construction of Cumberland road. [Washington, 1832] 8 p. MB.   16204

---- Report on Claim of John Lacy. Committee on Naval Affairs. Jan. 5, 1832. Reports of Committees, No. 139, 22d Cong., 1st sess., Vol. I. Recommends allowance of claim of petitioner for losses sustained by him on contract to furnish labor on Government property, being the result of the failure on the part of the United States to perform its share of the contract; Bill reported. [Washington, 1832] 2 p. MB.   16205

---- Report on Claim of John McDowell. Com. on Revolutionary Claims. Feb. 14, 1832. Reports of Committees, No. 287, 22d Cong., 1st sess., Vol. II. Recommends allowance of claim of petitioner for commutation of half-pay; Bill reported. [Washington, 1832] 1 p. MB.   16206

---- Report on Claim of John Rhea. Judiciary Committee. Feb. 9, 1832. Reports of Committees, No. 282, 22d Cong., 1st sess., Vol. II. Adverse to claim of petitioner for land in Alabama. [Washington, 1832] 4 p. MB.   16207

---- Report on Claim of John S. Fleming. Committee on Rev. Claims. Jan. 16, 1832. Reports of Committees, No. 190, 22d Cong., 1st sess., Vol. I. Recommends allowance of claim of petitioner as assignee of John Syme for flour furnished the Army; Bill reported. [Washington, 1832] 3 p. MB.   16208

---- Report on Claim of John Steele. Committee on Commerce. Apr. 11, 1832. Reports of Committees, No. 441, 22d Cong., 1st sess., Vol. III. Adverse to claim of petitioner, collector at Philadelphia, for refundment of money advanced for clerk-hire, etc. [Washington, 1832] 2 p. MB.   16209

---- Report on Claim of John Thomas. Com. on Revolutionary Claims. Jan. 4, 1832. Reports of Committees, No. 129, 22d Cong., 1st sess., Vol. I. Recommended that petitioner be granted commutation of half-pay for life; Bill reported. [Washington, 1832] 1 p. MB.   16210

---- Report on Claim of Joseph Brown. Committee on Indian Affairs. Feb. 17, 1832. Reports of Committees, No. 311, 22d Cong., 1st sess., Vol. II. Recommends payment of petitioner for lands taken by the Cherokee Indians; Bill reported. [Washington, 1832] 2 p. MB.   16211

---- Report on Claim of Joseph W. Torrey. Committee on the Judiciary. Jan. 25, 1832. Reports of Committees, No. 49, 22d Cong.,

1st sess., Vol. I. Recommends allowance of claim of petitioner for professional services as attorney of Michigan; Bill reported. [Washington, 1832] 1 p. MB.
                                    16212
---- Report on Claim of Joshua Kennedy. Committee on Claims. Mar. 9, 1832. Reports of Committees, No. 357, 22d Cong., 1st sess., Vol. III. Recommends rejection of Senate bill allowing compensation to Joshua Kennedy for property destroyed by the Creek Indians. [Washington, 1832] 4 p. MB.   16213

---- Report on Claim of Josiah Barker. Com. on Private Land Claims. Jan. 13, 1832. Reports of Committees, No. 187, 22d Cong., 1st sess., Vol. I. Recommends allowance of claim of petitioner to land in Louisiana as assignee of Madame Hinson; Bill reported. [Washington, 1832] 1 p. MB.   16214

---- Report on Claim of Lemuel Cook. Committee on Claims. Jan. 21, 1832. Reports of Committees No. 228, 22d Cong., 1st sess., Vol. II. Adverse to allowance of claim of petitioner for building destroyed by the British in 1813. [Washington, 1832] 7 p. MB.
                                    16215
---- Report on Claim of Leonard Holly. Committee on Military Affairs. Apr. 3, 1832. Reports of Committees, No. 423, 22d Cong., 1st sess., Vol. III. Recommends grant of bounty land to petitioner; Bill reported. [Washington, 1832] 1 p. MB.   16216

---- Report on Claim of Margaret Meade. Com. on Foreign Affairs. Feb. 10, 1832. Reports of Committees, No. 316, 22d Cong., 1st sess., Vol. II. Recommends that a board of commissioners be constituted to act upon the claim

of petitioner, as executrix of Richard W. Meade, against the Spanish Government. [Washington, 1832] 213 p. MB.   16217

---- Report on Claim of Mitchell Robertson. Com. on Revolutionary Claims. July 3, 1832. Reports of Committees, No. 499, 22d Cong., 1st sess., Vol. V. Recommends allowance of claim for services; Disallows claim for pension; Bill reported. [Washington, 1832] 1 p. MB.   16218

---- Report on Claim of N. A. Ware. Com. on Private Land Claims. Feb. 7, 1832. Senate Docs., No. 49, 22d Cong., 1st sess., Vol. I. Recommends allowance of claim of petitioner to land in Louisiana; Bill reported. [Washington, 1832] 1 p. MB.
                                    16219
---- Report on Claim of Nathan Carver. Committee on Claims. Mar. 2, 1832. Reports of Committees, No. 342, 22d Cong., 1st sess., Vol. III. Recommends that petitioner be allowed compensation for medical services to soldiers; Adverse to claim for horse and equipments captured; Bill reported. [Washington, 1832] 2 p. MB.   16220

---- Report on Claim of Parsons & Thorndike. Committee on Commerce. Feb. 15, 1832. Reports of Committees. No. 300, 22d Cong., 1st sess., Vol. II. Adverse to claim for reimbursement of extra duties paid by petitioners. [Washington, 1832] 5 p. MB.
                                    16221
---- Report on Claim of Peregrine Gardner. Committee on Claims. Jan. 3, 1832. Reports of Committees, No. 127, 22d Cong., 1st sess., Vol. I. [Washington, 1832] 1 p. DNA; MB.   16222

---- ---- ---- Dec. 28, 1832.

Reports of Committees, No. 15, 22d Cong. , 2d sess. Recommends allowance of claim of petitioner for horse and equipments lost in the United States Service; Bill reported. [Washington, 1832] 2 p. MB. 16223

---- Report on Claim of Peter Foster. Com. on Revolutionary Claims. Jan. 4, 1832. Reports of Committees, No. 130, 22d Cong. , 1st sess. , Vol. I. Recommends that petitioner be allowed commutation of half-pay for life; Bill reported. [Washington, 1832] 1 p. MB. 16224

---- Report on Claim of Philip Hickey. Committee on Claims. Feb. 29, 1832. Reports of Committees, No. 338, 22d Cong. , 1st sess. , Vol. III. Recommends that claim of petitioner for value of timber taken by the United States from his land be referred to the Third Auditor for adjudication; Bill reported. [Washington, 1832] 2 p. MB. 16225

---- Report on Claim of R. L. Livingston. Com. on Revolutionary Claims. Feb. 2, 1832. Reports of Committees, No. 254, 22d Cong. , 1st sess. , Vol. II. Recommends allowance of claim of petitioner as executor of Walter Livingston for loss on contract to furnish rations to the Army occasioned by fault on the part of the Government; Bill reported. [Washington, 1832] 18 p. MB. 16226

---- Report on Claim of Representatives of T. Coffin. Com. on Rev. Claims. Jan. 17, 1832. Reports of Committees, No. 198, 22d Cong. , 1st sess. , Vol. I. Adverse to claim of petitioners for further payment on vessel chartered by the Government and destroyed by the British. [Washington, 1832] 1 p. MB. 16227

---- Report on Claim of Reuben Wilkinson. Com. on Ways and Means. Jan. 30, 1832. Reports of Committees, No. 243, 22d Cong. , 1st sess. , Vol. II. Recommends allowance of compensation for depredations by the Creek Indians on the property of petitioner; Bill reported. [Washington, 1832.] 5 p. MB. 16228

---- Report on Claim of Richard Bagnall. Committee on Claims. Dec. 14, 1832. Reports of Committees, No. 3, 22d Cong. , 2d sess. Recommends allowance of claim of petitioner for bricks furnished the Navy; Bill reported. [Washington, 1832] 2 p. MB. 16229

---- Report on Claim of Richard Hardesty. Committee on Claims. Apr. 30, 1832. Reports of Committees, No. 457, 22d Cong. , 1st sess. , Vol. III. Recommends compensation to petitioner for extra work on Cumberland road and damage to property; Bill reported. [Washington, 1832] 2 p. MB. 16230

---- Report on Claim of Richard Wall. Com. on Revolutionary Claims. Feb. 14, 1832. Reports of Committees, No. 288, 22d Cong. , 1st sess. , Vol. II. Recommends allowance of claim of petitioner for prize-money; Bill reported. [Washington, 1832] 1 p. MB. 16231

---- Report on Claim of Riddle, Becktill & Headington. Com. on Claims. Jan. 4, 1832. Reports of Committees, No. 135, 22d Cong. , 1st sess. , Vol. I. Recommends allowance of claim of petitioner for interest on bill of exchange received in payment for shoes furnished the Quartermaster's Dept. ; Bill reported. [Washington, 1832] 2 p. MB. 16232

---- Report on Claim of Robert

Kaine. Committee on Claims.
Jan. 17, 1832. Reports of Committees, No. 195, 22d Cong.,
1st sess., Vol. I. Adverse to
claim of petitioner for arrears of
pay; Recommends allowance of
pay for equipments lost in the
service; Bill reported. [Washing-
ton, 1832] 2 p. MB.   16233

---- Report on Claim of S. Q.
Richardson. Committee on
Claims. Feb. 17, 1832. Reports
of Committees, No. 315, 22d
Cong., 1st sess., Vol. II. Adverse to payment of petitioner
for horse and equipments lost in
the Army. [Washington, 1832]
5 p. MB.   16234

---- Report on Claim of S.
Thompson. Committee on Claims.
Feb. 17, 1832. Reports of Committees, No. 305, 22d Cong.,
1st sess., Vol. II. Recommends
that petitioner be remunerated for
blankets furnished the Army; Bill
reported. [Washington, 1832] 1 p.
MB.   16235

---- Report on Claim of Samuel
May. Committee on Claims. July
5, 1832. Reports of Committees,
No. 501, 22d Cong., 1st sess.,
Vol. V. Recommends passage of
bill reimbursing claimant for
losses sustained by the destruc-
tion of storehouse by the British.
[Washington, 1832] 2 p. MB.
                           16236
---- Report on Claim of Samuel
Mecker. Committee on Claims.
Mar. 12, 1832. Reports of Com-
mittees, No. 364, 22d Cong., 1st
sess., Vol. III. Adverse to claim.
[Washington, 1832] 1 p. MB.
                           16237
---- Report on Claim of Single-
ton & Andrews. Com. on Priv.
Land Claims. Jan. 20, 1832. Reports of Committees, No. 221,
22d Cong., 1st sess., Vol. I.
Recommends allowance of claim

of petitioners to land in Louisiana; Bill reported. [Washington,
1832] 1 p. MB.   16238

---- Report on Claim of Sterling
Johnston. Committee on Claims.
Jan. 27, 1832. Reports of Committees, No. 240, 22d Cong.,
1st sess., Vol. II. Adverse to
claim of petitioner for injury to
his property caused by grading
the Cumberland road. [Washing-
ton, 1832] 2 p. MB.   16239

---- Report on Claim of Sylvester Havens. Committee on Claims.
Apr. 23, 1832. Reports of Committees, No. 452, 22d Cong.,
1st sess., Vol. III. Recommends
refundment of amount paid by
Sylvester Havens on note in favor
of the United States. [Washington,
1832] 1 p. MB.   16240

---- Report on Claim of T. E.
& W. M. Stansbury. Committee
on Claims. Dec. 19, 1832. Reports of Committees, No. 9, 22d
Cong., 2d Sess. Adverse to allowance of claim of petitioners
for property destroyed by the
British. [Washington, 1832] 4 p.
MB.   16241

---- Report on Claim of Thomas
Richardson. Committee on
Claims. Mar. 7, 1832. Reports
of Committees, No. 353, 22d
Cong., 1st sess., Vol. III. Recommends that claim of petitioner
for money due him as sutler
from certain soldiers be referred to the accounting officers
of the Treasury; Bill reported.
[Washington, 1832] 1 p. MB.
                           16242
---- Report on Claim of W. D.
Achen. Committee on Claims. Apr.
13, 1832. Reports of Committees,
No. 443, 22d Cong., 1st sess.,
Vol. III. Adverse to claim of petitioner, agent for preservation
of live-oak, for per diem allow-

ance and keep of horse. [Washington, 1832] 1 p. MB.   16243

---- Report on Claim of Whitford Gill. Committee on Claims. Dec. 17, 1832. Reports of Committees, No. 4, 22d Cong., 2d sess. Recommends allowance of claim of petitioner for value of boat captured by the British; Bill reported. [Washington, 1832] 2 p. MB.
16244

---- Report on Claim of William Arbuthnot. Committee on Claims. Feb. 15, 1832. Reports of Committees, No. 285, 22d Cong., 1st sess., Vol. II. Adverse to claim of petitioner for value of property destroyed by the British during the late war. [Washington, 1832] 9 p. MB.   16245

---- Report on Claim of William Baker. Committee on Claims. May 21, 1832. Reports of Committees, No. 480, 22d Cong., 1st sess., Vol. V. Adverse to claim of petitioner, sutler in the Army, for money alleged to be due him from deceased soldiers. [Washington, 1832] 19 p. MB.
16246

---- Report on Claim of William Eadus. Committee on Claims. Mar. 26, 1832. Reports of Committees, No. 414, 22d Cong., 1st sess., Vol. III. Adverse to claim of petitioner for compensation for house destroyed by the British. [Washington, 1832] 23 p. MB.
16247

---- Report on Claim of William S. Anderson. Committee on Claims. Mar. 12, 1832. Reports of Committees, No. 360, 22d Cong., 1st sess., Vol. III. Recommends allowance of claim of petitioner for horse lost in the army; Bill reported. [Washington, 1832] 3 p. MB.   16248

---- Report on Claim of William Smith. Committee on Claims.

Apr. 30, 1832. Reports of Committees, No. 456, 22d Cong., 1st sess., Vol. III. Recommends compensation to petitioner for horse lost in the United States service; Bill reported. [Washington, 1832] 2 p. MB.   16249

---- Report on Claims for Property Destroyed at Detroit. Select Com. Mar. 17, 1832. Reports of Committees, No. 393, 22d Cong., 1st sess., Vol. III. Recommends payment of claims for property destroyed by the British and Indians after the surrender of Detroit; Bill reported. [Washington, 1832] 3 p. MB.   16250

---- Report on Claims of D. Haselton and W. Palmer. Com. on Claims, Mar. 2, 1832. Reports of Committees, No. 343, 22d Cong., 1st sess., Vol. III. Recommends allowance of compensation for work performed in construction of light-house at Portsmouth, New Hampshire; Bill reported. [Washington, 1832] 3 p. MB.   16251

---- Report on Claims of S. Gordon and Ann V. Llewellyn. Apr. 6, 1832. Reports of Committees, No. 432, 22d Cong., 1st sess., Vol. III. Committee on Public Lands reports that there is no need of legislation to secure petitioners in their rights to land claimed. [Washington, 1832] 2 p. MB.   16252

---- Report on Claims of State of Virginia. Select committee. Jan. 16, 1832. Reports of Committees, No. 191, 22d Cong., 1st sess., Vol. I. Recommends reimbursement of the State of Virginia for moneys advanced to pay State militia engaged in the defence of the country; Bill reported. [Washington, 1832] 66 p. MB.   16253

---- Report on Claims to Lands
under Spanish Titles. Com. on
Public Lands. July 11, 1832. Reports of Committees, No. 508,
22d Cong., 1st sess., Vol. V.
Reasserts the claim of the United
States that no part of the territory between the Mississippi and
the Perdido Rivers lies within
Florida or was in the possession
of Spain, and that the United
States is not bound to confirm
titles to land within those limits
granted by the Spanish Government. [Washington, 1832] 6 p.
MB.   16254

---- Report on Clerks in Land
Office. Committee on Public
Lands. Jan. 23, 1832. Senate
Docs., No. 45, 22d Cong., 1st
sess., Vol. I. Relative to clerks
in the General Land Office and
their compensation. [Washington,
1832] 4 p. MB.   16255

---- Report on Clerks in the
Navy Department. Secretary Levi
Woodbury. Jan. 2, 1832. House
Ex. Docs., No. 34, 22d Cong.,
1st sess., Vol. II. Transmitting
list of clerks employed in the
Navy Dept. during the year 1831.
[Washington, 1832] 2 p. MB.
                             16256

---- Report on Clerks in the
Post-Office Department. P. M.
Gen. W. T. Barry. Jan. 5, 1832.
House Ex. Docs., No. 49, 22d
Cong., 1st sess., Vol. II. List
of clerks employed in the Post-
Office Dept. during the year 1831.
[Washington, 1832] 3 p. MB.
                             16257

---- Report on Clerks in the
State Department. Secretary E.
Livingston. Jan. 3, 1832. House
Ex. Docs., No. 30, 22d Cong.,
1st sess., Vol. II. Transmitting
list of clerks employed in the
State Dept. during the year 1831.
[Washington, 1832] 2 p. MB.
                             16258

---- Report on Clerks in the
Treasury Department. Sec. Louis
McLane. Jan. 10, 1832. House
Ex. Docs., No. 47, 22d Cong.,
1st sess., Vol. II. Transmitting
list of clerks employed in the
Treasury Dept. during the year
1831. [Washington, 1832] 8 p.
MB.   16259

---- Report on Clerks in War
Department. Jan. 6, 1832. House
Ex. Docs., No. 48, 22d Cong.,
1st sess., Vol. II. List of clerks
employed in the War Dept. during
the year 1831. [Washington, 1832]
2 p. MB.   16260

---- Report on Coins and Currency. Select Committee on
Coins. June 30, 1832. Reports of
Committees, No. 496, 22d Cong.,
1st sess., Vol. V. Reports a bill
for establishing the value of
United States coins and for regulating the operations of the Mint.
[Washington, 1832] 41 p. MB.
                             16261

---- Report on Commerce and
Navigation. Secretary Louis Mc-
Lane. Mar. 2, 1832. House Ex.
Docs., No. 230, 22d Cong., 1st
sess., Vol. V. Transmitting reports on the commerce and navigation of the United States for the
year ending Sept. 30, 1831.
[Washington, 1832] 314 p. MB.
                             16262

---- Report on Commercial Regulations. Committee on Commerce. Dec. 21, 1832. Reports
of Committees, No. 12, 22d
Cong., 2d sess. Reports a bill
to amend and explain a certain
section of the tariff law. [Wash-
ington, 1832] 3 p. MB.   16263

---- Report on Congressional
Documents. Gales & Seaton. Jan.
4, 1832. Senate Docs., No. 16,
22d Cong., 1st sess., Vol. I.
Transmitting two volumes of a
compilation of Congressional doc-

uments. [Washington, 1832] 2 p.
MB.   16264

---- Report on Construction of
Canal. Com. on Internal Im-
provements. Apr. 13, 1832. Re-
ports of Committees, No. 446,
22d Cong., 1st sess., Vol. III.
Recommends grant of land to the
State of Illinois for the purpose
of constructing a canal from Lake
Michigan to the Illinois River.
[Washington, 1832] 20 p. MB.
                                 16265
---- Report on Construction of
Forts. Secretary Lewis Cass.
Mar. 22, 1832. House Ex. Docs.,
No. 179, 22d Cong., 1st sess.,
Vol. IV. Transmitting informa-
tion relative to prices of materi-
als and labor at Fort Hamilton,
New York, and Fort Adams,
Rhode Island. [Washington, 1832]
2 p. MB.   16266

---- Report on Contingent Expenses of House. Clerk M. St.
Clair. Dec. 3, 1832. Ex. Docs.,
No. 4, 23d Cong., 2d sess.,
Vol. I. Showing expenditures
from the contingent fund of the
House of Representatives for the
year 1832. [Washington, 1832]
5 p. MB.   16267

---- Report on Contingent Expenses of the Military Academy. Sec.
L. Cass. Jan. 7, 1832. House
Ex. Docs., No. 50, 22d Cong.,
1st sess., Vol. II. Transmitting
statement of expenditures from
the contingent fund of the Military
Academy. [Washington, 1832]
5 p. MB.   16268

---- Report on Contingent Expenses of the Navy. Sec. Levi Woodbury. Dec. 14, 1832. Ex. Docs.,
No. 15, 22d Cong., 2d. sess.,
Vol. I. Statement of contingent
expenses of the Navy for year
ending Sept. 30, 1832. [Washing-
ton, 1832] 13 p. MB.   16269

---- Report on Corps of Mounted
Rangers. Com. on Military Affairs. Dec. 28, 1832. Reports of
Committees, No. 17, 22d Cong.,
2d sess. Bill reported converting
the corps of Mounted Rangers into a regiment of dragoons.
[Washington, 1832] 2 p. MB.
                                 16270
---- Report on Culture of Tropical Plants. Committee on Agriculture. Apr. 26, 1832. Reports
of Committees, No. 454, 22d
Cong., 1st sess., Vol. III. Reports bill setting apart tract of
land in Florida for the cultivation of tropical plants. [Washing-
ton, 1832] 24 p. MB.   16271

---- Report on Cumberland Road.
Secretary Lewis Cass. Jan. 11,
1832. House Ex. Docs., No. 52,
22d Cong., 1st sess., Vol. II.
Transmitting estimates of amounts
necessary to repair road from
Cumberland to Wheeling. [Wash-
ington, 1832] 5 p. MB.   16272

---- ---- ---- Feb. 9, 1832.
Senate Docs., No. 58, 22d Cong.,
1st sess., Vol. II. Report of
progress during the year 1831 in
the construction of the Cumberland
road west of Zanesville, Ohio.
[Washington, 1832] 2 p. MB.
                                 16273
---- Report on Customs Officers.
Sec. L. McLane. Apr. 18, 1832.
House Ex. Docs., No. 213, 22d
Cong., 1st sess., Vol. V.
Transmitting statement of the
emoluments and expenditure of
officers of the customs during the
year 1831. [Washington, 1832]
10 p. MB.   16274

---- Report on Discharged Seamen. Sec. Levi Woodbury. Feb.
1, 1832. Senate Docs., No. 46,
22d Cong., 1st sess., Vol. I.
Statement of number of seamen
discharged at foreign naval stations from July 1, 1827, to Dec.

31, 1831; Number returned to the United States at Government expense; Amount paid for transportation. [Washington, 1832] 2 p. MB.   16275

---- Report on Drawbacks. Sec. L. McLane. Jan. 4, 1832. Senate Docs., No. 20, 22d Cong., 1st sess., Vol. I. Statement showing amount of drawback on salted provisions; Vessels engaged in exporting the same; Quantity of beef, pork, and fish exported from 1791 to 1830. [Washington, 1832] 6 p. MB.   16276

---- ---- ---- Apr. 6, 1832. Senate Docs., No. 120, 22d Cong., 1st sess., Vol. III. Statement relative to amount of drawbacks, premiums, and bounties paid on exported fish, pork, and beef; Allowance to fishing vessels since the year 1789; Quantity of beef, fish, and pork annual exported. [Washington, 1832] 11 p. MB.
                              16277
---- Report on Duties. Sec. L. McLane. Jan. 9, 1832. Senate Docs., No. 25, 22d Cong., 1st sess., Vol. I. Statement showing the amount of duties that would be returnable to merchants of the United States under the provisions of the Senate bill fixing duties on imports. [Washington, 1832] 4 p. MB.   16278

---- ---- ---- July 14, 1832. Ex. Docs., No. 301, 22d Cong., 1st sess., Vol. VI. Transmitting annual statement of the net revenue collected on woollens and cottons, manufactures of iron, etc. [Washington, 1832] 8 p. MB.   16279

---- Report on Duties on Imports. Committee on Finance. Jan. 9, 1832. Senate Docs., No. 24, 22d Cong., 1st sess., Vol. I. Statement showing existing duties on imports and those proposed to be laid and repealed by Senate bill No. 72; Report from Secretary of Treasury showing amount of duties for the year 1829 on articles enumerated in the bill. [Washington, 1832] 11 p. MB.   16280

---- ---- Sec. L. McLane. Apr. 16, 1832. Senate Docs., No. 129, 22d Cong., 1st sess., Vol. III. Transmitting correspondence relative to construction of laws levying duties on imports. [Washington, 1832] 9 p. MB.   16281

---- Report on Election of Charles C. Johnson. Com. on Elections. Apr. 13, 1832. Reports of Committees, No. 444, 22d Cong., 1st sess., Vol. III. Petitioner, Joseph Draper, contests the right of Charles C. Johnson to a seat in the House of Representatives; Majority of committee recommends that the seat of Charles C. Johnson be declared vacant and that there be a new election; Minority reports that the sitting member is entitled to his seat. [Washington, 1832] 10 p. MB.   16282

---- Report on Employes in Custom-Houses. Sec. Louis McLane. Apr. 9, 1832. House Ex. Docs., No. 202, 22d Cong., 1st sess., Vol. V. Transmitting information relative to persons employed in the custom-houses of the principal cities of the United States. [Washington, 1832] 12 p. MB.   16283

---- Report on Errors in the Census. Sec. Edward Livingston. May 24, 1832. House Ex. Docs., No. 244, 22d Cong., 1st sess., Vol. VI. Transmitting statement concerning errors in returns of the fifth census. [Washington, 1832] 2 p. MB.   16284

---- Report on Expenditures in War Department. Com. on Expenditures. July 10, 1832. Reports of Committees, No. 507, 22d Cong., 1st sess., Vol. III. Reports that a careful examination has been made of the accounts of the contingent expenditures of the War Dept. [Washington, 1832] 2 p. MB. 16285

---- Report on Expenditures of War Department. Sec. Lewis Cass. Feb. 27, 1832. House Ex. Docs., No. 134, 22d Cong., 1st sess., Vol. IV. Transmitting statement showing amount appropriated and expended for the War Dept. for the year 1831. [Washington, 1832] 17 p. MB. 16286

---- Report on Expenses of Foreign Missions. Com. on Foreign Affairs. Feb. 27, 1832. Reports of Committees, No. 331, 22d Cong., 1st sess., Vol. III. Reports two bills regulating the expenses of foreign missions. [Washington, 1832] 6 p. MB. 16287

---- Report on Expenses of Indian Treaty. Sec. Lewis Cass. Mar. 24, 1832. House Ex. Docs., No. 181, 22d Cong., 1st sess., Vol. IV. Transmitting report of the Second Auditor on the expenses of holding a treaty with the Cherokee Indians during the months of August and September 1830. [Washington, 1832] 4 p. MB. 16288

---- Report on Expenses of Land Offices. Sec. Louis McLane. Mar. 9, 1832. House Ex. Docs., No. 160, 22d Cong., 1st sess., Vol. IV. Transmitting statement of sums paid to register and receiver of each land office during the year 1831. [Washington, 1832] 6 p. MB. 16289

---- Report on Expenses of the Judiciary. Sec. Louis McLane. Dec. 17, 1832. Senate Docs.,

No. 9, 22d Cong., 2d Sess., Vol. I. Transmitting report showing expenses of each judicial district of the United States from 1826 to 1831. [Washington, 1832] 13 p. MB. 16290

---- Report on Fees of United States Officers. Sec. Louis McLane. June 14, 1832. Ex. Docs., No. 148, 22d Cong., 2d sess., Vol. III. Transmitting report on fees of district attorneys and other officers of United States courts. [Washington, 1832] 30 p. MB. 16291

---- Report on Foreign Plants. Sec. Louis McLane. Apr. 6, 1832. House Ex. Docs., No. 198, 22d Cong., 1st sess., Vol. V. Transmitting information relative to the introduction of foreign trees and plants into the United States. [Washington, 1832] 23 p. MB. 16292

---- Report on Fortifications. Sec. Lewis Cass. Dec. 28, 1832. Ex. Docs., No. 24, 22d Cong., 2d sess., Vol. I. Transmitting report on fortifications and other defences in the State of Maine. [Washington, 1832] 4 p. MB. 16293

---- Report on Frauds on the Revenue. Sec. Louis McLane. Apr. 6, 1832. House Ex. Docs., No. 199, 22d Cong., 1st sess., Vol. V. Transmitting information relative to condemnation of smuggled goods and frauds on the public revenues. [Washington, 1832] 63 p. MB. 16294

---- Report on Frauds upon the Revenue. Sec. L. McLane. May 2, 1832. Senate Docs., No. 139, 22d Cong., 1st sess., Vol. III. Transmitting information relative to frauds upon the Treasury by importing sugar in the form of syrup. [Washington, 1832] 18 p. MB. 16295

---- Report on Government of
District of Columbia. Committee
on D. C. Feb. 28, 1832. Reports
of Committees, No. 337, 22d
Cong., 1st sess., Vol. III. Adverse to allowing the District of
Columbia a Delegate in Congress
or a local Legislature. [Washing-
ton, 1832] 9 p. MB.   16296

---- Report on Grant of Land to
Jacob Thompson. Com. on Public
Lands. Jan. 10, 1832. Reports
of Committees, No. 40, 22d
Cong., 1st sess. Adverse to
grant of land to Jacob Thompson,
a Choctaw Indian, under treaty
with the Choctaw Nation. [Wash-
ington, 1832] 1 p. MB.   16297

---- Report on Growth and Manufacture of Silk. Com. on Agriculture. Jan. 20, 1832. Reports
of Committees, No. 222, 22d
Cong., 1st sess., Vol. I. Recommends an appropriation to aid
in the culture and manufacture of
silk; Bill reported. [Washington,
1832] 15 p. MB.   16298

---- Report on Hall of Representatives. Select committee. June 30,
1832. Reports of Committees, No.
495, 22d Cong., 1st sess., Vol.
V. Recommends that the Commissioner of Public Buildings be directed to make certain alterations
in the Hall of Representatives during the recess of Congress. [Wash-
ington, 1832] 7 p. MB.   16299

---- Report on Immigration. Sec.
Edward Livingston. June 22, 1832.
House Ex. Docs., No. 293, 22d
Cong., 1st sess., Vol. VI.
Transmitting report of immigra-
tion into the United States during
the year ending Sept. 30, 1831;
Age; Sex; Nationality. [Washington,
1832] 42 p. MB.   16300

---- Report on Import Duties.
Secretary L. McLane. Dec. 10,

1832. Ex. Docs., No. 7, 22d
Cong., 2d sess., Vol. I. Statement of duties and drawbacks on
articles imported into the United
States and re-exported during the
years 1829, 1830, and 1831.
[Washington, 1832] 38 p. MB.
                           16301
---- Report on Imports. Sec.
Louis McLane. July 14, 1832.
Ex. Docs., No. 302, 22d Cong.,
1st sess., Vol. VI. Transmitting
statement showing invoice of prime
cost of merchandise in countries
whence imported. [Washington,
1832] 99 p. MB.   16302

---- Report on Imprisonment for
Debt. Select committee. Dec. 15,
1832. Reports of Committees, No.
5, 22d Cong., 2d sess. Recommends abolition of imprisonment
for debt in cases coming under
the jurisdiction of the Federal
courts; Bill reported. [Washington,
1832] 13 p. MB.   16303

---- Report on Improvement in
Washington. Com. on District of
Columbia. Feb. 15, 1832. Reports of Committees, No. 291,
22d Cong., 1st sess., Vol. II.
Reports that it is just and expedient that Pennsylvania avenue
should be improved at the expense
of the General Government. [Wash-
ington, 1832] 23 p. MB.   16304

---- Report on Improvement of
St. Louis and Louisville Road.
Apr. 3, 1832. Senate Docs., No.
117, 22d Cong., 1st sess., Vol.
III. Committee on Roads and Canals recommends passage of bill
for improvement of road. [Wash-
ington, 1832] 4 p. MB.   16305

---- Report on Indian Annuities.
Secretary Lewis Cass. May 22,
1832. House Ex. Docs., No. 242,
22d Cong., 1st sess., Vol. VI.
Transmitting information relative
to Indian annuities; Amount of

payments made during the years 1830 and 1831. [Washington, 1832] 19 p. MB. 16306

---- ---- ---- Dec. 20, 1832. Senate Docs., No. 39, 22d Cong., 2d sess., Vol. I. Transmitting statement showing annuities to Indians payable in 1833. [Washington, 1832] 7 p. MB. 16307

---- Report on Indian Contract with Sam Houston. Select committee. July 5, 1832. Reports of Committees, No. 502, 22d Cong., 1st sess., Vol. V. Exonerates the Secretary of War, John H. Eaton, from the charge of having corruptly given to Sam Houston a contract to supply emigrant Indians with rations. [Washington, 1832] 75 p. MB. 16308

---- Report on Indian Depredations in Georgia. Com. on Indian Affairs. Feb. 20, 1832. Reports of Committees, No. 317, 22d Cong., 1st sess., Vol. II. Recommends that the proper accounting officers of the Treasury be authorized to settle the claims of citizens of Georgia on account of depredations on their property by the Creek Indians. [Washington, 1832] 2 p. MB. 16309

---- Report on Indian Expenditures. Sec. Lewis Cass. Mar. 22, 1832. House Ex. Docs., No. 180, 22d Cong., 1st sess., Vol. IV. Transmitting copies of accounts of expenditures for the benefit of the Indians from Aug. 1, 1830, to Oct. 21, 1831. [Washington, 1832] 128 p. MB. 16310

---- Report on Indian Lands. Sec. Lewis Cass. Mar. 16, 1832. House Ex. Docs., No. 172, 22d Cong., 1st sess., Vol. IV. Transmitting a report upon the country west of the Mississippi reserved for the Indians. [Washington, 1832]

15 p. MB. 16311

---- Report on Indian Trading Licenses. Sec. L. Cass. Feb. 20, 1832. House Ex. Docs., No. 121, 22d Cong., 1st sess., Vol. IV. Transmitting list of licenses granted during the year ending Sept. 30, 1831, to trade with Indians. [Washington, 1832] 6 p. MB. 16312

---- Report on Insolvent Debtors. Sec. Louis McLane. Jan. 12, 1832. House Ex. Docs., No. 54, 22d Cong., 1st sess., Vol. II. Transmitting list of applicants under act for relief of insolvent debtors of the United States. [Washington, 1832] 9 p. MB. 16313

---- Report on Internal Improvements. Com. on Internal Improvements. Mar. 28, 1832. Reports of Committees, No. 416, 22d Cong., 1st sess., Vol. III. Reports bill making appropriations for the completion of certain roads and canals. [Washington, 1832] 4 p. MB. 16314

---- Report on Land Claimed by Indiana. Committee on Public Lands. June 7, 1832. Senate Docs. No. 158, 22d Cong., 1st sess., Vol. III. Adverse to granting claim of State of Indiana for certain land. [Washington, 1832] 7 p. MB. 16315

---- Report on Land Claims. Committee on Private Land Claims. Dec. 29, 1832. Reports of Committees, No. 18, 22d Cong., 2d sess., Recommends refundment of money paid for public land in Mississippi by Joseph Guedry, Edward Lambert, Michael Leboeuf, and John Vavaseur, said land having been already disposed of by the United States. [Washington, 1832] 1 p. MB. 16316

---- ---- Secretary Louis Mc-
Lane. Apr. 6, 1832. House Ex.
Docs., No. 197, 22d Cong., 1st
sess., Vol. V. Transmitting reports from the register and receiver of the land office in Alabama upon the subject of claims
to land. [Washington, 1832] 4 p.
MB.   16317

---- Report on Land Offices in
Arkansas. Sec. Louis McLane.
Jan. 23, 1832. House Ex. Docs.,
No. 87, 22d Cong., 1st sess.,
Vol. III. Transmitting copies of
instructions to registers and re-
ceivers of public moneys in Ar-
kansas. [Washington, 1832] 4 p.
MB.   16318

---- Report on Live-Oak. Secretary Levi Woodbury. Dec. 14,
1832. Ex. Docs., No. 23, 22d
Cong., 2d sess., Vol. I. Statement of live-oak growing on public lands; On private lands;
Quantity on hand. [Washington,
1832] 59 p. MB.   16319

---- Report on Live-Oak for the
Navy. Sec. Levi Woodbury. Mar.
19, 1832. House Ex. Docs., No.
178, 22d Cong., 1st sess., Vol.
IV. Transmitting information relative to the supply of live-oak, and
to the agents for procuring the
same. [Washington, 1832] 53 p.
MB.   16320

---- Report on Louisiana Sugar
Refinery. Legislature of Louisiana. Mar. 22, 1832. House Ex.
Docs., No. 220, 22d Cong., 1st
sess., Vol. V. Transmitting copies of reports made by the committee appointed to examine the
Louisiana sugar refinery. [Wash-
ington, 1832] 2 p. MB.   16321

---- Report on Memorial of A. R.
Woolley. Com. on Military Af-
fairs. Feb. 4, 1832. Reports of
Committees, No. 269, 22d Cong.,

1st sess., Vol. II. Memorialist
represents that he was an officer
in the Army and has been tried
by court-martial and dismissed
the service; Asks justice from
Congress; Committee recommends
that he have leave to withdraw his
papers. [Washington, 1832] 11 p.
MB.   16322

---- Report on Memorial of Alexandria Canal Company. Mar.
30, 1832. Reports of Committees,
No. 419, 22d Cong., 1st sess.,
Vol. III. Committee on Internal
Improvements recommends national subscription to stock of company; Bill reported. [Washington,
1832] 34 p. MB.   16323

---- Report on Memorial of Choctaw Indians. Com. on Public
Lands. Feb. 24, 1832. Reports of
Committees, No. 328, 22d Cong.,
1st sess., Vol. II. Recommends
grant of land to John Harlan; Bill
reported. [Washington, 1832] 2 p.
MB.   16324

---- Report on Memorial of Citizens of Alabama. Com. Private
Land Claims. Feb. 6, 1832. Reports of Committees, No. 272,
22d Cong., 1st sess., Vol. II.
Recommends that memorialists be
allowed to purchase certain lands
in Alabama at the minimum rate;
Bill reported. [Washington, 1832]
1 p. MB.   16325

---- Report on Memorial of Citizens of Illinois. Com. on Public
Lands. Jan. 17, 1832. Reports of
Committees, No. 196, 22d Cong.,
1st sess., Vol. I. Recommends
that county of Peoria be allowed
to purchase public land upon which
seat of justice is situated; Bill reported. [Washington, 1832] 2 p.
MB.   16326

---- Report on Memorial of Heirs
of J. Lawrence. Com. on Rev.

Claims. Feb. 17, 1832. Reports of Committees, No. 366, 22d Cong., 1st sess., Vol. III. Recommends compensation to petitioners on account of services of John Lawrence as Minister to France, and that certain allowances be made in his accounts as an Army officer; Bill reported. [Washington, 1832] 2 p. MB. 16327

---- Report on Memorial of Insurance Companies. Com. Ways and Means. May 29, 1832. Reports of Committees, No. 486, 22d Cong., 1st sess., Vol. V. Recommends appropriation to pay judgments against the United States in favor of the memorialists on account of tea seized, and to pay their counsel fees and expenses in bringing suit; Bill reported. [Washington, 1832] 2 p. MB. 16328

---- Report on Memorial of J. Burrows. Com. on District of Columbia. Feb. 20, 1832. Reports of Committees, No. 318, 22d Cong., 1st sess., Vol. II. Recommends the paving of F and G streets, Washington; Bill reported. [Washington, 1832] 1 p. MB. 16329

---- Report on Memorial of Jesse Bell. Committee on Public Lands. Mar. 17, 1832. Reports of Committees, No. 388, 22d Cong., 1st sess., Vol. III. Recommends exchange of land certificate held by petitioner; Bill reported. [Washington, 1832] 2 p. MB. 16330

---- Report on Memorial of John F. Lewis. Committee on Finance. Jan. 30, 1832. Senate Docs., No. 38, 22d Cong., 1st sess., Vol. I. Recommends refundment to memorialist of certain duties paid on matting; Bill reported. [Washington, 1832] 1 p. MB. 16331

---- Report on Memorial of Jos-

eph Eaton. Com. on Military Affairs. Jan. 3, 1832. Reports of Committees, No. 92, 22d Cong., 1st sess., Vol. I. Recommends reimbursement to petitioner of amount paid for quarters while a surgeon in the Army; Bill reported. [Washington, 1832] 1 p. MB. 16332

---- Report on Memorial of Legislative Council of Michigan. Jan. 6, 1832. Reports of Committees, No. 145, 22d Cong., 1st sess., Vol. I. Committee on Territories recommends the establishment of a territorial government for the inhabitants of Michigan west of the lake; Bill reported. [Washington, 1832] 9 p. MB. 16333

---- Report on Memorial of Legislature of Arkansas. Com. on Public Lands. Feb. 21, 1832. Reports of Committees, No. 321, 22d Cong., 1st sess., Vol. II. Adverse to request of memorialists for indemnification to certain settlers in Arkansas for losses sustained from the Indians. [Washington, 1832] 2 p. MB. 16334

---- ---- Post-Office Com. Mar. 14, 1832. Reports of Committees. No. 374, 22d Cong., 1st sess., Vol. III. Recommends an appropriation to construct post-roads through Arkansas; Bill reported. [Washington, 1832] 2 p. MB. 16335

---- Report on Memorial of Legislature of Ohio. Com. on Public Lands. Feb. 17, 1832. Reports of Committees, No. 312, 22d Cong., 1st sess., Vol. II. Recommends grant of land to the State of Ohio to aid in the education of the deaf and dumb; Bill reported. [Washington, 1832] 4 p. MB. 16336

---- Report on Memorial of New York Board of Health. Jan. 20, 1832. Reports of Committees, No.

226, 22d Cong. , 1st sess. , Vol.
II. Memorialists ask that Congress constitute a sanitary commission to visit Europe for the
purpose of investigating the
causes, prevention, and cure of
the Asiatic cholera; Committee
on Foreign Affairs recommends
that the subject be referred to the
Committee on Commerce. [Wash-
ington, 1832] 53 p. MB.   16337

---- Report on Memorial of Stephen Pleasanton. Judiciary Committee. Jan. 24, 1832. Senate
Docs. , No. 32, 22d Cong. , 1st
sess. , Vol. I. Recommends allowance to memorialist of extra
compensation for services as
Commissioner of Revenue while
holding the office of Fifth auditor; Bill reported. [Washington,
1832] 1 p. MB.   16338

---- Report on Memorial of
Trustees of Columbian College.
Feb. 27, 1832. Reports of Com-
mittees, No. 334, 22d Cong. ,
1st sess. , Vol. III. Committee
on the District of Columbia rec-
ommends a donation by the United
States to the Columbian College.
[Washington, 1832] 3 p. MB.
                             16339
---- Report on Memorial of W.
& J. Hardridge. Com. on Priv.
Land Claims. Jan. 16, 1832. Re-
ports of Committees, No. 192,
22d Cong. , 1st sess. , Vol. I.
Recommends issuance of land
patents to memorialists; Bill reported. [Washington, 1832] 1 p.
MB.   16340

---- Report on Mileage to Members of Congress. Com. Pub.
Expenditures. Feb. 27, 1832. Reports of Committees, No. 332.
22d Cong. , 1st sess. , Vol. III.
Recommends adoption of Post-
Office estimate of distances in
computation of mileage; Bill reported. [Washington, 1832] 1 p.

MB.   16341

---- Report on Mode of Settling Public Accounts. Committee on Finance.
Apr. 30, 1832. Senate Docs. , No.
138, 22d Cong. , 1st sess. , Vol.
III. Recommends that the offices
of the Second Auditor and Second
Comptroller be not abolished.
[Washington, 1832] 2 p. MB.
                             16342
---- Report on National Armories. Secretary Lewis Cass. Mar.
10, 1832. House Ex. Docs. , No.
170, 22d Cong. , 1st sess. , Vol.
IV. Transmitting statement of expenditures made at national armories during the year 1831.
[Washington, 1832] 5 p. MB.
                             16343
---- Report on National Road.
Secretary Lewis Cass. Jan. 28,
1832. House Ex. Docs. , No. 83,
22d Cong. , 1st sess. , Vol. III.
Transmitting information relative
to repairs of road from Grand
Bay to Prairie du Chien. [Wash-
ington, 1832] 2 p. MB.   16344

---- Report on Navy Appropriations. Secretary Levi Woodbury.
Feb. 1, 1832. House Ex. Docs. ,
No. 91, 22d Cong. , 1st sess. ,
Vol. III. Transmitting statement
of appropriations for the Navy for
the year 1831. [Washington, 1832]
12 p. MB.   16345

---- Report on Navy Contingent
Fund. Secretary Levi Woodbury.
Jan. 13, 1832. House Ex. Docs. ,
No. 59, 22d Cong. , 1st sess. ,
Vol. II. Transmitting abstract of
expenditures from the contingent
fund of the Navy for the year
ending Sept. 30, 1831. [Washing-
ton, 1832] 17 p. MB.   16346

---- Report on Navy Contracts.
Committee on Claims. Feb. 3,
1832. Reports of Committees,
No. 266, 22d Cong. , 1st sess. ,
Vol. II. Adverse to giving author-

ity to the Secretary of the Navy to make any increased payment on contracts. [Washington, 1832] 2 p. MB.   16347

---- ---- Secretary Levi Woodbury. Jan. 4, 1832. House Ex. Docs., No. 31, 22d Cong., 1st sess., Vol. II. Transmitting statement of contracts for the naval service during the year 1831. [Washington, 1832] 15 p. MB.   16348

---- Report on Navy Officers. Secretary Levi Woodbury. Feb. 27, 1832. House Ex. Docs., No. 132, 22d Cong., 1st sess., Vol. IV. Transmitting statement showing date of commission and rank of each lieutenant employed on vessels of war. [Washington, 1832] 4 p. MB.   16349

---- ---- ---- June 13, 1832. Ex. Docs., No. 307, 22d Cong., 1st sess., Vol. VI. Transmitting list of lieutenants in the Navy, and sea service performed by each since his promotion. [Washington, 1832] 13 p. MB.   16350

---- Report on Navy Pension Fund. Commissioners of the fund. Feb. 28, 1832. House Ex. Docs., No. 129, 22d Cong., 1st sess., Vol. IV. Transmitting list of applicants for Navy pensions. [Washington, 1832] 2 p. MB.   16351

---- ---- Secretary Levi Woodbury. Dec. 4, 1832. Ex. Docs., No. 5, 22d Cong., 2d sess., Vol. I. Transmitting report on Navy pension fund, Navy hospital fund, and privateer pension fund. [Washington, 1832] 12 p. MB.   16352

---- Report on Navy Pensions. Commissioners of Navy pension fund. Feb. 28, 1832. Senate Docs. No. 77, 22d Cong., 1st sess., Vol. II. Recommends that widows

and orphans of seamen be placed on the pension-rolls. [Washington, 1832] 2 p. MB.   16353

---- Report on Navy Ration. Sec. Levi Woodbury. Jan. 28, 1832. House Ex. Docs., No. 81, 22d Cong., 1st sess., Vol. II. Transmitting statement relative to a change in the rations now furnished to seamen. [Washington, 1832] 2 p. MB.   16354

---- Report on Negro Colonization. Committee on Foreign Relations. Feb. 7, 1832. Reports of Committees, No. 277, 22d Cong., 1st sess., Vol. II. Adverse to national aid to the project of the colonization of negroes. [Washington, 1832] 13 p. MB.   16355

---- Report on Newspaper Postage. Com. on Post-Office and Post-Roads. May 19, 1832. Senate Docs., No. 147, 22d Cong., 1st sess., Vol. III. Adverse to passing Senate bill No. 199, to repeal postage on newspapers. [Washington, 1832] 11 p. MB.   16356

---- Report on Officers in the Pay Dept. Com. on Military Affairs. Dec. 28, 1832. Reports of Committees, No. 16, 22d Cong., 2d sess. Bill reported regulating the rank and pay of officers of the Pay Dept. of the Army. [Washington, 1832] 3 p. MB.   16357

---- Report on Patents. Sec. E. Livingston. Jan. 3, 1832. House Ex. Docs., No. 39, 22d Cong., 1st sess., Vol. II. Statement of persons to whom patents have been granted during the year 1831; Nature of inventions. [Washington, 1832] 58 p. MB.   16358

---- Report on Payment of Treasury Certificates. Com. on Rev. Claims. Feb. 17, 1832. Reports of Committees, No. 310, 22d

450 United States

Cong., 1st sess., Vol. II. Recommends payment of Treasury certificates held by John Caldwell, Thomas Gordon, and Nicholas Scammon; Bill reported. [Washington, 1832] 2 p. MB.
16359

---- Report on Pension Applications. Sec. Lewis Cass. Feb. 16, 1832. House Ex. Docs., No. 120, 22d Cong., 1st sess., Vol. IV. Transmitting list of persons who have made application for pension or increase of pension. [Washingon, 1832] 9 p. MB. 16360

---- ---- ---- Dec. 28, 1832. Senate Docs., No. 20, 22d Cong., 2d sess., Vol. I. Transmitting list of persons who have made application for pension or increase of pension. [Washington, 1832] 8 p. MB. 16361

---- Report on Pension Laws. Committee on Revolutionary Pensions. Jan. 26, 1832. Reports of Committees, No. 238, 22d Cong., 1st sess., Vol. II. Recommends sundry amendments of the pension laws. [Washington, 1832] 9 p. MB. 16362

---- Report on Pensions. Secretary Levi Woodbury. Feb. 28, 1832. House Ex. Docs., No. 135, 22d Cong., 1st sess., Vol. IV. Relative to pensions chargeable to the privateer pension fund. [Washington, 1832] 1 p. MB. 16363

---- Report on Petition for Payment for Land. Committee on Claims. Jan. 30, 1832. Reports of Committees, No. 241, 22d Cong., 1st sess., Vol. II. Recommends allowance of compensation for land purchased by the Secretary of the Navy of Randall Allis, Timothy Twitchell, and John L. Williams. [Washington, 1832] 1 p. MB. 16364

---- Report on Petition of A. Gamble. Com. on Private Land Claims. Jan. 10, 1832. Reports of Committees, No. 152, 22d Cong., 1st sess., Vol. I. Recommends exchange of land granted to petitioner; Bill reported. [Washington, 1832] 2 p. MB.
16365

---- Report on Petition of A. Gotthilf. Select Committee on Patent Laws. May 1, 1832. Reports of Committees, No. 462, 22d Cong., 1st sess., Vol. IV. Petitioner asks patent as agent of Richard Bill, for mode of preserving timber; Committee recommends that he have leave to withdraw his papers. [Washington, 1832] 1 p. MB.
16366

---- Report on Petition of A. Hitchcock. Com. on Revolutionary Pensions. Jan. 3, 1832. Reports of Committees, No. 111, 22d Cong., 1st sess., Vol. I. Recommends allowance of pension to petitioner; Bill reported. [Washington, 1832] 1 p. MB. 16367

---- Report on Petition of A. Holmes. Com. on Revolutionary Pensions. Jan. 3, 1832. Reports of Committees, No. 114, 22d Cong., 1st sess., Vol. I. Recommends allowance of pension to petitioner; Bill reported. [Washington, 1832] 1 p. MB. 16368

---- Report on Petition of A. Peebles. Com. on Revolutionary Pensions. Jan. 3, 1832. Reports of Committees, No. 102, 22d Cong., 1st sess., Vol. I. Recommends petitioner to favorable consideration. [Washington, 1832] 1 p. MB. 16369

---- Report on Petition of Abijah Crane. Committee on Pensions. Mar. 1, 1832. Senate Docs., No. 84, 22d Cong., 1st sess., Vol. II. Recommends allowance of pension to petitioner; Bill reported. [Washington, 1832] 1 p. MB. 16370

---- Report on Petition of Abijah Fisk. Committee on Invalid Pensions. Jan. 18, 1832. Reports of Committees, No. 200, 22d Cong., 1st sess., Vol. I. Recommends allowance of pension to petitioner; Bill reported. [Washington, 1832] 2 p. MB. 16371

---- Report on Petition of Abner Smith. Com. on Revolutionary Pensions. Jan. 4, 1832. Reports of Committees, No. 133, 22d Cong., 1st sess., Vol. I. Recommends allowance of compensation to petitioner on account of services in the Army; Bill reported. [Washington, 1832] 1 p. MB. 16372

---- Report on Petition of Abraham A. Massias. Com. on Military Affairs. Jan. 12, 1832. Reports of Committees, No. 176, 22d Cong., 1st sess., Vol. I. Recommends payment of judgment obtained against petitioner, while an officer in the Army, for imprisonment of a British subject. [Washington, 1832] 18 p. MB. 16373

---- Report on Petition of Abraham Forbes. Com. on Private Land Claims. Jan. 27, 1832. Reports of Committees, No. 239, 22d Cong., 1st sess., Vol. II. Recommends grant of land to petitioner for services in Army; Bill reported. [Washington, 1832] 1 p. MB. 16374

---- Report on Petition of Alfred Baldwin. Com. on Invalid Pensions. Feb. 8, 1832. Reports of Committees, No. 278, 22d Cong., 1st sess., Vol. II. Recommends that petitioner be indemnified for impressment into the Army while a minor; Bill reported. [Washington, 1832] 1 p. MB. 16375

---- Report on Petition of Amos Sheffield et al. Com. on Commerce. Apr. 7, 1832. Reports of Committees, No. 433, 22d Cong., 1st sess., Vol. III. Recommends that petitioners be allowed the bounty paid to vessels engaged in the cod fishery; Bill reported. [Washington, 1832] 2 p. MB. 16376

---- Report on Petition of Amos W. Brown. Com. on Private Land Claims. Feb. 1, 1832. Reports of Committees, No. 253, 22d Cong., 1st sess., Vol. II. Recommends grant of bounty land to petitioner; Bill reported. [Washington, 1832] 1 p. MB. 16377

---- Report on Petition of Andrew Cushman. Committee on Pensions. Mar. 12, 1832. Senate Docs., No. 100, 22d Cong., 1st sess., Vol. II. Recommends allowance to petitioner of arrears of pension; Bill reported. [Washington, 1832] 1 p. MB. 16378

---- Report on Petition of Andrew F. Perry. Com. on the Judiciary. Mar. 20, 1832. Reports of Committees, No. 399, 22d Cong., 1st sess., Vol. III. Adverse to granting prayer of petitioner to be discharged in part from a debt due by him to the United States as receiver of public moneys. [Washington, 1832] 6 p. MB. 16379

---- Report on Petition of Andrew Marschalk. Committee on Pensions. Mar. 6, 1832. Senate Docs., No. 93, 22d Cong., 1st sess., Vol. II. Recommends that prayer of petitioner for grant of land for military services be not granted. [Washington, 1832] 1 p. MB. 16380

---- Report on Petition of Ann M. Barron. Com. on Revolutionary Claims. Feb. 17, 1832. Reports of Committees, No. 307, 22d

Cong., 1st sess., Vol. II. Recommends allowance of half-pay
to petitioner on account of services of William Barron; Bill reported. [Washington, 1832] 2 p.
MB.   16381

---- Report on Petition of Anthony Bollerman. Committee on
Commerce. Mar. 6, 1832. Reports of Committees, No. 350,
22d Cong., 1st sess., Vol. III.
Recommends that petitioner be allowed reduction of duties on dam-
aged ginghams imported; Bill reported. [Washington, 1832] 1 p.
MB.   16382

---- Report on Petition of Anthony Hussey. Committee on Naval Affairs. May 17, 1832. Reports of Committees, No. 477,
22d Cong., 1st sess., Vol. V.
Recommends allowance of prize-
money to petitioner as administrator of Joseph Rowe; Bill reported. [Washington, 1832] 3 p.
MB.   16383

---- Report on Petition of Asa
Hoyt. Committee on Invalid Pensions. Jan. 19, 1832. Report of
Committees, No. 208, 22d Cong.,
1st sess., Vol. I. Recommends
allowance of half-pay pension to
petitioner; Bill reported. [Wash-
ington, 1832] 1 p. MB.   16384

---- Report on Petition of Asher
Huntington. Com. on Invalid Pensions. Feb. 2, 1832. Reports of
Committees, No. 264, 22d Cong.,
1st sess., Vol. II. Recommends
allowance of arrears of pension
to petitioner; Bill reported. [Wash-
ington, 1832] 1 p. MB.   16385

---- Report on Petition of B.
Burlingame. Com. on Invalid
Pensions. Jan. 13, 1832. Reports
of Committees, No. 186, 22d
Cong., 1st sess., Vol. I. Rec-
ommends allowance of pension to

petitioner; Bill reported. [Wash-
ington, 1832] 1 p. MB.   16386

---- Report on Petition of Benjamin Dow. Committee on Invalid
Pensions. Jan. 25, 1832. Reports
of Committees, No. 232, 22d
Cong., 1st sess., Vol. II. Recommends allowance of pension to
petitioner; Bill reported. [Wash-
ington, 1832] 1 p. MB.   16387

---- Report on Petition of Benjamin Fitch. Com. on Invalid Pensions. Feb. 29, 1832. Report of
Committees, No. 349, 22d Cong.,
1st sess., Vol. III. Recommends
increase of pension to petitioner;
Bill reported. [Washington, 1832]
2 p. MB.   16388

---- Report on Petition of Benjamin Grover. Com. on Invalid
Pensions. Jan. 19, 1832. Reports
of Committees, No. 214, 22d
Cong., 1st sess., Vol. I. Recommends allowance of pension to
petitioner; Bill reported. [Wash-
ington, 1832] 1 p. MB.   16389

---- Report on Petition of Bradford Steele. Committee on Pensions. Feb. 23, 1832. Senate
Docs., No. 70, 22d Cong., 1st
sess., Vol. II. Recommends that
name of petitioner be placed on
the pension-roll; Bill reported.
[Washington, 1832] 1 p. MB.
                           16390

---- Report on Petition of C.
Drish. Com. on Revolutionary
Claims. Feb. 15, 1832. Reports
of Committees, No. 289, 22d
Cong., 1st sess., Vol. II. Recommends payment to petitioner,
as legal representative of Christian Ish, of certificate issued to
the latter for services to the
Government; Bill reported. [Wash-
ington, 1832] 2 p. MB.   16391

---- Report on Petition of C.
Lambert. Com. on Revolutionary

Pensions. Jan. 3, 1832. Reports of Committees, No. 110, 22d Cong., 1st sess., Vol. I. Recommends allowance of pension to petitioner; Bill reported. [Washington, 1832] 1 p. MB.   16392

---- Report on Petition of Caleb Church. Com. on Revolutionary Pensions. Jan. 10, 1832. Reports of Committees, No. 170, 22d Cong., 1st sess., Vol. I. Recommends allowance of pension to petitioner; Bill reported. [Washington, 1832] 1 p. MB.   16393

---- Report on Petition of Calvin Pinkham. Committee on Rev. Pensions. May 14, 1832. Reports of Committees, No. 473, 22d Cong., 1st sess., Vol. V. Recommends restoration of petitioner to pension-rolls. [Washington, 1832] 1 p. MB.   16394

---- Report on Petition of Carey Clark. Committee on Invalid Pensions. Jan. 19, 1832. Reports of Committees, No. 213, 22d Cong., 1st sess., Vol. I. Recommends increase of pension to petitioner; Bill reported. [Washington, 1832] 1 p. MB.   16395

---- Report on Petition of Charles Ludlow. Committee on Claims. Feb. 15, 1832. Reports of Committees, No. 301, 22d Cong., 1st sess., Vol. II. Adverse to granting release to petitioner as surety for Robert C. Ludlow, purser in the Navy. [Washington, 1832] 9 p. MB.   16396

---- Report on Petition of Chiefs of Choctaw Nation. Com. on Claims. Jan. 30, 1832. Reports of Committees, No. 246, 22d Cong., 1st sess., Vol. II. Recommends grant of land to Joseph Dukes, teacher of Indian school; Bill reported. [Washington, 1832] 2 p. MB.   16397

---- Report on Petition of Citizens of Louisiana. Select committee. Jan. 25, 1832. Reports of Committees, No. 233, 22d Cong., 1st sess., Vol. II. Recommends that claims to land in Louisiana under the De Bastrop grant be referred to the courts for adjudication. [Washington, 1832] 6 p. MB.   16398

---- Report on Petition of Citizens of Missouri. Com. on Territories. July 14, 1832. Reports of Committees, No. 512, 22d Cong., 1st sess., Vol. V. Recommends cession of territory to the State of Missouri to rectify a mistake in running boundary-line; Bill reported. [Washington, 1832] 1 p. MB.   16399

---- ---- Com. Private Land Claims. Feb. 17, 1832. Reports of Committees, No. 303, 22d Cong., 1st sess., Vol. II. Recommends confirmation of land title of petitioners; Bill reported. [Washington, 1832] 2 p. MB.   16400

---- Report on Petition of Citizens of Portland, Maine. Com. on Commerce. May 9, 1832. Reports of Committees, No. 468, 22d Cong., 1st sess., Vol. V. Recommends construction of marine hospital at Portland; Bill reported. [Washington, 1832] 1 p. MB.   16401

---- Report on Petition of Coleman Fisher. Com. on Private Land Claims. Jan. 31, 1832. Reports of Committees, No. 250, 22d Cong., 1st sess., Vol. II. Recommends grant of land to petitioner; Bill reported. [Washington, 1832] 1 p. MB.   16402

---- Report on Petition of D. Felton. Com. on Revolutionary Pensions. Jan. 3, 1832. Reports of Committees, No. 98, 22d Cong.,

1st sess., Vol. I. Recommends restoration of name of petitioner to pension-roll. [Washington, 1832] 1 p. MB.   16403

---- Report on Petition of D. Hendricks. Committee on Pensions. May 4, 1832. Senate Docs. No. 140, 22d Cong., 1st sess., Vol. III. Recommends that prayer of petitioner for pension be not granted. [Washington, 1832] 18 p. MB.   16404

---- Report on Petition of Daniel Burr. Committee on Pensions. Mar. 2, 1832. Senate Docs., No. 82, 22d Cong., 1st sess., Vol. II. Recommends that name of petitioner be placed on the pension-roll. Bill reported. [Washington, 1832] 1 p. MB.   16405

---- Report on Petition of Daniel Fuller. Com. on Invalid Pensions. Mar. 2, 1832. Reports of Committees, No. 347, 22d Cong., 1st sess., Vol. III. Recommends allowance of pension to petitioner; Bill reported. [Washington, 1832] 1 p. MB.   16406

---- Report on Petition of Daniel Johnson. Committee on Military Affairs. Jan. 3, 1832. Reports of Committees, No. 83, 22d Cong., 1st sess., Vol. I. Recommends that petitioner be compensated for non-fulfillment of contract on the part of the United States relative to his apprenticeship at the Harper's Ferry armory; Bill reported. [Washington, 1832] 1 p. MB.
16407

---- Report on Petition of Daniel Palmer. Com. on Invalid Pensions. Feb. 2, 1832. Reports of Committees, No. 262, 22d Cong., 1st sess., Vol. II. Reports petition for increase of pension without recommendation. [Washington, 1832.] 1 p. MB.   16408

---- Report on Petition of Daniel Stoddard. Com. on Invalid Pensions. Jan. 19, 1832. Reports of Committees, No. 209, 22d Cong., 1st sess., Vol. I. Recommends allowance of pension to petitioner; Bill reported. [Washington, 1832] 1 p. MB.   16409

---- Report on Petition of Daniel W. Coxe. Com. on Private Land Claims. Jan. 12, 1832. Reports of Committees, No. 178, 22d Cong., 1st sess., Vol. I. Recommends that petitioner be allowed to test his title to certain lands in Louisiana in the courts; Bill reported. [Washington, 1832] 2 p. MB.   16410

---- Report on Petition of Daniel Wyman. Committee on Pensions. Mar. 2, 1832. Senate Docs., No. 89, 22d Cong., 1st sess., Vol. II. Recommends that name of petitioner be restored to the pension-roll; Bill reported. [Washington, 1832] 1 p. MB.   16411

---- Report on Petition of David Beard. Committee on the Judiciary. July 9, 1832. Senate Docs., No. 179, 22d Cong., 1st sess., Vol. III. Reports bill granting petitioner partial compensation for goods forfeited to the United States on account of violation of the revenue laws. [Washington, 1832] 3 p. MB.   16412

---- Report on Petition of David Brooks. Com. on Revolutionary Pensions. Feb. 6, 1832. Reports of Committees, No. 273, 22d Cong., 1st sess., Vol. II. Recommends allowance of pension to petitioner; Bill reported. [Washington, 1832] 1 p. MB.   16413

---- Report on Petition of David Clap. Committee on Invalid Pensions. Jan. 19, 1832. Reports of Committees, No. 204, 22d Cong.,

1st sess., Vol. I. Recommends allowance of pension to petitioner; Bill reported. [Washington, 1832] 1 p. MB.   16414

---- Report on Petition of E. Foster. Committee on Commerce. Feb. 16, 1832. Reports of Committees, No. 302, 22d Cong., 1st sess., Vol. II. Recommends refundment of excess of duties paid by petitioner; Bill reported. [Washington, 1832] 1 p. MB.   16415

---- Report on Petition of E. Magruder. Com. on Revolutionary Claims. Jan. 3, 1832. Reports of Committees, no. 97, 22d Cong., 1st sess., Vol. I. Recommends allowance to petitioner of amount of commutation for services of her late father, Reynold Hillary, an officer in the Revolutionary army; Bill reported. [Washington, 1832] 1 p. MB.   16416

---- Report on Petition of E. Plympton. Com. on Revolutionary Pensions. Jan. 10, 1832. Reports of Committees, No. 160, 22d Cong., 1st sess., Vol. I. Recommends allowance of pension to petitioner; Bill reported. [Washington, 1832] 1 p. MB.   16417

---- Report on Petition of E. Weed. Com. on Revolutionary Pensions. Jan. 3, 1832. Reports of Committees, No. 112, 22d Cong., 1st sess., Vol. I. Recommends allowance of pension to petitioner; Bill reported. [Washington, 1832] 1 p. MB.   16418

---- Report on Petition of Ebenezer Breed. Committee on Commerce. Mar. 19, 1832. Reports of Committees, No. 398, 22d Cong., 1st sess., Vol. III. Petitioner claims refundment of duties paid on wines destroyed by burning of Government warehouse; Committee recommends that petitioner have leave to withdraw his papers. [Washington, 1832] 2 p. MB.   16419

---- Report on Petition of Edgar Freeman. Com. on Invalid Pensions. Jan. 19, 1832. Reports of Committees, No. 207, 22d Cong., 1st sess., Vol. I. Recommends allowance of pension to petitioner; Bill reported. [Washington, 1832] 1 p. MB.   16420

---- Report on Petition of Edmund Brooke. Com. on Revolutionary Claims. Jan. 19, 1832. Reports of Committees, No. 219, 22d Cong. 1st sess., Vol. I. Recommends allowance to petitioner of commutation of pay; Bill reported. [Washington, 1832] 1 p. MB.   16421

---- Report on Petition of Elijah S. Bell. Committee on Claims. Mar. 21, 1832. Reports of Committees, No. 403, 22d Cong., 1st sess., Vol. III. Adverse to purchasing from petitioner buildings erected by him on United States land. [Washington, 1832] 5 p. MB.   16422

---- Report on Petition of Elisha Hammond. Com. on Rev. Pensions. Mar. 13, 1832. Reports of Committees, No. 373, 22d Cong., 1st sess., Vol. III. Recommends allowance of pension to petitioner; Bill reported. [Washington, 1832] 1 p. MB.   16423

---- Report on Petition of Eloy Segura et al. Com. on Priv. Land Claims. Mar. 16, 1832. Reports of Committees, No. 383, 22d Cong., 1st sess., Vol. III. Recommends that each petitioner be granted a quarter-section of land; Bill reported. [Washington, 1832] 1 p. MB.   16424

---- Report on Petition of Enelia Cox. Committee on Claims. May

7, 1832. Reports of Committees, No. 467, 22d Cong., 1st sess., Vol. V. Recommends that petitioner, widow of John P. Cox, late paymaster, be refunded amount of money paid by him to the United States on account of Government funds stolen from him; Bill reported. [Washington, 1832] 3 p. MB.   16425

---- Report on Petition of Executors of J. C. Edwards, Select Com. Pat. Laws. May 1, 1832. Reports of Committees, No. 461, 22d Cong., 1st sess., Vol. IV. Petitioners ask extension of patent for improvement in water-wheel; Committee recommends that they have leave to withdraw papers. [Washington, 1832] 1 p. MB.
16426

---- Report on Petition of Executors of T. Worthington. Com. on Judiciary. Jan. 13, 1832. Reports of Committees, No. 181, 22d Cong., 1st sess., Vol. I. Recommends that petitioners be relieved from liability of Thomas Worthington as surety for Samuel Finley, late receiver of public moneys; Bill reported. [Washington, 1832] 3 p. MB.   16427

---- Report on Petition of F. M. Arredondo. Com. on Foreign Affairs. Jan. 20, 1832. Reports of Committees, No. 223, 22d Cong., 1st sess., Vol. I. Reports bill extending the authority of judges of the courts in Florida to the examination of claims for property lost or destroyed during the war in East Florida. [Washington, 1832] 31 p. MB.   16428

---- Report on Petition of Flournoy & Ward. Com. on Public Lands. Jan. 10, 1832. Reports of Committees, No. 151, 22d Cong., 1st sess., Vol. I. Recommends that petitioners be granted the right to exchange certain land;

Bill reported. [Washington, 1832] 1 p. MB.   16429

---- Report on Petition of Francis Barnes. Com. on Claims. May 17, 1832. Reports of Committes, No. 475, 22d Cong., 1st sess., Vol. V. Recommends that petitioner be reimbursed for losses sustained in furnishing whiskey to the Navy; Bill reported. [Washington, 1832] 17 p. MB.   16430

---- Report on Petition of Francis Du Coing. Com. on Invalid Pensions. Jan. 10, 1832. Reports of Committees, No. 157, 22d Cong., 1st sess., Vol. I. Recommends allowance of pension to petitioner; Bill reported. [Washington, 1832] 2 p. MB.   16431

---- Report on Petition of Francis Jacobs. Com. on Invalid Pensions. Feb. 15, 1832. Report of Committees, No. 293, 22d Cong., 1st sess., Vol. II. Recommends that petitioner be placed on the pension-rolls. [Washington, 1832] 1 p. MB.   16432

---- Report on Petition of G. Flanjac. Com. on Private Land Claims. Feb. 6, 1832. Reports of Committees, No. 270, 22d Cong., 1st sess., Vol. II. Recommends compensation to petitioner for his land sold by the United States; Bill reported. [Washington, 1832] 1 p. MB.
16433

---- Report on Petition of George Chinn. Committee on Claims. Feb. 17, 1832. Reports of Committees, No. 305, 22d Cong., 1st sess., Vol. II. Recommends allowance of additional rations to petitioner for services as lieutenant on board revenue-cutter; Bill reported. [Washington, 1832] 1 p. MB.   16434

---- Report on Petition of George

E. Tingle. Committee on Territories. Jan. 25, 1832. Reports of
Committees, No. 235, 22d Cong.,
1st sess., Vol. II. Recommends
that petitioner be allowed compensation for services under the Territorial government of Florida;
Bill reported. [Washington, 1832]
1 p. MB.   16435

---- Report on Petition of George
Field. Com. on Invalid Pensions.
Mar. 2, 1832. Reports of Committees, No. 346, 22d Cong., 1st
sess., Vol. III. Recommends allowance of pension to petitioner;
Bill reported. [Washington, 1832]
1 p. MB.   16436

---- Report on Petition of George
Gordon. Com. on Private Land
Claims. Apr. 5, 1832. Reports
of Committees, No. 428, 22d
Cong., 1st sess., Vol. III. Recommends confirmation of land title
to petitioner as assignee of Matthew Ramy; Bill reported. [Wash-
ington, 1832] 2 p. MB.   16437

---- Report on Petition of George
Gray. Committee on Patents. Apr.
20, 1832. Reports of Committees,
No. 451, 22d Cong., 1st sess.,
Vol. III. Petitioner prays for ex-
tension of patent for improvement
in ship deck lights; Committee
recommends that petitioner have
leave to withdraw his papers.
[Washington, 1832] 2 p. MB.
                            16438
---- Report on Petition of George
H. Jennings. Committee on
Claims. Mar. 26, 1832. Reports
of Committees, No. 408, 22d
Cong., 1st sess., Vol. III. Rec-
ommends compensation to petitioner for attendance as witness in
United States court; Bill reported.
[Washington, 1832] 2 p. MB.
                            16439
---- Report on Petition of Good-
man Noble. Com. on Rev. Pen-
sions. Mar. 15, 1832. Reports

of Committees, No. 379, 22d
Cong., 1st sess., Vol. III. Recommends allowance of pension to
petitioner; Bill reported. [Wash-
ington, 1832] 1 p. MB.   16440

---- Report on Petition of Grievo
Drummond. Com. on Invalid Pensions. Jan. 10, 1832. Reports of
Committees, No. 154, 22d Cong.,
1st sess., Vol. I. Recommends
allowance of pension to petitioner;
Bill reported. [Washington, 1832]
1 p. MB.   16441

---- Report on Petition of H. A.
De Saussure. Com. Revolutionary
Claims. Apr. 6, 1832. Reports
of Committees, No. 429, 22d
Cong., 1st sess., Vol. III. Recommends allowance to petitioner,
as executor of Alexander Garden,
of interest on commutation-money;
Bill reported. [Washington, 1832]
2 p. MB.   16442

---- Report on Petition of H. G.
Spafford. Select Committee on
Patents. Mar. 6, 1832. Reports
of Committees, No. 351, 22d
Cong., 1st sess., Vol. III. Petitioner asks for letters patent on
a new discovery in mechanics,
specifications to remain secret
during the continuance of the patent; Committee reports bill providing that specifications be kept
secret for four years. [Washing-
ton, 1832] 9 p. MB.   16443

---- Report on Petition of Hartwell W. Vick. Com. on Public
Lands. Mar. 17, 1832. Reports
of Committees, No. 427, 22d
Cong., 1st sess., Vol. III. Recommended refundment of purchase-
money paid United States for land
which had already been granted;
Bill reported. [Washington, 1832]
2 p. MB.   16444

---- Report on Petition of Heard
Brackett. Committee on Invalid

Pensions. Jan. 19, 1832. Reports
of Committees, No. 217, 22d
Cong., 1st sess., Vol. I. Recommends allowance of pension to
petitioner; Bill reported. [Washing-
ton, 1832] 1 p. MB.   16445

---- Report on Petition of Heirs
of D. McNeil. Com. on Rev.
Claims. Feb. 17, 1832. Reports
of Committees, No. 309, 22d
Cong., 1st sess., Vol. II. Recommends commutation of seven
years' half-pay to petitioners;
Bill reported. [Washington, 1832]
1 p. MB.   16446

---- Report on Petition of Heirs
of E. Anderson. Committee on
Claims. May 5, 1832. Reports of
Committees, No. 465, 22d Cong.,
1st sess., Vol. V. Petitioner
claims damages on account of
protest of drafts paid him for rations furnished United States
troops; Committee reports
bill for payment of claim with
interest. [Washington, 1832]
4 p. MB.   16447

---- Report on Petition of Heirs
of E. Meade. Com. Revolutionary Claims. July 7, 1832. Reports of Committees, No. 504,
22d Cong., 1st sess., Vol. V.
Recommends allowance of five
years' full pay to petitioners;
Bill reported. [Washington, 1832]
2 p. MB.   16448

---- Report on Petition of
Heirs of Elijah Winter. Com. on
Public Lands. Mar. 22, 1832.
Reports of Committees, No. 405,
22d Cong., 1st sess., Vol. III.
Majority reports bill to adjust
claim of petitioners for confirmation of title to land in Arkansas; Minority reports bill allowing petitioners to institute suit in
equity. [Washington, 1832] 40 p.
MB.   16449

---- Report on Petition of Heirs
of Henry Field. Mar. 10, 1832.
Reports of Committees, No. 358,
22d Cong., 1st sess., Vol. III.
The Committee on Revolutionary
Claims recommends allowance to
petitioners of seven years' half-
pay; Bill reported. [Washington,
1832] 1 p. MB.   16450

---- Report on Petition of Heirs
of J. and T. Pettigrew. Indian
Com. Mar. 22, 1832. Reports of
Committees, No. 406, 22d Cong.,
1st sess., Vol. III. Recommends
indemnification to petitioners for
negroes and other property taken
by the Creek Indians; Bill reported. [Washington, 1832] 24 p.
MB.   16451

---- Report on Petition of Heirs
of J. B. Vallery. Com. Priv.
Land Claims. Feb. 23, 1832.
Reports of Committees, No. 323,
22d Cong., 1st sess., Vol. II.
Recommends that petitioner's title to land in Louisiana be confirmed; Bill reported. [Washing-
ton, 1832] 1 p. MB.   16452

---- Report on Petition of Heirs
of J. Knight. Com. on Invalid
Pensions. Jan. 11, 1832. Reports
of Committees, No. 173, 22d
Cong., 1st sess., Vol. I. Recommends allowance of pension to
petitioner; Bill reported. [Wash-
ington, 1832] 1 p. MB.   16453

---- Report on Petition of Heirs
of J. M. Gregory. Apr. 3, 1832.
Reports of Committees, No. 421,
22d Cong., 1st sess., Vol. III.
Committee on Revolutionary
Claims recommends allowance of
seven years' half-pay to petitioners; Bill reported. [Washington,
1832] 1 p. MB.   16454

---- Report on Petition of Heirs
of John Campbell. Com. on Rev.
Claims. Jan. 20, 1832. Reports

of Committees, No. 220, 22d Cong., 1st sess., Vol. I. Recommends closing accounts of John Campbell, late deputy quartermaster-general; Bill reported. [Washington, 1832] 4 p. MB.   16455

---- Report on Petition of Heirs of John Wilson. Com. on Rev. Claims. Jan. 13, 1832. Reports of Committees, No. 183, 22d Cong., 1st sess., Vol. I. Recommends allowance of half-pay to petitioners; Bill reported. [Washington, 1832] 1 p. MB.   16456

---- Report on Petition of Heirs of John Winston. Com. on Rev. Claims. Mar. 23, 1832. Reports of Committees, No. 407, 22d Cong., 1st sess., Vol. III. Recommends allowance of five years' full pay to petitioners in lieu of half-pay for life; Bill reported. [Washington, 1832] 1 p. MB.   16457

---- Report on Petition of Heirs of Matthew Lyon. Com. on the Judiciary. Jan. 20, 1832. Reports of Committees, No. 218, 22d Cong., 1st sess., Vol. I. Recommends return of fine to petitioner, who was found guilty of libel under the sedition law; Bill reported. [Washington, 1832] 2 p. MB.   16458

---- Report on Petition of Heirs of P. Thornton. Com. on Rev. Claims. May 14, 1832. Reports of Committees, No. 470, 22d Cong., 1st sess., Vol. V. Recommends allowance to petitioners of five years' full pay; Bill reported. [Washington, 1832] 1 p. MB.   16459

---- Report on Petition of Heirs of Richard Livingston. Feb. 24, 1832. Reports of Committees, No. 329, 22d Cong., 1st sess., Vol. III. Committee on Revolu-

tionary Claims recommends grant of bounty land to petitioners; Bill reported. [Washington, 1832] 2 p. MB.   16460

---- Report on Petition of Heirs of Samuel J. Axson. Apr. 7, 1832. Reports of Committees, No. 436, 22d Cong., 1st sess., Vol. III. Committee on Revolutionary Claims recommends allowance to petitioners of five years' full pay; Bill reported. [Washington, 1832] 1 p. MB.   16461

---- Report on Petition of Heirs of T. Frothingham. Dec. 20, 1832. Reports of Committees, No. 11, 22d Cong., 2d sess. The Committee on Revolutionary Claims recommends allowance of claim of petitioners for building destroyed by the British; Bill reported. [Washington, 1832] 3 p. MB.   16462

---- Report on Petition of Heirs of T. Taylor. Com. Revolutionary Claims. June 26, 1832. Reports of Committees, No. 493, 22d Cong., 1st sess., Vol. V. Recommends allowance to petitioners of five years' full pay; Bill reported. [Washington, 1832] 1 p. MB.   16463

---- Report on Petition of Heirs of T. Wallace. Com. Revolutionary Claims. Feb. 23, 1832. Reports of Committees, No. 325, 22d Cong., 1st sess., Vol. II. Recommends that petitioner be allowed commutation of five years' full pay. Bill reported. [Washington, 1832] 1 p. MB.   16464

---- Report on Petition of Heirs of W. Pollard. Com. on Priv. Land Claims. Feb. 15, 1832. Reports of Committees, No. 299, 22d Cong., 1st sess., Vol. II. Recommends that petitioner be confirmed in his title to lot of

land in Mobile; Bill reported.
[Washington, 1832] 1 p. MB.
16465

---- Report on Petition of Heirs
of Wm. Young. Com. on Indian
Affairs. Mar. 17, 1832. Reports
of Committees, No. 389, 22d
Cong., 1st sess., Vol. III. Recommends payment to petitioners
for services of William Young in
taking the census; Bill reported.
[Washington, 1832] 1 p. MB.
16466

---- Report on Petition of Henrietta Barnes. Com. Revolutionary
Claims. July 2, 1832. Reports of
Committees, No. 498, 22d Cong.,
1st sess., Vol. V. Recommends
allowance to petitioner of commutation of pay due her father Allen
Lathrop; Bill reported. [Washing-
ton, 1832] 1 p. MB.   16467

---- Report on Petition of Henry
Blodget. Com. on Invalid Pensions. Feb. 2, 1832. Reports of
Committees, No. 260, 22d Cong.,
1st sess., Vol. II. Recommends
that petitioner be restored to pension-rolls; Bill reported. [Wash-
ington, 1832] 1 p. MB.   16468

---- Report on Petition of Henry
Click. Committee on Invalid Pensions. Feb. 2, 1832. Reports of
Committees, No. 263, 22d Cong.,
1st sess., Vol. II. Recommends
allowance of pension to petitioner;
Bill reported. [Washington, 1832]
1 p. MB.   16469

---- Report on Petition of Henry
Darling. Committee on Commerce. Mar. 12, 1832. Reports of
Committees, No. 361, 22d Cong.,
1st sess., Vol. III. Recommends
remission of penalty for salt
smuggled by the captain of a fishing vessel owned by petitioner;
Bill reported. [Washington, 1832]
1 p. MB.   16470

---- Report on Petition of Hiram

Ingram. Committee on Commerce.
Apr. 13, 1832. Reports of Committees, No. 445, 22d Cong., 1st
sess., Vol. III. Adverse to prayer
of petitioner for refundment of
tonnage duties on vessel owned by
him. [Washington, 1832] 2 p.
MB.   16471

---- Report on Petition of Hugh
Beard. Com. on Private Land
Claims. Jan. 24, 1832. Reports
of Committees, No. 229, 22d
Cong., 1st sess., Vol. II. Recommends granting request of petitioner for exchange of land certificate; Bill reported. [Washing-
ton, 1832] 1 p. MB.   16472

---- Report on Petition of Isaac
Moore. Com. on Rev. Pensions.
May 17, 1832. Reports of Committees, No. 476, 22d Cong., 1st
sess., Vol. V. Recommends allowance of pension to petitioner;
Bill reported. [Washington, 1832]
1 p. MB.   16473

---- Report on Petition of J.
Bradford. Com. on Private Land
Claims. Feb. 6, 1832. Reports of
Committees, No. 274, 22d Cong.,
1st sess., Vol. II. Recommends
confirmation of land title of petitioner; Bill reported. [Washing-
ton, 1832] 1 p. MB.   16474

---- Report on Petition of J. C.
Bondrean. Com. on Private Land
Claims. Mar. 16, 1832. Reports
of Committees, No. 385, 22d
Cong., 1st sess., Vol. III. Recommends confirmation of land title
of petitioner; Bill reported. [Wash-
ington, 1832] 1 p. MB.   16475

---- Report on Petition of J.
Campbell. Com. on Revolutionary
Pensions. Jan. 10, 1832. Reports
of Committees, No. 167, 22d
Cong., 1st sess., Vol. I. Recommends allowance of pension to petitioner; Bill reported. [Washing-

ton, 1832] 1 p. MB.   16476

---- Report on Petition of J. Crosby. Com. on Revolutionary Pensions. Jan. 3, 1832. Reports of Committees, No. 119, 22d Cong., 1st sess., Vol. I. Recommends that petitioner be allowed the benefits of the act of March 18, 1818; Bill reported. [Washington, 1832] 1 p. MB.   16477

---- Report on Petition of J. Du Commun. Committee on Military Affairs. Jan. 4, 1832. Reports of Committees, No. 125, 22d Cong., 1st sess. Vol. I. Recommends allowance of pension to petitioner for services as teacher at the Military Academy; Bill reported. [Washington, 1832] 1 p. MB.   16478

---- Report on Petition of J. F. Hertzog. Com. on Private Land Claims. Dec. 22, 1832. Reports of Committees, No. 13, 22d Cong. 2d sess. Recommends confirmation of title of petitioner to land in Louisiana; Bill reported. [Washington, 1832] 1 p. MB.   16479

---- Report on Petition of J. Fogg. Com. on Revolutionary Pensions. Jan. 3, 1832. Reports of Committees, No. 109, 22d Cong., 1st sess., Vol. I. Recommends allowance of pension to petitioner. [Washington, 1832] 1 p. MB.   16480

---- Report on Petition of J. Guild. Com. on Revolutionary Pensions. Jan. 10, 1832. Reports of Committees, No. 158, 22d Cong., 1st sess., Vol. I. Recommends restoration of name of petitioner to pension-roll; Bill reported. [Washington, 1832] 1 p. MB.   16481

---- Report on Petition of J. Hawes. Com. on Revolutionary Pensions. Jan. 3, 1832. Reports of Committees, No. 106, 22d Cong., 1st sess., Vol. I. Recommends claim of petitioner to the favorable consideration of Congress. [Washington, 1832] 1 p. MB.   16482

---- Report on Petition of J. Hedges. Committee on Public Lands. Feb. 17, 1832. Reports of Committees, No. 304, 22d Cong., 1st sess., Vol. II. Recommends that petitioner be allowed to locate certain tract of land; Bill reported. [Washington, 1832] 1 p. MB.   16483

---- Report on Petition of J. Jordan. Com. on Revolutionary Pensions. Jan. 10, 1832. Reports of Committees, No. 159, 22d Cong., 1st sess., Vol. I. Recommends allowance of pension to petitioner; Bill reported. [Washington, 1832] 1 p. MB.   16484

---- Report on Petition of J. L. Lobdell. Com. on Private Land Claims. Feb. 23, 1832. Reports of Committees, No. 324, 22d Cong., 1st sess., Vol. II. Recommends that petitioner be confirmed in his title to land in Louisiana; Bill reported. [Washington, 1832] 1 p. MB.   16485

---- Report on Petition of J. Mitchell. Com. on Revolutionary Pensions. Jan. 3, 1832. Reports of Committees, No. 121, 22d Cong., 1st sess., Vol. I. Recommends allowance of pension to petitioner; Bill reported. [Washington, 1832] 1 p. MB.   16486

---- Report on Petition of J. Polhemus. Com. on Revolutionary Claims. Feb. 7, 1832. Reports of Committees, No. 275, 22d Cong., 1st sess., Vol. II. Recommends that petitioner be granted commutation of half-pay; Bill reported. [Washington, 1832] 2 p.

MB.   16487

---- Report on Petition of J.
Richmond. Com. on Revolutionary
Pensions. Jan. 4, 1832. Reports
of Committees, No. 132, 22d
Cong., 1st sess., Vol. I. Reports
bill for relief of petitioner.
[Washington, 1832] 1 p. MB.
                                  16488
---- Report on Petition of J.
Rodgers. Committee on Indian
Affairs. May 5, 1832. Reports of
Committees, No. 464, 22d Cong.,
1st sess., Vol. V. Recommended
compensation to petitioner for
services rendered in connection
with treaty concluded with the
Cherokee Indians; Bill reported.
[Washington, 1832] 2 p. MB.
                                  16489
---- Report on Petition of J.
Scrivener. Committee on Naval
Affairs. Feb. 15, 1832. Reports
of Committees, No. 290, 22d
Cong., 1st sess., Vol. II. Rec-
ommends payment of transporta-
tion money to petitioner; Bill reported. [Washington, 1832] 1 p.
MB.   16490

---- Report on Petition of J.
Thorne and Lawson & Brice.
Com. on Commerce. Jan. 10,
1832. Reports of Committees, No.
172, 22d Cong., 1st sess., Vol.
I. Adverse to granting remission
of duties asked for by petitioners.
[Washington, 1832] 2 p. MB.
                                  16491
---- Report on Petition of J.
Tremble. Com. on Invalid Pen-
sions. Feb. 15, 1832. Reports on
Committees, No. 292, 22d Cong.,
1st sess., Vol. II. Recommends
allowance of pension of petitioner;
Bill reported. [Washington,1832]
1 p. MB.   16492

---- Report on Petition of J. Vinyard. Com. on Revolutionary Pensions. Jan. 3, 1832. Reports of
Committees, No. 103, 22d Cong.,

1st sess., Vol. I. Recommends
allowance of pension to petitioner.
[Washington, 1832] 1 p. MB.
                                  16493
---- Report on Petition of J.
Winchester. Com. on Revolutionary Pensions. Jan. 3, 1832. Reports of Committees, No. 105,
22d Cong., 1st sess., Vol. I.
Recommends allowance of pension
to petitioner. [Washington, 1832]
1 p. MB.   16494

---- Report on Petition of James
Caulfield. Com. on Private Land
Claims. Feb. 28, 1832. Reports
of Committees, No. 336, 22d
Cong., 1st sess., Vol. III. Recommends that petitioner be authorized to enter at Government
prices certain land purchased
from the Indians; Bill reported.
[Washington, 1832] 1 p. MB.
                                  16495
---- Report on Petition of James
Clark. Com. on Pensions. Mar.
12, 1832. Senate Docs., No. 99,
22d Cong., 1st sess., Vol. II.
Recommends restoration of name
of petitioner to the pension-rolls;
Bill reported. [Washington, 1832]
1 p. MB.   16496

---- Report on Petition of James
H. Brewer. Committee on Claims.
Mar. 26, 1832. Reports of Committees, No. 409, 22d Cong., 1st
sess., Vol. III. Recommends allowance of witness fees to petitioner as compensation for losses
sustained by detention on sub-
poena. [Washington, 1832] 1 p.
MB.   16497

---- Report on Petition of James
L. Stokes. Com. on Private Land
Claims. Jan. 20, 1832. Reports
of Committees, No. 225, 22d
Cong., 1st sess., Vol. II. Recommends that petitioner be allowed to complete purchase of
land; Bill reported. [Washington,
1832] 1 p. MB.   16498

---- Report on Petition of James Vanderburgh. Com. on Rev. Pensions. Mar. 15, 1832. Reports of Committees, No. 375, 22d Cong., 1st sess., Vol. III. Recommends allowance of pension to petitioner; Bill reported. [Washington, 1832] 1 p. MB. 16499

---- Report on Petition of Jane M. Lawrence. Com. on Invalid Pensions. Jan. 19, 1832. Reports of Committees, No. 216, 22d Cong., 1st sess., Vol. I. Recommends allowance of pension to petitioner as widow of Jonathan Lawrence; Bill reported. [Washington, 1832] 1 p. MB. 16500

---- Report of Petition of Jane Thornton. Com. on Revolutionary Claims. Jan. 6, 1832. Reports of Committees, No. 143, 22d Cong., 1st sess., Vol. I. Recommends allowance to petitioner of commutation of pay on account of services of her husband, John Thornton; Bill reported. [Washington, 1832] 2 p. MB. 16501

---- Report on Petition of Jared E. Groce. Committee on Public Lands. Jan. 20, 1832. Reports of Committees, No. 224, 22d Cong., 1st sess., Vol. II. Recommends exchange of land title of petitioner; Bill reported. [Washington, 1832] 1 p. MB. 16502

---- Report on Petition of Jesse Cunningham. Com. on Invalid Pensions. Jan. 19, 1832. Reports of Committees, No. 202, 22d Cong., 1st sess., Vol. I. Reports bill for relief of petitioner. [Washington, 1832] 1 p. MB. 16503

---- Report on Petition of Job Wood. Committee on Invalid Pensions. Apr. 7, 1832. Reports of Committees, No. 434, 22d Cong., 1st sess., Vol. III. Recommends allowance of pension to petitioner;

Bill reported. [Washington, 1832] 1 p. MB. 16504

---- Report on Petition of Joel Thomas. Com. on Private Land Claims. Jan. 10, 1832. Reports of Committees, No. 148, 22d Cong., 1st sess., Vol. I. Recommends that petitioner be confirmed in title to land; Bill reported. [Washington, 1832] 1 p. MB. 16505

---- Report on Petition of Joel Wright. Committee on the Judiciary. Jan. 3, 1832. Reports of Committees, No. 95, 22d Cong., 1st sess., Vol. I. Recommends that petitioner be released from a balance due on recognizance to the United States. [Washington, 1832] 1 p. MB. 16506

---- Report on Petition of John Bills. Com. on Private Land Claims. Feb. 29, 1832. Reports of Committees, No. 340, 22d Cong., 1st sess., Vol. III. Recommends that petitioner be confirmed in his title to land in Louisiana. [Washington, 1832] 1 p. MB. 16507

---- Report on Petition of John Blake. Committee on Pensions. Mar. 1, 1832. Senate Docs., No. 83, 22d Cong., 1st sess., Vol. II. Recommends that petitioner be allowed arrears of pension; Bill reported. [Washington, 1832] 1 p. MB. 16508

---- Report on Petition of John Bonny. Committee on Rev. Pensions. Mar. 15, 1832. Reports of Committees, No. 378, 22d Cong., 1st sess., Vol. III. Recommends allowance of pension to petitioner; Bill reported. [Washington, 1832] 1 p. MB. 16509

---- Report on Petition of John Boon. Committee on Rev. Pen-

sions. Mar. 13, 1832. Reports of
Committees, No. 368, 22d Cong.,
1st sess., Vol. III. Recommends
allowance of pension to petitioner;
Bill reported. [Washington, 1832]
1 p. MB.   16510

---- Report on Petition of John C.
Williams. Com. on Private Land
Claims. Jan. 17, 1832. Reports
of Committees, No. 197, 22d
Cong., 1st sess., Vol. I. Recommends that claimant be confirmed in his title to land as legal representative of Fielding
Barham; Bill reported. [Washing-
ton, 1832] 1 p. MB.   16511

---- Report on Petition of John
D. Howard. Com. on Rev. Pensions. Jan. 3, 1832. Reports of
Committees, No. 100, 22d Cong.,
1st sess., Vol. I. Recommends
allowance of pension to petitioner;
Bill reported. [Washington, 1832]
1 p. MB.   16512

---- Report on Petition of John
D. Sloat. Committee on Foreign
Affairs. May 14, 1832. Reports
of Committees, No. 471, 22d
Cong., 1st sess., Vol. V. Recommends compensation to petitioner for taking refugees on
board his vessel in Peru; Bill
reported. [Washington, 1832]
1 p. MB.   16513

---- Report on Petition of John
Kaime. Committee on Invalid
Pensions. Feb. 2, 1832. Reports
of Committees, No. 257, 22d
Cong., 1st sess., Vol. II. Recommends allowance of pension to
petitioner; Bill reported. [Wash-
ington, 1832] 1 p. MB.   16514

---- Report on Petition of John
Miller. Committee on Invalid
Pensions. Jan. 19, 1832. Reports
of Committees, No. 203, 22d
Cong., 1st sess., Vol. I. Rec-
ommends allowance of arrears of

pension to petitioner; Bill reported. [Washington, 1832] 1 p. MB.
                                16515

---- Report on Petition of John
R. Rappleye. Com. on Invalid
Pensions. Jan. 19, 1832. Reports
of Committees, No. 211, 22d
Cong., 1st sess., Vol. I. Recommends allowance of increase
and arrears of pension to petitioner; Bill reported. [Washing-
ton, 1832] 1 p. MB.   16516

---- Report on Petition of John
Scott. Com. on Invalid Pensions.
Feb. 15, 1832. Reports of Committees, No. 297, 22d Cong.,
1st sess., Vol. II. Recommends
allowance of pension to petitioner;
Bill reported. [Washington, 1832]
1 p. MB.   16517

---- Report on Petition of John
Slaughbough. Com. on Private
Land Claims. Feb. 21, 1832.
Reports of Committees, No. 322,
22d Cong., 1st sess., Vol. II.
Recommends that land title of pe-
titioner be changed; Bill reported.
[Washington, 1832] 1 p. MB.
                                16518

---- Report on Petition of John
Taylor. Committee on Invalid
Pensions. Feb. 2, 1832. Reports
of Committees, No. 258, 22d
Cong., 1st sess., Vol. II. Recommends allowance of arrears
of pension to petitioner; Bill reported. [Washington, 1832] 1 p.
MB.   16519

---- Report on Petition of John
Thompson. Committee on Claims.
Dec. 14, 1832. Reports of Committees, No. 2, 22d Cong., 2d
sess. Recommends compensation
to petitioner for damages sustained by being arrested, in the
performance of a Government contract, by a United States officer;
Bill reported. [Washington, 1832]
1 p. MB.   16520

---- Report on Petition of John Webber. Committee on Claims. Apr. 9, 1832. Reports of Committees, No. 435, 22d Cong., 1st sess., Vol. III. Recommends additional compensation to petitioner for services in taking the census; Bill reported. [Washington, 1832] 2 p. MB.   16521

---- Report on Petition of Jonas Youman. Committee on Rev. Pensions. March 19, 1832. Reports of Committees, No. 397, 22d Cong., 1st sess., Vol. III. Recommends allowance of pension to petitioner; Bill reported. [Washington, 1832] 2 p. MB.   16522

---- Report on Petition of Jonathan Bean. Com. on Invalid Pensions. Jan. 12, 1832. Reports of Committees, No. 177, 22d Cong., 1st sess., Vol. I. Recommends that petitioner be allowed pension. [Washington, 1832] 1 p. MB.   16523

---- Report on Petition of Jonathan Pearce. Com. Revolutionary Pensions. Jan. 3, 1832. Reports of Committees, No. 122, 22d Cong. 1st sess., Vol. I. Recommends allowance of pension to petitioner; Bill reported. [Washington, 1832] 1 p. MB.   16524

---- Report on Petition of Joseph Durfee. Com. on Rev. Pensions. Mar. 13, 1832. Reports of Committees, No. 370, 22d Cong., 1st sess., Vol. III. Recommends allowance of pension to petitioner; Bill reported. [Washington, 1832] 1 p. MB.   16525

---- Report on Petition of Joseph Nourse. Com. on the Judiciary. May 19, 1832. Senate Docs., No. 146, 22d Cong., 1st sess., Vol. III. Recommends extra compensation to petitioner for disbursement of funds; Bill reported. [Washington, 1832] 1 p. MB.
16526

---- Report on Petition of Joseph V. Garnier. Com. on the Judiciary. Mar. 2, 1832. Reports of Committees, No. 344, 22d Cong., 1st sess., Vol. III. Recommends allowance to petitioner of fees as clerk of the Territory of Missouri; Bill reported. [Washington, 1832] 1 p. MB.   16527

---- Report on Petition of Josiah Barker. Com. on Private Land Claims. Mar. 16, 1832. Reports of Committees, No. 384, 22d Cong., 1st sess., Vol. III. Recommends confirmation of land title of petitioner; Bill reported. [Washington, 1832] 1 p. MB.
16528

---- Report on Petition of Judith Thomas. Com. on Invalid Pensions. Jan. 10, 1832. Reports of Committees, No. 156, 22d Cong., 1st sess., Vol. I. Recommends allowance of five years' half-pay to petitioner; Bill reported. [Washington, 1832] 1 p. MB.
16529

---- Report on Petition of Keene & Martin. Com. on Private Land Claims. Jan. 10, 1832. Reports of Committees, No. 166, 22d Cong., 1st sess., Vol. I. Recommends exchange of land granted to petitioner; Bill reported. [Washington, 1832] 1 p. MB.   16530

---- Report on Petition of L. Houston. Com. on Revolutionary Pensions. Jan. 3, 1832. Reports of Committees, No. 101, 22d Cong., 1st sess., Vol. I. Recommends allowance of pension to petitioner. [Washington, 1832] 1 p. MB.   16531

---- Report on Petition of Lester Morris. Com. on Revolutionary Pensions. Dec. 22, 1831. Reports of Committees, No. 23, 22d Cong., 1st sess., Vol. I. Recommends that name of petitioner be restored in pension-roll; Bill re-

ported. [Washington, 1832] 1 p.
MB.   16532

---- Report on Petition of Levi
Brown. Com. on Invalid Pensions.
Feb. 15, 1832. Reports of Committees, No. 295, 22d Cong., 1st
sess., Vol. II. Recommends allowance of pension to petitioner;
Bill reported. [Washington, 1832]
1 p. MB.   16533

---- Report on Petition of Levi
Strong. Com. on Invalid Pensions.
Mar. 2, 1832. Reports of Committees, No. 348, 22d Cong., 1st
sess., Vol. III. Recommends allowance of pension to petitioner;
Bill reported. [Washington, 1832]
1 p. MB.   16534

---- Report on Petition of Lothario Donelson. Com. on Rev.
Pensions. Mar. 15, 1832. Reports of Committees, No. 380,
22d Cong., 1st sess., Vol. III.
Recommends allowance of pension
to petitioner; Bill reported. [Wash-
ington, 1832] 1 p. MB.   16535

---- Report on Petition of Louis
F. de Les Dernier. Jan. 10,
1832. Reports of Committees, No.
169, 22d Cong., 1st sess., Vol.
I. Committee on Revolutionary
Pensions recommends allowance of
pension to petitioner; Bill reported.
[Washington, 1832] 1 p. MB.
                             16536
---- Report on Petition of Louis
Pellerm. Com. on Priv. Land
Claims. Feb. 10, 1832. Reports
of Committees, No. 284, 22d
Cong., 1st sess., Vol. II. Rec-
ommends that title of petitioner to
land in Louisiana be confirmed;
Bill reported. [Washington, 1832]
1 p. MB.   16537

---- Report on Petition of Luther
L. Smith. Com. on Private Land
Claims. Feb. 2, 1832. Reports
of Committees, No. 255, 22d

Cong., 1st sess., Vol. II. Recommends that petitioner be allowed to purchase at minimum
price tract of land claimed by him
in Louisiana; Bill reported. [Wash-
ington, 1832] 1 p. MB.   16538

---- Report on Petition of M.
Higgins. Com. on Revolutionary
Pensions. Jan. 3, 1832. Reports
of Committees, No. 113, 22d
Cong., 1st sess., Vol. I. Recommends allowance of pension to
petitioner; Bill reported. [Wash-
ington, 1832] 1 p. MB.   16539

---- Report on Petition of M. Mc-
Causland. Com. on Invalid Pensions. Mar. 2, 1832. Reports of
Committees, No. 345, 22d Cong.,
1st sess., Vol. III. Recommends
allowance of pension to petitioner;
Bill reported. [Washington, 1832]
1 p. MB.   16540

---- Report on Petition of Maj.
Gen. A. Macomb. Com. on Military Affairs. Dec. 18, 1832.
Reports of Committees, No. 6,
22d Cong., 2d sess. Asks additional compensation for military
services and that the amount be
allowed as an offset to his liability as surety for Samuel Cham-
plain, paymaster; Committee recommends that he be relieved from
liability; Bill reported. [Washing-
ton, 1832] 2 p. MB.   16541

---- Report on Petition of Manuel Crecy. Com. on Invalid Pensions. Feb. 15, 1832. Reports of
Committees, No. 294, 22d Cong.,
1st sess., Vol. II. Recommends
allowance of pension to petitioner;
Bill reported. [Washington, 1832]
1 p. MB.   16542

---- Report on Petition of Martin
Parker. Committee on Invalid Pensions. Apr. 3, 1832. Reports of
Committees, No. 424, 22d Cong.,
1st sess., Vol. III. Recommends

allowance of pension to petitioner; Bill reported. [Washington, 1832] 1 p. MB.   16543

---- Report on Petition of Martin Smith. Com. on Invalid Pensions. Feb. 2, 1832. Reports of Committees, No. 261, 22d Cong., 1st sess., Vol. II. Recommends allowance of arrears of pension to petitioner; Bill reported. [Washington, 1832] 1 p. MB.   16544

---- Report on Petition of Nathan Durkee. Com. on Revolutionary Pensions. Jan. 10, 1832. Reports of Committees, No. 168, 22d Cong., 1st sess., Vol. I. Recommends allowance of pension to petitioner; Bill reported. [Washington, 1832] 1 p. MB.   16545

---- Report on Petition of Nathaniel Patten. Com. on the Judiciary. Feb. 28, 1832. Reports of Committees, No. 335, 22d Cong., 1st sess., Vol. III. Recommends allowing credit to petitioner in his accounts as postmaster for value of postage-stamps, etc., stolen. [Washington, 1832] 1 p. MB.   16546

---- Report on Petition of Nehemiah M. Badger. Com. on Invalid Pensions. Jan. 19, 1832. Reports of Committees, No. 210, 22d Cong., 1st sess., Vol. I. Recommends allowance to petitioner of arrears and increase of pension; Bill reported. [Washington, 1832] 1 p. MB.   16547

---- Report of Petition of Nelson Miller. Com. on Revolutionary Pensions. Jan. 3, 1832. Reports of Committees, No. 123, 22d Cong., 1st sess., Vol. I. Recommends allowance of pension to petitioner; Bill reported. [Washington, 1832. [Washington, 1832] 1 p. MB.   16548

---- Report on Petition of New England and Mississippi Land Company. Jan. 18, 1832. Senate Docs., No. 29, 22d Cong., 1st sess., Vol. I. Recommends refundment of money paid the United States for land; Bill reported. [Washington, 1832] 7 p. MB.   16549

---- Report on Petition of Nicholas Hart. Committee on Public lands. Jan. 10, 1832. Reports of Committees, No. 153, 22d Cong., 1st sess., Vol. I. Recommends grant of land to petitioner; Bill reported. [Washington, 1832] 1 p. MB.   16550

---- Report on Petition of Noah Miller. Com. on Invalid Pensions. Jan. 10, 1832. Reports of Committees, No. 155, 22d Cong., 1st sess., Vol. I. Recommends allowance of pension to petitioner; Bill reported. [Washington, 1832] 1 p. MB.   16551

---- Report on Petition of Officers of the Army. Com. on Military Affairs. Feb. 18, 1832. Reports of Committees, No. 313, 22d Cong., 1st sess., Vol. II. Recommends compensation for losses sustained by petitioners in consequence of the burning of Fort Delaware; Bill reported. [Washington, 1832] 8 p. MB.   16552

---- Report on Petition of Oliver May. Com. on Revolutionary Pensions. Jan. 3, 1832. Reports of Committees, No. 120, 22d Cong., 1st sess., Vol. I. Recommends allowance of pension to petitioner; Bill reported. [Washington, 1832] 1 p. MB.   16553

---- Report on Petition of P. & E. Greorley. Com. on Ways and Means. Feb. 24, 1832. Reports of Committees, No. 327, 22d Cong., 1st sess., Vol. III. Recommends remission of duties to petitioners on salt destroyed; Bill reported. [Washington, 1832] 1 p. MB.   16554

---- Report on Petition of P. Green. Com. on Post-Office and Post-Roads. Jan. 12, 1832. Reports of Committees, No. 179, 22d Cong., 1st sess. Vol. I. Recommends allowance of half-pay pension to petitioner on account of injuries received in carrying the mail; Bill reported. [Washington, 1832] 3 p. MB.
16555

---- Report on Petition of P. McCormick. Com. on Private Land Claims. Jan. 12, 1832. Reports of Committees, No. 175, 22d Cong., 1st sess., Vol. I. Recommends that petitioner be confirmed in title to land; Bill reported. [Washington, 1832] 2 p. MB.   16556

---- Report on Petition of P. Sprague and D. Kaiff. Com. on Commerce. Feb. 3, 1832. Reports of Committees, No. 268, 22d Cong., 1st sess., Vol. II. Recommends allowance to petitioners of the bounty paid to vessels engaged in the cod fishery; Bill reported. [Washington, 1832] 1 p. MB.   16557

---- Report on Petition of P. Yarnell and S. Mitchell. Com. on Claims. Jan. 27, 1832. Reports of Committees, No. 252, 22d Cong. 1st sess., Vol. II. Adverse to releasing petitioners from performance of contract to supply military posts with provisions. [Washington, 1832] 2 p. MB.
16558

---- Report on Petition of Paul Ducharme. Com. on Public Lands. Mar. 12, 1832. Reports of Committees, No. 363, 22d Cong., 1st sess., Vol. III. Adverse to claim of petitioner to land. [Washington, 1832] 3 p. MB.   16559

---- Report on Petition of Peter Bargy et al. Com. on Claims. Jan. 25, 1832. Reports of Committees, No. 231, 22d Cong., 1st sess., Vol. II. Recommends allowance of compensation to Peter Bargy, Stephen Norton, and Hiram Wolverton for services in removing obstructions in the Savannah River; Bill reported. [Washington, 1832] 3 p. MB.   16560

---- Report on Petition of Philip Slaughter. Com. on Revolutionary Claims. Feb. 21, 1832. Reports of Committees, No. 320, 22d Cong., 1st sess., Vol. II. Recommends allowance to petitioner of interest on commutation of half-pay; Bill reported. [Washington, 1832] 7 p. MB.   16561

---- Report on Petition of R. Clarke. Com. on Revolutionary Pensions. Jan. 3, 1832. Reports of Committees, No. 117, 22d Cong., 1st sess., Vol. I. Recommends allowance of pension to petitioner; Bill reported. [Washington, 1832] 1 p. MB.   16562

---- Report on Petition of R. Gibbs. Com. on Revolutionary Pensions. Jan. 3, 1832. Reports of Committees, No. 104, 22d Cong., 1st sess., Vol. I. Recommends allowance of pension to petitioner. [Washington, 1832] 1 p. MB.   16563

---- Report on Petition of R. Weatherhead. Com. on Private Land Claims. Feb. 7, 1832. Reports of Committees, No. 276, 22d Cong., 1st sess., Vol. II. Recommends that petitioner be permitted to purchase certain public lands; Bill reported. [Washington, 1832] 1 p. MB.   16564

---- Report on Petition of R. Wilmott. Com. on Revolutionary Claims. Mar. 8, 1832. Reports of Committees, No. 355, 22d Cong., 1st sess., Vol. III. Recommends allowance of five years' full pay to petitioner in lieu of half-pay for life. [Washington, 1832] 1 p. MB. 16565

---- Report on Petition of Rebecca Blodget. Com. on the Judiciary. May 4, 1832. Senate Docs., No. 141, 22d Cong., 1st sess., Vol. III. Bill reported granting petitioner compensation for right of dower in land purchased by the United States for post-office in Washington. [Washington, 1832] 3 p. MB. 16566

---- Report on Petition of Remington Arnold, jr. Com. on Commerce. Mar. 21, 1832. Reports of Committees, No. 404, 22d Cong., 1st sess., Vol. III. Recommends that petitioner be paid bounty allowed to vessels engaged in cod fishery; Bill reported. [Washington, 1832] 1 p. MB. 16567

---- Report on Petition of Representatives of J. Knight. Dec. 19, 1832. Reports of Committees, No. 8, 22d Cong., 2d sess. The Committee on Invalid Pensions recommends allowance of pension to petitioners; Bill reported. [Washington, 1832] 1 p. MB. 16568

---- Report on Petition of Representatives of John P. Wagnon. Jan. 18, 1832. Reports of Committees, No. 199, 22d Cong., 1st sess., Vol. I. Committee on Revolutionary Claims recommends commutation of half-pay to petitioners; Bill reported. [Washington, 1832] 1 p. MB. 16569

---- Report on Petition of Richard W. Hamilton. Com. on Commerce. Apr. 12, 1832. Reports of Committees, No. 442, 22d Cong., 1st sess., Vol. III. Recommends payment of salary to petitioner as collector at Pensacola; Disallows claim for expenses; Bill reported. [Washington, 1832] 2 p. MB. 16570

---- Report on Petition of Robert Alexander. Com. on Invalid Pensions. Jan. 19, 1832. Reports of Committees, No. 212, 22d Cong., 1st sess., Vol. I. Recommends increase of pension to petitioner; Bill reported. [Washington, 1832] 1 p. MB. 16571

---- Report on Petition of Robert Eaton. Com. on Ways and Means. Jan. 4, 1832. Reports of Committees, No. 136, 22d Cong., 1st sess., Vol. I. Recommends refundment to petitioner of fines paid on account of informalities in the importation of salt; Bill reported. [Washington, 1832] 1 p. MB. 16572

---- Report on Petition of Robert Kean. Committee on Invalid Pensions. Jan. 19, 1832. Reports of Committees, No. 215, 22d Cong., 1st sess., Vol. I. Recommends allowance of pension to petitioner; Bill reported. [Washington, 1832] 1 p. MB. 16573

---- Report on Petition of Robert Reynold. Com. on Rev. Pensions. Mar. 21, 1832. Reports of Committees, No. 400, 22d Cong., 1st sess., Vol. III. Recommends allowance of pension to petitioner; Bill reported. [Washington, 1832] 1 p. MB. 16574

---- Report on Petition of Roswell Hunt. Com. on Invalid Pensions. Feb. 2, 1832. Reports of Committees, No. 265, 22d Cong., 1st sess., Vol. II. Recommends allowance of pension to petitioner; Bill reported. [Washington, 1832] 1 p. MB. 16575

---- Report on Petition of S. Bliss. Com. on Revolutionary

Pensions. Jan. 10, 1832. Reports
of Committees, No. 161, 22d
Cong., 1st sess., Vol. I. Recommends allowance of pension to
petitioner; Bill reported. [Wash-
ington, 1832] 1 p. MB.   16576

---- Report on Petition of S.
Chase. Com. on Revolutionary
Pensions. Jan. 3, 1832. Reports
of Committees, No. 116, 22d
Cong., 1st sess., Vol. I. Recommends allowance of pension to
petitioner; Bill reported. [Wash-
ington, 1832] 1 p. MB.   16577

---- Report on Petition of S.
Frothingham. Com. on Rev. Pensions. Jan. 3, 1832. Reports of
Committees, No. 99, 22d Cong.,
1st sess., Vol. I. Recommends
restoration of name of petitioner
to pension-roll. [Washington,
1832] 1 p. MB.   16578

---- Report on Petition of S.
Harding. Com. on Revolutionary
Pensions. Jan. 10, 1832. Reports
of Committees, No. 164, 22d
Cong., 1st sess., Vol. I. Recommends allowance of pension to
petitioner; Bill reported. [Wash-
ington, 1832] 1 p. MB.   16579

---- Report on Petition of S.
Townsend. Com. on Revolutionary
Pensions. Jan. 10, 1832. Reports
of Committees, No. 162, 22d
Cong., 1st sess., Vol. I. Recommends allowance of pension to
petitioner; Bill reported. [Washing-
ton, 1832] 1 p. MB.   16580

---- Report on Petition of Samuel Andrews. Committee on Pensions. Mar. 7, 1832. Senate
Docs., No. 95, 22d Cong., 1st
sess., Vol. II. Recommends restoration of name of petitioner to
the pension-rolls; Bill reported.
[Washington, 1832] 1 p. MB.
                          16581
---- Report on Petition of Samuel

Dubose. Com. on Claims. Jan.
16, 1832. Reports of Committees,
No. 193, 22d Cong., 1st sess.,
Vol. I. Recommends that petitioner be credited as administrator of Elias D. Dick for moneys
paid out by the latter while an officer in the Army; Bill reported.
[Washington, 1832] 2 p. MB.
                          16582
---- Report on Petition of Samuel Eastforth. Com. on Rev. Pensions. Mar. 15, 1832. Reports of
Committees, No. 376, 22d Cong.,
1st sess., Vol. III. Recommends
allowance of pension to petitioner;
Bill reported. [Washington, 1832]
1 p. MB.   16583

---- Report on Petition of Sarah
Coleman. Com. on Naval Affairs.
Feb. 20, 1832. Reports of Committees, No. 319, 22d Cong., 1st
sess., Vol. II. Recommends allowance to petitioner of prize-
money due her late brother, John
Coleman; Bill reported. [Washing-
ton, 1832] 1 p. MB.   16584

---- Report on Petition of Sidney
Wishart. Com. on Revolutionary
Claims. July 13, 1832. Reports
of Committees, No. 509, 22d
Cong., 1st sess., Vol. V. Recommends payment to petitioner of
commutation on account of military service of Thomas Wishart.
[Washington, 1832] 1 p. MB.
                          16585
---- Report on Petition of Simeon
Bullock. Com. Revolutionary Pensions. Jan. 3, 1832. Reports on
Committees, No. 124, 22d Cong.,
1st sess., Vol. I. Recommended
allowance of pension to petitioner;
Bill reported. [Washington, 1832]
1 p. MB.   16586

---- Report on Petition of Simon
Deloach. Com. on Invalid Pensions. Feb. 15, 1832. Reports
of Committees, No. 296, 22d
Cong., 1st sess., Vol. II. Rec-

ommends allowance of pension to petitioner; Bill reported. [Washington, 1832] 1 p. MB.   16587

---- Report on Petition of Sinclair D. Gervais. Com. on Public Lands. Mar. 17, 1832. Reports of Committees, No. 387, 22d Cong., 1st sess., Vol. III. Petitioner bought public land, made part payment; On failure to pay balance of purchase-money the land reverted to the United States; Prays that a certificate be issued to him for the amount paid; Committee reports general bill covering this class of cases. [Washington, 1832] 2 p. MB.   16588

---- Report on Petition of Stephen Hawkins. Jan. 10, 1832. Reports of Committees, No. 171, 22d Cong., 1st sess., Vol. I. Committee on Revolutionary Pensions recommends allowance of pension to petitioner; Bill reported. [Washington, 1832] 1 p. MB.   16589

---- Report on Petition of Sureties of Nicholas Schrader. Com. on Claims. Mar. 21, 1832. Reports of Committees, No. 401, 22d Cong., 1st sess., Vol. III. Adverse to relieving petitioners from liability on bond of Nicholas Schrader for the payment of taxes on distilled spirits. [Washington, 1832] 3 p. MB.   16590

---- Report on Petition of Sureties of William Estis. Com. on the Judiciary. Jan. 25, 1832. Reports of Committees, No. 237, 22d Cong., 1st sess., Vol. II. Recommends that petitioners, Wm. Saunders and Wm. R. Porter, be released from judgment recovered against them as sureties for Wm. Estis, paymaster; Bill reported. [Washington, 1832] 1 p. MB.   16591

---- Report on Petition of T. Chapman. Committee on the Judi-

ciary. Apr. 24, 1832. Senate Docs., No. 140, 22d Cong., 1st sess., Vol. III. Recommends that petitioner, collector of customs of South Carolina, be allowed share of value of vessel seized by him and condemned; Bill reported. [Washington, 1832] 13 p. MB.   16592

---- Report on Petition of T. Reynolds. Com. on Private Land Claims. Feb. 6, 1832. Reports of Committees, No. 271, 22d Cong., 1st sess., Vol. II. Recommends grant of land to petitioner; Bill reported. [Washington, 1832] 2 p. MB.   16593

---- Report on Petition of T. Triplett. Com. on Revolutionary Claims. Jan. 3, 1832. Reports of Committees, No. 96, 22d Cong., 1st sess., Vol. I. Recommends allowance to petitioner of commutation for half-pay; Bill reported. [Washington, 1832] 1 p. MB.   16594

---- Report on Petition of Theodore Owens. Committee on the Judiciary. Jan. 30, 1832. Reports of Committees, No. 245, 22d Cong., 1st sess., Vol. II. Recommends additional compensation to petitioner for services in taking the fifth census. [Washington, 1832] 1 p. MB.   16595

---- Report on Petition of Thos. Ball. Com. on Invalid Pensions. Feb. 15, 1832. Reports of Committees, No. 298, 22d Cong., 1st sess., Vol. II. Recommends allowance of pension to petitioner; Bill reported. [Washington, 1832] 1 p. MB.   16596

---- Report on Petition of Thos. Buford. Com. on Military Affairs. Apr. 3, 1832. Reports of Committees, No. 422, 22d Cong., 1st sess., Vol. III. Recommends reimbursement to petitioner of

472   United States

money advanced to relieve the
necessities of certain American
prisoners; Bill reported. [Wash-
ington, 1832] 1 p. MB.   16597

---- Report on Petition of Thos.
Chapman. Committee on the
Judiciary. June 30, 1832. Reports of Committees, No. 494,
22d Cong., 1st sess., Vol. V.
Recommends that petitioner, executor of Thos. Chapman, late
collector of customs in South
Carolina, be allowed to share of
value of brig seized by the latter
and condemned; Bill reported.
[Washington, 1832] 2 p. MB.
                              16598
---- Report on Petition of Thos.
Cooper. Committee on the Judiciary. Jan. 30, 1832. Reports
of Committees, No. 244, 22d
Cong., 1st sess., Vol. II. Recommends refundment to petitioner of amount of fine paid for violation of the sedition law; Bill
reported. [Washington, 1832]
6 p. MB.   16599

---- Report on Petition of Thos.
Minor. Com. on Revolutionary
Claims. July 6, 1832. Reports
of Committees, No. 503, 22d
Cong., 1st sess., Vol. V. Recommends allowance of five years'
full pay to petitioner; Bill reported. [Washington, 1832] 1 p.
MB.   16600

---- Report on Petition of Trustees of Transylvania University.
Select com. Jan. 4, 1832. Reports of Committees, No. 138,
22d Cong., 1st sess., Vol. I.
Recommends that national aid be
granted to the Transylvania
University to enable it to repair
buildings injured by fire; Bill
reported. [Washington, 1832]
2 p. MB.   16601

---- Report on Petition of W. A.
Tennille. Com. on Invalid Pen-

sions. Jan. 13, 1832. Reports
of Committees, No. 185, 22d
Cong., 1st sess., Vol. I. Recommends allowance of pension to
petitioner; Bill reported. [Wash-
ington, 1832] 1 p. MB.   16602

---- ---- Military Committee.
Feb. 23, 1832. Senate Docs.,
No. 71, 22d Cong., 1st sess.,
Vol. II. Recommends that petitioner be granted additional compensation for disbursing money
for the Quartermaster's Dept.;
Bill reported. [Washington,
1832] MB.   16603

---- Report on Petition of W.
Davis. Com. on Revolutionary
Pensions. Jan. 3, 1832. Re-
ports of Committees, No. 118,
22d Cong., 1st sess., Vol. I.
Recommends allowance of pension
to petitioner; Bill reported.
[Washington, 1832] 1 p. MB.
                              16604
---- Report on Petition of W.
Howell. Com. on Revolutionary
Pensions. Jan. 3, 1832. Re-
ports of Committees, No. 107,
22d Cong., 1st sess., Vol. I.
Recommends allowance of pension
to petitioner. [Washington, 1832]
1 p. MB.   16605

---- Report on Petition of W.
Johnson. Com. on Revolutionary
Pensions. Jan. 3, 1832. Reports of Committees, No. 115,
22d Cong., 1st sess., Vol. I.
Recommends allowance of pension
to petitioner; Bill reported.
[Washington, 1832] 1 p. MB.
                              16606
---- Report on Petition of W.
McMillan. Com. on Revolutionary Pensions. Jan. 2, 1832. Report of Committees, No. 147,
22d Cong., 1st sess., Vol. I.
Recommends restoration of petitioner to pension-roll; Bill reported. [Washington, 1832] 2 p.
MB.   16607

---- Report on Petition of Walton & De Graff. Com. on Ways and Means. Mar. 19, 1832. Reports of Committees, No. 394, 22d Cong., 1st sess., Vol. III. Recommends that claim of petitioners for transportation of ordnance be referred for settlement to the Secretary of the Treasury; Bill reported. [Washington, 1832] 3 p. MB.   16608

---- Report on Petition of Ward & Tickler. Committee on the Judiciary. July 14, 1832. Reports of Committees, No. 513, 22d Cong., 1st sess., Vol. V. Petitioners purchased public lands; After payment deficit in title was discovered; Committee reports bill for relief. [Washington, 1832] 2 p. MB.   16609

---- Report on Petition of William Brackett. Com. on Invalid Pensions. Apr. 3, 1832. Reports of Committees, No. 425, 22d Cong., 1st sess., Vol. III. Recommends allowance of pension to petitioner; Bill reported. [Washington, 1832] 1 p. MB.   16610

---- Report on Petition of William Gallop. Com. on Invalid Pensions. Jan. 19, 1832. Reports of Committees, No. 206, 22d Cong., 1st sess., Vol. I. Recommends allowance of pension to petitioner; Bill reported. [Washington, 1832] 1 p. MB.   16611

---- Report on Petition of Wm. Huntington. Com. on Rev. Pensions. Mar. 15, 1832. Reports of Committees, No. 377, 22d Cong., 1st sess., Vol. III. Recommends allowance of pension to petitioner; Bill reported. [Washington, 1832] 1 p. MB.   16612

---- Report on Petition of William Ledman. Com. on Military Pensions. Feb. 2, 1832. Reports of Committees, No. 259, 22d Cong., 1st sess., Vol. II. Recommends allowance of pension to petitioner; Bill reported. [Washington, 1832] 1 p. MB.   16613

No entry.   16614

---- Report on Petition of William Marbury. Com. on Private Land Claims. Jan. 11, 1832. Reports of Committees, No. 174, 22 Cong., 1st sess., Vol. I. Recommends that petitioner be allowed to purchase public lands improved by him at usual price; Bill reported. [Washington, 1832] 1 p. MB.   16615

---- Report on Petition of William Osborn. Committee on Ways and Means. Jan. 21, 1832. Reports of Committees, No. 227, 22d Cong., 1st sess., Vol. II. Recommends that petitioner be allowed a drawback on certain merchandise exported; Bill reported. [Washington, 1832] 1 p. MB.   16616

---- Report on Petition of Z. Bartlett. Committee on Revolutionary Pensions. Jan. 10, 1832. Reports of Committees, No. 163, 22d Cong., 1st sess., Vol. I. Recommends allowance of pension to petitioner; Bill reported. [Washington, 1832] 1 p. MB.   16617

---- Report on Petition of Zebulon Wade. Committee on Invalid Pensions. Jan. 19, 1832. Reports of Committees, No. 205, 22d Cong., 1st sess., Vol. I. Recommends allowance of pension to petitioner; Bill reported. [Washington, 1832] 1 p. MB.   16618

---- Report on Petition of Zepha-

niah Halsey. Com. on Rev. Pensions. Mar. 17, 1832. Reports of
Committees, No. 390, 22d Cong.,
1st sess., Vol. III. Recommends
allowance of pension to petitioner;
Bill reported. [Washington, 1832]
1 p. MB.   16619

---- Report on Petitions for Con-
firmation of Land Title. Mar.
12, 1832. Reports of Committees,
No. 362, 22d Cong., 1st sess.,
Vol. III. Committee on Public
Lands report adversely to confir-
mation of land titles of James
Porlier, Alexander Gardipierre,
John B. Vine, and Joseph Jour-
dain. [Washington, 1832] 2 p.
MB.   16620

---- ---- Mar. 16, 1832. Reports
of Committees, No. 382, 22d
Cong., 1st sess., Vol. III. Committee on Private Land Claims
recommends that petitioners, Isaac
Thomas and William M. Wilson,
be confirmed in titles to land;
Bill reported. [Washington, 1832]
MB.   16621

---- Report on Petitions for Georgia Lands. Committee on the Judiciary. Jan. 25, 1832. Reports of
Committees, No. 236, 22d Cong.,
1st sess., Vol. II. Adverse to
claim of petitioners to lands in
Georgia granted to the Tennessee
Company. [Washington, 1832] 2 p.
MB.   16622

---- Report on Petitions for Pension. Committee on Invalid Pensions. Apr. 3, 1832. Reports of
Committees, No. 426, 22d Cong.,
1st sess., Vol. III. Recommends
allowance of pension to Benjamin
Goodridge, John P. Read, Benjamin Calhoun, David A. Ames,
Anthony Murray, Peter Bradley,
and Oliver Herrick. [Washington,
1832] 5 p. MB.   16623

---- ---- ---- May 14, 1832.

Reports of Committees, No. 474,
22d Cong., 1st sess., Vol. V.
Recommends allowance of pension
to Moses Cremeens, David Pearson, David King, John O'Neal,
and Joseph Lynn. [Washington,
1832] 4 p. MB.   16624

---- ---- ---- Dec. 19, 1832.
Reports of Committees, No. 7,
22d Cong., 2d sess. Recommends
allowance of pension to Joseph
Chamberlain, Jesse Cunningham,
William Ledman, Joseph Linn,
Oliver Herrick, Robert McCaus-
land, John Taylor, Martin Smith,
Henry Click, Zebulon Wade, Thomas Phillips, Daniel Fuller, Benjamin Goodrich, John P. Reed, Jonathan Bean, George Field, Roswell Hunt, Benjamin Burlingame,
Asher Huntington, and Heard
Brackett; Bills reported. [Wash-
ington, 1832] 10 p. MB   16625

---- ---- Committee on Revolu-
tionary Pensions. Feb. 18, 1832.
Reports of Committees, No. 314,
22d Cong., 1st sess., Vol. II.
Recommends allowance of pensions
to Samuel Youngs, Solomon Mills,
and Moses Sherwood; Bills report-
ed. [Washington, 1832] 2 p. MB.
                              16626
---- ---- ---- Mar. 12, 1832.
Reports of Committees, No. 365,
22d Cong., 1st sess., Vol. III.
Recommends allowance of pension
to Daniel Gray, Arnold Allen,
Jonathan Noakes, Levi Fay, Eli
Smith, Zeba Hayden, William Wait,
Laban Smith, Jeremiah Ware,
Simeon Moulton, David Marsten,
Ebenezer Seelye, Beriah Stiles,
Asa Holden, Nathaniel Bartlett,
Francis Cobb, William Hyland,
Zadoch Ingalls, Aaron Parks, and
Israel Bullock. [Washington, 1832]
10 p. MB.   16627

---- ---- ---- March 13, 1832.
Reports of Committees, No. 367,
22d Cong., 1st sess., Vol. III.

Recommends allowance of pension to Benjamin Sherman, Peter Sanborn, Samuel Barnes, Elijah Reckard, William Parden, Robert L. Tate, Asa Smith, William Dougherty, Jacob Loring, Caleb Steub, Ichabod Wood, James Little, Israel Hutchinson, and Spitsby Gregory. [Washington, 1832] 6 p. MB. 16628

---- ---- ---- ---- Reports of Committees, No. 369, 22d Cong., 1st sess., Vol. III. Recommends allowance of pension to Nathaniel Stewart, Asabel Gregory, Amon Marshall, Benjamin Carman, Hosea Tiffany, Thomas Tiffany, John Bain, and John James. [Washington, 1832] 5 p. MB 16629

---- ---- ---- ---- Reports of Committees, No. 371, 22d Cong., 1st sess., Vol. III. Recommends allowance of pension to Samuel Bacon, Isaac West, and Elihu Pond. [Washington, 1832] 2 p. MB. 16630

---- ---- ---- ---- Reports of Committees, No. 372, 22d Cong., 1st sess., Vol. III. Recommends allowance of pension to Edmund Richards, Comfort Goss, Isaac Morris, Elihu Morris, Archibald Shaw, John Logan, Reuben Finch, Jonathan Sturtevant, Francis Garnett, Benjamin Flinn, and Andrew Michael. [Washington, 1832] 4 p. MB. 16631

---- ---- ---- March 15, 1832. Reports of Committees, No. 381, 22d Cong., 1st sess., Vol. III. Recommends allowance of pension to Micah Skinner, Nell Whittaker, Nathaniel Montague, Charles Chamberlin, Abraham June, Samuel Burnett, Zachariah Saunders, Isaac Richardson, Isaac Fellows, Elias Chamberlin, Abner Ricard, Ebenezer Holmes, and Benjamin Jordan. [Washington, 1832] 5 p.

MB. 16632

---- ---- ---- March 17, 1832. Reports of Committees, No. 391, 22d Cong., 1st sess., Vol. III. Recommends allowance of pension to John Kidd and Jeremiah Adams; Bills reported. [Washington, 1832] 1 p. MB. 16633

---- ---- ---- March 19, 1832. Reports of Committees, No. 395, 22d Cong., 1st sess., Vol. III. Recommends allowance of pension to Randolph Newsom, Jesse Clark, William Spear, Pruim Ripley, Juvenal Winter, Oliver Parish, James Tuneur, Joseph Hews, Peter Van Orden, and John Percival. [Washington, 1832] 5 p. MB. 16634

---- ---- ---- ---- Reports of Committees, No. 396, 22d Cong., 1st sess., Vol. III. Recommends allowance of pension to Abner Morgan and Edward Herndon. [Washington, 1832] 2 p. MB. 16635

---- ---- ---- March 26, 1832. Reports of Committees, No. 410, 22d Cong., 1st sess., Vol. III. Recommends allowance of pension to George Beeler, Isaac Bullard, John Conklin, Christopher Doughty, Joseph Fox, Peter Gilman, James Graves, Isaac Olcott, John Shover, Sylvanus Simmons, and Thomas Taylor. [Washington, 1832] 4 p. MB. 16636

---- ---- ---- ---- Reports of Committees, No. 411, 22d Cong., 1st sess., Vol. III. Recommends allowance of pension to Abraham Lawrence, Jacobus Van Vorst, Peleg Weeden, James Miller, John W. Cook, Siloam Short, Orsamus Holmes, James Hereghtailing, Ezra Allen, and Grindal Chase. [Washington, 1832] 5 p. MB. 16637

---- ---- ---- ---- Reports of
Committees, No. 412, 22d Cong.
1st sess., Vol. III. Recom-
mends allowance of pension to
Theophilus Norris, Amos Allen,
James Osborn, and Geden Wood-
ruff. [Washington, 1832] 2 p.
MB.   16638

---- ---- ---- April 11, 1832.
Reports of Committees, No. 438,
22d Cong., 1st sess., Vol. III.
Recommends allowance of pen-
sion to John Lowell, Levi Tracy,
Jacob Hiler, Job Phillips, and
Ephraim Hunt. [Washington, 1832]
3 p. MB.   16639

---- ---- ---- ---- Reports of
Committees, No. 439, 22d Cong.
1st sess., Vol. III. Recommends
allowance of pension to David
Harson, Hiram Huntington, and
Eleazar Owen. [Washington, 1832]
2 p. MB.   16640

---- ---- ---- May 14, 1832.
Reports of Committees, No. 472,
22d Cong., 1st sess., Vol. V.
Recommends allowance of pension
to John Fox, Jacob Fleischer,
Michael Spatz, and Adam Gram-
lin. [Washington, 1832] 1 p.
MB.   16641

---- ---- ---- May 18, 1832.
Reports of Committees, No. 479,
22d Cong., 1st sess., Vol. V.
Recommends allowance of pension
to William Cole, David Parshall,
and Samuel Clark. [Washington,
1832] 2 p. MB.   16642

---- Report on Petitions for
Prize-Money. Committee on
Claims. Feb. 24, 1832. Reports
of Committees, No. 330, 22d
Cong., 1st sess., Vol. III. Rec-
ommends allowance of prize-
money to petitioners, heirs of
Andrew Nelson and Parnell Boyce;
Bill reported. [Washington, 1832]
1 p. MB.   16643

---- Report on Petitions of Road
Commissioners. Committee on
Public Lands. Feb. 24, 1832.
Reports of Committees, No. 341,
22d Cong., 1st sess., Vol. III.
Adverse to grant of land to J. F.
Stratton, Seely Neale, and Orin
White as compensation for laying
out National Road; Minority re-
ports in favor of petitioners.
[Washington, 1832] 3 p. MB.
                             16644
---- Report on Post-Office Con-
tracts. Postmaster-General W.
T. Barry. April 18, 1832. House
Ex. Docs., No. 212, 22d Cong.,
1st sess., Vol. V. Transmitting
statement of contracts made by
the Post-Office Department during
the year 1831. [Washington, 1832]
31 p. MB.   16645

---- Report on Post-Office Revenues. Postmaster-General W. T.
Barry. Dec. 18, 1832. Ex. Docs.,
No. 18, 22d Cong., 2d sess.,
Vol. I. Statement of net amount
of postage accruing at each post-
office in the United States for the
year ending March 31, 1832.
[Washington, 1832] 95 p. MB.
                             16646
---- Report on Post-Office Sup-
plies. Postmaster-General W. T.
Barry. June 25, 1832. House Ex.
Docs., No. 292, 22d Cong., 1st
sess., Vol. VI. Statement concerning contracts for blanks, paper, etc., for the use of the Post-
Office Department. [Washington,
1832] 2 p. MB.   16647

---- Report on Postage. Post-
master-General W. T. Barry.
Jan. 10, 1832. House Ex. Docs.,
No. 55, 22d Cong., 1st sess.,
Vol. II. Transmitting statement of
gross amount of postage on news-
papers and pamphlets for the
year ending June 30, 1831.
[Washington, 1832] 3 p. MB.
                             16648
---- Report on Postal Revenue.

Postmaster-General W. T. Barry.
May 22, 1832. House Ex. Docs.,
No. 262, 22d Cong., 1st sess.,
Vol. VI. Transmitting statement
of amount of postage accruing at
each post-office in each State and
Territory during the year ending
March 31, 1831. [Washington,
1832] 92 p. MB.   16649

---- Report on Pre-emption
Claims. Committee on Public
Lands. Jan. 3, 1832. Reports of
Committees, No. 94, 22d Cong.,
1st sess., Vol. I. Recommends
allowing right of pre-emption to
lands in Florida to Mary Daws,
Robert Bond, James Partridge,
and J. J. Smith; Bill reported.
[Washington, 1832] 1 p. MB.
                          16650

---- Report on Printing Public
Documents. Jan. 9, 1832. Senate
Docs., No. 22, 22d Cong., 1st
sess., Vol. I. Recommends al-
lowance of extra compensation to
Printer for House documents
printed by order of the Senate.
[Washington, 1832] 2 p. MB.
                          16651

---- Report on Printing United
States Laws. Committee on the
Judiciary. July 12, 1832. Reports
of Committees, No. 510, 22d
Cong., 1st sess., Vol. V. Recommends passage of Senate bill
providing for the publication of a
stereotype edition of the laws of
the United States. [Washington,
1832] 5 p. MB.   16652

---- Report on Printing United
States Statutes. Library Committee. March 13, 1832. Senate
Docs., No. 102, 22d Cong., 1st
sess., Vol. II. Report propositions of Richard Peters for printing a stereotype edition of the
laws. [Washington, 1832] 5 p.
MB.   16653

---- Report on Proposed Canal.
Secretary Lewis Cass. March 23,

1832. House Ex. Docs., No. 185,
22d Cong., 1st sess., Vol. IV.
Transmitting report on the practicability of constructing a canal
across the peninsula of Florida.
[Washington, 1832] 58 p. MB.
                          16654
---- Report on Proposed Land
Office. Committee on Public
Lands. March 17, 1832. Reports
of Committees, No. 392, 22d
Cong., 1st sess., Vol. III. Adverse to establishment of a land
office at Columbus, Mississippi.
[Washington, 1832] 2 p. MB.
                          16655
---- Report on Protested Bills
of Exchange. Committee on Foreign Affairs. May 5, 1832. Reports of Committees, No. 466,
22d Cong., 1st sess., Vol. V.
Communicating to the House all
the information obtainable on the
subject. [Washington, 1832] 7 p.
MB.   16656

---- Report on Public Improvements. Commissioner Jos. Elgar.
Dec. 13, 1832. Ex. Docs., No.
11, 22d Cong., 2d sess., Vol. I.
Statement of expenditures of the
appropriations for public improvements in the city of Washington
for the year 1832. [Washington,
1832] 5 p. MB.   16657

---- Report on Public Lands.
Commissioner Elijah Hayward.
May 9, 1832. Senate Docs., No.
142, 22d Cong., 1st sess., Vol.
III. Statement showing donations
of public lands to the several
States and Territories and to in-
dividuals. [Washington, 1832] 2 p.
MB.   16658

---- ---- Committee on Public
Lands. April 16, 1832. Senate
Docs., No. 128, 22d Cong., 1st
sess., Vol. III. Recommends that
it is inexpedient to reduce the
price of public lands or to cede
them to new States; Statement

showing dividend to each State in
the apportionment of public lands.
[Washington, 1832] 19 p. MB.
                                    16659
---- ---- ---- April 17, 1832.
Reports of Committees, No. 448,
22d Cong., 1st sess., Vol. III.
Committee is of opinion that it
wouldn't be inexpedient to grant
the public lands to the States in
which they are situated. [Wash-
ington, 1832] 32 p. MB.   16660

---- ---- ---- May 18, 1832.
Senate Docs., No. 145, 2d Cong.,
1st sess., Vol. III. Recommends
amendment of bill so as to reduce price of public lands; Does
not favor the principle of dividing among the states the proceeds
of sales of public lands. [Wash-
ington, 1832] 20 p. MB.   16661

---- ---- ---- Dec. 11, 1832.
Reports of Committees, No. 1,
22d Cong., 2d sess. Recommends
that grants of land be made to
surviving officers and soldiers of
the Revolution, or to the heirs of
those who died in the service.
[Washington, 1832] 8 p. MB.
                                    16662
---- ---- Secretary Louis Mc-
Lane. April 6, 1832. House Ex.
Docs., No. 196, 22d Cong., 1st
sess., Vol. V. Transmitting reports showing quantity of public
lands granted for internal improvements and for educational
and charitable purposes. [Wash-
ington, 1832] 4 p. MB.   16663

---- ---- ---- July 10, 1832.
Senate Docs., No. 182, 22d
Cong., 1st sess., Vol. III.
Transmitting report relative to
the deduction of certain expenditures in calculating net proceeds
of sales of public lands. [Wash-
ington, 1832] 2 p. MB.   16664

---- Report on Public Printing.
Committee on the Judiciary. Jan.

4, 1832. Reports of Committees,
No. 137, 22d Cong., 1st sess.,
Vol. I. Recommends that proposals be invited for publishing a
stereotype edition of the laws
and treaties of the United States.
[Washington, 1832]   3 p. MB.
                                    16665
---- Report on Publication of
Diplomatic Correspondence. Mar.
9, 1832. Reports of Committees,
No. 356, 22d Cong., 1st sess.,
Vol. III. The Joint Committee on
the Library reports bill making
appropriation to publish diplomatic correspondence from 1783 to
1789. [Washington, 1832] 3 p.
MB.   16666

---- Report on Purchase of Island
in Delaware River. Judiciary
Committee. April 12, 1832. Senate Docs., No. 124, 22d Cong.,
1st sess., Vol. III. Reports,
with amendments, bill to secure
title to island in Delaware River
upon which Fort Delaware is situated. [Washington, 1832] 19 p.
MB.   16667

---- Report on Pursers in the
Navy. Secretary Levi Woodbury.
Jan. 9, 1832. Senate Docs., No.
42, 2d [sic] Cong., 1st sess., Vol.
I. Statement of rate of percentage
allowed pursers on articles furnished to seamen; Highest compensation received by any purser;
Amount of expenditures by pursers on which commissions are
charged. [Washington, 1832] 6 p.
MB.   16668

---- Report on Receipt and Expenditures. Secretary Louis Mc-
Lane. Dec. 5, 1832. Ex. Docs.,
No. 3, 22d Cong., 2d sess., Vol.
I. Public revenues and expenditures; Public debt; Estimate of
public revenues and expenditures
for the year 1833. [Washington,
1832] 56 p. MB.   16669

---- ---- ---- Dec. 21, 1832. Senate Docs., No. 15, 22d Cong. 2d sess., Vol. I. Transmitting a report of the annual receipts and expenditures of the Government since 1789. [Washington, 1832] 23 p. MB.   16670

---- Report on Reduction of Foreign Missions. Com. on Foreign Affairs. Jan. 12, 1832. Reports of Committees, No. 180, 22d Cong., 1st sess., Vol. I. Adverse to encroaching on the prerogatives of the Executive by reducing the number of first-class foreign missions. [Washington, 1832] 3 p. MB.   16671

---- Report on Regulations in Post-Office Department. Post-Office Com. April 20, 1832. Reports of Committees, No. 450, 22d Cong., 1st sess., Vol. III. Committee is of the opinion that the regulations of the Post-Office Department are sufficient to guard against irregularities, and that no legislation on the subject is necessary. [Washington, 1832] 2 p. MB.   16672

---- Report on Relief of Augustine Taney. Committee on Claims. June 12, 1832. Reports of Committees, No. 490, 22d Cong., 1st sess., Vol. V. Recommends passage of bill compensating Augustine Taney for house destroyed by the British. [Washington, 1832] 2 p. MB.   16673

---- Report on Relief of E. Magruder. Committee on Private Land Claims. May 9, 1832. Reports of Committees, No. 469, 22d Cong., 1st sess., Vol. V. Recommends rejection of bill allowing petitioner to exchange land purchased of the Government. [Washington, 1832] 5 p. MB.   16674

---- Report on Relief of Elias

Earle. Committee on the Judiciary. Feb. 28, 1832. Reports of Committees, No. 359, 22d Cong., 1st sess., Vol. III. Recommends passage of bill to relieve Elias Earle, executor, from liability as surety for Adam Carruth, contractor, to furnish arms to the United States. [Washington, 1832] 2 p. MB.   16675

---- Report on Relief of Executor of Ellis Earle. Committee on Judiciary. Jan. 10, 1832. Senate Docs., No. 26, 22d Cong., 1st sess., Vol. I. Recommends passage of bill relieving him from liability as surety of Adam Carruth, contractor to furnish arms. [Washington, 1832] 2 p. MB.   16676

---- Report on Relief of Executors of James Roddey & Co. Committee on Claims, June 4, 1832. Reports of Committees, No. 487, 22d Cong., 1st sess., Vol. V. Bill provides for paying executors of James Roddey & Co., portion of amount claimed to be due on Government contracts; Committee recommends an amendment referring the claim to the Secretary of the Treasury for decision on principles of equity. [Washington, 1832] 21 p. MB.   16677

---- Report on Relief of Guy W. Smith. Committee on Claims. May 28, 1832. Reports of Committees, No. 483, 22d Cong., 1st sess., Vol. V. Proposes amendment to empower the Secretary of the Treasury to decide on the amount of money stolen from Guy W. Smith while receiver at the land office. [Washington, 1832] 2 p. MB.   16678

---- Report on Relief of Stephen Pleasanton. Committee on Claims. July 5, 1832. Reports of Committees, No. 511, 22d Cong., 1st sess., Vol. V. Recommends rejection of bill allowing claimant additional compensation for disbursement of money while Fifth Auditor. [Washington, 1832] 4 p. MB.   16679

---- Report on Relief of Sylvia Posner. Committee on Claims. June 12, 1832. Reports of Committees, No. 489, 22d Cong., 1st sess., Vol. V. Recommends passage, with amendments, of bill to compensate Sylvia Posner for house burned by United States troops. [Washington, 1832] 2 p. MB.   16680

---- Report on Relief of Trustee of T. H. Smith & Son. Judiciary Committee. May 26, 1832. Reports of Committees, No. 482, 22d Cong., 1st sess., Vol. V. Recommends that the Secretary of the Treasury be authorized to compromise the claim of the United States against Thomas H. Smith & Son for unpaid duties. [Washington, 1832] 2 p. MB.   16681

---- Report on Remission of Duties on Salt. Committee on Ways and Means. Feb. 24, 1832. Reports of Committees, No. 326, 22d Cong., 1st sess., Vol. III. Recommends remission of duties on salt destroyed belonging to N. & Dana & Co. and P. & E. Greerley; Bill reported. [Washington, 1832] 2 p. MB.   16682

---- Report on Resolution concerning the Tariff. Committee on Manufactures. March 30, 1832. Senate Docs., No. 116, 22d Cong., 1st sess., Vol. III. Recommends reduction of duties on teas, coffees, drugs, and other articles imported from foreign countries not coming into competition with productions of the United States. [Washington, 1832] 4 p. MB.   16683

---- Report on Return of Duties. Secretary L. McLane. April 24, 1832. House Ex. Docs., No. 216, 22d Cong., 1st sess., Vol. V. Transmitting statement of cases in which the Secretary of the Treasury has authorized a return of duties under the act of May 28, 1830, for the relief of certain importers. [Washington, 1832] 2 p. MB.   16684

---- Report on Revolutionary Survivors. Secretary Lewis Cass. June 15, 1832. Senate Docs., No. 170, 22d Cong., 1st sess., Vol. III. Statement relative to construction of act for relief of surviving officers and soldiers of the Revolution. [Washington, 1832] 8 p. MB.   16685

---- Report on Right of Debenture. Secretary Louis McLane. April 13, 1832. House Ex. Docs., No. 209, 22d Cong., 1st sess., Vol. V. Relative to extending the right of debenture to merchandise imported into Key West from other than foreign ports. [Washington, 1832] 2 p. MB.   16686

---- Report on River Surveys. Secretary Lewis Cass. June 30, 1832. Ex. Docs., No. 306, 22d Cong., 1st sess., Vol. VI. Transmitting report of survey of the Delaware and Raritan Rivers. [Washington, 1832] 6 p. MB.   16687

---- Report on Roanoke Inlet. Committee on Internal Improvements. March 29, 1832. Reports of Committees, No. 417, 22d Cong., 1st sess., Vol. III. Recommends incorporation of a company to reopen Roanoke Inlet; Bill reported. [Washington, 1832] 34 p. MB.   16688

---- Report on Salaries of Territorial Officers. Committee on Territories. Jan. 30, 1832. Reports of Committees, No. 242, 22d Cong., 1st sess., Vol. II. Recommends increase of salaries of Governor and judges in Arkansas; Bill reported. [Washington, 1832] 2 p. MB.   16689

---- Report on Sales of Condemned Clothing. Secretary Levi Woodbury. Mar. 15, 1832. Senate Docs., No. 103, 22d Cong., 1st sess., Vol. II. Statement showing average cost of clothing condemned, price for which sold, losses sustained by the United States on such sales during the last ten years. [Washington, 1832] 4 p. MB.   16690

---- Report on Salt in Public Stores. Secretary Louis McLane. Feb. 28, 1832. House Ex. Docs., No. 131, 22d Cong., 1st sess., Vol. IV. Transmitting statement showing quantity lying in the public stores January 1, 1831. [Washington, 1832] 2 p. MB.   16691

---- Report on Senate Bill to Adjust Claims of South Carolina. Committee on Claims. Jan. 6, 1832. Reports of Committees, No. 141, 22d Cong., 1st sess., Vol. I. Recommends that bill be rejected. [Washington, 1832] 70 p. MB.   16692

---- Report on Senate Contingent Fund. Sec. of the Senate Walter Lowrie. Dec. 3, 1832. Senate Docs., No. 2, 22d Cong., 2d sess., Vol. I. Statement of expenditures from the contingent fund of the Senate during the year 1832. [Washington, 1832] 3 p. MB.   16693

---- Report on Small-Pox among the Indians. Secretary Lewis Cass. March 29, 1832. House Ex. Docs., No. 190, 22d Cong., 1st sess., Vol. V. Transmitting information relative to small-pox

among the Indians. [Washington, 1832] 9 p. MB.   16694

---- Report on Statue of Washington. Joint Committee on the Library. April 30, 1832. Reports of Committees, No. 459, 22d Cong., 1st sess., Vol. III. Recommends that an appropriation be made for a pedestrian statue of Washington. [Washington, 1832] 1 p. MB.   16695

---- Report on Suits against United States Officers. Committee on Claims. April 9, 1832. Reports of Committees, No. 437, 22d Cong., 1st sess., Vol. III. Adverse to claims of----Twiggs, J. M. Street, and S. W. Kearney for expenses incurred in defending suits brought against them for acts done in the performance of their official duties. [Washington, 1832] 7 p. MB.   16696

---- Report on Surgeons in the Army. Secretary Lewis Cass. Jan. 7, 1832. House Ex. Docs., No. 63, 22d Cong., 1st sess., Vol. II. Transmitting documents to accompany bill (H. R. 295) to increase the number of surgeons and assistant surgeons in the Army. [Washington, 1832] 2 p. MB.   16697

---- Report on Survey. Secretary Levi Woodbury. Dec. 19, 1832. Ex. Docs., No. 19, 22d Cong., 2d sess., Vol. I. Transmitting report of survey of Narragansett Bay. [Washington, 1832] 3 p. MB.   16698

---- Report on Survey for Canal. Secretary Lewis Cass. May 12, 1832. Senate Docs., No. 143, 22d Cong., 1st sess., Vol. III. Transmitting report of survey for canal to connect Lake Michigan and the Wabash River, Indiana. [Washington, 1832] 19 p. MB.   16699

---- ---- ---- May 24, 1832. House Ex. Docs., No. 245, 22d Cong., 1st sess., Vol. VI. Transmitting report of survey for canal to connect Lake Michigan with the Illinois River. [Washington, 1832] 7 p. MB. 16700

---- Report on Survey for Railroad. Secretary Lewis Cass. Feb. 28, 1832. House Ex. Docs., No. 133, 22d Cong., 1st sess., Vol. IV. Transmitting report of survey for railroad from Portage Summit to Ohio River. [Washington, 1832] 19 p. MB. 16701

---- Report on Survey of Allegheny River. Acting Secretary John Robb. June 8, 1832. House Ex. Docs., No. 265, 2d Cong., 1st sess., Vol. VI. Transmitting report of survey of the Allegheny River from Pittsburgh to French Creek. [Washington, 1832] 12 p. MB. 16702

---- Report on Survey of Canal. Secretary Lewis Cass. Feb. 27, 1832. House Ex. Docs., No. 130, 22d Cong., 1st sess., Vol. IV. Transmitting report of survey and estimates for a canal to connect the Highwassee and Ocoa Rivers. [Washington, 1832] 1 p. MB. 16703

---- Report on Survey of Harbor. Secretary Lewis Cass. Jan. 28, 1832. House Ex. Docs., No. 86, 22d Cong., 1st sess., Vol. III. Transmitting report on survey of harbor of Westbrook, Connecticut. [Washington, 1832] 5 p. MB. 16704

---- Report on Survey of National Road. Sec. Lewis Cass. Feb. 6, 1832. House Ex. Docs., No. 149, 22d Cong., 1st sess., Vol. IV. Transmitting report of survey of road from Portsmouth, Ohio to Linville Mountain, North Carolina. [Washington, 1832] 32 p. MB. 16705

---- Report on Survey of the Hudson River. Secretary Lewis Cass. Mar. 30, 1832. House Ex. Docs., No. 189, 22d Cong., 1st sess., Vol. V. Transmitting report on survey for the improvement of the Hudson River. [Washington, 1832] 29 p. MB. 16706

---- Report on Survey of Wabash River. Secretary Lewis Cass. April 12, 1832. House Ex. Docs., No. 208, 22d Cong., 1st sess., Vol. V. Transmitting report of surveys and estimates for improving the navigation of the Wabash River. [Washington, 1832] 14 p. MB. 16707

---- Report on Surveys. Secretary Lewis Cass. Jan. 11, 1832. House Ex. Docs., No. 51, 22d Cong., 1st sess., Vol. II. Transmitting report of surveys and estimates by the War Department since March 4, 1829. [Washington, 1832] 6 p. MB. 16708

---- ---- ---- May 17, 1832. House Ex. Docs., No. 239, 22d Cong., 1st sess., Vol. VI. Transmitting report of surveys of certain roads and canals in Pennsylvania. [Washington, 1832] 11 p. MB. 16709

---- Report on Surveys of Rivers and Harbors. Com. Int. Improvements. June 23, 1832. Reports of Committees, No. 491, 22d Cong., 1st sess., Vol. V. List of works of internal improvement that appear to deserve examination by the Corps of Engineers. [Washington, 1832] 4 p. MB. 16710

---- Report on Tariff. Secretary of Senate. June 30, 1832. Senate Docs., No. 174, 22d Cong., 1st sess., Vol. III. Transmitting statement of present and proposed tariffs. [Washington, 1832] 45 p. MB. 16711

---- Report on Tariff Duties. Secretary L. McLane. April 27, 1832. House Ex. Docs., No. 222, 22d Cong., 1st sess., Vol. V. Relative to the adjustment of tariff duties; Submits copy of proposed bill to amend the present tariff laws. [Washington, 1832] 16 p. MB.   16712

---- Report on the Bank of Lake Erie. Secretary Louis McLane. Jan. 11, 1832. House Ex. Docs., No. 53, 22d Cong., 1st sess., Vol. II. Statement relative to debt due the United States by the Bank of Lake Erie. [Washington, 1832] 4 p. MB.   16713

---- Report on the Census. Secretary E. Livingston. Jan. 3, 1832. House Ex. Docs., No. 28, 22d Cong., 1st sess., Vol. II. Transmitting report showing the number of inhabitants in each State under the fifth census. [Washington, 1832] 2 p. MB.
                              16714
---- Report on the Coast Survey. Superintendent F. R. Hassler. July, 1832. Library of the Coast Survey. To Secretary McLane, of the Treasury Department, presenting the principles and views of the plan of operation for the survey of the coast as adopted in 1807. [Washington, 1832] 9 p. MB.   16715

---- Report (on the expediency of reducing the price of public lands and of ceding them to the several states, etc.) [Washington, 1832] MH.   16716

---- Report on the Fifth Census. Secretary Edward Livingston. Jan. 17, 1832. House Ex. Docs., No. 58, 22d Cong., 1st sess., Vol. II. Transmitting copies of instructions, regulations, and forms furnished to marshals and assistants. [Washington, 1832] 2 p. MB.
                              16717

---- ---- ---- Jan. 28, 1832. House Ex. Docs., No. 84, 22d Cong., 1st sess., Vol. III. Transmitting information relative to erroneous returns of slaves under the fifth census. [Washington, 1832] 2 p. MB.   16718

---- ---- ---- Feb. 10, 1832. House Ex. Docs., No. 103, 22d Cong., 1st sess., Vol. III. Transmitting corrected census returns from the southern district of New York. [Washington, 1832] 5 p. MB.   16719

---- Report on the Military Establishment. Secretary Lewis Cass. Dec. 8, 1832. Ex. Docs., No. 6, 22d Cong., 2d sess., Vol. I. Transmitting report on the revision of the acts of Congress relating to the military establishment. [Washington, 1832] 37 p. MB.   16720

---- Report on the Militia. Secretary Lewis Cass. Feb. 6, 1832. House Ex. Docs., No. 98, 22d Cong., 1st sess., Vol. III. Transmitting abstract of returns for the year 1831 of the United States militia. [Washington, 1832] 6 p. MB.   16721

---- Report on the Mint. Secretary Louis McLane. Feb. 13, 1832. House Ex. Docs., No. 115, 22d Cong., 1st sess., Vol. IV. Transmitting report of assays of foreign gold and silver coins made at the Mint during the year 1831. [Washington, 1832] 2 p. MB.   16722

---- ---- ---- June 28, 1832. Ex. Docs., No. 296, 22d Cong., 1st sess., Vol. VI. Transmitting statements showing the transactions of the United States Mint during the year 1831. [Washington, 1832] 5 p. MB.   16723

---- ---- Select Committee. Mar.
17, 1832. Reports of Committees,
No. 420, 22d Cong., 1st sess.,
Vol. III. Reports bills amending
the laws governing the United
States Mint and regulating the value of coins. [Washington, 1832]
71 p. MB.   16724

---- Report on the Ordnance Department. Colonel G. Bomford.
Mar. 19, 1832. House Ex. Docs.,
No. 177, 22d Cong., 1st sess.,
Vol. IV. Relative to the number
of officers, arsenals, and depots
belonging to the Ordnance Department. [Washington, 1832] 4 p.
MB.   16725

---- Report on the Patent Laws.
Select Committee on Patent Laws.
Apr. 30, 1832. Reports of Committees, No. 458, 22d Cong.,
1st sess., Vol. III. Petitioners
ask for passage of law allowing
certain aliens to take out patents;
Committee has already reported a
general bill covering this class of
cases. [Washington, 1832] 1 p.
MB.   16726

---- Report on the Petition of
Chastalain & Pouvert. Com. on
Commerce. Jan. 4, 1832. Reports of Committees, No. 134,
22d Cong., 1st sess., Vol. I.
Recommends that petitioners be
not charged duty on portion of
cargo of vessel destroyed by fire;
Bill reported. [Washington, 1832]
1 p. MB.   16727

---- Report on the Public Debt.
Secretary Louis McLane. Jan. 25,
1832. Senate Docs., No. 36, 22d
Cong., 1st sess., Vol. I. Statement of amount of three per cent
stock at the time of the passage
of the sinking fund act of 1817;
Market price of said stock; Amount
purchased under the act; Annual
payment on account of public debt
from 1817 to 1831. [Washington,

1832] 3 p. MB.   16728

---- Report on the Remission of
Duties. Secretary L. McLane.
Jan. 4, 1832. House Ex. Docs.,
No. 37, 22d Cong., 1st sess.,
Vol. II. Transmitting statement
of cases in which return of duties
has been authorized under the act
of March 2, 1831. [Washington,
1832] 2 p. MB.   16729

---- Report on the Sinking Fund.
Commissioners of the fund. Feb.
7, 1832. House Ex. Docs., No.
93, 22d Cong., 1st sess., Vol.
III. Statement of funds received
during the year 1831 and applied
in payment of the interest and
principal of the public debt.
[Washington, 1832] 9 p. MB.
                                 16730
---- ---- Committee on Finance.
Feb. 7, 1832. Senate Docs., No.
50, 22d Cong., 1st sess., Vol. I.
Recommends that there be no action on the subject by Congress
at the present session. [Washington, 1832] 27 p. MB.   16731

---- Report on the Tariff. Committee on Manufactures. May 23,
1832. Reports of Committees,
No. 481, 22d Cong., 1st sess.,
Vol. V. Recommends a modification of the laws on the subject of
the tariff; Bill reported. [Washington, 1832] 36 p. MB.   16732

---- ---- Committee on Ways and
Means. Feb. 8, 1832. Reports of
Committees, No. 279, 22d Cong.,
1st sess., Vol. II. Majority of
the committee recommends that
the protective system be abandoned; Minority is of opinion that
the protective system is interwoven with the best interests of
the country. [Washington, 1832]
33 p. MB.   16733

---- ---- ---- Dec. 28, 1832.
Reports of Committees, No. 14.

22d Cong., 2d sess. Recommends modification and reduction of the duties on imports; Bill reported. [Washington, 1832] 24 p. MB.   16734

---- ---- Secretary Louis McLane. June 4, 1832. House Ex. Docs., No. 264, 22d Cong., 1st sess., Vol. VI. Transmitting information showing the prices at different periods of the principal articles of merchandise protected by the tariff. [Washington, 1832] 28 p. MB.   16735

---- ---- ---- July 2, 1832. Senate Docs., No. 178, 22d Cong., 1st sess., Vol. III. Transmitting statement showing amount and rate of duties under present tariff and that proposed under bill S. 167 and bill S. 190. [Washington, 1832] 15 p. MB.   16736

---- Report on the United States Bank. Committee on Ways and Means. Feb. 9, 1832. Reports of Committees, No. 283, 22d Cong., 1st sess., Vol. II. Recommends renewal of charter of United States Bank, with modifications; Bill reported. [Washington, 1832] 70 p. MB. 16737

---- ---- Secretary Louis McLane. Dec. 10, 1832. Senate Docs., No. 4, 22d Cong., 2d sess., Vol. I. Transmitting report of the agent appointed to examine the accounts of the United States Bank. [Washington, 1832] 33 p. MB.   16738

---- ---- ---- Dec. 11, 1832. Senate Docs., No. 6, 22d Cong., 2d sess., Vol. I. Transmitting monthly statements of the Bank of the United States from June to November 1832. [Washington, 1832] 37 p. MB. 16739

---- Report on Treasury Bal-

ances. Comptroller Joseph Anderson. Jan. 6, 1832. House Ex. Docs., No. 41, 22d Cong., 1st sess., Vol. II. List of balances on the books of the Fourth Auditor remaining unaccounted for more than three years prior to September 30, 1830. [Washington, 1832] 40 p. MB. 16740

---- ---- ---- Dec. 11, 1832. Ex. Docs., No. 138, 22d Cong., 2d sess., Vol. III. Balances on the books of the Second Auditor which have remained due and unpaid for more than three years prior to September 30, 1832. [Washington, 1832] 111 p. MB.   16741

---- Report on Treasury Contracts. Secretary Louis McLane. Feb. 9, 1832. House Ex. Docs., No. 144, 22d Cong., 1st sess., Vol. IV. Transmitting statement of contracts authorized by the Treasury Department in 1831. [Washington, 1832] 20 p. MB.   16742

---- Report on United States Bank. Secretary Louis McLane. Jan. 23, 1832. Senate Docs., No. 31, 22d Cong., 1st sess., Vol. I. Statement of debts due bank from individuals and bodies corporate; List of directors of the bank and its branches; Number of shares of stock held by citizens; Amount of specie in bank. [Washington, 1832] 103 p. MB.   16743

---- ---- ---- Feb. 29, 1832. Senate Docs., No. 78, 22d Cong., 1st sess., Vol. II. Stating the reasons why orders drawn by presidents of branch banks on the cashier of the United State Bank and issued as currency are received by revenue officers in payment of dues to the Government. [Washington, 1832]

10 p. MB.   16744

---- ---- ---- Dec. 12, 1832.
Ex. Docs., No. 9, 22d Cong.,
2d sess., Vol. I. Transmitting correspondence from the
United States Bank on the subject of payment of the three per
cent stock of the United States.
[Washington, 1832] 13 p. MB.
                         16745
---- ---- Select Committee.
Apr. 30, 1832. Reports of Committees, No. 460, 22d Cong.,
1st sess., Vol. IV. Giving results of inspection of the books
and examination of the proceedings of the bank and its branches, and as to whether any provisions of the charter have been
violated, or whether there have
been any circumstances of mis-
management against which future
legislation might guard. [Wash-
ington, 1832] 572 p. MB.
                         16746
---- Report on Unproductive
Post-Roads. P. M. General W.
T. Barry. May 25, 1832.
House Ex. Docs., No. 243, 22d
Cong., 1st sess., Vol. VI.
Transmitting information relative to unproductive post-roads;
Routes; Cost of transportation;
Proceeds. [Washington, 1832]
6 p. MB.   16747

---- Report on Vacant Lands in
Tennessee. Committee on Public Lands. Jan. 24, 1832. Reports of Committees, No. 230,
22d Cong., 1st sess., Vol. II.
Recommends that vacant public
lands in Tennessee be ceded to
that State for the support of
schools; Bill reported. [Wash-
ington, 1832] 25 p. MB. 16748

---- Report on Vessels of War.
Secretary Levi Woodbury. May
3, 1832. House Ex. Docs., No.
228, 22d Cong., 1st sess., Vol.
V. Transmitting information

relative to vessles of war arriving at each naval depot; Number
of vessels built and repaired;
Number of men recruited.
[Washington, 1832] 12 p. MB.
                         16749
---- Report on Virginia Military
Land Warrants. Committee on
Public Lands. Jan. 31, 1832.
Reports of Committees, No. 249,
22d Cong., 1st sess., Vol. II.
Recommends that holders of
military land warrants issued by
the State of Virginia be permitted
to locate on public lands; Bill
reported. [Washington, 1832]
7 p. MB.   16750

No entry.   16751

---- Report on War Claims.
Committee of Claims. Mar. 16,
1832. Reports of Committees,
No. 386, 22d Cong., 1st sess.,
Vol. III. Adverse to any additional legislation to compensate
owners of property for losses
sustained from the British during
the war of 1812. [Washington,
1832] 36 p. MB.   16752

---- Report on War Department
Contracts. Secretary Lewis
Cass. Jan. 30, 1832. House
Ex. Docs., No. 89, 22d Cong.,
1st sess., Vol. III. Transmitting statement of contracts made
by the War Department during the
year 1831. [Washington, 1832]
45 p. MB.   16753

---- ---- ---- Feb. 24, 1832.
House Ex. Docs., No. 125, 22d
Cong., 1st sess., Vol. IV.
Transmitting information concerning contracts for cannon and can-
nonshot from the year 1820 to the
present time. [Washington, 1832]
5 p. MB.   16754

---- Report on Weights and Measures. Secretary Louis McLane.
June 28, 1832. Ex. Docs., No.

299, 22d Cong., 1st sess., Vol.
VI. Comparison of weights and
measures of length and capacity
at the various custom-houses of
the United States, made by Ferd.
Rod. Hassler. [Washington, 1832]
131 p. MB.   16755

---- Report on Weights and
Measures in Custom-Houses. Sec.
L. McLane. June 20, 1832. Senate Docs., No. 168, 22d Cong.,
1st sess., Vol. III. Transmitting
comparative statement of weights
and measures used in the custom-
houses of the United States.
[Washington, 1832] 128 p. MB.
                              16756
---- Report on Wool Imported.
Secretary Louis McLane. June 8,
1832. House Ex. Docs., No. 267,
22d Cong., 1st sess., Vol. VI.
Statement of quantity and value
of wool imported from Turkey,
the Levant, and Egypt from 1826
to 1831, inclusive. [Washington,
1832] 2 p. MB.   16757

---- Report relative to Army Officers. Committee on Military
Affairs. Feb. 8, 1832. Reports
of Committees, No. 286, 22d
Cong., 1st sess., Vol. II. Recommends that the practice of de-
taching captains from the command of their companies be dis-
continued. [Washington, 1832]
3 p. MB.   16758

---- Reports made to the Senate
and to the House of Representatives by committees of those
houses, on the propriety of disposing of the public lands to
those states in which they lie.
May 3, 1832...Washington, 1832.
22d Cong., 1st sess., H.R. No.
448. 32 p. OClWHi.   16759

---- Reports of Committees on
French Spoliation Claims. Jan.
31, 1832. Senate Docs., No. 51,
22d Cong., 1st sess., Vol. I.

Reports on the subject of the
claims of individuals for indem-
nity for spoliations by the French
Government prior to the 30th of
September, 1800, made by the
committees of the Senate and
House of Representatives from
April 22, 1802, to February 22,
1830. [Washington, 1832] 91 p.
MB.   16760

---- Residences of Land Officers.
Jan. 24, 1832. Library of the Interior Department. Registers and
receivers required to live at the
place where local land office is
located. [Washington, 1832] 1 p.
MB.   16761

---- Resolution against the Tariff. Citizens of Rhode Island.
May 31, 1832. Senate Docs., No.
162, 22d Cong., 1st sess., Vol.
III. In opposition to the bill proposed by the Secretary of the
Treasury reducing the duties on
imports. [Washington, 1832] 2 p.
MB.   16762

---- Resolution amending the
Constitution. Mr. Root. Mar. 2,
1832. Reports of Committees,
Resolution No. 3, 22d Cong., 1st
sess., Vol. V. Proposing an
amendment to the Constitution
changing the mode of election of
President and Vice-President.
[Washington, 1832] 1 p. MB.
                              16763
---- Resolution authorizing the
President of the United States to
contract for a full length Pedestrian Statue of George Washington. April 25, 1832. Agreeably to
notice given, Mr. Poindexter
asked and obtained leave to bring
in the following bill; which was
read, and passed to a second
reading. Apr. 26, 1832. Read a
second time, and referred to the
Committee on the Library. May
2, 1832. Reported without amendment. [Washington, 1832] 1 p.

488   United States

(S. 4) DNA; MB.   16764

---- Resolution concerning Rules
of the House. Mr. Sutherland.
June 30, 1832. Reports of Committees, Resolution No. 8, 22d
Cong., 1st sess., Vol. V. Proposing various amendments to the
rules of the House. 1 p. MB.
                         16765
---- Resolution concerning the
Mint. Mr. Wilde. Mar. 26, 1832.
Reports of Committees, Resolution No. 7, 22d Cong., 1st sess.,
Vol. V. Requesting Committee on
Coins to inquire into the expediency of authorizing prompt payment in coin for bullion delivered
at the Mint. [Washington, 1832]
8 p. MB.   16766

---- Resolution directing the distribution of a compilation of Congressional Documents. June 9,
1832. Mr. Frelinghuysen, from
the Joint Committee on the Library, reported the following resolution; which was read, and
passed to a second reading:
[Washington, 1832] 3 p. (S. 6)
DNA; MB.   16767

---- Resolution directing the purchase of Peale's original portrait
of Washington. June 23, 1832.
Mr. Frelinghuysen, from the
Joint Committee on the Library
of Congress, reported the following resolution; which was read,
and passed to a second reading:
[Washington, 1832] 1 p. (S. 8)
DNA; MB.   16768

---- Resolution distributing certain copies of the Secret Journals
of the old Congress, reported the
following resolution; which was
read, and passed to a second
reading: [Washington, 1832] 2 p.
(S. 3) DNA; MB.   16769

---- Resolution for Disposal of
Public Lands. Legislature of In-

diana. Jan. 26, 1832. Senate
Docs., No. 72, 22d Cong., 1st
sess., Vol. II. That State representation in Congress be requested to procure passage of law
for disposing of public lands in
tracts of forty acres. [Washing-
ton, 1832] 1 p. MB.   16770

---- Resolution for Improvement
of Rivers. Legislature of Indiana.
Feb. 3, 1832. Senate Docs., No.
76, 22d Cong., 1st sess., Vol.
II. That State representation in
Congress be requested to procure
an appropriation for the improvement of Wabash and White Rivers.
[Washington, 1832] 1 p. MB.
                         16771
---- Resolution for Revolutionary
Pensions. New York Legislature.
Jan. 27, 1832. Senate Docs.,
No. 109, 22d Cong., 1st sess.,
Vol. II. That State representation
in Congress be instructed to use
their exertions to have the pension laws so modified as to allow
pensions to all the surviving officers and soldiers of the Revolution. [Washington, 1832] 1 p. MB.
                         16772
---- Resolution of the Legislature
of Maine, against rechartering the
Bank of the United States, Mar.
15, 1832. Read, and committed
to the Committee of the Whole
House on the State of the Union,
to which is committed the bill
(H. R. No. 365) to renew and
modify the charter of the Bank
of the United States. Washington,
Pr. by Duff Green, 1832. R.
                         16773
---- Resolution on Jurisdiction of
Supreme Court. Mr. Pendleton.
Jan. 3, 1832. Reports of Com-
mittees, Resolution No. 2, 22d
Cong., 1st sess., Vol. V. Rela-
tive to the passage of a bill to
regulate the jurisdiction of the
United States Supreme Court.
[Washington, 1832] 1 p. MB.
                         16774

---- Resolution on Protection to Indians. Senator Frelinghuysen. Feb. 2, 1832. Senate Docs., No. 43, 22d Cong., 1st sess., Vol. I. That the United States is bound by treaty stipulations to protect the Cherokee Nation from all intrusion upon their territory; That it is the duty of the President to enforce the stipulations of said treaties. [Washington, 1832] 1 p. MB.   16775

---- Resolution on the Tariff. Senator Clay. Jan. 9, 1832. Senate Docs., No. 23, 22d Cong., 1st sess., Vol. I. That the existing duties upon imports not coming into competition with similar articles produced within the United States ought to be abolished, except those on wines and silks. [Washington, 1832] 1 p. MB.   16776

---- ---- Senator Wilkins. Mar. 23, 1832. Senate Docs., No. 111, 22d Cong., 1st sess., Vol. III. That the Secretary of State be requested to report the laws and regulations of foreign countries relative to duties on imports which tend to counteract the duties now imposed by law on importations into the United States. [Washington, 1832] 1 p. MB.   16777

---- ---- ---- ---- Senate Docs., No. 112, 22d Cong., 1st sess., Vol. III. That the Secretary of the Treasury be requested to report the present credits on duties on imports, and expediency of providing for reduction thereof, and on expediency of making such alteration in existing laws as to provide for resumption of ad valorem duties. [Washington, 1832] 1 p. MB.   16778

---- Resolution relative to Debate. Senator Foote. Jan. 25, 1832. Senate Docs., No. 35, 22d Cong.,

1st sess., Vol. I. That no motion shall be debated until seconded, nor debate be permitted until the President shall have announced to Senate the subject under consideration. [Washington, 1832] 1 p. MB.   16779

---- Resolution relative to Public Lands. Legislature of Indiana. Feb. 3, 1832. Senate Docs., No. 73, 22d Cong., 1st sess., Vol. II. That State representation in Congress be requested to obtain a cession to the State of unsold public lands in Indiana. [Washington, 1832] 1 p. MB.   16780

---- Resolution relative to State Rights. Legislature of Pennsylvania. Dec. 20, 1832. Ex. Docs., No. 19, 22d Cong., 2d sess., Vol. I. Affirming the doctrine that the laws of the United States are the supreme law of the land, and that no State has the power to nullify them. [Washington, 1832] 2 p. MB.   16781

---- Resolution relative to United States Bank. Mr. Clayton. Feb. 23, 1832. Resolution No. 4, 22d Cong., 1st sess., Vol. V. That a select committee be chosen to examine into the affairs of the United States Bank; Amendment submitted by Mr. Wayne. [Washington, 1832] 4 p. MB.   16782

---- Resolution relative to United States Territory. Mr. Archer. Mar. 16, 1832. Reports of Committees, Resolution No. 5, 22d Cong., 1st sess., Vol. V. Requesting the President to inform the House whether the subjects of any foreign Power have taken possession of any portion of United States territory on the Pacific Ocean. [Washington, 1832] 1 p. MB.   16783

---- Resolutions against recharter

of U.S. Bank. Legislature of
Missouri. Dec. 28, 1832. Senate
Docs., No. 78, 22d Cong., 2d
sess., Vol. I. Adverse to renew-
al of charter of United States
Bank. [Washington, 1832] 1 p.
MB.   16784

---- ---- Maine Legislature.
Feb. 23, 1832. House Ex. Docs.,
No. 169, 22d Cong., 1st sess.,
Vol. IV. In opposition to the re-
newal of the charter of the United
States Bank. [Washington, 1832]
1 p. MB.   16785

---- ---- New York Legislature.
Mar. 6, 1832. House Ex. Docs.,
No. 155, 22d Cong., 1st sess.,
Vol. IV. In opposition to renewal
of the charter of the United States
Bank. [Washington, 1832] 1 p.
MB.   16786

---- Resolutions against Reduc-
tion of Duties on Woollens. Rhode
Island Legislature. May 14, 1832.
House Ex. Docs., No. 236, 22d
Cong., 1st sess., Vol. VI.
Against reduction of duties on
woollen goods. [Washington, 1832]
1 p. MB.   16787

---- Resolutions against Removal
of Remains of George Washington.
Feb. 20, 1832. House Ex. Docs.,
No. 124, 22d Cong., 1st sess.,
Vol. IV. Resolutions of Legislature of Virginia in opposition to
the removal of the remains of
George Washington. [Washington,
1832] 2 p. MB.   16788

---- Resolutions against the Tariff. May 29, 1832. Senate Docs.,
No. 165, 22d Cong., 1st sess.,
Vol. III. Protesting against passage of bill to reduce duties on
imports proposed by the Secretary
of the Treasury. [Washington,
1832] 2 p. MB.   16789

---- ---- Citizens of New Hamp-

shire. June 9, 1832. House Ex.
Docs., No. 288, 22d Cong., 1st
sess., Vol. VI. Against the tariff
bill proposed by the Secretary of
the Treasury. [Washington, 1832]
2 p. MB.   16790

---- ---- Citizens of New Jersey.
June 1, 1832. Senate Docs., No.
164, 22d Cong., 1st sess., Vol.
III. Protesting against the bill
proposed by the Secretary of the
Treasury reducing the duties on
imports. [Washington, 1832] 2 p.
MB.   16791

---- ---- Citizens of Waterbury,
Conn. May 28, 1832. House Ex.
Docs., No. 260, 22d Cong., 1st
sess., Vol. VI. Against the passage of the tariff bill proposed by
the Secretary of the Treasury.
[Washington, 1832] 1 p. MB.
                                 16792

---- ---- Massachusetts Wool-
growers and manufacturers. May
20, 1832. House Ex. Docs., No.
269, 22d Cong., 1st sess., Vol.
VI. Against the passage of the
tariff bill proposed by the Secretary of the Treasury. [Washington,
1832] MB.   16793

---- Resolutions for a Canal.
Legislature of Louisiana. Mar.
23, 1832. House Ex. Docs., No.
219, 22d Cong., 1st sess., Vol.
V. Urging that a survey be made
as to the practicability of a canal
from Fort St. Philip to Breton Island. [Washington, 1832] 1 p.
MB.   16794

---- Resolutions for Pensions to
Revolutionary Soldiers. Mar. 9,
1832. House Ex. Docs., No. 182,
22d Cong., 1st sess., Vol. IV.
The Legislature of Maine requests
passage of a law granting pensions
to the surviving soldiers of the
Revolution. [Washington, 1832]
2 p. MB.   16795

United States   491

---- Resolutions for Recharter of U. S. Bank. Bank of Brownsville. Feb. 27, 1832. House Ex. Docs., No. 141, 22d Cong., 2d sess., Vol. IV. Favoring the renewal of the charter of the United States Bank. [Washington, 1832] 2 p. MB. 16796

---- ---- Bank of Steubenville. Feb. 21, 1832. House Ex. Docs., No. 167, 22d Cong., 1st sess., Vol. IV. Asking that charter of the United States Bank be modified and renewed. [Washington, 1832] 2 p. MB. 16797

---- ---- Delaware Legislature. Feb. 1, 1832. House Ex. Docs., No. 94, 22d Cong., 1st sess., Vol. III. In favor of the renewal of the charter of the United States Bank. [Washington, 1832] 1 p. MB. 16798

---- ---- Legislature of Louisiana. Mar. 16, 1832. House Ex. Docs., No. 218, 22d Cong.,1st sess., Vol. V. Favoring renewal of the charter of the United States Bank. [Washington, 1832] 1 p. MB. 16799

---- ---- State Bank of New York. Feb. 27, 1832. House Ex. Docs., No. 140, 22d Cong., 1st sess., Vol. IV. Asking that the charter of the United States Bank be renewed. [Washington, 1832] 1 p. MB. 16800

---- Resolutions for Reduction of the Tariff. Legislature of Maine. Mar. 7, 1832. House Ex. Docs., No. 183, 22d Cong., 1st sess., Vol. IV. Favoring reduction of duties on imports. [Washington, 1832] 2 p. MB. 16801

---- Resolutions for Revolutionary Pensions. Legislature of Pennsylvania. Mar. 16, 1832. House Ex. Docs., No. 187, 22d Cong., 1st sess., Vol. V. Requesting modification of pension laws so as to include all the surviving soldiers of the Revolution. [Washington, 1832] 1 p. MB. 16802

---- Resolutions moved in Committee of the Whole. Dec. 10, 1832. Reports of Committees, Resolution No. 1, 22d Cong., 2d sess. Resolutions for reference of portions of the President's message. [Washington, 1832] 2 p. MB. 16803

---- Resolutions on Commissioner of General Land Office. Mr. Wickliffe. Mar. 17, 1832. Reports of Committees, Resolution No. 6, 22d Cong., 1st sess., Vol. V. Directing the Committee on the Judiciary to investigate and report whether the Commissioner of the General Land Office was officially called upon to fix the boundaries of a new land district in Michigan. [Washington, 1832] 2 p. MB. 16804

---- Resolutions on Internal Improvements. Legislature of Georgia. Dec. 21, 1832. Ex. Docs., No. 91, 22d Cong., 2d sess., Vol. II. Deprecating the exercise by Congress of the power to carry out a system of internal improvements. [Washington, 1832] 2 p. MB. 16805

---- Resolutions on Public Lands. Mr. Clay of Alabama. Dec. 11, 1832. Reports of Committees, Resolution No. 2, 22d Cong., 2d sess. Directing the Committee on Public Lands to inquire into the expediency of reducing the price of certain public lands and of ceding public lands to the States; Amendments by Mr. Williams, Dec. 18, and by Mr. Wickliffe, Dec. 19. [Washington, 1832] 2 p. MB. 16806

---- Resolutions on Removal of
Public Officers. Senator Ewing.
Jan. 31, 1832. Senate Docs., No.
41, 22d Cong., 1st sess., Vol.
I. That the practice of removing
public officers for any other purpose than that of securing a faithful execution of the laws is hostile to the spirit of the Constitution; That it is inexpedient for
the Senate to consent to the appointment of any person to a va-
cancy resulting from a removal
for no sufficient cause. [Washing-
ton, 1832] 1 p. MB.   16807

---- Resolutions on Steamboat
Explosions. Legislature of Louisiana. May 2, 1832. House Ex.
Docs., No. 226, 22d Cong., 1st
sess., Vol. V. Transmitting report of the Joint Committee on
the subject of steam-boiler explosions, and requesting that experiments be made to test the
value of J. O. Blair's system for
generating steam so as to avoid
explosions. [Washington, 1832]
12 p. MB.   16808

---- Resolutions on Tariff and
United States Bank. Citizens of
Pennsylvania. June 25, 1832.
House Ex. Docs., No. 291, 22d
Cong., 1st sess., Vol. VI. In
favor of the protective system
and of the renewal of the charter
of the United States Bank. [Wash-
ington, 1832] 5 p. MB.   16809

---- ---- Legislature of Pennsylvania. June 6, 1832. Senate Docs.
No. 161, 22d Cong., 1st sess.,
Vol. III. Resolutions in favor of
a protective tariff, and asking
renewal of charter of the United
States Bank. [Washington, 1832]
2 p. MB.   16810

---- Resolutions on Tariff, Internal Improvements, etc. Legislature of New Hampshire. June
22, 1832. Senate Docs., No. 53,

22d Cong., 2d sess., Vol. I.
Favoring a reduction of the tariff,
and opposing the adoption of a
system of internal improvements
at the national expense. [Wash-
ington, 1832] 9 p. MB.   16811

---- Resolutions on the Tariff.
Citizens of Brooklyn. June 14,
1832. House Ex. Docs., No. 279,
22d Cong., 1st sess., Vol. VI.
Protesting against the reduction
of duties on articles coming into
competition with American manufactures. [Washington, 1832] 2 p.
MB.   16812

---- ---- Citizens of Connecticut. June 11, 1832. Senate Docs.,
No. 169, 22d Cong., 1st sess.,
Vol. III. In favor of the protective system. [Washington, 1832]
1 p. MB.   16813

---- ---- ---- June 19, 1832.
Senate Docs., No. 175, 22d
Cong., 1st sess., Vol. III. Fav-
oring the protective system.
[Washington, 1832] 2 p. MB.
                           16814

---- ---- Citizens of New York.
June 9, 1832. House Ex. Docs.,
No. 270, 22d Cong., 1st sess.,
Vol. VI. Favoring a rearrange-
ment of the tariff system during
the present session of Congress.
[Washington, 1832] 4 p. MB.
                           16815

---- ---- ---- June 11, 1832.
House Ex. Docs., No. 281, 22d
Cong., 1st sess., Vol. VI.
Against any reduction in the du-
ties on articles coming into com-
petition with American products.
[Washington, 1832] 2 p. MB.
                           16816

---- ---- ---- ---- Senate Docs.,
No. 166, 22d Cong., 1st sess.,
Vol. III. Favoring the protective
system, and in opposition to the
bill proposed by the Secretary of
the Treasury to reduce duties on
imports. [Washington, 1832] 2 p.

MB.   16817

---- ---- Citizens of Pennsylvania. June 14, 1832. Senate Docs., No. 172, 22d Cong., 1st sess., Vol. III. In favor of the protective system. [Washington, 1832] 2 p. MB.   16818

---- ---- ---- June 19, 1832. House Ex. Docs., No. 294, 22d Cong., 1st sess., Vol. VI. Against any reduction of the duty on imports. [Washington, 1832] 2 p. MB.   16819

---- ---- Citizens of Pittsburgh. June 9, 1832. House Ex. Docs., No. 285, 22d Cong., 1st sess., Vol. VI. Against any tariff law to lessen the protection now afforded American industries. [Washington, 1832] 2 p. MB.   16820

---- ---- Legislature of Connecticut. May 14, 1832. House Ex. Docs., No. 282, 22d Cong., 1st sess., Vol. VI. Favoring the protective system. [Washington, 1832] 2 p. MB.   16821

---- Resolutions on the Tariff and United States Bank. Citizens of Pennsylvania. June 7, 1832. Senate Docs., No. 171, 22d Cong., 1st sess., Vol. III. In favor of the protective system and of a renewal of the charter of the United States Bank. [Washington, 1832] 2 p. MB.   16822

---- Resolutions on the Tariff, etc. Legislature of Vermont. Nov. 7, 1832. Senate Docs., No. 51, 22d Cong., 2d sess., Vol. I. Adverse to modification of the tariff; In favor of internal improvements and of renewal of charter of United States Bank. [Washington, 1832] 3 p. MB.   16823

---- ---- ---- Dec. 18, 1832. Ex. Docs., No. 21, 22d Cong.,

2d sess., Vol. I. Favoring the system of protection to American industry, the renewal of the charter of the United States Bank, internal improvements, etc. [Washington, 1832] 3 p. MB.   16824

---- Resolutions on Trade with British Colonies. Senator Sprague. Feb. 8, 1832. Senate Docs., No. 52, 22d Cong., 1st sess., Vol. I. That the arrangement made with Great Britain by the Executive relative to the colonial trade violates the principle of reciprocity; That the proclamation of the President opening United States ports to British vessels was not authorized by act of May 29, 1830. [Washington, 1832] 1 p. MB.   16825

---- Resolutions passed at a meeting of the citizens of New Canaan, Fairfield County, Connecticut, in favor of the protective system. June 30, 1832. Laid on the table and ordered to be printed. Washington, Pr. by Duff Green, 1832. R.   16826

---- Resolutions passed at the meeting of the inhabitants of Sharon, Connecticut, in favor of the protective system, etc. June 23, 1832 laid on the table, and ordered to be printed by Duff Green, Washington, 1832. R.   16827

---- Resolutions relative to Nullification. Legislature of Illinois. Dec. 26, 1832. Ex. Docs., No. 103, 22d Cong., 2d sess., Vol. II. Disapproving the nullification doctrines of the South Carolina convention. [Washington, 1832] 2 p. MB.   16828

---- Resolutions relative to Secession. Legislature of South Carolina. Dec. 20, 1832. Senate Docs., No. 24, 22d Cong., 2d sess., Vol. I. Declaring the re-

cent proclamation of the President denying the right of secession to be unconstitutional. [Washington, 1832] 2 p. MB.
16829

---- Resolutions relative to State Rights. Legislature of Georgia. Dec. 22, 1832. Ex. Docs., No. 92, 22d Cong., 2d sess., Vol. II. Favoring the calling a convention to amend the Constitution so as to determine the relative rights of the General Government and the States. [Washington, 1832] 2 p. MB.
16830

---- ---- Legislature of South Carolina. Dec. 13, 1832. Ex. Docs., No. 59, 22d Cong., 2d sess., Vol. II. Favoring a call of a general convention of the States to determine questions of disputed power between the States and the General Government. [Washington, 1832] 2 p. MB.
16831

---- Resolutions relative to Tariff and United States Bank. Legislature of Pennsylvania. June 7, 1832. House Ex. Docs., No. 266, 22d Cong., 1st sess., Vol. VI. Favoring the protective system and the renewal of the charter of the United States Bank. [Washington, 1832] 2 p. MB.
16832

---- Resolutions relative to the Constitution. Legislature of Georgia. Dec. 12, 1832. Senate Docs., No. 23, 22d Cong., 2d sess., Vol. I. In favor of a convention of the people for the purpose of making amendments. to the constitution. [Washington, 1832] 2 p. MB.
16833

---- Resolutions relative to the Tariff. Citizens of Delaware. June 2, 1832. House Ex. Docs., No. 259, 22d Cong., 1st sess., Vol. VI. Against any modification of the present tariff. [Washington, 1832] 3 p. MB.
16834

---- Returns of Banks of District of Columbia. Secretary Louis McLane. Jan. 23, 1832. House Ex. Docs., No. 69, 22d Cong., 1st sess., Vol. II. Transmitting returns of the banks of the District of Columbia for the year 1831. [Washington, 1832] 10 p. MB.
16835

---- Rules of the Navy department, regulating the civil administration of the navy of the United States... Washington, Pr. at the Globe office, 1832. 73 p. CU; DLC; MB; PHi; RNR.
16836

---- Sales of military reservations. On Monday, the 3d Sept. next, 10 o'clock, A. M. will be sold at public auction, the military reservations within the City of Detroit, and on the River Rouge. Detroit, 1832. Broadside. MiD-B.
16837

---- School Lands. Dec. 16, 1832. Library of the Interior Department. Additional instructions in regard to selections of school lands. [Washington, 1832] MB.
16838

---- Selections of School Lands. Aug. 30, 1832. Library of the Interior Department. Circular relating to selections of school lands under act of May 20, 1826. [Washington, 1832] 2 p. MB.
16839

---- Senate Documents, Twenty-second Congress, Second Session. From Dec. 3, 1832. Vol. I. Docs Nos. 1 to 84, inclusive. Pr. by Duff Green. Vol. II, Doc. No. 85. Report on a system of civil and criminal law for the District of Columbia. [Washington, 1832] MB.
16840

---- Senate Journal, Twenty-second Congress, Second Session. Dec. 3, 1832. From Dec. 3, 1832, to Mar. 2, 1833. Vice-President, John C. Calhoun, of

South Carolina; President of the
Senate pro tempore, Hugh L.
White, of Tennessee, elected De-
cember 3, 1832; Secretary of the
Senate, Walter Lowrie, of Penn-
sylvania. Washington, Pr. by
Duff Green [1832] 357 p. MB;
MdBP; PPAmP; R.   16841

---- Soldiers of the Revolution.
Memorial in behalf of certain
soldiers of the Revolutionary
Army, Dec. 13, 1832. Referred
to the Committee on Revolutionary
Claims. Washington, Pr. by Duff
Green, 1832. 2 p. R.   16842

---- Standard Weights and Measures. Mar. 5, 1832. Library of
the Coast Survey. An enumera-
tion of the objects and statements
desirable to form a collection of
standard weights and measures of
foreign countries for the Department of State of the United States.
[Washington, 1832] 3 p. MB.
                           16843
---- Statement of Apportionment
of Representation. Jan. 4, 1832.
House Ex. Docs., No. 36, 22d
Cong., 1st sess., Vol. II. Statement showing the apportionment
of representation in the House of
Representatives under the first,
second, third, and fourth census-
es. [Washington, 1832] 8 p. MB.
                           16844
---- Statement of Apportionment
of Representatives. Mr. Clayton.
Apr. 14, 1832. Senate Docs.,
No. 127, 22d Cong., 1st sess.,
Vol. III. Statement of apportionment of Representatives from
1792 to 1832, inclusive. [Wash-
ington, 1832] 4 p. MB.   16845

---- ---- Mr. Webster. Apr. 13,
1832. Senate Docs., No. 126,
22d Cong., 1st sess., Vol. III.
Statement relative to the apportionment of Representatives under
the fifth census. [Washington,
1832] 5 p. MB.   16846

---- Statement of Apportionment
of Representatives under Fifth
Census. Feb. 14, 1832. House
Ex. Docs., No. 105, 22d Cong.,
1st sess., Vol. IV. [Washington,
1832] 1 p. MB.   16847

---- Statement of Appropriations.
July 14, 1832. Ex. Docs., No.
305, 22d Cong., 1st sess. Appropriations made during the
first session of the Twenty-second Congress. [Washington, 1832]
32 p. MB.   16848

---- ---- Secretary Louis Mc-
Lane. Apr. 6, 1832. House Ex.
Docs., No. 200, 22d Cong., 1st
sess., Vol. V. Transmitting
statement of appropriations for
fortifications, light-houses, public debt, internal improvements,
and pensions for the years 1830
and 1831. [Washington, 1832]
3 p. MB.   16849

---- Statement of Duties. Secretary Louis McLane. Apr. 12,
1832. Senate Docs., No. 125,
22d Cong., 1st sess., Vol. III.
Statement showing duties that
would be repealed in case bill
(S. 167) to repeal in part duties
on imports should become a law.
[Washington, 1832] 4 p. MB.
                          16850
---- Statement of Imports. Secretary of Senate. Mar. 23, 1832.
Senate Docs., No. 110, 22d Cong.,
1st sess., Vol. II. Alphabetical
list of all articles imported into
the United States; Duties imposed
thereon; Articles free of duty.
[Washington, 1832] 65 p. MB.
                          16851
---- Statement of Representation
in Congress. Senator Clayton.
Mar 5, 1832. Senate Docs., No.
91, 22d Cong., 1st sess., Vol.
II. Statement showing representative numbers of people of United
States at each census; Ratio of
representation; Number of Rep-

resentatives. [Washington, 1832] 4 p. MB. 16852

---- ---- Senator Webster. Mar. 6, 1832. Senate Docs., No. 92, 22d Cong., 1st sess., Vol. II. Statement concerning the ratio of representation in Congress under the fifth census. [Washington, 1832] MB. 16853

---- Statement of the Judiciary Fund. Senator Smith. Mar. 28, 1832. Senate Docs., No. 114, 22d Cong., 1st sess., Vol. III. Statement of appropriations and expenditures for the judicial fund from 1824 to 1831, inclusive. [Washington, 1832] 1 p. MB. 16854

---- Statement regarding the Tariff. Secretary of Senate Walter Lowrie. May 15, 1832. Senate Docs., No. 144, 22d Cong., 1st sess., Vol. III. Comparative statement of present and proposed tariff. [Washington, 1832] 56 p. MB. 16855

---- Statement relative to Foreign Missions. Mar. 1, 1832. House Ex. Docs., No. 146, 22d Cong., 1st sess., Vol. IV. List of secretaries of legation and consuls who have performed duties of chargé d'affaires and who have applied for or will apply for additional compensation. [Washington, 1832] 1 p. MB. 16856

---- Statement relative to Indian Annuities. Feb. 27, 1832. House Ex. Docs., No. 127, 22d Cong., 1st sess., Vol. IV. Showing number and amount of Indian annuities now payable under treaty stipulations. [Washington, 1832] 7 p. MB. 16857

---- Statement relative to Report on Commerce and Navigation. Secretary McLane. Feb. 18, 1832. Senate Docs., No. 67, 22d Cong.,

1st sess., Vol. II. Giving the reasons why the report on commerce and navigation has not yet been transmitted to Congress. [Washington, 1832] 6 p. MB. 16858

---- Statements of United States Bank. Secretary Louis McLane. Jan. 12, 1832. Senate Docs., No. 27, 22d Cong., 1st sess., Vol. I. General statement of bank; Offices of discount and deposit; Capital stock; Dividends unclaimed; Redemption of public debt; Deposits. [Washington, 1832] 73 p. MB 16859

---- ---- ---- Mar. 1, 1832. House Ex. Docs., No. 147, 22d Cong., 1st sess., Vol IV. Transmitting semi-annual statements of the Bank of the United States and its various offices. [Washington, 1832] 66 p. MB. 16860

---- ---- ---- Mar. 5, 1832. Senate Docs., No. 96, 22d Cong., 1st sess., Vol. II. Monthly statements of the United States Bank for January and February, 1832; Funded debt; Bills discounted on personal security; Domestic and foreign bills of exchange; Amount due State banks. [Washington, 1832] 13 p. MB. 16861

---- ---- ---- June 4, 1832. Senate Docs., No. 156, 22d Cong., 1st sess., Vol. III. Transmitting monthly statements of the United States Bank for March, April, and May. [Washington, 1832] 19 p. MB. 16862

---- Statements relative to the Bank of England. Apr. 12, 1832. House Ex. Docs., No. 203, 22d Cong., 1st sess., Vol. V. Statement of notes of the Bank of England in circulation on Saturday of every week from Aug. 6, 1831, to Feb. 4, 1832; Statement of the coinage of Great Britain. [Washington, 1832] 2 p. MB. 16863

---- Summary Statement of Commerce of United States for Year ending Sept. 30, 1831. May 14, 1832. House Ex. Docs., No. 238, 22d Cong., 1st sess., Vol. VI. [Washington, 1832] 21 p. MB.
16864

---- Surveys--Road--Uniontown to Pittsburg--Canal--Conneaut Creek to Erie. Canal Ohio River to Lake Erie--Pennsylvania. May 18, 1832. Referred to the Committee on Internal Improvements. Washington, Pr. by Duff Green, 1832. 11 p. R.
16865

---- Territory of Wisconsin; report of the committee on the territories...submitted by Mr. Kerr. Dec. 6, 1832, [Washington, 1832] 9 p. (U.S., 22d Cong., 1st sess. House doc. 145) WHi.
16866

---- Unconfirmed Land Titles in Missouri. Nov. 7, 1832. Library of the Interior Department. Instructions to the commissioners charged with examination of all unconfirmed claims to lands in Missouri founded on foreign titles. [Washington, 1832] 3 p. MB.
16867

---- Vermont--Tariff. Memorial of citizens of the State of Vermont, in public meeting at Windsor. May 31, 1832. Read and referred to a committee of the Whole House on the State of the Union. Washington, Pr. by Duff Green, 1832. 8 p. R.
16868

---- ---- Bennington. Memorial of citizens of Vermont, on the subject of the tariff. June 16, 1832. Referred to a committee of the Whole House on the State of the Union. Washington, Pr. by Duff Green, 1832. 2 p. R. 16869

---- William Gray, William Davis and Ge A. Scherpf, Apr. 30, 1832 ..Report Washington, Pr. by Duff Green, 1832. 1 p. R.
16870

---- Wool imported from Smyrna. Letter from the Secretary of the Treasury, in reply to a resolution of the House of Representatives, of the 6th instant, in relation to the quantity and value of wool imported from Smyrna. June 9, 1832. Referred to the Committee of the Whole House on the State of the Union. Washington, Pr. by Duff Green, 1832. 2 p. R.
16871

United States Anti-Masonic Convention. Baltimore, 1831.
Proceedings of 2nd United States anti-masonic convention held at Baltimore, Sept. 1831, journal and reports, nomination of candidates for President and vice president of the United States, letters of acceptance, resolutions and the address of people. Boston, the convention, 1832. 88 p. IaCrM; MWA; MeB; NjP; WHi.
16872

The United States Baptist annual register and almanac for 1833. By I. M. Allen. Philadelphia, T. W. Ustick [1832] InU; KyLoS; MB; NcWfC; ViW.
16873

[United States] Catholic Almanac; or Laity's directory for the year 1833-1837. Baltimore, J. Myres, 1832-[1836] 120 p. CtY; DLC; MHi; NHi; OOC.
16874

The universal songster. A collection of the most fashionable, popular, sentimental, comic, patriotic and naval songs... New York, J. H. Turney, 1832. 243 p. LNH; NN; OClWHi.
16875

Upham, Charles Wentworth, 1802-1875.
A discourse delivered on the anniversary of the association of the first parish in Hingham, auxiliary to the American Unitarian Association, July 8, 1832. By Charles W. Upham...Hingham,

Pr. by Jedidiah Farmer, 1832.
22 p. CSmH; CtSoP; MBAU;
NjR; NNUT.   16876

---- Discourse, on the anniversary of the Ancient and Honorable Artillery Company, June 4,
1832. By Charles Wentworth
Upham. Junior Pastor of the
First Church in Salem. Salem,
Press of Foote & Brown, 1832.
38 p. CSmH; DLC; MB-FA; MHi;
PHi.   16877

---- Lectures on witchcraft, com-
prising a history of the delusion
in Salem, in 1692. By Charles
W. Upham... 2d ed. Boston,
Carter & Hendee, 1832. 300 p.
DLC; MB; NNUT; OkU; ViU;
WHi.   16878

Upham, Thomas Cogswell, 1799-
1872.
Elements of mental philosophy,
abridged and designed as a text
for academies and high schools.
By Thomas Cogswell Upham.
3d ed. Boston, W. Hyde & Co.,
1832. 600 p. CtHC; IEG; MiU;
NjP; OMC.   16879

Utica, New York.
An act to incorporate the City
of Utica, passed Feb. 13, 1832.
36 p. NUt; NUtHi.   16880

---- Laws and ordinances of the
Common Council of the city of
Utica, passed April 1832. Pub. by
order of the Common Council.
Utica, Pr. by E. A. Maynard,
1832. 52 p. NUt.   16881

---- Baptist Church. Maternal
Association.
Constitution and address of the
Maternal Association, of the Bap-
tist Church and Society in Utica.
Formed April, 1832. Utica,
Press of Bennett & Bright, 1832.
8 p. PScrHi.   16882

---- Trinity Church.
Constitution of Trinity Church,
Utica Education Society organized
Feb. 20, 1832. Auburn, Press of
the Society for Promoting Chris-
tian Knowledge. 8 p. NUt.
                             16883
Utica Directory...1832, arranged
in five parts... by Elisha Harring-
ton. Utica, E. A. Maynard, 1832.
NHi; NN; NUT.   16884

V

Vale, G[ilbert] 1788-1866.
Cometarium, or The astronomy
of comets, with a particular account of that comet of 1832, which
approaches nearer to the earth
than any other comet is known
ever to have done. By G. Vale...
To which is added a description
of Kile's planetarium and cometarium... New York, Pr. by
Evans & Brooks, 1832. 15, [1] p.
DLC; ICJ; MB; MH; NNC. 16885

Value, Victor.
Experience consulted; or, Rational system of teaching modern
languages. Philadelphia, 1832.
192 p. MH; PPAmP; RPB.16886

Van Doren, J. Livingston.
English grammar and chart for
parsing the English language.
New York, 1832. 22 p. NBLHi.
                             16887

Van Heythuysen, Frederick Miles,
comp.
The equity draftsman, being a
selection of forms of pleadings
in suits in equity. Originally compiled by F. M. Van Heythuysen...
Rev. and enl., with numerous additional forms and practical notes.
By Edward Hughes... From 2d
London ed. New York, O. Halsted, 1832. 952 p. CU; GU-L;
NjR; PP; WaU.   16888

Vanhook, C.
The sick man's companion, or,
The preserver of health, treat-
ing diseases common to this
country, according to the most
successful practice. To which is
added a short and comprehensive
description of the medicines
used in the practice, and their
doses... By Dr. C. Vanhook, of
Vincennes, state of Indiana. Vincennes, Ind., Pr. by E. Stout,
at the office of the "Western
Sun," 1832. 76 p. InHi.   16889

Vans, William, b. 1763.
Life, [by himself] Boston,
1832. MBAt.   16890

Vergennes, Vermont.
Great sheriff's sales at Vergennes. On Wednesday, the 11th
day of July, and Monday, the
16th in Stant,... Vergennes, July
2, 1832. Middlebury, Pr. at the
American office [1832] Broadside.
VtArHi.   16891

Vergilius Maro, Publius.
Bucolica, Georgica, et Aeneis.
Accedunt Clavis Metrica, Notulae
Anglicae, et Quaestiones. Cura
B. A. Gould. In Usum Scholae
Bostoniensis. Bostoniae, Hilliard,
Gray, Little et Wilkins, 1832.
ICP; MB.   16892

---- Opera. Interpretatione et
notis illustravit Carolus Ruaeus.
Ed. 6a in America stereotypis impressa; cum novissima Parisiensi
diligenter collata, caeterisque
hactenus editis longe emendatior.
Huic editioni accessit Clavis Vir-
giliana. Philadelphia, J. Allen,
1832. 568, (2), 106 p. "Vita,"
p. v-xii. MH.   16893

---- Publii Virgilii Maronis opera; or, The works of Virgil;
with copious notes... Designed for
the use of students in the colleges, academies, and other semi-

naries in the United States... By
the Rev. J. G. Cooper. 3d stereotype ed. New York, N. & J.
White, 1832. 2 v. GHi; LNL;
MdBe; PPL-R; ViRu.   16894

---- ---- New York, Collins,
1832. KyLo.   16895

Vermont.
Acts passed by the Legislature
of the State of Vermont, at their
October session, 1832. Pub. by
authority. Montpelier (Vt.), Pr.
by Knapp & Jewett, 1832. 124 p.
IaU-L; MdBB; Nj; Nv; TxU.
                          16896

---- Directory and rules of the
House of Representatives for the
present session. Montpelier, Pr.
by Knapp & Jewett, 1832. 8 p.
MH; NN.   16897

---- Governor's speech. Gentlemen of the Council and Gentlemen of the House of Representatives: the freemen having a second time failed to elect a chief
magistrate of this State, I have
again been called to the discharge
of the duties of that office by
your suffrages, etc. Montpelier,
Oct. 19, 1832. Broadside. 16898

---- Journal of the General Assembly of...; at their session
begun and holden at Montpelier,
in the County of Washington, on
Thursday, 13th of Oct., A.D.
1832. Danville, Eben'r Eaton
[1832] Mi.   16899

---- Reports of cases argued and
determined in the Supreme Court
of the State of Vermont. Reported
by the judges of said court, agreeably to a statute law of the State.
St. Albans, Pr. by J. Spooner,
1832. 621 p. Ia; MBU-L; Mn;
No; PPiAL; T.   16900

Vermont miniature register, for
the year of our Lord, 1833; being

the first after bissextile, and of
the independence of the United
States the fifty-seventh. Astro-
nomical calculations by Marshall
Conant. Windsor, Richards &
Tracy [1832] 152 p. MH; NN;
VtHi.   16901

Vermont Temperance Society.
Washington County.
     An appeal to the people of
Washington County upon the subject of temperance. By a committee of the Washington County
Temperance Society. Jan. 2,
1832. 8 p. Gilman.   16902

Verplanck (Gulian Crommelin)
1786-1870.
     Discourses and addresses on
subjects of American history,
arts, and literature. New-York,
1832. BrMus.   16903

Verri, Alessandro, 1741-1816.
     Roman nights; or The tomb of
the scipios, by Alessandro Verri,
... New York, Peabody & Co.,
1832. 2 Vols. MBL; NNG. 16904

Very, Nathaniel.
     First and second epistles of
Nathaniel Very to Mr. E. C----.
Boston, The Investigator Office,
1832. 8 p. MWA.   16905

Vethake, Henry.
     Introductory lecture on politi-
cal economy, delivered at Clinton Hall, before the New York
Young Men's Society, Dec. 22,
1832. New York, 1832. 28 p.
WHi.   16906

Viaud, M. Pierre.
     The surprising, yet real and
true voyages and adventures of
M. Pierre Viaud, a French sea
captain... Lewistown, Pa., C.
Bell & Sons, 1832. 252 p.
MdBLC; N.   16907

The Victim of Indulgence: by a

teacher of youth for the amusement and instruction of her pupils.
Founded on facts. "Fatal effects
of luxury and ease we drink our
poison, and we eat disease, in-
dulge our senses at our reason's
cost, till sense is pain and reason hurt or lost." Boston, Hilliard, Gray & Co., 1832. 140 p.
DLC; ICBB.   16908

Vincent, Nathaniel.
     The Spirit of Prayer. By Na-
thaniel Vincent, A. M...With an
introductory essay, by Enoch
Pond. Boston, Peirce & Parker,
1832. 189 p. DLC; MAub; MeBat.
                               16909
A vindication of the divine purpose in relation to the existence
of sin. New Haven, Baldwin &
Treadway, 1832. 48 p. MWA.
                               16910
Vinton, Samuel Finley, 1792-1862.
     A speech delivered at Jackson
Court House, Ohio, September
17th, 1832, by Samuel F. Vinton,
to the people of that county. Gallipolis, Pr. by J. J. Coombs,
1832. 15 p. CSmH; MB.   16911

Virginia.
     Acts passed at a General As-
sembly of the commonwealth of
Virginia, begun and held at the
Capitol, in the City of Richmond,
on Monday, the fifth day of De-
cember, in the year of our Lord,
one thousand eight hundred and
thirty-one, and of the common-
wealth the fifty-sixth. Richmond,
Thomas Ritchie, 1832. 346 p.
IaU-L; L; MdBB; MdHi; Mi-L;
NNLI; Nj; Nv; T; W; WvW-L.
                               16912
---- Journal of the Senate, of the
Commonwealth of Virginia...
Richmond, Pr. by John Warrock,
1832. Vi.   16913

---- The laws now in force, which
relate to the duties of the over-
seers of the poor, or which con-

cern the poor; published under
the direction of the auditor of
public accounts, pursuant to an
act passed the 4th day of January, 1832. Richmond, Pr. by
Samuel Shepherd & Co., 1832.
40 p. Ct; MH-L.   16914

---- A list of lands... vested in
the president and directors of the
Literary fund. [Richmond, Pr.
by T. W. White, 1832] [20] p.
DLC; RPB.   16915

---- The resolution moved by
Mr. Goods... on the subject of
the colored population of the commonwealth... n.p., 1832. 22 p.
IU.   16916

---- ...Resolutions of 1798...
Washington, 1832. 82 p. ScC.
                          16917
---- Sketch of the laws passed
at the session of 1831-32. 1832.
2 p. PPAmP.   16918

Virginia and Kentucky resolutions of 1798 and 1799; with Jefferson's original draught thereof; also, Madison's report, Calhoun's address, resolutions of the
several states in relation to state
rights, with other documents in
support of the Jeffersonian doctrines of 1798... Washington,
Jonathan Elliott, 1832. CU; MoK;
PPL; ScSp; ViU.   16919

Virginia and North Carolina almanac for the year of our Lord
1832. Being bissextile or leap-
year, and fifty-sixth of American
independence. By David Richardson, of Louisa County, Va. Richmond, Pr. by John Warrock
[1832] 36 p. DLC; InU; MWA; Vi;
ViRVal.   16920

The vocal annual, or Singer's own
book for 1832. A collection of the
newest & most popular songs of
the day. Boston, F. S. Hill, 1832.

8, 280 p. MHi; NcD; PU.   16921

Voget, L.
    Life of Geshe Margaret Gott-
fried, executed at Bremen in Germany in May, 1831 for having
poisoned her parents, children,
and brother; her two husbands,
and another person. Translated
by E. Frederici... Gettysburg,
Pa. [1832?] 79 p. DLC; PHi.
                          16922
The voice of the people and the
facts, in relation to the rejection
of Martin Van Buren, by the U.S.
Senate. Albany, Pr. by Packard
& Van Benthuysen, 1832. 47 p.
DLC; MH; NjR; OClWHi; PPL-R.
                          16923
---- New York, Pr. at the Standard office, 1832. 35 p. CSmH;
DLC; MB; PPL; WHi.   16924

Volksfreund und Hagerstauner
Calender auf das Jahr 1833...
zum sechs und dreyssigstenmal
herausgegeben. Hagerstaun, Johann Gruber [1832] 30 p. CLU;
MWA; MdHi; PHi; PPG.   16925

Voltaire, François Marie Arouet
de, 1694-1778.
    Histoire De Charles XII. Roi
De Suede. Par Voltaire. Edition
stéréotype,... quatrième édition,
revue et corrigée. Charles De
Belvr, 102 Broadway, New York,
Charles de Behr, 1832. 285 p.
C-S; MoU; WaU.   16926

The volunteer; devoted to promotion of revivals, evangelical doctrines, and Congregationalism.
Boston, 1832. 2 vols. MB; MHi;
RP.   16927

Vose, John, 1766-1840.
    A compendium of astronomy;
intended to simplify and illustrate
the principles of the science, and
give a concise view of the motions and aspects of the great
heavenly luminaries. Adapted to

the use of common schools, as
well as higher seminaries. By
John Vose... Boston, Carter,
Hendee & Co., 1832. 180 p.
ICP; MB; NbU; NUt; TxU. 16928

Vulpius, Christian August, 1762-
1827.
The history of Renaldo Rinal-
dini, captain of banditti, from
the German Vulpius... Boston,
n.p., 1832. 3 vols. CtMW;
KyDC; KyLxT; MH; MWal. 16929

W

Wainwright, Jonathan Mayhew,
1792-1824.
Music of the Church. Boston
[1832] MB.   16930

Wakefield, Samuel, 1799-1895.
The Christian's Harp. Containing a choice selection of
psalm and hymn tunes. Pittsburgh, Pa., Johnston and Stockton, 1832. 200 p. ODaB. 16931

Wakefield, Mass. First Baptist
Church.
Ecclesiastical record. Boston,
J. Howe, 1832. 24 p. MH.
                                16932
Walker, George, 1772-1847.
The three Spaniards. A ro-
mance. By George Walker. Exe-
ter, J. C. Gerrish, 1832. 203 p.
CtY; LNH; Nh; ViU; VtStjF.
                                16933
Walker, James, 1794-1874.
A discourse, delivered at the
ordination of the Rev. Ephraim
Peabody, over the First Congre-
gational Church in Cincinnati,
May 20, 1832. Cincinnati, Hub-
bard & Edmands, 1832. 45 p.
CSmH; InU; OClWHi; PHi; RPB.
                                16934
---- On moral temperance. [Bos-
ton, 1832] 9 p. MH; MH-AH.
                                16935
---- On the exclusive system.

By James Walker. 3d ed. Pr.
for the American Unitarian Association. Boston, Gray & Bow-
en, 1832. 34 p. CBPac; ICMe;
MeB; MH; NjR.   16936

---- Unitarianism, vindicated
against the charge of not going
far enough. 3d ed. Boston, Gray
& Bowen, 1832. 24 p. CBPac;
DLC; ICMe; MB-FA; MMeT-Hi.
                                16937
Walker, John, 1732-1807.
Cobb's abridgment of J. Walker's critical pronouncing dictionary, and expositor of the English
language, carefully compiled from
the London quarto editions, published under the inspection of the
author; in which Mr. Walker's
principles of orthography and
pronunciation are strictly followed... to which are prefixed
concise principles of pronunciation, and rules for accentuation
and the division of words; with an
appendix, containing a class of
words which are in common use
in this country, and not found in
Walker's dictionary. Particularly
designed for the use of schools
... Hartford, Conn., S. Andrus,
1832. 440 p. DLC.   16938

---- Critical pronouncing dictionary, and expositor of the English
language. Abridged for the use of
schools. To which is annexed,
an abridgment of Walker's Key to
the pronunciation of Greek, Latin, and Scripture proper names.
Boston, Lincoln & Edmands, C.
(Ewer) and J. H. A. Frost, 1832.
MH.   16939

---- ---- Lunenburg, Mass., Edmund Cushing, 1832. 448 p.
MFiHi; VtStjF.   16940

---- ---- Philadelphia, Griggs
& Dickinson, 1832. 413 p.
MiDSH; OClWHi; USIC.   16941

Walker, Joseph, 1792-1851.
Infant Baptism, a gospel doctrine. By Joseph Walker, pastor of a Pedobaptist Church in Paris Maine. Norway, William E. Goodnow, 1832. 36 p. MdBJ; MeIIi; MeLewB.   16942

Walker, S. C.
New Latin reader... Boston, Richardson, Lord, & Holbrook, etc., 1832. DLC; MH; MiU.
16943
Walker, Timothy, 1806-1856.
An address delivered before the Union Literary Society of Miami University, on the twenty-fifth of September at their anniversary celebration. Cincinnati, Corey & Fairbank, 1832. 26 p. MB; NNUT; OC; PPAmP; WHi.
16944
Wallis, William.
The western gentleman's farrier; containing remedies for the different diseases to which horses are incident in the western & south western states.... To which is added an appendix; containing receipts for the cure of many diseases to which horses, cattle, sheep and hogs are liable, ...Dayton, O., E. Lindsly, at the office of the Republican, 1832. 168 p. ODa.   16945

Walmsley, Amasa E., 1806-1832.
Life and confession of Amasa E. Walmsley, who was tried and convicted before the Honorable Supreme Court of Rhode Island of the murder of John Burke and Hannah Frank, in Burrillville, R. I. Sept. 11, 1831 and by said court sentenced to be hanged. Taken from his own mouth, in presence of Stephen Wilmarth... Providence, 1832. 16 p. DLC; NHi; RHi; RPB; RPE.   16946

Walsh, Michael, 1763-1840.
Book-keeping, suited to the business of traders, farmers, and mechanics. Mostly by single entry... To which is added A key to certain parts of the Mercantile arithmetic. By Michael Walsh, A. M. Boston, Carter, Hendee & co., 1832. 78 p. MB; MH; T.   16947

Walton, Isaac, 1593-1683.
The lives of Donne, Wotton, Hooker, Herbert, and Sanderson. By Isaac Walton. With some account of the author and his writing's... Boston, Hilliard, Gray & Co.; Cambridge, Brown, Shattuck & Co., 1832. 2 vols. KyDC; MdBP; NNS; PHC; RNR.   16948

---- ---- New York, Protestant Episcopal press, 1832. 450 p CtHT; InID; MsJPED; NGH; ViU.
16949
Walton's Vermont Register and Farmer's Almanac... 1833... Montpelier, J. S. Walton [1832] 123 p. Ct; DLC; MHi; MWA; OO.
16950
Wanostrocht, Nicolas, 1745-1812.
A grammar of the French language, with practical exercises by N. Wanostrocht, LL. D., stereotyped from the last London ed. to which is added, a very comprehensive table of contents; and an alphabetical arrangement of the irregular verbs, with reference to the places where they are conjugated with alterations, additions, and improvements; and a scheme for parsing also, a treatise on French versification, by M. De Wailly, member of the National Institute of France, &c. &c. Boston, Carter, Hendee & Co., 1832. 447 p. MH; WGr.   16951

Wardlaw, Ralph, 1779-1853.
A dissertation on the scriptural authority, nature, and uses of infant baptism. By Ralph Wardlaw, D. D. 1st Amer. ed. Boston, Peirce & Parker; New York, H. C. Sleight, 1832. 158 p. CtHC;

ICT; KyLoP; LNB; NjP; OMC;
MeBat; PPPrHi.   16952

Ware, Henry, 1794-1843.
   The combination against intemperance explained and justi-
fied. An address delivered before
the Cambridge Temperance Society, Mar. 27th, 1832. By Henry Ware, jr. Boston, The Boston Temperance Society, 1832. 12
p. CSmH; DLC; ICMe; MH; MdBJ;
NN.   16953

---- ---- 2d ed. Boston, Boston Temperance Society, 1832.
12 p. CtHWatk; MHi; MNtCA;
MPeaI; MWA.   16954

---- ---- 3d ed. Boston, Boston
Temperance Soc., 1832. 12 p.
CBPac; ICU; MH; MHi; NNUT.
                             16955
---- ---- 4th ed. [Boston] The
Boston Temperance Society, 1832.
12 p. Ct; MB; MH; OCIWHi;
PPPrHi.   16956

---- ---- 5th ed. Boston, 1832.
MB.   16957

---- ---- Cambridge, Hilliard
and Brown, 1832. 16 p. DLC;
ICMe; MH; PPPrHi; WHi. 16958

---- The faith once delivered to
the saints. See American Unitarian Association.

---- On the formation of the
Christian character. Addressed
to those who are seeking to lead
a religious life. By Henry Ware,
Jr. 7th ed. Cambridge, Hilliard
and Brown; Boston, Carter and
Hendee, 1832. 176 p. CtHC;
LNH; MH-AH; PPM.   16959

---- ---- 8th ed. Boston, Hilliard, Gray & Co., etc., etc.
1832. 176 p. IP; KyBC; MH;
NbOM; OMC.   16960

---- Outline of the Testimony of
Scripture against the Trinity. By
Henry Ware, Jr. No. 58. 1st
series. American Unitarian Association. Boston, Gray & Bowen,
1832. 22 p. ICMe; MCon; MeB;
NjR; RP.   16961

---- ---- 2d ed. Pr. for the
American Unitarian Association.
Boston, Charles Bowen, 1832.
22 p. CBPac; GHi; ICMe; MMeT;
FDeS.   16962

Ware, William.
   The Antiquity and revival of
Unitarian Christianity. By Willi-
am Ware. 2d ed. Boston, Gray
& Bowen, 1832. 28 p. CBPac;
ICMe; MNF; MeBat; RP. 16963

Ware, Mass. East Evangelical
Church.
   Articles of faith and covenant,
together with a historical sketch
of the East Evangelical Church in
Ware. [Brookfield, 1832] 12 p.
WHi.   16964

[Warner, Aaron]
   Memoir of Florence Kidder,
who died in Medford, Mass.,
April, 1832. Aged eleven years.
Boston, Peirce & Parker; New
York, H. C. Sleight, 1832. 71 p.
DLC; IaDuU-ScM; MBAt; MBC;
MWA.   16965

Warner, Henry Whiting, d. 1875.
   A discourse on legal science,
before the corporation of the
New-York Law Institute. New
York, G. and C. and H. Carvill,
1832. 43 p. PPAmP; ScU. 16966

Warren, Edward, 1804-1878.
   Sketch of The Progress of the
malignant or epidemic cholera,
from its arrival in America...
By Edward Warren, M.D. Boston, Carter, Hendee & Co., 1832.
40 p. DLC; ICMe; MHi; NNNAM;
OC; PPL.   16967

[Warren, Samuel] 1807-1877.
The diary of a late physician.
D. New York, New York, n.p.,
1832. 2 vols. AzPh; KyCov;
MWA.   16968

Washington, George, 1732-1799.
Farewell address to the people of the U.S. Sept., 1796; Centennial anniversary, 1832. Reading, 1832. 1 p. PHi.   16969

---- Valedictory address to the
people of the United States. Pub.
in Sept., A.D. 1796. Pr. in pursuance of a resolution of the Senate of Pennsylvania... Harrisburg,
Pr. by Henry Welsh, 1832. 16 p.
InU; MB; NjR; PLFM; PU. 16970

---- Washington's Abschieds-
addresse an das Volk der Ver-
eingten Staateb; Bekanntgemacht
im September, A.D. 1796... Harrisburg, 1832. 16 p. PHi. 16971

Washington, District of Columbia.
Laws of the corporation of the
City of Washington, passed by
the twenty-ninth Council, 1831-32.
Pr. by order of the Council.
Washington, Pr. by Way & Gid-
eon, 1832. 53 p. IN-SC; MdBB.
                            16972
---- Board of Common Council.
Rules of order for the board
of common council of the City of
Washington... Washington City,
1832. 8 p. MdBJ.   16973

---- Citizens.
Republican meeting of the citizens of Washington City friendly
to the re-election of Andrew Jackson to the presidency July 24,
1832. n.p. 1832. 24 p. WHi.
                            16974
Washington almanac, 1832. Philadelphia, Jos. McDowell [1832]
PHi.   16975

Washington College, Hartford,
Conn. See Trinity College,

Hartford, Conn.

Washington County Grammar
School. Montpelier, Vermont.
Catalogue of the trustees,
teachers and students connected
with the Washington County Grammar School, Montpelier, Vermont,
during the year ending July 25,
1832. Montpelier, Pr. by E. P.
Walton [1832] 8 p.   16976

The Washington literary gazette;
a miscellany of literature and the
fine arts. V.1- Dec. 5, 1832.
Washington, [D. Green] 1832-
Weekly (irregular). DLC; NcD.
                            16977
Washington Lyceum.
Constitution of the Washington
Lyceum. Adopted Nov. 25, 1831.
Washington, P. Force, 1832. 7 p.
MB.   16978

The Washington Society, Charleston, S.C.
Address of the Washington Society to the people of South Carolina. Charleston, Pr. by J.S.
Burges, 1832. 8 p. DLC; MHi;
PU; ScU; TxU.   16979

Washington's birthday centennial
celebration; committee of arrangement, order of procession &c.
Philadelphia, 1832. 1 p. PHi.
                            16980
[Waterbury, Jared Bell] 1799-1876.
Advice to a young Christian
on the importance of aiming at an
elevated standard of piety. By a
village pastor. With an introductory essay, by the Rev. Dr. Alexander, of Princeton, N.J. 6th
ed., rev. and cor. New York,
G. & C. & H. Carvill, 1832. 196
p. MH; MeB; NSyU.   16981

Waterbury, Conn. First Congregational Church.
Articles of faith and church
covenant (with members) 1832.
New Haven, 1832. 32 p. CtSoP.
                            16982

Waterland, Daniel.
Regeneration stated and explained according to scripture and antiquity. By Rev. Daniel Waterland, D. D. 2d Amer. ed. Newburyport, Charles Whipple, 1832. 23 p. LNB; MBC; NNG.
16983

Watkins, N.
Female preaching defended. Added, a sermon: By Miss N. Watkins. Albany, 1832. 24 p. MH-AH; RPB.   16984

Watson, John Fanning, 1780-1860.
Historic tales of olden time; concerning the early settlement and advancement of New York and state. For the use of families and schools. Illus. with plates. New York, Collins & Hannay, 1832. 214 p. MB; MdBS; NNS; OMC; PCC.   16985

Watson, Richard, 1781-1833.
Apology for the Bible, letters addressed to Thomas Paine, author of Age of reason. Also, Leslie's short and easy methods with the deists. New York, Emory, 1832. 226 p. IU; IaDmD; MsJMC.   16986

---- A biblical and theological dictionary, explanatory of the history, manners, and customs of the Jews, and neighbouring nations, with an account of the most remarkable places and persons mentioned in sacred scripture, an exposition of the principal doctrines of Christianity, and, notices of Jewish and Christian sects and heresies. New York, Waugh and Mason, 1832. CBPSR; GHi; NcD; PLT; TJaL.   16987

---- Conversations for the young: designed to promote the profitable reading of the Holy Scriptures. By Richard Watson, author of "Theological institutes,"

&c. from the last London ed....
New-York, B. Waugh & T. Mason, for the Methodist Episcopal Church, Pr. by J. Collord, 1832. 300 p. CtMW; GEU-T; ICBB; MoS; WuU.   16988

---- The life of the Rev. John Wesley...founder of the Methodist societies. By Richard Watson ...1st Amer. official ed., with translations and notes by John Emory. New-York, J. Emory & B. Waugh for the Methodist Episcopal Church, 1832. 323 p. IaBo; KyHi; NNUT; OHi; ViAl.   16989

---- Theological institutes; or A view of the evidences, doctrines, morals and institutions of Christianity. By Richard Watson... Stereotype ed., complete in 1 vol. New-York, J. Emory & B. Waugh for the Methodist Episcopal Church, 1832. 663 p. ArSsJ; InID; MH; NNUT; ViRut.   16990

Watts, Isaac, 1674-1748. See also Bible.

---- Additional hymns to the supplement of Winchell's Watts. Boston, James Loring, & Lincoln & Edmands, 1832. 36 p. MH-AH; MiD-B.   16991

---- An arrangement of the Psalms, Hymns, and spiritual songs of the Rev. Isaac Watts... to which is added, a supplement of more than three hundred hymns of Dr. Watts, adapted to public worship. By James M. Winchell ...Imp. by the addition of two hundred hymns. Boston, J. Loring, etc. [c1832] OCH; OO; PCA; ViRU; WHi.   16992

---- Discourses on the love of God, and its influence on all the passions, with a discovery of the right use and abuse of them in matters of religion. Also, a de-

vout meditation annexed to each
discourse. New York, Turney,
1832. 231 p. GEU-T; ICU; MB;
PCA; WBeloC. 16993

---- First catechism. Philadelphia, L. Johnson, 1832. 8 p.
DLC; MWA; Mi; PPPrHi. 16994

---- A guide to prayer: or A
free and rational account of the
gift, grace and spirit of prayer,
with plain directions how every
Christian may attain them. New
Haven, N. Whiting, 1832. 252 p.
IEG; KWiU; T. 16995

---- The improvement of the
mind; or A supplement to the art
of logic, containing a variety of
remarks and rules for the attain-
ment and communication of useful knowledge in religion, in the
science, and in common life.
Baltimore, J. J. Harrod, 1832.
281 p. AWaJ; MoSU-M; OCh;
PWaybu; ViSwc. 16996

---- ---- To which are added a
discourse on the education of
children and youth; and short essays on various subjects. By
Isaac Watts, D.D New York,
Betts & Anstice, 1832. 396 p.
MAbD; NCH. 16997

---- ---- New York, B. Waugh
& T. Mason, Methodist Episco-
pal Church, 1832. 192 p. CoDI;
CtEhad. 16998

---- ---- With corrections, questions and supplement. By Joseph
Emerson... Rev. stereotype ed.
Boston, J. Loring, 1832. 234 p.
GDC; KyLxT; MiU; OkU; IaB.
16999
---- Second catechism, with
proofs. Philadelphia, L. Johnson,
1832. 47 p. DLC. 17000

Waugh, B. and T. Mason, firm,
publishers.

An alphabetical catalogue of
books published and sold under
the patronage of the Methodist
Episcopal Church by B. Waugh
and T. Mason. New York [1832]
34 p. TxDaM. 17001

Wayland, Francis, 1796-1865.
An Address, delivered before
Providence Association for the
Promotion of Temperance, Oct.
20, 1831. By Francis Wayland,
D.D. President of Brown Univer-
sity. Pub. at the request of the
Board of Managers. 3d ed. Bos-
ton, Lincoln & Edmands, 1832.
24 p. CBPSR; KyLoS; NjR; OCHP;
PCA. 17002

[Wayland, Jane]
Recollections of a beloved sister, addressed to her own children. New York, 1832. NN; RP.
17003
Wayne, [James Moore?]
Speech of Mr. Wayne on the
Panama mission. Washington,
1832. PPL-R. 17004

Webb, George James.
"The moon shines bright."
Boston, 1832. MB. 17005

---- When from the Sacred Gar-
den driven; (aria). The words, an
extract from "Art," written by C.
Sprague. Music composed by G.
J. Webb. Boston [1832?] 5 p.
MH; MNF. 17006

Webber, Samuel, 1797-1880.
An introduction to English
grammar, on an analytical plan,
adapted to the use of students in
colleges and the higher classes
in schools and academies. By
Samuel Webber... Cambridge,
Hilliard and Brown; Boston, Carter & Hendee, 1832. 116 p.
CtHWatk; MH; MsNF; NNC; WU.
17007
Weber, William M.
The Heart Changed By Divine

Grace, or, The Protestant Episcopal Church vindicated in her
views of spiritual influences; in
a letter to the parishioners of
Emmanuel Church, Little Falls.
Auburn, Pr. at the C. K. Society's Press, 1832. 27 p. LNB;
N; PPM.   17008

Webster, Daniel, 1782-1852.
    Speech in the Senate of the
United States, on the President's
Veto of the Bank Bill, July 11,
1832. Boston, I. E. Hinckley &
Co., 1832. 32 p. InU; MH; Nh-
Hi; OO; RPB.   17009

---- Speech of the Hon. Daniel
Webster at the National Republi-
can Convention, in Worcester,
Oct. 12, 1832. Boston, Stimpson,
& Clapp, 1832. 43 p. CtHT;
IaB; MH; NNUT; ScCC.   17010

---- Speeches in the Senate upon
the question of renewing the charter of the bank of the United
States. Delivered May 25, and 28,
1832. Washington, Gales & Seaton, 1832. 16 p. ICU; MdHi; Nh-
Hi; OClWHi; PPL; T.   17011

Webster, James, 1803-1854.
    Facts concerning anatomical in-
struction in Philadelphia. By
James Webster, M. D.... Philadelphia, Feb. 1832. 24 p. IEN-M;
MdBM; NBMS; PHi; PU.   17012

Webster, Noah, 1758-1843.
    An American dictionary of the
English language. 10th ed. New
York, 1832. 1011 p. MH; MiU;
OMC.   17013

---- A dictionary of the English
language. Abridged from the
American dictionary for the use
of primary schools and the count-
ing house. By Noah Webster,
LL. D. New York, N. & J. White,
1832. 537 p. CtMW; MH; Nh;
PWaybu.   17014

---- ---- 9th ed. New York, N.
& J. White, 1832. 536 p. NhD;
RPB.   17015

---- ---- 10th ed. New York,
White, 1832. 536 p. OO; T.
                           17016

---- The elementary spelling
book; being an improvement on
the American spelling book. By
Noah Webster, LL. D. Boston,
Carter, Hendee & Co.; Brattleboro Power press office, 1832.
168 p. NNC.   17017

---- ---- Burlington, Vt., Chauncey Goodrich, 1832. 168 p. NN;
VtU.   17018

---- History of the United States,
to which is prefixed a brief his-
torical account of our [English]
ancestors, from the dispersion at
Babel, to their migration to
America, and of the conquest of
South America, by the Spaniards.
By Noah Webster, LL. D. New
Haven, Durrie & Peck; Louisville,
Ky., Wilcox, Dickerman & Co.,
1832. 324 p. DLC; ICU; LNH;
MBC; NN; WHi.   17019

Webster's calendar of the Albany
almanack for the year of Our
Lord 1833 being (till July 4th) the
fifty-seventh year of American
Independence calculated for the
meridian of Albany, N. Y., by
Edwin E. Prentiss. Albany, Websters & Skinners [1832] 36 p.
DLC; InU; M; MWA; NN.   17020

---- 2d ed. MB; MWA; MnU.
                           17021
Weeks, William Raymond.
    A letter on protracted meet-
ings; addressed to the church in
Paris, by William R. Weeks...
Utica, Press of William Williams,
1832. 16 p. CSmH; DLC; MiU-C;
NjP; PPPrHi.   17022

Weems, Mason Locke, 1760?-1825.

The life of George Washington;
with curious anecdotes equally
honourable to himself, and ex-
emplary to his young country-
men; embellished with six engravings... Philadelphia, Joseph
Allen, 1832. 228 p. CtSoP; KHi;
MnU; OClWHi; PHi.   17023

Welker, Martin.
   Farm life in critical Ohio sixty years ago. Wooster, Clapper,
1832. 36 p. OO.   17024

Wells, Bezaleel.
   An address to the churchmen
of the United States on the difficulties in the diocese of Ohio.
n.p. [1832?] 19 p. MH.   17025

Wells, Charles.
   Inaugural address as Mayor of
Boston, 1832-33. MBC.   17026

Wells, Seth Youngs.
   Thomas Brown and his pre-
tended history of the Shakers.
Correspondence between Seth
Youngs Wells of Shakers, New
York and Professor Benjamin Sil-
liman of Yale College, New Haven.
n.p., n.p., 1832? NBuG. 17027

Welsh, Jane Kilby.
   Familiar lessons in mineralogy and geology, designed for the
use of young persons and lyceums... By Jane Kilby Welsh...
Boston, Clapp & Hull, 1832-33.
2 vols. CoU; MA; NNE; PPAN;
TxH.   17028

Wentworth, Thomas, 1568-1628.
   The office and duty of executors. By Thomas Wentworth...
with the supplement of H. Cur-
son and notes of the late Serjeant
Wilson and others; from the 14th
London ed., rev. by Henry Jeremy... with references to the
English common law reports and
to Amer. decisions by E. D. Ingraham. Philadelphia, P. H.

Nicklin & T. Johnson, 1832.
547 p. CLSU; GU-L; NcD; PPB;
TU.   17029

Wesley, John, 1703-1791.
   An Extract of the Christian's
pattern.... See Imitatio Christi.

---- Imitatio Christi. See under
title.

---- The journal of the Rev.
John Wesley, A.M... first complete... Amer. ed. from the latest
London ed., with the last corrections of the author; comprehending
also numerous translations and
notes, by John Emory. New York,
Emory & B. Waugh, 1832. 2
vols. ICMc; NoCC; NcU, OrBe;
WHi.   17030

---- Sermons on several occa-
sions. By Rev. John Wesley.
New York, J. Emory & B.
Waugh, 1832. 2 vols. GDecA;
MdBD; NcWfc; OO; PLT.   17031

---- The works of the Rev. John
Wesley... 1st Amer. complete and
standard ed., from the latest
London ed., with the last corrections of the author: comprehending also numerous translations,
notes, and an original preface,
&c. by John Emory. New York,
Waugh & Mason, 1832. 7 vols.
ArCH; CLSU; GDC; MnSH; TxGR.
                           17032

West Pennsylvania Synod. See
Evangelical Lutheran Synod of
West Pennsylvania.

Westbrook Seminary and Junior
College. Portland, Me.
   By-laws, Westbrook Seminary,
1831. Portland, Thomas Todd,
1832. 12 p. MeHi.   17033

The western almanac, for 1832:
being leap-year and the 56th-57th
of American independence. Calculated for the meridian of Ro-

chester, and will serve for the western part of New York and Pennsylvania, northern part of Ohio, and Upper Canada. Batavia, Sherman and Parker [1832] 12 l. CSmH. 17034

---- Geneva, J. Bogert, 1832. 12 l. NN. 17035
---- Rochester, Hoyt, Porter & Co., 1832. NRMA. 17036

Western Bank of Philadelphia.
An Act to establish the Western Bank of Philadelphia. Approved April 23, 1832. Philadelphia, Pr. by Peter Hay & Co., 1832. 33 p. P; PPN. 17037

The Western Farmer's Almanac for 1833. Calculated by the Rev. John Taylor. Pittsburgh, Pa., H. Holdship & Son [1832] 36, 36 p. CSmH; DLC; MWA; WHi; WvU. 17038

The Western medical gazette. Conducted by Doctors Eberle, Mitchell, Staughton, and Bailey. [Cincinnati, O.] John Stapleton, Dec. 1832-[April, 1835] CtU-M; DSG; OCIWHi; PLF; TxU. 17039

Western Reserve almanac. Cleveland [1832] MWA. 17040

Western Reserve University, Cleveland, Ohio.
Catalogue of the officers and students of Western Reserve College, December, 1832. n.p., [1832] 8 p. N. 17041

Western shield, and literary messenger. v. 1; Aug. 8, 1832-Nov. 23, 1833. Cincinnati, R. C. Langdon, 1832-33. 416 p. DLC. 17042
Western University of Pennsylvania. See Pittsburgh. University.

Westliche "Vaterlandsfreund"

and Cantoner calender. Canton, Ohio, Peter Kaufmann [1832] MWA. 17043

Westminister Assembly of Divines.
The Assembly's Shorter Catechism. Pittsburgh, 1832. PPiRPr. 17044

---- A key to the shorter catechism; containing catechetical exercises, a paraphrase, and a new and regular series of proofs on each answer. 3d Amer. (stereotyped) from 5th Edinburgh ed. New York, J. Leavitt; Boston, Crocker & Brewster, 1832. 216 p. MBC; NjP; OCIWHi. 17045

Weybosset Bank, Providence.
Charter granted June 1831. Providence, 1832. 8 p. RHi. 17046
Whately, Richard, 1787-1863.
Elements of Logic. Comprising the substance of the article in the encyclopaedia Metropolitana; with additions, &c. By Richard Whatley, D.D. From the 4th London ed. New York, William Jackson, 1832. 335 p. ICU; FDcS; MH; MiU; NjR; PPiW. 17047

---- Elements of rhetoric. Comprising the substance of article in the Encyclopaedia Metropolitana... By Richard Whately, D.D. Cambridge, Brown, Shattuck & Co.; Boston, Hilliard, Gray, and Co., 1832. 347 p. IaHi; KyLoS; MdBD; NNG; OO; PPF. 17048
---- Historic doubts relative to Napoleon Buonaparte. By Richard Whately, D.D... From the 4th London ed. Cambridge, Brown, Shattuck & Co., 1832. 39 p. CtSoP; ICMe; MH; PHi; RP. 17049
Wheaton, Henry, 1785-1848.
Enquiry into the validity of the British claim to a right of visita-

tion and search of American vessels suspected to be engaged in the African slave-trade. By Henry Whaton, LL. D. Philadelphia, Lea & Blanchard, 1832. 151, 12 p. LNH.   17050

Wheelock, Alonzo.
King James' version. A sermon by... Wheelock... for the third anniversary of the American Bible Union... New York, Oct. 10, 1832. New York, American Bible Union [1832?] 20 p. OCIWHi.   17051

[Whelpley, Samuel] 1766-1817.
The triangle: a series of numbers upon three theological points, enforced from various pulpits in the city of New York. By Investigator. New York, O. Halsted, 1832. 396 p. CtMW; DLC; MH-AH; NCH; PPL. 17052

Whig against Tory; or, The military adventures of a shoe maker. A tale of the revolution for children. Hartford, S. Andrus, 1832. 104 p. DLC; ICU; RPB.   17053

White, Gilbert, 1720-1793.
The natural history of Selborne. By the late Rev. Gilbert White, A. M. , fellow of Oriel College. Oxford. With additions by Sir William Jardine. Philadelphia, Carey & Lea, 1832. 342 p. GAuY; ICJ; MdW; PReaHi; TNP; ViRu.   17054

White, Hugh Lawson, 1773-1840.
Speeches in the Senate of the United States, June 1832, on the bill to re-charter the Bank of the United States. Washington, 1832. 22 p. DLC; PU; T; WHi. 17055

White, James.
A complete system of farriery. 2d Amer. ed. from 10th London ed. Pittsburg, Henry Holdship & Son, 1832. NIC-V.   17056

[White, Josiah]
To the committee on corporations of the Senate (re. complaints against the Lehigh Coal and Navigation Company). [Harrisburg, Pr. by Hamilton & Son, 1832] 12 p. MH-BA; P.   17057

White, Seneca.
Ki noh shuh, nr wen ne un, na da wi sem nyo qurh. nas hr ne a nent yo yot dub, gr non no noh ka. do shoo wl da ku, skr a, noh da wen nyer a, sehne use has he na, tik ne, skr a. By Seneca White, Pr. at the Republican Press, 1832. 45 p.
17058

White, Thomas.
Treatise on the diseases of the teeth, and the cause of those diseases, with directions for preventing their occurrence. Lexington, Ky. , Savary & Co. , 1832. 23 p. ICU; UofPDent.   17059

White, William, 1748-1836.
The case of the Episcopal Churches in the United States considered... Philadelphia, David C. Claypoole, 1832. 35 p. DLC; MB.   17060

---- An Episcopal charge, on the subject of revivals, delivered before the forty-eighth convention of the diocese of Pennsylvania, and address to the clerical members of the convention. Philadelphia, J. Harding, 1832. 21 p. MH; NGH; NNG; NNUT; ScU.
17061

---- ---- Wilmington, Repr. by J. Newton Harker, 1832. 19 p. N.   17062

---- Of the increase of the church, a sermon preached before the Domestic and foreign missionary society of the Protestant Episcopal Church... Oct. 22, 1832... New York, Protestant Episcopal Press, 1832. 20 p.

MdBD; NNG; PHi; RPB.   17063

---- A sermon on the beneficial
influence of the gospel ministry:
delivered before the convention of
the Protestant Episcopal Church
of the State of Delaware, on the
9th day of June 1832. Pr. at the
request of the convention. Wilmington, Del., Pr. by R. & J.
B. Porter, 1832? 16 p. DeWi;
N; NGH; PHi.   17064

Whitehead, George, 1636-1723.
   Memoirs of George Whitehead;
a minister of the Gospel in the
Society of Friends... written by
himself, and published after his
decease, in the year 1725.... al-
so introductory observations.
By Samuel Tuke... Philadelphia,
Nathan Kite, 1832. 2 vols. MH;
NcD; PPF; OO.   17065

Whitman, Bernard, 1796-1834.
   Address delivered May 30,
A.D. 1832, at the dedication of
the Masonic Temple in Boston.
By Bernard Whitman. Cambridge,
E. W. Metcalf & Co., 1832. 44 p.
CtHT; DLC; IaCrM; MH; NNUT.
                         17066
---- An answer to "Eliphalet
Pearson's letter to the candid."
By Bernard Whitman. Boston,
Christian Register office, 1832.
32 p. CBPSR; ICU; MH; NNUT;
RPB.   17067

---- Village sermons: doctrinal
and practical. By Bernard Whitman. Boston, Leonard C. Bowles,
1832. 292 p. CBPac; IEG; MH;
NhPet; RPB.   17068

Whitman, Ezekiel, 1776-1866.
   Memoir of John Whitman and
his descendants. By Ezekiel Whit-
man. Portland, Charles Day &
Co., 1832. 44 p. DLC; MB; Nh-
Hi; OClWHi; PPM.   17069

Whitman, Jason, 1799-1848.

An address delivered before
the York County Temperance Society at Alfred, Feb. 15, 1832.
By Jason Whitman, pastor of the
second parish in Saco. Saco, W.
J. Condon, 1832. 24 p. MH; MWA;
NNUT.   17070

---- Religious excitement not the
result of special divine influence.
A sermon, preached at the ordi-
nation of the Rev. Edward H.
Edes; as minister of the First
Congregational Society in Eastport,
Me., Nov. 15, 1831. Boston,
Bowles, 1832. 72 p. CBPac; MB;
MPiB; NNUT; RPB.   17071

Whitney, Reuben M., d. 1845.
   Memorial to the honorable
House of Representatives United
States, in relation to the charges
made against him, as a witness
before the committee of investigation into the affairs of the Bank
of the United States. Washington,
1832. 52 p. MWA; PHi; OCl; ScU;
WHi.   17072

Whittemore, Thomas, 1800-1861.
   Notes and illustrations of the
parables of the New-Testament,
arranged according to the time in
which they were spoken. By
Thomas Whittemore. Boston, Pub.
by the author, 1832. 277, (2) p.
DLC; KKcBT; MiU; NCH; OHi.
                         17073
---- Parable of New Testament.
Boston, Pub. by the author, 1832.
381 p. GMar; NSyU.   17074

---- A sermon delivered at the
funeral of the Rev. Alfred V.
Bassett, pastor of the Universalist Society in Dedham. Boston,
Pr. at the Trumpet Office, 1832.
(3), 4-16 p. MMeT; MW; Nh-Hi;
RPB.   17075

[Whittier, John Greenleaf] 1807-
1892.
   Molly Pitcher. A poem...

Boston, Carter & Hendee, 1832.
27 p. CSt; DLC; MBAt; PHC;
TxU; WHi.					17076

Whittingham, William R.
	A sermon preached in St.
Luke's Church, New York, on
Friday, Aug. 3, 1832, the day of
public humiliation and prayer...
by the Rev. Wm. R. Whittingham,
A.M. ...New-York, Pr. at the
Protestant Episcopal Press, 1832.
38 p. InID; MWA; NNG; NNNAM;
PPPrHi.					17077

Whittlesey, Frederic, 1799-1851.
	Abduction and murder of Wil-
liam Morgan. An interesting and
authentic narrative of the abduc-
tion and probable murder of Wil-
liam Morgan, by Free-masons, in
the state of New York, Sept. 1826.
Being the report of a committee,
appointed by the National Anti-
Masonic Convention, assembled at
Philadelphia, Sept. 11, 1830.
Hallowell, Pr. at the Maine Free
Press Office, 1832. 24 p. MWA.
					17078
Whittlesey, Joseph.
	Sermon on the disease of Mrs.
Sarah Palmer. New York, 1832.
16 p. MBC.					17079

Wickliffe, Robert, 1775-1859.
	The Shakers. Speech of Robert
Wickliffe. In the Senate of Ken-
tucky--Jan. 1831. On a bill to repeal an act of the General Assembly of the state of Kentucky,
entitled "an act to regulate civil
proceedings against certain com-
munities having property in common." [Frankfort, Ky., A. G.
Hodges, 1832] 32 p. Ct; ICN;
MPiB; NBuG; WHi.					17080

Wilcox, Richard.
	To the President of the United
States, and the members of both
Houses of Congress, on the sub-
ject of the tariff. By Richard
Wilcox, Engineer, City of New-

York. [New York, 1832?] 8 p.
DLC; NN.					17081

[Wilcox, Thomas] 1622-1687.
	Choice drops of honey from
the rock Christ. Exeter (N.H.),
Stephen H. Piper, 1832. 9-98 p.
MB; NhD.					17082

---- ---- New-Haven, Jeremy L.
Cross, 1832. [9]-96 p. CtY; MB.
					17083
Wilde, Richard Henry, 1789-1849.
	Speech of Mr. Wilde, of Geor-
gia, on the bill to alter and
amend the several acts imposing
duties on imports. Delivered in
the House of Representatives, on
the 12th and 13th days of June,
1832. Washington, Pr. by Gales
& Seaton, 1832. 36 p. MWA;
MdHi; TxU.					17084

---- Speech on the currency, delivered in the House of Representatives, on the 20th & 21st of
March, 1832. [Washington, 1832]
24 p. DLC; MB; MWA; OC1FRB;
WHi.					17085

Wilder, James Humphrey.
	An oration delivered at the re-
quest of the young men of Hingham...Hingham, J. Farmer,
1832. 36 p. MHing; RPB.	17086

Wilkins, John Hubbard, 1794-
1861.
	Elements of astronomy, illus-
trated with plates, for the use of
schools and academies, with questions. By John H. Wilkins, A.M.
Stereotype ed. Boston, Hilliard,
Gray, Little & Wilkins, 1832.
152 p. CU; ICBB; IaU; InHan;
NjP.					17087

Wilkins, William, 1778-9-1865.
	An address delivered before the
Literary societies of Jefferson
College, at the annual commence-
ment, Sept. 27, 1832. By the
Hon. Wm. Wilkins. Pittsburgh,

Pr. by D. & M. Maclean, 1832.
22 p. DLC; KyLx; PHi; PWW;
ScU; ViU.   17088

Willard, Emma (Hart), 1787-
1870.
Abridgment of the History of
the United States; or, Republic of
America. Accompanied with maps.
By Emma Willard. New York,
N. & J. White, 1832. 300 p.
NTEW.   17089

[Willard, Samuel] 1776-1859.
Essays on the philosophy of instruction, or The nurture of
young minds. Greenfield, A.
Phelps, 1832. 41 p. MH; PHi.
                17090
---- General class book; or, Interesting lessons in prose and
verse on a great variety of subjects; combined with an epitome
of English orthography and pronunciation... By the author of the
Franklin Primer and the Improved
reader. 6th ed. Greenfield, Mass.,
A. Phelps; Boston, Carter, Hendee & Co.; Crocker & Brewster;
New York, David Felt and J. & N.
White, 1832. 324 p. MNF; MNHi.
                17091
Willets, Jacob.
The scholar's arithmetic.
Poughkeepsie, P. Potter, 1832.
191 p. MiU.   17092

William Prince & Son, Flushing,
L. I.
Annual catalogue of fruit and
ornamental trees and plants, cultivated at the Linnaean botanic
garden and nurseries, 1832-33.
Providence, W. Marshall & Co.,
1832. 1 vol. KyDC; RP.   17093

William Weston; or The reward of
perseverance. Hingham, C. & E.
B. Gill. Boston, Leonard C.
Bowles, 1832. 123 p. DLC; ICBB.
                17094
Williams, Ara.
A universal vocabulary of prop-

er names, ancient and modern together with classes of people, religious, national, and philosophical, and titles, ecclesiastical and
civil among Christians, Jews,
Mahometans, and Pagans... Cincinnati, E. Deming, 1832. 536 p.
InEvC; InU; LNH; OO.   17095

Williams, Benjamin P.
An address delivered at the
dedication of the School house
called Eliot Hall on Jamaica Plain.
By Benjamin P. Williams. Boston, Gray & Bowen, 1832. 24 p.
ICMe; ICN; MBNEH; MH; MWA.
                17096
Williams, Catherine Read (Arnold), 1790-1872.
Aristocracy; or, The Holbey
family; a national tale... By Mrs.
C. R. Williams... Providence,
Pr. by J. Knowles, 1832. 312 p.
DLC; ICU; MnU; PU; TxDaM.
                17097
Williams, Edward Vaughan, 1797-
1875.
A treatise on the law of executors and administrators. By Edward Vaughan Williams... with
notes and references to the de-
cisions of the courts of this coun-
try, by Francis J. Troubat...
Philadelphia, R. H. Small, 1832.
2 vols. CoU; ICLaw; Ky; NcU;
TxU.   17098

Williams, Edwin, 1797-1854.
The new universal gazeteer or
geographical dictionary, derived
from the latest & best authorities,
being part 2 of, The treasury of
knowledge and library of reference... New York, James Conner,
1832. 432 p. DLC; MPiB; NBu;
OHi; PPL.   17099

---- The Politician's Manual; or,
Statistical Tables. Prepared by
Edwin Williams. 2d ed. New York,
Wm. Stodart, 1832. 36 p. DLC;
MB; MH; PHi.   17100

---- United States Tariff. The
new tariff act, or rates of duties
on imports into the United States.
Passed July, 1832. With an alphabetical arrangement of articles,
and comparative rates of duties
thereon, by the Tariffs of 1828
& 1833. Prepared by Edwin Williams...2d ed. New York, Pr.
by Elliott & Hegeman, 1832. 36,
2 p. MWA; NN.   17101

Williams, James R.
    A treatise on the institution,
nature, and design of the Lord's
Supper. Baltimore, John J. Harrod, 1832. 84 p. LNB; MWA;
MeBP.   17102

Williams, John, 1792-1858.
    The life and actions of Alex-
ander the Great. By the Rev. J.
Williams, A.M. New York,
J. & J. Harper, 1832. 351 p.
MWo; NPtw; OAsht; TN; VtBrt.
                           17103
Williams, Thomas, 1787-1846.
    Missionaries to be wise and
harmless. A sermon delivered
in Wiscasset, June 27, 1832, be-
fore the Maine Missionary Soci-
ety, at their 25th anniversary.
By Thomas Williams, pastor of
the Congregational Church in
Foxcroft. Portland, Pr. by A.
Shirley, 1832. 48 p. CBPSR;
MBC; MH; MWA; MeBat.   17104

---- Sermons in a series of vol-
umes, by Thomas Williams, Vol.
II. Providence, Marshall &
Brown, 1832. 352 p. MBeHi;
MH; MeBat; PLT.   17105

Williams' Calendar, or the Utica
Almanack for 1833. Astronomi-
cal calculations by Edwin E.
Prentiss. Utica, N.Y., William
Williams [1832] 32 p. MWA; NHi;
NN; NUt; WHi.   17106

Williams College. Williamstown,
Mass.

Catalogue of the officers and
students of Williams College, and
of the Berkshire Medical institution connected with it, Oct. 1832.
[Pittsfield, 1832] 8 p. NNNAM;
OCHP.   17107

Williamson, William Durkee,
1779-1846.
    The history of the state of
Maine; from its first discovery,
A.D. 1602 to the separation A.D.
1820 inclusive. By Wm. D. Williamson... Hallowell [Me.] Glazier, Masters & Co. 1832. 2 vols.
CtSoP; ICN; LU; MB; MeAu.
                           17108
Williamstown, Mass. First Congregational Church.
    Articles of faith and form of
covenant. Williamstown, 1832.
24 p. MBC.   17109

Willis, William, 1794-1870.
    An address to the Teachers
of the Sunday school in the First
Parish, Portland. Delivered June
2, 1832. Portland, Pub. by request of the teachers, 1832. 23 p.
CBPac; ICMe; MH; MeHi. 17110

Willison, John, 1680-1750.
    An example of plain catechiz-
ing, upon the assembly's shorter
catechism... By the Rev. Mr.
John Willison. Pittsburg, J. Wilson, 1832. 288 p. ICP; IEG;
MWA; PPPrHi; PPins.   17111

Willson, James Renwick, 1780-
1853.
    Prince Messiah's claims to
dominion over all governments;
and the disregard of his authority
by the United States in the Federal constitution. Albany, Packard, 1832. 48 p. MBC; NCH; NN;
NjR; PPPrHi; RPB.   17112

Wilson, Caroline (Fry), 1787-
1846.
    The Listener, by Caroline
Fry, author of "The Assistant of

Education. " &c. From the 2d
London ed. rev. Philadelphia,
Latimer & Co. , 1832. 2 vols.
MH; NT; PPA; RP; ViAL.   17113

Wilson, Daniel, 1778-1858.
The evidences of Christianity;
stated in a popular and practical
manner, in a course of lectures,
(on the authenticity, credibility,
devine authority, and inspiration
of the New Testament) delivered
in the parish church of St. Mary,
Islington... Boston, Crocker &
Brewster; New York, J. Leavitt,
1832. 2 vols. MiU.   17114

Wilson, John.
The history of Switzerland,
from B. C. 110 to A. D. 1830. By
John Wilson. Philadelphia, Carey
& Lea, 1832. 288 p. CtHT; IP;
PPA; TxU; WvW.   17115

Wilson, Thomas, 1663-1755.
Sacra privata, or The private
meditations and prayers of Thomas Wilson. To which is added,
A short introduction for the true
understanding of the Lord's Supper. Philadelphia, Towar & Hogan, etc. , etc. , 1832. 187 p.
ICP; MDeeP; MH; PPL; ScCMu.
                          17116
Winchell, James Manning, 1791-
1820.
An arrangement of the psalms,
hymns, and spiritual songs of the
Rev. Isaac Watts... See Watts,
Isaac, 1674-1748.

Winchester and Potomac Rail
Road Co.
First annual report of the
president and directors... Win-
chester, Office of the Winchester
Virginian, 1832. 48 p. MH-BA;
MdHi; NN.   17117

Winebrenner, John, 1797-1860.
A prayer meeting and revival
hymn book or a selection of the
best psalms and hymns and spir-

itual songs from various authors,
for the use of social prayer meetings and revivals of religion.
6th ed. , enl. By John Winebrenner, V. D. M. Harrisburg, Pr.
by Jacob Baab, 1832. 406, (16) p.
RPB.   17118

Wines, Enoch Cobb, 1806-1879.
Two years and a half in the
navy: or, Journal of a cruise in
the Mediterranean and Levant,
on board of the U. S. frigate Constellation, in the years 1829,
1830, and 1831. By E. C. Wines.
Philadelphia, Carey & Lea, 1832.
2 vols. IP; MH; Nj; PPA; Vi.
                          17119
Winslow, George Erving.
Essay on the nature, symptoms, and treatment of Asiatic
cholera. New York, Sleight &
Robinson, 1832. 70 p. MdUM;
NBMS; OCHP; PaHosp; ScU.
                          17120
Winslow, Hubbard.
A compendious history of the
First parish in Dover; taken from
the sermons preached on the
first Sabbath in January, 1831,
by Rev. H. Winslow... Dover,
(N. H.), C. C. P. Moody, 1832.
16 p. Nh; Nh-Hi.   17121

Winthrop, Grenville Temple.
Trial by a court martial of
Lieut. Col. Grenville Temple
Winthrop, on charges preferred
against him by Adjutant Gen. Wil-
liam H. Sumner, in pursuance of
orders from... Levi Lincoln, gov-
ernor of the commonwealth of
Massachusetts... Boston, Carter,
Hendee, 1832. 456 p. Ct; M;
OCLaw; PPB; Vi; W.   17122

Wirt, Mrs. Elizabeth Washington
(Gamble), 1784-1857.
Flora's dictionary, by a lady.
Baltimore, Lucas, 1832. 192 p.
CSmH; LNH; MoS; RPB; TxU.
                          17123
Wirt, William, 1772-1834.

The letters of the British spy.
By William Wirt... 10th ed. rev.
and cor. To which is prefixed a
biographical sketch of the author.
New York, J. & J. Harper, 1832.
GDC; KU; OMC; PPA; TxU; WHi.
                              17124
---- Sketches of the life and character of Patrick Henry, by William Wirt of Richmond, Virginia;
5th ed., cor. by the author. New
York, McElrath & Bangs, 1832.
443 p. GEU; KyU; MAnP; PU;
WaSp.   17125

[Wisner, Benjamin Blydenburg]
1794-1835.
  Review of "The new divinity
tried" or An examination of Rev.
Mr. Rand's strictures on a ser-
mon delivered by the Rev. C. G.
Finney, on Making a new heart.
Boston, Peirce & Parker, 1832.
44 p. Ct; KyDC; MBC; MH;
MWA; PPPrHi.   17126

[Wistar Institute of Anatomy and
Biology, Philadelphia.]
  Catalogue of the Anatomical
museum of the University of
Pennsylvania, with a report to
the Museum committee of the
trustees. Nov. 1832. ..2d ed.
Philadelphia, L. R. Bailey, 1832.
                              17127
Witherspoon, Mr.
  Speech of Mr. Witherspoon delivered in the House of Representatives, of the State of Alabama, Dec. 1832... (N. p., 1832?)
16 p. ScU.   17128

Withington, Leonard, 1789-1885.
  Puritan morals defended: a
discourse delivered at the dedication of the Crombie Street Church
in Salem... and the installation of
the Rev. William Williams, Nov.
22, 1832. Salem, Mass., Warwick Palfray, 1832. 36 p. IEG;
MBC; NjR; RPB; WHi.   17129

---- The soul of man, a sermon

preached at the Tabernacle
Church, Salem, Mass., April 22,
1832. By Leonard Withington...
Pub. by request of the Tabernacle Church, Salem, Whipple &
Lawrence, Pr. by J. H. Buckingham, Newburyport, 1832. 22 p.
Ct; ICMe; M; MHi; OO; WHi.
                              17130
Withy, George.
  An affectionate farewell address to Friends in North America... New-York, Mahlon Day,
1832. NHi.   17131

Woburn [Mass.] Association for
the Promotion of Temperance.
  Constitution. Rules and regulations of the Woburn Association
for the Promotion of Temperance.
Boston, Press of Peirce & Parker, 1832. 16 p. MWo.   17132

---- First Congregational Church.
  Regulations of First Congrega-
tional Church in Woburn. Charles-
town Square, Pr. by William W.
Wheildon, 1832. 14 p. MWo.
                              17133
Wood, George, 1789-1860.
  Opinions of George Wood and
Nathaniel Saxton, Esq., as to the
question whether the New Hope,
Delaware bridge company have
banking privileges. New York,
Sleight & Robinson, pr., 1832.
16 p. NjR.   17134

---- The Society of Friends vindicated: being the arguments of the
counsel of Joseph Hendrickson,
in a cause decided in the Court
of Chancery of the state of New
Jersey, between Thomas L.
Shotwell, complainant, and Joseph Hendrickson and Stacy Decow,
defendants. By George Wood and
Isaac H. Williamson, counsellors
at law. To which is appended the
decision of the court. Trenton,
N.J., P. J. Gray, 1832. 167,
90 p. Ct; DLC; MB; MWA; PPA.
                              17135

Wood, John.
  First book for primary
schools. Boston, Munroe and
Francis, 1832. 120 p. CtY; MH.
                              17136
Wood, Nicholas.
  A practical treatise on rail-
roads and interior communication
in general.... By Nicholas Wood.
1st Amer., from 2d London ed.
Philadelphia, Carey & Lea, 1832.
600 p. DLC; GHi; ICJ; MoKU;
RPB; ViU.   17137

Wood, Samuel.
  Addresses for Sunday Schools
by the Rev. Samuel Wood, B. A.
from the London ed. Boston, B.
H. Greene, 1832. 152 p. ICBB;
MB; MeBat; MH.   17138

Wood, Thomas.
  Germs of thought; or Rudiments of knowledge intended to
promote mental & religious improvement of youth. New York,
Waugh and T. Mason, 1832. 212 p.
NSyU; OO.   17139

[Woodbridge, W. C.]
  Report of the committee on the
propriety of studying the Bible in
the institutions of a Christian
country, presented to the Literary
Convention at New York. Boston,
1832. 24 p. MBC; MidbC; Vt.
                              17140
Woodbridge, William Channing,
1794-1845.
  Rudiments of geography, on a
new plan designed to assist the
memory by comparison and classification. Accompanied with an
atlas; by William C. Woodbridge.
A new ed., enl., cor., and imp.
Hartford, Oliver D. Cooke & Co.,
1832. 208 p. DLC; OClWHi;
PWcHi.   17141

---- ---- 15th ed., with preparatory lessons for beginners. Hartford, Oliver D. Cooke, & Co.,
1832. vi, 208 p. front. MFHi;

MH; NjR; OClWHi.   17142

---- ---- 16th ed., enl., cor.,
and imp. with preparatory lessons,
a series of questions, etc. Hartford, Cooke, 1832. 208 p. PP.
                              17143
---- School atlas; an improved
edition in which the four quarters
of the globe are drawn on the
same scale and appear in their
natural connection and comparative size; with additional maps,
questions, etc. Atlas on a new
plan exhibiting the prevailing religions, forms of government, degrees of civilization and comparative size of towns, rivers, and
mountains. 15th ed. Hartford,
Oliver D. Cooke & Co, 1832.
CtY; Nh.   17144

---- A system of universal geog-
raphy, on the principles of com-
parison and classification. 4th ed.
Hartford, Oliver D. Cooke & Co.,
1832. 336, 4, 24 p. ICPNA; TNP.
                              17145
Woods, Alva.
  Address to the students of the
University of Alabama, delivered
December 19, 1832. (Tuscaloosa?
1832?) 7 p. AU; MH.   17146

Wood's Almanac for 1833. Calcu-
lations by Joshua Sharp. New
York, Samuel Wood & Sons [1832]
DLC; MWA; NNA; NHi; PPL-R.
                              17147
Woonsocket Company.
  Charter of the Woonsocket
Company granted by the General
Assembly Jan. 1832. Providence,
Pr. by William Marshall & Co.,
1832. 4 p. MH-BA; RHi. 17148

Worcester, Henry Aiken.
  A dissertation on The Principles
of Moral Government and the
Atonement. By... Boston, John
Allen, 1832. 27 p. MBC; OUrC;
PBa.   17149

Worcester 519

Worcester, Joseph Emerson, 1784-1865.
A comprehensive pronouncing and explanatory dictionary of the English language, with pronouncing vocabularies of classical and Scripture proper names. Burlington, C. Goodrich, 1832. 400 p. CL; VtMidSM. 17150

---- Elements of geography, with an atlas. Ancient and modern. New ed. Boston, Hilliard, Gray & Co., 1832. 324 p. DLC; ICP; KyBvU; MB; MH; NNMuCN. 17151

---- Elements of history, ancient and modern: with historical charts. By J. E. Worcester. Boston, Hilliard, Gray, Little & Wilkins, 1832. 403 p. MB; NcSalL. 17152

---- Modern atlas. Boston, Hilliard, Gray & Co. [1832] MH. 17153

Worcester, Leonard.
An address on female education. Delivered at Newark, Mar. 28, 1832. By Leonard Worcester ... [Newark, N.J., 1832] 16 p. DLC; ICMe; NNUT. 17154

Worcester, Noah.
A friendly review of remarkable extracts and popular hypothesis relating to the sufferings of Christ. By Noah Worcester... Cambridge, Hilliard and Brown, 1832. 55 p. IEG; MB; MHi; Nh-Hi; NNUT. 17155

Worcester, Samuel, 1793-1844.
A primer of the English language for the use of families and schools. Hallowell, Glazier, Masters & Co., 1832. 72 p. MB; MH. 17156

---- The Psalms, Hymns and Spiritual song of Rev. Isaac Watts. See Watts, Isaac, 1674-1748.

---- Remarks on several common errors concerning the writings of

Emanuel Swedenburg; contained principally in two pamphlets, which are used for opposing the new Jerusalem. Boston, John Allen, 1832. 76 p. IEG; MBC; MeBat; Nh-Hi; PBa; PCC. 17157

---- A second book for reading and spelling. New ed. Boston, Richardson, Lord and Holbrook, 1832. 144 p. MH. 17158

---- A third book for reading and spelling, with simple rules and instructions for avoiding common errors. Boston, Carter & Hendee, 1832. 240 p. DLC; MLy; OMC; RPB. 17159

Worcester, Samuel Austin, 1798-1859.
Cherokee hymns compiled from several authors and revised. By S. A. Worcester and E. Boudinot. ...Pr. for the American Board of Commissioners for Foreign Missions. 3d ed. New Echota [Ga.], John Candy, 1832. DLC. 17160

Worcester, Samuel Thomas, 1804-1882.
Sequel to spelling book. Boston, Lilly, Wait, Colman & Holden, 1832. MH. 17161

Worcester [Mass.] County Auxiliary Colonization Society.
Report of the managers of the Worcester County Auxiliary Colonizing Society, at the annual meeting, held in Worcester, Dec. 14, 1832. Worcester, M. Spooner, and Co., 1832. 12 p. MWA; MdBJ; MiU; NNC; PHi. 17162

---- Baptist Church.
Articles of Faith and Covenant, adopted by several Baptist Churches in the County of Worcester, Pr. by Moses W. Grout, 1832. 23 p. MWA; MNtcA; MWHi; MiD-B; NRAB; RNHi. 17163

---- Mutual Fire Society.
    Constitution. See under the
Society.

---- West Association.
    A manual of family prayers,
prepared by the association.
Brookfield, 1832. 72 p. MH-AH.
                            17164

Worcester Agricultural Society.
    Catalogue of members of The
Worcester Agricultural Society.
Incorporated in 1833. Arranged
by towns. Worcester, Pr. by
Moses W. Grout, 1832. 34 p.
MWA; MWH.   17165

Working-man's calendar for 1833.
Concord, Marsh, Capen, and
Lyon [1832] MWA; NhHi.   17166

The Working-Man's Companion.
The rights of industry: addressed
to the Working-men of the United
Kingdom, by the author of "The
Results of Machinery." 1st Amer.
ed. Philadelphia, Carey & Hart;
Boston, Carter, Hendee & Bab-
cock, 1832. 213 p. ICU; MWA;
Mi; NBP; NjR.   17167

Working-men's Shield. See
Western Shield and Literary Messenger.

Wright, Elizur.
    A lecture on tobacco, deliv-
ered in the chapel of the Western
Reserve College, Hudson, O.,
May 29, 1832. Cleveland, Pr. by
order of the students, 1832. 14 p.
C.   17168

Wright, Joshua Grainger.
    Oration delivered 4th July,
A.D. 1832, at the Presbyterian
Church in Wilmington, N.C. Wil-
mington, 1832. 12 p. NcU.
                            17169
Wright, Samuel Osgood.
    An historical discourse deliv-
ered at Malden, Mass., on

Thanksgiving Day, Dec. 1, 1831.
Sketch of the history of that town
from its settlement to the present time. Boston, Light & Harris,
1832. 36 p. MBAt; MHi; Nh-Hi;
RPB; WHi.   17170

Wright, Theodore S.
    Pastoral letter addressed to
the Colored Presbyterian Church
in the city of New York. New
York, Sears, 1832. 8 p. PPPrHi.
                            17171
Wylie, Andrew.
    An address delivered to the
graduates in Indiana college, at
the late commencement, by A.
Wylie, D.D. president. Bloomington, Ia., 1832. 8 p. In; InU.
                            17172
Wylie, Samuel B.
    Two sons of oil; or, The faith-
ful witness for magistracy &
ministry upon a scriptural basis.
Montgomery, N.Y., Thomas,
1832. 96 p. PPPrHi.   17173

Wyman, William.
    A new collection of select
hymns; for worship in prayer,
conference, and camp meetings.
Lowell, 1832. MB.   17174

Wyss, Johann David, 1743-1818.
    ...The Swiss family Robinson;
or, Adventures of a father and
mother and four sons on a desert
island... New York, Harper,
1832. 2 vols. CtHT; ICU; NcD;
ScCliTO; TJoV.   17175

                X Y Z

Yale University.
    Catalogue of books belonging
to the Society of Brothers in Uni-
ty. Yale College, Sept. 1832.
New Haven, Pr. by Whitmore &
Minor, 1832. 39 p. CtY; MB;
PPAmP.   17176

---- Catalogue of officers and

students in Yale College 1832-
33. New Haven, Pr. by Baldwin & Treadway Co. [1832] 32 p.
MeAug; NIC; PPL; PPPrHi.
17177
---- A catalogue of the members
of the Linonian Society of Yale
College. New Haven, Pr. by
Whitmore & Minor, 1832. 30 p.
Ct; DLC; MB; MH; NjR; PPAmP.
17178
---- Catalogues of the officers
and graduates...1832. New Haven,
1832. NIC.   17179

---- Catalogus...in Collegio
Yalensi, Novi Portus... Hezekia
Howe et soc., typographis
(1832) 78 p. MeHi.   17180

---- Dec. 20, 1832. Sir - On the
27th day of November, 1832, the
presidents of three banks...de-
cided...that the several subscrip-
tions are...obligatory...[New
Haven, Yale College, 1832] 2 l.
CtY.   17181

---- Directions and regulations
relative to Yale College wood and
woodyards. [New Haven? 1832]
broadside. CtY.   17182

---- The laws of Yale College
enacted by presidents and fellows.
New Haven, Pr. by Baldwin and
Treadway, 1832. 45 p. Ct; CtY;
MeAug; MeBat; NjP.   17183

---- Regulations of the South
hall, Yale College. [New Haven?
1832] broadside. CtY.   17184

---- A statement of facts per-
taining to the case of Yale College... [New Haven? 1832] 4 p.
CtY.   17185

---- To the citizens of New Haven.
It is now generally known, that
during the late year, a plan was
formed and put into operation, to
raise, by private donations, an

adequate fund for Yale College...
[New Haven? 1832] broadside.
CtY.   17186

The Yankee; or Farmer's Almanack for 1833. By Thomas Spofford. Boston, Willard Felt &
Co. [1832] MWA; MPeHi; WaSP;
WHi.   17187

Yates, Christopher C.
Observations on the epidemic
now prevailing in the city of New
York, called the Asiatic or spasmodic cholera; with advice to the
planters of the south, for the
medical treatment of their slaves.
2d ed., to which is added...New
York, Collins & Hannay, 1832.
57 p. MWA; NjR; OCGHM; PU;
RNR.   17188

Young, Alexander, 1800-1854.
Evangelical Unitarianism
adapted to The poor and un-
learned. By Alexander Young.
Boston, Gray & Bowen, 1832.
20 p. ICMe; MiGr.   17189

---- ---- 2d ed. Boston, Gray,
and Bowen, 1832. 28 p. CSPac;
ICMe; MB-FA; MB-HP; MMeT-
Hi.   17190

Young, James Hamilton.
Mitchell's travellers guide
through the United States. See
under Mitchell, Samuel Augustus.

Young, John Radford, 1799-1885.
An elementary treatise on Algebra, theoretical and practical:
with attempts to simplify some of
the more difficult parts of the
science...By J. R. Young, 1st
Amer. ed., with additions and
improvements: by Samuel Ward,
jr. Philadelphia, Carey & Lea,
1832. 352 p. CtMW; IU; MH; PU;
ViU.   17191

Young, Samuel, 1789-1850.
Considerations on the Bank of

the United States; in which its repugnance to the Constitution, its hostility to the rights of the states and the liberties of the citizen, are briefly discussed. Albany, Pr. by Packard & Van Benthuysen, 1832. 30 p. CtY; ICU; MH-BA; MWA; NN; T. 17192

The young lady's own book: A manual of intellectual improvement and moral deportment. By the author of The young man's own book. Philadelphia, Key, Miekle & Biddle, 1832. 361 p. ICMe; MH; PU; Mi; TxU; WyU. 17193

The young man's own book: a manual of politeness, intellectual improvement and moral deportment, calculated to form the character on a solid basis, and to insure respectability and success in life... Philadelphia, Key, Meikle and Biddle, 1832. 320 p. CtMW; MB; MH; OCl; PPi. 17194

The Young Mechanic. See Boston mechanic and journal of the useful arts and sciences.

The Young men's advocate. v. 1; Feb. 23, 1832-Feb. 14, 1833. New York, For the New-York young men's society by M'Elrath & Bangs [etc.] 1832-33. 17195

The Young Voyager to the south seas... New Haven, Hezekiah Howe & Co., and Whitmore & Minor for Durrie & Peck, 1832. 2 vols. MH; PP. 17196

Youngs, James, comp.
A history of the most interesting events in the rise and progress of the Methodism in Europe and America... 2d ed. New Haven, Daniel McLeod, 1832. 468 p. OClWHi. 17197

Youth's companion, and weekly family visitor; New York. April 1,

1832-March 22, 1834. DLC; IaHi; MWA; NjN; NjR. 17198

The Youth's instructer in natural history. New York, E. Bliss, 1832. 7 v. DLC; MLex. 17199

Youth's literary gazette. Philadelphia, Dec. 1, 1832-[Nov. 22, 1832] CtY; DLC; ICU; MB; MWA; PP. 17200

Zanesville, O. Bank of Zanesville.
The charter of the bank of Zanesville. Incorporated by act of assembly, in 1832. [Zanesville?] Pr. at the Messenger office, 1832. 22 p. OCHP. 17201

Zavala, Lorenzo de.
Ensayo Historico de las Revoluciones De Megico, Desde 1808 hasta 1830. Vol. 2. New York, Elliott & Palmer, 1832. NN; NmU; TxU. 17202

Zünd, Johann Joseph.
Handbuch der Pferde-und Viehharzney-Kunde, in besonderer Beziehung auf innerliche Krankheiten, Heilmittellehre, Wundarzney, Geburtshülfe u. s. w., für den Landmann und Pferdebesitzen. 1te Aufl. Philadelphia, gedruckt für den Verfasser Von H. Hary, 1832. MH; MiU-C; PU-V; U of PDent. 17203

Zeuner, Charles, 1795-1857.
The American harp, being a collection of new and original church music arranged and composed by Charles Zeuner. Boston, Oliver Ditson & Co., 1832. 378, (17) p. CtMW; ICN; MH; PPPrHi; WHi. 17204

---- Corner-stone march. Boston, 1832. MB. 17205

Zimmerman, John G.
Solitude, by John G. Zimmerman, with the life of the author.

In two parts. Baltimore, Geo.
McDowell & son, 1832. 312 p.
KPea; MdHi; MoSU; PLT; WLac.
                                    17206
Zschokke, Heinrich, 1771-1848.
    Abaellino, the brave of Venice.
Translated from the German by
M. G. Lewis, Woodstock, Vt.,
Rufus Colton, 1832. 159 p. VtHi.
                                    17207